Please remember that this is a library book,
and that it belongs only temporarily to each
person who uses it. Be considerate. Do
not write in this, or any, library book.

Introduction to
CRIMINOLOGY

Second Edition

Hugh D. Barlow

Southern Illinois University
Edwardsville

 Little, Brown and Company
Boston   Toronto

Alex Inkeles, Series Advisor

Library of Congress Catalog Card No. 80-81437

ISBN 0-316-081159

9 8 7 6 5 4 3 2 1

MV

Published simultaneously in Canada
by Little, Brown & Company (Canada) Limited

Printed in the United States of America

Text Acknowledgments

The author gratefully acknowledges permission to quote material from the following sources.

James Boyd, excerpt from "The Ritual of Wiggle: From Ruin to Reelection." Reprinted with permission from *The Washington Monthly,* September 1970. Copyright 1970 by The Washington Monthly Co., 1611 Connecticut Ave., N.W., Washington, D.C. 20009.

Donald R. Cressey, abridged from pp. x–xi, 163–164, 175–178, 248, 250, and 251–252 in *Theft of the Nation.* Copyright © 1969 by Donald R. Cressey. Reprinted by permission of Harper & Row, Publishers, Inc.

Cyrus Gordon, from *Hammurabi's Code.* Copyright © 1957 by Cyrus Gordon. Reprinted by permission.

Stewart L. Hills, from *Crime, Power, and Morality* (Scranton, Pa.: Chandler Publishing Co., 1971). Reprinted by permission.

Francis A. J. Ianni, *Black Mafia: Ethnic Succession in Organized Crime.* Copyright © 1974 by Francis A. J. Ianni. Reprinted by permission of Simon & Schuster, a Division of Gulf & Western Corporation.

James A. Inciardi, excerpts from *Careers in Crime,* © 1975 Rand McNally College Publishing Company, Chicago. Reprinted by permission.

Burton M. Leiser, from *Liberty, Justice and Morals.* Reprinted with permission of Macmillan Publishing Co., Inc. Copyright © 1973 by Burton M. Leiser.

Peter Letkemann, *Crime as Work,* © 1973. Reprinted by permission of Prentice-Hall, Inc., Englewood Cliffs, New Jersey.

Richard Quinney, excerpted from *Criminology: Analysis and Critique of Crime in America.* Copyright © 1975, 1970 by Little, Brown and Company (Inc.). Reprinted by permission.

Walter C. Reckless, from *The Crime Problem,* 5th edition. Copyright © 1973 by Goodyear Publishing Company. Reprinted by permission.

Ralph Salerno and John S. Tompkins, excerpt from *The Crime Confederation: Cosa Nostra and Allied Operations in Organized Crime.* Copyright © 1969 by Ralph Salerno and John S. Tompkins. Reprinted by permission of Doubleday & Company, Inc.

Edwin H. Sutherland and Donald R. Cressey, from *Criminology,* 9th ed. (Philadelphia: Lippincott, 1974). Reprinted by permission.

Photograph Acknowledgments appear on page 518.

To my Mother

Preface

This text is written for the beginning student in criminology. As in the first edition, my goal is to provide an overview of the field that students will find readable and interesting, and that will stimulate discussion about topics clearly in the forefront of the public mind: rape and other violence, crime in corporate and legislative suites, the legislation of morality, the methods and consequences of punishment, criminal justice policy, and others.

In this edition I have retained the emphasis on history and societal reactions to crime, firmly believing that both are crucial for a proper grasp of the subject and the scholarly endeavors that bear upon it. In addition, I still believe that most criminology texts fail miserably when it comes to giving the student an understanding of what goes on when people "do" the things we call crime.

There are also some major revisions. Apart from updating the evidence wherever possible (to 1978 for most official data), I have written new sections on family violence — including child abuse and rape in marriage — on reactions to occupational crime, on victimization and self-report studies, on biogenic theories of crime; and on the prosecution, sentencing, and punishment of criminal suspects and offenders. I have also made greater use of tables, charts, and diagrams.

The single most significant change is the addition of a new chapter on the consequences of punishment. It seemed to me that in the first edition I had not adequately addressed the question: What does criminal punishment actually accomplish? Some people believe that punishment prevents or reduces criminality; others are skeptical of its preventive effects and assert instead that punishment actually *produces* crime. As yet there are no definitive answers to most of the questions that surround the issue. In the new chapter I discuss various possibilities, focusing on deterrence, rehabilitation and reform, and the effects of imprisonment.

I am still indebted to those who helped with the first edition. This edition has benefited from the insights of Professors Eugene Fappiano and J. Corzine, and the assistance of Greg Waugh, and Debby Long, Kristen Milligan, Sally Azim, and Kathy King. I also want to thank Professors Tony Jones and Krishnan Namboodiri for providing me with the opportunity to spend more time on my revisions than would otherwise have been possible.

I especially wish to acknowledge those at Little, Brown who helped make the first edition a success and whose support has been invaluable. Katie Carlone and Cynthia Chapin deserve my special thanks. Finally, there is again my substantial debt to my family, grown now by the addition of Melissa.

Contents

Part I

Criminology: Theory and Method

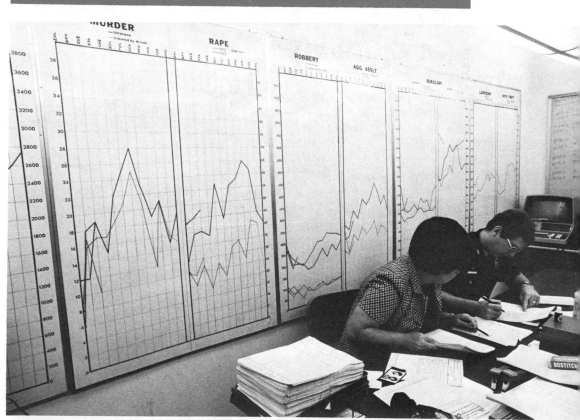

Crime, Criminal Law, and Criminals

Few people would contest the assertion that there is a crime problem in America. This does not mean, however, that everyone agrees on exactly what the problem is — or, for that matter, its solution. Consider these findings, drawn from recent studies:

Three million juveniles were arrested in 1977.

In 1978, there were 8,700 Americans killed and 280,000 injured in fires, with a total of $5 billion in property losses. Many of these fires were deliberately set.

The most frequent victims of personal and household crimes are young, poor, black males.

More than 10 percent of robbery and burglary victims are subject to severe and sometimes long-term emotional problems.

Rape is the fastest rising crime of violence.

The average loss from a single computer crime (e.g., use of computer technology to defraud) is $430,000; the risk of prosecution is only 1 in 22,000.

Forty-six percent of people surveyed in Boston, and 44 percent of those sampled in Buffalo, felt unsafe going out alone at night in their own neighborhoods. Of those groups, 61 percent and 57 percent, respectively, felt that their chances of being attacked or mugged had increased in recent years.

A 1977 Gallup poll showed that nearly one in five high school students in a national sample feared for their safety at school.

Among juveniles, female arrest rates from 1967 to 1976 rose 68 percent, while male arrest rates rose 30 percent.

Six men are arrested for every woman apprehended. The ratio of male to female prisoners is 21:1.

Between 1.4 and 1.9 million American children are at risk of being physically abused by another family member.

In 1974, 80 percent of convicted felons in Florida were given probation as part of or all of their sentence.

The United States has the highest homicide rate and the highest rate of imprisonment of any industrialized democracy.[1]

The list could go on. These are just a few of the findings that are reflected in people's perceptions of the crime problem. Naturally, people tend to regard crimes that affect them as the most important ones. Some react to the extensive involvement of young people in crime or the rapid rise and high cost of occupational crimes like computer theft and the leniency with which the criminal justice system deals with white-collar offenders. Many people fear they will be victims of violent crime — with apparent good reason if they are poor, young, and black. Some view the real crime problem as the breakdown of order in the nation's schools, where early delinquencies could perhaps be prevented. Others are incensed by the extensiveness of child abuse, including sexual assaults by other family members. Certain people assert that crime is largely a problem of males overplaying their masculinity and prizing strength and aggression above all. Still others see the rising crime rate in terms of the failure of the judicial system.

An area of concern to many officials is the habitual offender who makes crime a career. Whereas most people implicated in crimes are amateurs and opportunists, it has become evident that the bulk of robberies, burglaries, and other "street" crimes are committed by a relatively small number of repeat offenders. The suggestion that some criminals may commit hundreds of thousands of crimes during their careers seems a bit farfetched, but offenders who commit three or four hundred crimes a year are certainly not unusual.[2] They are considered the major target of law enforcement efforts in many jurisdictions.

If different people see the problem of crime differently, it is also true that they often define *crime* in different ways. What exactly is a crime? Some people define crime to include acts that harm innocent victims;

others include so-called victimless behaviors — use of illicit drugs, prostitution, homosexual acts between consenting adults — in their definition of crime. Yet others favor a broad conception: crimes, they say, are acts that violate "society's" rules. Criminologists tend to be more precise when they define the terms *crime* and *criminal,* but this does not mean there is complete agreement on a single definition.

Defining Crime

Let us consider first what is commonly called the "legal" or "legalistic" definition of crime. While the specific words used vary from time to time, it generally goes something like this: *Crime is a human act that violates the criminal law.*

This definition has two important components. First, crime involves *behavior;* second, this behavior is identified in terms of *law.* The concepts of law and crime have long been linked in people's minds.[3] Contemporary definitions speak of *criminal law,* however, and thus point to a special type of law with which crime is to be identified.

According to that law, a number of specific criteria must normally be met for an act to be considered a crime and the perpetrator a criminal. First, there must be *conduct* (mere thoughts, no matter how terrible, are not crimes). Second, the conduct must constitute a *social harm;* that is, be injurious to the state (or "the people"). Third, the conduct must be *prohibited by law.* Fourth, the conduct must be performed *voluntarily.* Fifth, the conduct must be performed *intentionally* (the issue here is criminal intent, expressed in the concept of *mens rea,* meaning guilty mind). Sixth, the harm must be *causally related* to the conduct. Finally, the conduct must be *punishable by law* (in fact, the punishment must be specified in advance of the conduct).

ARGUMENTS FOR AND AGAINST THE LEGALISTIC DEFINITION

Over the years, scholars have debated the pros and cons of the legalistic definition. Among those who favor this definition are Jerome Michael and Mortimer Adler, who assert that the legalistic definition is "the only possible definition of crime."[4] Why? In their view the definition is precise and unambiguous and identifies the heart of the subject, namely, its relation to law. Three other common observations are: (1) the legalistic definition recognizes a common thread binding instances of human conduct (they are legally identified as criminal); (2) the word *crime* is reserved for a class of acts to which stigma is attached by virtue of their illegality — to alter the definition to include other types of rule-breaking behavior would needlessly broaden the scope of this stigmatization; and (3) this definition identifies clear-cut boundaries for criminology, which distinguish it from the study of other areas of nonconformity and "deviance."

These arguments have not impressed some experts. In the thirties, Thorsten Sellin argued for a more universally applicable definition that would encompass any violation of what he called "conduct norms." Noting that legal rules are only a part of the more general body of social norms regulating behavior, and that laws tend to vary over time and space, Sellin suggested that the legal criterion invoked in definitions of crime was at best artificial and arbitrary, and at worst ignored other socially significant actions that are in conflict with the "general social interest."[5] Sellin thought criminologists should study not just illegal acts, but any and all conduct that represents violation of group norms.

Other critics have pointed out that the notion of social harm is often invoked in delineating acts that are the proper concern of criminal law. In his discussion of criminal law, Jerome Hall observes that the notion of social harm is central to legal conceptions of crime.[6] But what about acts that are harmful yet not identified in law as crimes? Should they not also be treated as crimes?

Some criminologists take issue with the legalistic definition more for what it implies than for its substance. This is an important issue, for definitions have implications for the kinds of questions we ask. When we define crime as violation of criminal law, our efforts to understand and explain crime are inevitably drawn to such questions as: "Why do people engage in behavior that violates the law?" and "What is the extent of violation?" Attention is drawn away from such questions as: "Why are the laws what they are?" "How did they come about?" "Who created them?" and "What purposes do they serve?" The law side of the coin is considered primarily as a formal cause of crime — it "creates" crime by identifying acts that violate it — and not as an integral part of the crime picture that in itself needs critical analysis. By treating law as a given, and thus largely irrelevant for the explanation of crime as behavior, we may fall into the trap of mysticizing the concept of law: The law is the law, no person is above it, all people are subject to it, and who is to question its existence? If our definition of crime leads us in this direction, some scholars argue, our understanding of crime will never be complete.[7]

MODIFICATIONS OF THE LEGALISTIC DEFINITION

Some authors have suggested modifications of the traditional legalistic definition. Walter Reckless, for example, suggests that we should limit our attention to only those illegal acts that have been reported to the police:

> To the question: What constitutes crime? the modern criminologist must answer that crime exists when a violation of the criminal code is reported. Otherwise, the phenomenon is a non-reported violation, and we are not sure philosophically whether a non-reported violation is a phenomenon at all. A star might fall in the heavens, but if no one saw it and reported it and got

confirmation from others who saw it, then the star did not fall in fact. So the fact of crime is the reporting of a violation of a criminal code. Anything else is not a crime in fact.[8]

Other authors limit crime even more, namely, to those acts for which an offender has been caught, tried, and punished.[9] In effect they are saying that the significance of crime as a legal phenomenon lies not so much in the idea that an act happens to violate the law but, rather, *in the quality the act takes on when the machinery of law acts upon it*. Some laws on the books, for example, are never enforced; in these cases it makes little sense to treat the illegal act as a crime. On paper the act is a crime; but as part of social experience it is not. As Roscoe Pound noted many years ago, *law in action* is the appropriate focus for those interested in the reality of law.[10] Law in action involves the activities of those who create and enforce criminal law.

The Labeling Perspective Definitions that refer to those who administer the law underscore, at least implicitly, the idea that crimes are distinguished from other acts *precisely because they have been defined as crimes by those in a position to react to them*.[11] The activities of those who administer the criminal law lead to the imposition of the label "crime" on a behavior, at which point the behavior in question becomes part of the crime scene. While those who create the law do, in fact, impose labels on behavior, the social significance of a given act is in the reactions it calls forth. If you rob someone, the responses others make to your behavior create a social reality quite different from that created when you engage in some other activity.

The idea that crimes are identifiable in terms of the reactions to them is not new. Emile Durkheim, one of the fathers of sociology, noted that a crime is "every act which, in any degree whatever, invokes against its author the characteristic reaction we term punishment."[12] Speaking on the more general topic of deviance, Howard Becker more recently observed that

> . . . deviance is *not* a quality of the act the person commits, but rather a consequence of the application by others of rules and sanctions to an "offender." The deviant is one to whom the label has been successfully applied; deviant behavior is behavior that people so label.[13]

Pursuing this reasoning, what makes behavior distinctive is the kinds of reactions it calls forth. The distinctive thing about *criminal* behavior is that the behavior in question has been labeled crime.[14]

When labeled crime, behavior is transformed into criminal behavior, and the actor may be transformed into a criminal. This transformation is called *criminalization*. The opposite process — when the label "criminal" is removed from an action, event, or person — is called *decriminalization*. For those who favor the *labeling perspective*, as it is often called, why and how the transformation occurs is crucial for an understanding of crime. How people perceive the actions of others, and what they do about it, are issues of considerable interest to the criminologist.

Yet it is not merely a matter of linking reactions to acts. The acquisition of criminal status may have little to do with the act that happens to be performed. Instead, it may have a lot to do with the attributes or characteristics of the person whose behavior is under scrutiny.[15] By the same token, withholding criminal status may have more to do with the person than with his or her behavior. From recent history we can recall that many considered President Nixon a noncriminal despite the overwhelming evidence of "high crimes and misdemeanors." Why?

From the labeling perspective, crime is treated as *status* rather than behavior. But who ascribes this status to acts? Certainly, in the broadest sense, we all do. Based on our experiences, our knowledge, and our feelings about things, our perceptions may lead us to define certain actions as crimes. This category of crime can be called "natural" crime, to distinguish it from "legal" crime.[16]

If we restrict ourselves to crime as legal status, then we are in effect treating acts as crimes *only when they are so labeled by those who create and administer the criminal law.* We are once again reminded that criminal law plays an important part in the determination of crime, but here it is clearly more than a "formal" cause of crime. Apart from anything else, criminal law *in action* sets the conditions under which labels can be applied, and it restricts, in theory if not always in practice, the range of behaviors that can be appropriately defined as crime.

When we view it in this way, crime actually has five distinct meanings.[17] The five levels of meaning depend upon the stage in the legal process that we are considering. Legislatures and other agencies, whose job it is to *create* legal definitions of behavior, provide us with formulations of criminal law. These formulations identify acts that violate them, and which therefore are crimes. But those who *enforce* the criminal law also define crime. The act of arrest applies the crime label at another stage of the legal process. Persons who are not arrested escape the imposition of the crime label on their actions at this and any subsequent stages. While in terms of the first stage their behavior might be a crime, it is not a crime at the arrest stage, since no arrest is made.

In the *prosecution* and *conviction* stages, specific interpretations of conduct are again made within the framework of criminal law. The personal and social ramifications of labeling at these stages are, needless to say, different from those at earlier stages. Finally, we can identify a fifth stage during which *punishment* is meted out. Conduct reaching this stage may be said to constitute crime at all levels of meaning.

Bearing these conceptual distinctions in mind, we can now define crime. *Crime is a label that is attached to human conduct by those who create and administer the criminal law.*

Social Control and Law

We have seen that crime and law are intertwined. Now is an appropriate time to look more closely at law in general, and criminal law in particular. Criminal law as a type of law is generally regarded as a relatively recent development in legal systems. While no specific date of origin can be identified, criminal law in the Western world developed from already existing systems of law some two thousand years ago and began to take shape in the later years of the Roman Empire. Before tracing the development of criminal law, let us examine the nature of law in general.

In any social group, efforts are made to ensure that members behave predictably and in accordance with the expectations and evaluations of others. These efforts are at the heart of *social control* and their success is thought to be indispensable to orderly group life. It is difficult to imagine how group life could endure if members simply acted impulsively or in continued violation of the expectations of others.

Social control appears in different guises. It may involve facial expressions, gestures, language, threats, gossip, ridicule, ostracism. It may take the form, in part at least, of written rules backed by force, or it may consist largely of unwritten rules passed on by word of mouth, by example, or even unconsciously, with little more than social disapproval of nonconformity. Sometimes conformity is promoted through the use of rewards ("positive sanctions"), sometimes through the use of penalties ("negative sanctions").

Law is a type of social control. It is an example of what we call *formal* social control, described here by F. James Davis:

> Formal social control is characterized by (1) explicit rules of conduct, (2) planned use of sanctions to support the rules, and (3) designated officials to interpret and enforce the rules, and often to make them.[18]

A classic definition of law was written by German sociologist Max Weber:

> An order will be called *law* if it is externally guaranteed by the probability that coercion (physical or psychological), to bring about conformity or avenge violation, will be applied by a *staff* of people holding themselves specially ready for that purpose.[19]

Weber contends that law has three essential features, which, taken together, distinguish it from other normative orders such as *custom* and *convention*. First, regardless of whether an individual wants to obey rules or does so out of habit, pressures to conform must be *external,* in the form of actions or threats of action by others. Second, these external actions or threats are of a specific kind: they involve coercion or force. Third, those who carry out the coercive threats are persons whose official role is enforcing the law. When this staff or administrative body is part of an agency of political authority, then Weber speaks of "state" law.

Customs and conventions differ from law because they do not involve one or more of these features. Customs are rules *of* conduct that people follow "without thinking," or as Weber puts it, with unreflective imitation. These customary rules of conduct are called usages, and there is no sense of "oughtness," or obligation, about them. On the other hand, conventions are rules *for* conduct, and they do involve a question of obligation. Pressures to conform are brought to bear on rule-breakers, and these usually involve some form of disapproval. However, unlike law, a conventional order "lacks specialized personnel for the implementation of coercive power."[20]

A number of prominent scholars adhere to the essentials of Weber's definition of law, but take issue with two major points. First, some suggest that by emphasizing coercion Weber ignores other, possibly more important considerations that influence people to conform to obligatory rules. It has been argued that the authoritative character of legal rules prompts a special kind of obligation not dependent on the use or threat of force.[21] H. L. A. Hart writes that coercion is only one guarantee of conformity, and in fact is less important as a characteristic of law than subjective evaluations on the basis of which individuals " 'apply' the rules themselves to themselves."[22]

Weber appears to have been quite aware of these issues. People, he said, obey laws for a variety of reasons — sometimes because of an emotional commitment to them, sometimes through fear of disapproval, sometimes because it is in their interests to do so, and sometimes simply out of habit. Many laws are obeyed because we feel it is our duty to obey them, and this feeling seems to articulate a special kind of obligation that is built into authority relations.[23] But Weber makes it clear that the question of why people obey obligatory rules is really irrelevant for a definition of law. The existence of a coercive apparatus in no way precludes the possibility that noncoercive pressures are more important in guaranteeing obedience. Most important in distinguishing legal systems from other methods of social control is that coercion is available and may be used by an authorized staff to ensure conformity or avenge violation.

The second objection is over the special staff. Some critics claim that Weber's definition unnecessarily restricts the use of the term *law* in cross-cultural and historical contexts. Rather than use the word *staff,* which implies an organized administrative apparatus that may not exist in certain nonliterate and primitive societies, some suggest using a less restrictive term. Jack P. Gibbs offers "special status," E. Adamson Hoebel mentions persons possessing "a socially recognized privilege," and Ronald L. Akers says simply, "a socially authorized third party."[24] Law in America, of course, provides for specific "officers" to administer and enforce it, and its very creation is the task of appointed and elected officials operating within the framework of an established political system. Still, we should bear these suggestions in mind when studying societies other than our own.

Criminal Law

Criminal law is a specific type of law:

> The criminal law . . . is defined conventionally as a body of specific rules regarding human conduct which have been promulgated by political authority, which apply uniformly to all members of the classes to which the rules refer, and which are enforced by punishment administered by the state.[25]

This definition identifies four critical features of criminal law: *politicality, penal sanction, specificity,* and *uniformity.* Briefly stated, *politicality* invokes the notion of political authority. Generally, it means that we include in criminal law only those rules created and enforced by authorized agents of the state.

Penal sanction "refers to the notion that violators will be punished or at least threatened with punishment by the state."[26] *Specificity* points at the specific rather than general character of rules: "The criminal law . . . generally gives a strict definition of a specific act."[27] *Uniformity* refers to the applicability of criminal laws and the way they are used. Such laws apply to all persons for whom they are relevant and must be applied without regard for personal status or prestige.

Sutherland and Cressey realize the difficulties surrounding attempts to apply this definition in the real world. Criminal law in action rarely seems to come up to this ideal characterization, and some of the distinctions are essentially arbitrary or ambiguous.[28] Rather than retain the definition simply because it is conventional, some authors have taken steps to improve upon it.

In his definition of criminal law, Quinney leaves out any reference to uniformity. Criminal law is apparently not considered uniformly applicable by those who create and administer it, nor is it applied uniformly. Thus, it is somewhat pointless and misleading to include uniformity in the definition. Quinney also disagrees with the inclusion of penal sanction, pointing out that while criminal law contains provisions for the use of punitive sanctions, actual enforcement practices are quite another thing.[29]

Some authors question whether criminal law need be linked with the concept of political community or, even more narrowly, the state. When we think of a political community, we generally have in mind something on the order of Weber's classic conceptualization:

> . . . a separate "political" community is constituted where we find (1) a territory; (2) the availability of physical force for its domination; and (3)

communal action which . . . regulates the interrelations of the inhabitants of the territory.[30]

Hartjen has recently suggested that the notion of political community is not essential to the definition of criminal law:

> . . . whether or not we want to stipulate that the rules of criminal law are created or enforced by a body that falls within some criteria designating it as a political group or are the result of some informal ad hoc procedure carried out by the group at large is really irrelevant. The character of the group that takes action against another person's conduct is significant only for the particular case being studied. In some societies no specific body politic exists. The members of such a society, however, can act as a political body as they respond in concert against one of their members. The important point is that it is the act of creating some rule providing that the offender will be punished in the name of the group that generates the possibility of crime. The sociological reality of crime is located in the application of punishment, in the *act* of enforcing the rule. Criminal law provides a standard and an excuse for defining another's behavior as crime. As such it makes crime a *possible reality.*[31]

In summary, then, criminal law *encompasses specialized rules, created by those with the authority and power to do so, which contain provisions for punishments to be administered in the name of the group, community, or society.* Further, unlike tort or civil law, which requires that the victim make a complaint, *these rules may be enforced without the invitation or implied consent of the victim, or any interested third party.*[32]

Origins and Development of Criminal Law

Much of what we know about the origins and development of criminal law has come through the efforts of legal historians and cultural anthropologists. Classic historical works such as *Ancient Law* by Sir Henry Sumner Maine and *The Growth of Criminal Law in Ancient Greece* by George Calhoun provide us with important interpretative accounts of early law.[33] Twentieth-century anthropologists have added to the store of knowledge by drawing attention to rule making, rule breaking, and rule enforcement in primitive societies. Works by A. R. Radcliffe-Brown, Bronislaw Malinowski, E. Adamson Hoebel, and E. E. Evans-Pritchard are among the best known.[34]

THE DECLINE OF PRIMITIVE LAW

It is generally agreed that "primitive law" — the system of rules and obligations in preliterate and semiliterate societies — represents the foundation upon which modern legal systems arose. Primitive law contains three important features: (1) acts that injured or wronged others were considered "private wrongs," that is, injuries to particular individuals rather than the group or tribe as a whole (exceptions to this were acts deemed harmful to the entire community; for example, aiding an enemy or witchcraft); (2) the injured party or his family typically took personal action against the wrongdoer, a kind of self-help justice; (3) this self-help justice usually amounted to retaliation in kind. Blood feuds were not uncommon under this system of primitive justice.

Strongly entrenched customs and traditions, the relative autonomy of the family, homogeneity of the population and its activities, and other features of primitive society were undermined as technological progress and a growing division of labor ushered in social heterogeneity and increasing organizational complexity. Growing differences in wealth, prestige, and power found consolidation in new patterns of authority and decision making. The rise of chieftains and kings set the stage for centralization of political authority, establishment of territorial domain, and the emergence of sovereign authority and the civil state. The handling of disputes slowly moved out of the hands of the family and into the hands of the sovereign and, subsequently, the state. So, too, the creation of legal rules became the prerogative of central authority.

These changes did not happen overnight. Criminal law as we know it today is a product of centuries of change. The earliest known code of written law dates back to the twenty-first century B.C. This is the code of Ur-Nammu, the Sumerian king who founded the Third Dynasty of Ur. The famous Code of Hammurapi (sometimes spelled Hammurabi) was discovered in 1901 in Susa, near the Persian Gulf. This code dates from around 1650 B.C. Other ancient codes of law include the Twelve Tables of Rome, the Mosaic Code, the laws of ancient Greece, and the laws of Tacitus. All these codes show strong ties with the self-help justice typical of more primitive eras. As Maine notes, early penal law was primarily the law of torts (or private wrongs). The Twelve Tables treated theft, assault, and violent robbery as *delicta* (private wrongs) along with trespass, libel, and slander. The person, not the state or the public, was the injured party.[35]

The maturing legal systems of ancient Greece and Rome moved steadily toward the formulation of offenses against the state (public wrongs, or *crimena*) and the establishment of machinery for administration and enforcement. According to Maine, the legislative establishment of permanent criminal tribunals around the first century B.C. represented a crucial step in the emergence of "true criminal law."

One of the most interesting features of these early codes is the number of activities they cover. The Code of Hammurapi is particularly wide ranging. The laws covered such diverse areas as kidnapping, unsolved crimes, price fixing, rights of military personnel, the sale of liquor, marriage and the family, inheritance, and slavery.[36] The contents of these early codes suggest four important observations: (1) most laws are products of prevailing social, political, and economic condition; (2) some laws articulate long-established customs and traditions and can be thought of as formal restatements of existing mores; (3) some laws reflect efforts to regulate and coordinate increasingly complex social relations and activities; and (4) some laws display prevailing ethical and moral standards and show close ties to religious ideas and sentiments.

MALA PROHIBITA AND MALA IN SE

There has been much legal debate concerning the connection between law and morality. In the minds of some scholars, law is based on ethical beliefs, and criminal codes are a sort of catalogue of sins. But others have argued that there is much in our criminal codes that bears no obvious connection with ethics or morality. In what sense, for example, are laws prohibiting certain forms of drug use or certain kinds of business activities matters of sin?

Laws were once indistinguishable from the general code governing social conduct. As primitive societies became more complex, law and justice were identified as concepts that regulated the moral aspects of social conduct. Even the extensive legal codes of Greece and Rome fused morality with law. And in some languages, Hungarian for example, the word for *crime* means not only an act that is illegal but one that is evil or sinful.[37] In time criminal codes expanded and laws were passed to regulate activities in business, politics, the family, social services, and even our intimate private lives. The connection between law and morality became less clear, and people categorized crimes as *mala prohibita* — meaning evil because they are forbidden — or *mala in se* — meaning evil in themselves. *Mala prohibita* crimes would include drug offenses, traffic violations, antitrust violations, and embezzlement; examples of *mala in se* crimes, acts that are inherently evil, include rape, murder, arson, and robbery.

INTERESTS AND THE DEVELOPMENT OF LAW

As we have learned more about the history of criminal law, particularly by analyzing past legal decisions, another important facet of its development has received growing attention. This is the role interests play in the creation, content, and enforcement of legal rules.

One of the first scholars to systematically discuss the importance of interests in formulating law was Roscoe Pound. According to Pound, law helps to adjust and harmonize conflicting individual and group interests:

Looked at functionally, the law is an attempt to satisfy, to reconcile, to harmonize, to adjust these overlapping and often conflicting claims and demands, either through securing them directly and immediately, or through securing certain individual interests, or through delimitations or compromises of individual interests, so as to give effect to the greatest total of interests, or to the interests that weigh the most in our civilization, with the least sacrifice of the scheme of interests as a whole.[38]

Pound's view suggests that the laws of heterogeneous and pluralistic societies are best understood as efforts at *social compromise,* with the maintenance of social order and harmony a priority.

The interest theory of sociological jurisprudence offered by Pound has been attacked in recent years for its emphasis on compromise and harmony, and for its suggestion that there will be consensus where important social interests are concerned. According to Quinney,

> society is characterized by diversity, conflict, coercion, and change, rather than by consensus and stability. Second, law is a *result* of the operation of interests, rather than an instrument that functions outside of particular interests. Though law may control interests, it is in the first place created by interests. Third, law incorporates the interests of specific persons and groups; it is seldom the product of the whole society. Law is made by men, representing special interests, who have the power to translate their interests into public policy. Unlike the pluralistic conception of politics, law does not represent a compromise of the diverse interests in society, but supports some interests at the expense of others.[39]

Quinney seems to be asking us to imagine that all criminal laws reflect special interests and the exercise of power in support of them. But in what sense are laws prohibiting murder, arson, or incest, special interest laws? And what of laws that are probably not in the interests of those in a position to influence policy, such as those prohibiting influence peddling and political corruption?

While asserting the connection between conflict, power, and criminal law, we should first acknowledge the distinction between *mala in se* and *mala prohibita* crimes. Conflict between interests and the exercise of power are more relevant to crimes of the latter sort. (This will become evident when we discuss the historical development of certain offenses.) Second, conflict between interests and the exercise of power in defense of special interests are important in the application of criminal definitions to people. Historically, those low in status, social prestige, or power have usually found themselves labeled criminals most often and punished most severely for their crimes. Many early legal codes contained special provisions specifying different reactions according to distinctions of status. The more powerful were the more privileged. Finally, conflict and power help explain why some activities are not crimes. This is especially evident in matters relating to business and government practices and environmental pollution.

Anglo-American Criminal Law

Criminal law in the United States draws from Greek, Mosaic, and Roman law, but its major roots lie in English law. The common law of England can be traced to the reign of Henry II (1154–1189). For centuries English law had been a system of tribal justice, the primitive law of private wrongs and self-help retaliation. As feudalism took hold in the eighth and ninth centuries, Anglo-Saxon society underwent important changes. The family lost its autonomy; kings and kingdoms emerged; and the blood feud was replaced by a system of material compensation (usually money), directed by individuals with special status — by king, lord, or bishop. Equally important, political unification was under way, as territorial acquisitions of the new kings transformed a patchwork of small kin-dominated domains into fewer, larger kingdoms. With the Norman conquest of 1066, complete political unification was but a short step away.

The Normans centralized their administrative machinery, including that concerned with law. During the reign of Henry II, new legal procedures emerged, including a court of "common law" administered in the name of the crown and dispensing justice to all (except the nobility and the clergy, who remained special cases for special dispensation). But most important, during this period certain acts were identified as offenses against king and country ("Breaches of the King's Peace"), and with them the curtain was raised on modern criminal law.[40]

By the time the Puritans arrived in New England, criminal law was firmly established in England, and the new colonists imported its essential features virtually intact. Not only was the machinery of imposition and enforcement similar to that in the mother country, but the laws themselves departed little from those found in England.[41] By the time the Declaration of Independence was signed, adjustments in law and the legal system were already taking place. Over the next 200 years both substantive and procedural features of the criminal law were slowly "Americanized."

The distinction between *procedural* and *substantive* criminal law draws attention to two basic issues in law: (1) how the authorities handle matters of law and deal with law violators — the question of procedure; and (2) the content of the specific rules making up the body of criminal law — the question of substance. The rules embodied in American criminal law, substantive and procedural, come from four sources: (1) federal and state constitutions; (2) decisions by courts (common law or case law), including decisions of precedent and Supreme Court rulings; (3) administrative regulations, those policy decisions employed by agencies on the federal, state, and local levels as they carry out their legal duties; and (4) statutory enactments by legislatures.

Procedural rules govern the way we officially handle matters of criminal law. They are applicable at all stages of the legal process. They govern the different groups involved in the handling of offenses and offenders — the police, the prosecution and defense, the courts, and those who administer punishment. They shape the administration of criminal justice and help determine whether given acts and individuals will be officially identified as criminal, how offenders will be "processed," and what will happen to them if found guilty of a crime. Procedural aspects of criminal law are vital to the study of crime, criminals, and legal sanctions. They set the tone for the process of criminalization and provide us with insights into criminal law in action.

The Criminal

We have defined crime and criminal law, but who is the "criminal"? Paul Tappan used this question as the subject of a paper some years ago, drawing attention to the fact that criminologists disagree on whom they have in mind when they speak of the criminal.

Differences of opinion over the definition of the criminal mirror some of the disputes over the definition of crime. Some scholars identify criminals in terms of strict legal considerations, while others emphasize the antisocial character of their behavior or their involvement in the skills, techniques, attitudes, and life-styles of repetitive law violators.

From the standpoint of criminal law, a criminal is an individual who is legally capable of conduct that violates the law and who can be shown to have actually and intentionally engaged in that conduct. If it cannot be demonstrated that the person committed the illegal act, or that he or she was capable of committing it — for example, by meeting requirements of age and mental condition — or that the act was intentional (or the result of negligence), then the person is not legally a criminal. Emphasizing the legalistic view, Tappan suggests "only those are criminal who have been adjudicated as such by the courts."[42]

A conception of the criminal more in keeping with our definition of crime would stress that even though people are ostensibly innocent of crime until proven guilty, those suspected of violating the law are treated in a special way by the machinery of justice. People who are investigated by the police, people who are arrested, people who end up in court, and people who are convicted and punished, all are in fact treated as if they belonged to the same category, that of the law violator. The moment that the machinery of criminal law bears down on anyone, that person is singled out for special consideration. Accordingly, we can define the criminal as *a person whose conduct has been labeled a crime by those who create and administer the criminal law.*

Once a person is identified as a criminal, he or she is treated as one by those charged with the responsibility of creating and administering the system of criminal justice. The label can be applied at different stages in the legal process, from the point where criminal conduct is created in law to the point where punishment ends. In addition, the label often stays with people even after they have paid the price for their officially recognized behavior. The stigma associated with the criminal label is an important facet of the crime scene. When friends or associates know an individual has been labeled a criminal by agencies of law, *and treat him*

Bored teenagers make easy targets for the imposition of delinquent or criminal labels by police.

in a special way because of this knowledge, then to all intents and purposes his social identity becomes that of a criminal.

You may be wondering: Why emphasize the activities of those who enforce the law when surely a person is a criminal because of something he or she does, not because of something the enforcers do? That would be the same as saying that people are what they do, regardless of what others do to them. If we take this position, we underemphasize the social dimension of human existence; we fail to take into account the extent to which the attitudes, knowledge, ideas, and actions of others give meaning to an individual's behavior. The idea of the "criminal" is created by people. It is something we impute to another's behavior. That person's behavior is not criminal until we say it is by our words or deeds. On its own, the physical act that a person performs is only that, a physical act. Even its meaning to the actor himself is dependent on his previous experiences and the course of his life's learning as a social being.

It seems, then, that we are partly what we do and partly what others do to us. We are criminal not simply because we break the law, but because those who make official judgments about our behavior decide to treat us as criminal and act on that decision. Remember, discretion is involved in applying the criminal label, and power and social position can influence the decision. If we are young, or black, or poor, or less well educated, or living in the inner-city slums, we are more susceptible than others to having the status of criminal assigned to us. In America people with these characteristics turn up in crime statistics more often than we would expect on the basis of their numbers in the total population. Why? In part because the police concentrate their energies in areas of towns and cities where such people are likely to be found. Also because the actions of legal agencies are inherently political actions and stem from decision making and the exercise of power as part of the American political process. Those individuals with the characteristics identified above are generally excluded from the political process and are in effect without voice in the creation and enforcement of criminal law. As relatively powerless members of society, they are more susceptible to actions that identify their behavior as "deviant."

If criminals are identified strictly on the basis of their actions, then most of us are probably criminals. Whether we take office supplies home, lie a little on our tax returns, have sexual intercourse out of wedlock, drink alcohol while under age, open another's mail, gamble, put slugs in vending machines, engage in some kind of fraudulent activity, or commit murder, robbery, assault, or arson may matter little according to the letter of the law. It matters a great deal from the standpoint of social experience, however, for the criminal label will be applied in the last four situations far more often than in the others. Ultimately, the decision to apply the label is wholly in the hands of those we charge with the responsibility of creating and administering the criminal law.

This may suggest that we need only study the creation and application of criminal definitions in order to grasp the "real" crime scene. But what about those actions and people who escape societal reactions and remain secret as far as the law is concerned?[43] Should these be ignored in criminology? The answer is no. Our definitions of *crime* and *criminal* do not exclude the rule-creation and application processes, but neither do they lead us to ignore the behavioral elements in crime. The criminologist who focuses only on crime as status and on the people to whom the label has been applied looks at merely a part of the crime scene. Crime is also behavior in the sense that it constitutes a human activity. The criminologist is therefore interested in explaining the occurrence of that behavior. Why do people kill? and why are some people more likely to be killed than others? How is the behavior we call crime distributed throughout the population? Is criminal activity random or does it follow a pattern? If patterned in a certain way, why? Questions such as these are not incompatible with our definitions.

References

1. *LEAA Newsletter,* vol. 8 (Washington, D.C.: U.S. Government Printing Office, 1979); U.S. Department of Justice, *Boston: Public Attitudes About Crime: A National Crime Survey Report,* No. SD-NCS-C-20, and *Buffalo: Public Attitudes About Crime,* No. SD-NCS-C-21 (Washington, D.C.: U.S. Government Printing Office, 1979); Lee H. Bowker, "Women and Crime: An International Perspective," paper presented at the Ninth World Congress of Sociology, Uppsala, Sweden, August 1978; Nicolette Parisi, Michael R. Gottfredson, Michael J. Hindelang, and Timothy J. Flanagan, *Sourcebook of Criminal Justice Statistics* (Washington, D.C.: U.S. Government Printing Office, 1979); "Teenagers Fear School Violence," *St. Louis Post-Dispatch* (December 21, 1977), p. 5F; Linda Singer, "Women and the Correctional System," *American Law Review* 11 (1973), pp. 295–308; Richard J. Gelles and Murray A. Straus, "Violence in the American Family," *Journal of Social Issues* 35 (1979), p. 15; Andrew T. Scull, *Decarceration* (Englewood Cliffs, N.J.: Prentice-Hall, 1977), p. 47.
2. For higher estimates, see Samuel Yochelson and Stanton E. Samenow, *The Criminal Personality* (New York: Jason Aronson, 1976), pp. 221–25.
3. See Herbert A. Bloch and Gilbert Geis, *Man, Crime, and Society,* 2nd ed. (New York: Random House, 1970), pp. 14–15; and Richard Quinney, *The Problem of Crime* (New York: Dodd, Mead, 1970), pp. 16–19.
4. Jerome Michael and Mortimer Adler, *Crime, Law, and Social Science* (New York: Harcourt, Brace, 1933), p. 2.
5. Thorsten Sellin, *Culture Conflict and Crime* (New York: Social Science Research Council, 1938), pp. 17–32.
6. Jerome Hall, *General Principles of Criminal Law* (Indianapolis: Bobbs-Merrill, 1960), pp. 14–26.
7. For some views on this see the articles by Richard Quinney and by Herman and Julia Schwendinger in *Issues in Criminology* 7 (1972).
8. Walter Reckless, *The Crime Problem* (New York: Appleton-Century-Crofts, 1950), p. 8.
9. Richard Korn and Lloyd McCorkle, *Criminology and Penology* (New York: Holt, 1957), p. 46.
10. Roscoe Pound, *Interpretations of Legal History* (New York: Macmillan, 1923), especially Chapter 3.
11. Quinney, *The Problem of Crime,* pp. 5–6.
12. Emile Durkheim, *The Division of Labor in Society* (New York: Free Press, 1964), p. 70.
13. Howard S. Becker, *The Outsiders: Studies in the Sociology of Deviance* (New York: Free Press, 1963), p. 9.
14. Clayton Hartjen, *Crime and Criminalization* (New York: Praeger, 1974), pp. 5–8.
15. Austin T. Turk, *Criminality and Legal Order* (Chicago: Rand McNally, 1969), pp. 9–10.
16. Quinney, *The Problem of Crime,* pp. 7–8.
17. Quinney presents a discussion of the first four stages in *The Problem of Crime;* the fifth is added here.
18. F. James Davis, "Law as a Type of Social Control," in *Society and the Law,* ed. F. James Davis, Henry H. Foster, Jr., C. Ray Jeffery, and Eugene Davis (New York: Free Press, 1962), p. 43.
19. Max Weber, *Law in Economy and Society,* trans. and ed. by Max Rheinstein (Cambridge, Mass.: Harvard University Press, 1954), p. 2.
20. Ibid., p. 27.
21. Philip Selznick, "Sociology of Law," *International Encyclopedia of the Social Sciences,* vol. 9 (New York: Macmillan and the Free Press, 1968), pp. 50–59. See also Selznick, *Law, Society, and Industrial Justice* (New York: Russell Sage Foundation, 1969), pp. 4–8.
22. See Jack P. Gibbs, "Definitions of Law and Empirical Questions," *Law and Society Review* 2 (1968), pp. 431–32.
23. See Weber, *Law in Economy and Society,* pp. 15, 21, 37, chapter 5, and pp. 322–37.
24. Jack P. Gibbs, "Crime and the Sociology of Law," *Sociology and Social Research* 51 (1966), p. 29; E. Adamson Hoebel, *The Law of Primitive Man* (Cambridge, Mass.: Harvard University Press, 1954), p. 28; and Ronald L. Akers, "Towards a Comparative Definition of Law," *Journal of Criminal Law, Criminology, and Police Science* 56 (1965), p. 306.
25. Edwin H. Sutherland and Donald R. Cressey, *Criminology,* 9th ed. (Philadelphia: Lippincott, 1974), p. 4.
26. Ibid., p. 7.
27. Ibid., p. 6.
28. Ibid., pp. 4–8.
29. Quinney, *The Problem of Crime,* p. 16.
30. Weber, *Law in Economy and Society,* p. 339.
31. Hartjen, *Crime and Criminalization,* p. 20.
32. Gibbs, "Crime and the Sociology of Law," p. 33.
33. Maine, *Ancient Law,* 10th ed. (London: John Murray, 1905); Calhoun, *The Growth of Criminal Law in Ancient Greece* (Berkeley: University of California Press, 1927).
34. A. R. Radcliffe-Brown, *The Andaman Islanders* (New York: Free Press, 1948); Hoebel, *The Law of Primitive Man,* and *The Cheyenne Way* (Norman: University of Oklahoma Press, 1941); Bronislaw Malinowski, *Crime and Custom in Savage Society* (New York: Harcourt, Brace, 1926); and E. E. Evans-Pritchard, *The Nuer* (Oxford: Clarendon Press, 1940).
35. Maine, *Ancient Law,* pp. 341–42.
36. See Cyrus H. Gordon, *Hammurapi's Code:*

Quaint or Forward Looking? (New York: Rinehart, 1957).

37. See Stephen Schafer, *Theories in Criminology* (New York: Random House, 1969), chapter III.

38. Roscoe Pound, "A Survey of Social Interests," *Harvard Law Review* 57 (1943), p. 39; see also his *Social Control through Law* (New Haven: Yale University Press, 1942).

39. Richard Quinney, *The Social Reality of Crime* (Boston: Little, Brown, 1970), p. 35. For a less "radical" view see Turk, *Criminality and Legal Order*, pp. 31–32.

40. On the development of criminal law in England see C. Ray Jeffery, "The Development of Crime in Early English Society," *Journal of Criminal Law, Criminology, and Police Science* 47 (1957), pp. 647–66.

41. See Roscoe Pound, "The Development of American Law and Its Deviation from English Law," *Law Quarterly Review* 67 (1951), pp. 49–66. See also Kai T. Erickson, *Wayward Puritans* (New York: J. Wiley, 1966) for an in-depth look at law and crime in Puritan New England.

42. Paul W. Tappan, "Who Is the Criminal?" *American Sociological Review* 12 (1947), p. 100.

43. For more on "secret deviance" see Becker, *The Outsiders*, pp. 19–22.

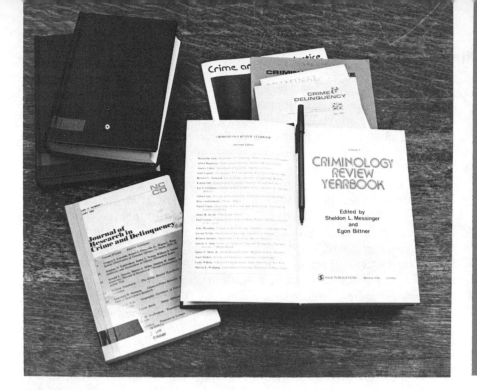

Criminology Past and Present: Theoretical Perspectives

Criminology is a relatively young field of study, dating back roughly a hundred years. Most criminologists today receive their academic training in the social sciences, usually taking degrees in sociology. The pioneers in the new field, however, were trained in other disciplines. Cesare Lombroso (1835–1909) was a physician and surgeon; Raffaele Garofalo (1852–1934) was a professor of law and a magistrate; Enrico Ferri (1856–1929) was a criminal lawyer and member of the Italian parliament; and Gustav Aschaffenburg (1866–1944) was a psychiatrist, as was William Healy (1869–1965), one of the American pioneers.

Criminology gained its place in American academe between 1920 and 1940. During these years textbooks covering the developing field began to appear. These books were primarily the work of sociologists, with Maurice Parmelee, Edwin H. Sutherland, John L. Gillin, Philip A. Parsons, and Fred E. Haynes leading the way.[1] Though sociology has been recognized as the "home" of academic criminology, persons from a wide variety of disciplines continue to make important contributions to the field. And criminology has also benefited from the knowledge and insights of those with little or no academic training but plenty of experience with some aspect of the crime scene.

What Is Criminology?

Today, criminology is an established academic subject of study, but this does not mean that criminologists agree on a definition of the field. Those authors of criminology texts who offer a definition (not all do) rarely offer the same one. True, most textbooks depict criminology as the *scientific study of crime as a social phenomenon;* but in more detailed explication important differences emerge. The authors of one current text argue that criminology is "committed to the achievement of an understanding of the roots and manifestations of *different aspects of behavior that violate criminal law*" (italics added).[2] The authors of another text assert that "criminology is concerned with the *immediate application of knowledge to programs of social order and crime control*" (italics added).[3] Some criminologists would strongly disagree with these statements.

While it is comforting to believe that science can be divorced from values or prejudices, this is simply not true. Values enter scientific activity at many points because human beings subscribe to values, and the assumptions and beliefs that go along with them. In criminology, as in other fields of scientific inquiry, we see the impact of values and beliefs in the decisions made about what to investigate, what questions to ask, and what to do with the knowledge acquired. We see the impact of values, also, in how criminologists conceptualize their field and its subject matter. The differences of opinion over the proper definition of *crime* and *criminals* reflect in part the intrusion of values.

This is not wrong. But it warns us not to expect consensus when we seek definitions of criminology. About the only thing on which criminologists do agree is that criminology today is vastly different from what it was 100, 50, or even 25 years ago. And it is different in large part because different values have been expressed in the work criminologists have done and in the questions they have asked.

Conservative, Liberal-Cynical, and Radical Criminology

Don C. Gibbons and Peter Garabedian discuss the competing value-perspectives that have shaped criminology over the years. They identify three major perspectives: conservative, liberal-cynical, and radical (sometimes called "critical").[4]

FROM CONSERVATIVE TO LIBERAL-CYNICAL CRIMINOLOGY

Conservative criminology gained ascendancy in America with the early writings of Parsons, Gillin, and Parmelee, who were among the American pioneers in sociological criminology. Gibbons includes among the conservative criminologists such later contributors as Harry Barnes and Negley Teeters, whose text *New Horizons in Criminology* became a best-seller.

As Gibbons and Garabedian see it, conservative criminology incorporates the following: (1) criminal law is a given and is interpreted as the codification of prevailing moral precepts; (2) in accordance with this view, criminals are looked upon as morally defective; (3) the questions appropriate for the criminologist to study include "How are morally defective persons produced?" and "How can society better protect itself against criminals?"; (4) when dealing with etiological questions conservative criminologists advocate the multifactor approach, emphasizing a combination of personality and biological and environmental factors; and (5) conservative criminology tends to have "*faith in the ultimate perfectability of the police and criminal justice machinery.*"[5]

According to Gibbons and Garabedian, liberal-cynical criminology emerged along with the more sophisticated sociological analyses of crime that began to appear during the 1940s and early 1950s. Because liberal-cynical criminology has dominated the field over the past thirty years, we might also call it "mainstream" criminology.

Early liberal criminology retained the emphasis on offenders and their behavior and attempted to explain crime in terms of either social structure or social process (rarely both). There are three major versions of liberal criminology. *Control* theory states that crime and delinquency result "when an individual's bond to society is weak or broken."[6] When this occurs, conformity to social rules is undermined; a decline in social control follows, allowing more room for individual deviance. *Strain* theory suggests that when people find they cannot achieve valued goals through conventional (i.e., legitimate) means they experience stress and frustration, which in turn may lead to rule-violating behavior. Delinquency and crime are seen as normal adaptations to conditions of discontinuity between means and ends.[7]

The third version of liberal criminology, *cultural (or subcultural) deviance* theory, draws attention to the manner in which people become criminal as they interact with their immediate social environment. This type of theory asserts that delinquency and crime represent *conformity*, but conformity to definitions that are deviant when viewed from the standpoint of the dominant culture. A useful way of looking at this version of liberal criminology is simply to say that "lawbreaking is the result of ordinary learning processes occurring within a crimogenic culture."[8]

More recently, liberal criminology has moved away from the earlier emphasis on crime as behavior and on the offender toward an emphasis on crime as *status* and on the processes of making and enforcing criminal laws. According to the new liberal criminology, society is characterized by conflict, and criminality is the product of power differentials and the struggle to defend group and individual interests. Society's criminals are those who lack power and are unsuccessful in the struggle to defend their interests — lower-class people, blacks, the young, the poor, and other minorities. Criminal law and its enforcement are products of institutionalized power differentials and reflect the ability of some groups to criminalize those who deviate from the standards the powerful support.[9]

Gibbons and Garabedian find the cynical aspect of liberal criminology most often in discussions of the criminal justice system and correctional institutions:

> The sociologist brings to the analysis of these structures the inside dopester's awareness that social organizations are often "screwed up." That is, he knows about all kinds of complex organizations that operate in ways quite different from those sketched in organizational charts or manuals of procedure. This growing sophistication of criminological analysis has been paralleled by a marked decline in the criminologist's faith in the perfectability of the legal-correctional machinery.[10]

The cynical criticism focuses on the failure of police and courts to live up to ideals of justice; the lack of real efforts to treat and rehabilitate offenders; and the failure of juvenile justice both to follow the basic rules of due process and to achieve its long-standing goals of individualized treatment and child care.

RADICAL (OR CRITICAL) CRIMINOLOGY

The liberal-cynical criminologist is skeptical about the perfectability of crime control efforts, and locates crimogenic forces in the basic structure and institutions of society, but he still retains a belief in the continued viability of American society in its present form. In radical criminology such a belief is absent. Further, the radical criminologist rejects the liberal reformism that, it is claimed, "has helped to create probation and parole, the juvenile court system, reformatories and halfway houses, the indeterminate sentence, adjustment and diagnostic centers, public defenders, youth service bureaus," all of which "have served to strengthen the power of the State over the poor, Third World communities and youth."[11]

Gibbons and Garabedian summarize the major thrust of radical criminology, in its most extreme form during the early 1970s:

> First, it is alleged that a relatively small bunch of corporate officials, government leaders, and military men comprise a close-knit power structure bent upon exploiting "the people," both in the United States and in formally colonialized nations elsewhere. Laws have been created as devices for compelling the masses to remain docile. The police are "pigs" who are the mercenaries of oppression, serving as the hired lackeys of powerful interests. Exploitation is most severe in the case of blacks, Chicanos, and other ethnic minorities. Black convicts are political prisoners being held captive as innocent victims of a corrupt, capitalistic, exploitative society. Finally, the police are involved in deliberate policies of genocide, in which they have embarked

upon systematic attempts to murder those Black Panthers and others who have dared to fight against the exploitative system.[12]

More moderate radical criminologists shade into the newer brand of liberal-cynical criminology, but still view crime and the criminal as manifestations of the exploitative character of monopoly capitalism. Unless the present political-economic structure of American capitalistic society is changed, they argue, criminality as we know it today will remain, and the legal machinery will continue to undermine the interests of the people while consolidating those of the rulers.

The Rise of Positivism

The birth of criminology is usually traced to nineteenth-century European scholarship. By the latter half of that century the scientific revolution was well under way. The armchair philosophizing that for centuries had dominated learned discourse on the nature of man and society was replaced by the logic and methodology of objective, empirical science. Observation, measurement, and experimentation became the basic tools of the scientific method, and their use in the study of human behavior and social phenomena heralded the development of disciplines we now take for granted — biology, anthropology, psychiatry, psychology, sociology, and statistics. Europe, if not yet the world, had entered the age of positivism, and crime became one of the phenomena now placed under the microscope of science.

Actually, the notion that crime could be studied objectively through the methods of science had received support early in the nineteenth century in the works of André Michel Guerry and Adolphe Quetelet who, in the 1830s, published important studies of variations in rates of crime and delinquency.[13] These authors linked patterns in crime rates (calculated per capita) to other social, demographic, and ecological variables. As Leon Radzinowicz has observed, "for the first time in history crime became thought of as a social fact moulded by the very environment of which it was an integral part."[14] This was an important break with the classical theorists, who viewed criminal behavior as stemming from man's exercise of free will and his rational pursuit of pleasure (see chapter 13). But equally important, Guerry and Quetelet demonstrated that tools of scientific analysis could be used productively to study crime.

The major impetus to the rise of positivistic criminology was provided by Charles Darwin's work on animal evolution.[15] Darwin's interpreters argued that man's behavior is largely determined by his place on the evolutionary scale and his constant battle with other men for survival. The impact of these factors on an individual was considered to be a matter for empirical investigation; but in any case, behavior was to be understood as a consequence of forces largely beyond individual control.

The Search for the Criminal Type

Influenced by the scientific revolution and the theory of evolution, positivistic criminology took shape in the hands of Cesare Lombroso. A physician attached first to the army and later to prisons and asylums, Lombroso found himself in a position to observe and examine thousands of individuals, many of whom came before him precisely because they were "deviants." Profoundly influenced by the evolutionary doctrine, Lombroso searched for physiological evidence that would provide the link between human behavior, especially its deviant forms, and biological forces.[16]

In 1870 Lombroso found what he took to be evidence of *atavism* (that is, a biological throwback to a more primitive evolutionary state) in the criminals he was studying. This led him to claim a major discovery, that some persons are born criminals and can be identified by certain physical stigmata or anomalies. Among the stigmata observed by Lombroso were an asymmetrical cranium, a receding chin, a low forehead, too many fingers, a sparse beard, low sensitivity to pain, large ears, protruding lips, and peculiarities of the eye. The presence of certain combinations of these stigmata, Lombroso argued, is evidence of a personality predisposed to criminal behavior.

But the born criminal was not the only type of criminal identified by Lombroso, nor did he argue that crime was solely the result of biological forces. He distinguished other categories of criminals, including *insane criminals* (idiots, imbeciles, alcoholics, and others exhibiting degeneracy), *criminaloids* (who had less pronounced physical stigmata and biological degeneracy but were drawn into occasional crime by situational or environmental factors), and *criminals by passion* (who were neither atavistic nor products of degeneracy but were drawn into crime by love, politics, offended honor, or other emotional pressures). The core of his theory was biological, but Lombroso recognized the importance of precipitating situational and environmental factors. He mentioned poverty, emigration, food prices, police corruption, and the changing nature of the law as among the nonbiological determinants of criminal conduct.[17] It was not, however, until one of his followers, Enrico Ferri, undertook his own studies of criminals that the impact of environmental forces received serious attention in positivistic criminology.[18]

Notwithstanding considerable and sometimes bitter criticism of his research methods and his conclusions, Lombroso's ideas had a tremendous impact on the emerging field of criminology. One of the most telling results of his work was the impetus it gave to further research on the individual criminal offender.[19] For more than fifty years scholars in numerous disciplines concentrated their efforts on the criminal. Experts in physiology and physical anthropology, in psychology and psychiatry zeroed in on the offender in attempts to formulate detailed classifications of criminals and to distinguish them from noncriminals.

Many felt strongly that such research would identify traits and characteristics peculiar to criminals. But some were not convinced that the positivists, emphasizing biological factors in the etiology of crime, had really proved their case. These doubters set out to disprove the earlier claims or demonstrate the inadequacies of previous research methodologies. An English physician, Charles Goring, spent nearly ten years seeking to "clear from the ground the remains of the old [Lombrosian] criminology, based on conjecture, prejudice, and questionable observations."[20] Following his careful statistical analysis of data collected on thousands of convicts, Goring concluded that *there is no such thing as a physical criminal type.*"[21]

Goring's conclusion, however, did not stop the search; the urge to demonstrate a connection between criminal behavior and biological traits was still strong. The American anthropologist Earnest A. Hooton studied 13,873 male criminals from ten different states, as well as 3,023 assorted civilians, and claimed to have reestablished the organic inferiority of criminals. Hooton did see environmental factors as precipitating influences, but he clung to the idea of an underlying connection between physical types and criminal behavior. And he even claimed to have demonstrated that physical type is linked to type of criminal behavior: thin, tall men tend to commit murder and robbery; short, heavy men are prone to commit sex and assaultive crimes; and small men commit theft and burglary.[22]

Researchers between 1880 and 1940 piled up what they claimed to be hard evidence of a causal link between criminal behavior and heredity. As Elmer Johnson notes, belief in the biological inheritance of crime has been based on one of two assumptions: (1) that the criminal act itself is inherited, that is, biological structure is somehow connected with behavior; or (2) that "the inheritance of crime is viewed as a propensity, tendency, or mental predisposition which is part of the physical endowment."[23] Studies reflecting these views were conducted on identical twins, on feeblemindedness, on body types, on glandular secretions, and on a host of constitutional variables.[24] And in recent years, research on chromosomal abnormality (the so-called XYY pattern, found in a number of prisoners, including some notorious offenders such as Richard Speck) has been offered as further support for the link between heredity and criminal behavior.[25]

Intelligence and Race   The 1970s have witnessed a renewed interest in biological theories of criminal behavior. The relationship of race and intelligence to crime is once more a popular topic for elaboration and discussion in scientific circles; no less so in criminology.

The new edition of Vold's classic *Theoretical Criminology* (1979; prepared by Thomas Bernard) discusses in some detail the contributions of studies linking race and intelligence with criminal behavior.[26] Much of the work has focused on academic performance rather than broader concepts of intelligence. The basic finding is that boys with lower aptitude or intelligence are more likely to be involved in delinquency and crime, as reported by the police or by their own admission. In a recent review of the evidence, Hirschi and Hindelang argue that intelligence is directly related to delinquency, and they call for renewed efforts to incorporate that fact into criminological theory.[27]

Although there is a developing consensus that intelligence and delinquency are related, eyebrows are raised when the discussion turns to race. We are all very sensitive to racial matters, especially when there is any suggestion that one racial group is innately inferior to another. Some scholars believe that as much as 80 percent of intelligence is inherited. When blacks score consistently lower on intelligence tests than whites, these researchers reach the following conclusion: blacks are less intelligent because they are blacks.[28] When we then observe that blacks are overrepresented in almost every statistic on serious crime (especially violent offenses),[29] it is easy to conclude that differences in criminality between blacks and whites are the result of genetic differences in intelligence (or some other mental trait to which it relates).

Few criminologists go this far, recognizing, perhaps, that the genetic contribution to intelligence is still in doubt. Most do acknowledge that there is a relationship between race and crime as well as one between intelligence and crime; however, they look for evidence of environmental differences (neighborhood, upbringing, schools, economic conditions, and so on) that might account for this correlation. Some scientists argue that intelligence tests are biased in favor of middle-class whites, leaving black students at a disadvantage. Others blame the relatively greater incidence of black criminality on biases in the criminal justice system: blacks are more likely to be arrested than whites. This tendency might be interpreted in a different way: rather than being the object of discrimination by law enforcement officials, it is the less intelligent offender who is likely to be caught. The evidence for this is not at all compelling, but the idea persists in some circles.[30]

We are a long way from categorical answers to the intelligence-race-criminality puzzle. Bernard is correct in cautioning that "low intelligence" will probably not get much mileage as an explanation of crime in general: "It does not account for fluctuations in crime rates in the population at large or within a specific group, and it fails to take into account white collar crime, organized crime (particularly its leadership), and political crime — all of which require considerable intellectual ability."[31]

Psychogenic Approaches Other investigators, meanwhile, were pursuing the psychogenic approach to criminality, in which the emphasis is on linking criminal behavior to mental states, especially mental disease, mental disorders, pathologies, and emotional problems. Evidence in support of such a connection came from research on personality defects and disorders in delinquents, on mental disease in prisoners, on parent-child interactions, on the psychopathic personality and its cousin the sociopathic personality, and on the subconscious (or unconscious) repression of drives and desires.[32]

Recently, the work of Yochelson and Samenow has been received with much fanfare. *The Criminal Personality* records the authors' research at St. Elizabeths Hospital in Washington, D.C., over more than a decade.[33] Their goal was to change the behavior of 240 criminals, mostly hard-core adult offenders. Their work is especially noteworthy, not only because it breaks with traditional psychiatry, but because it advocates the position that criminal behavior is a manifestation of the offender's exercise of free will, rather than of environmental influence:

> It is not the environment that turns a man into a criminal. Rather, it is a series of choices that he makes starting at a very early age. . . . There is a continuity in his thinking and action regardless of setting. . . . Crime does not come to him; he goes to it. . . . He seeks out other delinquents. . . . By the time he is apprehended, he has more than likely committed hundreds, if not thousands, of offenses. . . . The excitement that is involved [in crime] is what is important. . . .[34]

Throughout their account, Yochelson and Samenow stress the calculating, hedonistic personality of their subjects. In this they remind us of the classical school of criminological thought, as seen in the works of Beccaria and Bentham (see chapter 13). The authors firmly believe that crime can be deterred, but whereas conventional views of deterrence stress the use of external threats and sanctions (such as stiff penalties, rigorously applied), Yochelson and Samenow favor the development of internal deterrents to crime: deter the person from *thinking* in criminal ways and you will reduce the likelihood of his *acting* in criminal ways.

Although we cannot give a detailed account of Yochelson and Samenow's thesis here, we should nevertheless be alerted to some major problems with their work. Bernard has criticized their methodology:

> The assertion is made that criminals think in a certain way, and this statement is supported with several examples to illustrate it. That format has no scientific validity, since literally any statement can be made in a similar way. One can say: "All criminals come from bad home environments — for example, Joe's father beat him and his mother drank. . . ." and so on. No terms are operationally defined, no indication is given as to how it was ascertained that all these thinking patterns were present in all the 240 subjects involved in the experiment, or why it is thought that these traits, which are found in a highly selected population . . . would be found in the general population of criminals.[35]

Even more alarming, from the standpoint of theory, is the fact that whereas the authors repeatedly assert that crime is a consequence of the way criminals think, they do not say how that thinking arises in the first place. Since environmental influences are apparently ruled out, one is tempted to believe that it must be something in the criminal's biological makeup. But why do Yochelson and Samenow emphasize that "what is particularly striking is that *siblings* within the same home can turn out so differently" (italics added)?[36] If the root cause of criminal thinking is neither environmental nor biological, then what is it? The answer is unclear.

Some difficulties and problems are common to much of the biogenic and psychogenic research that has been done. On the conceptual level, vagueness and ambiguity seem to be the rule rather than the exception. Even when concepts have been defined with care, problems have plagued the effort to move from the theoretical to the empirical level. In psychogenic research, concepts such as intelligence, psychopathy, sociopathy, feeblemindedness, and drives have been bandied about even though experts disagree on how to define them, let alone measure them. Another conceptual problem is that crime has received a restrictive, behavioristic conception and little attention has been paid to its relativity or the manner in which it is created. An underlying assumption seems to have been that something constant and inherent in behavior distinguishes the criminal from the noncriminal. Also, some authors have tended to wish away the interaction between environmental forces and the biological or psychological. Their thinking has been shaped by a belief in the existence of a single, basic cause of crime, or else they have conveniently sidestepped the problem of separating one realm of etiological influence from another. This has plagued the research on heredity and crime in particular. Even when environmental influences are acknowledged, separating them from biological influences proves virtually impossible.[37]

Criticisms of the methodological strategies used in biogenic and psychogenic research have been many. Experimental research has often lacked the essential control group without which the impact of variable manipulation cannot be properly assessed. When control groups have been used, they have been either too small or unrepresentative of the population as a whole. The problem of unrepresentativeness has also plagued much of the research trying to identify traits or characteristics of offenders based on samples of prisoners or juvenile delinquents. Such samples are rarely, if ever, representative of all offenders to which the research relates. Further, it is not always clear precisely how some samples were produced — this has been a major criticism of William Sheldon's work on body types and temperament[38] — and many scholars have succumbed to temptation and generalized on the basis of evidence drawn from extremely small samples. In addition, the desire to find the cause or causes of crime has led too many scholars to assert causality on the basis of findings of mere statistical association.

Some critics take exception to an entire field of criminological research on methodological grounds, as in the case of psychoanalysis. George Vold has written: "A methodology under which only the patient knows the 'facts' of the case, and only the analyst understands the meaning of those 'facts' as revealed to him by the patient, does not lend itself to external, third person, impersonal verification or to generalizations beyond the limits of any particular case."[39] For those who believe that crime can and should be the object of verifiable scientific analysis such a criticism is a devastating indictment of the psychoanalytical approach, and it leads them to reject the approach and its findings.

Multifactor Approaches

A long-standing criticism of the early biogenic and psychogenic approaches to crime has been that much of the work centered around the search for a single factor (or single set of like factors) that could be shown to account for all criminal behavior. Thus, biological degeneracy, or feeblemindedness, or psychopathy was held up as the single cause of crime. Yet if feeblemindedness, or poverty, or broken homes, or race was the only cause of crime, the other factors could not also be. The result was "much rancor and argument among the theorists whose approach to the problem of crime was mutually antagonistic."[40] Theorists held steadfastly to their views despite competing evidence piled up through the research efforts of their colleagues.

The multifactor approach in criminology grew out of the discrepancies and arguments attending the single-factor tradition of the early days. Its adherents argued for an approach to crime that would reconcile the disparate orientations and generate an explanation of crime based on an assessment of the contributions made by a variety of factors. The underlying assumption was that crime is the product of many factors — biological, psychological, social — and that different crimes will be the result of different combinations of factors. Hence the "proper" approach in criminology is an eclectic one emphasizing the identification and analysis of multiple factors.

Ferri and many other early criminologists recognized some of the inadequacies of the single-factor approach and in their own work sought to identify a variety of crimogenic factors. But the multifactor approach gained its momentum from the research efforts of William Healy, the English scholar Cyril Burt, and Sheldon and Eleanor Glueck.

Healy engaged in a five-year study of nearly 1,000 delinquency cases brought before juvenile court authorities.[41] He was interested solely in the identification of any "causal factor" present among his subjects. The result was a list of 138 distinct delinquency factors, most of which were psychological, though some were biological or social-environmental. Clearly influenced by Healy's work, Burt pursued a similar investigation in England, and he found no less than 170 distinct delinquency factors, which he classified into nine major categories.[42] For their part, the Gluecks published a series of studies focusing on sociocultural, biological, and psychological factors in a search for correlates of delinquency. In their best-known work, *Unraveling Juvenile Delinquency,* the Gluecks matched 500 "delinquents" with 500 "nondelinquents" on a number of dimensions, including residence, age, and general intelligence.[43] They then looked for delinquency factors in an extensive analysis of social background, home life, physical characteristics, intellectual ability, psychiatric states, emotion, and temperament. They concluded that while a host of different factors show statistical associations with delinquency, the major causes of delinquency are problems in the home (parental separation or prolonged absence; parental drunkenness and other physical or mental ailments; poor home management; lack of child supervision; or little show of affection toward child or children).

CRITICISMS OF THE MULTIFACTOR APPROACH

The multifactor approach has not gone without criticism. The most frequent criticisms were those advanced some years ago by Albert K. Cohen.[44] While recognizing that the approach made a useful contribution to criminology through the compilation of factors associated with delinquency, Cohen took it to task for three reasons. First, advocates of the approach have tended to eschew the search for integrated theories of criminality, arguing that such efforts are futile given the multiplicity of factors associated with crime. By the same token, they have rejected as too narrow and particularistic the explanations offered by their colleagues. Cohen observed, however, that they seem to have confused explanation *by means of a single theory* with single-factor explanations. A list of factors associated with crime is not an explanation of crime; nor does a single theory necessarily explain crime in terms of a single factor. Theories are concerned with *variables* (aspects or characteristics of things that vary with respect to other aspects or characteristics) not factors, and a single theory usually incorporates a number of different variables. To explain crime we need theories, which consist of logically related statements asserting particular relationships among a number of variables.

Second, Cohen objected to a major assumption of the multifactor approach, namely, that factors have intrinsic crime-producing qualities. Factors found statistically associated with crime are often asserted to cause crime, or to be one cause among others. Each factor is presumed to carry a fixed amount of crimogenic power. But, argues Cohen, not only do factors have no intrinsic crime-producing qualities, but they should not be confused with causes. Causal power cannot be assumed on the basis of a discovery that a certain factor, or combination of factors, shows a statistical association with crime.

Finally, Cohen observed that many, if not most, multifactor studies have run afoul of the "evil causes evil" fallacy. The fallacious notion is that evil consequences (crime) must have evil precedents (biological pathologies, low IQ, pathological mental states, sordid living conditions). Sutherland and Cressey make the following observation on this point and bring to mind some of the issues mentioned earlier in connection with liberal-cynical criminology:

> Thus, when we "explain" crime or almost any other "social problem," we tend merely to catalog a series of sordid and ugly circumstances which any "decent citizen" would deplore, and attribute causal power to those circumstances. In criminology, this fallacious procedure might stem from a desire to eradicate crime without changing other existing conditions which we cherish and esteem; that is, criminologists tend to identify with the existing social order and seek "causes" of crime in "factors" which might be eliminated without changing social conditions which they hold dear, or which may be safely deplored without hurting anyone's feelings.[45]

Despite its shortcomings, the multifactor approach has remained a major research orientation in criminology.[46]

MULTIFACTOR RESEARCH IN SOCIOLOGICAL CRIMINOLOGY

Sociological investigations of crime and delinquency factors have given considerable attention to the so-called sins of cities.[47] Much of the work focusing on crime-producing features of city environments has come out of the specialty known as *human ecology,* which is the study of the relationship between human beings and the physical and social space they occupy. Ecological studies of crime came into their own during the early twentieth century, and were especially prominent at the University of Chicago. But even before that time, interest in criminal ecology had been growing, spurred on by the research of Quetelet and Guerry and two monumental nineteenth-century English works — Henry Mayhew's *London Labour and the London Poor* and Charles Booth's *Life and Labour of the People of London.*

Led by Robert E. Park and E. W. Burgess, sociologists at the University of Chicago published a series of studies uncovering numerous environmental correlates of crime and delinquency.[48] The label "delinquency (or delinquent) areas" was introduced and applied to those areas of Chicago displaying the highest delinquency rates. Upon examination, these areas were found to be close to the central business district and to be areas of population transition. They were chararacterized by slum conditions, overcrowding, mobility and migration, physical deterioration, concentrations of black and foreign-born residents, concentrated poverty, lack of home ownership, lack of locally supported community organizations, and concentrations of unskilled and unemployed workers.[49] Later work showed that these areas also had high rates of school truancy, young-adult crime, infant mortality, tuberculosis, and mental disorder.

Research findings from other cities — for example, Boston, Cincinnati, and Philadelphia — supported the earlier claims that crime and delinquency-producing factors were inherent in communities experiencing population transition and social disorganization.[50] In a report to the 1931 National Commission on Law Observance and Enforcement, Clifford Shaw — the major figure in delinquency area studies — summarized the process of delinquency concentration:

> In the process of city growth, the neighborhood organizations, cultural institutions and social standards in practically all of the areas adjacent to the central business district and the major industrial centers are subject to rapid change and disorganization. The gradual invasion of these areas by industry and commerce, the continuous movement of the older residents out of the area and the influx of newer groups, the confusion of many divergent cultural standards, the economic insecurity of the families, all combine to render difficult the development of a stable and efficient neighborhood organization for the education and control of the child and the suppression of lawlessness.[51]

Social Structural Theories of Crime and Delinquency

Human ecologists look at the impact of social and physical environments on the behavior of individuals and groups. In broader terms, their work is part of sociologists' continuing interest in the impact of *social structure* — the organization of social relationships and group interactions — on behavior.

Theories of crime and delinquency emphasizing social structure have sought to explain crime as normal rather than abnormal or pathological social behavior. By *normal,* sociologists mean that something is a characteristic feature of social life. The idea that crime is normal was first developed by Emile Durkheim, the nineteenth-century French sociologist:

> Crime is present not only in the majority of societies of one particular species but in all societies of all types. There is no society that is not confronted with the problem of criminality. Its form changes; the acts thus characterized are not the same everywhere; but, everywhere and always, there have been men who have behaved in such a way as to draw upon themselves penal repression. . . . There is . . . no phenomenon that presents more indisputably all the symptoms of normality, since it appears closely connected with the conditions of all collective life.[52]

If crime is normal, why is it not distributed evenly throughout society? This is the basic question underlying social structural theories of crime. These theories have sought to explain variations in *rates* of criminality; that is, in criminality as an attribute of a population rather than as a characteristic of an individual.

MEANS, GOALS, AND OPPORTUNITIES

In *Suicide,* Durkheim used the term *anomie* (sometimes spelled *anomy*) to refer to a social condition in which "normlessness" prevails; that is, in which the system of regulations and restraint has broken down such that individuals suffer a loss of external guidance and control in their goal-seeking endeavors.[53] The structure regulating social relationships is disrupted and social cohesion and solidarity are undermined. According to Durkheim, anomie is most likely during periods of rapid social change, when traditional norms prove ineffective in regulating human conduct but new modes have not yet been accepted.

Robert K. Merton has extended and elaborated on Durkheim's notion of anomie, making it the central feature of a *strain* theory of crime.[54] In Merton's view, pressures are exerted on some segments of society to engage in crime, and these pressures relate directly to structural arrangements conducive to a state of anomie. Merton argues that all social structures establish institutionalized means for the attainment of culturally supported goals. These means and goals, however, are not always in a state of harmony or integration. In some societies there may be much stress on goals and little concern with the prescribed means for achieving them; in others there may be a ritualistic concern with the means to achieve goals but little emphasis on the goals themselves. In between these polar situations are varying states of means-goals integration.

Looking at American society — and we should note that he was writing in the 1930s — Merton argues that a state of anomie exists because goals receive structural emphasis, but the means to achieve them do not. He describes America as a society with an inordinate emphasis on success goals, represented mainly by the possession and consumption of goods and services that are held up as achievable by all. Not all segments of society, however, have the same access to these goals, for the institutionalized means are not distributed evenly throughout the population. Rather, structural arrangements are such that certain segments of the population — especially blacks, the lower classes, and the poor — are routinely denied access to legitimate means of achievement. The accepted routes to success — a good education, the "right" background, promotions, managerial and other skilled jobs — typically are not the routes open to such people.

What happens? In Merton's view a number of "modes of adaptation" are possible. One is *conformity,* or acceptance of the prevailing state of affairs. A second is *innovation,* in which the goals are accepted while the means are rejected and alternatives are substituted in their place. A third is *ritualism,* in which socially approved means are given particular emphasis and cultural goals more or less rejected. A fourth is *retreatism,* a rejection of both culturally suported goals and institutionalized means. Finally there is *rebellion,* a rejection of means and ends coupled with the substitution of new means and goals — in other words, an attempt to introduce a new social order.[55]

Merton offers his category of *innovation* in support of the argued link between anomie and crime (mostly property crime). The innovator, in rejecting institutionalized means and substituting alternatives, is likely to find that the new means are illegal ones, and his actions crimes. Innovation is thus the key mode of adaptation in Merton's theory of anomie and crime, and he uses it to explain the high crime rates among lower-class, poor segments of the population. Their disadvantaged status coupled with the high cultural priority given to pecuniary success as a dominant goal for all make high rates of crime a "normal outcome" for those segments of the American population.[56]

LOWER-CLASS CRIMINALITY

Ecological studies of crime and Merton's theory of anomie and deviance made much of the high rates of crime officially observed among the lower classes. From 1940 to 1960 lower-class criminality received considerable sociological interest, and a number of theories were advanced purporting to explain the high crime rates. Most of these theories retained a social structural emphasis, though they differed in some important specifics.

Delinquent Subcultures or Cultural Deviancy   A number of theories during this period focused on what is called the "delinquent subculture." Any heterogeneous society is likely to have a parent or dominant culture and a number of different subcultures (see pages 120–123 for a fuller discussion of subcultures). The *dominant culture* consists of the beliefs, attitudes, symbols, ways of behavior, meanings, ideas, values, and norms shared by those who regularly make up the membership of a society; *subcultures* differ from the dominant culture and consist of the beliefs and values shared by members of identifiable subgroups of the society. The differences between a subculture and the parent culture and between subcultures themselves are a function of differences in life experiences and social conditions.

According to the authors of one important theory in criminology, a *delinquent subculture* "is one in which certain forms of delinquent activity are essential for the performance of the dominant roles supported by the subculture. It is the central position accorded to specifically delinquent activity that distinguishes the delinquent subculture from other deviant subcultures."[57] In terms of the subculture's norms, values, and expectations, delinquent activity is supported as right and proper and assumes a central place in the life-style of the membership.

Based on research with lower-class delinquent gangs, a number of authors have offered subcultural theories of delinquency. Albert K. Cohen, for example, suggests that high rates of lower-class delinquency reflect a basic conflict between lower-class youth subculture and the dominant middle-class culture. The delinquent subculture arises as a reaction to the dominant culture that effectively discriminates against lower-class members of society. Exhorted in school and elsewhere to strive for middle-class goals and behave according to middle-class values (be orderly, clean, responsible, ambitious, and so forth), lower-class youths find that their socialization experiences have not prepared them for the challenge. They become "status frustrated" as a result of their inability to meet middle-class standards and goals, and in reaction turn to delinquent activities and form delinquency-centered groups as an alternative to status, autonomy, and control. The resulting delinquency is characterized by Cohen as *nonutilitarian* (they steal, for example, "for the hell of it"), *malicious* (they derive "enjoyment in the discomfort of others"), and *negativistic* (they take pride in doing things precisely because they are wrong by middle-class standards).[58]

An alternative theory of delinquency is offered by Richard A. Cloward and Lloyd E. Ohlin. In *Delinquency and Opportunity,* these authors begin with the theories of Durkheim and Merton and argue that "marked discrepancies between culturally induced aspirations . . . and the possibilities for achieving them by legitimate means" exist for certain segments of the population, especially the youth of the lower classes. This condition produces pressures toward the formation of delinquent subcultures:

> Our hypothesis can be summarized as follows: The disparity between what lower class youth are led to want and what is actually available to them is the source of a major problem of adjustment. Adolescents who have formed delinquent subcultures, we suggest, have internalized an emphasis upon conventional goals. Faced with limitations on legitimate avenues of access to these goals, and unable to revise their aspirations downward, they experience intense frustrations; the exploration of nonconformist alternatives may be the result.[59]

Cloward and Ohlin find three major kinds of delinquent subcultures in which the bulk of delinquents participate. *Criminal subcultures* — characterized by illegal money-making activities and often providing a stepping-stone toward adult criminal careers — tend to arise in those lower-class slum areas with relatively stable accommodative relationships between adult carriers of conventional and criminal values and with relatively well-organized age hierarchies of criminal involvement. The latter condition provides the young with criminal role models and encourages their recruitment into instrumental crime; the former condition is illustrated by established adult roles such as "fixer" and "fence," and helps encourage and facilitate involvement in illegal money-making activities as the appropriate alternative route to success goals.

The *conflict subculture,* dominated by gang fighting and acts of violence, arises in disorganized slum areas with weak social controls, an absence of institutionalized channels to success goals, either legitimate or illegitimate, and a predominance of personal failure. Violence is a route to status besides being a release for pent-up frustrations. The *retreatist subculture,* marked by the prevalence of drug use and addiction, emerges as an adaptation for some lower-class youths when they have failed in both the criminal or conflict subcultures, or have failed to take good advantage of either the legitimate or illegitimate opportunity structures. Members of this subculture disengage from the competitive struggle for success goals.

Lower-Class Life and "Focal Concerns"   Social structural theories of lower-class criminality owe much to Walter B. Miller's contribution.[60] Focusing primarily on youthful gangs, Miller argues that lower-class cultural prescriptions and expectations encourage delinquent behavior. Developing in response to structural patterns such as material and social deprivation or female-led households, lower- or working-class culture emphasizes certain issues or themes. These themes then come to command widespread attention, and a high degree of emotional commitment is attached to them. These "focal concerns" include "toughness," "trouble" (a concern to avoid entanglements with the authorities), "smartness" (being able to con, or outwit, others; being able to hustle), "autonomy" (remaining free from domination or control by other people), and "excitement" (avoiding routine and monotony; getting kicks).

Merely to engage in some of the activities shaped by these focal concerns is to be delinquent, for the law, reflecting the dominant standards of middle-class society, has defined them as such. But even when given a choice, the "deviant" activity (frequently illegal) is often considered the most attractive because reference-group norms and peer-group pressures point to it as a means of acquiring prestige, status, and respect.

To summarize, these theories purport to show a relationship between the organization or structure of society and the behavior of people. The almost exclusive focus on lower-class delinquency obviously limits the scope of the theories, and no author claims to have advanced a theory of crime or delinquency that is applicable to all types of crime and all types of offenders in all situations. Yet by emphasizing lower-class criminality as the focus for criminological theory, they give encouragement to those who persist in viewing crime as a lower-class phenomenon. In addition, these theorists have not concerned themselves with the problematic nature of crime or delinquency, but have chosen instead to accept the objective existence of crime and criminals, and to assume that these differ inherently from noncrimes and noncriminals. These theories make conflicting claims, and, though every theory can claim some empirical support, *no single theory can claim an abundance in its favor.*[61] The fact is that we are still a long way from a social structural explanation of crime, or even of lower-class delinquency. The value of these theories lies in their identification of some of the routes to delinquency (as behavior) and in their efforts to relate social structure to patterns of human conduct. That they have also served to shift the emphasis in criminology away from the individual offender and the idea that he or she is somehow abnormal or defective is also important.

Social Process Theories

A common observation regarding social structural theories is that they fail to explain why some of those exposed to a particular "crime-producing" structure are not criminals or delinquents, and why some of those not so exposed do commit crimes or delinquent acts. Criminologists who view crime from a *social process* perspective try to answer those questions.

Social process theories are concerned with the steps individuals go through in acquiring temporary or permanent attributes. In criminology, social process theories attempt to describe and explain the processes by which individuals become criminals. They deal with the links between an individual's immediate social world and his motivations, perceptions, self-conceptions, attitudes, and behavior. An underlying assumption is that criminal behavior can be analyzed within the same theoretical framework as noncriminal behavior. A common theme in many social process theories is that, like any other kind of social behavior, criminal behavior is learned; accordingly, they place much emphasis on the manner in which learning takes place and on the factors thought to affect the content of learning.

DIFFERENTIAL ASSOCIATION

In the 1939 edition of *Principles of Criminology,* Edwin H. Sutherland introduced the *theory of differential association.* According to this theory, which has remained unchanged but for some slight modifications made in 1947, criminal behavior patterns are acquired through processes of interaction and communication just as are other behavior patterns. The principle of differential association accounts for the behavior pattern acquired through these processes. Individuals acquire criminal behavior patterns because they are exposed to situations in which the learning of definitions favorable to lawbreaking outweighs the learning of definitions unfavorable to lawbreaking. The theory as a whole consists of the following nine statements or propositions:

1. Criminal behavior is learned.
2. Criminal behavior is learned in interaction with other persons in a process of communication.
3. The principal part of the learning of criminal behavior occurs within intimate personal groups.

4. When criminal behavior is learned, the learning includes (a) techniques of committing the crime, which are sometimes very complicated, sometimes very simple; and (b) the specific direction of motives, drives, rationalizations, and attitudes.
5. The specific direction of motives and drives is learned from definitions of the legal codes as favorable or unfavorable.
6. A person becomes delinquent because of an excess of definitions favorable to violation of law [the principle of differential association].
7. Differential associations may vary in frequency, duration, priority, and intensity.
8. The process of learning criminal behavior by association with criminal and anticriminal-patterns involves all of the mechanisms that are involved in any other learning.
9. While criminal behavior is an expression of general needs and values, it is not explained by those general needs and values, since noncriminal behavior is an expression of the same needs and values.[62]

Two important observations should be made about this theory. First, the theory of differential association purports to explain noncriminal as well as criminal behavior. That is, noncriminal behavior emerges because of an excess of definitions unfavorable to law violation. Second, the theory can be used to explain variations in crime rates as well as individual criminality. While the theory focuses on how individuals come to engage in criminal behavior, a compatible explanation of variations in crime rates is possible. Donald R. Cressey argues as follows:

> The differential association statement . . . is a "principle of normative conflict" which proposes that high crime rates occur in societies and groups characterized by conditions that lead to the development of extensive criminalistic subcultures. The principle makes sense of variations in crime rates by observing that modern societies are organized for crime as well as against it, and then observing further that crime rates are unequally distributed because of differences in the degree to which various categories of persons participate in this normative conflict.[63]

Accordingly, high crime rates are predicted for areas and groups having a social organization with extensive exposure to definitions favorable to law violation and with a high probability that such definitions will be learned by a significant proportion of the population.

It is fair to say that the theory of differential association must be counted as one of the most influential contributions to modern criminology. This is not to say that it has not come under fire. Few theories have been subjected to more extensive criticism. The points of contention have been many, ranging from objections to words and individual propositions to the theory as a whole. Among the major criticisms are: (1) the theory is stated in language which is at times neither precise nor clear; (2) major concepts, such as "definitions favorable to law violation," cannot be measured; (3) because they cannot be measured the theory cannot be tested; (4) the theory does not take into account personality traits, personality factors, or psychological variables in criminal behavior; and (5) the theory does not explain the "differential response" patterns that emerge when different individuals are exposed to the same situation.[64]

C. Ray Jeffery has raised many questions concerning differential association theory. For example, if criminality is learned it must first exist; what accounts for that first criminal act? How are crimes of passion to be explained? How do we account for criminal behavior in people who have had no prior contact with criminals or their attitudes?[65]

Modifications of Differential Association Theory   Daniel Glaser has argued that a theory of criminal behavior based on patterns of association must acknowledge the complexity of association itself, which he claims Sutherland's theory does not do. Accordingly, Glaser proposed that Sutherland's theory be reconceptualized to place greater emphasis on the identification processes that go on in all forms of interaction between an individual and his environment (including himself). The term *differential identification* was used to identify the core process in Glaser's scheme. "A person," he argued, "pursues criminal behavior to the extent that he identifies himself with real or imaginary persons from whose perspective his criminal behavior seems acceptable."[66] The individuals' particular associations provide them with opportunities for identification with others. During the course of interaction, the individual selects persons with whom he will identify, and these serve as models for his own behavior. But this selection also occurs in contexts other than the immediate groups to which an individual belongs. Hence Glaser acknowledges what Sutherland did not: the possibility that portrayal of criminal roles in mass media is linked with the adoption of criminal behavior patterns. The theory of differential identification considers relevant any and all features of a person's world to the extent that they affect his choice of others with whom to identify.

Among the notable efforts to rework Sutherland's theory of differential association is the contribution of Robert Burgess and Ronald Akers.[67] These authors attempted a restatement of the theory based on a body of modern learning theory asserting that behavior is learned through a process called *operant conditioning*. According to this view, social actions are repeated (or not repeated) as a consequence of their association in the actor's mind with punishing or rewarding experiences. If the response has been punished in the past, the tendency is not to repeat the particular behavior; if, however, the response has been rewarded, the behavior in question has been *reinforced* and will tend to be repeated. The notion of reinforcement is central, then, to the explanation of the learning of social behavior. Applied to criminal behavior, the operant conditioning–reinforcement theory advanced by Burgess and Akers asserts that people engage in crime because it has been more highly reinforced in the past

THE DIFFERENTIAL ASSOCIATION–REINFORCEMENT THEORY OF CRIMINAL BEHAVIOR

1. Criminal behavior is learned according to the principles of operant conditioning.
2. Criminal behavior is learned both in nonsocial situations that are reinforcing or discriminative and through that social interaction in which the behavior of other persons is reinforcing or discriminative for criminal behavior.
3. The principal part of the learning of criminal behavior occurs in those groups which comprise the individual's major source of reinforcements.
4. The learning of criminal behavior, including specific techniques, attitudes, and avoidance procedures, is a function of the effective and available reinforcers, and the existing reinforcement contingencies.
5. The specific class of behaviors which are learned and their frequency of occurrence are a function of the reinforcers which are effective and available, and the rules and norms by which these reinforcers are applied.
6. Criminal behavior is a function of norms which are discriminative for criminal behavior, the learning of which takes place when such behavior is more highly reinforced than noncriminal behavior.
7. The strength of criminal behavior is a direct function of the amount, frequency, and probability of its reinforcement.

SOURCE: Robert L. Burgess and Ronald L. Akers, "A Differential Association–Reinforcement Theory of Criminal Behavior," *Social Problems* 14:2 (Fall 1966), adaptation of table 1, p. 146. Copyright 1966 by the Society for the Study of Social Problems. Reprinted by permission.

than other behavior. That some people become criminals while others do not they explain by noting that all people do not go through the same socialization process, during which the reinforcement of criminal and other social behavior occurs, nor are they exposed to the same nonsocial situations of reinforcement.[68] (For a complete statement of the Burgess and Akers theory, see box above).

Attempts have been made to test Sutherland's original theory — which is no easy venture — but the outcomes, not to mention methodologies, have been inconsistent. What support has been shown for the theory has not been strong.[69] For the differential association–reinforcement theory of Burgess and Akers, results have generally shown more promise.[70] In addition, where Sutherland is primarily concerned with the appearance or acquisition of behavior, Burgess and Akers deal with both appearance and maintenance. Consider the opiate user. According to the differential association–reinforcement theory, individuals *become* drug users because the reinforcing effects of the drug itself combine with social reinforcements such as peer group approval. They *continue* as users for the same reasons; however, if addiction occurs, use is further reinforced because it allows the addict to avoid the distress of withdrawal. If an addict succeeds in breaking his physiological dependence on the drug, however, he may yet *relapse* into its use because reinforcements gained through association with others are once again combined with the reinforcing effects — the "jolt," "kick," euphoria — of the drug. And so the cycle continues.[71]

SELF-CONCEPT IN CRIMINOLOGY

The theories reviewed in the preceding section share a common emphasis in that they draw attention to socialization processes. Learning, communication, and interaction are key elements in socialization, and it is through these mechanisms that individuals acquire the personal organization, or personality, that marks them as human beings.[72] Personal organization consists of many things, including motivations, ideas and beliefs, perceptions, feelings about things, preferences, attitudes, values, self-control and inhibitions, and an awareness or sense of self.

In dealing with the question, "Why do people behave the way they do?" psychologists, social psychologists, and sociologists have long asserted a connection between personality and behavior. While their perspective on the connection will be shaped in part by their particular discipline, scholars in these fields have generally agreed that a sense of self, or self-concept, is an element in personal organization deserving serious attention in efforts to explain behavior. In criminology, interest in self-concept gained momentum during the 1950s and remains strong today.

One of the major contributors to theory and research linking self-concept with delinquent and criminal behavior has been Walter Reckless.[73] Reckless has pursued the argument that the individual confronted by choices of action will feel a variety of "pulls" and "pushes." The pulls are environmental factors — such as adverse living conditions, poverty, lack of legitimate opportunities, abundance of illegitimate opportunities, or family problems — that serve to pressure the individual away from the norms and values of the dominant society. The pushes take the form of internal pressures — hostility, biopsychological impairments, aggressiveness, drives, or wishes — that may also divert the individual away from actions supported by dominant values and norms.

But not all people faced with the same pulls and pushes become delinquent or criminal. To explain why some do not, Reckless advances the idea of *containment*. According to Reckless, there are two kinds of containment, inner and outer:

> Inner containment consists mainly of self components, such as self-control, good self-concept, ego strength, well-developed superego, high frustration tolerance, high resistance to diversions, high sense of responsibility, goal orientation, ability to find substitute satisfactions, tension-reducing rationalizations, and so on. These are the inner regulators.
>
> Outer containment represents the structural buffer in the person's immediate social world which is able to hold him within bounds. It consists of such items as a presentation of a consistent moral front to the person, institutional reinforcement of his norms, goals, and expectations, the existence of a reasonable set of social expectations, effective supervision and discipline (social controls), provision for reasonable scope of activity (including limits and responsibilities) as well as for alternatives and safety-valves, opportunity for

acceptance, identity, and belongingness. Such structural ingredients help the family and other supportive groups contain the individual.[74]

In Reckless's view, it is the inner control system, primarily self-concept, that provides a person with the strongest defense against delinquency involvement. Commenting on the results of a follow-up study of white schoolboys in high-delinquency areas in Columbus, Ohio, Reckless and Dinitz observe:

> In our quest to discover what insulates a boy against delinquency in a high delinquency area, we believe we have some tangible evidence that a good self-concept, undoubtedly a product of favorable socialization, veers slum boys away from delinquency, while a poor self-concept, a product of unfavorable socialization, gives the slum boy no resistance to deviancy, delinquent companions, or delinquent subculture. We feel that components of the self strength, such as a favorable concept of self, act as an inner buffer or inner containment against deviancy, distraction, lure, and pressures.[75]

The work of Reckless and his associates has not gone without criticism.[76] Interest in self-concept and its connection with criminality, however, has remained very much alive in some circles. One interesting theoretical contribution bearing on self-concept comes from David Matza and Gresham Sykes. Matza, in *Delinquency and Drift,* argues that individuals are rarely committed to or compelled to perform delinquent or criminal behavior.[77] Rather, they drift into and out of it, retaining a commitment neither to convention nor to crime.

In Matza's view, delinquency does not reflect commitment to values and norms that oppose those of the dominant society. In addition, delinquents are never totally immune from the demands for conformity made by the dominant social order. At most they are merely flexible in their commitment to them. In a joint publication, Sykes and Matza argue that evidence shows that if delinquents do form subcultures in opposition to dominant society, they are surprisingly weak in their commitment to them. They show guilt and shame though one would expect none; they "frequently" accord respect and admiration to the "really honest" person and to law-abiding people in their immediate social environment; and they often draw a sharp line between appropriate victims and those who are not fair game; all of which suggests that "the virtue of delinquency is far from unquestioned."[78] In terms of the dominant normative order, the delinquent appears to be both conforming and nonconforming.

Sykes and Matza argue that in order to practice nonconformity, the delinquent must somehow handle the demands for conformity to which he accords at least some recognition. In the view of these authors he handles those demands *by neutralizing them in advance of violating them.* That is, he redefines his contemplated action, putting it in the category of "acceptable" if not "right" behavior. The authors identify five "techniques of neutralization" that facilitate the juvenile's drift into delinquency: (1) *denial of responsibility* ("such-and-such causes me to do it; I am helpless"); (2) *denial of injury* ("my action won't hurt anyone"); (3) *denial of the victim* ("so-and-so deserves it"); (4) *condemnation of the condemners* ("those who condemn me are worse than I am"); and (5) *appeal to higher loyalties* ("my friends come first, so I must do it"). Yet Sykes and Matza caution us:

> Techniques of neutralization may not be powerful enough to fully shield the individual from the force of his own internalized values and the reactions of conforming others, for as we have pointed out, juvenile delinquents often appear to suffer from feelings of guilt and shame when called into account for their deviant behavior. And some delinquents may be so isolated from the world of conformity that techniques of neutralization need not be called into play. Nonetheless, we would argue that techniques of neutralization are critical in lessening the effectiveness of social controls and that they lie behind a large share of delinquent behavior.[79]

The Labeling Process and Its Impact

Up to this point, we have focused on crime and delinquency as behavior, and on people who commit crimes and the distinctions between them and those who do not. The questions "What causes or influences criminal behavior?" and "What factors are associated with committing crime or becoming criminals?" have been underlying concerns in the work we have reviewed. However, the conception of crime and the criminal that underlies such questions is not the only one that has been recognized. Rather than viewing crime as illegal behavior and the criminal as one who engages in it, some criminologists have argued for definitions that draw attention to the labeling behavior of those in a position to react to the existence and actions of others. Crime is a label attached to behavior, and the criminal is one whose behavior has been labeled crime. Crime is thus problematic and a question of social definitions. Nothing intrinsic in behavior makes it a crime.

Labeling theory, or the societal reactions approach, gained immense popularity in the fields of crime and deviance during the 1960s. Sociologists Howard Becker, Kai Erickson, and John Kitsuse helped develop interest in it.[80] Labeling theory ranks today as a major perspective in sociology. In its applications to the crime scene, labeling theory has been used to explain why individuals continue to engage in activities that others define as criminal, why individuals become career criminals, why the official data on crime and criminals look the way they do, why crime waves occur, why law enforcement is patterned the way it is, why criminal stereotypes emerge and persist, and why some groups in society have a better chance of being punished, and punished more severely, than others.

The labeling process begins early in life as significant others — parents, teachers, peers — react to a child's behavior. By the time the teenage years are reached, the child may have already adopted a deviant or delinquent self-image.

LABELING AND "SECONDARY DEVIATION"

Though labeling theory gained popularity only recently, precedents for it were established by the important contributions of Frank Tannenbaum and Edwin Lemert. Forty years ago, Tannenbaum pointed out that society's efforts at social control may actually help create precisely what those efforts are meant to suppress: crime.[81] By labeling individuals as "delinquents" or "criminals," and by reacting to them in a punitive way, Tannenbaum argued, the community encourages those individuals to redefine themselves in accordance with the community's definition. A change in self-identification (or self-concept) may occur, such that the individual "becomes" what others say he is. As Tannenbaum describes the process:

> From the community's point of view, the individual who used to do bad and mischievous things has now become a bad and unredeemable human being. From the individual's point of view there has taken place a similar change. He has gone slowly from a sense of grievance and injustice, of being unduly mistreated and punished, to a recognition that the definition of him as a human being is different from that of other boys in his neighborhood, his school, street, community. This recognition on his part becomes a process of self-identification and integration with the group which shares his activities. It becomes, in part, a process of rationalization; in part, a simple response to a specialized type of stimulus. The young delinquent becomes bad because he is defined as bad and because he is not believed if he is good. There is a persistent demand for consistency in character. The community cannot deal with people whom it cannot define. Reputation is this sort of public definition.[82]

Even if the individual acts in ways normally defined as good, his goodness will not be believed. Once stigmatized, he or she finds it extremely difficult to get rid of the label "delinquent" or "criminal." As Erickson notes in *Wayward Puritans,* "The common feeling that deviant persons never really change . . . may derive from a faulty premise; but the feeling is expressed so frequently and with such conviction that it eventually creates the facts which later 'prove' it to be correct."[83]

Societal reaction to crime and delinquency helps turn individuals away from an image of themselves as basically "straight" and respectable and toward an image of themselves as deviant. In discussing the impact of the labeling process, Lemert uses the term *secondary deviation* to refer to the norm-violating behavior associated with the individual's acquired status as a deviant and his ultimate acceptance of it.[84] Lemert thinks secondary deviation emerges from a process of reaction and adjustment to the punishing and stigmatizing actions of significant others, such as schoolteachers, parents, and law enforcement officials. While initially the individual engages for a short time in deviant acts that he regards as incompatible with his true self (suggesting the need for the techniques of neutralization discussed earlier), he eventually comes to accept his new identity as a deviant and is well on the road toward a career in deviance. Lemert pictures the process:

> The sequence of interaction leading to secondary deviation is roughly as follows: (1) primary deviation [initial acts of deviance prompted by any number of reasons]; (2) social penalties; (3) further primary deviation; (4) stronger penalties and rejections; (5) further deviation, perhaps with hostilities and resentments beginning to focus upon those doing the penalizing; (6) crisis reached in the tolerance quotient, expressed in formal action by the community stigmatizing of the deviant; (7) strengthening of the deviant conduct as a reaction to the stigmatizing and penalties; (8) ultimate acceptance of deviant social status and efforts at adjustment on the basis of the associated role.[85]

Whether an individual moves from primary to secondary deviation depends greatly on the degree to which others' disapproval finds expression in concrete acts of punishment and stigmatization. In a recent article, Lemert notes: "While communication of invidious definitions of persons or groups and the public expression of disapproval were included [in earlier discussions] as part of the societal reaction, the important point was made that these had to be validated in order to be sociologically meaningful. Validation was conceived as isolation, segregation, penalties, supervision, or some kind of organized treatment."[86]

Lemert's work, and that of his followers, has helped identify the processes that encourage a self-identity conducive to repetitious involvement in crime.[87] Summarizing the viewpoint, Stuart Hills notes:

> The effects of criminal stigmatization may not only transform the identity of the offender in the eyes of others, but also reshape to some degree the offender's own self-image, and may impel him into various behavior patterns that will further confirm his negative public identity, increasing the probability of further criminal processing and harsher penalties. The imprisoned drug addict released on parole, for example, may find jobs difficult to secure and may be denied access to the very kinds of legitimate conventional opportunities that he needs to demonstrate his "fitness" to reenter society and effectively remove the label of "dope fiend." Skepticism, suspicion, and withdrawal of trust are likely to prevail long after the offender has "paid his debt to society."[88]

In one attack on labeling theory, Charles Wellford argues that many of its key assumptions are not supported by the bulk of available evidence. In addition, he asserts that the averred connection between punitive reactions, changes in self-concept, and secondary deviation is "a simplistic view of behavior causation, one that stresses the explanation of intellectual as opposed to behavioral characteristics of the subject."[89] According to Wellford, the claim that changes in self-concept produce changes in behavior has yet to be demonstrated. He prefers to view behavior as situationally determined, and, citing research on prisonization (see chapter 13), argues that crime may well occur quite independently of the actor's self-concept. Wellford's viewpoint is yet to be substantiated, however.

CONFLICT, AUTHORITY, AND POWER

A common observation regarding societal reactions to crime is that certain individuals and groups are more likely to suffer the ignominy of being stigmatized as criminals an' to be subjected to punitive sanctions than others. As a general rule, those lacking wealth, prestige, and political influence are more likely to be labeled criminal, to be convicted of criminal offenses, and to be punished by incarceration (this is treated in detail in chapters 11–15). By the same token, those *victims* of crime who lack wealth, prestige, and political influence are less likely than others to receive justice at the hands of the authorities (for an example, see the discussion of historical developments in criminal theft on pages 169–172).

These observations remind us that the crime scene cannot be divorced from the basic social, political, legal, economic, and historical arrangements that characterize a society, nor from the values or action patterns that characterize its members. But they also remind us that a comprehensive grasp of the crime scene requires that we go beyond such questions as "Why do people commit crimes?" Questions of equal importance are "Why have certain activities been designated crimes and others not?" "Why are certain segments of the population more likely than others to suffer criminal labeling and stigmatization?" and "Why are official reactions to crime patterned in a particular way?"

The *conflict perspective* in criminology has sought answers to questions like these, and in doing so has enlarged our understanding of the crime scene. Proponents of the perspective differ on specific issues, but their work shares a common interest in the consequences of group differences in power and influence and the conflicts that arise as groups seek to fulfill their interests. Charles McCaghy points out:

> Basic to any conflict perspective is the assumption that whichever groups can exert the greatest influence on the legislative and the enforcement processes are most assured that their interests will be protected. What is illegal depends upon the outcome of struggles between concerned parties. Who is treated as criminal depends upon the bureaucratic interpretation of both law and behavior.[90]

Austin Turk has developed one of the most promising theoretical treatments of crime and criminalization from the conflict point of view.[91] He begins by rejecting the conception of crime as behavior, arguing instead that criminality is a *status* acquired during the course of interaction between norm creators, interpreters, and enforcers (lawmakers, police, prosecution, judges, and others in positions of legal authority) and the general public. He then constructs a theory to explain and predict *criminalization,* the acquisition of criminal status. In Turk's view, criminology needs a theory stating "the conditions under which cultural and social differences between authorities and subjects will probably result in conflict, the conditions under which criminalization will probably occur in the course of conflict, and the conditions under which the degree of deprivation associated with becoming a criminal will probably be greater or lesser."[92]

Turk argues that conflict between groups is most likely when what people say ought to be (cultural norms) corresponds to a high degree with what they actually do (social norms) *for both authorities and subjects* regarding a particular activity. For example, if the authorities hold that use of marijuana is wrong and abstain from its use themselves, but a group of subjects holds that use of marijuana is acceptable and consume it themselves, then conflict is likely, for there is no room for compromise. In such a case, Turk argues, the authorities are likely to resort to coercion in order to get their way. Conflict is least likely when neither authorities nor subjects display high congruence between what they think should be and how they actually behave. In such cases the particular issue provokes little or no conflict, for it is more symbolic than anything else and both sides leave plenty of room for modifications and adjustments.

Other factors affecting the probability of conflict include the degree to which those having an illegal attribute or engaging in an illegal act are *organized,* and their degree of *sophistication.* Sophistication here means "knowledge of patterns in the behavior of others which is used in attempts to manipulate them."[93] Conflict is more probable, Turk argues, the less organized and sophisticated the norm resisters are.

Turk argues that the probability of criminalization depends on *power differences* between authorities and subjects and upon the *realism of moves* (the tactical skills employed by the opposing parties) in the conflict situation. The probability of criminalization is greater the more power differences favor enforcers over norm resisters, and the less realistic the moves adopted by the latter. Turk argues that any move is likely to be unrealistic that (1) increases the visibility of the attribute or behavior perceived as offensive by the norm enforcers; (2) draws attention to additional offensive attributes or violates an even more significant norm of the authorities; (3) increases consensus among the various levels of enforcers by, for example, turning opposition to a particular rule into an attack on "the whole system"; or (4) increases the power difference in favor of the enforcers.[94]

In addition to the theory itself, Turk suggests what kinds of data are relevant for empirical tests and submits some of his own findings in tentative support of some of the theory's predictions. As it stands now, the theory still awaits careful test and evaluation, but it must be counted as a significant contribution to the efforts to unravel the puzzles of the crime scene. If nothing else, Turk's effort represents one of the best examples of theory construction in criminology, and has served to alert us to some of the critical issues serious students of crime must confront in their efforts to comprehend variations in criminality. Foremost among these issues is the nature of the relationships among those who create, interpret, and enforce legal norms and those who are subject to their decisions and actions. Crime has no objective reality apart from the meanings attached to it, and criminality is an expression of those meanings and the actions that give them life. Turk has reminded us that criminality is a product of social interaction; as such, its patterns and variations reflect those that characterize relations between the people who come in contact with each other as political authorities and political subjects.

The brand of criminology known as radical or critical criminology cannot be ignored as a force in this field; nor should it be. In this section I shall present a glimpse of what radical criminology is, and describe what it offers to students of crime.

THE MARXIAN HERITAGE

While Karl Marx said little about crime, radical criminology recognizes a substantial debt to this nineteenth-century scholar. The substance and the intent of Marx's work have had considerable influence on those writers who identify themselves with radical criminology. His ideas about the nature of man, the nature of society, and social relations under capitalism, and the nature of social change provide a framework for the analysis of crime. And his desire to strip away the myths and "false consciousness" created and fostered by those in power has become a major thrust of the radical perspective.

Marx's social theory provides some of the themes and ideas that hold an important place in critical criminology.[95] First is Marx's view that the mode of economic production — the manner in which relations of production are organized — determines in large part the organization of social relations, that is, the structure of individual and group interaction. Under a capitalistic mode of production social relations are structured differently than under the mode of production found in feudal societies. Accordingly, to "know" society we must first understand how the forces of material production are organized.

In addition, Marx believed that those who own and control the means of production are in a position to control the lives of others. They have the power, for they are the ones who control the most basic of socially meaningful human activities: work. But more than this, Marx asserts that this ruling class also controls the formulation and implementation of moral and legal norms, and even ideas. As he put it in *The German Ideology:* "The ideas of the ruling class are in every epoch the ruling ideas. . . . The class which has the means of material production at its disposal, has control at the same time over the means of mental production."[96]

In advanced capitalistic societies, Marx identifies two great classes — the *bourgeoisie,* owners of the means of production (capital); and the *proletariat,* sellers of their ability to work. Inevitably, the interests of these two classes are bound to conflict, for capitalism places them in a relationship of asymmetrical exchange and exploitation. From the standpoint of the bourgeoisie, survival and growth depend on success in the competition over scarce resources and the drive for maximization of profits. For the proletariat, survival depends on the ability to sell themselves as workers. But since the ruling class controls production it controls work. The worker is thus a pawn in the game of competition and profit maximization that the bourgeoisie inevitably must play. Relations between the two classes are marked by the bourgeoisie's exploitation of the worker, just as the chess player exploits his pawns in the effort to beat his opponent.

This relationship affects law — and by extension, crime. Legal rules and the relations they support flow from the "material conditions of life," that is, the conditions produced by relations of production.[97] When the economic structure of society changes, law and crime change. Since the dominant class controls the instruments of law creation and implementation, legal rules and enforcement practices are shaped by, and supportive of, the interests of that class. Yet, as Marx and Engels point out, the image of law presented to the masses depicts law as the "will of the people." This "juridical illusion" is fostered by the ruling class as part of the effort to undermine the formation of sentiments of opposition and resistance.[98]

Some authors point out that Marx's method, more than anything else, helped shape contemporary radical criminology.[99] It is a critical method in the sense that it encourages not only the attempt to know the "real" reality, but also the attempt to think negatively. As Richard Quinney describes it:

> A critical mode of inquiry is a radical philosophy — one that goes to the roots of our lives, to the foundations and the fundamentals, to the essentials of consciousness. In rooting out presuppositions we are able to assess every actual and possible experience. The operation is one of demystification, removing the myths created by the official reality. Conventional experience is revealed as a reification of the social order, exposing the underside of official reality. . . .
>   A critical philosophy lets us break with the ideology of the age, for built into critical thinking is the ability to think negatively. This *dialectical* form of thought, by being able to entertain an alternative, allows us to question current experience and better understand what exists. Instead of merely looking for an objective reality, we are interested in negating the established order, which will make us better able to understand what we experience. By applying this dialectic in our thought we can comprehend and surpass the present.[100]

Important to Marx's critical thought was his refusal to separate man from his society. Man is a social product and cannot be understood apart from society. But man is also a product of history, for society is shaped by the past as well as the present. In the view of Marx and the radical criminologists, social relations must be examined in their historical context.

WILLEM BONGER ON CRIME AND ECONOMIC CONDITIONS

Though Marx said little about crime in particular, Willem Bonger sought to apply various of Marx's theoretical arguments to the crime scene in capitalistic societies. In *Criminality and Economic Conditions* (published in English in 1916), Bonger observed that capitalistic societies appear to have considerably more crime than precapitalistic societies.[101] Furthermore, during the era of economic development that ushered in capitalism, crime rates increased steadily. Since he recognized that "men behave" and in doing so may commit crimes (acts punishable by those in political authority), Bonger's underlying concern was to account for change in man. He considered man to be a product of his social environment, "which is determined in its turn by the mode of production."[102]

Under capitalism, Bonger argued, the characteristic trait of man is self-interest (egoism). Given the emphasis on profit maximization and competition, and the fact that social relations are class-structured and geared to economic exchange, capitalistic societies spawn intra- and interclass conflicts as individuals seek to survive and prosper. Interclass conflict is one-sided, however, since those who own and control the means of production are in a position to coerce and exploit their less fortunate neighbors. Criminal law, as one instrument of coercion, is used by the ruling class to protect its position and interests. Criminal law "is principally constituted according to the will of" the dominant class, and "hardly any act is punished if it does not injure the interests of the dominant class."[103] Behavior threatening the interests of the ruling class is designated criminal.

Since social relations are geared to competition, profit seeking, and the exercise of power, considerations of mutual support and reciprocity are subordinated to egoistic tendencies. These tendencies lead, in Bonger's view, to a weakening of altruistic sentiment and internal restraint. Both the bourgeoisie and proletariat become prone to crime. The working class is subject to further demoralization, however, because of its inferior exchange position and its exploitation at the hands of the ruling class. As Bonger describes it: "Long working hours and monotonous labor brutalize those who are forced into them; bad housing conditions contribute also to debase the moral sense, as do the uncertainty of existence, and finally absolute poverty, the frequent consequence of sickness and unemployment."[104]

In Bonger's view, economic conditions that induce egoism, coupled with a system of law creation and enforcement controlled by the capitalist class, account for (1) higher crime rates in capitalistic societies than in other societies; (2) crime rates increasing with industrialization; and (3) official crime as predominantly a working-class phenomenon.

Bonger's analysis has a number of major weaknesses. First, he sees a direct causal link between economic conditions and all crime. He does admit the possibility that some criminal acts may be due to psychic disturbance and degeneracy in the individual, but he ends by relating these to underlying economic causes.[105] Second, his use of arrest data in the major part of his analysis is questionable. More than anything else these data reflect the behavior of social control agencies, not those who commit crimes. While appropriate for analyses of the implementation and enforcement of criminal law, Bonger uses arrest data as well to demonstrate the egoism of individuals who have acted antisocially by committing crimes. Third, the important precipitating variable in his scheme, egoism, is not itself measured, but is inferred from the existence of what it presumes to explain, namely, crime. Apparently, where there is crime there is egoism, for where there is egoism there is crime. This gets us nowhere. Even if we accept the proposed link between egoism and crime, we must remember that crimes may be entirely unselfishly motivated: how would we categorize the mother who shoplifts under the pressure of family hunger?

These and other criticisms combine with the failure of subsequent research to uniformly bear out the contention that economic conditions are underlying causes of crime to leave Bonger's theory with few supporters.[106] Even so, he must be credited with making an important attempt to apply Marxian theory to criminality, and with drawing the attention of criminologists to social conflict, class struggles, power, interests, economic conditions, and exploitation as possible determinants of crime.[107]

RADICAL CRIMINOLOGY TODAY

Proponents of the radical perspective today rarely mention Bonger.[108] Yet, like him, they hold that capitalism itself provides us with vital clues to why the crime scene looks as it does in the capitalist West. Some predict a significant reduction in criminality once capitalism is replaced by socialism. In America, the dawn of the 1970s saw the first systematic statements on crime from the perspective of radical criminology. The observations of David M. Gordon and Richard Quinney illustrate this "new" perspective.[109]

According to David Gordon, the radicals view most crime as a rational response to the structure of institutions, including the legal, on which capitalistic societies are based. Crime is "a means of survival in a society within which survival is never assured." Gordon finds three types of crime in America as the best examples of this rationality: ghetto crime, organized crime, and corporate, or white collar, crime. These types offer a chance at survival, status, or respect in a society geared to competitive forms of social interaction and characterized by substantial inequalities in the distribution of social resources, wealth, political power, and so on.

Involvement in different types of crime is explained by class position. Those in the upper socioeconomic classes have access to jobs where paper transactions, lots of money, and unobtrusive communication are important features. Illegal opportunities are manifest in the many forms of white-collar crime. Those in the lower classes, especially those who are "raised in poverty," do not have easy access to money and nonviolent means to manipulate it. Accordingly, illegal activities tend to be the sort that involve taking things by force or physical stealth. As far as the relative violence of crimes is concerned, Gordon attributes this in part to class biases of the state:

> . . . I would argue that the biases of our police, courts, and prisons *explain* the relative violence of many crimes. . . . For a variety of historical reasons . . . we have a dual system of justice in this country; the police, courts, and prisons pay careful attention to only a few crimes. It is only natural, as a result, that those who run the highest risks of arrest and conviction may have to rely on the threat or commission of violence in order to protect themselves. Many kinds of ghetto crimes generate violence, for instance, because the participants are severely prosecuted for their crimes and must try to protect themselves however they can. Other kinds of ghetto crimes, like the numbers racket, are openly tolerated by the police, and those crimes rarely involve violence.[110]

The duality of American public justice is seen in the fact that the state tends to ignore certain kinds of crime — most notably corporate and white-collar crimes — while it concerns itself "incessantly" with crimes among the poor, which, Gordon notes, usually victimize the poor themselves. According to the author, we can understand this duality only if we view the state through the radical perspective. First of all, government in a capitalistic society exists primarily to serve the interests of the capitalist class, and preservation of the system itself is the priority. So long as power and profits are not undermined the offenses that tend in general to harm members of other classes receive little interest. Second, even though offenses of the poor tend to harm others who are poor, they are collectively viewed as a threat to the stability of the system and the interests of the ruling class. Furthermore, an "uppity" lower class is a dangerous class, and the spread of ghetto crime (conveniently identified with blacks) to other parts of the nation's cities heightens the fears of the affluent classes who are in a position to influence policy (for more on crime and public policy see chapter 15).

Richard Quinney's recent work has set down in more detailed fashion some of the major theoretical arguments of radical criminology. Dealing with the problem of crime in America, Quinney urges us to recognize the links between the nature of our society, its criminal laws, conceptions of crime, and crime control practices. Quinney sets down six propositions that make up a critical-Marxian theory, which, he argues, strips away the "official reality" of crime and uncovers what he calls the "social reality of crime." The social reality of crime is a reality constructed out of conflict and the exercise of power, and consists of the meanings people attach to events and activities as they interact as social beings. The theory's propositions are:

1. *The Official Definition of Crime:* Crime as a legal definition of human conduct is created by agents of the dominant class in a politically organized society.

2. *Formulating Definitions of Crime:* Definitions of crime are composed of behaviors that conflict with the interests of the dominant class.
3. *Applying Definitions of Crime:* Definitions of crime are applied by the class that has the power to shape the enforcement and administration of criminal law.
4. *How Behavior Patterns Develop in Relation to Definitions of Crime:* Behavior patterns are structured in relation to definitions of crime, and within this context people engage in actions that have relative probabilities of being defined as criminal.
5. *Constructing an Ideology of Crime:* An ideology of crime is constructed and diffused by the dominant class to secure its hegemony.
6. *Constructing the Social Reality of Crime:* The social reality of crime is constructed by the formulation and application of definitions of crime, the development of behavior patterns in relation to these definitions, and the construction of an ideology of crime.[111]

Proposition 1 is a definition and proposition 6 a composite of the first five propositions; accordingly, Quinney identifies the body of his theory in the four middle propositions.

Quinney calls these propositions a theory, but a careful reading leaves unclear precisely what they explain. Furthermore, the theory offers no specific predictions about variations in the phenomena with which it deals. Such deficiencies are not peculiar to Quinney's work, nor are they found only among those who subscribe to the radical perspective. However, they certainly do not help the cause, especially that of a critical theory that will "demystify" our understanding of crime. But even if we ignore problems of theory construction, we find other difficulties in the work of Gordon, Quinney, and the radical-critical perspective.

CRITICAL VIEWS OF RADICAL CRIMINOLOGY

Radical criminology has stirred up considerable debate, which tells us that the perspective is something to be reckoned with. It also means that opinions differ, reminding us once again that criminology is a vibrant field. No criminologist claims to have all the answers to questions about crime, and most accept that the sorts of questions they ask are not the only ones worth raising.[112]

Interestingly, a criticism lodged against some proponents of the new criminology is that they have failed to allow for differences in studying crime. In a recent symposium reviewing an English contribution to radical criminology, Paul Rock observed: *"The New Criminology*'s master vision makes no provisions for a division of intellectual labor. It does not recognize the possibility that the study of deviancy is not always enhanced by the imposition of one grand scheme upon all its subordinate projects."[113] While proponents of the new perspective are quick to condemn mainstream liberal criminology for its intellectual domination of the field, their own position seems to advocate replacing one kind of domination with another. In Quinney's view, a "critical philosophy" should now dominate the field. Consider what he has said about the most recent product of mainstream liberal criminology:

> In retrospect, conflict theory was misguided at best, and perhaps at worst a mistake. Even on its own terms, conflict theory could account for merely the surface phenomena of social and political life, ignoring the dynamic forces which make conflict possible. The theories that became known as conflict theories could not get the deeper meaning of conflict in contemporary society. Conflict theory as thus formulated served to mystify reality. What is needed in its place is a *critical philosophy.* . . . Conflict theory . . . was merely another bourgeois academic enterprise.[114]

Unfortunately, Quinney's own work does not deliver on the promise made on behalf of his critical philosophy.

Some radical criminologists would have us believe that some criminals are "real" and presumably that some are not real. According to the recently formed Union of Radical Criminologists, "the real criminals govern this society [America] and are protected by its laws."[115] Who are these people? Does this mean that "real" criminals are only to be found in America? It is unlikely that the answer to the second question would be yes. But the first question cannot be answered easily, and it is an especially important one, for the answer should tell us who are the appropriate objects of criminological interest for the Union.

Yet, as Gibbons has pointed out, the work of Quinney and others does not make clear just who are the governors, and hence the "real" criminals.[116] Sometimes the image conjured up is one of a small group of powerful individuals in constant touch who determine the destinies of the rest of us. At other times the image suggests a category of people broad enough to include almost everybody. But beyond this, what makes this category of people "real" criminals? The answer to this remains thoroughly in doubt.

The emphasis on class interests in the formulation of criminal definitions has been criticized for two reasons. On one hand is the uncertainty as to what the word *class* means and serious doubt that, in a sociological sense, classes can be said to exist in America. On the other hand is the fact that certain crimes, such as rape, murder, or child molesting, are surely condemned by society as a whole rather than by the ruling class alone. Are we to ignore such crimes as an appropriate object of criminological theory and research?

Indeed, Gibbons suggests that radical criminology tends to "gloss over" the "real pains" caused by *mala in se* crimes, and to "romanticize" the behavior of the person who commits them:

> This is the sort of thing that is involved when members of the "Hell's Angels" are viewed as "noble ruffians" or when the rapist activities of Eldridge

Cleaver are glossed over by some. Although rape may be a form of symbolic revenge conducted by persons who feel the sting of racial discrimination, the fact remains that innocent persons are victimized by rapists. Some convoluted logic is required in order to transform the rape victim into an appropriate target for someone who wishes to make a symbolic gesture against repression. Rape is rape, whatever the motives of the rapist.[117]

Does this mean we should not consider the new radical criminology a significant contribution to the field? Not at all. It means, partly, that the radicals have important problems to iron out. None of the criticisms mentioned is a fatal flaw. As a matter of fact, we must credit the radical perspective with bringing to the forefront issues deserving careful consideration and constant reappraisal. One of these is the utility of alternative theoretical perspectives in improving our understanding of the crime scene. The interest in Marxian theory encourages serious criminologists to familiarize themselves with its potentialities in the study of crime. The radical criminologist asks us to look at crime in new ways and suggests how we might do so, making a challenge to established ideas that ought not to be ignored. Learning decays unless new ideas are forthcoming. That these ideas sometimes conflict with strongly held beliefs, values, and predispositions does not make them any less important. The same is true of the information gathered by those whose perspectives depart from our own. Radical criminology, with its concern with the exercise of power in defense of ruling interests, has brought forth facts about the crime scene that otherwise might not have been supplied in a systematic way. Such information adds to our store of knowledge, and should not be ignored or set aside on ideological grounds.

Future Trends   The status of radical criminology among the competing theoretical orientations of the field seems less secure today than it was at the beginning of the 1970s. This is not surprising, for that decade began at a time of social and political unrest. The radical vision offered hope of relief for those feeling the exploitation and oppression (real and imagined) of monopoly capitalism. With the end of American involvement in Vietnam and with the demise of the Nixon era, things quieted down considerably. Inflation, high oil prices, and crime in the streets eventually replaced the counterculture, political repression, and war as issues of pressing concern to most Americans. A law-and-order reaction to the rebellion of the 1960s was setting in, not just among so-called middle Americans, but also on college campuses and in the inner cities. The appeal of radical Marxian theory has to some extent been undermined by these changes.

The radicalization of criminological thinking may itself have sparked a counterreaction on the part of those in a position to affect the discipline:

> As criminology has radicalized and politicized, authorities and those in positions of power have reinforced their own commitments to the status quo,

convinced themselves of the limited practical contributions of research, and solidified their resistance to self-exposure. By announcing its assumptions regarding the role of social agencies, the new criminology has precipitated an already serious crisis of confidence in the discipline's ability to deal fairly with the problem of crime and criminality. Politicalization has met with counter-politicalization.[118]

In addition, there were claims in academic circles that both labeling theory and critical criminology had been leading theory and research too far away from the criminal. We know a tremendous amount about the social control apparatus and its personnel, Stanton Wheeler has claimed, but we know little more about the criminal offender now than we knew twenty-five years ago.[119] Others have questioned whether the newer brands of criminology offer hope of a better explanation of crime and criminality than can be expected from more traditional approaches.[120]

In short, it seems likely that the next few years will see a return to many of the questions about crime that were previously thought to be important. We may even find serious efforts to resurrect the ideas of classical theory — that the criminal is rational, hedonistic, and capable of being deterred. That is the focus of Yochelson and Samenow's work and has long been a major thrust of the decision-making models advanced by economists and decision theorists interested in crime. It has, finally, been the cornerstone of all deterrence theory and research (see chapter 14).

Summary

In this chapter we have reviewed some of the major theoretical perspectives on crime that have marked the development of criminology up to the present. The early perspectives emphasized crime as behavior and sought explanations in characteristics of individual offenders. Criminals were presumed to be somehow different from other people and were thought by many to be morally defective. The criminal, it was argued, must be a product of some sort of biological or psychic degeneracy.

As sociological interest in crime grew, the search for causes led to investigation of the social environment. While at first there was still considerable interest in the individual as the unit of analysis, the emphasis shifted to the impact of social conditions. Although the multifactor approach supported a search for crime-producing factors in the realms of biology and psychology as well, the die was cast: from the 1930s on, sociology came to dominate criminology as an academic field of study.

In sociological criminology, the question "Why do people commit crimes?" was answered first by looking at the impact of social structure on group life. Theories linking anomic conditions to crime gained considerable attention, as did those that argued that certain structural conditions are conducive to the formation of delinquent subcultures wherein crime becomes an accepted and supported aspect of life. As these theories gained prominence, Edwin Sutherland offered a *social process* view of criminality. In his differential association theory he argued that, like any other form of social behavior, criminal behavior is learned through interaction. Hence there grew an interest in the processes by which individuals become criminals.

The social structural and early social process theories shared in common the view that crime is a normal rather than a pathological condition. The criminal, furthermore, is not morally defective but is, instead, much like anyone else. The fact that some segments of the population have higher crime rates than others reflects not a tendency toward ''sickness'' or ''moral defectiveness'' but different social experiences and conditions. These theoretical perspectives also shared the long-standing view that there *is* something called crime, which is different from noncrime and can be studied objectively.

Later social process theorists rejected this view, treating crime as problematic instead. The labeling theorists took the view that crime is nothing more than a label attached to conduct and people, and what needs to be explained is variations in labeling behavior. Crime came to be thought of as a status applied to behavior, not as a particular kind of act. Accordingly, the processes of making and enforcing criminal laws began to receive central attention. The imposition of criminal labels explains why there are criminals, and the fact that some groups display higher rates of criminality than others has come to be explained largely in terms of social conflict. The conflict theories of the 1960s drew attention away from crime as behavior and toward the activities of those in a position to impose the criminal label. Radical-critical criminology, an outgrowth of the conflict perspective, has adopted a largely Marxian view of social relations in capitalistic societies. The emphasis is on the exercise of power in defense of ruling-class interests and the status quo.

Obviously we have not yet reached the point where we can hold any single theory to be the explanation of crime. One reason is that people do not agree on what we mean by crime, the phenomenon to be explained. We only achieve an incomplete grasp of the crime scene if we treat crime as either behavior or status, but not both. To understand the crime scene we must ask not only why certain activities, people, and groups come to be labeled criminals, but also why people engage in such activities. We need to understand not only why armed robbery is a crime, and why armed robbery is reacted to in certain ways, but also why some people commit armed robbery and others do not. A theory of criminology that focuses only on crime as status, and on the processes and effects of conferring that status, is as inadequate, in my view, as one that focuses only on why and how people behave in ways defined as criminal.

References

1. See Walter C. Reckless, "American Criminology," *Criminology: An Interdisciplinary Journal* 8 (1970), pp. 4–20.
2. Herbert A. Bloch and Gilbert Geis, *Man, Crime, and Society,* 2nd ed. (New York: Random House, 1970), p. 79.
3. Edwin H. Sutherland and Donald R. Cressey, *Criminology,* 9th ed. (Philadelphia: Lippincott, 1974), p. 3.
4. Don C. Gibbons and Peter Garabedian, "Conservative, Liberal, and Radical Criminology: Some Trends and Observations," in *The Criminologist: Crime and the Criminal,* Charles E. Reasons, ed. (Pacific Palisades, Calif.: Goodyear, 1974), pp. 51–65; Don C. Gibbons, "Emerging Perspectives in Criminology," unpublished paper.
5. Gibbons and Garabedian, "Conservative, Liberal, and Radical Criminology," p. 52.
6. Travis Hirschi, *Causes of Delinquency* (Berkeley: University of California Press, 1971), p. 16.
7. See Gresham M. Sykes, "The Future of Criminality," *American Behavioral Scientist* 15 (1972), pp. 409–19.
8. Gibbons and Garabedian, "Conservative, Liberal, and Radical Criminology," p. 53.
9. Major contributors to the emphasis on power are Austin T. Turk, *Criminality and Legal Order* (Chicago: Rand McNally, 1969); Richard Quinney, *The Social Reality of Crime* (Boston: Little, Brown, 1970); Stuart L. Hills, *Crime, Power, and Morality* (Scranton, Penn.: Chandler, 1971); and William J. Chambliss, ed. *Criminal Law in Action* (Santa Barbara, Calif.: Hamilton, 1975).
10. Gibbons and Garabedian, "Conservative, Liberal, and Radical Criminology," p. 55.
11. Tony Platt, "Prospects for a Radical Criminology in the United States," *Crime and Social Justice* 1 (1974), p. 3.
12. Gibbons and Garabedian, "Conservative, Liberal, and Radical Criminology," p. 57.
13. André Michel Guerry, *Essai sur la Statistique Morale* (Paris, 1833); Adolphe Quetelet, *Sur l'Homme et le Dévélopment de Ses Facultés ou Essai de Physique Sociale* (Paris, 1835).
14. Leon Radzinowicz, *Ideology and Crime* (New York: Columbia University Press, 1966), p. 35.
15. See George B. Vold, *Theoretical Criminology* (New York: Oxford University Press, 1958), p. 27.
16. For a discussion of his writings see Marvin E. Wolfgang, "Pioneers in Criminology: Cesare Lombroso (1835–1909)," *Journal of Criminal Law, Criminology and Police Science* 52 (1961), pp. 361–91. The major English translation of Lombroso's work is his *Crime, Its Causes and Remedies* (Boston: Little, Brown, 1911).
17. Marvin E. Wolfgang, "Cesare Lombroso," in *Pioneers in Criminology,* ed. Hermann Mannheim (London: Stevens, 1960), p. 207.
18. For one of the best discussions of Ferri's work see Thorsten Sellin, "Enrico Ferri," in Mannheim, *Pioneers in Criminology.*
19. Thorsten Sellin, "The Lombrosian Myth in Criminology," *American Journal of Sociology* 42 (1937), pp. 898–99.
20. Charles Goring, *The English Convict: A Statistical Study* (London: His Majesty's Stationery Office, 1913), p. 18.
21. Ibid., p. 173.
22. Earnest A. Hooton, *Crime and the Man* (Cambridge, Mass.: Harvard University Press, 1939); also his *The American Criminal: An Anthropological Study* (Cambridge, Mass.: Harvard University Press, 1929).
23. Elmer H. Johnson, *Crime, Correction, and Society,* 2nd ed. (Homewood, Ill.: Dorsey, 1974), pp. 206–7.
24. For identical twin and other biological studies see M. F. Ashley Montague, "The Biologist Looks at Crime," *The Annals* 217 (1941), pp. 46–57. Two major studies on feeblemindedness were Richard L. Dugdale, *The Jukes* (New York: Putnam, 1877), and Henry H. Goddard, *The Kallikak Family* (New York: Macmillan, 1912). See also George Vold, *Theoretical Criminology* (1958), pp. 75–89. One of the first studies on body types was Ernst Kretschmer, *Physique and Character* (New York: Harcourt, Brace, 1926). William H. Sheldon was a major contributor to body type research: see his *Varieties of Human Physique* (New York: Harper and Row, 1940); *Varieties of Temperament* (New York: Harper and Row, 1942); and *Varieties of Delinquent Youth* (New York: Harper and Row, 1949). An early work on glandular secretions was Louis Berman's "Crime and the Endocrine Glands," *American Journal of Psychiatry* 12 (1932); for recent discussions see Saleem A. Shah and Loren H. Roth, "Biological and Psychophysiological Factors in Criminality," in *Handbook of Criminology,* ed. Daniel Glaser (Chicago: Rand McNally, 1974).
25. For discussions of the XYY "theory" see Theodore R. Sarbin and Jeffrey E. Miller, "Demonism Revisited: The XYY Chromosomal Anomaly," *Issues in Criminology* 5 (1970), pp. 195–207; Richard G. Fox, "The XYY Offender: A Modern Myth?" *Journal of Criminal Law, Criminology, and Police Science* 62 (1971), pp. 59–73; and Ernest B. Hood, "Behavioral Implications for the XYY Genotype," *Science* 179 (1973), pp. 139–50.
26. George B. Vold, *Theoretical Criminology,* 2nd

ed. Prepared by Thomas J. Bernard (New York: Oxford University Press, 1979), pp. 87–97. (This edition will hereafter be identified by "(1979)" to distinguish it from the 1958 edition.)

27. Travis Hirschi and Michael J. Hindelang, "Intelligence and Delinquency: A Revisionist Review," *American Sociological Review* 42 (1977), pp. 572–87.

28. See A. R. Jenson, "How Much Can We Boost IQ and Scholastic Achievement?" *Harvard Educational Review* 39 (1969), pp. 1–123; Robert Gordon, "Prevalence: Datum in Delinquency Measurement and Its Implications for the Theory of Delinquency," in Malcolm W. Klein, ed., *The Juvenile Justice System* (Beverly Hills, Calif.: Sage, 1976), pp. 201–84.

29. See Michael J. Hindelang, "Race and Involvement in Common Law Personal Crimes," *American Sociological Review* 43 (1978), pp. 93–109; and Michael J. Hindelang, Travis Hirschi, and Joseph G. Weis, "Correlates of Delinquency: The Illusion of Discrepancy Between Self-Report and Official Measures," *American Sociological Review* 44 (1979), especially pp. 999–1002.

30. See Vold, *Theoretical Criminology* (1979), p. 90; Hirschi and Hindelang, "Intelligence and Delinquency," pp. 582–83. On the matter of criminal justice bias, see Carl E. Pope, "Race and Crime Revisited," *Crime and Delinquency* 25 (1979), especially 354–56, for review of the inconsistent findings; see also chapters 11 and 12 in this text.

31. Vold, *Theoretical Criminology* (1979), p. 97.

32. For work in the psychogenic vein see Vold, *Theoretical Criminology* (1958); Stephen Schafer, *Theories in Criminology* (New York: Random House, 1969), chapter IX; Richard W. Nice, ed. *Criminal Psychology* (New York: Philosophical Library, 1962), chapter IX; Gregory Zilboorg, *The Psychology of the Criminal Act and Punishment* (New York: Harcourt, Brace, Jovanovich, 1954); David Abrahamsen, *Crime and the Human Mind* (New York: Columbia University Press, 1945); David Abrahamsen, *The Psychology of Crime* (New York: Columbia University Press, 1960); H. J. Eysenck, *Crime and Personality* (Boston: Houghton Mifflin, 1964); Gordon Trasler, *The Explanation of Criminality* (London: Routledge and Kegan Paul, 1962); and Gordon P. Waldo and Simon Dinitz, "Personality Attributes of the Criminal: An Analysis of Research Studies, 1950–1965," *Journal of Research in Crime and Delinquency* 4 (1967), pp. 185–202.

33. Samuel Yochelson and Stanton E. Samenow, *The Criminal Personality,* vols. 1 and 2 (New York: Jason Aronson, 1976, 1977).

34. Ibid., vol. 1, pp. 247–48.

35. Vold, *Theoretical Criminology* (1979), p. 155.

36. Yochelson and Samenow, *The Criminal Personality,* p. 247.

37. Richard Korn and Lloyd W. McCorkle, *Criminology and Penology* (New York: Holt, Rinehart and Winston, 1959), pp. 202–4.

38. See Juan B. Cortes and Florence M. Gatti, *Delinquency and Crime: A Biopsychosocial Approach* (New York: Seminar Press, 1972), p. 8.

39. Vold, *Theoretical Criminology* (1958), p. 125.

40. Schafer, *Theories in Criminology,* p. 221.

41. William Healy, *The Individual Delinquent: A Textbook and Prognosis for All Concerned in Understanding Offenders* (Boston: Little, Brown, 1915).

42. Cyril Burt, *The Young Delinquent* (London: University of London Press, 1925).

43. Sheldon and Eleanor Glueck, *Unraveling Juvenile Delinquency* (New York: Commonwealth Fund, 1950).

44. Albert K. Cohen, "Juvenile Delinquency and the Social Structure" (Ph.D. diss., Harvard University, 1951). pp. 5–13.

45. Sutherland and Cressey, *Criminology,* p. 61.

46. See Stephen Schafer, *Introduction to Criminology* (Reston, Va.: Reston Publishing Co., 1976), p. 85.

47. A phrase borrowed from Wilbert E. Moore, "Social Aspects of Economic Development," in *Handbook of Modern Sociology,* ed. Robert E. L. Faris (Chicago: Rand McNally, 1964), p. 905.

48. See Nels Andersen, *The Hobo* (Chicago: University of Chicago Press, 1923); Frederic M. Thrasher, *The Gang: A Study of 1313 Gangs in Chicago* (Chicago: University of Chicago Press, 1927); Clifford R. Shaw, *Delinquency Areas* (Chicago: University of Chicago Press, 1931); Clifford R. Shaw, *Jackroller: The Natural History of a Delinquent Career* (Chicago: University of Chicago Press, 1931); and Clifford R. Shaw and Henry D. McKay, *Juvenile Delinquency and Urban Areas* (Chicago: University of Chicago Press, 1942).

49. See Shaw, *Delinquency Areas.*

50. See Shaw and McKay, *Juvenile Delinquency and Urban Areas.* For supporting and conflicting evidence from England, see Terence Morris, *The Criminal Area* (New York: Humanities Press, 1958).

51. *Report on the Causes of Crime,* vol. 2, no. 13 (Washington, D.C.: U.S. Government Printing Office, 1931), p. 387. Quoted in Martin R. Haskell and Lewis Yablonsky, *Crime and Delinquency* 2nd ed. (Chicago: Rand McNally, 1974), p. 582.

52. Emile Durkheim, *The Rules of Sociological Method,* 8th ed., trans. Sarah A. Solovay and John H. Mueller (New York: Free Press, 1964), pp. 65–66.

53. Emile Durkheim, *Suicide,* trans. John A. Spauld-

ing and George Simpson (London: Routledge and Kegan Paul, 1952).

54. Robert K. Merton, "Social Structure and Anomie," *American Sociological Review* 3 (1938), pp. 672–82. See also his *Social Theory and Social Structure* (New York: Free Press, 1957), chapters 4 and 5.

55. Haskell and Yablonsky have added a sixth mode of adaptation, "dropping out," but it is unclear how this departs significantly from Merton's "retreatism." See their *Crime and Delinquency,* p. 580.

56. Merton, *Social Theory and Social Structure,* p. 146.

57. Richard A. Cloward and Lloyd E. Ohlin, *Delinquency and Opportunity: A Theory of Delinquent Gangs* (New York: Free Press, 1960), p. 7.

58. Albert K. Cohen, *Delinquent Boys: The Culture of the Gang* (New York: Free Press, 1955).

59. Cloward and Ohlin, *Delinquency and Opportunity,* p. 86.

60. See Walter B. Miller, "Lower Class Culture as a Generating Milieu of Gang Delinquency," *Journal of Social Issues* 14 (1958), pp. 5–19; William C. Kvaraceus and Walter B. Miller, *Delinquent Behavior: Culture and the Individual* (Washington, D.C.: National Education Association, 1959).

61. Apart from the evidence collected by the authors of these various theories, the following is a sample of research bearing upon social structural theories: Albert J. Reiss, Jr., and A. Lewis Rhodes, "The Distribution of Juvenile Delinquency in the Class Structure," *American Sociological Review* 26 (1961), pp. 720–32; Irving Spergel, "Male Young Adult Criminality, Deviant Values, and Differential Opportunities in Two Lower Class Negro Neighborhoods," *Social Problems* 10 (1963), pp. 237–50; John P. Clark and Eugene P. Wenninger, "Socio-Economic Class and Area as Correlates of Illegal Behavior among Juveniles," *American Sociological Review* 27 (1962), pp. 826–34; Roland J. Chilton, "Continuities in Delinquency Area Research: A Comparison of Studies for Baltimore, Detroit, and Indianapolis," *American Sociological Review* 29 (1964), pp. 71–83; James F. Short, Jr., "Gang Delinquency and Anomie," in Marshall B. Clinard, ed., *Anomie and Deviant Behavior* (New York: Free Press, 1964), pp. 98–127; La Mar T. Empey and Maynard L. Erickson, "Hidden Delinquency and Social Status," *Social Forces* 44 (1966), pp. 546–54; Edgar Epps, "Socioeconomic Status, Race, Level of Aspiration, and Juvenile Delinquency; A Limited Empirical Test of Merton's Conception of Deviation," *Phylon* 28 (1967), pp. 16–27; Delbert S. Elliot, "Delinquency, School Attendance, and Dropout," *Social Problems* 13 (1966), pp. 307–14.

62. Sutherland and Cressey, *Criminology,* pp. 75–77.

63. Ibid., p. 89.

64. For critical evaluations of differential association theory see: Daniel Glaser, "The Differential Association Theory of Crime," in *Human Behavior and Social Process,* ed. Arnold M. Rose (Boston: Houghton Mifflin, 1962), pp. 425–42; Sheldon Glueck, "Theory and Fact in Criminology: A Criticism of Differential Association," *British Journal of Delinquency* 7 (1956), pp. 92–109; Reed Adams, "The Adequacy of Differential Association Theory," *Journal of Research in Crime and Delinquency* 11 (1974), pp. 1–8. Donald R. Cressey, "Epidemiology and Individual Conduct: A Case from Criminology," *Pacific Sociological Review* 3 (1960), pp. 47–58, is a response to the criticisms and a clarification of Sutherland's theory.

65. C. Ray Jeffery, "An Integrated Theory of Crime and Criminal Behavior," *Journal of Criminal Law, Criminology, and Police Science* 49 (1959), pp. 533–52.

66. Daniel Glaser, "Criminality Theories and Behavioral Images," *American Journal of Sociology* 61 (1956), pp. 433–44. For research evidence see Victor Matthews, "Differential Identification: An Empirical Note," *Social Problems* 15 (1968), pp. 376–83; and J. R. Stratton, "Differential Identification and Attitudes toward the Law," *Social Forces* 46 (1967), pp. 256–62.

67. Robert L. Burgess and Ronald L. Akers, "A Differential Association–Reinforcement Theory of Criminal Behavior," *Social Problems* 14 (1966), pp. 128–47.

68. For comments on the theory see Reed Adams, "Differential Association and Learning Principles Revisited," *Social Problems* 20 (1973), pp. 458–70.

69. See James F. Short, Jr., "Differential Association as a Hypothesis: Problems of Empirical Testing," *Social Problems* 8 (1960), pp. 14–25; Harwin L. Voss, "Differential Association and Reported Delinquent Behavior: A Replication," *Social Problems* 12 (1964), pp. 78–85; Albert J. Reiss, Jr., and A. Lewis Rhodes, "An Empirical Test of Differential Association Theory," *Journal of Research in Crime and Delinquency* 1 (1964), pp. 5–18.

70. Major studies are cited in Adams, "Differential Association and Learning Principles Revisited," p. 465.

71. See Ronald L. Akers, Robert L. Burgess, and Weldon T. Johnson, "Opiate Use, Addiction, and Relapse," *Social Problems* 15 (1968), pp. 459–69.

72. The term "personal organization" is borrowed from Melvin L. DeFleur, William V. D'Antonio, and Lois B. DeFleur, *Sociology: Human Society* (Glenview, Ill.: Scott, Foresman, 1973), p. 127.

73. See Walter C. Reckless and Simon Dinitz, "Pioneering with Self-Concept as a Vulnerability Factor in Delinquency," *Journal of Criminal Law, Criminology, and Police Science* 58 (1967), pp. 515–23; Walter Reckless, "A New Theory of Delinquency and Crime," *Federal Probation* 25 (1961), pp. 42–46, reprinted in Reckless, *The Crime Problem*, 5th ed. (Englewood Cliffs, N.J.: Prentice-Hall, 1973), pp. 55–57; Walter Reckless and Shlomo Shoham, "Norm Containment Theory as Applied to Delinquency and Crime," *Excerpta Criminologica* 3 (1963), pp. 637–44; see also Walter Reckless, Simon Dinitz, and Barbara Kay, "The Self Component in Potential Delinquency and Potential Nondelinquency," *American Sociological Review* 22 (1957), pp. 566–67.

74. Reckless, *The Crime Problem*, pp. 55–56.

75. Reckless and Dinitz, "Pioneering with Self-Concept," p. 517.

76. See Michael Schwartz and Sandra S. Tangri, "A Note on Self-Concept as an Insulator against Delinquency," *American Sociological Review* 30 (1965), pp. 922–26; Sandra S. Tangri and Michael Schwartz, "Delinquency Research and the Self-Concept Variable," *Journal of Criminal Law, Criminology, and Police Science* 58 (1967), pp. 182–94.

77. David Matza, *Delinquency and Drift* (New York: J. Wiley, 1964).

78. Gresham M. Sykes and David Matza, "Techniques of Neutralization: A Theory of Delinquency," *American Sociological Review* 22 (1957), pp. 664–70.

79. Ibid., pp. 669–70.

80. See Howard S. Becker, *The Outsiders: Studies in the Sociology of Deviance* (New York: Free Press, 1963); Kai T. Erickson, "Notes on the Sociology of Deviance," *Social Problems* 9 (1962), pp. 307–14, also his *Wayward Puritans: A Study in the Sociology of Deviance* (New York: J. Wiley, 1966); and John I. Kitsuse, "Societal Reactions to Deviant Behavior: Problems of Theory and Method," *Social Problems* 9 (1962), pp. 247–56.

81. Frank Tannenbaum, *Crime and the Community* (New York: Columbia University Press, 1938).

82. Ibid., pp. 17–18.

83. Erickson, *Wayward Puritans*, p. 17.

84. See Edwin M. Lemert, *Social Pathology* (New York: McGraw-Hill, 1951), pp. 75–77; also Lemert, *Human Deviance, Social Problems, and Social Control*, 2nd ed. (Englewood Cliffs, N.J.: Prentice-Hall, 1972).

85. Lemert, *Social Pathology*, p. 77.

86. Edwin M. Lemert, "Beyond Mead: The Societal Reaction to Deviance," *Social Problems* 21 (1974), p. 457.

87. Don C. Gibbons recognizes a substantial debt to Lemert in his own work on the development of criminal careers; see Gibbons, *Society, Crime,* *and Criminal Careers*, 2nd ed. (Englewood Cliffs, N.J.: Prentice-Hall, 1973), p. 210.

88. Hills, *Crime, Power, and Morality*, p. 50.

89. Charles Wellford, "Labelling Theory and Criminology: An Assessment," *Social Problems* 22 (1975), p. 342. For other criticisms of labeling theory, see Arnold Birenbaum and Edward Sagarin, *Norms and Human Behavior* (New York: Praeger, 1976), pp. 116–25.

90. Charles H. McCaghy, *Deviant Behavior: Crime, Conflict, and Interest Groups* (New York: Macmillan, 1976), p. 89.

91. Austin T. Turk, *Criminality and Legal Order* (Chicago: Rand McNally, 1969). See also his "Conflict and Criminality," *American Sociological Review* 31 (1966), pp. 338–52.

92. Turk, *Criminality and Legal Order*, p. 53.

93. Ibid., pp. 58–59.

94. Ibid., p. 72.

95. For recent views of Marxism's applicability to criminology, and a sampling of Marx's own observations, see Ian Taylor, Paul Walton, and Jock Young, eds., *Critical Criminology* (London: Routledge and Kegan Paul, 1975), pp. 44–57 and 203–43.

96. Karl Marx and Frederick Engels, *The German Ideology* (New York: International Publishers, 1947), p. 39.

97. See Karl Marx, *A Contribution to the Critique of Political Economy* (London: Lawrence and Wishart, 1971), p. 20.

98. See Marx and Engels, *The German Ideology*, pp. 58–62.

99. For example, Taylor, Walton, and Young, *Critical Criminology*, p. 45.

100. Richard Quinney, *Criminology*, 2nd ed. (Boston: Little, Brown, 1979), pp. 17–18.

101. Willem Bonger, *Criminality and Economic Conditions* (Boston: Little, Brown, 1916). A shortened version has been published recently by Indiana University Press (1969) with an introduction by Austin T. Turk.

102. Ibid., p. 33 (1969 ed.).

103. Ibid., pp. 379–80 (1916 ed.).

104. Ibid., p. 195 (1969 ed.).

105. Ibid., p. 182 (1969 ed.).

106. For a review of the criticisms of Bonger's theory see Turk's introduction to the 1969 edition. For reviews of the pertinent research see Leon Radzinowicz, "The Influence of Economic Conditions on Crime," *Sociological Review* 33 (1941); also his "Economic Pressures," in *The Criminal in Society*, ed. Leon Radzinowicz and Marvin E. Wolfgang (New York: Basic Books, 1971), pp. 420–42; also Donald R. Taft and Ralph W. England, Jr., *Criminology*, 4th ed. (New York: Macmillan, 1964), pp. 120–35.

107. For further discussion of Bonger's work see J. M. Van Bemmelen, "William Adrian Bonger," in Mannheim, *Pioneers in Criminology*.

108. An exception is found in Taylor, Walton, and Young, *The New Criminology.*

109. See David M. Gordon, "Capitalism, Class, and Crime in America," *Crime and Delinquency* 19 (1973), pp. 163–86; and his "Class and the Economics of Crime" *Review of Radical Economics* 3 (1971), pp. 51–75. See also Quinney, *Criminology,* pp. 37–91; Quinney, *Critique of Legal Order* (Boston: Little, Brown, 1974); and Quinney's "The Ideology of Law: Notes for a Radical Alternative to Legal Oppression," *Issues in Criminology* 7 (1972), pp. 1–35.

110. Gordon, "Class and the Economics of Crime," p. 61.

111. From Richard Quinney, *Criminology: Analysis and Critique of Crime in America* (Boston: Little, Brown, 1975), pp. 37–41.

112. This section relies heavily on Don C. Gibbons, "Emerging Perspectives in Criminology," and Gresham M. Sykes, "The Rise of Critical Crimi-nology," *Journal of Criminal Law and Criminology* 65 (1974), pp. 206–13.

113. "Feature Review Symposium," *The Sociological Quarterly* 14 (1973), p. 595. The symposium reviewed Taylor, Walton, and Young, *The New Criminology.*

114. Ibid., pp. 591–92.

115. Cited by Quinney, Ibid., p. 593.

116. Gibbons, "Emerging Perspectives in Criminology," pp. 16–17.

117. Ibid., p. 15.

118. Paul C. Friday, "Changing Theory and Research in Criminology," *International Journal of Criminology and Penology* 5 (1977), p. 166.

119. Stanton Wheeler, "Trends and Problems in the Sociological Study of Crime," *Social Problems* 23 (1976), pp. 525–34.

120. See William V. Pelfrey, "Mainstream Criminology: More New than Old," *Criminology* 17 (1979), pp. 323–29.

Getting a Line on Crime: The Production and Use of Data

Most authors of criminology texts make a special point of warning readers about the many pitfalls encountered in the compilation and use of data on crime. These warnings usually contain strong words about the inadequacies of crime statistics. Here are some typical remarks drawn from three recent texts:

> The statistics about crime and delinquency are probably the most unreliable and most difficult of all social statistics.[1]

> Crime statistics are among the most unreliable and questionable social facts.[2]

> Crime statistics contain numerous labyrinths to trap the incautious, even when presented with the purest of intentions.[3]

These warnings refer to the data compiled and reported by those who are administrators of criminal law. Unquestionably, for some purposes official statistics are woefully inadequate, if not downright useless. The data represent no more than what official agencies know and care to report. To understand the meaning and limitations of crime data we must first know something about how the data are produced.

People create crime and people produce information about it. The production of data on crime and criminals begins when an evaluation by someone results in the label "crime" being attached to a piece of behavior. This label may have no legal meaning, for people do not always know the precise legal definitions of crimes. Nevertheless, if the label "crime" is attached to an activity, then the activity is criminal for the person making the evaluation.

Sometimes an activity escapes the scrutiny of others and remains known only to the actor himself. When this happens, the activity in question must be regarded as unknown and unknowable; it can never become part of the data on crime. In other words, to become part of a potential body of data on crime, an activity must be labeled "criminal," or at least "possibly criminal," by someone other than the actor himself.

PRODUCING OFFICIAL DATA: AN ILLUSTRATION

Suppose that 10,000 actions occur in an hour. Of these actions, only 9,000 are ever known to anyone other than the person responsible for them. These 9,000 actions become eligible for evaluation by others; the other 1,000 are "lost." When the 9,000 known activities are evaluated by someone, there are three possibilities: (1) the actions are labeled "noncrimes"; (2) they are labeled "crimes"; or (3) they are labeled "possible crimes." This does not mean that people go around calling things "noncrimes" or "possible crimes" in the real world. The three possibilities are merely categories into which we can divide evaluations. By implication, when a person does not think of an activity as a crime or a possible crime, it is a noncrime.

Imagine that of 9,000 known actions, 8,600 are evaluated as "noncrimes." As with the 1,000 activities that were lost, these are never going to appear in the data on crime. Now we have 400 activities left. At this point we come to an important question: who does the labeling? If the evaluator is also an administrator of criminal law (a policeman, lawyer, or judge), the label "crime" takes on new significance. It is now an official label, and the behavior in question becomes part of the *official data on crime*. By the same token, when an administrator of criminal law applies the label "criminal" to a person, that action produces part of the official data on criminals.

Not all activities or people considered criminal by members of the general public will be so labeled by officials. Sometimes this is because they are not criminal according to legal definitions. But the reasons may have nothing to do with strict legal rules. For example, discretion is an important facet of police work, and sometimes the exercise of police discretion results in the criminal label not being applied, even when existing legal definitions call for it. When this happens, these acts or people will not appear as part of the official record on crime, *but they do remain part of a potential pool of data on crime.* They comprise, along with other acts and people that have been labeled criminal by someone, the *unofficial data on crime and criminals*. (In a moment we shall discuss how this seemingly lost information on crime can be recovered by the criminologist.)

To become part of the *official* data on crime, activities must be known to legal officials and must be appropriately labeled by them. Activities become known to the police, and hence become eligible for official labeling as crimes, in two ways. The most common way is for a member of the public to notify the police of a "crime" or "possible crime." The less common way is for the police to directly witness an activity that they then label crime. Police rely heavily on citizens bringing suspected crimes to their attention.[4] This means that most actions that eventually become official crimes do so only because they have been evaluated as "crimes" or "possible crimes" by the public, who then bring them to the attention of the police. Here we see the importance of unofficial (public) evaluations and behavior in the production of *official* crime data.

To return to the hypothetical situation, suppose that of the 400 "crimes" or "possible crimes," 150 come to the attention of the police in one way or another. (For reasons discussed in a moment, 250 of the unofficial crimes are "lost" to the production of official crime data.) Yet not all of the 150 activities known to the police will necessarily be labeled crime; some will be screened out. Imagine that 50 of the 150 activities are screened out — as far as the police are concerned, these are "noncrimes." This leaves 100 activities, each of which has been evaluated as crime by the police. These 100 crimes make up the pool of official data on crime; they are called, appropriately enough, "crimes known to the police." Figure 3.1 summarizes what we have said so far.

The production of official data on criminals starts when activities are first labeled "crime" or "possible crime" by someone. The hypothetical illustration has 400 activities to which persons can be linked as "criminals" or "possible criminals" by someone. However, more than one person may have committed the act in question. On the other hand, the same individual may have committed more than one "crime." If the former is generally the case, data will show more criminals than instances of criminal activity; if the latter holds, data will show fewer criminals than "crimes." This warns us not to expect a one-to-one relationship between activities and people. Even though the illustration has 400 possible crimes, 600 criminals may be involved, or then again only 250. Generally speaking, even if every known crime were solved by the identification of those responsible, the number of "crimes" and the number of "criminals" would probably not be the same. Since the police do not solve every known crime, we usually find many more official crimes than offi-

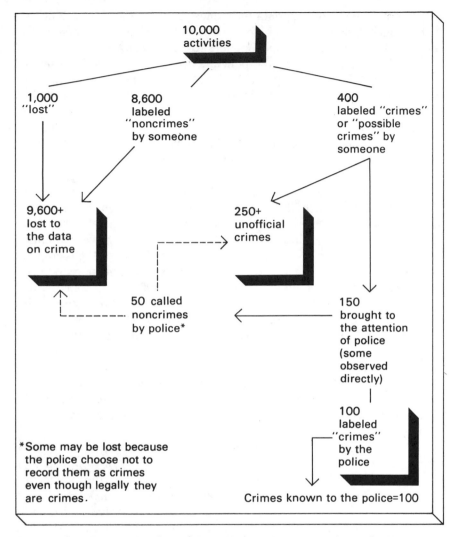

Figure 3.1 *The production of data: "crimes known to the police"*

cial criminals. Accordingly, we should not expect to find the 100 "crimes known to the police" in figure 3.1 matched with 100 "criminals known to the police."

THE POLICE ROLE IN DATA PRODUCTION

Some of the "crimes" and "possible crimes" that come to police attention fail to make it into the official record. This is because the police may decide not to officially acknowledge an incident as a crime. This decision shapes not only the official data on crimes, but also those on criminals.[5] If the police officially record an activity as a crime, the person who performed the activity becomes eligible for the official label "criminal" and is subject to scrutiny by the police, as well as others in the criminal justice system. If the activity is not officially recorded as crime, then the individual is lost to official statistics on arrests, charges, adjudication, and sentencing.

Studies of police labeling behavior have produced some interesting findings regarding the kinds of things that influence decisions about those incidents brought to police attention. We have learned that the police respond to public pressures and are extremely sensitive to the possibility of criticism. If they feel that prevailing public sentiments call for less or more attention to specific kinds of crime, they adjust their labeling practices accordingly. One example of this occurred in England some years ago. During the 1950s and early 1960s much public and private attention was focused on the issue of homosexuality and the law. A government commission was established to look into the matter and make recommendations regarding public policy. The so-called Wolfendon Report recommended the decriminalization of homosexual activity between consenting adults in private (a recommendation that has since become law). But the interesting thing is this: in a ten-year period from the mid-1950s to the mid-1960s, official records of arrests for "gross indecency between males" fell off by more than 50 percent. The decline was not due to a corresponding decline in the incidence of the behavior itself but, rather, to changes in police behavior. Under the national spotlight, the police were apparently less willing to take official action than they had been in the past.[6]

One of the major determinants of police labeling behavior is the legal seriousness of the offense. Looking at police actions in Boston, Chicago, and Washington, D.C., Donald Black discovered that "the police officially recognize proportionately more legally serious crimes than legally minor crimes."[7] Suspected felonies were officially recorded as crimes 72 percent of the time, compared to only 53 percent of the time in the case of suspected misdemeanors. Even so, the fact that around a quarter of the suspected felonies were not officially recognized by the police leaves little doubt that factors other than seriousness come into play.

In the same study, Black discovered that the likelihood of official labeling was influenced by: (1) the *demeanor* of the complainant — those more deferential toward the police were more successful in getting their complaints officially recorded; (2) the complainant's apparent *preference* for formal or informal action — those asking for formal action tended to get that action; and (3) the *relational distance* between the suspect and the complainant — acts committed by strangers were more likely to be officially recognized as crimes than acts committed by members of the complainant's family or by close friends or acquaintances.

In their work the police are often required to make on-the-spot evaluations of events and people. Customary departmental rules and policies together with work norms generated by the officers themselves support considerable discretion in the determination of what action to take. Studies indicate that the legal character of an activity is no guarantee that official action will be taken. It is in making arrests that the police formally apply the criminal label, but those who make up the pool of official arrest data are sometimes there for reasons other than the legal character of their actions. When we look at official arrest figures we have to remember that those arrested have not necessarily committed the act for which they were apprehended. In dealing with the complex demands of their work, "the police attempt to accomplish their job with a minimum of strain and . . . the effort leads to the selection of law violators *not* according to legal prescriptions alone."[8] Factors that influence the police in their decisions to arrest someone include the person's age, sex, demeanor, prior contacts with the police, and reputation and respect within the community.[9] In sum, the official record on crime and criminals is shaped by police decisions, which in turn are influenced by factors that may have nothing to do with criminal law. Knowing how and why police decisions are made becomes one of the keys to understanding the official crime picture.

One other aspect of official compilation of data on crime deserves our attention and ties in with what we have been discussing: the falsification and manipulation of official records. Even if we grant the impact of situational variables on police decisions, the records that become part of the official data on crime may also be affected by "in-house" decisions that have nothing to do with street contacts, complainants, and officer discretion.

The police exist and work within a political and economic environment that places its own demands on their behavior and decision making.[10] Two constant pressures on any police department are financial security and bureaucratic survival and growth. Besides the fact that police departments cost money to operate, they are like other organizations in that self-perpetuation comes high on the list of priorities. In their dealings with the political and business leadership police executives strive to meet these pressures by demonstrating on the one hand that service is successful, and on the other that there are continuing financial and personnel needs.

One way to demonstrate needs is to show that without certain resources the community will suffer. Suppose you are a police chief and you want additional equipment. You have been told that money is tight, and any additional funds will be allocated only on the basis of most urgent needs. How do you meet the requirement? One way is to manipulate crime and arrest data so that it looks as if, instead of reducing or containing crime, your department is being swamped by it. Such manipulations can take a number of forms. Skolnick found that one of the police departments he studied would periodically manipulate the data on crimes "cleared by arrest."[11] In America (as in some other countries) the police tally the proportion of known crimes cleared by arrest (*clearance rate*). "Cleared by arrest" does not mean that the person arrested is proven guilty. Rather, the police consider a case solved for their purposes when an arrest has been made. In order to make the crime problem appear overwhelming and so demonstrate the need for patrol cars (or additional personnel), you might manipulate the clearance rate so that the *ratio of arrests to known crimes* appears *lower* than it actually is. For example, suppose your department had actually arrested 2000 suspects during the year. Instead of reporting this figure you report only 1500 arrests. If there were 10,000 reported crimes over the same period, a ratio of 1500 to 10,000 would indicate greater difficulties in the areas of detection and arrest than would the true ratio of 2000 to 10,000. As police chief you could achieve the same end by ordering fewer arrests in the first place, but the risks are greater with this method because it is more likely that people will catch on. In any case, if the politicians are interested in helping defend the community against criminals, you argue, they must pay for devices that help raise the clearance rate.

Just as the police may on occasion manipulate crime data to make their needs appear urgent, they may also manipulate the data to make their department look good. This may mean underreporting certain known offenses, as was the case in New York City in 1966.[12] It may mean manipulation of the clearance rate so that the ratio of arrests to known crimes is *higher* than it actually is.[13] This practice is most likely to occur, it seems, in police departments whose administrators are political appointees or elected by the public. To keep their jobs they must demonstrate progress in combating crime. By the same token, administrators may come under pressure from city and state officials who see their own jobs in jeopardy when crime gets out of hand. A little manipulation for the mayor or governor may be called for.

Unfortunately, we have no way of assessing how much data is lost or created through police falsification and manipulation. With computerized techniques of data recording and dissemination, it may now be more difficult for individual departments to manipulate the records after they have been initially compiled. But even then, department officials can still order their men to "go slow" or speed up on arrests, thus providing another means to the same end. Lacking accurate ways of assessing the situation, we have to remember that what is reported by the police may be quite different from what is actually known or recorded by them.

English sociologist Dennis Chapman has enumerated some additional reasons that police underreport crime: first, much crime occurs in family and organizational settings. A good deal (perhaps most) of such crime tends not to be reported to the police in the first place, and when the police do know of possible crimes, they find it difficult to penetrate the institutional privacy of these settings.[14] Second, the detection of crime is in part a function of the "social range of the police, who are drawn from the lower middle class and the working class and, in addition, find their social relations restricted by their occupation. . . . In general, the effectiveness of the police can be expected to decline as the social-class area of the problem is raised. . . ."[15] Third, crimes differ in the degree to which they can be readily concealed. Crimes involving symbols and paper — embezzlement, fraud, political corruption, and the like — tend to be greatly underreported in comparison to acts of violence and other forms of theft because those crimes are less easily concealed. Fourth, patrolling practices of the police coupled with middle-class concerns with privacy make it less likely that crimes in middle-class neighborhoods will be recorded. This helps explain why the official police data show a preponderance of lower-class crime.

How We "Lose" and "Find" Crime Data

The hypothetical situation presented in the opening section of this chapter purposely emphasizes that a considerable proportion of the potential official data on crime is "lost." Some potential data are lost because those who have committed a crime were clever enough to conceal their activities from others. Some potential data are missed because people are not too observant. While it is impossible to estimate the amount of data lost as a result of these two situations, studies indicate it is probably substantial. Recent evidence on "disappearing money" shows that Americans cannot account for the disappearance of billions of dollars each year. In a significant proportion of cases, the money has apparently been stolen.[16]

LOSING DATA THROUGH NONREPORTING

Much information on crime is lost because individuals simply do not bring suspicious events to the attention of police. Estimates in recent years indicate that even with serious crimes such as robbery, rape, and burglary, a considerable proportion of offenses are not brought to police attention — perhaps as high as 75 percent.[17] Most often cited are the figures compiled from a survey of 10,000 households conducted in 1965 and 1966 on behalf of the President's Commission on Law Enforcement and the Administration of Justice. Many more people responding to this survey reported having been victimized than official statistics would indicate should be the case. Apparently, many victims of crime do not report their experiences to the police. *Victimization rates* (the number of incidents in which persons are victims of crime per 100,000 people) were around 3½ times the crime rate officially published for rape, triple the rate published for burglary, and about double the official rates for robbery and aggravated assault.[18] Other recent studies of victimization support the general findings of this first study, namely, that official rates are significantly lower than rates of victimization for most crimes. One exception is auto theft. Here, official rates and victimization rates are similar. This is largely because victims must report the offense to collect insurance.

One might think that failure to report criminal incidents to the police results because people are generally unaware that what has happened is a crime. While this may be true in some cases, it is unlikely with such incidents as robbery, burglary, and interpersonal violence. In fact, there is ample evidence that even if a person recognizes that he or she is the victim of a crime, or a witness to one, there is no guarantee that the police will be notified. In the case of some offenses — especially shoplifting, forgery, and employee theft — the probability that they will be reported is so low that statistics make them appear infrequent when they are, in reality, among the most numerous offenses.

Why, of all people, do the victims of crime not report their victimization to the police? Though there are a number of reasons, two of the more common explanations given by the victims themselves are that they felt "nothing could be done anyway," or they felt that the police would not want to be bothered with their problems. Another reason often given is that the incident was a private matter, and the victim would rather keep it that way.[19] Can you think of other reasons why victims might not report offenses to the police?

It is not only victims who fail to report actions they have identified as "crimes" or "possible crimes." People who witness or simply hear about a possible crime may also avoid reporting it to the police. Again the reasons vary. Albert Biderman found, for example, that while the major reason given by the subjects in his investigation was that they did not want to get involved, other reasons included belief that the police already knew about the incident, fear that the offender would seek some kind of revenge if he found out who had reported his behavior, and simple lack of knowledge as to what to do.[20]

FINDING DATA WITH VICTIMIZATION STUDIES

The information lost through nonreporting can be recovered in some measure by *victimization studies*. These studies employ questionnaires designed to find out whether interview subjects have been victims of crimes during a certain period, and if so, how often and of which crimes. A typical series of questions might read as follows:

> *Item:* During the last 12 months, did anyone break into or somehow illegally get into your home, garage, or another building on your property?
> YES ____ how many times? _____
> NO ____

Current fact-finding techniques only scratch the surface of child abuse and other family offenses.

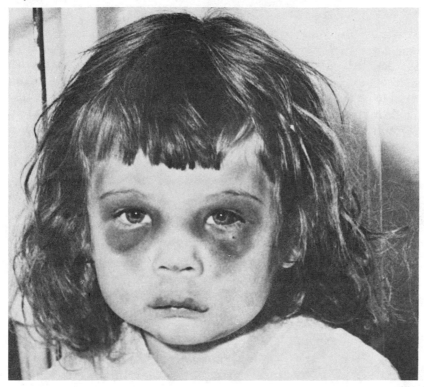

Item: Other than the incidents just mentioned, did you find a door jimmied, a lock forced, or any other signs of an *attempted* break in?
YES ____ how many times? _____
NO ____

Item: During the last 12 months, did anyone take anything directly from you by using force, such as by a stickup, mugging, or threat?
YES ____ how many times? _____
NO ____

Item: Did anyone *try* to rob you by using force or threatening to harm you?
YES ____ how many times? _____
NO ____

Item: Did anyone beat you up, attack you or hit you with something, such as a rock or bottle?
YES ____ how many times? _____
NO ____

Item: Were you knifed, shot at, or attacked with some other weapon by anyone at all (other than incidents already mentioned)?
YES ____ how many times? _____
NO ____

Item: Did anyone *try* to attack you in some other way?
          YES ____ how many times? _____
          NO ____ [21]

These are "screening" questions that prepare the interviewer for more detailed questioning on the incidents mentioned by the respondents. This more detailed questioning is designed to pin down exactly what happened. On superficial glance an incident may look like a crime but turn out not to be one; it may look like a burglary when in fact it was "merely" vandalism. In addition, detailed questioning about the incidents can provide the researcher with information on the characteristics of offenses, the actions of the offender, the actions of the victim, the extent of the injury or loss, and so forth. This information can be invaluable in helping

Table 3.1 Victimizations by type of crime, 1974, 1976, and 1978

TYPE OF CRIME	1974	1976	1978
Crimes of violence (combined)			
Number	5,510,000	5,599,000	5,941,000
Rate[a]	33.0	32.6	33.7
Rape			
Number	163,000	145,000	171,000
Rate[a]	1.0	0.8	1.0
Robbery			
Number	1,199,000	1,111,000	1,038,000
Rate[a]	7.2	6.5	5.9
Aggravated assault			
Number	1,735,000	1,695,000	1,708,000
Rate[a]	10.4	9.9	9.7
Simple assault			
Number	2,413,000	2,648,000	3,024,000
Rate[a]	14.4	15.4	17.2
Crimes of theft			
Number	15,889,000	16,519,000	17,050,000
Rate[a]	95.1	96.1	96.8
Household burglary			
Number	6,720,600	6,663,400	6,704,000
Rate[b]	93.1	88.9	86.0
Motor vehicle theft			
Number	1,358,400	1,234,600	1,365,100
Rate[b]	19.1	16.5	17.5

SOURCE: U.S. Department of Justice, "Criminal Victimization in the United States: Summary Findings of 1977–1978 Changes in Crime and Trends Since 1973," SD-NCS-13A (Washington, D.C.: U.S. Government Printing Office, 1979), Table 1.

a. Number per 1,000 population age 12 and over.
b. Number per 1,000 households.

Table 3.2 Percent of victimizations reported to police, 1978

TYPE OF CRIME	TOTAL	RELATIONAL DISTANCE	
		STRANGER	NONSTRANGER
Crimes of violence (combined)	44.2%	45.7%	41.6%
Rape	48.8	49.9	45.8
Robbery	50.6	52.3	44.6
Aggravated assault	52.8	52.4	53.4
Crimes of theft	24.6	—	—
Household burglary	47.1	—	—
Motor vehicle theft	66.1	—	—

SOURCE: U.S. Department of Justice, "Criminal Victimization in the United States: Summary Findings of 1977–1978 Changes in Crime and Trends Since 1973," SD-NCS-13A (Washington, D.C.: U.S. Government Printing Office, 1979), table 3.

us understand victim experiences with crime, and the nature of criminal activities themselves.

Under the auspices of the federal government, national victimization data have been collected each year since 1973 by the *National Crime Survey*. Table 3.1 shows some of the findings of this survey for three different years. Table 3.2 presents estimates of the percentage of offenses *reported to the police* in 1978. Included is a comparison of reporting behavior for victimizations involving strangers and nonstrangers. Offenses involving strangers are, on the whole, more likely to be reported. Notice also that motor vehicle theft was reported in the largest percentage of cases. This is easily explained: insurance claims may well be jeopardized if the loss is not reported to the police.

SELF-REPORTED CRIMINALITY

In addition to victimization studies, lost data may be recovered by asking members of the public to tell about their own involvement in criminal activities. The idea behind these "self-report" studies is to establish more reasonable estimates of the extent of criminality. The feeling has long been that official statistics give us only the tip of the iceberg. Self-report studies provide us with a means to uncover the remainder of the iceberg — the so-called hidden criminality.

The self-report technique commonly employs a questionnaire listing a variety of deviant, delinquent, and illegal activities. Respondents are asked to check if they have engaged in any of them during a specified period of time, say, the past year. Self-report studies have usually focused on adolescents because it is recognized that much crime and delinquency in this population remains hidden from official records and because rep-

SELF-REPORTED DELINQUENCY ITEMS FROM THE 1977 NATIONAL YOUTH SURVEY

[The following behavior items were designed to tap delinquent or criminal behavior as reported by interview respondents. It should be noted that the National Youth Survey items cover a more extensive list of behaviors than have most previous questionnaires. The researchers wanted a set of items that was both comprehensive and representative of the range of delinquent acts. This list of 47 acts may well become the standard for future self-report measures.]

Self-reported Delinquency and Drug-Use Items as Employed in the National Youth Survey

How many times in the last year have you:
1. purposely damaged or destroyed property belonging to your *parents* or other family *members.*
2. purposely damaged or destroyed property belonging to a *school.*
3. purposely damaged or destroyed *other property* that did not belong to you (not counting family or school property).
4. stolen (or tried to steal) a *motor vehicle,* such as a car or motorcycle.
5. stolen (or tried to steal) something worth more than $50.
6. knowingly bought, sold or held stolen goods (or tried to do any of these things).
7. thrown objects (such as rocks, snowballs, or bottles) at cars or people.
8. run away from home.
9. lied about your age to gain entrance or to purchase something; for example, lying about your age to buy liquor or get into a movie.
10. carried a hidden weapon other than a plain pocket knife.
11. stolen (or tried to steal) things worth $5 or less.
12. attacked someone with the idea of seriously hurting or killing him/her.
13. been paid for having sexual relations with someone.
14. had sexual intercourse with a person of the opposite sex other than your wife/husband.
15. been involved in gang fights.
16. sold marijuana or hashish ("pot," "grass," "hash").
17. cheated on school tests.
18. hitchhiked where it was illegal to do so.
19. stolen money or other things from your *parents* or *other members of your family.*
20. hit (or threatened to hit) a *teacher* or other adult at school.

resentative samples are readily available for interviewing in school settings.

With adolescents as their targets, self-report questionnaires invariably include acts that would not be crimes if committed by adults (see box above). Furthermore, it is now recognized that these questionnaires tap generally trivial delinquency and crime, rather than the serious street crime emphasized in official statistics.[22] In a study by Martin Gold, the 10 percent "most delinquent" group included a boy whose admitted delinquent activities from age 12 were as follows:

> . . . he and a friend had knocked down a tent in a neighbor boy's back yard — the aftermath of an earlier mud fight.
> That winter, he had shoplifted gum a few times from a neighborhood store.
> On turning 13, he had begun to lie regularly about his age to cashiers at movie theaters.
> In June, 1961, he had shoplifted a cartridge belt from a hardware store and later given it to a friend.
> The month after, he had taken an address book from a department store.

21. hit (or threatened to hit) one of your *parents.*
22. hit (or threatened to hit) other *students.*
23. been loud, rowdy, or unruly in a public place (disorderly conduct).
24. sold hard drugs, such as heroin, cocaine, and LSD.
25. taken a vehicle for a ride (drive) without the owner's permission.
26. bought or provided liquor for a minor.
27. had (or tried to have) sexual relations with persons against their will.
28. used force (strong-arm methods) to get money or things from other *students.*
29. used force (strong-arm methods) to get money or things from a *teacher* or other adult at school.
30. used force (strong-arm methods) to get money or things from *other people* (not students or teachers).
31. avoided paying for such things as movies, bus or subway rides, and food.
32. been drunk in a public place.
33. stolen (or tried to steal) things worth between $5 and $50.
34. stolen (or tried to steal) something at school, such as someone's coat from a classroom, locker, or cafeteria, or a book from the library.

35. broken into a building or vehicle (or tried to break in) to steal something or just to look around.
36. begged for money or things from strangers.
37. skipped classes without an excuse.
38. failed to return extra change that a cashier gave you by mistake.
39. been suspended from school.
40. made obscene telephone calls, such as calling someone and saying dirty things.

How often in the last year have you used:
41. alcoholic beverages (beer, wine, and hard liquor).
42. marijuana — hashish ("grass," "pot," "hash").
43. hallucinogens ("LSD," "Mescaline," "Peyote," "Acid").
44. amphetamines ("Uppers," "Speed," "Whites").
45. barbiturates ("Downers," "Reds").
46. heroin ("Horse," "Smack").
47. cocaine ("Coke").

SOURCE: Delbert S. Elliott and Suzanne S. Ageton, "Reconciling Race and Class Differences in Self-Reported and Official Estimates of Delinquency," *American Sociological Review* 45 (1980), pp. 108–109. Reprinted by permission.

In the summer of 1961, he and a friend had helped themselves to several beers from his friend's refrigerator.

In late August, 1961, he and another friend had twice raided an orchard not far from R's home, taking ripe pears and unripe apples and grapes. They ate the first, and threw the rest at various targets.

In September, 1961, he had lifted a hunting knife from a sporting-goods store just for something to do. "We took it back the next day, snuck it back in."

He regularly carried a hunting knife under his jacket "for protection" when he went collecting on Friday nights on his paper route.[23]

Bearing in mind, then, that most self-report studies measure less, rather than more, serious crime and delinquency in supposed "nondelinquent" populations, the findings nevertheless show widespread involvement in behavior that is in technical violation of the law. In most studies, more than 75 percent of those surveyed admit having committed at least one illegal act, and most admit more than one. While self-report studies confirm the overrepresentation of males in criminal activities, they also show that females are heavily implicated in trivial criminality.[24] What is also confirmed in these studies, for both juveniles and adults, is that a small portion of those surveyed admit committing the bulk of serious offenses. A survey of 646 California inmates (whose criminality had already been established in legal proceedings) found that one-fourth of the sample admitted committing 65 percent of the burglaries, 58 percent of the robberies, 48 percent of the drug sales, and 46 percent of the auto thefts.[25]

Self-report studies are not without their methodological problems. Three common sources of error are: (1) those who agree to answer questions may be markedly different from those who refuse, which leaves in doubt the representativeness of any sample of persons interviewed; (2) those who do take part may conceal their previous involvement in crime; or (3) they may exaggerate their participation crime — for example, by "admitting" acts they had not committed or admitting more serious crimes than they had in fact committed.[26] Another problem relates to the wording of items in the questionnaires. Respondents can be expected to have a hard time relating their previous conduct to legal descriptions of offenses. Accordingly, the usual ploy is to phrase items in everyday language and to include examples by way of illustration. Unfortunately, the translation of legal offense categories into everyday language is not always easy, and some respondents may be left wondering whether a specific act they committed should be counted when it does not exactly fit the illustrations.[27]

Despite the difficulties, most criminologists accept self-report studies as a major means of identifying the extent and nature of hidden criminality. It appears on balance that a good deal of faith can be placed in the results of these investigations.[28] While it is virtually impossible to guarantee that concealment or lying will not occur, the general feeling seems to be that most of those interviewed tell the truth. Since the estimates of the proportion of crimes that go undetected and unacted upon range up to more than 90 percent for juveniles, self-report investigations are vital when it comes to finding out about youthful crime.[29]

The FBI Uniform Crime Reports

Certain kinds of data are clearly inappropriate for some types of research problems in criminology. You would not, for instance, go to official data sources for an accurate count of the rate of criminal behavior. Instead you might supplement official records with information compiled from the pool of unofficial data found in victimization and self-report studies. On the other hand, if you want to find out about police reactions to crime, what better place could you start than with the police themselves?

The scientific enterprise being what it is, decisions to use one data source over another are often geared not so much to the known or suspected inadequacies of available data but, rather, to the fact of their availability. Research costs time and money, two commodities not always in good supply. This being the case, many criminologists use already available data even though they fully realize the pitfalls in doing so. In recent years efforts have been made in the social sciences to establish and stock data banks containing a wide range of information, most of which has been acquired through the efforts of individual researchers pursuing various investigations. The University of Michigan has one such data bank. Using the information contained there (which is not always possible) enables a researcher to shed light on a problem where the use of official statistics would be less satisfactory.

It remains true, nevertheless, that official, readily accessible sources of data turn up time and again in works on crime (this text included). The most widely used official data on crime are found in the FBI's *Uniform Crime Reports,* published annually by the Department of Justice. Begun over forty years ago, these reports came about in the effort to meet growing demands from many quarters that crime data be systematically collected and made accessible to those with an interest in the subject. At first, only the largest police departments sent their records to the FBI. Now, even though the program is still voluntary for police agencies, the FBI claims to receive crime information from law enforcement agencies representing more than 95 percent of the total national population.

The use of computer-based systems of information storage and retrieval has become a major feature of police operations. By means of these systems, many states now act as collecting agencies for the national Uniform Crime Reporting Program. Instead of reporting directly to the FBI, local and county police agencies now send their crime data to the responsible state agency, which then forwards the information, via computer, to the FBI. Some states have laws making it mandatory for all police agencies to participate in the recording and reporting of crime information, and many states provide assistance in data collection. In 1978, forty-three states acted as collection agencies for the national program.

Tables 3.3 to 3.6 and figure 3.2, presented in the next few pages, are samples of what is available in the annual *Uniform Crime Reports.* Today the reports contain information on the number and rate of crimes reported by the police (crime *rate* is the number of reported crimes per 100,000 people), on arrests, and on other topics ranging from crime on university campuses, to the killing of police officers, and law enforcement employment statistics. A major portion of the report deals with data on a select number of offenses — called Part I, or Index, offenses. These data are presented for the nation as a whole, for states, for standard metropolitan statistical areas (SMSAs), for cities of various sizes, for suburbs, and for rural areas. The Part I offense list was established some years ago as an index of serious crime, the idea being that the dimensions of the crime problem could best be assessed from year to year by keeping track of

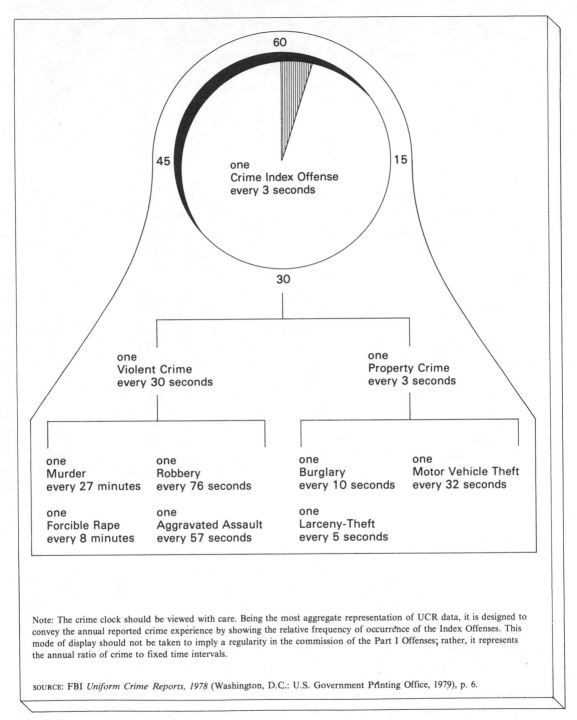

Figure 3.2 Crime Clock, 1978

Table 3.3 Index of crime, United States, 1978

AREA	POPULA-TION[a]	CRIME INDEX TOTAL	VIOLENT CRIME[b]	PROPERTY CRIME[b]	MURDER AND NON-NEGLIGENT MAN-SLAUGHTER	FORCIBLE RAPE	ROBBERY	AGGRA-VATED ASSAULT	BUR-GLARY	LARCENY-THEFT	MOTOR VEHICLE THEFT
United States total	218,059,000	11,141,334	1,061,826	10,079,508	19,555	67,131	417,038	558,102	3,104,496	5,983,401	991,611
Rate per 100,000 inhabitants	....	5,109.3	486.9	4,622.4	9.0	30.8	191.3	255.9	1,423.7	2,743.9	454.7
Standard metropolitan statistical area	159,388,199										
Area actually reporting[c]	99.0%	9,282,753	925,984	8,356,769	15,683	58,168	395,892	456,241	2,573,406	4,900,044	883,319
Estimated total	100.0%	9,356,438	930,629	8,425,809	15,740	58,468	397,219	459,202	2,592,698	4,942,712	890,399
Rate per 100,000 inhabitants	....	5,870.2	583.9	5,286.3	9.9	36.7	249.2	288.1	1,626.7	3,101.1	558.6
Other cities	25,890,583										
Area actually reporting[c]	96.3%	1,085,750	71,060	1,014,690	1,299	3,901	12,490	53,370	256,604	699,591	58,495
Estimated total	100.0%	1,129,850	73,882	1,055,968	1,347	4,059	12,963	55,513	267,110	728,152	60,706
Rate per 100,000 inhabitants	....	4,363.9	285.4	4,078.6	5.2	15.7	50.1	214.4	1,031.7	2,812.4	234.5
Rural	32,786,218										
Area actually reporting[c]	93.8%	627,488	54,255	573,233	2,302	4,332	6,394	41,227	233,778	300,828	38,627
Estimated total	100.0%	655,046	57,315	597,731	2,468	4,604	6,856	43,387	244,688	312,537	40,506
Rate per 100,000 inhabitants	....	1,997.9	174.8	1,823.1	7.5	14.0	20.9	132.3	746.3	953.3	123.5

SOURCE: FBI, *Uniform Crime Reports, 1978* (Washington, D.C.: U.S. Government Printing Office, 1979), p. 38.

a. Populations are Bureau of the Census provisional estimates as of July 1, 1978.

b. Violent crimes are offenses of murder, forcible rape, robbery, and aggravated assault. Property crimes are offenses of burglary, larceny-theft, and motor vehicle theft.

c. The percentage representing area actually reporting will not coincide with the ratio between reported and estimated crime totals, since these data represent the sum of the calculations for individual states which have varying populations, portions reporting, and crime rates.

Table 3.4 Index of crime, United States, 1969–1978

POPULATION[a]	CRIME[b] INDEX TOTAL	VIOLENT[c] CRIME	PROPERTY[c] CRIME	MURDER AND NON-NEGLIGENT MAN-SLAUGHTER	FORCIBLE RAPE	ROBBERY	AGGRA-VATED ASSAULT	BURGLARY	LARCENY-THEFT	MOTOR VEHICLE THEFT
Number of offenses:										
1969										
201,385,000	7,410,900	661,870	6,749,000	14,760	37,170	298,850	311,090	1,981,900	3,888,600	878,500
1970										
203,235,298	8,098,000	738,820	7,359,200	16,000	37,990	349,860	334,970	2,205,000	4,225,800	928,400
1971										
206,212,000	8,588,200	816,500	7,771,700	17,780	42,260	387,700	368,700	2,399,300	4,424,200	948,200
1972										
208,230,000	8,248,800	834,900	7,413,900	18,670	46,850	376,290	393,090	2,375,500	4,151,200	887,200
1973										
209,851,000	8,718,100	875,910	7,842,200	19,640	51,400	384,220	420,650	2,565,500	4,347,900	928,800
1974										
211,392,000	10,253,400	974,720	9,278,700	20,710	55,400	442,400	456,210	3,039,200	5,262,500	977,100
1975										
213,124,000	11,256,600	1,026,280	10,230,300	20,510	56,090	464,970	484,710	3,252,100	5,977,700	1,000,500
1976										
214,659,000	11,304,800	986,580	10,318,200	18,780	56,730	420,210	490,850	3,089,800	6,270,800	957,600
1977										
216,332,000	10,935,800	1,009,500	9,926,300	19,120	63,020	404,850	522,510	3,052,200	5,905,700	968,400
1978										
218,059,000	11,141,300	1,061,830	10,079,500	19,560	67,130	417,040	558,100	3,104,500	5,983,400	991,600

Rate per 100,000 inhabitants:[d]

Year										
1969	3,680.0	328.7	3,351.3	7.3	18.5	148.4	154.5	984.1	1,930.9	436.2
1970	3,984.5	363.5	3,621.0	7.9	18.7	172.1	164.8	1,084.9	2,079.3	456.8
1971	4,164.7	396.0	3,768.8	8.6	20.5	188.0	178.8	1,163.5	2,145.5	459.8
1972	3,961.4	401.0	3,560.4	9.0	22.5	180.7	188.8	1,140.8	1,993.6	426.1
1973	4,154.4	417.4	3,737.0	9.4	24.5	183.1	200.5	1,222.5	2,071.9	442.6
1974	4,850.4	461.1	4,389.3	9.8	26.2	209.3	215.8	1,437.7	2,489.5	462.2
1975	5,281.7	481.5	4,800.2	9.6	26.3	218.2	227.4	1,525.9	2,804.8	469.4
1976	5,266.4	459.6	4,806.8	8.8	26.4	195.8	228.7	1,439.4	2,921.3	446.1
1977	5,055.1	466.6	4,588.4	8.8	29.1	187.1	241.5	1,410.9	2,729.9	447.6
1978	5,109.3	486.9	4,622.4	9.0	30.8	191.3	255.9	1,423.7	2,743.9	454.7

SOURCE: FBI, *Uniform Crime Reports, 1978* (Washington, D.C.: U.S. Government Printing Office, 1979), p. 39.

a. Populations are Bureau of Census provisional estimates as of July 1, except April 1, 1970, census.

b. Due to rounding, the offenses may not add to Crime Index totals.

c. Violent crimes are offenses of murder, forcible rape, robbery, and aggravated assault. Property crimes are offenses of burglary, larceny-theft, and motor vehicle theft.

d. Crime rates calculated prior to rounding number of offenses.

Table 3.5 Total estimated arrests, United States, 1978[a]

TOTAL[b]	10,271,000	Sex offenses (except forcible rape and prostitution)	69,100
Murder and nonnegligent manslaughter	19,840	Drug abuse violations	628,700
Forcible rape	29,660	Opium or cocaine and their derivatives	83,100
Robbery	148,930	Marijuana	445,800
Aggravated assault	271,270	Synthetic or manufactured narcotics	17,200
Burglary	511,600	Other—dangerous nonnarcotic drugs	82,500
Larceny-theft	1,141,800		
Motor vehicle theft	161,400	Gambling	55,800
		Bookmaking	5,400
Violent crime[b]	469,700	Numbers and lottery	8,200
Property crime[b]	1,814,700	All other gambling	42,200
Crime Index total	2,284,000	Offenses against family	56,900
		Driving under the influence	1,268,700
Other assaults	468,600	Liquor laws	376,400
Arson	19,000	Drunkenness	1,176,600
Forgery and counterfeiting	77,200	Disorderly conduct	715,200
Fraud	262,500	Vagrancy	49,300
Embezzlement	8,100	All other offenses (except traffic)	1,883,800
Stolen property; buying, receiving, possessing	118,200	Suspicion (not included in total)	22,900
Vandalism	235,300	Curfew and loitering law violations	83,100
Weapons; carrying, possessing, etc.	157,900	Runaways	182,100
Prostitution and commercialized vice	94,200		

SOURCE: FBI, *Uniform Crime Reports, 1978* (Washington, D.C.: U.S. Government Printing Office, 1979), p. 186.

a. Arrest totals based on all reporting agencies and estimates for unreported areas.
b. Because of rounding, items may not add to totals.

certain serious offenses. (What is serious and what is not serious is a matter of conjecture; certainly, the FBI's index should not be taken as the definitive statement.) The Index offenses are homicide (murder and nonnegligent manslaughter), forcible rape, robbery, aggravated assault, burglary, larceny-theft, and auto theft. Arson was added to the list in 1979. The appendix, on page 515, presents the FBI definitions of all the offenses dealt with in its reports. According to the FBI, the fundamental objective of the *Uniform Crime Reports* "is to produce a reliable set of criminal statistics on a national basis for use in law enforcement administration, operation, and management." The data may also be used, we are told, for professional and scholarly research, and "as a reference source for the public as an indicator of the crime factor in our society."[30]

Those who use the FBI's reports certainly get an indication of crime, but what sort of an indication is it? We know from our earlier discussion that it provides no accurate measure of how many crimes are actually committed, nor can we believe that the American crime scene is accurately described. At best the FBI data provide us with indications of what is officially recognized as crime and reported to the FBI. In that sense the data provide us with a means of assessing the contours of some aspects of the American crime scene as seen through the eyes of the police and other official agencies. Since these contours are the ones readily given the public via the mass media, these are also the contours of the American "crime problem," as it is brought to public attention.

Many difficulties face those who try to use official data such as that published by the FBI. One problem concerns the use of official data for comparative purposes. Sooner or later most scientific research becomes comparative research. Animals, diseases, gases, rocks, stars, people, and crimes are compared along one dimension or another in the search for generalizations, laws, predictions, and explanations. Criminology is no exception. But comparative research on crime using official data is beset with difficulties.

First of all, the criminal law definitions of offenses vary. This is a particularly vexing problem in international comparisons; but even in America, in spite of the efforts by the FBI and by lawyers interested in uniform penal codes, we are not entirely free of the problem. The difficulty is this: (1) different jurisdictions may treat different things as crimes, so what is crime in one state or country may not be in another; and (2) one jurisdiction may define a particular type of crime, say auto theft, differently from another, so what they report as auto theft may not be quite the same thing.

Second, comparisons over time are especially hazardous to make. For one thing, the FBI's own offense classification system has not remained uniform over the years. In both 1958 and 1974, for instance, a number of definitional changes were made, rendering comparisons of figures before and after these dates rather difficult. In addition to this problem is the

ARREST TABULATIONS

Arrest statistics are collected monthly from contributing law enforcement agencies. In using these arrest figures, it's important to remember that the same person may be arrested several times during one year for the same type or for different offenses. Each arrest is counted. Further, the arrest of one person may solve several crimes and in other instances two or more persons may be arrested during the solution of one crime.

Arrests are primarily a measure of law enforcement activity as it relates to crime.

Arrest data, while primarily a measure of law enforcement activity, is also a gauge of criminality when used within its limitations as must be done with all forms of criminal statistics including court and penal.

SOURCE: FBI, *Uniform Crime Reports, 1978* (Washington, D.C.: U.S. Government Printing Office, 1979), p. 185.

Table 3.6 Total arrest trends, sex, 1969–1978 (3,608 agencies; 1978 estimated population 114,764,000)

OFFENSE CHARGED	MALES						FEMALES					
	TOTAL			UNDER 18			TOTAL			UNDER 18		
	1969	1978	PERCENT CHANGE	1969	1978	PERCENT CHANGE	1969	1978	PERCENT CHANGE	1969	1978	PERCENT CHANGE
TOTAL	4,195,086	4,424,628	+5.5	975,556	1,074,142	+10.1	659,638	917,618	+39.1	252,296	297,099	+17.8
Murder and nonnegligent manslaughter	7,777	8,988	+15.6	845	960	+13.6	1,453	1,582	+8.9	85	97	+14.1
Forcible rape	11,705	15,877	+35.6	2,355	2,643	+12.2	......	141	......	......	48	......
Robbery	55,827	74,035	+32.6	17,833	23,773	+33.3	3,534	5,739	+62.4	1,148	1,707	+48.7
Aggravated assault	79,565	117,849	+48.1	12,718	20,082	+57.9	11,274	17,818	+58.0	1,675	3,459	+106.5
Burglary	198,496	261,321	+31.7	108,128	139,524	+29.0	9,001	17,289	+92.1	4,709	8,974	+90.6
Larceny-theft	312,139	459,261	+47.1	169,722	209,342	+23.3	115,194	224,850	+95.2	53,239	84,445	+58.6
Motor vehicle theft	97,101	78,724	−18.9	56,705	41,202	−27.3	5,465	7,545	+38.1	3,153	4,446	+41.0
Violent crime[a]	154,874	216,749	+40.0	33,751	47,458	+40.6	16,261	25,280	+55.5	2,908	5,311	+82.6
Property crime[b]	607,736	799,306	+31.5	334,555	390,068	+16.6	129,660	249,684	+92.6	61,101	97,865	+60.2
Crime Index total	762,610	1,016,055	+33.2	368,306	437,526	+18.8	145,921	274,964	+88.4	64,009	103,176	+61.2

Offense												
Other assaults	193,664	226,830	+17.1	31,438	43,942	+39.8	26,422	37,226	+40.9	7,263	11,256	+55.0
Arson	6,280	8,881	+41.4	4,076	4,800	+17.8	606	1,264	+108.6	345	519	+50.4
Forgery and counterfeiting	22,895	27,621	+20.6	2,721	4,058	+49.1	7,058	13,107	+85.7	802	1,775	+121.3
Fraud	39,467	64,514	+63.5	1,850	2,669	+44.3	14,058	44,803	+218.7	455	1,130	+148.4
Embezzlement	3,839	3,050	−20.6	131	434	+231.3	1,064	1,112	+4.5	57	145	+154.4
Stolen property; buying, receiving, possessing	29,562	55,350	+87.2	10,514	20,545	+95.4	2,801	7,222	+157.8	819	2,035	+148.5
Vandalism	81,028	122,801	+51.6	59,703	72,645	+21.7	6,417	11,401	+77.7	4,068	6,024	+48.1
Weapons; carrying, possessing, etc.	68,936	84,753	+22.9	12,441	14,546	+16.9	4,802	7,424	+54.6	596	921	+54.5
Prostitution and commercialized vice	7,816	19,588	+150.6	236	814	+244.9	27,499	40,806	+48.4	617	1,748	+183.3
Sex offenses (except forcible rape and prostitution)	36,044	35,154	−2.5	7,020	6,515	−7.2	5,932	3,497	−41.0	2,190	687	−68.6
Drug abuse violations	145,864	298,220	+104.5	35,182	72,412	+105.8	29,062	51,185	+76.1	10,075	14,756	+46.5
Gambling	50,010	32,928	−34.2	1,309	1,297	−.9	4,366	3,293	−24.6	44	68	+54.5
Offenses against family and children	41,521	20,638	−50.3	531	1,109	+108.9	4,232	3,152	−25.5	181	732	+304.4
Driving under the influence	277,972	500,299	+80.0	3,112	11,370	+265.4	19,296	49,170	+154.8	138	1,301	+842.8
Liquor laws	153,995	155,295	+.8	49,182	54,268	+10.3	22,825	29,255	+28.2	10,129	16,069	+58.6
Drunkenness	1,178,850	626,369	−46.9	32,652	21,399	−34.5	88,822	51,785	−41.7	4,680	3,666	−21.7
Disorderly conduct	422,959	380,070	−10.1	84,138	71,301	−15.3	65,645	76,902	+17.1	16,697	15,055	−9.8
Vagrancy	67,818	16,633	−75.5	6,279	2,733	−56.5	7,305	4,092	−44.0	1,099	573	−47.9
All other offenses (except traffic)	468,358	637,951	+36.2	129,137	138,131	+7.0	87,362	130,013	+48.8	39,889	39,518	−.9
Suspicion (not included in totals)	72,802	10,070	−86.2	15,805	3,232	−79.6	12,697	1,682	−86.8	2,574	553	−78.5
Curfew and loitering law violations	69,788	45,499	−34.8	69,788	45,499	−34.8	17,192	11,355	−34.0	17,192	11,355	−34.0
Runaways	65,810	46,129	−29.9	65,810	46,129	−29.9	70,951	64,590	−9.0	70,951	64,590	−9.0

SOURCE: FBI, *Uniform Crime Reports, 1978*, p. 189.

a. Violent crimes are offenses of murder, forcible rape, robbery, and aggravated assault.
b. Property crimes are offenses of burglary, larceny-theft, and motor vehicle theft.

question of crime rate computation itself. Rates are used for comparative purposes since they express the number of reported crimes in proportion to some base, thus making comparisons more meaningful. Population is traditionally used in the computation of rates: the number of reported crimes in say, Chicago, is multiplied by 100,000 and divided by the population of the city. Now, accurate figures on population are notoriously difficult to arrive at. Even census figures amount to estimates rather than true numbers. But official crime rates for many years were figured using population data from the most recent past census. Since the national census is conducted every ten years, this meant that crime rate figures for 1959, for example, were based on a population figure for 1950. Obviously, if both crime and population are on the increase, but *only* crime increases are taken into account, the rates for a year like 1959 will be substantially higher than for 1950; but much of the rate increase might disappear if the corresponding population increases were taken into account.[31]

Another difficulty is the composition or structure of the population. Suppose, for example, you are comparing two states, and you find that the crime rate in state X is higher than that in state Y. Suppose also that in state X a larger proportion of the population is under age 21 than in state Y. Part of the difference in rates could, then, be due to differences in the age composition of the two state populations. Unless you have accurate ways to assess population structure (and this includes racial composition, sex composition, and so forth) your comparisons lend themselves to faulty interpretations. The problem would be solved if those responsible for the publication of official crime rates could provide us with rates specific to certain population groups, that is, age-specific rates, sex-specific rates, and so on. Armed with this information we could make better comparisons from place to place and time to time.

These are not the only difficulties facing those who would do comparative research on crime. Variations and changes in data recording technology, in police policy and practice, and in public sentiments hamper efforts to do such research and to make constructive interpretations of crime patterns and trends. Yet comparative analysis is very important in criminology. We are not going to uncover the complexities of the crime scene if we cannot compare one time with another and one place with another. It is hoped, therefore, that efforts continue to be made in ironing out problems in this area.

Official Data on the Criminal Justice System

Suppose you wanted to know how many Americans were serving time in the nation's prisons, the reasons they were there, and how long they had been there. Suppose you wanted to know about the physical, social, and health conditions in jails. Or suppose you were interested in comparing the social characteristics of those in prison with those in community-based correctional programs and those on parole and probation. Where would you look to find out?

It was not until very recently that the authorities displayed any interest at all in the compilation of national data on the processing of suspects and offenders. However, the Law Enforcement Assistance Administration (LEAA) has helped turn things around. With its financial backing, much research on the criminal justice system has now been undertaken. In 1970 a much-needed *National Jail Census* was conducted by the United States Bureau of the Census. This study covered all aspects of jail operations, including facilities, programs, inmate populations, physical conditions, and day-to-day use. Its findings were a startling revelation for those who thought that inhumane conditions were largely a thing of the past and that jails were meant to be places where the *guilty* are punished. Certainly, jails are a punitive experience for those in them; but the jail census found that of 160,863 persons being held on the census date, less than half were actually serving sentences; the remainder were awaiting trial or some kind of postconviction action.[32]

The LEAA has sponsored other fact-finding surveys of correctional institutions in America. In 1972, a more detailed survey of the nation's jails was undertaken, and in 1974 a census of state prison populations was carried out.[33] The criminologist interested in the confinement side of the legal process finds a wealth of information in these reports. Yet they are likely to be "one shot" affairs rather than an annual event, and hence are of limited value for longitudinal research.

If you want to find out about imprisonment from year to year, the United States Bureau of Prisons' National Prisoner Statistics series is a useful data source. However, these bulletins, together with a few special reports, provide only gross data on an extremely limited number of issues.[34] Far broader in their coverage of criminal justice issues are the recent volumes compiled by the Criminal Justice Research Center of Albany, New York.[35] Under a grant from LEAA, this center has put together a *Sourcebook of Criminal Justice Statistics* dealing with the most recent data compiled by both governmental and private agencies. It includes information on just about every aspect of the criminal justice system as well as on public attitudes toward criminal justice topics. Annual editions have been published since 1973, and it is hoped that the effort continues.

For scholars interested in keeping track of research efforts sponsored by private and public agencies, the LEAA's National Institute of Law Enforcement and Criminal Justice (NILECJ) maintains a Reference and Dissemination Division. This division manages the distribution of information and related services through its National Criminal Justice Reference Service (NCJRS), an international clearinghouse. Bulletins are published on a regular basis and, together with the *Justice Assistance*

A SAMPLING OF CURRENT JOURNALS DEALING WITH CRIME AND JUSTICE[a]

American Criminal Law Review
American Journal of Sociology
American Sociological Review
British Journal of Criminology
Canadian Journal of Criminology
Corrections Today (formerly American Journal
  of Corrections)
Crime and Delinquency
Crime and Social Justice
Criminology: An Interdisciplinary Journal
Federal Probation
Journal of Criminal Justice

Journal of Criminal Law and Criminology
Journal of Police Science and Administration
Journal of Research in Crime and Delinquency
Judicature
Law and Society Review
Social Problems

— plus a host of law journals and a variety of practice-oriented magazines and journals focusing on particular occupations and professions.

a. Not all these journals deal *only* with crime-related topics.

News (formerly the *LEAA Newsletter*), provide up-to-date feedback on who's doing what in criminal justice research and in criminology generally. Government-sponsored research alone is now touching on all areas of crime and justice — victimization, parole, police practices, prisons, prosecution, homicide, organized crime, rape, deterrence, burglary, juvenile justice, alternatives to prison, white-collar crime, and more.

Needless to say, not all criminological research deals with problems for which available data are appropriate. If you are not interested in aggregate phenomena such as crime rates or rates of imprisonment, then official data will probably be irrelevant. You certainly would not find much on the social organization of burglary by thumbing through the *Uniform Crime Reports* (but see pages 193–196).[36] Sometimes it is both necessary and desirable to collect your own data according to a specific research design. Scholars and practitioners recognize the need to keep abreast of development in the field, so they belong to professional associations such as the American Society of Criminology and the Academy of Criminal Justice Sciences. They also read the journals relevant to their interests — there are now a good many of these available (see box above). In this way they are kept aware of theoretical advances, new methodologies, and new evidence.

When it comes to the broad spectrum of criminological issues and problems no one kind of data will serve our needs. Criminology is a growing and changing field; new perspectives and new interests call for new methodologies, new data, new lines of inquiry. Throughout the remainder of this text you will see tradition and innovation side by side in the continuing quest for insights and explanations. If we recognize the limitations of available (usually official) data on the crime scene, if we bear in mind that they provide us with some information on some aspects of our subject, and if we know when *not* to use them, then we will no doubt find an important place for them in our enterprise. Certainly, we should continue to strive for the systematic, routine collection and dissemination of national, state, and local crime data. Because the task is both monumental and expensive, it will likely be government agencies which will continue to do the job for us.

In subsequent chapters you will have occasion to consider official statistics as these bear upon different topics. Don't be afraid to challenge them, bearing in mind the discussion in this chapter. I have tried to present official data in such a way as to minimize misunderstanding and misinterpretation; I hope the effort has been successful. Where it is possible to do so I have coupled official data with findings from in-depth studies by individual criminologists, who are less hampered by official constraints (which is not to say that they have no such constraints). We do our subject an injustice if we do not know something about how crime, criminals, and criminal justice appear in their official guises. In many important respects the official crime scene *is* the crime scene.

References

1. Edwin H. Sutherland and Donald R. Cressey, *Criminology*, 9th ed. (Philadelphia: Lippincott, 1974), p. 25.
2. Don C. Gibbons, *Society, Crime, and Criminal Careers*, 2nd ed. (Englewood Cliffs, N.J.: Prentice-Hall, 1973), p. 100.
3. Herbert A. Bloch and Gilbert Geis, *Man, Crime, and Society*, 2nd ed. (New York: Random House, 1970), pp. 111–12.
4. See Donald J. Black, "Production of Crime Rates," *American Sociological Review* 35 (1970), pp. 735–36.
5. Black, "Production of Crime Rates," p. 736.
6. Nigel Walker, *Crime, Courts, and Figures* (Baltimore: Penguin Books, 1971), p. 27.
7. Black, "Production of Crime Rates," p. 746.
8. See Wayne R. LaFave, *Arrest: The Decision to Take a Suspect into Custody* (Boston: Little, Brown, 1965); Irving Piliavin and Scott Briar, "Police Encounters with Juveniles," *American Journal of Sociology* 70 (1964), pp. 206–14; Arthur L. Stinchcombe, "Institutions of Privacy in the Determination of Police Administrative Practices," *American Journal of Sociology* 69 (1963), pp. 150–60; William J. Chambliss and John T. Liell, "The Legal Process in the Community Setting," *Crime and Delinquency* 12 (1966), pp. 310–17.
9. Chambliss and Liell, "The Legal Process in the Community Setting," p. 317.
10. Jerome H. Skolnick, *Justice without Trial: Law Enforcement in a Democratic Society* (New York: Wiley, 1966); Austin T. Turk, *Criminality and Legal Order* (Chicago: Rand McNally, 1969); Michael Banton, *The Policeman in the Community* (London: Tavistock, 1964).
11. Skolnick, *Justice Without Trial*, pp. 164–81.
12. Marvin E. Wolfgang, *Crimes of Violence*, A Report to the President's Commission on Law Enforcement and the Administration of Justice (Washington, D.C.: U.S. Government Printing Office, 1967), p. 33.
13. Skolnick, *Justice Without Trial*, pp. 172–73.
14. Dennis Chapman, *Sociology and the Stereotype of the Criminal* (London: Tavistock, 1968), pp. 10–11.
15. Ibid.
16. See Michael Fooner, "Money and Economic Factors in Crime and Delinquency," *Criminology* 8 (1971), p. 335.
17. See Wesley G. Skogan, "Dimensions of the Dark Figure of Unreported Crime," *Crime and Delinquency* 23 (1977), pp. 41–50.
18. The President's Commission on Law Enforcement and the Administration of Justice, *The Challenge of Crime in a Free Society* (Washington, D.C.: U.S. Government Printing Office, 1967), p. 21.
19. See Albert J. Reiss, Jr., "Public Perceptions and Recollections about Crime, Law Enforcement, and Criminal Justice," in *Studies in Crime and Law Enforcement in Major Metropolitan Areas*, vol. 1, sect. 1, Report to the President's Commission on Law Enforcement and the Administration of Justice: *Field Surveys III*. Also see Albert Biderman, Louise A. Johnson, Jennie McIntyre,

and Adrianne W. Weir, *Report on a Pilot Study in the District of Columbia on Victimization and Attitudes toward Law Enforcement*, Report to the President's Commission: *Field Surveys I;* and Richard Block, "Why Notify the Police?: The Victim's Decision to Notify the Police of an Assault," *Criminology* 4 (1974), pp. 555–69. Richard O. Hawkins, "Who Called the Cops?: Decisions to Report Criminal Victimization," *Law and Society Review* 7 (1973), pp. 427–44.

20. Biderman *Report on Victimization*.

21. Appendix 1, p. 3, of *Criminal Victimization Surveys in Eight American Cities: A Comparison of 1971/1972 and 1974/1975 Findings*. National Crime Survey Report No. SD-NCS-C-5 (Washington, D.C.: U.S. Government Printing Office, 1976).

22. See Michael J. Hindelang, Travis Hirschi, and Joseph G. Weiss, "Correlates of Delinquency: The Illusion of Discrepancy Between Self-Report and Official Measures," *American Sociological Review* 44 (1979), pp. 995–1014. See also Delbert S. Elliott and Suzanne S. Ageton, "Reconciling Race and Class Differences in Self-Reported and Official Estimates of Delinquency," *American Sociological Review* 45 (1980), p. 107.

23. Martin Gold, *Delinquent Behavior in an American City* (Belmont, Calif.: Brooks/Cole, 1970), p. 30. Quoted in Hindelang, Hirschi, and Weis, "Correlates of Delinquency," p. 997.

24. For self-report studies consult Austin L. Porterfield, "Delinquency and Its Outcome in Court and College," *American Journal of Sociology* 44 (1943), pp. 199–208; James S. Wallerstein and Clement Wyle, "Our Law-abiding Lawbreakers," *Federal Probation* 25 (1947), pp. 107–12; James F. Short, Jr., and F. Ivan Nye, "Reported Behavior as a Criterion of Deviant Behavior," *Social Problems* 5 (1957–1958), pp. 207–13; Short and Nye, "Extent of Unrecorded Juvenile Delinquency: Tentative Conclusions," *Journal of Criminal Law, Criminology, and Police Science* 49 (1958), pp. 296–302; Robert A. Dentler and Lawrence J. Monroe, "Social Correlates of Early Adolescent Theft," *American Sociological Review* 26 (1961), pp. 733–43; Ronald L. Akers, "Socio-Economic Status and Delinquent Behavior, A Retest," *Journal of Research in Crime and Delinquency* 1 (1964), pp. 38–46; Harwin L. Voss, "Socioeconomic Status and Reported Delinquent Behavior," *Social Problems* 13 (1966), pp. 314–24.

25. *LEAA Newsletter* 9 (1979–1980), p. 8.

26. Walker, *Crimes, Courts, and Figures*, p. 37.

27. See John Blackmore, "The Relationship Between Self-Reported Delinquency and Official Convictions Amongst Adolescent Boys," *British Journal of Criminology* 14 (1974), p. 173.

28. See Robert H. Hardt and George E. Bodine, *Development of Self-Report Instruments in Delinquency Research*, Youth Development Center, Syracuse University, 1965; John P. Clark and L. L. Tifft, "Polygraph and Interview Validation of Self-reported Deviant Behavior," *American Sociological Review* 31 (1966), pp. 516–23; David P. Farrington, "Self-Reports of Deviant Behavior: Predictive and Stable?" *Journal of Criminal Law and Criminology* 64 (1973), pp. 99–110; H. B. Gibson, Sylvia Morrison, and D. J. West, "The Confession of Known Offences in Response to a Self-reported Delinquency Schedule," *British Journal of Criminology* 10 (1970), pp. 277–80.

29. Maynard L. Erickson and Lamar T. Empey, "Court Records, Undetected Delinquency and Decision-Making," *Journal of Criminal Law, Criminology, and Police Science* 54 (1963), p. 4.

30. FBI, *Uniform Crime Reports, 1974* (Washington, D.C.: U.S. Government Printing Office, 1975), p. 2.

31. See Daniel Bell, "The Myth of Crime Waves," in Bell, *The End of Ideology*, rev. ed. (New York: Free Press, 1962), pp. 151–74.

32. Law Enforcement Assistance Administration, *National Jail Census, 1970: A Report on the Nation's Local Jails and Types of Inmates* (Washington, D.C.: U.S. Government Printing Office, 1970), pp. 10–11.

33. Law Enforcement Assistance Administration, *The Nation's Jails* (Washington, D.C.: U.S. Government Printing Office, 1975). Law Enforcement Assistance Administration, *Census of State Correctional Facilities, 1974, Advance Report* (Washington, D.C.: U.S. Government Printing Office, 1975).

34. The special reports published by the U.S. Bureau of Prisons as part of the National Prisoner Statistics series are entitled: *Characteristics of State Prisoners, 1960; Prisoners Released from State and Federal Institutions, 1960; State Prisons: Admissions and Releases, 1964; State Prisons: Admissions and Releases, 1970;* and *Profile of State Prison Inmates; Sociodemographic Findings from the 1974 Survey of State Correctional Facilities*. All are available from the U.S. Government Printing Office, Washington, D.C.

35. The most recent edition is Timothy J. Flanagan, Michael J. Hindelang, and Michael R. Gottfredson, eds., *Sourcebook of Criminal Justice Statistics — 1978* (Washington, D.C.: U.S. Government Printing Office, 1979).

Part II

Crimes and Criminal Offenders

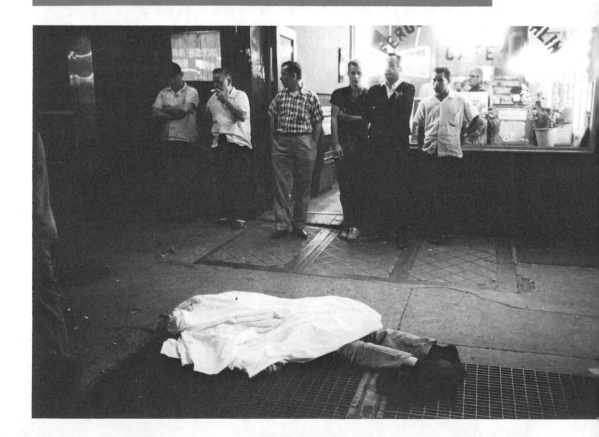

4

Interpersonal Violence

The world is no stranger to violence. The last eighty years have witnessed two world wars; the mass extermination of millions of Jews; the worldwide killing of countless political enemies; the mass destruction caused by the slaughter of Olympic athletes in Munich; and the strife in Northern Ireland, in Africa, and in the Near and Far East. And the list could go on.

In America, violence is everyday fare. Over the last few years Americans have been witness to the assassination of presidents and civil rights leaders; riots and the killing of student dissenters; labor violence; and armored cars in Chicago during the Democratic National Convention of 1968. Not so long ago there was the spectacle of lynch mobs, the violence of the Ku Klux Klan, and the rampages of Hell's Angels. Today we hear of torture and killings in the nation's jails and prisons; we hear of child abuse, hidden and yet apparently on the increase; we await the next account of a plane hijacking, a kidnapping, a sniper wreaking havoc, or a mass murder.

Those of us who have not experienced violence directly can do so vicariously. Books, films, television programs, news stories, and comic strips all keep us in daily touch with violence. Even our language is replete with the imagery of violence, as death itself is conjured up in a host of ways:

A well used tennis ball is "dead"; a playoff in a golf match is called "sudden death"; a marksman is a "dead shot"; a player in any game who falls behind is a "dead duck" . . . ; we say "he slays me" of a comedian; a "dying cause" or a "dead issue" for a lost proposition; a bill was "killed" in committee; the "dead" of night; he was caught "dead to rights"; "let's kill some time," or "he murdered the music," or the team was "slaughtered," etc. . . .[1]

In this chapter our focus will be on interpersonal violence. Attention is restricted to situations in which the victim is another human being, rather than a nonhuman object as in the case of vandalism. Likewise, we shall not consider suicide. Also, and in contrast to the National Commission on the Causes and Prevention of Violence, we shall exclude rape and robbery. While both these crimes involve interpersonal violence, they differ in significant ways from the offenses to be discussed here, and are reserved for discussion in later chapters. As used in this chapter, *violence* is defined simply as the use of physical force by one or more human beings against one or more others during the course of face-to-face interaction.

Violence in Historical Perspective

Most authors agree that a better understanding of the present is accomplished through awareness of the past. Certainly, violence is not something unique to the twentieth century. Human history bears witness to its occurrence throughout the ages. So long as physical force remains an option in man's repertoire of actions, it may surface at any time.

Looking back in time, violence is found in primitive societies just as it is in civilized societies. Under primitive law, acts of physical aggression were typically handled privately by the injured party or his kinfolk. Redress of grievances was often sought through bloody retaliation. If, as was sometimes the case, this violent retaliation was viewed by the original offender as an offense in itself, a bloody feud was likely to result. Feuds thus begun might last for a short time or they might last for generations. Feuds are not uncommon in some societies even today.[2]

In ancient Rome, a civilized society by the standards of its day, violence was met with violence. The eye-for-an-eye conception of proper retaliation was invoked in the Twelfth Tables. However, not all judicial violence was in retaliation for other violence: anyone who stole by night was subject to death at the hands of the injured party. As A. W. Lintott describes things: "a general belief that private force was a proper instrument to execute private justice seems to have been in evidence at the time of the Twelve Tables." Also, "violence that was used to secure a man's natural or legal rights was recognized as a perfectly proper way of freeing him from undeserved restrictions."[3] The Romans, Lintott suggests, were used to violence, and the upper classes in particular placed no great value on human life. Indeed, toward the end of the Republic, bands of strong-arm thugs roamed the streets acting on orders from their upper-class retainers.

In the Middle East, the Code of Hammurapi identified various acts of violence: kidnapping children, assaulting parents, and assaults resulting in miscarriage. The punishments for these offenses varied. If someone kidnapped another's son he was executed; if a boy struck his father his hand was cut off; if an assailant caused a miscarriage, he was punished according to the victim's status — the higher her status the more severe the penalty. Generally speaking, whenever an offense injured a person of higher status than the offender the punishment was accordingly more severe. Women were regarded as socially inferior to men and the laws reflected this. The Code of Hammurapi reads "If a man's wife has caused the death of her husband because of another male, they shall impale that woman on a stake."[4] No such law appears to have existed for cases of a man killing his wife for the sake of another woman. Interpersonal violence in early human civilizations was matched, if not exceeded, by violence in punishment. Emile Durkheim paints the following gruesome picture of retributive justice under early law:

> In many ancient societies, death pure and simple did not constitute the supreme punishment. For the most atrocious crimes it was augmented with additional tortures to make it all the more frightful. Thus, the Egyptians, besides hanging and beheading, also favored burning at the stake, torturing with hot coals, and crucifixion. . . . The Code of Manou distinguished between simple death, as in beheading, and death with aggravation. There were seven kinds of the latter: empalement, fire, drowning, crushing under the feet of an elephant, hot oil poured in the mouth and ears, being torn to pieces by dogs in public, and being cut up into pieces with razor-sharp knives.[5]

With the development of English criminal law, violence as a means to punish other violence slowly moved out of the hands of private individuals and into the hands of the state. Violence became the prerogative of the state, which means it became outlawed as something members of society could adopt in handling their affairs. It is interesting to consider why violence became legal and permissible in most situations only when perpetrated by the state. The answer lies partly in the political processes that accompanied the developing Norman grip on English society during the twelfth and thirteenth centuries. Since the Normans were in effect occupation forces, and interested in consolidating their hold over the country, one of the first things on their agenda was to secure control over the routine use of force. The new rulers slowly wrested from the English barons their traditional control over the use of force in their jurisdictions:

> To replace the confusion of feudalism, national rulers set about destroying the old instrumentalities of coercion and control. Private armies and bands of

retainers were abolished; manorial courts were squeezed out of existence; local bodies of law were absorbed or overridden. . . . The national political authorities were intent on establishing a monopoly over the forms of violence, or, stated otherwise, the exercise of violence was being converted into a national function.[6]

This did not mean a declining role for violence in everyday affairs. On the contrary, English life was marked until at least the eighteenth century by the ready use of violence. Violence surfaced not merely in wars and disputes among political foes, both common events, but also in sports, from the earlier jousting matches to cock fighting, wrestling, and other pastimes; in the routine affairs of governments and the judicial system; and in the efforts of peasants and outlaws to make a living. Notwithstanding its condemnation under law, physical aggression found expression in myriad forms. We might think that the modern world is violent; but medieval England was no paradise of domestic tranquillity.

VIOLENCE IN AMERICAN HISTORY

The Puritans came to America largely to escape the violence associated with efforts to suppress their free exercise of religious preferences. Perhaps because of this, violence by New Englanders was generally a rare thing. Violence in the name of justice, however, was not. Consider what happened during the celebrated Salem witch hunts. In one year alone more than a score of deaths resulted from this repressive episode in criminal justice — and more were to die before the witch scare died down.[7]

Some people believe violence is never right, that it is immoral and without justification no matter what the circumstances. Others think violence can be justified, though only under exceptional circumstances, such as for the purposes of self-defense or collective defense. Others contend that violence can be justified by its accomplishments: a greater good or the prevention of a greater evil.[8] Much of the violence that has marked America's history has been justified, if not glorified, on the grounds that it brought about important, constructive changes in American society. The revolutionary war, the Civil War, the Indian wars, frontier vigilante justice, and labor violence have been called examples of positive violence.[9] That thousands of people were killed, maimed, orphaned, and left homeless has been played down; the ends have been used to justify the means.

During the nineteenth century, instrumental violence, that is, violence used to achieve an ulterior purpose, became a way of life in America. Riots plagued the major cities; feuds erupted in Kentucky, Virginia, West Virginia, and Texas; guerrilla bands roamed the Midwest in search of glory and fortune; outlaws plundered the frontier regions of the country; citizens formed groups of vigilantes for the ostensible purpose of establishing law and order; workers seeking the right to unionize took to the streets and were met by police and hired thugs; lynch mobs plagued the South and dealt their own brand of justice; and the mass destruction of Native Americans continued. Wherever they surfaced, situations of conflict seemed destined to result in violence.[10]

The ready resort to violence as a problem-solving device continued into the twentieth century. The labor movement was marked by violence as it confronted stubborn bosses and like-minded politicians. Especially violent were the clashes in the country's mining areas. In one mining strike — against the Colorado Fuel and Iron Company, from 1913 to 1914 — more than thirty men, women, and children lost their lives in the fighting between the two sides.[11] Then, too, the first half of the twentieth century witnessed new forms of violence: during and after Prohibition, gangland killings became a routine event in some cities, Chicago in particular; the Ku Klux Klan became a national organization and brought its hatred and prejudice to bear on blacks, Catholics, Jews, and "radical" whites in brutal beatings and killings.

But the historical American experience with individual rather than group acts of violence is difficult to pin down because of the lack of national statistics dealing with past levels and trends. In their report to the National Commission on the Causes and Prevention of Violence (hereafter called the National Commission), Mulvihill and Tumin argue that "there is no unequivocal evidence to suggest that recent levels and trends of violence per capita are significantly greater than in the more historical past."[12] Given the post–revolutionary war levels of group violence, a reasonable expectation would be that individual acts of violence were at high, not low, levels and followed an upward, not downward, trend during the nineteenth century. Mulvihill and Tumin conclude:

> If any general reported trend can be hypothesized, the available evidence suggests an initial high level of violence slowly rising in the late 19th century, perhaps leveling off for a period, rising to a new peak shortly after the turn of the 20th century, and then declining somewhat thereafter. The question of whether or not Americans have historically shown a propensity or impulse to acts of violence remains difficult to answer.[13]

Homicide and Assault: The Current Picture

Most experts agree that violent crime has been on the increase in America during recent years. The National Commission found about a 47 percent increase in the official rates for murder and nonnegligent manslaughter between 1958 and 1968. Rates for aggravated assault showed even higher increases, around 100 percent.[14] FBI data confirm that aggravated assault rates continued to rise during the 1970s, although more slowly.[15] The most recent four-year period for which information is available shows recorded rates increasing 19 percent (see figure 4.1). In the case of murder, rates actually fell slightly over this same 1974–1978 period. However, it is too early to tell whether we shall continue to enjoy a decline in rates of homicidal violence.

HOMICIDE

Official rates of murder and nonnegligent manslaughter vary around the country. New England states typically have the lowest rates, while states

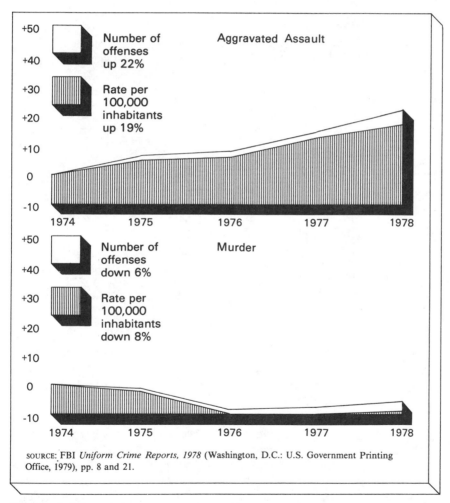

SOURCE: FBI *Uniform Crime Reports, 1978* (Washington, D.C.: U.S. Government Printing Office, 1979), pp. 8 and 21.

Figure 4.1 Trends in aggravated assault and murder, 1974–1978 (% change over 1970)

Table 4.1 U.S. homicide rates per 100,000 population, by region, 1978

NORTHEAST	6.9	NORTH CENTRAL	7.1
New England: Connecticut, Maine, Massachusetts, New Hampshire, Rhode Island, Vermont	3.6	*East North Central:* Illinois, Indiana, Ohio, Michigan, Wisconsin	7.9
Middle Atlantic: New York, New Jersey, Pennsylvania	8.0	*West North Central:* Iowa, Kansas, Minnesota, Missouri, Nebraska, North Dakota, South Dakota	5.1
SOUTH			
South Atlantic: Delaware, Florida, Georgia, Maryland, North Carolina, South Carolina, Virginia, West Virginia	11.6	WEST	9.5
		Mountain: Arizona, Colorado, Idaho, Montana, Nevada, New Mexico, Utah, Wyoming	7.8
East South Central: Alabama, Kentucky, Tennessee, Mississippi	10.9	*Pacific:* California, Hawaii, Oregon, Washington, Alaska	10.1
West South Central: Oklahoma, Texas, Arkansas, Louisiana	10.9 13.2	UNITED STATES RATE: 9.0 homicides per 100,000 population	

SOURCE: FBI, *Uniform Crime Reports, 1978* (Washington, D.C.: U.S. Government Printing Office, 1979), pp. 40–44.

in the South lead the country (see table 4.1). Rates also vary by size of city. The highest rates are found in cities with over 250,000 population, and rates tend to decline along with city size. Homicide is primarily a large-city phenomenon. However, for many years, rural rates have been slightly higher than the rates for many small- and medium-sized cities. The reason seems to be that the distance from and quality of medical services in rural areas render assaults more likely to turn into homicides. We are reminded again that it may be mostly fortuitous that an assault does not end up a homicide.

More detailed information about official homicides is found in arrest data. Fortunately, official statistics on homicides are among the best available. It is rare that homicides go unreported, and it is also rare that a suspect is not apprehended and charged with the crime. Police departments generally take great pride in their ability to solve homicides, which is made possible by the existence of a corpse and the typical circumstances of the crime. Certainly, the clearance rate for homicide is markedly better than that for any other Index crime (see figure 4.2).

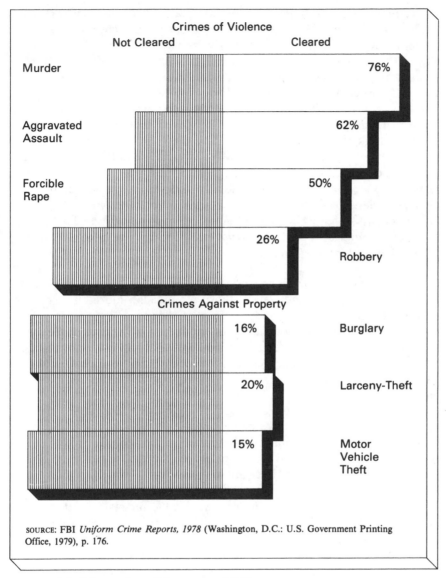

Figure 4.2 Crimes cleared by arrest, 1977

More than half of the arrests for homicide occur in cities over 250,000; of all those arrested, more than 80 percent are males and more than half are under age 25. Blacks are arrested around 50 percent of the time, and more than one-third are under age 18. According to recent FBI data, around 20 percent of those homicides on which information is available are committed in the course of another felony crime, most often rape, robbery, or burglary. In most of these cases, the arrested suspect is white.

The most common homicide situation starts when the parties to the fatal interaction are involved in an argument or altercation, often over matters that might appear relatively trivial to many people. Quarrels over money, over girls, in bars, and sundry other situational disputes are the precipitating circumstances in most homicides. The FBI estimates that around 50 percent of all known homicides follow this pattern, with a third of these occurring within the family. Family homicides mostly involve a spouse killing a spouse, but on occasion children are the killers or victims.

The victims of homicides, national data show, are preponderantly male and usually young adults under 35. Most victims are of the same race and socioeconomic status as the offender, which most often means black and relatively poor. Most likely, the offender and victim know each other as relatives, friends, or acquaintances. In sum, official national data suggest that if you are a young black male living in one of the nation's larger cities you have a better chance than anyone else of being arrested for homicide or of being the victim of one.

Urban Studies While official statistics on homicide are valuable for assessing gross patterns and trends, those who wish a more complete picture will find a number of in-depth urban studies to which they can turn. The pioneering study of homicide was conducted by Marvin Wolfgang in the mid-1950s. Wolfgang looked at homicides that had come to the attention of Philadelphia police from 1948 to 1952. He investigated a host of variables, including race, sex, age, temporal patterns, spatial patterns, motives, and offender-victim relationships.[16]

Since the publication of Wolfgang's study quite a few other urban investigations of homicide have been done. In America, the settings for these investigations have included Houston, Chicago, Detroit, Atlanta, and greater Cleveland.[17] With few exceptions, these studies tend to confirm the following observations about homicide: (1) young black adult males are most likely to be identified as offenders and victims; (2) offenders and victims tend to be of low socioeconomic status and to reside in inner-city slums; (3) homicides usually occur during the late evening and early morning hours of the weekend; (4) around half of the known homicides occur in either the offender's or the victim's home; (5) homicides do not follow consistent seasonal patterns — they do not, as prevalent myth would have it, occur more often during the hot months of the year; (6) offenders and victims are usually acquainted and often live in the same immediate neighborhood; and (7) strangers are killed most often during the commission of another felony, such as robbery or burglary.

Studies in Atlanta and Chicago provide us with some interesting observations regarding trends in homicide. Though tentative at this point, three conclusions seem warranted on the basis of the evidence from these studies: (1) the homicide offender is getting younger — the proportion of offenses committed by persons under age 25 has been rising; (2) interracial homicides seem to be on the increase, though the increases are small in both Chicago and Atlanta; and (3) the proportion of homicides involving strangers has been increasing.[18] It will be interesting to see whether future studies in other cities confirm these apparent trends.

Guns and Alcohol   According to the FBI, over 60 percent of all homicides recorded in 1978 were committed with a firearm; handguns were the weapon in 49 percent of all homicides. The picture has remained virtually unchanged since 1970.

Some claim that if Americans could not readily acquire guns there would be less killing; others argue that the availability of guns has no bearing on homicide rates — that people kill, not guns. The debate on the issue is fierce and seems unlikely to be resolved in the near future. Since guns are a fact of life in America and have been a prominent possession for at least two centuries, those in favor of civilian disarmament come up against the opposition of tradition as well as contrary opinions and beliefs. Their position is made more difficult by the opposition of powerful interest groups such as the National Rifle Association (NRA) and the highly profitable gun industry, which earns an estimated $2 billion a year.[19]

What are the facts? Would as many homicides occur if guns were banned or strict controls were instituted making possession of firearms difficult and limited? What if we outlaw only handguns? Would we see less violent crime if we did what countries such as England have done, namely, place major restrictions on gun acquisition and ownership and set severe penalties for violations of gun laws?

Clearly these are complex questions, and, as might be expected, they have no simple answers. Insofar as scholars have investigated guns and violence, the evidence indicates beyond a reasonable doubt that the availability of guns is a factor in homicide. Other things being equal, and assuming there simply were no guns, we could anticipate an immediate reduction in the proportion of assaults resulting in death. According to most experts, the chances of dying from a gunshot wound are one in five, compared to one in twenty for knives and other stabbing or cutting instruments. But guns are available. The effect of availability was established by a 1976 study of homicides in Detroit. It concluded that guns were a factor in that city's rising homicide rates, and that the availability of firearms, especially handguns, contributed to yearly homicide levels.[20]

Other evidence cited in support of the connection between gun availability and homicide rates concerns regional variations in these two phenomena. George Newton and Franklin Zimring point out that known weapon ownership rates are highest in the South: 59 percent of all households owned weapons in 1968. On the other hand, only 33 percent of all households in the East owned firearms.[21] In 1967, the official homicide rate for the South was almost 10 per 100,000 people; for the East it was just over 4 per 100,000 people.[22]

Most homicides occur in the heat of an argument between acquaintances. Alcohol and firearms are often present as situational factors.

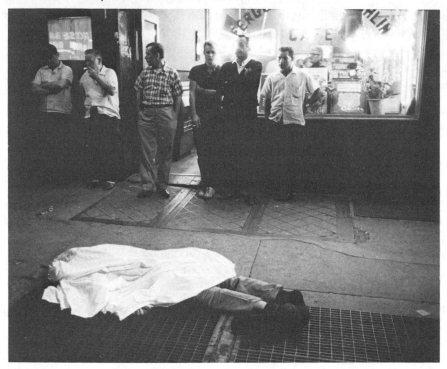

Just as guns turn up as the weapon used in most homicides, so alcohol turns up as a situational feature in most homicides. According to research findings of the past few years, alcohol has been found to be present in a majority of homicide incidents. Wolfgang, for example, found that in Philadelphia alcohol was present in either the offender or victim or both in 63.6 percent of his 588 homicide cases. Other studies have found alcohol to be present in similar or greater proportions.[23] More often than not, both offender and victim had been drinking immediately prior to or during the fatal interaction.

Does this mean that alcohol in some way caused the subsequent killing? Most authors recognize the statistical association between presence of alcohol and homicides but do not speak of the relationship in causal terms. True, alcohol, is a psychoactive drug (see page 282), meaning it produces mental changes in most people who consume it. What kind of changes and how extensive they are will depend upon numerous factors, including the quantity consumed, the physiological state of the consumer, the consumer's tolerance for the drug, and whether or not he or she has just eaten. Summarizing their review of the literature, Mulvihill and Tumin conclude:

It cannot be overemphasized that the relationship between alcohol and crime is a highly complex one. Only occasionally can one say with certainty that a violent crime would not have been committed if the offender had not been drinking. Therefore, while the relationships indicated . . . between alcohol and violent crimes are highly suggestive, they cannot, of course, be construed as causal connections. . . . It has been pointed out, however, that a causal relationship does appear to exist in many instances between alcohol and violence. For example, when a man kills his best friend over a trivial situation, drunkenness often appears as a direct factor. On the other hand, although many serious crimes may be committed by drunk persons, more often drunkenness is only one of several complicating factors. It must also be remembered that most men who drink or who are drunk *do not* commit serious crimes, and particularly do not commit homicide. . . . One must keep in mind that even if alcohol appears to be a necessary element in some instances of homicide, it is clearly not necessary for all of them. Further, it is important to bear in mind that alcohol use does not automatically or necessarily lead to violence.[24]

In short, alcohol is best viewed as one likely precipitating factor in violence. To the extent that alcohol lowers social inhibitions and fosters in many cases a reduction of anxiety and guilt, people who are or have been drinking and are involved in some sort of dispute may find themselves acting more aggressively than otherwise would have been the case. The dispute may have erupted anyway, and the individuals concerned may well have been tempted to seek a violent solution; with the situational influence of alcohol missing, however, fear, anxiety, guilt, and social inhibitions are there to serve as constraints.

Victim Precipitation There is growing evidence that many homicide victims precipitate their own deaths. Many years ago Hans Von Hentig underscored the importance of victim precipitation. In a landmark book, *The Criminal and His Victim,* Von Hentig argued that killers are often driven to murder as much by their victim's activities as by their own inclination.[25] This is most likely to occur when those involved know each other and are attuned to each other's personality. Tensions and mutual aggravations may reach the point where both personalities see reconciliation only through violence; this can occur suddenly or develop over a long period of time. In any event, the violence is to be understood as an outcome of actions and responses by both parties and not merely those of the subsequent slayer.

A standard definition of victim precipitation is given by Marvin Wolfgang:

The term *victim-precipitated* is applied to those criminal homicides in which the victim is a direct, positive precipitator in the crime. The role of the victim is characterized by his having been the first in the homicide drama to use physical force directed against his subsequent slayer. The victim-precipitated cases are those in which the victim was the first to show and use a deadly weapon, to strike a blow in an altercation — in short, the first to commence the interplay of resort to physical violence.[26]

Examples given by Wolfgang, taken from Philadelphia police files, will serve to illustrate typical situations of victim-precipitated homicide:

> During a lover's quarrel, the male (victim) hit his mistress and threw a can of kerosene at her. She retaliated by throwing the liquid on him, and then tossed a lighted match in his direction. He died from the burns.

And again:

> A victim became incensed when his eventual slayer asked for money which the victim owed him. The victim grabbed a hatchet and started in the direction of his creditor, who pulled out a knife and stabbed him.[27]

Estimates of the number of victim-precipitated homicides are difficult to make, because doing so requires intimate knowledge of the interaction before the killing took place. Since one party is dead, re-creation of the incident must rely on personal accounts by the killer and any witnesses who might be available. Estimates have nevertheless been made, and these range from around 25 percent of homicides to upwards of 50 percent. Evidence from Wolfgang, the National Commission, and elsewhere suggests that many victim-precipitated homicides occur when offender and victim know each other well. In addition, victim precipitation appears to occur more often when parties to the interaction are black and the victim is female.

Homicide on the International Scene   The United States is certainly not alone in experiencing violence in interpersonal relations. True, violence among group members is rare or seemingly nonexistent in some societies — the Arapesh of New Guinea, the Lepchas of Sikkim, the Eskimos, and the Zuni Indians are examples — but this is clearly the exception to the rule.

Nevertheless, the level of violence does vary from society to society. Regardless of legal definitions, some societies do seem to be more violence-prone than others. Table 4.2 shows rates of death by violence (mainly homicides) for thirty-three countries around the world. Whereas differences in classification and reporting practices may explain some of the variation, the more sizable differences are obviously a result of other factors.

The United States ranks first among highly industrialized countries and has done so for many years. When compared to America, European countries generally show much lower rates, as in fact do most nations for which data are available. Over the last few years, however, some countries have shifted position relative to one another. Wars, internal strife, and changing social conditions may well be responsible for these shifts. When compared with similar data for 1960, the figures show, for example,

Table 4.2 Violent death rates for selected countries, circa 1970[a]

COUNTRY	RATE	COUNTRY	RATE
Mexico[b]	46.7	Ireland	3.4
Chile	38.1	England and Wales[b]	3.2
South Africa (blacks)	32.6	Australia[b]	3.2
Colombia[c]	22.3	Portuguese Guinea	3.2
Guatemala	21.5	Mozambique	2.9
Kenya	11.4	Kuwait	2.8
United States	11.2	Federal Republic of Germany	2.6
Israel[b]	10.1	Japan	2.5
Venezuela[b]	9.7	Denmark	2.5
Panama[b]	9.3	France	2.5
Scotland[b]	5.7	Belgium[c]	2.4
Finland	4.7	Austria[b]	2.1
South Africa (whites)	4.3	Greece	1.9
Poland[b]	4.3	New Zealand	1.8
Sweden	4.3	Italy	1.4
Bulgaria[b]	3.6	Spain	0.6
Canada[b]	3.5	German Democratic Republic	0.5

SOURCE: United Nations, *Demographic Yearbook* (N.Y.: United Nations Publishing Service, 1973). Copyright, United Nations 1973. Reproduced by permission.

a. Rates are number of deaths per 100,000 population; they include homicides and deaths due to external causes such as riots, terrorism, and operations of war. They do not include auto fatalities.
b. Data are for the year 1971.
c. Data are for the year 1969. All others are for 1970.

that Ireland has overtaken England and Wales; New Zealand has dropped below Belgium, Sweden, and Denmark; the United States has passed Panama; and Scotland has moved from a relatively low rate (0.7 per 100,000 population) in 1960 to a relatively high rate (5.7 per 100,000 population) in 1970.[28]

Homicide is most often a crime of passion; it is rarely a planned thing committed in cold blood. In other countries, as in America, murders tend to occur in situations of interpersonal tension and hostility. A study of murder in Great Britain found, for instance, that more than half of the murders committed by persons not found insane or who had not afterward committed suicide (usually a fairly high proportion of killers in that country) occurred during or as a result of a passionate, highly charged exchange with the victim.[29] Similar findings exist for other countries.

Needless to say, heated personal exchanges do not normally result in physical assaults, let alone killings. But when they do we find that homicide situations around the world share some other common features. First, offenders are likely to be male, young (under 30), and of relatively low socioeconomic status. Second, they are likely to have known the victim, as a relative, friend, or acquaintance. Third, in countries with racial or ethnic heterogeneity, the offender and victim are usually of the same race or ethnic group. Fourth, many homicides appear to be victim-precipitated, especially when the victim is male or the offender is female. The actions of the victim, in many different cultures, are often instrumental in creating the aura of violence characteristic of homicide.[30]

AGGRAVATED ASSAULT

Aggravated assault is not as well researched as homicide. What we know about it, however, suggests a striking resemblance to homicide. Pittman and Handy, the National Commission, and other sources agree that these two offense categories are alike in many important respects.[31] This should not surprise anyone, for the essential difference between the two is the existence of a corpse.

Those arrested for aggravated assault are disproportionately young black males who come from lower socioeconomic backgrounds and reside in the inner cities of the nation's large urban centers. The victims also tend to fit this characterization. As with homicides, aggravated assaults often occur inside the home or around bars and street corners. Not surprisingly, knives are the weapons most often used (were guns the weapons most frequently used, assaults would often become homicides).

As with homicide, it is estimated that quite a number of violent assaults are victim-precipitated. While accurate figures are difficult to secure — partly because aggravated assaults often escape the attention of the authorities — it seems that the victim's actions are often instrumental in generating the atmosphere of violence that makes physical assault more likely to occur. Insinuating gestures and language may be all that is needed to provoke a violent outcome in interpersonal relations.[32]

In sum, homicides and violent assaults are much alike in many respects. This means that in all probability satisfactory explanations of the one are also good explanations of the other. The key to unlocking the mysteries of homicide and aggravated assault lies in explaining why personal violence occurs and is patterned in certain ways.

FAMILY VIOLENCE

We have already seen that many homicides and assaults occur in family settings. If there are still doubts that violence is widespread in the American family, consider the following facts. In Detroit, 50 percent of all homicides are domestic. Boston police receive an average of 45 calls a day — that's 17,277 a year — involving family disputes. Nationally, an estimated 1.4 to 1.9 million children are at risk of physical abuse by other family members. Indeed, "a person is more likely to be hit or killed in his or her own home by another family member than anywhere else or by anyone else."[33]

The contours of family violence appear to be consistent with those of homicide and assault. Most incidents occur during arguments or other heated exchanges; offensive remarks or moves are made by one party, invoking retaliation from the other. The interaction moves inexorably toward violence, perhaps acting out an internecine drama that has occurred many times before. If weapons are used the result is invariably serious injury or death. Often it is the victim who first uses violence.

Death is less frequent when the victims of violence are children. Nevertheless, the potential for serious injury is always there, finding expression in brain damage, skull and bone fractures, internal injuries, and other severe traumas. A nationwide survey of 2,143 families found that, during the year preceding the survey, over 20 percent had experienced parental assaults on children involving throwing or hitting with some object, and kicking, biting, or hitting with fists.[34] While this sort of violence can be found in all social classes, the weight of the evidence indicates that it is more common in families of lower socioeconomic status. In general, domestic violence appears to reproduce the uneven class representation found in official statistics on homicides and assaults. It does not appear that this finding can be accounted for in differential reporting practices or police recording behavior.[35]

Explaining Violence

Violence has absorbed the attention of scholars and laymen for centuries. These days probably few of us do not have some pet theory to explain its occurrence in humans. In the world of scholarly research, many different theories have been advanced to explain human aggression, with biologists, psychologists, psychiatrists, anthropologists, and sociologists tending to dominate the discussion. Let us briefly review some of the more prominent explanations of human violence and then turn to the contributions of sociological criminology.[36]

HUMANS ARE INSTINCTIVELY AGGRESSIVE

One prominent theory in biological circles is that humans are by nature, or instinctively, aggressive. This argument has been helped along by influential studies of animal behavior. Konrad Lorenz's book, *On Aggression,* may be taken as a case in point.[37] According to Lorenz, nature has armed animals with an instinct for aggression for three reasons: (1) to ensure that stronger animals succeed in mating the most desirable females of their kind, thus helping to perpetuate "good" qualities in future generations; (2) to ensure that each individual has sufficient physical space for securing food, raising the young, and so on (defense of physical space is called *territoriality*); and (3) to maintain hierarchies of dominance, and through them a stable, well-policed society.

While it is conventional to refer to humans as unique in the animal kingdom, some scholars agree that "human behavior is not radically discontinuous from that of other species."[38] Not a few biologists, zoologists, primatologists, and anthropologists are convinced that we can learn a lot about human behavior from the behavior of lower species, particularly the higher primates (monkeys and apes). Equally important, they encourage us to conceive of human behavior along the same lines that they conceptualize the behavior of other mammals — as the product of a complex interplay of biological and environmental factors.

Pierre van den Berghe, who advocates a biosocial approach to aggression in humans, argues that "there is no reason to assume that our biological make-up does not affect our behavior when it so clearly affects that of other species."[39] Van den Berghe, Lorenz, and others argue that humans, like animals, have predispositions to aggression that are innate, that is, biologically grounded. Though few authors claim to have found conclusive proof of this, a good indication is the discovery that aggression is a universal behavior pattern within a species. Historical and cross-cultural studies have left little doubt that this is true of man, despite widely differing habitats, technologies, and cultures. Additional indications are the established relationship between the male hormone testosterone and aggression, and the discovery of "aggression centers" in the human brain.[40]

One promising approach drawn from evolutionary theory has been advanced by Robert L. Burgess, explaining variations in child abuse and family violence.[41] He suggests that humans seek to increase the probability that their genes are represented in successive generations. Parents have limited resources, however, and must therefore exercise discretion when investing them in relatives and offspring. Accordingly, parents will tend to invest most in those *genetic* relatives who show the best prospects of surviving and reproducing, and least in nongenetic relatives and/or those genetic offspring who show the worst prospects of surviving and reproducing. We should expect greater abuse and neglect of these latter children and relatives.

Burgess offers some evidence in tentative support of this theory. Studies here and abroad have shown that (1) child abuse is more prevalent in families with stepchildren, and the stepparent is usually identified as the abuser; (2) child abuse is inversely related to socioeconomic status, especially income and education; (3) child abuse is twice as prevalent in families with four or more children as it is in those with fewer; (4) single-parent families are at greater risk of violence than two-parent families; and (5) abuse and neglect are more likely when children have mental or physical impairments or deficiencies.

As noted on page 27, the so-called XYY chromosomal abnormality has been advanced as an explanation of violent behavior in some people. This rare abnormality (the normal chromosomal combination in males is one X and one Y chromosome) is most likely to be found among tall white males. It has been linked to severe violence among some convicted criminals and persons who have been classified as mentally retarded or defective. However, as things stand now many important questions remain. One has to do with the fact that the abnormality is almost unheard of in blacks, tempting Mulvihill and Tumin to ask: "Are we to believe that Negro violence cannot be accounted for by XYY chromosomes, but that white violence can?"[42] Concluding their analysis of this and other "born violent" explanations of human violence, Mulvihill and Tumin observe:

> Under specific circumstances, some individuals are more likely than others to become criminals or violent as a result of biological makeup. But it is never "given" in the "nature" of any individual that he will be criminal or law abiding, pacific or violent, cooperative or competitive, selfish or altruistic. All these are complex forms of social behavior, which depend upon the social and cultural milieu of the developing individual.[43]

TRIGGERS AND INHIBITORS

To say that man has an innate predisposition toward aggression is not to say that it will surface in action, nor does it explain different levels and types of aggression. The general feeling among many scholars is that both *triggers* and *inhibitors* can affect the actual display of aggression. Knowing what these are and the conditions under which they come into play is crucial for an understanding of actual aggression and its variations within a species.

Lorenz argues that man exhibits not only high levels of aggression but also high levels of homicidal aggression toward others of his species. In Lorenz's view, the homicidal violence of man, much more common than the intraspecies homicidal violence of other mammals, is explained by the absence of built-in inhibitors capable of counterbalancing his "technology of destruction."[44] Scholars have shown that other mammals have built-in control systems that serve to inhibit the display of aggression, especially deadly violence. Sometimes the inhibitors consist of a lack of fighting equipment — claws, fangs, tusks, or large and powerful limbs. Sometimes they take the form of inbred inhibitory mechanisms that trigger action rituals — for example, the rituals of defeat (turning away, bowing, crouching) that permit the victor in intraspecies fighting to stop short of fatal injury to his opponent.

Some psychiatrists believe that we develop internal inhibitors as we go through the early stages of childhood. According to Freud and his followers, the individual psyche is composed of three parts: the ego, the id, and the superego. The motive force behind behavior is found in our drives or "instincts," as Freud called them; these are innate, and are considered part of the id. There are sex drives, aggression drives, even death drives. As we develop from infancy, we come into contact with others, and through that contact our superego emerges. The superego consists of the social ideals, rules, and "morals" that are internalized as we undergo socialization. "The ego is that part of the psyche that 'listens' to the wishes of the id and the approval or objection of the superego and decides what sort of behavior will result."[45]

The key to the expression of aggressive drives in violence lies, according to the psychoanalytical view, in how the three parts of the psyche work in relationship to each other. Disorder can occur, and when it does the "disturbed" or "sick" person may become violent. A number of possibilities are offered as causes of this disorder:

> The id may overflow with violent drives: the individual hates too much, enjoys pain too much, or wants to destroy himself. Sometimes the id is just too much for the ego to control, and the individual breaks out into violent behavior. . . . Alternatively, the superego may be extremely overformed or underformed. If the superego tries to quash *all* expression of dislike or hatred, and to quell all fantasies about violence, the individual may build up a greater and greater reserve of unfulfilled desire, until he can no longer control himself. Then he becomes violent. If the superego is underdeveloped, the individual simply sees nothing wrong with violence; he will use it whenever the occasion seems to call for it. In the underdeveloped superego, we are not dealing with a "sick" man at variance with his environment; we are rather dealing with a sick environment which has encouraged violence as the "normal" mode of response.[46]

Many psychiatrists — whether subscribing to the Freudian view or not — see in parent-child relationships the seeds of emotional disorders, hence violence. In their report to the National Commission, Bernard Chodorkoff and Seymour Baxter argue that the "love bonds" between parent and child are especially important in the regulation of aggressive drives: "The absence or rupture of human bonds has a permanent effect on the capacity to regulate aggressive behavior. This implies that the eradication of the source of later destructive behavior could be made possible by providing stable human relationships for each child in his development."[47] Excessive physical disciplining by parents may not only undermine these bonds, but may also impart a message to the youngster: violence has its place in relationships with loved ones. The oft-cited observation that child abusers were themselves abused as children might be borne in mind here.

While psychiatrists may have much to tell us about aggression and violence among those who are "disturbed" or "sick," their work has not proved very helpful in sorting out the reasons for variations in the level and types of violence for whole populations and societies. Indeed, some question the applicability of the psychiatric approach to even extreme forms of aggression such as murder, for, they point out, available evidence does not indicate that known violent offenders suffer from mental disorders as a rule. Summarizing the findings of investigations into mental disorders among murderers, psychiatrist Donald Lunde argues:

> I cannot emphasize too strongly the well-established fact that mental patients, in general, are no more murderous than the population at large. While it should not be surprising to find that psychotic killers have been previously hospitalized for treatment of psychosis, *the incidence of psychosis among murderers is no greater than the incidence of psychosis in the total population*. Furthermore, the percentage of murderers among former mental patients is actually slightly *lower* than that among persons who have never been in a mental hospital. Crimes committed by the mentally ill tend to receive disproportionate publicity, which reinforces a widespread myth about mental illness and violence.[48]

THE "FRUSTRATION-AGGRESSION" HYPOTHESIS

A prominent psychological explanation of human violence is the so-called *frustration-aggression hypothesis*. As orginally presented in the 1930s, the essential idea was that "the occurrence of aggressive behavior always presupposes the existence of frustration, and contrariwise, . . . the existence of frustration always leads to some form of aggression."[49] According to John Dollard and his colleagues at Yale, frustration arises whenever something interferes with an individual's attempt to reach some goal or end.

The idea that frustration and aggression have some kind of fixed causal relationship soon came under attack, and later modifications of the theory have taken some criticisms into account. Today it is recognized that the actual display of aggression may be inhibited by either internalized norms or external controls, even though the impulse for aggression is strong following some frustrating experience. Further, it is recognized that frustrations can be cumulative, one experience adding to another, and that they can remain active over a long period of time. It is also acknowledged that people perceive frustrations in varying ways, with those deemed arbitrary or unreasonable most likely to trigger aggressive responses. In addition, it is recognized that responses to frustrations can be learned, just like any other social behavior, and that what is learned will have a lot to do with socialization practices, which themselves differ from group to group and society to society. For example, "Some families teach their children to respond aggressively to insult, while others teach their children to turn away from insults and ignore them."[50] In short, aggressive actions are not an automatic consequence of frustration, and whether or not they will occur or take a certain form depends upon numerous factors, many of them firmly rooted in the conditions of social life.

As children grow up they quickly learn that violence has its place in social life.

LEARNING VIOLENCE

If violence is something we learn, then how do we learn to be violent (or conversely, nonviolent)? A major school of thought in social psychology is founded on the work of Albert Bandura and his colleagues, which emphasizes learning through imitation and modeling.[51] Through experiments with children and adults, Bandura has accumulated impressive evidence that individuals pick up the behavior patterns of those they are taught to respect and learn from. Whether observed in the flesh or via visual media, the behavior of aggressive models is readily imitated by experimental subjects when they are placed in situations similar to those observed. In one well-known experiment, Bandura played a film depicting a woman sitting on, beating, kicking, and hacking an inflatable doll. After witnessing the film, nursery school children both duplicated the woman's actions and performed their own aggressive acts when placed in a room with a similar doll.

Experiments such as these seem to establish the existence of immediate imitation. But how enduring are the behavior patterns learned through modeling, and how similar must modeling and future situations be to bring them forth? Categorical answers to these questions are still wanting, but tentative evidence gathered by Bandura and others suggests that aggressive behavior patterns learned through modeling remain part of our repertoire of social responses over time, and that people tend to generalize from the initial modeling situation to other, quite dissimilar situations — for example, from a situation in which the target of aggression is an inanimate doll to one in which the target is another human being.[52]

The theories of social learning through imitation and modeling are highly controversial in social psychology, but it is generally agreed that rewards and punishments play a crucial role in the learning and expression of behavior patterns. Bandura himself helped substantiate the connection, for in some of his experiments he demonstrated that subjects are more likely to repeat activities when the model has been rewarded than when not rewarded (or actively punished). Other scholars, too many to cite, attest to the importance of rewards and punishments; in fact, we all could if we were to reflect upon why we do the things we do.

The connection between rewards and behavior can be stated in simple terms: people tend to repeat activities for which they are rewarded; conversely, they tend not to repeat activities for which they have not been rewarded or have been openly punished.[53] But since we can *think* of doing many things without actually doing them, and hence receive neither rewards nor punishments for them, it is clear that our own experience of rewards or punishments is not a necessary ingredient in the formulation of our behavior patterns. Rather, we can anticipate whether a certain action will reward us or punish us by learning about what happens when others do it.

REWARDS FOR VIOLENCE

One might think that physical aggression directed against one's fellows could hardly have any rewards, actual or anticipated. After all, we think of ourselves as civilized people, and civilized people simply do not reward violence. But we would be quite wrong to think that. The truth is that violence offers abundant rewards, and we learn about some very early in life.

We learn, for example, that violence wins wars, and winning wars is rewarding (or so it seems to many). We learn that violence can be used as a rule-enforcing technique, to the benefit of those interested in upholding rules — parents, police, courts, or governments. We learn that violence can sometimes help us get our way — the schoolyard bully uses it to advantage. We learn that "respectables" pat you on the back when you use violence against someone acknowledged as an enemy by those same "respectables" — in broader terms, groups support insider-versus-outsider aggression. We learn from history books that violence helped make America what it is today — in broader terms, violence can bring the reward of constructive social change. We learn that successful use of violence can confer status, authority, and power — it could be in the context of sports ("where might Muhammad Ali be today if . . . ?"), or school life, or street life, or political life (assassinations bring instant recognition, and often much more).[54]

This brief list certainly does not exhaust the reward possibilities associated with physical aggression. The point to remember, however, is that violence is rewarded and we have plenty of opportunities to learn that. But just as we learn that violence can bring rewards, we also learn about the costs of being violent. There are contingencies to the use of violence and learning them is the other side of the coin. William Goode looks at these contingencies from the standpoint of a growing boy: "A boy is punished more for using violence on a girl than on a boy, on a younger boy than on a boy his own age, on a teacher than on a stranger; more for imposing his will by violence than for defending his rights."[55] It is not enough, therefore, to speak only of rewards and violence; we must also think of the costs of violence, and if these outweigh the former, violence is less likely to occur, other things being equal.

To recapitulate, contemporary thoughts on violence run all the way from the idea that humans are violent (or at least aggressive) by nature to the idea that they learn violence during normal social development. To explain why violence finds expression in deeds rather than remaining merely a possibility, we find theorists arguing that biologically grounded "triggers," psychic disorders, frustrations, tendencies to imitate, or actual and anticipated rewards act to bring it forth. Though I have of necessity presented only some views, and treated them superficially at that, it should be clear that we are still a long way from any agreed-upon explanation of human violence. The task of trying to account for the characteristics of criminal violence remains. Some specific questions might refresh our memories. Why are lower-class, inner-city black males disproportionately identified as homicide offenders and victims? Why is the typical homicide a crime situation involving people who know each other? Why are homicide rates so much higher in the South than elsewhere in the United States? Why do homicide rates vary from country to country, and why is homicidal violence considerably more prevalent in certain countries than in most others?

Subcultures of Violence

When it is found that certain forms of behavior are not randomly distributed in cities, around the country, or among populations, efforts to explain the patterns inevitably center on sociological variables, that is, variables pertaining to group life and its conditions. In sociological criminology, a prominent body of theory purporting to explain variations in rates of violent crime has emerged in recent years, and the focus is on what are termed *subcultures of violence*.

Drawing heavily on contributions from anthropology, sociology, and psychology, Marvin Wolfgang and Franco Ferracuti sought in the 1960s to integrate the existing body of knowledge on group life and violence into a single theoretical framework in terms of which differential rates of criminal violence might be explained. In 1967 they published *The Subculture of Violence,* now a classic work in criminology.[56]

In brief, their thesis goes as follows. First, a distinction is made between planned, premeditated, or psychotic violence and the so-called passion crimes of violence. Arguing that probably no more than 5 percent of all known homicides (an estimate for assaults is not given) are manifestations of premeditation or psychosis, their interest lies in explaining variations in passion homicides, those occurring in the heat of interpersonal drama and tension. Next, the authors make it clear that their arguments are meant to apply to differences in rates of violence in populations rather than to individual acts of violence committed by particular persons.

With these distinctions made, the authors turn to the notion of culture. Any heterogeneous society, they argue, is likely to have a dominant, or parent, culture consisting of beliefs, values, attitudes, ideas, ways of behaving, meanings, evaluations, and expectations that are shared in varying degrees by those who regularly make up the membership of the society. In America, the dominant culture is commonly characterized as the culture of white, middle-class society.

In addition to the dominant culture a society may have various subcultures. While never completely different from the parent culture, these subcultures consist of values, norms, and life-styles, some of which depart more or less from the dominant culture. Sometimes these subcultures are merely different from the parent culture — the Amish settlements are a case in point — and sometimes they may be directly at variance with the dominant culture — the hippie culture of the 1960s or delinquent subcultures, for example. Wolfgang and Ferracuti identify various of these "contracultures," though they do not concern themselves with why they arose in the first place.[57]

Different life conditions, opportunities, and social histories — in short, different life experiences and life chances — tend to be the hallmarks of subcultures. As individuals are born into and become a part of one of the various groups in society, they come to share, more or less, the culture peculiar to their group. Through the socialization process they are encouraged to adopt ways of behaving supported by the subculture. They become acclimatized to the group culture, and how well they are submerged in it determines how close or distant their contact with the dominant culture will tend to be. This implies that their actions will differ from those of other people in situations that have special significance to the subculture. For example, those persons involved in a subculture stressing materialistic, status-striving orientations can be expected to engage in activities aimed at making money and getting ahead. In contrast, those who are involved in a subculture stressing nonmaterialistic, nonstatus-conscious orientations would not be expected to engage in such activities.

Individuals and groups are said to belong to a subculture of violence to the extent that violence is supported and expected by the subculture in situations where it is not supported by the dominant culture or by other subcultures. Those who belong to a subculture of violence see violence as a significant element in their repertoire of action alternatives. Violence is an integral part of their way of life, and judgments are developed as to its proper use in interpersonal relations. When others define a situation as one in which violence is neither appropriate nor expected, members of a subculture of violence may define it as quite the opposite.

In concrete terms, what are some of the indications of the existence of a subculture of violence? First, it is marked by relatively high rates of violence (homicide, assault, child beating, or wife beating) for an identifiable group or collection of people. Second, violence is used in situations where violence is not common among other groups or collectivities. Third, members will be prepared for violence — exhibited by the carrying of weapons and other tactics of defense or strategies of confrontation. Fourth, it will have relatively high rates of violence among the young (who presumably would not be immune to the subculture, since they are raised in it). Fifth, relatively high rates of violence will persist over time — subcultures do not develop overnight nor do they disappear at the drop of a hat. Sixth, it will have relatively high rates of victim precipitation — if violence is a dominant theme in life, interacting parties are likely to be "keyed up" for its occurrence and ready to provoke each other. Finally, group members will have personal histories of involvement with or in violence — criminal records indicating repetitious lawbreaking of the violent kind might be indicative of such a history, though they would not tell us anything about persons who had managed to avoid contacts with the police or the stigma of an official record.

One more thing should be added to this list. The presumption of a subculture of violence leads one to anticipate that interpersonal violence will have predictable features. That is, far from being senseless and random, we can expect it to be patterned and quite rational given the existence of values, norms, and expectations governing its use. If it makes any sense at all to speak of cultures, the assumption has to be that we are dealing with shared cognitive and behavioral elements that together provide meaning, legitimation, and justification, and help stabilize group life. Actions that may appear senseless to outsiders are not so to group members, and it is precisely because they are predictable that they endure over time.

While Charles Whitman's violent rampage on the University of Texas at Austin campus some years ago and Richard Speck's massacre of eight nurses in Chicago were hailed as somehow indicative of the times, they did not indicate a subculture of violence. Martin Haskell and Lewis Yablonsky call such acts raw violence and argue that they do not flow from any readily comprehensible social conditions.[58] The following situation is much more what we would expect to see, given the existence of a subculture of violence:

> The female victim was fatally stabbed to death by the defendant. . . . Both the defendant and the victim were in a bar when they exchanged some words, apparently about a mutual male acquaintaince. Defendant then left the bar and shortly thereafter re-entered, having changed her clothes. . . . As the defendant walked through the bar . . . the victim hit her on the head with a beer bottle . . . and after this attack, defendant removed a paring knife from her brassiere and struck the victim an unknown number of times.
>
> Defendant's arrest record shows four previous arrests for violent attacks. Two arrests involved fights with her husband; once she threw an ashtray and cut him; another time she chased him with an ice pick. The other arrests involved attacks on bar patrons; one time she cut a man with a beer bottle and the second time she stabbed a man with a knife.[59]

We see in this illustration an offender-victim acquaintanceship, victim precipitation, weapons carried on the person, prior involvement in violence, and violence within the family. These are not the hallmarks of senseless, random violence but, rather, of a subculture of violence.

LOWER-CLASS LIFE-STYLES AND URBAN GANG VIOLENCE

The notion of a subculture of violence has been used to explain the predominance of lower-class, young, male (most often black), inner-city residents in homicide statistics, including those on victims. Commenting on homicides in Philadelphia, Wolfgang observes:

> . . . the significance of a jostle, a slightly derogative remark, or the appearance of a weapon in the hands of an adversary are stimuli differentially perceived and interpreted by Negroes and whites, males and females. Social expectations of response in particular types of social interaction result in differential "definitions of the situation." A male is usually expected to defend the name and honor of his mother, the virtue of womanhood . . . and to accept no derogation about his race (even from a member of his own race), his age, or his masculinity. Quick resort to physical combat as a measure of daring, courage, or defense of status appears to be a cultural expectation, especially for lower socioeconomic class males of both races.[60]

The lower-class urban gang provides the setting in which many inner-city residents feel their way around violence while they are growing up. The lower-class youth gang has been characterized as one in which ideals of toughness, masculinity, excitement, and reputation are given value priority and govern the gang-related activities of group members. Physical prowess is the mark of the youth with prestige among his peers; being able to "take care of yourself" when threatened or provoked distinguishes the "men from the boys," as does dominance over and conquest of females (an issue explored further in the section on rape in chapter 10.[61]

A provocative illustration of gang subcultures of violence is provided in a study of ninety-eight Puerto Rican males serving time for violent crimes. The author discovered the following features of gang life as described by his "informants":

1. Carrying weapons, for example, machetes, knives, or firearms, is common, accepted, and expected in his group, and these practices are sanctioned by the individual.
2. Fighting and other similar aggressive behavior is common in his social group.
3. Certain situations, especially related to gambling, reputation (personal and of his family), and honor are defined as provocative of violence.
4. The individual has witnessed fights in which weapons were used, and has been involved in such fights, directly or indirectly.[62]

We should at this point pause to acknowledge that opinions differ over the amount of violence in American urban youth gangs as well as its nature and role. During the past twenty years or so, a considerable amount of public attention and professional interest has been drawn to street violence and the juvenile gang. In the minds of many Americans, youth gangs are a particularly threatening aspect of city life. Fanned partly by sensational news stories, this conception of youth gangs has gained some additional support from recent studies, some of which contain accounts by gang members themselves. The Lynch Report by the attorney general of California, Lewis Yablonsky's *The Violent Gang,* and Hunter Thompson's *Hell's Angels* all appeared in the 1960s, and those who were so inclined could find in them support for the view that gangs and violence go together.[63]

In Yablonsky's opinion, the modern gang "reflects a brand and intensity of violence that differentiates it from earlier gang patterns." Gangs pose, in Yablonsky's view, an increasing threat to social tranquillity, personal safety, and public order. As he describes it, the violent gang emerges more or less spontaneously, without plan or premeditation, as a means to channel the aggressions of maladjusted individuals. Its members come together primarily "for emotional gratification, and violence is the theme around which all activities center."[64] The violence of which Yablonsky speaks is termed by him "irrational," "senseless," "unprovoked"; it is violence of a "kill for kicks" kind. Gang members are portrayed as "disturbed youths" of "limited social ability," and with "defective personalities."

This view has been challenged by others who have studied youth gangs in America. The alternative picture, also based on work carried out during the late 1950s and early 1960s, shows that violence does not figure prominently in gang activities, and when it does surface from time to time it is not senseless or irrational. After a careful review of the gang literature, Malcolm Klein concludes:

> Gang violence exists; it exists in almost every large urban area. . . . However, it seems clear that the public view of gang violence as an ever present, widely threatening phenomenon simply does not fit the facts. . . . Violence constitutes a small portion of gang activity and is commonly of low seriousness in its physical consequences.[65]

Walter Miller concludes one of his own studies in a similar vein:

> These data thus grant virtually no support to the notion that favored targets of gang attacks are the weak, the solitary, the defenseless, and the innocent; in most cases assaulters and assaultees were evenly matched; the bulk of assaultive incidents involved contacts between peers. . . . Violent crime was not a dominant activity of the gangs, nor a central reason for their existence.[66]

It is instructive to look more closely at Miller's study, for while it does not conclude that violence is a predominant theme in gang life, it does provide a picture of subcultural supports for violence.

Miller undertook his study in Boston. Intensive field observations were carried out over a period of two years per gang. Twenty-one gangs were studied, seven more intensely than the rest. The gangs were all from an inner-city slum area of the city, called simply "Midcity." Miller found that though assaultive behavior did occur, it did so far less frequently than other activities, some of which were criminal. Further, he discovered that violence was much more a matter of words than deeds. Gang members frequently expressed violent sentiments, but rarely carried them out — suggesting strongly the existence of norms governing the use of violence.

In the seven intensely studied gangs, Miller found that when members of these gangs engaged in assaultive behavior that could legally be classified as violent crime, they most often did so in a group. In all, eighty-eight violent crime incidents were observed over the two-year period, and most of the time weapons were not used, adults or women not assaulted, and the targets were themselves gang-affiliated. Injuries were most often cuts, scratches, and bruises.

Contrary to Yablonsky's findings, Miller discovered that gang violence did not appear to be erratic, unpredictable, or senseless. Violence, when approved by the group, was used as a means to achieve prestige, honor, and recognition — things that make up a gang member's "rep" — when other avenues were unsuccessful or closed off. This may seem senseless to middle-class adults, but then it is difficult for most "respectables" to grasp lower-class gang ideology:

> Gang members fight to secure and defend their honor as males; to secure and defend the reputation of their local area and the honor of their women; to

show that an affront to their pride and dignity demands retaliation. Combat between males is a major means to achieve these ends.[67]

CAREERS IN VIOLENCE

As if to contradict one of the essential expectations associated with subcultures of violence, namely, that those living within them have personal histories of violence, a number of authors have argued that the violent criminal is typically a "first-timer," or as Gibbons calls him, a "one-time loser."[68] Marshall Clinard and Richard Quinney have noted that murderers and assaulters generally do not have criminal careers. They "do not conceive of themselves as being real 'criminals': they seldom identify with crime, and criminal behavior is not a significant part of their life organizations."[69] Gibbons suggests that "one-time loser personal offenders exhibit non-criminal self images. Frequently, the violator himself reports his behavior to the police, due to the fact that, after it has occurred, he is contrite, guilt-ridden, and repentant."[70]

If the subculture of violence thesis has any merit, one indication would be group-centered patterns of repetitive involvement in violence, though not necessarily homicidal violence. Official records indicate on balance that most murderers have not been previously arrested or convicted for the same offense, and one recent study of 621 convicted murderers indicates that they have a lower "criminality level" than other prisoners.[71] However, the picture now emerging suggests that a majority of violent crime offenders do have histories of prior involvement in crimes, which often are interpersonal acts of violence (this includes rape and robbery).[72]

Aggravated assault gives more substantial evidence supporting the subculture theory of violent crime rates. In its analysis of persons arrested for aggravated assault from 1970 to 1972, the FBI reports 68 percent having prior arrest records for the same offense. In addition, those who committed aggravated assault showed the longest histories of identified criminal involvement of all offenders surveyed.[73] We should remain cautious in taking this evidence as in any way conclusive, recalling that official statistics may be more a measure of what the police do than what criminals do. Still, the National Commission concluded its own exhaustive and diverse investigations by saying: "most violent offenders have an extensive history of crime."[74] What remains to be established in a firm way is the degree to which this criminal history touches on violence. Judging from victimization and self-report studies, we are probably fairly safe in assuming that official criminal histories underreport, rather than overreport, prior involvement in interpersonal violence.

REGIONAL AND INTERNATIONAL VARIATIONS IN HOMICIDE

Wolfgang and Ferracuti apply the subculture of violence thesis to regional and international variations in homicide. They note with particular interest the extremely high rates of homicide in Mexico and Colombia. Between 1928 and 1963, 203,432 persons were arrested for homicide in Mexico. It has been said that in the Federal District of Mexico City, the risk of dying from homicide is greater than was the risk of being killed in London during the World War II blitzes. Wolfgang and Ferracuti observe:

> The high rates of criminal homicide in Mexico, the convergence of such social factors as male sex, membership of the working class, and a tradition of employing physical aggression, suggest that there exists in that country subcultural areas of violence. Where the use of violence is taken for granted and homicide is a common form of death, subcultural values encouraging the use of violence can surely be assumed to be present.[75]

Colombia, with a population of around 25 million, lost over a quarter of a million people to apparent homicides in less than two decades (1948–1965). The term *la violencia colombiana* has been applied to the violence there. This phenomenon apparently has its roots in social and political upheavals and certain long-standing cultural traditions:

> The most authoritative study of *La Violencia* . . . traces the reign of terror to political changes beginning in 1930 and to causes deep-rooted in Colombian temperament and tradition: (1) the ignorance and increasing poverty of the rural population which made them an easy prey to demagogues in both parties; (2) the violence of political, clerical, and anti-clerical fanaticism; (3) the corruption of local *politicos* and oppression by the police; (4) a passion for unrestrained freedom bordering on egocentricity; (5) hero-worship inspired by the courage and cruelty of the outlaw leaders that was regarded as evidence of virility — the traits of the juvenile delinquent transferred to adult gangsters; and (6) the hard, economic fact that, as the violence spread, there was no other way than banditry for the plainsman or farmer to earn a living after his own farm had been plundered and destroyed.[76]

We see here an important fact about subcultures of violence: they do not emerge and develop in a sort of vacuum that keeps them apart from the larger society. It seems that in Colombia, at least, *la violencia colombiana* grew out of and was shaped by societal conditions, not merely localized ones. Much the same is true, it appears, when we look at lower-class urban violence in America. As the National Commission observed:

> . . . if the poor, young, black male is conditioned in the ways of violence by his immediate subculture, he is also under the influence of many forces in the general dominant culture. [Violence] is a pervasive theme in the mass media. The frequency of violent themes in myriad forms in the media tends to foster permissive attitudes toward violence. Much the same can be said about guns in American society. The highest gun-to-population ratio in the world, the glorification of guns in our culture, and the television and movies' display of guns by heroes surely contribute to the scope and extent of urban violence.[77]

In more concrete terms, the very conditions of existence faced by black inner-city residents are a product of societal structure and process. Lack of opportunities, overcrowding, physical deterioration, poverty and unemployment, transient populations, police surveillance and harassment, and high rates of crime and victimization are among ghetto conditions; these are problems having local import but societal underpinnings. If subcultures of violence emerge and prosper against a backdrop such as this, the root causes lie in the general social condition and the history behind it.

In its application to regional variations in homicide rates, the subculture of violence thesis remains the subject of controversy. There are those who have argued that historical trends and conditions in the South — slavery, lynchings, post–Civil War adjustments, relative poverty, and pre–Civil War values — spawned a cultural condition in terms of which the relatively high rates of interpersonal violence can be explained. In its simplest form, the argument is that "Southernness" explains much of the difference in homicide rates between the South and elsewhere.[78] In support of the argument, John Shelton Reed suggests that (1) the South maintains laws that protect the rights of an individual to assault another in certain situations; (2) certain forms of violence are taken for granted in the South — they are seen as "natural"; (3) violence occurs more often in the South in situations identified there as demanding such action and less often than elsewhere in other situations: "The statistics show that the Southerner who can avoid both arguments and adultery is as safe as any other American, and probably safer"; (4) violence is found in the well-socialized Southerner, the upright citizen; and (5) violence is found in other areas of southern life, more so than in the North — for example, in country music, in literature, even in jokes.[79]

Societal Reactions to Violence

We have seen in this chapter that America and other countries have values and attitudes that support interpersonal violence. Some of these values and attitudes have their roots in America's history, with its wars, intergroup conflicts, frontier traditions, and physical hardships; other values and attitudes appear to be products of more localized conditions, such as those prevalent in our inner-city ghetto areas, where the struggle for survival has a decidedly physical character.

This is not to say that when asked about it, most Americans see nothing wrong with interpersonal violence or feel that violent criminals should be let off lightly. In fact, quite the opposite is true. Public sentiment supports swift and severe punishment for those who commit crimes of violence. Studies by Gibbons in San Francisco, Sellin and Wolfgang in Philadelphia, and surveys by national polling organizations confirm that Americans rate crimes of violence — especially homicides — as the most serious offenses, which merit severe penalties.[80] This is true regardless of sex, race, economic status, occupation, or other social characteristics of those interviewed.

However, while Americans may be concerned about violence, many are quick to point out that violence is sometimes quite acceptable, and even expected. In short, violence is accorded legitimacy in some situations while in others it is feared and condemned. Sandra Ball-Rokeach argues that violence is most often considered legitimate and justifiable (1) when it is used for certain instrumental purposes — self-defense, family security; (2) when it occurs out of a sense of duty or as a result of following orders — in war or in police work; and (3) when it occurs as a result of extenuating circumstances — accident, could not be helped, or extreme provocation.[81]

POLICE USE OF DEADLY FORCE

Surveys have shown that many people see a wide range of circumstances in which police violence can be justified. From the standpoint of the police this public support is vital, for it lends legitimacy to their use of force.[82] There are, of course, different levels of force. At one extreme are actions whose intent is not to inflict injury, although this may happen on occasion. An example is handcuffing. At the other extreme lies the use of deadly force, which in police work invariably means the firing of a gun. Happily, most police violence is not of this sort; in fact, it is relatively rare for the police to actually fire their weapons, let alone kill someone.

But it does happen, of course. In one recent nine-month period 32 civilians were killed by police in Chicago, 21 in New York, 13 in Philadelphia, 8 in Los Angeles, and 4 in Detroit.[83] National trend data indicate that police killing of civilians has increased in its yearly averages — from 240 in the period 1950 to 1959, to 268 from 1960 to 1969, to 342 from 1968 to 1976.[84]

Certain features of the typical police killing deserve comment. First, black males are seven to thirteen times more likely than white males to be killed by police.[85] Even when we look at the young (10 to 14 years old) and the old (65 and over), the picture remains the same. Paul Takagi found that "black youngsters and old men have been killed by the police at a rate 15 to 30 times greater than that of whites at the same age."[86] It appears that the racial difference cannot be adequately explained by reference to higher arrest rates for blacks. Blacks are killed by police more frequently than one would expect on the basis of arrests, even for serious felony crimes. Gerald Robin documents the largest discrepancy in the literature: in Philadelphia during the 1950s, at a time when blacks comprised 37.5 percent of the arrests for major felonies, they comprised 87.5 percent of civilian deaths at the hands of the police.[87] Less marked discrepancies have been found for other major cities.[88]

Second, while almost all police killings are lawful and labeled justifiable, a significant minority involve victims who actually have committed no crime at all (or if they have, the crime was legally classified as a misdemeanor). When the victim has committed a felony offense, the usual case in most studies, it is more often a property crime than a crime of violence. Most surprisingly, in many cases neither another citizen nor the police officer (or officers) involved is under threat of death or serious injury from the suspect; often the suspect is fleeing the scene when shot.[89]

The law in most states requires that one of three conditions be present for the police to use deadly force: (1) the suspect is engaged in a felony; or (2) he is fleeing the scene of a felony he has committed; or (3) he is resisting arrest and has placed the officer or a civilian in danger of serious injury or death. Recent court actions have indicated a trend toward narrowing the range of police discretion by limiting the use of deadly force to felony situations involving violence.[90] If followed conscientiously, this sort of change should reduce homicides by police.

Some police argue that further limiting the use of deadly force will increase the murder of police. This argument is understandable for an occupational group armed and trained for violence, but it misses the point. The reforms are not meant to tie police hands in the event of criminal violence, whether actual or threatened. Rather, they are meant to eliminate the use of deadly force in situations where the suspect is not threatening or using violence against them or others.

The picture of police homicides and nonfatal shootings drawn by recent research suggests that we might be witnessing the clash of two violent subcultures. On the one hand we have the subculture of police violence — a legitimized, supported subculture associated with the Establishment — and on the other, the inner-city subculture of the ghetto — an outlawed subculture at variance with the Establishment, and deemed a threat to it. Many inner-city black youths expect violence in their daily lives, not only from those who share their existence but also from those who do not. They come prepared for violence in their dealings with their friends and neighbors and find they must be prepared for it in their dealings with officials. And we have every reason to believe that violence reinforces violence. Surveys have shown that respondents who would accept relatively high levels of police violence are themselves likely to have been involved in violence, and accept it in a variety of interpersonal situations.[91]

It should come as no surprise, however, that for the most part blacks are less inclined than whites to support police violence. They tend, after all, to be its victims. Middle-class whites, on the other hand, shun the use of violence in their interpersonal relations but turn to the police for its use when culturally approved situations arise: "Individuals from 'nice' society will not direct personal violence against selected individuals. Rather, the police structure will be justified in violent reactions."[92] According to the middle-class view, violence has its place in society; at the very least we need it to protect ourselves from criminals.

Public support for police use of violence in dealing with the "criminal element" is one aspect of a theme that seems to have achieved a central place in our lives: catch the criminal at all costs. This theme is heavily pushed by current television shows dealing with "cops and robbers." Hardly an episode goes by without one of our favorite police heroes firing at some fast-disappearing suspect. While most professionals would likely laugh at the antics of the Kojaks, Starskys, and Hutches, these TV characters reinforce public images of the fast-shooting cop in pursuit of justice. More dangerous, perhaps, is their potential impact on young people who anticipate contacts with the "heat." If you're going to have dealings with the police — inevitable in some areas of our cities — it is best to be prepared for police violence, perhaps even a shoot-out. When all is said and done, "catch the criminal at all costs" is not a sound doctrine for either the public or police to follow. One clear consequence is police fatalities. National figures show police deaths occur most often during pursuit and arrest (see figure 4.3). As Rubin observes: "It would seem more prudent to allow [potentially resistant, armed suspects] to escape, as many criminals do anyway."[93]

VARIATIONS IN OFFICIAL REACTIONS TO HOMICIDE

In law and public opinion criminal homicide is the most serious offense a person can commit. In most American jurisdictions it carries with it the possibility of death as punishment. This does not mean that official reactions to homicide are therefore immune to the influence of nonlegal factors. On the contrary, it appears that what happens to homicide offenders depends, among other things, on who the criminal is and who the victim is.

Consider the findings of Harold Garfinkel and Guy B. Johnson.[94] Both authors studied homicide cases known to the police during the 1930s. Garfinkel investigated homicide indictments and convictions in North Carolina, and Johnson in both North Carolina and Virginia. They found that (1) blacks who killed whites were more likely to be indicted and convicted than whites who killed blacks; (2) blacks who killed whites were more likely to receive the death penalty than whites who killed blacks; and (3) blacks who killed other blacks were more likely to receive lighter sentences than blacks who killed whites.

In his investigation of sentence lengths for assorted crimes in Texas, Henry Allen Bullock discovered that regardless of type of plea and number of prior convictions, blacks received stiffer sentences than whites. However, he found that for murder, blacks tended to receive shorter sentences than whites who were convicted of the same offense. He suggested that this reversal in the case of homicide resulted from the fact that most homicides were intraracial (blacks killing blacks), and local mores tolerated, and perhaps even indulged, blacks in their mistreatment of each other. On the other hand, many of the other offenses affected white society, and in those cases, "local norms are less tolerant, for the

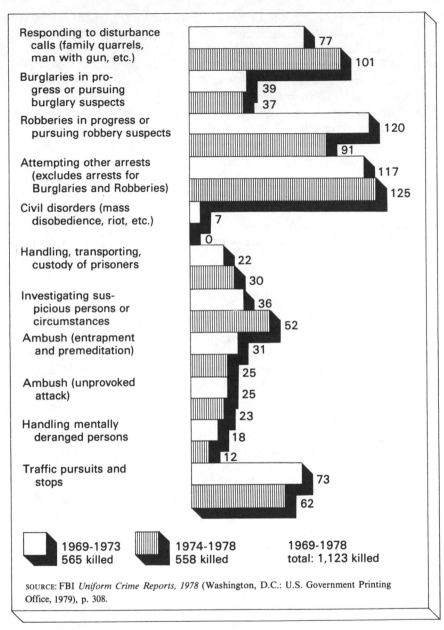

Responding to disturbance calls (family quarrels, man with gun, etc.) — 77 / 101

Burglaries in progress or pursuing burglary suspects — 39 / 37

Robberies in progress or pursuing robbery suspects — 120 / 91

Attempting other arrests (excludes arrests for Burglaries and Robberies) — 117 / 125

Civil disorders (mass disobedience, riot, etc.) — 7 / 0

Handling, transporting, custody of prisoners — 22 / 30

Investigating suspicious persons or circumstances — 36 / 52

Ambush (entrapment and premeditation) — 31 / 25

Ambush (unprovoked attack) — 25 / 23

Handling mentally deranged persons — 18 / 12

Traffic pursuits and stops — 73 / 62

1969–1973
565 killed

1974–1978
558 killed

1969–1978
total: 1,123 killed

SOURCE: FBI *Uniform Crime Reports, 1978* (Washington, D.C.: U.S. Government Printing Office, 1979), p. 308.

Figure 4.3 Situations in which law enforcement officers were killed, 1969–1978

motivation to protect white property and to protect 'white' society against disorder is stronger than the motivation to protect 'Negro' society."[95]

Criminologists who have studied the imposition of the death penalty generally agree that some of the variation is due to racial discrimination on the part of those responsible for criminal justice. On the whole, compared to other forms of punishment, the death penalty has been used relatively infrequently. From 1930 to 1976, 3,334 persons were executed for murder in the United States. Of these, however, just under 50 percent were blacks, a proportion far exceeding their representation in the population as a whole. It could be, of course, that these figures reflect the proportionately greater involvement of blacks in homicides. But careful studies indicate that whites are more likely than blacks to have their sentences commuted to life imprisonment.[96]

One recent study investigated the possibility that nonlegal variables might influence the decision to dismiss or prosecute a homicide offender.[97] Looking at the disposition of 125 "crime specific" homicides (that is, homicides occurring during the commission of another felony), the study found that the employment status and age of the offender, and the employment status of the victim, were influential factors in the decision. This was true even after such legal variables as prior criminal record had been taken into account. Young unemployed offenders who killed employed victims were more likely to be prosecuted than other offenders. Once again we see that official reactions are not accounted for solely by reference to the law.

Most questions about interpersonal violence have no clear-cut answers. In truth, the issues are complex and few criminologists would entertain hopes of finding a single theory in terms of which interpersonal violence can be understood and variations in its occurrence predicted.

Looking at serious acts of criminal violence — homicides and aggravated assaults — the bulk of theory and evidence points to some combination of cultural and situational elements as factors conducive to their occurrence. These elements are presented in the following outline. As you go down the list you are moving from more general influences to more specific, situational influences.[98]

1. **General cultural values and norms supportive of violence.** For example, frontier traditions; use of violence to settle intergroup disputes; use of violence for social control purposes; pervasive media interest in violence; ownership of guns.

2. **Subcultural values and norms supportive of violence.** For example, physical prowess as a sign of masculinity; violence as a means of status-advancement; violence as accepted and expected in goal-achievement; police acceptance of violence on the job.

3. **Situational frustrations and conflicts.** For example, unsuccessful attempts at goal achievement via nonviolent means; threats to masculinity,

honor, "rep"; challenges to authority (in the case of the police); quarrels, heated arguments among intimates; victim precipitation.

4. **Use of alcohol** (chronologically, this may precede number 3).

5. **Availability of weapon.**

References

1. Walter Bromberg, *The Mold of Murder: A Psychiatric Study of Murder* (Westport, Conn.: Greenwood Press, 1961), pp. 3–4.
2. See Marvin Wolfgang and Franco Ferracuti, *The Subculture of Violence* (London: Tavistock, 1967), pp. 280–82.
3. A. W. Lintott, *Violence in Republican Rome* (Oxford: Clarendon Press, 1968), pp. 26, 29.
4. Cyrus H. Gordon, *The Code of Hammurapi: Quaint or Forward Looking?* (New York: Holt, Rinehart, Winston, 1957), p. 14.
5. Emile Durkheim, "Deux Lois de L'Évolution Pénale," *Année Sociologique* IV (1900), pp. 70–71 (my translation).
6. Sheldon S. Wolin, "Violence and the Western Political Tradition," in Renatus Hartogs and Eric Artzt, *Violence: Causes and Solutions* (New York: Dell, 1970), p. 30.
7. Kai T. Erickson, *Wayward Puritans* (New York: Wiley, 1966), p. 149.
8. See Gerald Runkle, "Is Violence Always Wrong?" *The Journal of Politics* (1976), pp. 368–89, for a discussion of philosophical issues in the justification of violence.
9. See Richard Maxwell Brown, "Historical Patterns of Violence in America," in *Violence in America*, A Staff Report to the National Commission on the Causes and Prevention of Violence, eds. Hugh David Graham and T. Robert Gurr (Washington: D.C.: U.S. Government Printing Office, 1969), pp. 35–64.
10. See Brown, "Historical Patterns of Violence," for views of violence in America during the nineteenth century. See also Walter White, *Rope and Faggot: A Biography of Judge Lynch* (New York: Knopf, 1929); James E. Cutler, *An Investigation into the History of Lynching in America* (New York: Longmans, Green, 1905); Roger Lane, *Policing the City: Boston, 1822–1885* (Cambridge, Mass.: Harvard University Press, 1967); and Philip D. Jordon, *Frontier Law and Order* (Lincoln: University of Nebraska Press, 1970).
11. Cited in Brown, "Historical Patterns of Violence," p. 55.
12. Donald J. Mulvihill and Melvin M. Tumin, *Crimes of Violence*, A Staff Report to the National Commission on the Causes and Prevention of Violence, vol. 11 (Washington, D.C.: U.S. Government Printing Office, 1969), p. 49.
13. Ibid., p. 52.
14. Ibid., p. 58.
15. FBI, *Uniform Crime Reports, 1978* (Washington, D.C.: U.S. Government Printing Office, 1979), pp. 15, 20. Throughout the remainder of this chapter and the text as a whole, FBI data comes from this source unless otherwise noted.
16. Marvin E. Wolfgang, *Patterns in Criminal Homicide* (Philadelphia: University of Pennsylvania Press, 1958).
17. For Cleveland, see Robert G. Bensing and Oliver Schroeder, *Homicide in an Urban Community* (Springfield, Ill.: Thomas, 1960). Houston is studied in Alex D. Pokorny, "Human Violence: A Comparison of Homicide, Aggravated Assault, and Attempted Suicide," *Journal of Criminal Law, Criminology, and Police Science* 56 (1965), pp. 488–97; and his "A Comparison of Homicide in Two Cities," *Journal of Criminal Law, Criminology, and Police Science* 56 (1965), pp. 479–87. For Chicago, see Harwin L. Voss and John R. Hepburn, "Patterns in Criminal Homicide in Chicago," *Journal of Criminal Law, Criminology, and Police Science* 59 (1968), pp. 499–508; also Richard Block and Franklin E. Zimring, "Homicide in Chicago; 1965–1970," *Journal of Research in Crime and Delinquency* 10 (1973), pp. 1–12. Joseph C. Fisher writes about Detroit in "Homicides in Detroit: The Role of Firearms," *Criminology* 14 (1976), pp. 387–400. And Atlanta is studied in Robert S. Munford, Ross J. Kazer, Roger A. Feldman, and Robert R. Stivers, "Homicide Trends in Atlanta," *Criminology* 14 (1976), pp. 213–32.
18. Ibid., and Block and Zimring, "Homicide in Chicago."
19. See Robert Sherrill, *The Saturday Night Special* (Baltimore: Penguin Books, 1975), pp. 57–95.
20. Fisher, "Homicide in Detroit," pp. 397, 399.
21. George D. Newton and Franklin E. Zimring, *Firearms and Violence in American Life*, Consultant Report to the National Commission on the Causes and Prevention of Violence (Washington, D.C.: U.S. Government Printing Office, 1969), pp. 9–10.
22. Mulvihill and Tumin, *Crimes of Violence*, vol. 11, p. 70.
23. Wolfgang, *Patterns in Criminal Homicide*, p. 136.

See also Mulvihill and Tumin, *Crimes of Violence,* vol. 12, pp. 641–49.

24. Mulvihill and Tumin, *Crimes of Violence,* vol. 12, pp. 648–49.

25. Hans von Hentig, *The Criminal and His Victim* (New Haven: Yale University Press, 1948).

26. Wolfgang, *Patterns in Criminal Homicide,* p. 252.

27. Ibid., p. 253.

28. The 1960 data are in Wolfgang and Ferracuti, *The Subculture of Violence,* pp. 274–75.

29. Evelyn Gibson and S. Klein, *Murder, 1957–1968* (London: Her Majesty's Stationery Office, 1969), chapter II.

30. Some of the recent studies of violence in other countries include: Paul Bohannan, *African Homicide and Suicide* (Princeton, N.J.: Princeton University Press, 1960); Veli Verkko, *Homicides and Suicides in Finland and Their Dependence on National Character* (Copenhagen: G E C Gads Forlag, 1951); Kaare Svalastoga, "Homicide and Social Contact in Denmark," *American Journal of Sociology* 62 (1956), pp. 37–41; Richard Quinney, "Suicide, Homicide, and Economic Development," *Social Forces* 43 (1965), pp. 401–6; and Stuart Palmer, "Murder and Suicide in Forty Non-literate Societies," *Journal of Criminal Law, Criminology, and Police Science* 56 (1968), pp. 320–24.

31. David J. Pittman and William Handy, "Patterns in Criminal Aggravated Assault," *Journal of Criminal Law, Criminology, and Police Science* 55 (1964), pp. 462–70.

32. Mulvihill and Tumin, *Crimes of Violence,* vol. 11, p. 226.

33. The quote and reference to children at risk is from Richard J. Gelles and Murray A. Straus, "Violence in the American Family," *Journal of Social Issues* 35 (1979), p. 15. The Detroit and Boston data comes from U.S. Department of Justice Center for Women Policy Studies, "Violence in the Home Is a Crime Against the Whole Family" (Washington, D.C.: U.S. Government Printing Office, 1979).

34. Richard J. Gelles, "Violence Toward Children in the United States," *American Journal of Orthopsychiatry* 48 (1978).

35. See D. G. Gil, *Violence Against Children: Physical Abuse in the United States* (Cambridge, Mass.: Harvard University Press, 1970); Gelles and Straus, "Violence in the American Family"; and L. H. Pelton, "Child Abuse and Neglect: The Myth of Classlessness," *American Journal of Orthopsychiatry* 48 (1978), pp. 608–17.

36. In *Crimes of Violence,* vol. 12, Mulvihill and Tumin provide one of the few detailed reviews of prominent theories on interpersonal violence. Parts of this section rely heavily on their discussion.

37. Konrad Lorenz, *On Aggression* (New York: Bantam Books, 1971).

38. Pierre L. van den Berghe, "Bringing Beasts Back in: Toward a Biosocial Theory of Aggression," *American Sociological Review* 39 (1974), p. 777.

39. Ibid.

40. See ibid., and also Ronald H. Bailey, *Violence and Aggression* (New York: Time-Life Books, 1976), p. 30.

41. Robert L. Burgess, "Family Violence: Some Implications from Evolutionary Biology," paper presented to the annual meeting of the American Society of Criminology, Philadelphia, November 1979.

42. Mulvihill and Tumin, *Crimes of Violence,* vol. 12., p. 421.

43. Ibid., p. 424.

44. This term is used by van den Berghe in "Bringing Beasts Back in," p. 783.

45. Mulvihill and Tumin, *Crimes of Violence,* vol. 12. p. 460.

46. Ibid., pp. 460–61.

47. Bernard Chodorkoff and Seymour Baxter, "Psychiatric and Psychoanalytic Theories of Violence and Its Origins," in Mulvihill and Tumin, *Crimes of Violence,* vol. 13, p. 66 (appendix 23).

48. Donald T. Lunde, *Murder and Madness* (San Francisco: San Francisco Book Co., 1970), p. 93.

49. John Dollard, N. Miller, L. Doob, O. H. Mowrer, and R. R. Sears, *Frustration and Aggression* (New Haven: Yale University Press, 1939), p. 1.

50. Mulvihill and Tumin, *Crimes of Violence,* vol. 12, p. 436.

51. See Albert Bandura, *Aggression: A Social Learning Analysis* (Englewood Cliffs, N.J.: Prentice-Hall, 1973). For critical views see Leonard Berkowitz, *Aggression: A Social Psychological Analysis* (New York: McGraw-Hill, 1962).

52. See Bailey, *Violence and Aggression,* pp. 49–52.

53. For a more complex view of the connection see George C. Homans, *Social Behavior: Its Elementary Forms* (New York: Harcourt, Brace, and World, 1961).

54. For a fascinating collection of studies on assassinations, see William J. Crotty, ed., *Assassinations and the Political Order* (New York: Harper and Row, 1971).

55. William J. Goode, *Explorations in Social Theory* (New York: Oxford University Press, 1973), p. 162.

56. See note 2. above.

57. The term *contraculture* emphasizes elements of conflict between parent and subculture. For a discussion of this term see James W. Vander Zanden, *Sociology: A Systematic Approach,* 2nd ed. (New York: Ronald Press, 1970), pp. 47–49.

58. Martin R. Haskell and Lewis Yablonsky, *Crime and Delinquency,* 2nd ed. (Chicago: Rand McNally, 1974), p. 364.

59. David A. Ward, Maurice Jackson and Renee E. Ward, "Crimes of Violence by Women," in Mul-

vihill and Tumin, *Crimes of Violence*, vol. 13, p. 881 (appendix 17).

60. Wolfgang, *Patterns in Criminal Homicide*, pp. 188–89.

61. For a discussion of the "masculine ideal" see Jackson Toby, "Violence and the Masculine Ideal: Some Qualitative Data," *The Annals* 364 (1966), pp. 19–27.

62. Jaime Toro-Calder, "Personal Crimes in Puerto Rico," (M.A. thesis, University of Wisconsin, 1950); see also Marshall B. Clinard and Daniel J. Abbott, *Crime in Developing Countries* (New York: Wiley, 1973), pp. 59–60.

63. Lewis Yablonsky, *The Violent Gang* (New York: Penguin Books, 1966); Hunter S. Thompson, *Hell's Angels* (New York: Ballantine Books, 1966).

64. Yablonsky, *The Violent Gang*, p. 146.

65. Malcolm Klein, "Violence in American Juvenile Gangs," in Mulvihill and Tumin, *Crimes of Violence*, vol. 13, pp. 1449–50 (appendix 13).

66. Walter B. Miller, "Violent Crimes in City Gangs," *The Annals* 364 (1966), pp. 109–12.

67. Ibid., p. 112.

68. See Don C. Gibbons, *Changing the Lawbreaker* (Englewood Cliffs, N.J.: Prentice-Hall, 1965), pp. 116–17.

69. Marshall B. Clinard and Richard Quinney, *Criminal Behavior Systems: A Typology*, 2nd ed. (New York: Holt, Rinehart, and Winston, 1973), p. 28.

70. Gibbons, *Changing the Lawbreaker*, p. 116.

71. Gordon Waldo, "The 'Criminality Level' of Incarcerated Murderers and Non-Murderers," *Journal of Criminal Law, Criminology, and Police Science* 61 (1970), pp. 60–70.

72. See Wolfgang, *Patterns in Criminal Homicide*; Gibson and Klein, *Murder, 1957–1968;* and FBI, *Uniform Crime Reports, 1972* (Washington, D.C.: U.S. Government Printing Office, 1973).

73. FBI, *Uniform Crime Reports, 1972)*, pp. 36–38.

74. Mulvihill and Tumin, *Crimes of Violence*, vol. 12, chap. 12.

75. Wolfgang and Ferracuti, *The Subculture of Violence*, p. 280.

76. George Jackson Eder, "Urban Concentration, Agriculture, and Agrarian Reform," *The Annals* 360 (1965), p. 28.

77. See *To Establish Justice, To Insure Domestic Tranquility*, Final Report of the National Commission of the Causes and Prevention of Violence (Washington, D.C.: U.S. Government Printing Office, 1969), p. 37.

78. See Sheldon Hackney, "Southern Violence," in Hugh D. Graham and Ted R. Gurr eds., *The History of Violence in America* (Princeton, N.J.: Princeton University Press, 1969), pp. 505–27; Raymond Gastill, "Homicide and a Regional Subculture of Violence," *American Sociological Review* 36 (1971), pp. 157–62; and John Sheldon

Reed, "To Live . . . and Die . . . in Dixie: A Contribution to the Study of Southern Violence," *Political Science Quarterly* 86 (1971), pp. 429–43. For an opposing view, see Colin Loftin and Robert H. Hill, "Regional Subculture and Homicide: An Examination of the Gastill-Hackney Thesis," *American Sociological Review* 39 (1974), pp. 714–24.

79. John Shelton Reed, "Below the Smith and Wesson Line: Reflections on Southern Violence." Lecture to the Second Annual Hugo L. Black Symposium, University of Alabama at Birmingham, April 1977. For a recent critique of violent subculture theories see Alan J. Lizotte and David J. Bordua, "Firearms Ownership for Sport and Protection: Two Divergent Models," *American Sociological Review* 45 (1980), pp. 229–244.

80. See Thorsten Sellin and Marvin E. Wolfgang, *The Measurement of Delinquency* (New York: Wiley, 1964); Don C. Gibbons, "Crime and Punishment: A Study in Social Attitudes," *Social Forces* 47 (1969), pp. 391–97; and Peter H. Rossi, Emily Waite, Christine E. Bose, and Richard E. Berk, "The Seriousness of Crimes: Normative Structure and Individual Differences," *American Sociological Review* 39 (1974), pp. 224–37.

81. Sandra Ball-Rokeach, "The Legitimation of Violence," in *Collective Violence*, eds. James F. Short and Marvin E. Wolfgang (Chicago: Aldine, 1972), pp. 100–11.

82. In addition to Ball-Rokeach, "The Legitimation of Violence," see Monica D. Blumenthal, Robert L. Kahn, Frank M. Andrews, and Kendra B. Head, *Justifying Violence: Attitudes of American Men* (Ann Arbor, Mich.: Institute for Social Research, 1972); and William Gamson and James McEvoy, "Police Violence and Its Public Support," in Short and Wolfgang, *Collective Violence*, pp. 329–42. Also, William A. Westley, "The Escalation of Violence through Legitimization," *The Annals* 364 (1966), pp. 120–26.

83. Ralph Knoohuizen, Richard P. Fahey, and Deborah J. Palmer, *The Police and Their Use of Fatal Force in Chicago* (Evanston, Ill.: Chicago Law Enforcement Study Group, 1972).

84. Cynthia G. Sultan and Phillip Cooper, "Summary of Research on the Police Use of Deadly Force," in U.S. Department of Justice, *A Community Concern: Police Use of Deadly Force* (Washington, D.C.: U.S. Government Printing Office, 1979), p. 69. The data for 1950 to 1959 are from Gerald D. Robin, "Justifiable Homicide by Police Officers," in Marvin E. Wolfgang, ed., *Studies in Homicide* (New York: Harper and Row, 1967) pp. 88–100; Arthur L. Kobler, "Police Homicide in a Democracy," *Journal of Social Issues* 31 (1975), pp. 163–84.

85. See Sultan and Cooper, "Summary of Research on the Police Use of Deadly Force."

86. Paul Takagi, "Death by 'Police Intervention,' "

in U.S. Department of Justice, *Police Use of Deadly Force*, p. 34.

87. Robin, "Justifiable Homicide by Police Officers."
88. See Sultan and Cooper, "Summary of Research on the Police Use of Deadly Force."
89. See Sol Rubin, "Cops, Guns, and Homicides," *The Nation*, December 27, 1965.
90. Takagi, "Death by 'Police Intervention,' " p. 36.
91. See Blumenthal et al., *Justifying Violence*, pp. 65–68; also David L. Lange, Robert K. Baker, and Sandra J. Ball, *Mass Media and Violence*, Report to the National Commission on the Causes and Prevention of Violence (Washington, D.C. U.S. Government Printing Office, 1969), chapter 16.
92. Roy G. Francis, "Capow! An Argument and a Forecast," *Social Problems* XII (1965), p. 333.
93. Rubin, "Cops, Guns, and Homicides."
94. Harold Garfinkel, "Research Note on Inter- and Intra-Racial Homicides," *Social Forces* 27 (1949), pp. 369–81; Guy B. Johnson, "The Negro and Crime," *The Annals* 277 (1941), pp. 93–104.
95. Henry Allen Bullock, "Significance of the Racial Factor in Length of Prison Sentencs," *Journal of Criminal Law, Criminology, and Police Science* 52 (1961), p. 416.
96. See Marvin E. Wolfgang and Bernard Cohen, *Crime and Race* (New York: Institute of Human Relations Press, 1970), pp. 85–86.
97. Steven Barnet Boris, "Stereotypes and Dispositions for Criminal Homicide," *Criminology* 17 (1979), pp. 139–58.
98. For a similar treatment see Charles H. McCaghy, *Deviant Behavior: Crime, Conflict, and Interest Groups* (New York: Macmillan, 1976), p. 123.

Robbery: Theft by Violence

Activities that tend to include the display of physical force are called "heavy" crimes in street argot. As a rule, heavy crime involves the calculated, instrumental use of violence. Most typically, violence is threatened or used in order to deprive the victim of things of value — money, goods, or services. Examples of such crimes are armed robbery, strong-arm robbery, hijacking, piracy, and extortion.

Heavy Crime in History and Law

Activities of the theft-by-violence type are identified as crimes in some of the oldest known legal codes. Thus we find mention of robbery in Hammurapi's Code, in Roman law, and in the laws of various Anglo-Saxon kings. These early laws were rather vague in their references to robbery, however, and it is not always clear precisely what behavior the word *robbery* identified. Even so, in Anglo-Saxon and early Norman law robbery was quite distinct from mere theft, and those who interpreted the law paid particular attention to the violence of the offense. Indeed, one of Henry III's judges, Henry de Bracton, reminded his colleagues that whatever else robbery may be, it is still a form of theft.[1] Bracton's influence was substantial, and we find that after the middle of the thirteenth century robbery was treated in common law as *aggravated theft*.

It is interesting to note that the Anglo-Saxon and early Norman distinction between robbery and theft may have rested largely on a prevailing ethical judgment regarding the two sorts of activities and their perpetrators.[2] Theft was considered a dishonorable activity, and the thief was accorded little respect as a person. Those who steal do so by guile, cunning, stealth, and deceitfulness. Those who rob, on the other hand, do so through direct confrontation with the victim, who, as a result of the challenge, is given an opportunity to fight in defense of his possessions. At least the robber is open and honest in his work!

While similar views are apparently held by some robbers today, the prevailing theme expressed in dominant American culture is that robbery is one of the more heinous offenses. To explain why feudal England maintained a somewhat different view, one must look at the sociopolitical climate of the times. Physical confrontation permeated medieval England. It could be seen in the almost perpetual battles and wars being fought at home and abroad; it was encouraged as sport; and it had an integral role in the prevailing system of justice, whether in the form of self-help retaliation and feuding, or in the form of trial by ordeal and official punishments. If physical confrontation is an integral part of a society's way of life, the shape in which it comes and the kind of people who indulge in it may not matter much.

Bandits and Highwaymen While medieval England may have shown grudging respect for the robber and his trade, lawmakers lost little time in designating robbery as one of the more serious felony crimes, punishable by the death penalty. As far as the evidence allows, two major reasons can be advanced for this turn of events: one, concerning the frequency of offenses of the robbery type; the other, the nature of the victims.

During the thirteenth and fourteenth centuries, banditry and plundering appear to have gained in popularity as a means of subsistence for increasing numbers of oppressed and dispossessed serfs and peasants. These were hard times, made even harder by a pervasive inequality that kept the poor and lowly completely at the mercy of the rich and powerful. These were the times when tales about Robin Hood flourished, for the common people could find in his exploits solutions to their own miserable condition. Robin Hood did all the things they wanted to do, but could not.[3] But most of all, these were times of resistance and innovation: Resistance found shape in the largely unsuccessful peasant revolts; innovation found shape in banditry. Robin Hood provided the *modus operandi,* and bands of marauding robbers plied their trade around the countryside. Joined by out-of-work soldiers and men of fortune, the ranks of the robbers swelled as feudalism began to decay.

The victims were often the rich and the powerful. Though we have no way of knowing the actual distribution of robbery victims throughout the three great classes — nobility and landed gentry, churchmen, and peasantry — it is more than likely that most victims came from the first two classes. For one thing, these were the people most likely to travel from one part of the country to the next, making them easy prey for the robber whose territory was the field, the footpath, and the forest. Second, these were the people most likely to have things of value, or to have in their homes and churches possessions worth stealing. And third, these were the people at whose feet responsibility for the pervasive personal and collective troubles could be laid. What better victims could the robber find?[4]

The growing incidence of heavy crime and the high status of its victims probably account for the severity with which robbers were handled under law. And severely handled they were: the scaffold continually felt the weight of the highwayman and bandit. By the sixteenth century, robbers who challenged their victims in dwelling-houses and about public highways were denied "benefit of clergy." This simply meant that those who might previously have escaped the gallows because of birth or occupation now found it more difficult to do so.[5] The removal of benefit of clergy may have been related to the appearance of a new category of highway robbers. During the highwayman's golden age, which stretched from the early sixteenth century until the early eighteenth century, many highwaymen were of noble birth or substantial means. Their trade permitted such people the opportunity to humiliate their peers and political adversaries and make off with plunder in the process.[6] It is not surprising that those in power should have made certain that the "gentlemen robbers," as they were popularly called, did not escape full punishment for their audacity.

Piracy As the era of the highwayman declined, a new form of heavy crime made its appearance, this time on the high seas: piracy. Relatively unknown before the dawn of international sea trade and exploration, "Piracy emerged in the Western Hemisphere in response to a unique interaction of many natural and social events."[7] The exploitation of the New World provided rich cargoes, the plunder of which was made viable by the existence of well-situated islands that provided hiding and cover for the pirates, and by the increasing mastery of the sea made possible by developments in maritime technology. As navies grew, moreover, more and more seamen had sufficient knowledge of the sea to make piracy an option for the exercise of their skills.

But some of the same factors that helped piracy develop also ushered in its decline. Naval warfare, advances in technology, growth in national fleets, international maritime agreements, and the advance of civilization each helped to erect insurmountable obstacles to the buccaneer. His ships became outgunned, outmanned, and out-of-date; his escape routes and hiding places were controlled by treaties and regularly patrolling fleets; his seamen were pressed into legitimate service or volunteered for it; and the maritime frontiers were closed. The nineteenth century witnessed little piracy.

Frontier Outlaws   In nineteenth-century America, meanwhile, heavy crime was flourishing in the form of cattle rustlers, bank and train robbers, marauding bands of outlaws, and lone bandits in search of quick money. For in America, the frontier had been moving south and west, and with it went robbery, plunder, and violence. Just as robbery flourished in England during periods of social and political upheaval, so it did in America. The turbulent decades of the nineteenth century witnessed unprecedented personal and group lawlessness. First stagecoaches and then trains became the favorite targets of organized bands of outlaws and "road agents," as the highway robbers were called. Organized in gangs or operating alone, the road agents, American counterparts of the English highwayman, plied the countryside. For some of them this was a form of moonlighting. Their legitimate occupations were of all kinds, and some road agents were small-town marshals and deputies who could use their police cover to advantage: "A man skilled with a gun might serve as outlaw, sheriff, and hero of his people at various stages of his usually short-lived career as a social bandit."[8]

The sprouting mining camps on the edges of the western frontier became the scenes of numerous battles between miners and outlaws, and between miners themselves, as people sought easy wealth by robbing company or individual of gold and silver. The nineteenth century was also the era of bank robberies. From Montana, the Dakotas, and Minnesota in the north, to New Mexico and Texas in the south, few banks were secure.

These developments were in part mere extensions of America's experiences when the Mississippi valley was its western frontier. As Philip Jordon describes the Mississippi situation:

> Piracy and robbery increased with the spread of settlements. Both steamboats and river towns were looted not only by individuals but also by organized groups of desperadoes. The Chicester and Morrell gangs operated on the lower river, and the Timber Wolves and the Brown gang terrorized residents in Iowa, Illinois, and Missouri. Navou, the Mormon settlement, was felt by many to be the center of Middle Border crime. The steamer *Kentuckian* was robbed of $37,000 in September 1831, and a few months later a passenger on the *Peruvian* was robbed of a trunk containing $2,500. Such thefts could be multiplied many times over. St. Louis newspapers, as the decades advanced, regularly reported steamboat robberies.[9]

Frontier heavy crime reached its height following the conclusion of the Civil War. Thousands of discharged soldiers were left to their own devices, and many apparently found banditry a solution to their problems. Evidence shows, too, that some soldiers from the losing side organized themselves into bands of plundering outlaws whose major victims were initially "Yankee enemies."[10] As with the gentlemen robbers of seventeenth-century England, their crimes seem to have been motivated, in part at least, by a desire to get back at and humiliate those considered responsible for their loss of status and jobs and their financial woes.

Of the many factors that supported this era of heavy crime probably the most important was the ready availability and common use of firearms. Even as late as 1890 few states considered the carrying or drawing of firearms a serious offense. Another influence was the natural environment itself — its geographic size and physical contours. Not only did the frontier have miles and miles of unsettled land where outlaws could roam at will, but "the successful planning and execution of their crimes were made possible by the topography of confusing ranges of high mountains, segmented by wide deserts, and creviced with inaccessible canyons."[11] A final influence was the public sentiment of the period, one best summed up in the mystique surrounding the outlaws whose ties to the fallen Confederacy made them noble victims of tragic circumstance:

> Characteristic of the mystique surrounding the noble robber is that he begins his career not as a criminal but as a victim of injustice, that he rights wrongs, that he robs the rich to feed the poor, that he never kills except in self-defense or just revenge, that he never deserts his people, that he is admired, aided, respected by his compatriots, that he dies because of betrayal, and, finally, that he is regarded as invulnerable. . . . No sooner is the bandit killed than popular legend restores him to life.[12]

The Younger brothers, the Dalton boys, Frank and Jesse James, Henry Starr, and Sam Bass are but a few of the outlaws eulogized in folktales and popular songs. Even while the James brothers were carrying out their most ruthless robberies, observers were ready with explanations laying the blame anywhere but at the outlaws' feet.[13] This is certainly far from the popular sentiment regarding most robbers today.

With the dawn of the twentieth century, the era of the frontier outlaw was already on the wane. The frontier itself had disappeared as the railroads conquered the deserts, and urbanization took hold of strategic points throughout the entire country. Going, too, were some of the other conditions that had lent support to banditry. Large-scale unemployment vanished with World War I, law enforcement achieved unprecedented sophistication and professionalism, and the sociopolitical climate began to stabilize. While the depression years revived for a time some of the features of the bandit era, with John Dillinger, "Pretty Boy" Floyd, Bonnie and Clyde, and "Baby Face" Nelson playing key roles, the period from the late 1930s until the present saw the demise of frontier-style heavy crime.

In 1978 robbery made up only 4 percent of the total index crimes reported by the FBI, but accounted for over one-third of those index offenses involving interpersonal force. Robbery rates in the last decade or so have increased considerably over what they were in the early 1960s. In 1978 the robbery rate for the country as a whole was 191.3 recorded offenses per 100,000 people; the comparable rate in 1960 was 59.9 (see figure 5.1).

Caution must be exercised in dealing with any published data on crime, and this is particularly so in the case of robbery. Robbery comes in many forms, and general statements about the "robbery rate" tend to be misleading. All robberies and all robbery situations are not the same; to speak, then, of robbery does not mean that we are dealing with a homogeneous collection of situations and activities. To get a feel for some of the ways actual robberies differ, consider the robberies in the box on page 144. These robberies were reported to Washington, D.C., police in one twenty-four-hour period during December 1966. You can see differences in the location of the robberies, in the types of victims, in the methods used, in the weapons used, and in the amount of monetary loss. These are just a few of the ways in which robberies can be distinguished from one another.

Even though robberies take diverse forms and involve different circumstances, some features tend to be shared by many of the incidents on

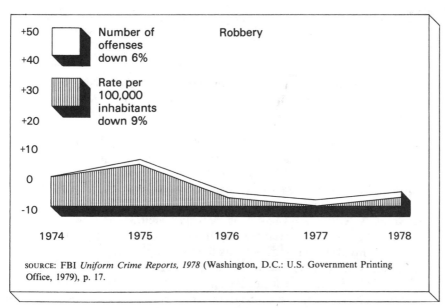

SOURCE: FBI *Uniform Crime Reports, 1978* (Washington, D.C.: U.S. Government Printing Office, 1979), p. 17.

Figure 5.1 Robbery, 1974–1978 (% change over 1974)

ONE DAY OF ROBBERY IN WASHINGTON, D.C., 1966

Friday, December 9:

9:15 a.m. Strongarm robbery, street, $2.

10:00 a.m. Armed robbery, liquor store, $1,500.

11:30 a.m. Pocketbook snatched with force and violence, street, $3.

12:30 p.m. Holdup with revolver, roofing company, $2,100.

2:40 p.m. Holdup with gun, shoe store, $139.

3:20 p.m. Holdup with gun, apartment, $92.

4:55 p.m. Holdup with gun, bank, $8,716.

6:25 p.m. Mugging, street, $5.

6:50 p.m. Holdup with revolver, tourist home, $30.

7:00 p.m. Strongarm robbery, street, $25.

7:05 p.m. Holdup with gun, auto in parking lot, $61.

7:10 p.m. Strongarm robbery, apartment house, $3.

7:15 p.m. Holdup with revolver (employee shot twice), truck rental company, $200.

7:25 p.m. Mugging street, $5.

7:50 p.m. Holdup with gun, transfer company, $1,400.

8:55 p.m. Holdup with shotgun, newspaper substation, $100.

10:10 p.m. Holdup with gun, hotel, $289.50.

10:15 p.m. Strongarm robbery, street, $120.

10:30 p.m. Holdup with gun, street, $59.50.

10:53 p.m. Strongarm robbery, street, $175.

11:05 p.m. Holdup, tavern, $40.

11:30 p.m. Strongarm robbery, street, $3.

11:55 p.m. Strongarm robbery, street, $51.

Saturday, December 10:

12:20 a.m. Strongarm robbery, street, $19.

1:10 a.m. Strongarm robbery, apartment house, $3.

3:25 a.m. Strongarm robbery, street, $25.

3:50 a.m. Holdup with knife, street, $23.

3:55 a.m. Holdup with gun, street, $25.

4:20 a.m. Robbery with intent to rape, street, 75 cents.

4:20 a.m. Holdup with gun, carryout shop, $80.

6:25 a.m. Holdup-rape, street, $20.

6:25 a.m. Holdup with gun, tourist home, no amount listed.

6:45 a.m. Holdup, street, $5.

7:30 a.m. Holdup with knife, cleaners, $300.

7:40 a.m. Strongarm robbery, street, $80.

SOURCE: President's Commission on Law Enforcement and the Administration of Justice, *The Challenge of Crime in a Free Society* (Washington, D.C.: U.S. Government Printing Office, 1967), p. 2.

---

which we have information. Data compiled by the FBI, as well as those produced by a number of in-depth studies of robbery,[14] indicate the following tendencies.

1. Robbery tends to occur most frequently in the more highly populated cities of the country. Larger cities experience higher rates than smaller cities, and the lowest rates are found in rural areas. In 1975, for example, the fifty-eight largest American cities accounted for around two-thirds of the reported robberies.

2. Robbery tends to involve offenders and victims who are strangers. While the percentages vary from city to city, estimates of the proportion of incidents involving strangers go as high as 90 percent.

3. Robbery offenders tend to be young males. Males between the ages of 15 and 25 predominate in arrest statistics for robbery. In addition, it seems that black males are more likely than white males to be identified as the offender in robbery incidents.

4. Robbery victims tend to be males over age 21. Males are much more likely than females to be the victims of robbery. Whereas offenders are more likely to be blacks, the most likely victims are white males.

5. Robbery tends to take place "on the street." While percentages will vary from city to city and from one part of a city to another, nationally, around 60 percent of recorded robbery incidents occur in the open — in alleys, outside bars, in streets, in parking lots, or in playgrounds.

6. The robbery offender tends to be in possession of a weapon. The most typical robbery is an armed robbery, that is, one in which a weapon other than the person's own body is present. However, weapons are rarely used to inflict injury.

7. The victim tends to be uninjured or only slightly injured during the commission of a robbery.

These seven features of robberies indicate the nature of the most typical robbery in day-to-day urban living. However, as stressed at the beginning of this section, it would be misleading to think of robbery in just these terms. In recent years criminologists have drawn attention to differences in robbery, and in the effort to make sense of them have suggested a number of robbery typologies or classifications. Let us then consider some of these typologies, and in doing so draw a more complete picture of robbery and the robbery offender.

Robbery Typologies

The two best-known typologies dealing with robbery are those by F. H. McClintock and Evelyn Gibson and by John Conklin. The first focuses on the circumstances in which the victim is attacked; the second on the robbery offender.

A TYPOLOGY OF ROBBERY CIRCUMSTANCES

McClintock and Gibson, in their London study, offer a fivefold classification of robbery circumstances.[15]

Group I: Robbery of persons who, as part of their employment, are in charge of money or goods. This group includes robbery of shops, banks, taxis, factories, offices, and other commercial establishments where money is likely to be handled on a regular basis by employees.

Group II: Robbery in the open following a sudden attack. Included here are street offenses such as mugging, yoking (putting an arm around the victim's neck from behind and pulling back on it), purse snatching, and other unprovoked, unexpected stickups.

Group III: Robbery on private premises. This includes robberies by persons who gained entry by force or who were disturbed by a member of the household after breaking and entering the premises.

Group IV: Robbery after preliminary association of short duration between victim and offender. This includes such situations as those in which the victim and offender have come together for purposes of prostitution or homosexual encounters, or in which they have been drinking together in a bar or at a party. In incidents involving prostitution, whether heterosexual or homosexual, the victim may be either the prostitute or the client.

Group V: Robbery after previous association of some duration between the victim and offender. This includes robbery by a friend, lover, or coworker.

Some of the advantages of a classification of this sort are listed by the authors:

> There are several advantages in a classification based on the circumstances in which the victim was attacked. It is sufficiently objective to be applied in any police area; it can include all crimes recorded by the police, and not only those in which an offender has been apprehended; and it indicates the vulnerability of different classes of person to attack.[16]

In the London study the authors found that groups I and II accounted for around 70 percent of the robbery incidents recorded by the police in both 1950 and 1957. Over that period, however, robberies of persons in charge of money or goods (group I) had increased more than those in group II. The authors speculate that London robbery is looking more and more like the work of professionals — those who seek out lucrative targets and, among other things, make robbery a steady source of income. Additional support for this speculation comes from data on the financial gains from group I robberies and police clearance rates:

> First, it emerges that in 1950 hauls valued at one hundred pounds or over [then equivalent to around $280] represented only ten percent of the total stolen; seven years later the proportion had gone up, though only slightly, to 13 percent; but nowadays [1961] twenty-five percent of all recorded robberies involve at least a hundred pounds. Secondly, it would appear, on the whole, that the more he steals, the better the thief now fares. Though in 1950 about half of those taking over 100 pounds were detected, in 1957 less than a sixth, and in 1960 less than a fifth were brought to justice. Thirdly, when larger thefts are considered, the success rate of the professional criminal becomes even more impressive. Nine out of the eleven robberies involving property valued at over 500 pounds in 1950 were not cleared up, twenty-nine out of the thirty in 1957 and thirty-two out of the thirty-seven in the first half of 1960.[17]

Differences Between Groups I and II The substantial differences between the robbery circumstances for groups I and II revolve around the robber, the victim, the method, and the losses. In robberies of persons in charge of money, the offender is likely to be older than his counterpart in the sudden attack situation (group II), where juveniles and young adults predominate. Often, it seems, the sudden attack robber is opportunistic, inexperienced, and casually involved in this form of violent theft. The victims come from all walks of life, and if women and children are the victims they are more likely to be found in sudden attack robberies. Violence, too, is more likely to occur in sudden attack robberies than in robberies of persons in charge of money, though the carrying of weapons is less likely to be seen in sudden attack robberies. (For more information on this, see pages 151–155.) The amount stolen is likely to be greater in robberies of persons in charge of money than in sudden attack situations. Sudden attack robberies are more likely to occur during the hours of darkness and in relatively isolated spots such as parks, alleys, and dimly lit streets. Understandably, robberies of persons in charge of money are most likely to occur during business hours and involve spatial patterns reflecting the location of businesses.

London and Philadelphia Data Compared Does the McClintock and Gibson typology help us make sense out of our information on robbery in American cities? How do American robberies compare with those in London in the late 1950s and early 1960s?

To date only one published application of the McClintock and Gibson typology has been made to robbery in America. This was done by Andre Normandeau as part of his larger study of robbery in Philadelphia.[18] Using a sample 10 percent of robbery incidents from 1960 to 1966, Normandeau discovered that, as in London, sudden attack robberies tend to involve young males who are unarmed and who strike lone victims in isolated places. However, he also found some important differences. Groups I and II accounted for over 70 percent of the robberies he investigated, as in London, but sudden attack robberies far outnumbered robberies of persons in charge of money as part of their jobs. In addition, sudden attack robberies in Philadelphia were much more likely to involve female victims than those in London.

How are we to interpret these differences? Normandeau comes to the tentative conclusion, which he admits is rather speculative, that London witnessed more organized robbery than Philadelphia. It is tentative and speculative since the data have to do with robbery incidents rather than robbery offenders; to find out about such things as organization, planning, decision making, and professionalism we need information about the robbers themselves that deals specifically with these issues. Neither the London nor the Philadelphia data really permit inferences about these dimensions of the robbery situation.

On the national scale there is some evidence that sudden attack robberies may be declining in relation to other categories, most notably groups I and III (robbery on private premises). FBI data covering 1974 to 1978 show bank robberies were up 43 percent and those of gas stations up 52

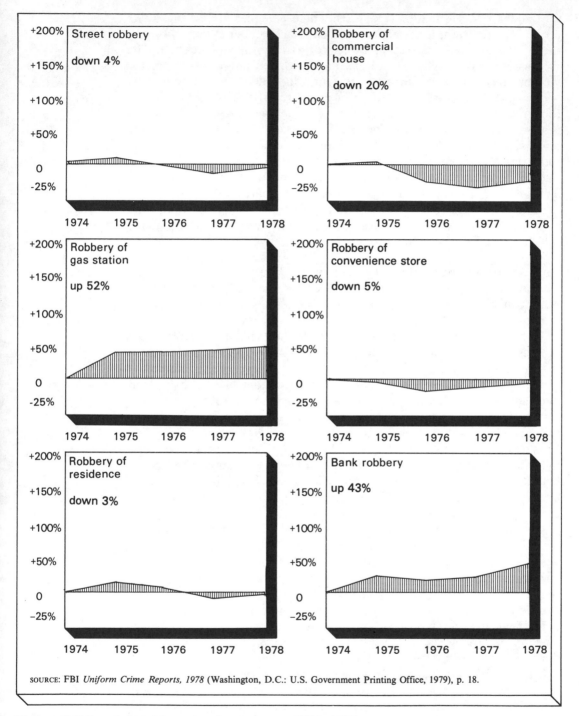

Figure 5.2 Trends in robbery, by circumstance, 1974–1978

percent, compared a 4 percent decline for street robberies, which are primarily of the sudden attack variety. Though the FBI does not use the McClintock and Gibson typology, the evidence seems to substantiate a relative decline in sudden attack incidents (see figure 5.2).

ROBBERY OFFENDERS

What type of people are robbers? Do they plan, premeditate, and organize their robberies? Do they use weapons, and if so, why? How do they carry out their robberies? Are they "one-time losers" when convicted, or do they have a history of involvement in robbery or in other criminal offenses? What happens to them when they are arrested and when they go to court? Do different types of robbers exist, and if so, do they commit different types of robberies?

These questions can only be answered with information about robbers themselves. An attempt to shed light on these questions is John Conklin's study of robbery in Boston. Focusing on the robbery offender, Conklin devised a typology of robbers on the basis of interviews with prison inmates. This typology was then used to make sense out of the data on robbery contained in police and court records.

The Professional Robber Conklin describes the professional robber as

> . . . the type of offender who reflects the image of the robber in the public's mind. He is portrayed in the media as the bandit who carefully plans his robbery, executes the crime with a group of accomplices, and steals large sums of money which are used to support a hedonistic life style. He exhibits a long-term deep-seated commitment to robbery as a means of getting money and carries out his holdups with skill and planning. . . .
>
> We will here define professionals as *those who manifest a long-term commitment to crime as a source of livelihood, who plan and organize their crimes prior to committing them, and who seek money to support a particular life style that may be called hedonistic.*[19]

According to Conklin two main types of professionals are involved in robbery: those who do it almost exclusively and those who are committed to some other form of crime (such as burglary) but may occasionally commit a robbery. The professional robber is one who engages in robbery exclusively, or almost exclusively, and for whom it is the main source of income. Professional robbers are probably the least numerous.

The Opportunist Robber Unlike the professional robber, the opportunist robber commits a variety of property crimes besides robbery; and though he does rob, it is a relatively infrequent activity for him. Also in contrast to professional robbers, opportunists rarely score in a big way, and the small amounts they do obtain are generally for spur-of-the-moment needs or to maintain their life-style or peer group image. The more favored targets for the opportunist are women with purses, drunks, cabdrivers, and people who walk alone on dark streets. Opportunists tend to be young black males, relatively inexperienced in serious crime, who come from lower-class slum backgrounds. Their robberies are mostly unplanned, haphazard affairs, and the decision to rob is often a sudden thing, influenced by momentary pressures and the availability of a vulnerable victim. The opportunist is commonly involved in a sudden attack robbery, and in the robbery of small shops. Conklin offers the following illustration as typical of the opportunist robber:

> One night, George and two friends stole a car. While driving around the city, one suggested that they get a little extra spending money. The driver stopped the car next to an elderly lady who was alone on the street. George got out and grabbed the lady's purse, then ran back to the car and the group drove away.[20]

These youths netted seventeen dollars and were eventually caught and charged with unarmed robbery.

The Addict Robber   This category is a rather peculiar one, for it includes those who are addicted to drugs and commit robberies in order to support their habits, and those who simply use drugs — most notably amphetamines, psychedelics, and assorted pills — and whose robberies may or may not be motivated by need for cash to buy more drugs. Conklin brings them together in this category because they share a low level of commitment to robbery — it is often considered a last resort, a dangerous, risky business — because they seem to engage in little planning or deliberation before they rob, and because they are likely to use the proceeds for drug purchases. Since they are not all addicts, the label seems a misnomer.

The relationship between drugs and robbery is difficult to assess, and most authorities are inclined to maintain that *nothing about drugs as a substance leads to robbery,* or to any crime for that matter. On the other hand, no one questions that those who are dependent on drug use, especially males, will rob to finance their habit when other avenues to cash appear closed off. The extent to which robbery is drug-related in this way is extremely hard to establish. Evidence does suggest that other property offenses — for example, burglary, shoplifting, and larceny — are more likely than robbery to be drug-related. In any event the horror stories we hear through the media about drugs and violent property crime probably overstate the issue. (In chapter 9 we will further investigate drugs and crime.)

The Alcoholic Robber   This is the least convincing of Conklin's four categories of robbers. Apart from the fact that it is based on interviews with only seven inmates and relies on their claims to having been drunk at the time of their robberies, nothing definitive emerges in Conklin's descriptions of the robber who typifies this category. He is painted as part opportunist, part addict, and above all as someone who is driven to his crime by the effects of alcohol. Perhaps because alcohol affects people differently, nothing in Conklin's account provides grounds for making any predictions about such things as motivation, method, and use of violence. Some of the alcoholic robbers he describes apparently committed their robberies to gain cash for drinking purchases, two took their victims' money as an afterthought, having first beaten them up, and one robbed to recover the money he had lost in a card game. The major issue throughout seems to be that alcohol somehow induced the offender to commit his robbery, and this is the key distinction between this and the second and third categories.

Conklin's typology is useful nevertheless because it helps us understand robbery from the standpoint of those who engage in it — why and how they do it and what happens to them — and because it helps us predict patterns of robbery and societal reaction to it on the basis of the differences between them. In America there seems to be little doubt that the bulk of robbers are opportunistic; however, it is also likely that addict robbers account for the highest rates of robbery when the categories are compared.

Violence in Robbery

Both legal and popular conceptions emphasize violence as a key feature of robbery. Whether actually used or merely threatened, physical force gives robbery its unique character as one type of criminal theft. Because force may be used, robbery is looked at with fear and apprehension. Robbery and assaultive crimes readily come to mind when people explain why they are afraid to go out alone at night, why they stay off the streets at night, and why they avoid talking to strangers. In his investigation of public conceptions of crime, Albert Biderman found that most of those interviewed in Washington, D.C., thought of crime in terms of personal attacks, and similar findings have been uncovered in other studies.[21] Prevailing beliefs concerning robbery, particularly in its more common street forms, appear to be little different from these 1950 observations by journalist Howard Whitman:

> The hoodlum will bash in your head with a brick for a dollar and ninety-eight cents. The police records of our cities are spotted with cases of "murder for peanuts" in which the victims, both men and women, have been slugged, stabbed, hit with iron pipes, hammers or axes, and in a few cases kicked to death — the loot being no more than the carfare a woman carried in her purse or the small change in a man's pocket.[22]

It is true that the kinds of things Whitman describes do occur in some robbery incidents. But how valid is this as a general description of robbery in America today? What role does violence play in robbery inci-

Most robbery is by amateurs who rarely plan their crimes and whose thefts, even when successful, bring them little profit.

dents? Why and when does the threat of violence become actual violence? Are robbers likely to injure or kill their victims as a general rule, or is physical assault a relatively rare occurrence in robbery?

We have already seen that on the whole robbery incidents do not result in physical injury to the victims. When injury does occur it is usually minor, requiring no hospitalization. The degrees of violence that can occur in a robbery incident range from threat alone to fatal assault. This means that the designation of robbery as a "crime of violence" — as is done, for example, by the FBI — tends to gloss over variations in the kind and degree of physical aggression actually found in particular robbery cases:

> There are many variations, ranging from an armed bank robbery in which several people are shot and injured to minor thefts such as purse snatching, where force or the threat of force is used. Dramatically profiling the lower end of the robbery spectrum was the report of an offense in which one of two

9-year-old boys twisted the arm of the other in the schoolyard in order to obtain 25 cents of the latter's lunch money. Because force was used, the police correctly recorded and counted the act as "highway robbery." . . . While these less serious events should be recorded, it does not seem reasonable to include them in the same category as the more serious offenses.[23]

The FBI now distinguishes between armed and unarmed robbery. According to its reports, robberies by persons who are armed with a weapon outnumber unarmed robberies about three to two. But this still tells us nothing about the actual use of violence, since the presence of a weapon does not mean that it will be used to inflict violence. Indeed, evidence from the National Commission and from Conklin's Boston study show that violence is *more likely to erupt in cases where the offender is unarmed than where he is armed.* In the eighteen cities covered by these studies violence only infrequently involved shooting or stabbing; it was far more likely to amount to kicking, shoving, beating, or knocking down.[24]

The tendency for violence to erupt in unarmed robbery incidents is not hard to explain. First, the offender places himself in a situation where he has no obviously deadly weapon with which to intimidate the victim. To impress upon the victim that he means business the robber may therefore resort to a display of actual violence. With a gun or knife present, such a display may be unnecessary — the victim is sufficiently intimidated to offer no resistance.[25]

Second, much unarmed robbery is of the sudden attack variety. A successful sudden attack robbery depends as much on the element of surprise and the speedy commission of the theft as it does upon intimidation. The opportunist robber, bent on getting as much as possible and then "splitting" uses violence in an instrumental way: it helps ensure that the victim is in no position to resist even if he or she wanted to do so, and it makes escape more likely. It may also lessen the chances that the victim will be clearheaded enough to "get the make on him" and identify him for the police.

While violence is most likely to occur in situations where the robber is unarmed, most robberies do involve the use of weapons. If weapons are present, why is force not used in most cases? We have already touched on one possible answer — the mere appearance of a weapon is sufficient to intimidate the victim and secure compliance with the robber's demands. If victim compliance is the key to use or nonuse of force in armed robberies, then we should expect to find the following two conditions in the typical armed robbery: (1) no victim resistance, or resistance so meek that a gesture with the weapon is all that is needed to secure compliance; and (2) a tendency for the robber to use force in cases where the victim offers more than meek resistance. Some evidence indicates that both these conditions hold. For example, Conklin found in Boston that most victims did not resist (more than 80 percent in both 1964 and 1968). When the victim did resist, however, robbers with knives were twice as likely to use force, and those with guns three times as likely, as in situations where the victim did not resist.[26]

But this is not the end of the story. Enough cases are left to indicate that compliance per se cannot adequately account for use or nonuse of force in armed robberies. Again using the Boston findings, more than half of those with firearms did not use force even though victims resisted. Conversely, around 15 percent of offenders with guns, and around a third of those with knives used force even with no resistance.

In such cases we must look more closely at the robber for possible explanations. What we have learned about offender types might shed some light on the issue. We know, for example, that the opportunist robber is neither continually involved in robbery nor committed to it as a career, and that his robbery is often unplanned. In the usual opportunist robbery (particularly when undertaken by a group of offenders) weapons are not used. But if the relatively inexperienced opportunist is armed, he may be frightened and confused by the confrontation or perhaps carried away with it. If he is frightened or confused, his use or nonuse of force may be a consequence of those factors likely to heighten his mental state — for example, the appearance of a third party, a counterthreat by the victim, an alarm going off, a weakening of resolve, or a conflict between his immediate desire and pressure from significant others. The opportunist may get carried away with his exploit and use force even if the victim does not resist. This may happen if friends are looking on or participating, or if he interprets the robbery confrontation and his use of a weapon as an opportunity to display toughness and machismo.[27] In such cases we may be seeing the impact of subcultural forces akin to those discussed in chapter 4. Since the opportunist is most likely to be of relatively low socioeconomic status, to have a history of delinquency, and to have spent much or all of his young life in slum or ghetto surroundings, he may well have come under the influence of a subculture of violence. In any event, for both the tough youth and the confused one, violence or its avoidance may have nothing to do with victim resistance. Remember, however, these interpretations are speculative.

To summarize, emphasis must again be placed on the general observation that most robbery incidents do not involve the use of violence, and certainly not the kind likely to result in serious injury. It seems clear that this is partly because most victims do not resist. If a trend develops toward more victim resistance, we may see an escalation in the use of violence. On the whole, however, we find few indications, if any, that robbers are particularly violence-prone, and while the subculture of violence perspective may help account for the use of violence in some incidents, robbers are perhaps best understood as people out for a fast buck, who cash in on the low probability that their victims will or can resist effectively.

Professional Robbers

Those who commit robbery as a steady source of income have some very special views on the use of force in their work. But before we get to these views we must distinguish between the professional criminal and one who commits crime habitually. Many robbers are habitual criminals in the sense that they engage in crime repetitively. They begin their careers in crime at an early age and remain largely unsophisticated in both choice of crime and methods used. As juveniles they quickly come to the attention of authorities, mostly for minor infractions of the law or because they are repetitively tagged as delinquent and incorrigible by parents, schools, and neighbors. Some may engage in robbery on a repetitive basis — evidence is considerable that a small core of repeaters is responsible for most robberies committed by juveniles. But the robberies these repeaters commit are often of the street variety — mugging, "rolling" drunks, purse snatching — or they involve small stores and corner gas stations. They are typically opportunists, and commitment to robbery is transitory if it exists at all. If they carry their criminal careers into adulthood, some may emerge as professionals in the long run, but most do not. The majority probably spend their early adulthood in and out of jails and in and out of opportunist crime.

George Vold has the following to say on the distinction between the professional and the habitual criminal:

> The professional criminal must be distinguished from the merely habitual one whose activity, while repetitive and habitual, has no other element of a profession. A lawyer "habitually" practices law; a doctor is in the habit of practicing medicine. We do not, however, speak of them as habitual lawyers or doctors, but as professional men of law or medicine. Similarly, the term "habitual criminal" is descriptive of a less specific and meaningful vocational identification with crime than is true of the professional. Such a person is often a repeater in crime, but essentially a failure in the practice of crime as a vocation and a way of life. He frequently gets caught, yet wants to work at crime and associate with other criminals, but often is not good enough to be trusted with any significant assignments. Consequently he sometimes has to work at legitimate employment between "jobs" and prison sentences. The merely habitual criminal, whose only accomplishment is that he has been caught several times, has no place and no status among truly professional criminals.[28]

Those offenders who repetitively engage in robbery will sometimes develop rudimentary strategies and tactics, and may undergo some training at the hands of more experienced peers. In Clifford Shaw's classic study of the "jackroller" (a person who robs drunks and skid-row bums), "Stanley," the subject of the study, tells us about his experiences in early twentieth-century Chicago:

> I went immediately to the News Alley, and there met an old pal that I had become acquainted with in St. Charles [Reformatory]. I showed him the bank roll, and that strengthened our friendship considerably. So we started to blow it in . . . and in a few days the dough was gone. I had tasted the life and found it sweet. But I was in a predicament, for I had no money, and you can't enjoy life without dough. My buddy, being an old "jackroller," suggested "jack-rolling" as a way out of the dilemma. So we started out to "put the strong arm" on drunks. We sometimes stunned the drunks by "giving them the club" in a dark place near a lonely alley. It was bloody work, but necessity demanded it — we had to live.

And later:

> I slept like a top that night, and the next morning I met Tony. We worked out a plan for "making drunks," which was crude, although it didn't seem so to us. . . .
>
>   That night Tony and I embarked on our tour of the slums after "live ones" (bums with money), which were fairly plentiful in that district at that season. The drunks who had recently come in from the labor camps would usually have money. . . . Tony and I continued to "make drunks" and to break into apartments for about three months, and then his brother ran into him on the street. . . . Tony had to go and that left me without a pal. I was very lonely. I met many of my old friends, and one of them, knowing of my success of "making drunks" and that Tony had left me, wanted to establish a partnership with me. Realizing that I would have "cold feet" if I went out alone to steal, I considered his offer and sized him up for the job. . . . Jack (that was his name) was a well-built, swarthy Kentucky lad of twenty-two years. I looked at his strong arms and shoulders with approval, and although he was not a polished city chap, he knew the ropes around the West Side, so I agreed to take him into partnership with me.[29]

While the habitual offender may skip from one type of activity to another, from legitimate enterprise to illegitimate enterprise, from burglary and shoplifting to mugging and assault, his involvement in criminal subcultures provides him with the argot (slang) and other trappings of the normative system, which help him feel at home among his fellows and provide group support for repetition in criminal activities. But to be a professional means to work at crime so that crime becomes work, a job, employment — a steady source of income. And professionalism means more than quasi-membership in a criminal subculture. It means developing skills, talents, know-how, competence, viewpoints, a way of life, and assorted rationalizations and justifications. It means weighing risks, choosing among alternatives, planning, using caution, and subscribing to a code of conduct. Vold comments, "Any worthwhile professional man is proud of the profession he practices and is loyal to the code of conduct required of him."[30] Professionalism in robbery means that robbery is a part of one's way of life.

Werner Einstadter has recently investigated the social organization of professional armed robbery. His informants were convicted robbers on parole in California. All of them had committed more than one armed robbery in the company of others, the robberies had been fully planned and calculated and were not incidental to some other form of crime, and all the subjects considered themselves robbers and had spent considerable time in that line of work.[31]

Among the features of professionalization that Einstadter discovered were the following. Proceeds are shared equally and anyone who participates gets his share. They usually have no financial backing, but meet expenses themselves or by committing a series of smaller robberies. If arrested a team member is on his own — he is under no obligation to keep quiet, nor are his colleagues under any obligation to help him. If he does "rat," however, he loses his share. The group has little cohesion, members come in and leave the team as occasion necessitates, and leadership roles are filled more or less at will. Members of the team and other professional robbers are expected to deal honestly with one another, at least insofar as it bears on the work itself. Members have a fatalistic attitude toward events that might transpire during a robbery; this is especially true of violence and of mistakes made by the inexperienced who have not yet learned the ropes:

> It's the "breaks" that count; you either have them or not. Fate is deemed to control the robber's destiny; when the cards are right, when the dice are right, when the *setup* is perfect, nothing can go wrong; but if luck is against you, "you haven't got a chance." It therefore becomes easy to excuse what would under normal circumstances be considered an unforgivable error.[32]

Other aspects of the professional robber's code and social organization concern cooperation, partnership consensus, planning the "hit," assigning roles (usually done on the basis of skill and knowledge), and decision making.[33] (On pages 174–181 we will have an opportunity to see how professionalism in robbery departs in some ways from professionalism in nonviolent theft.)

The kinds of robberies professionals usually commit are those likely to pay large dividends, though less lucrative jobs will be taken on if financial needs are pressing for one reason or another. The more lucrative jobs will be well-planned robberies, usually of commercial concerns, in which the partners work as a well-oiled team. This type of planned operation, as Einstadter calls it, only works when all contingencies are evaluated beforehand (fate rules anything else), when they have rehearsals or dry runs, when the target is fully studied, perhaps over a period of weeks, and when the partners know and trust each other well. The professional will be interested in banks, loan companies, drugstores, large super-markets, and liquor stores.

Although many professional robbers confine most of their work to the robbery of commercial establishments, some apparently specialize in the robbery of individuals. The professional purse snatcher, or "cutpurse," as he is called in the trade, is an example. Though looked down upon by many of his professional colleagues, some purse snatchers are quick to claim membership in the professional ranks, and like other professionals, they distinguish themselves from the opportunist, the amateur, and those not in robbery for a living.[34] One such professional cutpurse relates how the profession of purse snatching has been invaded by amateurs and other characters:

> Like many a once-honored trade, the traditional art of the cutpurse has fallen on evil times. The profession is now overrun with amateurs, heavy-handed louts of small talent and even smaller character who would be better em-ployed on a rock pile. Purse-snatching has become the catch-all of crime. It's a last resort for down-at-the-heel burglars, unemployed stick-up artists, and others who have lost the professional drive and are too lazy to go straight. It's a lark for high school kids, a source of party-money for juvenile delin-quents, a spur-of-the-moment thing for drunks — and for many it's the outlet for something dark and vicious inside of them.[35]

Today many of the forms of robbery that in the past were the primary activity of professionals are now committed as often, if not more often, by amateurs — those who are not familiar with the skills, techniques, and other professional aspects of career robbery. Bank robbery is an example. Whereas bank robbery was once a favorite of the professional, today we see growing indications that opportunists and other nonprofessionals are trying this extremely risky and difficult type of robbery. Much of the 79 percent increase in bank robberies reported by the FBI for the period 1970–1975 may be attributed to the nonprofessional. One study had this to say on the character of current bank robbery:

> Many of the violations . . . revealed that the robbers seldom made any well-defined plans as to their methods of operations or getaway. . . . One pair of armed robbers jumped from their car and dashed up to the doors of a bank only to find they were locked. . . . Twenty-four who attempted robberies were thwarted by bank employees who either refused to comply with their demands, screamed, or merely ducked behind their cages or calmly walked away. In one of these cases the bandit fled when the teller fainted, and in another, the teller advised the would-be bandit that she was going to faint and he told her to go ahead, then calmly walked out.[36]

As if in substantiation of the amateur status of many contemporary bank robbers, we continually read in the newspapers about robbers who hold up tellers while cameras take clear pictures of their undisguised faces, or who try to rob drive-up facilities where the tellers are protected by bulletproof glass and are sufficiently hidden from view that they can summon the police via silent alarm systems. Indications of amateurism in bank robbery are also found in estimates of the amounts of money lost in such robberies and in the arrest rates of the last few years. Not only are arrest rates higher now for bank robbery than for any other felony property crime, but the average amount lost has apparently decreased over the last few decades. In 1932, for example, 609 reported bank holdups netted their perpetrators an estimated $3,400,000. In 1967, 1,730 bank robberies resulted in losses of $3,323,000. Thus the average loss for 1932 was $5,583 compared to $1,921 in 1967. Of course, some of the decline is doubtless due to changes in banking procedures in the handling of cash. But a professional will know this and will not waste time on petty "scores" unless hard-pressed.

Working at Robbery

For any robber, the way the job is done in large part determines its success. We can learn more about the job of robbery by asking how professional, career robbers work. While professional robbers are less numerous than their amateur counterparts, they have been investigated more systematically, hence far more is known about their activities, work attitudes, and organization. In addition, the professional robber is important to study for he (rarely she) steals far more than the typical amateur and often has a lengthy career (despite concerted efforts to protect commercial establishments from him).

Since the professional makes robbery his work, he cannot afford to fail or get caught; therefore his emphasis on careful planning, anticipation of difficulties that might arise, assessment of risks, and teamwork. To get some idea of how career robbers pursue their work, we can look at four typical phases in the robbery attempt: going into partnership, setting up the robbery, the robbery itself, and the getaway.

GOING INTO PARTNERSHIP

First-time robbers, and even those who have robbed before, must often get a team together before embarking on a robbery or series of robberies. For those who have not before committed armed robbery, the usual kind of professional robbery, what moves them to get involved in this particular scene? It might be at the invitation of an acquaintance who has some experience in armed robbery and needs a partner; it might come up in the course of conversation between experienced thieves who are looking for a new "line"; and sometimes the decision to get involved in armed robbery comes after a careful assessment of what best serves a person's needs as he sees it:

When my partner and I decided to go into crime, the first thing we had to decide next was just what branch of crime to go into. You've got car theft, burglary, stealing, stealing money or rolling drunks, armed robbery, other things. . . .

. . . [I]n order to decide which branch we wanted to go into, since we were both inexperienced criminals at the time, we decided to do as much research as we could and find out which made the most money the fastest and that percentagewise was the safest. . . . We spent four days in the public library and we researched, and came up with armed robbery as the most likely for us. . . .

We found . . . that armed robbery is by far the best as getting away with it is concerned because, unlike burglary or breaking and entering, you don't take anything that you have to convert into cash, thereby putting something in somebody else's hands, and you're not taking anything but *money,* which is spendable in any damned place.[37]

Einstadter found that partnerships might evolve as a result of casual interaction between strangers who find they have similar backgrounds and interests:

. . . You meet some guy and you say, I like him, and he likes you, and so you start horsing around, well you don't know each other, really, you don't know anything about each other, but eventually it comes out, you know. You let slip, you ask him about something — how do you like what you're doing? — and he says — it's a whole lot better than doing time. Then I know, and I told him, yeah, and you're finally out on your backgrounds. So, we got to talking about an easier way to make money. . . . He says "I know a couple of guys, and we all got guns, and we can go out and hit a few places now and then. If we don't hit it heavy we won't get caught." So we started doing this stuff.[38]

When we are dealing with a group of robbers who have had some experience in this line of work, we find that they, too, formulate partnerships before going into particular jobs. Sometimes the initial impetus to engage in a series of jobs will come from a transient robber who happens to be in town and makes contact with others he knows. Here the choice of partners will probably be made on the basis of the kinds of skills needed for whatever jobs are in the air.[39]

SETTING UP THE SCORE

Once a partnership is set up — and this may occur after a prospective heist has surfaced — planning consumes the partnership's time and resources. Many arrangements have to be made. Those who have been in the game for some time will make sure that they have personnel lined up for contingencies that might arise — doctors in case of injuries, lawyers in case of trouble with the police, and bondsmen to pay bail money.[40]

The planning of the robbery may differ from one partnership to the next, but certain activities are typically involved. Among the things that must be set up are (1) the target — bank, supermarket, or liquor store; (2) role assignments for the job — someone to drive the getaway car, often called the "wheelman," someone to be the lookout, someone to be the "gunman," and someone to be his accomplice during the job; (3) stolen cars, false license plates, and routes to and from the robbery; (4) a place and time for splitting up the money; and (5) most important, "casing" the target and dry runs.

Casing the target may be done by the one who set up the robbery or by all members of the team. If done while driving around the area, attention will be paid to such factors as parking opportunities, entrances and exits, police patrols, and the movement of people into, out of, and around the target. Some groups even take special note of architectural arrangements:

> Bank robbers rely heavily on the architectural uniformity of banks. Banks are frequently located on street corners, and this is convenient for getaways. Glass doors permit the robber-doorman to see who is coming in, whereas, as a robber noted, the persons coming in have more difficulty seeing through the glass because of light reflection. The present trend toward low counters, possibly motivated by the bank officials' desire for a more personal and less prison-like atmosphere, is looked upon favorably by bank robbers.[41]

Quoting one of his interview subjects, Peter Letkemann continues:

> Well, sometimes, you see, you might have to jump the counter. Well, if you get some of these real high counters, well, they're tough to get over. Well, you lose a few seconds by getting over the counters, and some of these banks, like, they have these gates, like with — well you can't reach over and open them because the catch is too far down, so therefore you've got to jump over this counter, you see.[42]

During casing, attention is also paid to alarm systems, presence of guards, number of employees, and location of safes and cash registers. The timing of a robbery is also vital. If the job is in a small rural town robbers are likely to have additional time to carry it out, whereas in an urban setting there is greater risk of police intervention, not to mention the coming and going of customers and employees. The extent to which some robbers go in planning their jobs is well illustrated in the memoirs of Blackie Audett, who participated in nearly thirty bank robberies.[43] He sometimes purchased specially drawn-up plans from a man who made his living supplying robbers with complete information on the target and on routes to and from it, and who set up cars and other supplies for the job and any emergencies that might arise.

THE ROBBERY

Here again, the actual procedures used during a robbery will vary from one team to another and from one situation to another. If the job is in an urban area the robbers will typically do everything to avoid drawing attention to themselves, at least until the robbery is in progress. Thus they may park their cars in legal places so as to avoid the risks of police interest, or they may wait until they are inside the target before donning masks or other disguises. If the target is in a small town or village, no such restraints may be necessary:

> . . . we don't care about parking, whether or not. We drive right in front of the bank where the door is closest to it, even if it's on the sidewalk, and there's a thing that goes on the sidewalk. And if there's one there we go right on the sidewalk. Period! Because we figure that as soon as we open the door of the car, we assume that the alarm is going off right there.[44]

In getting to the bank or other target a common ploy is to use previously stolen vehicles whose plates have been removed or changed. These cars will then be ditched after the robbery. Often two such cars are used as security against any breakdowns or other problems. If the team has a member whose only job is to drive, he will stay with the car and keep its engine running, while also being in a position to sound the horn in the event of trouble.

Once inside the target, the team will have assigned roles that they are bound to adhere to if things are to go smoothly. "The work positions are determined by the central concern of the operation, namely speed."[45] One man may be assigned to watch the door and generally oversee the operation as it progresses, paying special attention to time. Another may have the sole job of keeping the employees and customers out of the way, and hence out of trouble. In smaller teams this important aspect of the job may be fulfilled by herding employees and customers into a room or vault that can be kept under surveillance but does not require the total attention of one man. In teams of four or more, two men can usually be allotted the specific tasks of collecting the cash.

Letkemann notes one important aspect of the robbery situation that must be handled especially well if the attempt is to succeed with maximum payoff and minimum trouble. He calls it *victim management,* and it has two dimensions: surprise and vulnerability; and establishing authority and managing tension.[46]

The matter of surprise is crucial. When confronted out of the blue employees and customers are more vulnerable than if they have been forewarned in some way as to what is about to happen. Surprise, and the accompanying temporary paralysis of the victims, allows the robbers to get matters under their control and saves precious minutes. Some robbers, in fact, make a point of hitting banks and stores when employees are most likely to be sleepy and dull — early in the morning and preferably on Monday. As they see it, anything adding to surprise works in their favor.

Once things are under way the robbers must maintain their control over the situation and manage the tensions that are bound to arise. The hysterical employee, the stubborn cashier, and the glory hunter each may react differently to the stress of robbery, and all must be controlled by the robber. How this is done will differ from one situation to the next, but the tools commanded by the robber are generally limited to voice commands, appearance, and the use of force. The robbers generally want to sound and look as if they mean business. As one robber put it: "They can tell by the sound of your voice, by what you say and how you go about things, whether or not you mean business. If you're shaky, they'll know."[47] Masks and hoods, besides concealing identity, also have a role to play in establishing authority and managing tension. To some robbers they are important because they help to maintain the shock effect produced by the surprise entrance; to others they are useful because they conceal facial expressions and thus make it less likely that victims will detect any anxiety the robber may feel.

The use of force in professional robbery generally extends only to pushing, shoving, and, on occasions, pistol whipping. Some robbers use an overt display of force as a means to maintain their authority and keep the situation under control. One of the first things they will do is attack an employee in the expectation that this move will convince others of their purpose and resolve. According to one robber, the technique his team used was this:

> So they are froze there — their reaction is one of extreme fear and they drop on the floor and sometimes we select the strongest person — the manager especially or another teller which is very big — a six-footer, or something like that, you know. And we won't say a word, we just walk up to him and smack him right across the face, you know, and we get him down. And once he's down the people, the girls especially, they look at him and say, "My God — big Mike, he's been smashed down like that — I'd better lay down too, and stay quiet."[48]

The use of violence by the professional robber is apparently governed by two considerations. The first concerns getting the job done as quickly and easily as possible. The second involves escape. The typical professional seems to have no doubt that if he has to, he will use force; if mere threat does not produce the desired results, the next step is violence. But he will avoid using his gun if he possibly can. Studies of violence among professional robbers concur in this. Apart from the fact that weapons usually make noise and thus attract attention, robbers have no particular desire to seriously injure or kill their victims — an attitude that may stem from the widely shared view that those from whom they actually take the money are not the real victims anyway. They hold no beef against the teller, the cashier, or the customer. As Einstadter puts it:

> The employee with whom the robbery encounter is made is considered to have nothing at stake since there is no personal loss for him; at most he is conceived of as an agent-victim. . . . [The robber] views the actual encounter

as an impersonal matter for in doing so he is not robbing a person but some amorphous mass — a bank, a supermarket, a loan company.[49]

It should be remembered that the robber is out for money, not blood. On those occasions when weapons are actually used, and these are rare, it is usually because the robber has been cornered or challenged by others with weapons, most notably, the police. "Although the robber will hesitate to use his gun on a civilian, confrontation by the police is seen as resulting inevitably in a 'shoot-out' "[50]

THE GETAWAY

The getaway is the most important phase of any robbery, for whether or not the attempt succeeds, the robbers must still escape if they expect to remain free. Those who have carefully planned their operations will have escape routes and contingency plans already mapped out.

As with the robbery itself, speed is paramount. The longer robbers remain at or near the scene, the greater the risks of apprehension. They usually drive stolen cars, which are abandoned at a prearranged point, and then transfer to a vehicle owned by one of the team. If all goes well the team may disperse for a time, move to a different town, or simply go underground until the "heat is off."

It is during the getaway that violence is most likely to erupt. And the violence may include shooting, running roadblocks, or taking hostages. Robbers will make every effort to clear the scene and get as far away as is necessary. Understandably, the skills of the wheelman are especially important in this phase of the operation. Not only must the getaway vehicle be in top running condition, but it must be close at hand with the engine running so that team members can hop in and clear the scene as soon as possible. Once in the car, the driver's skills and his maintenance of a cool head may mean the overall success of the job.[51]

When robbery is studied as work we find that it does not look so different from many legitimate business pursuits. The popular myth depicting robbery as a senseless, violent act of plunder perpetrated by equally senseless and violent individuals can be upheld on some occasions. But a robbery is more accurately pictured as having characteristics that lie on a number of continua, of which three of the more important are *planning, organizing,* and *skill at victim management.* Those who make robbery a regular pursuit are likely to be found in robberies at the high end of these continua; those who are opportunists, or who indulge in robbery in a repetitive but sporadic and unsystematic manner will be involved in robberies at the low end. Thus robberies committed by professionals tend to exhibit high levels of planning, organization, and victim-management skills; those committed by opportunists out for a fast buck will tend to exhibit little in the way of planning and organization, and it may be in robberies committed by such individuals that we find confusion, fear, and disorder when it comes to handling their own and the victims' stresses and tensions.

Reactions to Robbery

Official reactions to robbery are usually severe, and to this extent they parallel public sentiments.[52] While the police generally make arrests in less than 30 percent of the incidents that come to their attention,[53] the suspects who are arrested are almost always prosecuted.[54] When it comes to sentencing, robbers are more likely than other property offenders to get prison terms. The average length of sentence in state courts is exceeded only by that for homicide, and in federal courts, only kidnapping sentences are longer. More people in the nation's prisons are serving time for robbery than for any other offense. In 1974 nearly two-thirds of those inmates were black; in addition, almost 25 percent were under 20 years of age when admitted to prison.[55] Robbery is heavy crime indeed for the minority who are caught and convicted.

Where official and public sentiments show signs of parting somewhat is when we compare the robbery of commercial establishments, such as banks and loan companies, with the robbery of private individuals. It seems that those who rob institutions are more likely to be prosecuted and to receive long prison terms than those who rob individuals.[56] Yet the public seems less hostile toward the robbery of institutions than the robbery of individuals. Whereas Jesse James, the Dalton gang, and others (not to mention the "great train robbers" in England) are accorded a sympathetic hearing, the mugger is hated and feared. Robbery of institutions, like plunder in war, is more impersonal, its impact more diffuse.[57] When the victim is also viewed in a somewhat negative light — as banks and loan companies seem to be these days — perhaps the public cares less that they are sometimes the victims of crime. Yet to the authorities these establishments are the backbone of the American economic system. To rob them is to threaten the foundations of capitalism. Perhaps this explains the more punitive official reaction in the absence of corresponding public sentiments.

References

1. Sir Frederick Pollock and Frederick William Maitland, *The History of English Law,* vol. II, 2nd ed. (Cambridge: Cambridge University Press, 1968), p. 494.
2. Ibid.
3. For two of the best analyses of Robin Hood and medieval life see Maurice Keen, *The Outlaws of Mediaeval Legend* (London: Routledge and Kegan Paul, 1961); and P. Valentine, *The Truth about Robin Hood* (Linneys of Mansfield, 1969).
4. See Patrick Pringle, *Stand and Deliver: The Story of the Highwayman* (New York: Norton, n.d.); also Keen, *The Outlaws of Mediaeval Legend.*
5. William Blackstone, *Commentaries on the Laws of England,* vol. IV (Boston: Beacon Press, 1962), pp. 280–81.

6. Pringle, *Stand and Deliver;* also Charles J. Finger, *Highwaymen* (New York: McBride, 1923).

7. James A. Inciardi, *Careers in Crime* (New York: Rand McNally, 1975), p. 87.

8. Stanford M. Lyman and Marvin B. Scott, *The Drama of Social Reality* (New York: Oxford University Press, 1975), p. 139. See also Wayne Gard, *Frontier Justice* (Norman: University of Oklahoma Press, 1949), pp. 168–83.

9. Philip D. Jordon, *Frontier Law and Order* (Lincoln: University of Nebraska Press, 1970), pp. 102–3.

10. Ibid.

11. Inciardi, *Careers in Crime,* p. 91.

12. Lyman and Scott, *The Drama of Social Reality,* p. 139.

13. See Joseph W. Snell, "Introduction" to Frank Triplett, *The Life, Times, and Treacherous Death of Jesse James* (Chicago: Swallow Press, 1970), p. ix.

14. The in-depth studies include John E. Conklin, *Robbery and the Criminal Justice System* (Philadelphia: Lippincott, 1972); Donald J. Mulvihill and Melvin Tumin, with Lynn Curtis, *Crimes of Violence,* A Staff Report to the National Commission on the Causes and Prevention of Violence, vols. 11 and 12 (Washington, D.C.: U.S. Government Printing Office, 1969); Andre Normandeau, "Trends and Patterns in Crimes of Robbery" (Ph.D. diss., University of Pennsylvania, 1968); and Arnold Sagalyn, *The Crime of Robbery in the U.S.* (Washington, D.C.: National Institute of Law Enforcement and Administration of Justice, 1971).

15. F. H. McClintock and Evelyn Gibson, *Robbery in London* (London: Macmillan, 1961).

16. Ibid., p. 15.

17. Leon Radzinowicz, "Preface" to McClintock and Gibson, *Robbery in London,* p. x.

18. See Andre Normandeau, "Robbery in Philadelphia and London," *British Journal of Criminology* (1970), pp. 71–79.

19. John E. Conklin, *Robbery,* p. 63.

20. Ibid., p. 70.

21. Albert D. Biderman, Louise A. Johnson, Jennie McIntyre, and Adrianne W. Weir, *Report on a Pilot Study in the District of Columbia on Victimization and Attitudes toward Law Enforcement, Field Surveys I,* Report to the President's Commission on Law Enforcement and the Administration of Justice (Washington, D.C.: U.S. Government Printing Office, 1967).

22. Howard Whitman, *Terror in the Streets* (New York: Dial Press, 1951), p. 5.

23. Mulvihill and Tumin, *Crimes of Violence,* vol. 11, p. 25.

24. Ibid.; see also Conklin, *Robbery.*

25. Conklin, *Robbery,* p. 116.

26. Ibid., p. 117.

27. See Mulvihill and Tumin, *Crimes of Violence,* vol. 12, pp. 617–18.

28. George B. Vold, *Theoretical Criminology* (New York: Oxford University Press, 1958), p. 225.

29. Clifford R. Shaw, *The Jack-Roller: A Delinquent Boy's Own Story* (Chicago: University of Chicago Press, 1930), pp. 84–85 and 139–41.

30. Vold, *Theoretical Criminology,* p. 225.

31. Werner J. Einstadter, "The Social Organization of Armed Robbery," *Social Problems* 17 (1969), pp. 64–83.

32. Ibid., p. 69.

33. Ibid.

34. Ibid., p. 80.

35. Robert Dale, "Memoirs of a Contemporary Cutpurse," in Duane Denfeld, *Streetwise Criminology* (Cambridge, Mass.: Schenkman, 1974), pp. 73–74.

36. FBI, "Profile of a Robber," *Law Enforcement Bulletin* 34 (1965), p. 21.

37. Bruce Jackson, *Outside the Law: A Thief's Primer* (London: Macmillan, 1969), pp. 20–21.

38. Einstadter, "The Social Organization of Armed Robbery," p. 68.

39. Ibid.; see also Peter Letkemann, *Crime as Work* (Englewood Cliffs, N.J.: Prentice-Hall, 1973), p. 92.

40. Letkemann, *Crime as Work,* pp. 92–93.

41. Ibid., p. 94.

42. Ibid.

43. Blackie Audett, *Rap Sheet: My Life Story* (New York: William Sloane, 1945).

44. Letkemann, *Crime as Work,* p. 98.

45. Ibid.; see also Einstadter, "The Social Organization of Armed Robbery."

46. Letkemann, *Crime as Work,* pp. 107–16.

47. Ibid., p. 111.

48. Ibid., p. 110.

49. Einstadter, "The Social Organization of Armed Robbery," p. 80.

50. Letkemann, *Crime as Work,* p. 115.

51. Conklin, *Robbery,* p. 99.

52. See Thorsten Sellin and Marvin Wolfgang, *The Measurement of Delinquency* (New York: Wiley, 1964); and Don C. Gibbons, "Crime and Punishment: A Study in Social Attitudes," *Social Forces* 47 (1969), pp. 391–97.

53. FBI, *Uniform Crime Reports,* "Crimes Cleared by Arrest."

54. Kristen M. Williams, "The Effects of Victim Characteristics on the Disposition of Violent Crimes," in William McDonald, ed. *Criminal Justice and the Victim* (Beverly Hills, Calif.: Sage, 1976), pp. 177–213.

55. These data come from the following sources: Nicolette Parisi, Michael R. Gottfredson, Michael J. Hindelang, and Timothy J. Flanagan, *Sourcebook of Criminal Justice Statistics, 1978* (Washington, D.C.: U.S. Government Printing Office, 1979), p.

645; *Profile of State Prison Inmates*, National Prisoner Statistics, Special Report SD-NPS-SR-4 (Washington, D.C.: U.S. Government Printing Office, 1979).

56. Williams, "The Effects of Victim Characteristics."

57. Willem Bonger speaks of war as a "colossal robbery" in *Criminality and Economic Conditions*, ed., Austin T. Turk (Bloomington: Indiana University Press, 1969), p. 134.

6

Varieties of Nonviolent Theft

Theft comes in a multitude of forms and involves countless different situations and people. Legal and popular labels designating types of theft include shoplifting, pocket picking, burglary, petty larceny, grand larceny, check forgery, embezzlement, auto theft, fraud, confidence games, and many other crimes. Just three conditions are necessary to make a theft situation possible: there must be some goods or service that is capable of being stolen, there must be someone from whom it can be stolen, and there must be someone to do the stealing.

In industrialized nations of the West, theft is a daily occurrence. If we don't do it ourselves, then we are its victims, or we hear about thefts involving other people. Many of us may be the victims of theft without even knowing it. To put matters simply, theft is commonplace. But it would be a mistake to believe that something inherent in human beings leads them to steal; in some societies theft is almost unheard of.[1]

As one might expect, the character of theft is not uniform throughout different societies, nor has it remained uniform throughout the history of any single society. Theft is shaped by many factors, not the least of which are those determined by the prevailing culture. Where property or material possessions do not exist, people are unlikely to have any notion of stealing. What is more, the types of things that can be and are stolen, the methods used, and the kinds of people who are victims of theft all are influenced by culture, by the way people live and the attitudes and values held by them.

In a society where the acquisition and ownership of property are strongly supported, the violation of such rights meet with understandable condemnation. However, cultural values supporting the acquisition of material wealth may also provide supports for the very behavior that is condemned. If possession of material wealth is highly valued, then people may stop at nothing to accumulate such wealth. Whether they acquire possessions through channels deemed legitimate by the dominant culture, or whether they steal from others, may be less important than the fact that they do acquire these possessions. If we could all acquire whatever we wanted through culturally acceptable channels then theft might not exist. But when some people are systematically excluded from access to acceptable channels of acquisition, or cannot acquire what they want even with such access, then stealing may be an alternative avenue to material wealth. Though it has remained popular to think that thieves are primarily the poor and disadvantaged, our experience with theft shows that people from all walks of life, even those with all kinds of supposed advantages, may yet steal from others.

Historical Developments in Criminal Theft

As a criminal activity, theft has a long and interesting history. The creation and extension of theft laws, as well as their application, have been exercises in the control of behavior in conflict with the interests of certain segments of society.

Theft in early legal codes is a rather vague term, though few known codes did not have some laws identifying theft as punishable behavior. More interesting, perhaps, is that in many of these early codes efforts were made to distinguish between different methods of stealing and different classes of victims. On the question of methods, the Roman law of the Twelve Tables designated theft by night as a more serious offense than daylight theft. As for the victims, the Code of Hammurapi placed the interests of church and state above those of the citizenry as a whole: those who stole from temples or the king's palaces were punished by death, whereas stealing from a private citizen merely resulted in the payment of compensation.[2]

It is mainly in English law that we find the roots of modern criminal-law conceptions of theft. Even before the Norman conquest of 1066, theft was firmly established as an offense in Anglo-Saxon codes. We are familiar with the old adage "possession is nine points of the law," but in early English law, possession was virtually all the law. It was in terms of possession that theft was identified and the thief so labeled. Ownership was a notion quite alien to early English society. One did not own something; it was in one's possession. To identify theft it was necessary to show, first, that the thief did not have lawful possession of the object in question, and second, that the person who claimed lawful possession could rightly do so. In practical terms this meant that to establish theft it was important to produce the thief, and so his apprehension took on special importance in English law.

The tradition in Anglo-Saxon and early common law was for the person who claimed lawful possession to conduct pursuit of the suspected thief and challenge his right to possession. Akin to the "posse" of American frontier justice, the English chase was thus an integral part of the theft scene.[3] If the suspect was caught while transporting the stolen goods from the scene of the crime, then the theft was "manifest," and justice could be meted out swiftly and severely (and often was). If the chase was unsuccessful, or the lawful possessor had failed in his duty to conduct the pursuit, then the theft was "secret," and justice slow and tortuous. All things considered, it was certainly in the interest of the victim to catch the thief in the act of fleeing with the loot.

Another important aspect of common law conceptions of theft was a civil law violation, *trespass.* The common legal term for theft was then, and still is, *larceny,* and larceny was but an extension of trespass. Under earlier Roman law, larceny (*latrocinium*) covered almost any type of deceit and trickery, but this was not the case in England. Larceny involved *laying hands on another's possessions without his permission,* and this was what trespass amounted to: "Simply to lay a hand on a man's thing without his permission would be trespass, therefore it was argued that there could be no larceny without trespass."[4] Larceny went beyond trespass in the notion of *animus furandi* (intent to steal), and it was argued that trespass turned into larceny when the trespasser intended to steal from the victim. The notion of trespass is still retained in many state laws dealing with theft today.[5]

Where the objects of theft are concerned, the idea of "movable" possessions remained central in emerging criminal law; the old charge that the thief "stole, took, and carried away," implies as much. In medieval times the most prized movables were agricultural chattels — farm animals such as oxen, cows, horses, and pigs, which often also served as money. Not surprisingly, then, these were the movable possessions to which early theft laws most often applied. But the creators of law have never been bound by prevailing cultural definitions of what are valuable chattels. Indeed, one Anglo-Saxon king went so far as to declare: "Men shall respect everything the king wishes to be respected, and refrain from theft on pain of death and loss of all they possess."[6] Though this is putting the matter bluntly, the point is obvious: those who shape legal conceptions of what can be stolen are in a position to impose their own ideas about what is valuable, and to determine what will and will not be deemed an object capable of being stolen. The entire history of theft laws illustrates the role of interests in the designation of objects it is possible to steal.[7]

Once goods and services have been legally identified as possible to steal, the matter of their actual value in any given case has traditionally been irrelevant to the identification of theft. It matters little whether you steal a coat worth $5,000 or one worth only five cents — a theft has still been committed. But where value clearly *does* matter is in what happens to the thief. From at least Anglo-Saxon times, distinctions in theft have been based on the value of the property taken. Just as today many states treat theft under $50 (or some other figure) as petty theft, and anything over that as grand theft, similar distinctions have been made throughout the history of theft laws. The penalties for grand theft, a felony, have traditionally been more severe. If value is an indication of seriousness, which some undoubtedly believe, then such value distinctions may be justified on the grounds that they provide a workable solution to the problem of "making the punishment fit the crime." But some authors have argued that distinctions of value merely reflect the operation of class interests and ignore the fact that what to one person may be a great loss, to another may be a drop in the bucket. The more wealthy theft victims stand to realize more in the way of "justice" than the poorer classes, whose individual losses will more often fall below the misdemeanor/felony cutoff point.[8]

As you will have observed, criminal law is constantly changing. One reason for this is that existing legal formulations prove inadequate when confronted by changing social conditions and interests. Theft laws have for centuries undergone revision and extension, and one result is that new forms of theft and new means of committing theft have emerged from time to time. One particularly significant development in criminal theft occurred during the late 1400s, and it provides us an opportunity to see the impact on criminal law of emergent social conditions and interests.[9]

The "Carrier's Case" involved a man who was hired to carry some bales of merchandise to Southampton, an English port city. Instead of doing this he broke open the bales and took their contents. He was subsequently caught and charged with felony theft. As the larceny law then stood, however, his actions did not legally constitute theft: he had entered an agreement in good faith, and he thus had lawful possession of the bales. Under the possession rules he could not steal from himself (or by extension, from the merchant who hired him). After much debate a majority of the judges who handled the case finally found him guilty of felony theft, and in doing so extended the law of larceny to cover cases of "breaking bulk," as it was thereafter called (though for some time a carrier was still free to steal the contents, so long as he took the bales as well!).

Most of us would probably argue that the guilty verdict and attendant legal precedent sounds reasonable enough. After all, if I hire a truck driver to deliver goods for me I would hardly appreciate his stealing them and would doubtless desire satisfaction. But if no laws could be applied in my particular case, then what satisfaction could I hope to receive? To judge from the Carrier's Case, successful resolution of the problem would depend on how much pressure I could bring to bear on the legal machinery to protect my interests. It so happens that at the time of the Carrier's Case the judges were faced with a number of outside pressures:

> The most powerful forces at the time were interrelated very intimately and at many points: the New Monarchy and the *nouveau riche* — the mercantile class; the business interests of both and the consequent need for a secure carrying trade; the wool and textile industry, the most valuable by far in all the realm; wool and cloth, the most important exports; these exports and foreign trade; this trade and Southampton, chief trading city with the Latin countries for centuries; the numerous and very influential Italian merchants who brought English wool and cloth inland and shipped them from Southampton. The great forces of an emerging modern world, represented in the above phenomenon, necessitated the elimination of a formula which had outgrown its usefulness. A new set of major institutions required a new rule.[10]

And so, as William Chambliss recently argued, "The judges deciding the Carrier Case had, then, to choose between creating a new law to protect merchants who entrusted their goods to a carrier or permitting the lack of such legal protection to undermine trade and the merchant class economic interests. The court decided to act in the interests of the merchants despite the lack of a law."[11]

Revision and expansion of theft in law has continued to the present day. Many of the changes came about as a result of statutes designed to plug the gaps and crevices in prevailing common law standards. Embezzlement, for example, emerged in its modern form in 1799 when Parliament passed a statute to cover cases of servants misappropriating goods placed in their possession in the course of their employment. It was later extended to cover brokers, bankers, attorneys, and others in positions of trust as agents for third parties. But embezzlement statutes only covered the illegal transfer of possession. For cases of ownership fraudulently acquired — as when you sign over property to another after he has tricked you into doing so — the law remained inadequate until a statutory decree in 1861 created the offense of obtaining goods by false pretenses. This new offense was basically an extension of earlier common law crimes such as "larceny by trick and device," and the so-called cheats, many of which are today variations on the confidence-game theme.

The Prevalence and Distribution of Reported Theft

Much theft remains beyond the reach of bureaucratic data collection. Accordingly, national data on theft are extremely difficult to assess and interpret. To give some idea of the problem, recall that estimates of the true rate of burglary alone begin at more than three times the rate reported by the FBI. When we add to this the fact that only a relatively minute number of thefts are ever solved, our difficultues become obvious.

Published national data do give us some idea of the dimensions of the theft problem, at least from the standpoint of the criminal justice system. In 1978, burglary, larceny-theft, and motor vehicle theft accounted for 10,079,508 (more than 90 percent) of the 11,141,334 Index offenses reported by the FBI. Arrests numbered 1,814,700, or nearly 90 percent of total arrests for Index offenses. All three offenses showed steady increases during the 1960s, with burglary and larceny continuing to climb, though more slowly, during the 1970s. Motor vehicle theft tapered off and remained fairly stable with a rate of around 450 recorded incidents per 100,000 population. The published national data indicate other characteristics of these three Index offenses: (1) rural rates are substantially below those found in both cities and suburbs; (2) suburban rates have been increasing faster than large city rates; and (3) of those offenses reported, 20 percent or less in each of the three categories are cleared by arrest (see figure 4.2).

Auto theft is a rather peculiar category of offenses. The FBI includes in it the "unlawful taking" of motor vehicles, and like many states, thus encompasses in auto theft the mainly juvenile behavior known as joy-riding. Unlike theft, joyriding is not a predatory crime; it does not involve depriving the owner of a possession nor does it imply any gain of money or property. Suffice it to say that some of the FBI's figures on auto theft are accounted for by the stealing of automobiles for gain, but exactly how many cannot be assessed. Since good data on predatory auto theft are virtually impossible to secure, no ground is gained by speculating on its prevalence and distribution.

Before moving on to a more detailed investigation of burglary and theft, we should note that many theft-related offenses do not appear among the Index offenses. Included here are fraud, forgery, embezzlement, and a host of misdemeanor offenses. The statistics given above represent only the tip of the iceberg, and the data presented are in any case only an approximation of the true, but unknown, national picture.

Professionalism in Theft

Professionalism in theft has a history going back at least to Elizabethan times, when "conny-catching" (a type of swindling) was a full-time profession. Over the years other varieties of theft became the focus of professionalization, with shoplifting and pocket picking two of the more common ones. Much of what we know about professional theft and the professional thief has come from firsthand accounts by thieves (both practicing and reformed), many of which are of the "as told to" sort. Among the best known are *The Professional Thief,* edited by Edwin Sutherland; Ernest Booth's *Stealing through Life;* and the more recent accounts, *My Life in Crime,* reported by John Bartlow Martin, and *Box Man: A Professional Thief's Journey,* as told to William Chambliss. To those must be added an assortment of books and articles focusing on professionalism in specific types of theft — for example, confidence games, burglary, forgery, and pocket picking.[12]

PROFESSIONAL THEFT AS A WAY OF LIFE

By far the most influential work on professional theft has been Sutherland's *The Professional Thief.*[13] Sutherland used the written accounts of one professional thief ("Chic Conwell") to illustrate the complex assortment of behavior characteristics, attitudes, organizational features, subcultural patterns, and views of the world that together make up a way of life shared by professional thieves.

In describing the world to which he belonged, Chic Conwell tells us that professional thieves (1) "make a regular business of stealing"; (2) acquire their skills and professional know-how through tutelage by and association with already established professionals; (3) develop highly skilled work techniques, the most important of which is the "ability to manipulate people"; (4) carefully plan everything they do in connection with their business; (5) look upon themselves as different from amateurs, and superior to them, particularly those who indulge in sex crimes; (6) have a code of ethics that "is much more binding among thieves than that among legitimate commercial firms"; (7) are "sympathetic" and "congenial" with each other; (8) view successes and failures as "largely a matter of luck"; (9) have an established vocabulary of criminal slang, the main purpose of which is to enhance "we-feeling" and promote ease of intra-profession communication; (10) rarely engage in only one specialized form of theft (the notable exception being pickpockets, or "cannons"); and (11) usually operate in gangs, "mobs," or partnerships whose life span is generally short unless they are consistently successful.[14] Summarizing the substance of Conwell's account of professional theft, Sutherland offers this conception of the profession:

> The profession of theft is more than isolated acts of theft frequently and skillfully performed. It is a group way of life and a social institution. It has techniques, codes, status, traditions, consensus, and organization. It has an existence as real as that of the English language. It can be studied with relatively little attention to any particular thief. The profession can be understood by a description of the functions and relationships involved in this way of life. In fact, an understanding of this culture is a prerequisite to the understanding of the behavior of a particular professional thief.[15]

BECOMING A PROFESSIONAL THIEF

Sutherland's work describes the behavior system of professional theft as it appeared in the first quarter of the twentieth century, viewed through the eyes of one thief. We get a more complete and up-to-date picture of professionalism in theft if we also look at some more recent contributions to the literature. Consider first how one becomes a professional thief.

There is no one way to become a professional thief, and whether or not a thief makes the grade depends less on what or who he is or has been and more on how he is received by those who already make up the professional fraternity. Put bluntly, "one gets into the profession by acceptance."[16] Gaining acceptance represents the pinnacle of a maturation process for the emerging professional. During the process the newcomer will have learned to think, act, and be a professional thief. This means he must adopt those aspects of professionalism deemed important by those already in the fraternity, particularly those with whom he will spend much of his time.

One way an aspiring professional learns what is important is through others sharing with him the common store of knowledge. While no formal or extensive recruiting of new members into the profession goes on, the fraternity would die out if new members were not accepted on a fairly regular basis. It is through the process of sharing information that many take their first steps toward membership. In earlier days this sometimes took the form of systematic training and preparation, as when would-be pickpockets were formally schooled in the art, often at a young age and in groups.[17] Today tutelage is a much more informal process, and while training in technical skills can still involve rather formal procedures, such as apprenticeships, most of what is learned comes through continued association with professionals at work and play. Things are picked up, experienced, and discussed, but rarely taught. Simply by hanging around places where known professionals congregate, those interested will pick up details of the professional life-style, including many of the less tangible aspects:

> But later on . . . I started hanging around with professionals and learned from them that you didn't steal from a home or small place of business; you stole only from a big place that could afford it.[18]

Needless to say, association with professional thieves is governed by the life-style of the professional fraternity itself. One very important facet of this life-style is the tendency of professionals to live, "hang out," and work in particular localities. This provides the profession with a geographic and ecological identity. It also means that spending time in the same places provides a pretty good chance of forming associations with professionals, even for "straights" and the police. Just as the nineteenth-century cities boasted favored places where the criminal underworld congregated, so do most urban centers today. New York's Tenderloin, Five Points, and Satan's Circus have given way to a sixteen-block area around Times Square; London's Hoxton has been replaced by Soho.[19] The typical urban habitat of the professional is

> . . . composed of gambling and taxi dance halls, rooming houses and cheap hotels, houses of prostitution, third-rate bars, poolrooms, second-hand stores and pawn shops, or theatre, restaurant, and penny arcade complexes. Within these districts are the girls, the gaiety, and the excitement that attract victims of the pickpocket and confidence swindler. Every city has its *line*, its *tenderloin*, its *strip*. What is found in this area of the larger cities can also be found on a proportionate level in the smaller urban centers, the satellite cities, and the provincial county seats.[20]

The professional crooks spend much of their time in these areas, and they often reside in them if they are not on the move or have not yet reached the pinnacle of the profession and can afford a nice place in the suburbs. The specific hangout — bar, restaurant, poolroom, or barbershop — is partly a matter of custom, partly a matter of convenience, and sometimes a matter of security.[21] It is in such localities that association with professionals is most likely to occur, and that mutual confidences can take shape.

Most information sharing occurs when the criminals themselves can exercise some control over the process. This is contrasted with the situation in prisons, where some learning of the professional way of life also takes place. In prisons, convicted offenders are thrown together in confined spaces, and their interaction is geared to the constraints of formal prison arrangements, so what they do with whom is not entirely a matter of choice. It is in prison that many amateurs, opportunists or habitual thieves are exposed to aspects of professional crime, but the exposure has less of the voluntariness and freedom of that outside prison walls. However, what and how much is learned in prison still seem to depend greatly on the decisions of those in a position to share information. The popular idea that more experienced cons willingly and routinely teach others the skills and know-how of professional crime is far from the truth. It seems that learning comes primarily through friendship and acquaintanceship with imprisoned professionals, just as it does on the outside, and not infrequently those who share inside information with others do so with great caution and deliberation. Much consideration is given to who receives the information — whether he can be trusted, whether he will be a useful contact after release, and whether he shows promise.[22] On the whole, prisons undoubtedly do provide an important information service for would-be careerists and professionals. The specifics of what is learned, however, will vary according to patterns of friendship, modes of theft (some can be more easily learned about than others), and even the prison involved. Some prisons become known for the kinds of criminal skills and know-how that can be picked up.[23]

An individual becomes a professional thief not only by learning skills, argot, manners, and values, but also through his own endeavors in the field. What he comes to learn from others he must put into practice, and by doing so demonstrate that he deserves to be thought of by others as a professional. It is not until others accord him the status of professional that he can justifiably think of himself as a professional thief.

STATUS AND PRESTIGE

A key feature of professionalism noted by Sutherland is the maintenance of a system that confers status and prestige. Status distinctions are based on a variety of things: type of theft engaged in, skill and technical competence, success, connections, and commitment. As in any other profession, participants confer prestige and recognition upon each other and distinguish the entire fraternity from outsiders, those who do not belong.

Within the ranks of professional thieves, certain work specialties stand out as having high status. Confidence men and "box" men (safecrackers) have traditionally been considered at the top of the pecking order. Their work involves considerable skill and ability, and the payoffs can be substantial for those who succeed. Those who become known for their expertise in these areas are usually fully integrated into the professional subculture, for their work depends heavily on group effort, trust, connections, and esprit de corps. At the other end of the status hierarchy are those whose jobs usually have a small payoff, involve more modest levels of skill and risk, and whose victims are typically individuals or small businesses. Cannons (pickpockets), "boosters" (professional shoplifters), and small-time burglars are examples of low-status thieves. Here is how two thieves view shoplifting:

> A booster is just about the lowest thief there is. Nobody has much to do with them. I mean, I seen one yesterday as a matter of fact. I saw this one, then talked to this other guy who was a meter-robber; you know, a guy who robs parking meters. They make a lot of money. I was talking to this friend and he said he saw Charlie boosting the other day. I told him: "Gee, Charlie Jay? Man, I can remember when he was a real high-classed thief." "Oh," he said, "he's down at the bottom now." In our estimation he's down dragging bottom because he's boosting. And he used to be a real high-classed thief at one time.[24]

Status distinctions are maintained even within theft specialties. Confidence men who operate the more sophisticated, complex games (the "big con") consider themselves and are considered by others as superior to "short con" operators who go in for quick swindles and usually a small payoff. Similarly, burglars distinguish among themselves, with high prestige going to the "good burglar," who (1) is superior in technical skills;

(2) has a reputation for personal integrity; (3) tends to specialize in burglary; and (4) has been relatively successful in making money and staying out of prison.[25]

When professionals look at nonprofessionals — the opportunists, habitual amateurs, sex offenders, and those who use spur-of-the-moment violence — a variety of names are used to designate their inferior status. These are the "bums," "young punks," "squares," "hustlers," the "small-timers," "weirdos," and "amateurs." Unlike the professionals, their involvement in crime is unsystematic and sporadic, skills are minimal, and "anything goes." While some make it into the ranks of the professionals as they mature in crime, most do not. They remain bums in the eyes of professionals and, for that matter, the public and the police.

SELF-IMAGES AND WORLD VIEW

In distinguishing themselves from amateur thieves and other criminal offenders, professionals reinforce their feelings of importance and superiority, and in this way bolster their self-esteem while erecting barriers against encroachment by the unworthy. Yet professionals do not conceive of themselves only in terms of other criminals and other kinds of crime. Though they recognize that their life-style often places them in conflict with the larger society, they are nevertheless products of, and participants in, that society. Like other Americans, they brush their teeth, they wear clothes, they drive on the right side of the road, they are consumers, lovers, and (from their point of view) businessmen; they are concerned about prices, politics, war, the state of their country, and about their own successes and failures. But unlike some others, they are committed to work that continually brings them the threat of arrest, prosecution, and punishment in the name of the larger society. Though they are committed to crime as a profession, they have trouble accepting the idea that they are deviant, immoral, or unworthy of respect.

And so, like others of us who have difficulty reconciling what we like to think of ourselves with what others appear to think of us, the professional thief negotiates a path that at once emphasizes his or her adherence to the "American way" and devalues his critics and oppressors.[26] Here are some comments by professional thieves, which illustrate how the larger society is brought into focus along the path to self-respect and self-esteem:

A successful professional burglar: You might laugh, but I'm for law and order. I don't hurt anyone, and anyway most of the people who lose stuff are insured, and I could tell you about the way they inflate their losses. But this mugging on the streets and rapes, and the way they have to coddle those creeps makes me sick.[27]

A "short con" man: You know how it goes in this dog-eat-dog world. You got to take the other guy before he takes you. You know, the real sharpie outwits the marks [victims]. Of course, it all depends on how you get ahead. My way was no different from, say, a lawyer or businessman. You know, a lawyer has a license to steal. The cops should lay off con men. We don't hurt nobody. You can't con an honest man. . . . The cops should do their job and clear the streets of the muggers, heist men, hopheads, and the rest. Why, it's dangerous for a decent man like me to walk down the street at night.[28]

And, to illustrate that "my way" is not as foolish as "your way":

It looks so foolish to me to work for a living when I look at you. Take, like any official, any policeman, anything else, that's doing everything in the book and getting by with it, and here's you that's working your heart and soul out, if you miss three days at work you're three months behind — it looks so foolish.[29]

In sum, the professional thief can hold his head high, knowing that he is good at what he does, successful in it, and professional in how he does it. In his view, the main thing distinguishing him from so-called upright citizens is that some supercilious, if not misguided, public servants have chosen to outlaw him.

CONSENSUS AND PROFESSIONAL ETHICS

The survival of any profession depends in part on the maintenance of a normative system to which its members adhere and in terms of which they interpret their behavior and that of their colleagues. Professional theft is no exception. Consensual understandings are expressed as expectations about and evaluations of the conduct of one's fellows. For years, because they have their rules, maxims, and codes of ethics, as well as skills, high pay, and prestige, professional thieves have likened their fraternity to legitimate professions. Those who violate these rules and collective expectations are subject to the derision of their colleagues, and, as in other professions, are punished in various ways and with varying degrees of severity.

Professional expectations and evaluations cover a wide range of topics, probably more extensively than many legitimate professions. The topics include work activities, treatment of professionals and nonprofessionals, relationships with the larger society, and relationships with family and lovers. Some of the more prominent expectations for conduct among thieves are that members will deal honestly with one another, stick to their assigned roles, give aid to others in time of crisis, and pay their debts, whether it be for information, financial stakes, or other help. One of the long-standing principles of professionalism deals with informing or "snitching." A thief simply does not snitch on colleagues and expect to remain an honored and respected member of the professional fraternity, not to mention a healthy one.[30] They also have the time-honored imperative, "Never grift [take] on the way out."[31] This means that thieves will restrain their greed and take during a heist only what they can safely handle, and will avoid doing another job when they still have loot from a previous one.

Much of the consensus among thieves can be traced directly to their isolation from the larger society and the related need for solidarity in a hostile world. The "we-feeling" among career criminals provides a sense of solidarity and helps to maintain group identity and security. Argot has a special place here. The slang used and shared by thieves is an expression of togetherness and facilitates communication among members of the criminal subculture. Many of the terms used have a long history, some going back to Elizabethan days. By the adoption of an artificial language, professionals are "able to determine in only a few minutes of conversation with a stranger whether he is acquainted with the underworld, what rackets he has experience with, and whom he knows."[32] Needless to say, professionals are cautious in their use of criminal slang when there is a chance that it might draw attention to them. This consensus in language is especially important when thieves are on the move and when they are setting up "connections." With few exceptions, professionals rely on an extensive network of contacts among those within the fraternity as well as those peripheral to it. Such connections are important not only as avenues of information sharing but also as a pool of potential partners — or, if they are lawyers and bondsmen, a pool of potential help when the law strikes.[33]

While thieves clearly recognize the value of consensus, evidence indicates that much of the underworld code of honor among thieves may be crumbling. In his interviews with professional burglars, Shover found many spontaneous comments bemoaning the apparent decline of "the Code." In part this may be due to the fact that "the 'solid,' ethical career criminal seems to be giving way to the 'hustler,' an alert opportunist who is primarily concerned only with personal — as opposed to collective — security."[34] But adherence to any code is severely tested when the chips are down, and thieves are certainly no different from the rest of us in this regard. It appears that pressures of the moment, and practical considerations generally, lie at the heart of any particular acceptance or rejection of professional codes or consensual understandings. Loyalty may have existed in the old days, but as one thief put it: "There is no loyalty among thieves today. There's no such thing at all. They have absolutely no loyalty. They'll beat one another to the money, you know, anything they can, they beat one another for their girls, or anything."[35] When the rules are observed, when the code is followed, honor or loyalty may have little to do with it:

. . . honor among thieves? Well — yes and no. You do have some old pros who might talk about honor, but they're so well heeled and well connected they can afford to be honorable. But for most people, it's a question of "do unto others'' — you play by the rules because you may need a favor some-day, or because the guy you skip on, or the guy you rap to the cops about — you never know where he'll turn up. Maybe he's got something on you or maybe he ends up as your cellmate, or he says bad things about you — you can't tell how things could turn out.[36]

The "Fix"

Most career criminals spend considerable time and energy negotiating their way around trouble with the law. For the professional, confrontations with the machinery of law are treated as normal, expected features of a thief's way of life. As a professional, however, the thief acts so as to minimize the risk that confrontations will result in conviction and confinement. Whereas amateurs seem preoccupied with avoiding detection and arrest, professionals direct their energies to the avoidance of conviction. Letkemann found that experienced criminals "didn't particularly mind if the police 'knew' they had pulled a particular caper. The important factor for the experienced criminal was that 'they have nothing on me.' That is, there must be no evidence that will 'stand up' in court."[37]

The major method professionals employ to reduce the risks of conviction, and hence of confinement, is the "fix." The fix involves organization and resources, and it is the professional, as opposed to the amateur criminal, who is generally in a position to make it work. Basically, the fix works through manipulation of the judicial process. Efforts are made, therefore, to buy the help of those in a position to influence criminal proceedings. They include the police, lawyers, bondsmen, politicians, court personnel, and judges. Only one link in the chain of law enforcement need be diverted from its legally sanctioned path for the fix to work.

In most large cities, professional fixers handle many of the legal problems faced by organized thieves. These persons generally hold respectable positions within the administration of justice and are often associated with the prosecution. As holders of occupational positions within the legitimate work structure of society, fixers represent one of the more important connections between the profession of theft and the larger society. It is through this connection that organized theft helps guarantee its own survival. Without the fix, professional crime would lose one of its essential lines of defense against encroachment by organized repression.[38] What this means, of course, is that so long as individuals who claim membership in legitimate society, and are recognized as having such membership, engage in activities in support of acknowledged illegitimate pursuits, the distinction between what is legitimate and illegitimate itself remains vague and contestable. It is therefore not surprising to find many thieves arguing persuasively that what they do is not that different from what respectable people do.

The perpetuation of thief-fixer relationships depends upon a number of things. Obviously, if each pays off as expected, both parties meet the immediate demands of the relationship. From the standpoint of the fixer, this usually means money, but sometimes nonmonetary favors of one sort or another are involved. For the thief it means no conviction at all, or the lightest possible sentence. But apart from these more obvious considerations are questions of personal security and mutual trust (which is not the same as respect!). The successful thieves and fixers are those who keep tight lips, who do not divulge confidences, and who can be relied upon to fulfill their part of the bargain.

In making the most of fix possibilities, thieves display intimate knowledge of the ways of the world. They know, for example, that if it comes to a trial, court proceedings and sentence decisions may well be influenced by extraneous variables, such as the way in which their offense is handled by the media. So, some knowledgeable thieves use the fix in dealings with newspaper reporters.[39] By the same token, indirect methods sometimes work more productively and safely than blatant efforts to "put the fix in":

> If you were going to pay off a judge you wouldn't offer him any money, you do it indirectly. Say you had a big case coming up. If you're any kind of businessman at all, you don't put too much faith in your lawyer. Lawyers being what they are. So you go to your state committee man who don't hold any office at all, you go to your political boss and explain what your troubles are and you'd like to be pretty sure things were going to turn out all right and it would be worth so much if you could be sure things would turn out all right. He's the guy that put the judge's name on the ballot. So about 99 times out of a hundred when you come back to his office the next day he tells you, Don't worry about it, it'll cost five thousand, everything's gonna be taken care of.[40]

While some evidence indicates that use of the fix may be less productive and predictable than in the past, a recent study shows that of those professional criminals interviewed, all had employed the fix quite frequently, and generally with good results. The ratio of arrests to felony convictions was 100 to 5.8, and that of arrests to imprisonment for one year or more, 100 to 3.5.[41] The fix works for those who are in a position to use it, and will remain available as long as people are willing and able to manipulate the machinery of law for a price.

"Fencing" Stolen Property

Along with the fix, the "fence" is another of the essential ties between theft and the larger social structure. Without someone to receive and dispose of stolen property, theft, particularly professional theft, would face hard times. The fence fills this important role.

Despite the importance of fencing as one facet of criminal theft and its relationship with legitimate society, few criminology texts have much to say on the topic. One reason for this lies in the paucity of research on fencing and fences. Quite simply, very little is known. Recently, two authors have come up with some interesting reasons why so little attention has been paid to receiving stolen property.[42] One reason, they suggest, is that because fencing amounts to a rational, businesslike activity, it has none of the qualities of deviance traditionally emphasized in criminological theory and research. Another reason lies with the intangible nature of the crime of receiving. Not only does it have low visiblity, it seems to disappear on successful completion: "It is as though the conduct erases itself after execution so that, while a fundamental existence can be attested to (here, stolen property is fenced), any tangible evidence as to the conduct's independent existence is gone."[43] Then again, any detailed investigation of fencing is difficult because of functional requirements of secrecy and the maintenance of a legitimate front, not to mention the probability that neither those who use fences, nor those who buy from them, have any inclination toward opening things up for research that might later be used to help put them out of business — a good thing is a good thing.

Fencing has long been a troublesome issue in criminal law. Early English common law, with its emphasis on possession and trespass, found those who received stolen property to be guilty of "receiving larcenously" — a rather nebulous concoction designed to permit the law to act against persons who could not be dealt with under prevailing conceptions of larceny. It appears that the application of this label meant different things to different judges, and while the act itself was generally considered only a misdemeanor, at least one person is known to have been hanged for it in the fourteenth century.[44] After centuries of confusion, "receiving stolen goods" finally became an independent misdemeanor by statute in 1707, and in 1827 was made a felony.

In America, as in England, there are four elements in the criminal law conception of receiving: (1) the property must have been stolen, or, as some codes put it, "feloniously taken"; (2) the property must have been received or concealed, though in most states the receiver need not actually have seen or touched it; (3) the receiver must have accepted it with the knowledge (in some states, merely the belief) that it was stolen or feloniously taken; and (4) the property must be received with fraudulent or criminal intent.[45] As you can readily see from this list of legal requirements, it is no simple matter to demonstrate an actual case of receiving.

Recent federal efforts to combat fencing operations have led to new crime-fighting methods. The so-called sting antifencing operation was introduced in 1974 and had been tried in 46 cities by 1979. Typically, the police set up a bogus fencing operation using undercover officers and various electronic gadgets for monitoring transactions. "Customers" include thieves as well as amateur and professional fences. The Department of Justice estimates that some $226,582,045 in stolen property had been recovered by late 1979; in its turn, the government put up some $5.95 million in "buy" money. Not a bad return by any standards.

Even more important, we are told, is the fact that some 6,654 individuals have been indicted since the sting programs began, with an astounding conviction rate of 98 percent. Many of those arrested are career thieves and professional fences with extensive criminal histories. Cities that have used the sting appear to have experienced subsequent declines in rates of robbery, burglary, larceny, and auto theft — suggesting, perhaps, — that many of the "customers" have been arrested.[46]

Lay and Professional Fences. A useful place to begin to better understand fencing's relation to theft is with Jerome Hall's distinction between the professional and amateur, or lay, receivers. According to Hall:

1. The professional receiver *buys for the purpose of resale,* whereas the lay receiver buys for consumption.
2. Hence the professional receiver sells stolen merchandise, whereas the lay receiver *consumes* the goods.
3. The professional receiver operates a business; he deals in stolen commodities and is apt to be *in possession of a relatively large amount of such commodities, derived from different thefts and thieves, as a stock in trade; the lay receiver does not operate a business nor does he deal in or possess a large quantity of stolen commodities.*[47]

Lay receiving encompasses people from all walks of life and in all sorts of relationships with thieves. They are likely to be members of the family, friends, or acquaintances, and they may be plumbers, professors, or preachers. Lay receivers may be "square johns" or they may themselves be dabblers in theft or other crime.[48] The amateur thieves, from habitual ones to sporadic opportunists, will from time to time want or need to unload stolen items. It is likely they are not familiar with professional fences or professional fencing (even if they are, professionals may not want to be involved with them); this leaves them little recourse but to sell or give their merchandise to friends and acquaintances. They may, of course, hock their property, in which case they get a pittance for it and take considerable risks in doing so.

The professional thief and the professional fence are better organized, better equipped, and better placed than the amateur thief and the lay fence. Their relationship is one of mutual support and dependency. The continued rewarding existence of each depends on relations with the other. Because of their legitimate fronts, fences are in a position to provide a relatively secure outlet for stolen merchandise, but that outlet remains secure only as long as both parties maintain productive ties and respect each other's needs for secrecy and continued business. Many fences remain on the periphery of professional theft, but from time to time are useful sources of tips and information for working thieves. By acting as a source of information the fence can retain better control over his own enterprise, since he will know "what's coming down" and what goods will be available.[49] Obviously, this works to both his and the thief's advantage.

Apart from information, fences may also provide loans for thieves about to pull lucrative capers, and can put thieves in contact with each other, as well as with bondsmen and lawyers in a time of crisis. Quite often, fences have businesses in areas where criminals hang out — taverns, poolrooms, barbershops, and restaurants. Those fences are commonly not big money-makers in their legitimate pursuits but get their lucrative returns from fencing.

As with professional thieves, the fraternity of fences has gradations of status. One professional fence ("Morris") recently outlined some of the variations in fencing practices that become sources of status distinctions.[50] At the top of the fencing ladder is the "master" fence, whose organization, facilities, and bankroll permit him to handle the biggest jobs. Master fences deal with all kinds of merchandise and will be able at a moment's notice to arrange the disposal of a haul too big, or too general, for the more common "specialty" fence. Thieves who specialize in only certain types of merchandise — jewelry, furs, credit cards, or clothing — prefer to deal with fences who also specialize in the same goods. Morris estimates that in New York City alone there are some fifty fences who specialize in jewelry. At the bottom of the professional fence hierarchy are the neighborhood fences who are parts of the vast network of fencing operations within any large city. Their business is relatively small, yet indispensable for the run-of-the-mill professional thief whose own scores are small but require regular disposal.

In line with changing methods of doing business in the American economy, fences have adapted their illegal work to the requirements of legitimate exchange. For example, whereas credit cards used to be avoided like the plague, today they are a boon to the established fence. As Morris puts it:

> Years ago, if a thief picked up a credit card he would throw it away. He was afraid to use it because he didn't know how long it took before the stores found out the card had been stolen. Today it's worth anything from $50 to $200 to me, depending on when it was lifted. It takes at least five business days to get a hot sheet out on most stolen cards. My people can bang the hell out of one in three or four days.[51]

Morris estimates his income from fencing operations to be around $250,000 a year. We can see that his work has all the earmarks of a planned, rational, business enterprise. He makes money and survives in his fencing business (only one arrest in more than twenty years) because he effectively plays off the legal and illegal sides of American economic enterprise.

Specialization and Varieties of Theft

Professional thieves rarely spend all or even most of their time in one particular line of theft. The common exceptions to this general rule are professional shoplifters, pickpockets, and forgers ("paper hangers"). Explaining why most thieves spread their talents around, one professional thief had this to say:

> Stealing for a living isn't just being a burglar or stick-up man. You've got to be able to look around and recognize opportunities and be able to take advantage of them regardless of what the conditions are. A lot of people think once a stick-up man, always a stick-up man. Well, you can't run around stickin' up people every day of the week like a workin' man. Maybe something worthwhile sticking up only shows up every two or three months. In the meantime you're doing this and that, changing around, doing practically anything to make a dollar.[52]

Some, of course, develop interests and talents that lead them toward particular sorts of capers in preference to others. They "have a line."[53] Some thieves express an interest in the theft of only certain types of merchandise — for example, credit cards, jewelry, or furs — and others see their talents put to the most productive (and secure) use in one line of work — picking pockets, sneak theft, forgery, or con games. On the whole, however, it seems that for both practical and social reasons thieves are generalists rather than specialists. Some may even be adamantly opposed to specialization: it reduces the chances of remaining anonymous, and increases the risks of being fingered for a caper known to be their style. Professionals do give recognition to those who can say they "have a line," but this denotes their preference and skill rather than day-to-day activity. Letkemann suggests that concern with specialization is more likely to be found among aspiring young amateurs, and goes on: "It may be that they carry over to the criminal world some of the square criteria for assigning status."[54]

Those varieties of theft involving high levels of skill, organization, and planning, and those requiring substantial resources (some big cons) are usually outside the reach of the typical amateur. However, many types of theft attract both professionals and amateurs. Within these types, some of the major things distinguishing amateurs from professionals are arrest and conviction history, size of the heist, level of technical skill involved, and type of fencing arrangement employed. Amateurs tend to be arrested and convicted more often, to come away with smaller payoffs (or none), to employ little in the way of manipulative and technical skills, and to steal for themselves or for disposal via lay fences. Both professionals and amateurs are involved in burglary, sneak theft, forgery, and auto theft. Amateurs are rarely found in confidence swindling, counterfeiting, or extortion.

SHOPLIFTING

Sneak theft is a term commonly applied to those forms of theft that involve stealing from under the nose of the victim (or someone in the victim's employ). Sneak theft includes shoplifting, pickpocketing, "till tapping" (stealing from cash registers), and sneak house theft.

Of the many varieties of theft, few are more pervasive than shoplifting. Shoplifting is an activity many Americans have probably engaged in at least once in their lives. Shoplifting knows few restrictions: it cuts across lines of age, race, sex, economic status, and education. Shoplifting provides people from all walks of life the chance to get something for nothing. It has been estimated that the losses from shoplifting may reach $8 billion a year.[55]

Although shoplifting has been making headlines in recent years as businesses protest the pilfering American shopper, it is by no means a recent phenomenon. As long ago as 1726 a shoplifting crime wave was plaguing England:

> In the year 1726, shoplifters became so numerous and so detrimental to the shopkeepers, that they made application to the Government for assistance in apprehending the offenders; and in order thereto, offered a reward and a pardon for any who would discover their associates in such practice.[56]

Written accounts of shoplifting go back at least to the sixteenth century, and we have no reason to believe that pilfering does not have a history going back to the first days when merchants took to displaying wares for sale.

From an historical standpoint, methods of shoplifting appear to have changed little over the years. Certainly, techniques of shoplifting are influenced by the way of life in any particular society at any particular time. Prevailing modes of dress, the architecture of stores, the manner in which goods are displayed, and the overall character of the shopping experience will all have some bearing on how shoplifters operate. Yet shoplifters still employ time-honored methods: concealing items underneath their clothes, putting them in false-bottomed cases, "bad-bagging" them (placing in well-worn shopping bags), and using "booster boxes" (cartons and packages that appear sealed but in fact have an opening for receiving lifted items).[57]

Contemporary shoplifting shows close ties with its past in another respect. Within the multitude of shoplifters has long been a minority of

Sneak theft is one of the most prevalent forms of criminal theft. The major variety, shoplifting, cuts across age, sex, race, and class lines.

professionals — "boosters" and "heels," as they are often called in the trade — who make all or a part of their living in this line of work. The professional has appeared in the literature on shoplifting since 1597, when one chronicler described how professional troupes worked in Elizabethan times. Today professionalism still remains an important facet of this branch of theft.

Information on shoplifting is extremely difficult to come by. Since the behavior itself is but one kind of larceny in most jurisdictions, shoplifting does not appear in published statistics as a separate offense for which rates can be calculated. But even if it were recorded as a distinct offense, the data would likely be far from satisfactory. Adequate data are difficult to compile since store operators themselves have no accurate ways of assessing what is stolen, in how many separate incidents, and by whom. Most store data on pilferage is in the form of estimates based on inventory losses (called "shrinkage"), which include employee theft and a host of other business losses. A second source of data is the records kept by stores dealing with actual cases of shoplifting that have come to their attention during business hours (and many stores keep no records). Even if such records are regularly and systematically compiled, they would probably do no more than scratch the surface, since most shoplifting goes undetected and the matter of securing evidence of a lift is a complex one.

Mary Owen Cameron's classic study of shoplifting and other investigations over the past few years do, nevertheless, permit some tentative generalizations about what is taken, by whom, and with what results for the offender.[58] These studies indicate that women and children are the most frequent shoplifters, that most are pilferers who steal once or twice on a strictly amateur basis, and that no one social class has a monopoly on such activities. The amateur who occasionally pilfers a store usually takes items worth less than ten dollars, and the favored articles are bric-a-brac, food, toilet articles, clothing accessories, recreation items, and, with child shoplifters, school supplies.

Cameron's study indicates that professional shoplifting differs in significant ways from the much more common amateur variety. Boosters and heels (the latter are professionally involved in shoplifting as an almost exclusive means of livelihood) generally steal items worth more, do so with preplanning and practiced skill, and usually as part of a troupe, whose members may number as many as twelve to fifteen. Also in contrast to amateur pilferage (or "snitching"), professionals usually do not steal with the intention of keeping the items for themselves, but in order to sell them to a fence, who will give them a portion of the items' value in cash.

Reactions to Shoplifting   Reactions to shoplifting and shoplifters reveal the most intriguing facets of this criminal activity. Time and again studies indicate that though most shoplifters are never caught, those that are often face little more than a scolding, to be sent on their way after returning or paying for the merchandise. But the shoplifter's chances of being merely "told off" depend on age, sex, ability to pay, attitude, apparent breeding, and whether or not he or she is a known or suspected professional.

Overall, it appears that the value of the items taken is the best predictor of whether the shoplifter will get by with verbal scolding or whether the police will be notified and prosecution pursued. Michael Hindelang's study of the referral behavior of a California private security agency shows that in both 1963 and 1968 those who were most likely to be referred to the police by the victim had stolen items of relatively large value.[59] But in this same study it was discovered that when the value of the item was controlled, the nature of the goods and how they were concealed also figured in the picture. The person who stole liquor, cigarettes, or fresh meat had a better chance of being referred to the police than one who did not. The person who employed a method of concealment that left little room for doubt about illegal intentions again had a better chance of being referred to the police.

Why do many offenders get little more than a scolding when caught?

Since detection and arrest of shoplifters is commonly the responsibility of store personnel, who gets arrested, and what happens to them, will be influenced in part by the policies and attitudes held by those assuming that responsibility. Both in America and abroad the general store policy is caution and leniency. The primary objective is to deter shoplifting while avoiding anything that might hurt store business. Store management wants to avoid scenes on the shop floor that might adversely affect the attitudes and behavior of customers; equally, it wants to minimize the time and expense involved in carrying through official prosecution of suspects; and finally, it wants to avoid unnecessary publicity that might mark the store as unfriendly, or harsh, or as a place frequented by shoplifters.[60] If the store can recover the items or obtain payment for them through informal and discreet means, then its interests are at least partially met.

Other aspects of the informal approach should be borne in mind. Store management knows that on the whole most pilferers are amateurs, and, when confronted with their attempted theft, most are so shaken up they will do almost anything to avoid official attention. Further, they will probably refrain from stealing in that store, at least for a time. Studies have shown that typical pilferers are what the criminal subculture labels "square johns," who neither systematically involve themselves in criminal pursuits nor identify themselves as criminals, but adhere to dominant cultural values and spend most of their time in legitimate pursuits. When caught, amateurs (particularly adults) display their commitment to dominant conceptions of right and wrong and strenuously deny that they have done anything wrong or that they are criminals. Cameron reports the following as a typical verbal response from the amateur on being apprehended:

> I didn't intend to take the dress. I just wanted to see it in the daylight. Oh! what will my husband do! I *did* intend to pay for it. It's all a mistake. Oh! my God! what will mother say! I'll be glad to pay for it. See, I've got the money with me. Oh! my children! They can't find out I've been arrested! I'd never be able to face them again.[61]

Some pilferers dream up quite incredible excuses or explanations for their behavior: "The shop assistant took so long in coming"; "I thought my sister had paid for it"; "I only wanted to see whether things are properly supervised here."[62]

Another important reason management may react informally rather than formally to shoplifting has to do with the legal difficulties surrounding civilian arrest of persons suspected of misdemeanors. Since most shoplifters steal only enough to get charged with a misdemeanor, civilians are placed in a difficult situation, because many states have strict laws governing the conditions under which misdemeanor suspects may be apprehended. To arrest a misdemeanor suspect is to do so at peril because those who do may be subject to suits charging false imprisonment or false arrest.[63] Rather than face possible legal troubles, many stores approach a suspect discreetly and informally, playing down the fact that technically a civilian arrest is being made. Not surprisingly, retailers have in recent years brought considerable pressure to bear on legislatures to amend regulations dealing with the apprehension of suspected shoplifters. Many states now permit store personnel to detain suspects under certain broad conditions, and without fear of civil suits charging false arrest or imprisonment.[64] This may mean an increase in the official handling of pilferers, though considerations such as those we have reviewed will continue to play an important part in management decisions.

Consequences of Informal Reactions Informal handling of shoplifters may have important ramifications for the way shoplifting is viewed by those apprehended as well as by the general public. The fact that many shoplifters are generally upright citizens suggests that in order to engage in shoplifting in the first place — which they recognize as wrong and illegal — they may have convinced themselves that in their case it is not really theft, certainly not crime. We have already seen that such is indeed the way many apprehended amateurs conceive of their actions. How do they arrive at this conception? How is it that what they do is not crime but what someone else does — for example, robbery and burglary — is crime?

What we view as crime is partly influenced by prevailing cultural conceptions of crime and partly by the kinds of things that happen, or at least are expected to happen, to criminals. If we do things we expect will result in our being labeled criminal, then to be so labeled comes as no surprise and merely reinforces our conception of the act and ourselves as criminal. But if we are not sure that our actions are criminal, or if we have adopted the view that they are not, we will see no reason to alter our views when reactions to our acts fail to conform with what we know, assume, or expect will happen to "real" criminals doing "real" criminal things. And so, the upright citizen who occasionally shoplifts, and who when caught is treated informally and discreetly by store personnel, will be under little pressure to alter his or her conception of self and behavior. The ramification of this is that informal handling of shoplifters permits upright citizens, believers in the "American way," to retain the view that what they do is not criminal, and that the criminal is quite another kind of person.

Interestingly enough, American business practices may encourage amateur shoplifting in yet another way. Businesses spend billions of dollars every year on campaigns designed to convince Americans that they need and want items offered for sale. Already attuned to the values of an acquisitive society, Americans are constantly reminded to spend as much money as they can. We are continually exhorted to buy now, buy more, buy better (whatever that means), and pay later if we do not have the cash on hand. At Christmastime, when shoplifting is at its yearly peak, the glitter and the temptation are at their height. We come to learn that a successful, self-respecting American is one who can demonstrate in his consumption behavior that he has at least kept up with his fellows, if not gone ahead of them. Even if we cannot really afford an item we are discouraged from forgetting about it, and instead are extolled to find a way that we can afford it. Continually pushed to conceive of the meaning of life in material terms, Americans have adopted standards that measure a person by what he possesses, what he can afford, and what he consumes, rather than who he is and what he is. Among the casualties of an acquisitive society are values of fairness, dignity, decency, concern for others, and feelings of contentment and well-being, as Harry Bredemeier and Jackson Toby have argued.[65] For their part, retailers help to perpetuate the ethic of acquisitiveness:

> In department stores many of the symbols of status are dazzlingly arrayed before people who have been exhorted to desire them. Manufacturers employ skilled professional tempters (advertising agencies) to represent their products as necessary ingredients for the appearance of success.[66]

Small wonder, then, that many Americans see personal troubles largely in terms of access to and control over material things. In two nationwide surveys, Samuel Stouffer found that "the largest single block of personal worries involved concern over personal business or family economic problems."[67] Some of the typical worries expressed were:

> How to make a living for my family is my biggest worry. We've got the new home now if we can ever get it paid for.

> My children. They are too ambitious for our income; takes more money than we've got. And I work, too, in an office, to help out the income.

> Business conditions at the store worry me some. Trade is not as good as it was.

> Paying bills. My husband has been in the hospital and may have to go back again.

> I worry about my pension. Might not be enough to eat. Hard times now and no work. I want fixings for my new home, but things cost a lot.

> Trying to pay my honest and just debts.

> Money goes too fast. Food, it is so expensive. High rent. We are moving to California to see if we can get a better living there.

Why Shoplift?   When faced with failure in the bid to keep up material standards (an adult rather than juvenile concern) we have two basic options. We can withdraw entirely from the battle for access to and control over material wealth or we can try all the harder to win that battle. It is especially hard to withdraw when everything around us seems to confirm and reinforce the central place held by material things. In fact, Bredemeier and Toby argue, most Americans probably choose the latter option. If taken, the option of trying harder will lead us in one of three directions: (1) we can relentlessly pursue those culturally supported, institutionalized avenues to material acquisition; (2) we can reject those legitimized avenues and select alternatives; or (3) we can combine relentless pursuit of *some* legitimized avenues with the *rejection* of others. In these authors' view, the American solution to problems of acquisition revolves around three "governing principles": self-reliance (fend for yourself, "shop around"); competition (outperform or outshine those who are competing with you for rewards); and negotiated exchange (get as much as you can for as little as possible).[68] Americans who face apparent defeat in the race for material things can be expected to frame their choice of options around these three institutionalized mechanisms. We can relentlessly pursue or we can reject some or all of them.

The adult American who shoplifts on an amateur basis is perhaps best understood as one who, while pursuing the solution to his acquisitive problems in the "American way," finds it convenient or necessary from time to time to reject the idea of a negotiated exchange and overemphasize self-reliance, to the point where "taking care of number one" is an engrossing concern. It is easier for upstanding Americans to reject the idea of bargaining for acceptable terms of exchange if they perceive that they are in fact not in a position to bargain in the first place, or that no matter what they offer to negotiate, the terms are settled in the other's favor before the negotiation begins. Under these conditions the situation is itself in violation of the institutionalized principle. The feeling that retailers are to all intents and purposes "ripping us off" is simply an expression of defeat in negotiated exchange.[69] However, if you cannot win in the exchange, but you still need or desire that blouse, that bottle of liquor, those earrings, that wallet, or that food, things can be worked to your advantage through pursuit of self-reliance. Instead of defeat, temporary victory can be claimed when you fend for yourself and rip off the store. But through all this, your interpretation of what has happened, what you have done, remains appropriately American — you were merely being self-reliant under circumstances where the principle of negotiated exchange could not be satisfactorily followed. And so, as we saw earlier, the amateur adult shoplifters see themselves not as criminals, not as thieves, but instead as upholders of the "American way."

BURGLARY

Of all serious felonies burglary is the most common, and, to many Americans, one of the more frightening of crimes. Victims often report that they felt as if their very person had been violated. We cherish the privacy and security of our homes, and there is anger and resentment when these are breached. The victims of burglary come from all walks of life, though the poorer parts of American cities tend to bear the brunt of this assault on private property (see table 6.1).

Over the last few years the fears of middle-class homeowners have increased as suburban burglary rates have shot up. Communities have organized "crime watch" groups to patrol their neighborhoods in an attempt to protect themselves from the burglar, among other criminals.

Whether in the suburbs, in rural areas, or in cities, most burglaries are the work of relatively unskilled amateurs. They look for cash and for items that can be readily disposed of via lay fences and pawnshops. Their methods are scorned by professionals. The professional takes pride in his ability to gain entrance without force and noise and to pull a job speedily and profitably. The unskilled, often youthful burglars are called "door shakers," "kick-it-in men," "loidmen," and "creepers," names that reflect their amateur techniques.[70]

A number of research efforts during the past decade have aimed at

Table 6.1 Burglary incidents by census characteristics, 1972–1973[a]

CENSUS CHARACTERISTIC	PERCENTAGE OF INCIDENTS
Income	
Low	39.7%
Medium-Low	27.8
Medium-High	21.3
High	11.2
	100%
Educational level	
Low	40.5%
Medium-Low	31.8
Medium-High	18.8
High	8.8
	99%
Percentage of owner-occupied homes	
Low	34.6%
Medium-Low	30.5
Medium-High	20.5
High	14.4
	100%

SOURCE: Carl E. Pope, *Crime-Specific Analysis: The Characteristics of Burglary Incidents*. Analytic Report SD-AR-10 (Washington, D.C.: U.S. Government Printing Office, 1977), from table 11, p. 27.

[a] Based on 8,137 burglary incidents occuring between April 1972 and May 1973 in the following cities: San Francisco, Oakland, Los Angeles (city and county), San Diego, and Orange County, California.

identifying the major contours of burglary offenses and offenders. There is considerable agreement among them as to the main characteristics.[71] Burglary incidents tend to involve residences more frequently than commercial establishments; losses are moderate, usually well under $500; most are burglaries of cash and of cash-convertible items such as televisions, radios, and stereos; residential burglaries usually take place during the daytime, those of commercial establishments at night, often on weekends; most involve some sort of forced entry. It is perhaps significant that the clearance rate (proportion of incidents resulting in arrest) tends to be higher for burglaries where there is no loss at all or only a small one. Presumably these are uncompleted burglaries, and their numbers are higher than might be expected — up to 33 percent of all incidents in some studies.[72] They are often the work of amateurs who can't find what they want or who are discovered or frightened away before they have had a chance to start work.

Many offenders are under 18 years of age when arrested, with blacks tending to be overrepresented. Very few are female, but when women are involved they are more likely than men to work in partnerships or groups, although men frequently work in teams. Most adult burglars have prior arrest records, often for burglary.

When professionals work they choose targets that have been carefully cased, they work in well-oiled teams with each member assigned a specific role based on experience and expertise, and they work with quiet speed.[73] In search for a lucrative score, the professional must effectively deal with security systems. The ability to disarm alarms separates the good burglar from both the amateur and the aspiring professional.[74]

Once inside, there is the problem of finding whatever it is the burglar is after. If he is interested in cash, as many are, finding it is not always a simple matter. The skilled burglar applies the experience and know-how that lead him to anticipate the behavior of his victim:

> In commercial establishments, he may find it in the expected places, such as safes, cash registers, or in deliberately unexpected places, such as one shoe box among several hundred others. In residential dwellings, the burglar's task may be even more difficult, since the places where cash may be found are less predictable. A home does not have a cash register, nor, necessarily, a safe. Therefore, the burglar must make quick interpretations as to the most probable location of cash. The mental activity here is really a game of wits — or operating on the basis of reciprocal expectations. He proceeds on the assumptions he has regarding routine family behavior, and he anticipates uniformities in architecture as well as in styles of placing valuables.[75]

In professional burglary, safe men are at the top of the status hierarchy, and their work makes some of the greatest demands on a thief's skill. Safecracking has been explored in detail by Letkemann.[76] Among the basic tools and equipment are "grease" (nitroglycerine), made from a combination of sulphuric acid, nitric acid, and glycerine; soap, which must be pliable and is used for funneling the grease into the door; and "knockers and string," (detonators and fuses). The most common technique of safeblowing is the so-called jam shot, a procedure consisting of some ten coordinated steps that, if done correctly, make the door of the safe swing open on its hinges. When not done correctly, the door is blown off the safe, or worse, the door and safe buckle.

Professional safe men must keep up with technological advances if they are to stay in business, and those who have been long in the field recognize the importance of information sharing and connections. Safe men share information on jobs, on techniques, on new developments, and on any related aspects of their line. Letkemann suggests that the already fairly strong social bonds linking safe men have been strengthened as a result of greatly restricted access to dynamite (a ready source of grease), and the resulting need to make their own nitroglycerine: "It enabled leaders to screen new 'recruits' and necessitated the development of a stronger subculture based on mutual aid and group loyalty."[77]

Today sophisticated professional burglary has been swallowed up by the growing numbers of amateur burglaries committed by those in search of immediate economic rewards. While professional burglary is undoubtedly alive and well, it may be that increased security and decreased use of cash as a medium of exchange will help to drive all but the most organized and skilled burglars into other lines of work. The one thing about a professional is that he or she will endeavor to find an alternative way to stay in business, especially if that alternative permits the retention of self-conceptions in line with professionalism.

FORGERY

It is estimated that in any given year losses to forgery in America run from $500 million to $1 billion.[78] By far the most common form of forgery is "paper hanging." Paper hanging involves the use of bank checks when funds are insufficient to cover them, or when the signature has been forged. Since around 90 percent of all American money transactions are made with checks, a ready-made exchange climate exists within which forgery can flourish.[79] Actually, it is not just the abundant use of checks that provides a supportive environment for the check forger. Public attitudes regarding checks and their use, the ease with which paper hanging can be accomplished, the unwillingness of banks and stores to prosecute, and the hazy line between criminal intent and mistake all make for a supportive atmosphere. In many respects, the very things that provide support for shoplifting also encourage check forgery.

Checks are commonly seen as "like" money but not as "real" money, hence their misuse may escape the public censure that loss or theft of cash receives. In addition, checks are drawn on, and supplied by, relatively impersonal institutions, which, like department stores, provide services we have to use in order to meet prevailing cultural standards (or at least we think we do). As institutions to which we are beholden, but which are beyond our personal control, we, not they, stand as potential victims in the relationship. Those who would attempt to reverse this situation, however temporarily, may well receive a kind of quiet praise on the part of the public, for they have bucked the institutionalized situation of dependency. Two factors help to explain the seemingly pervasive public indifference to check forgery. First, it is not rare for a person to inadvertently cash or use a check without at that moment having sufficient funds to cover it. Second, check forgery does not have any of the earmarks of what we conventionally think of as a crime — it does not look like crime, so maybe it really is not.[80]

Banks and stores, which provide checks and checking services, also help support forgery. Because they are in a business dependent upon continued public good faith, they are unwilling to make too much of the typical case of check forgery. Rather than antagonize current or prospective clients, banks and stores are more likely to treat most paper hanging, on the surface at least, as mistakes or oversights rather than what they legally are — felonies. More privately, of course, they increase their efforts to ward off the forger. Commercial check cashers and issuers now find that insurance companies employ deductible clauses that can be invoked in cases of check forgery — another incentive for businesses to increase their vigilance.[81]

These and other features of our society provide an atmosphere in terms of which check forgery can be partly understood. Check forgery is easy to do (access to a check is virtually all that is needed). It can be readily explained away as a mistake or oversight. Checks are currently the major means of dealing in money, so few of us are surprised to see checks come into our lives or suspicious of those who use them. Paper hanging has none of the earmarks of crime. Official reaction to it by banks, stores, and police is at best ambivalent (arrests from 1960 to 1973 remained under 30,000 for each year, and the increase over those years hardly kept pace with population increases, let alone increases in the use of checks).

It should come as no surprise that the bulk of check forgers ("naive check forgers," as Edwin Lemert calls them) do not think of themselves as criminals, cannot believe that anyone would have the audacity to call them that ("I would never hurt anyone!"), and come up with ready excuses or rationalizations for their behavior (from the more obvious, "it was a mistake," to comments such as "no one is hurt by forgery because supermarkets make great profits and don't miss a little money lost through bad checks").[82] Although naive forgers are found in all socioeconomic classes, and include both men and women, blacks and whites, and all ethnic groups, the category of persons most often identified among forgers is that of the white male who holds a white-collar job and has little identified criminality in his history. In addition, when compared to other known felons, the convicted forger appears to have higher than average intelligence and to have begun his adventure in crime at a much later age — late twenties and early thirties.[83]

Studies of naive check forgery suggest two factors that together may help explain why some people pass hot checks. One factor is the impact of situational conditions and the importance of forgery as a psychological and behavioral mechanism for coping with stress produced in the situation. Lemert discovered that the typical instance of naive check forgery occurs when the offender is under pressure to come up with money — he may be out drinking with buddies, he may be in a strange town and need cash for some contingency or other, or he may be on a shopping spree. The pressures of the moment create a stress condition that demands resolution, or "closure," as Lemert calls it. The forger achieves closure by passing a bad check. He achieves closure because he has resolved the immediate problem — getting hold of cash or buying the item he wants.

But why forgery? Why not some other means of bringing the stressful situation to closure? Why not enlist the help of friends or family? The answer, it appears, lies with the fact that naive forgers commonly have experienced considerable social isolation in their personal histories. Many forgers have apparently experienced stressful and unproductive relationships with others that have progressively pushed them toward a condition of isolation relative to conventional social bonds. They are often estranged from their families, many have experienced difficulties in marriage (Lemert found divorce in 40 percent of his sample), some have encountered problems in employment and military service, and some have experienced gambling losses. As these situational pressures build, those who suffer them find themselves unwilling or unable to break the chain of personal troubles by enlisting the support and confidence of others. Instead, they seek closure of their immediate situation, but in a self-made manner (here we may again be witnessing the importance of the self-reliance principle noted in our discussion of shoplifting). Remember, however, that society has provided an exchange climate within which forgery is more easily and comfortably accomplished. Therefore, the choice of forgery as a closure device must be seen as a choice directed to some extent by this supportive exchange environment. One wonders what those who now pass hot checks would do if check forgery were not available to them, or if it carried the stigma of crime. If not one already, perhaps the naive forger would become a pilferer.

Not all paper hangers belong to the category of naive check forger; some are professionals (Lemert prefers the term *systematic forgers*). For the systematic forger, forgery provides a steady source of income and is treated in a highly businesslike manner.[84] While forgery was once a well-established part of the repertoire of professional theft, evidence today is that most systematic forgers are on the periphery of the fraternity of professional thieves. For one thing, they most often work alone, and therefore are not intimately wrapped up in the organizational facets of professionalism — they do not need connections, accomplices, financial stakes, fences, or other aspects of group support. Further, theirs is not a criminal activity requiring special skills and tutelage (although this is not true of the skilled counterfeiter).[85] In many ways, the professional forger is similar to the professional shoplifter. Moreover, some professional aspects of theft have become more vulnerable in the case of forgery because those who treat it seriously must now guard themselves against association with the more common habitual amateurs — for example, petty thieves, alcoholics, and other drug users — who cannot be trusted when the chips are down and who are not welcomed by the professional fraternity.[86]

No accurate estimates have been made of the proportion of forgery efforts attributable to professionals. In all probability, professionals account for a small number of the total incidents of paper hanging. But the systematic forger stands out in the size of his rewards from forgery and in the persistence with which he pursues this line of work. Bloch and Geis tell of a female systematic forger who claims to work a forty-hour week in her line and who can expect to make around $100 an hour if things go well.[87] One form of professional forgery requiring a little more planning and perseverance (not, according to Lemert, something many systematic forgers care for) is "check-kiting":

> *Check-kiting* is a swindle related to forgery that is directed against banks. This fraudulent operation involves the covering of bad checks with other bad checks. A professional bank swindler might open a series of checking accounts at scattered banks with deposits of $25. At *Bank Z* he cashes a $100 check drawn on *Bank X,* depositing $25 and pocketing $75. He then covers the *Bank X* check with a $250 check on *Bank Y,* depositing $125 and pocketing $125. This latter check on *Bank Y* is made good with a $500 check on *Bank Z,* with $300 deposited and $200 pocketed. Manipulations of this type have been executed by both individuals and organized groups of bank swindlers, with single operations accumulating thefts in excess of half a million dollars.[88]

CONFIDENCE GAMES

Swindlers have been around for centuries. It is said that wherever people want something for nothing, the swindler will also be found. Swindlers and confidence artists rely on the something-for-nothing attitude, and they often say "you can't cheat an honest man."

Variations on the con game are numerous: Inciardi notes that lists of different swindles compiled over the years show as many as 250 variations.[89] For at least 200 years two of the most common con games have been "ring dropping" and "purse dropping." Both involve simple techniques of victim manipulation, and both rely on the latter's greed, gullibility, and dishonesty. In ring dropping, for example, a worthless piece of jewelry is dropped by one member of the con team (the "roper" or "steerer") near a stranger (the victim or "mark"). A second member of the team (the "insideman") rushes forward to pick up the jewelry, and after showing it to the mark, agrees to share the proceeds if the stranger will sell it. The mark is persuaded to leave something of value with the insideman as security — a token of good faith. The climax of the game is obvious — the insideman absconds with the security, leaving the mark to discover that the jewelry is worthless.

The game just described is one variety of those swindles commonly referred to as "short cons." The aim in a short con is to fleece the mark of whatever he has with him at the time, or can get hold of in a matter of minutes. In a short con, the amount of preparation needed and the size of the take are generally small — it can be put into motion at a moment's notice and the score is usually a matter of dollars and cents.[90] Another common version of the short con is the "pigeon drop," which operates along lines similar to ring dropping but requires more manipulative abilities on the part of the confidence operator. In the typical pigeon drop, the victim is invited to share money that has supposedly been found by one member of the confidence partnership; but in order to qualify for a share the mark must first demonstrate good faith by putting up some of his or her own money.

The successful con artist must accomplish at least three things: (1) the mark must be made to feel that he can trust the con operator, (2) he must be made to believe that his own part in the enterprise will be rewarding to him; and, most important, (3) he must be convinced that in order to get that reward he has to part (temporarily, of course) with some of his own money. Clearly, a good deal of smooth talking and friendly persuasion on the part of the confidence team is usually necessary. This is where good con men excel.[91]

Those con men who set their sights on lucrative swindles, and are able and prepared to spend considerable time and energy in the preparation and performance of the swindle, go after the big con. Big-con operators are at the top of the hierarchy of professional crime, and their line of work involves considerable skill and ingenuity. Big-con operators are shrewd businesspeople whose special talents lie in their acting ability and their knowledge of the limits to which people can be pushed in search of a fast buck.[92] Big cons can reap large payoffs, as the experience of John Ernest Keely demonstrates:

> Keely, an ex-carnival pitchman, began a hoax in 1874 that reaped many fortunes and lasted for a quarter of a century. His nonexistent perpetual motion machine, "which would produce a force more powerful than steam and electricity," involved the financiers of many cities, the public of two continents, and the United States Secretary of War. Before his career ended, Keely had a 372-page volume written on his "discovery," over a million

dollars in cash, a life of luxury for twenty-five years, and an international reputation.[93]

Most big-con operators adhere to a sequence of steps, each of which must be successfully accomplished if the con is to go through. As each step is completed, it becomes more difficult for the con operators to abandon the enterprise, and more likely that the swindle will succeed. Gasser has outlined seven major steps in the sequence:

Step 1: *Tying into the mark* — finding a victim, gaining his confidence, getting him ready for step two.

Step 2: *Telling the mark the tale* — showing the victim what is at stake for him, and how he can get hold of it.

Step 3: *Initial money gaff* — letting the mark make some money to show how easy it is.

Step 4: *Putting the mark on the send* — sending the victim for money.

Step 5: *Playing the mark against the store* — fleecing him of his money.

Step 6: *Cooling out the mark* — see explanation below.

Step 7: *Putting the mark in the door* — getting rid of the victim.[94]

One of the most important steps in the sequence of events is "cooling out" the victim. Big-con operators recognize their vulnerability to the victim's passions once he has discovered that he has been duped. Accordingly, they build into their operating procedures a special step, the purpose of which is to reduce the chances that the mark will bring trouble down on their heads. They hope he will be convinced to forget the whole incident. The methods used for cooling out the mark vary, but on the whole they revolve around the victim's perception of himself and his own situation. Generally speaking, con men avoid the use of violence, even if it means losing the score.[95] How, then, do they cool out the mark?

One method is to create a twist in the con men–victim relationship whereby the victim becomes an apparent accessory to a felony (sometimes murder), and hence finds himself in a situation where he thinks he has committed a crime. From being a victim the mark now sees himself as a criminal offender, facing a prison sentence if caught. Of course, the whole situation is contrived; the con men stage a fake murder (or robbery or rape). But the effect can be devastating. Assuming himself to be an accessory to a serious crime, the victim is only too glad to forget the whole thing.[96]

Erving Goffman has discussed a second method of cooling out the mark. This method relies on "the art of consolation." Instead of generating fear in the victim, the con man helps to provide him with a redefinition of his situation and self so that he can feel more comfortable with the outcome of his experience at the hands of the con men.[97] By emphasizing, for example, that it was extremely hard to con him, or that he presented a real challenge, or that he was a cut above the usual mark, the con operators help the victim to retain a positive conception of self.

Although perhaps for higher stakes, it is rather like the situation in which a chess opponent who has just beaten you hastily proceeds to commend you on your play and the challenge you gave him. You have still lost the game, but you feel much better. Redefining the situation for the mark provides him with "a new set of apologies . . . [and] a new framework in which to see himself and judge himself."[98]

We should remind ourselves that confidence games do not survive in our society merely because some people have the talents to pull them off. Neither do they survive simply because some of us may be dishonest and gullible. For confidence games to persist there must be values that give special emphasis to personal acquisitiveness. As with shoplifting, forgery, and, indeed, any type of theft, the behavior itself cannot be understood solely in terms of the players or the immediate situation in which it occurs. Confidence games differ from other varieties of theft in that both offender and victim are after something for nothing, or relatively little. The con game represents a situation in which the principles of negotiated exchange and self-reliance are relentlessly pursued by all parties. And these are principles given cultural support in our society.

References

1. See Herbert A. Bloch and Gilbert Geis, *Man, Crime, and Society*. 2nd ed. (New York: Random House, 1970), pp. 272–73.
2. Cyrus H. Gordon, *Hammurapi's Code: Quaint or Forward Looking?* (New York: Holt, Rinehart and Winston, 1975), p. 4.
3. Sir Frederick Pollack and Frederick W. Maitland, *The History of English Law before the Time of Edward I*, vol. II, 2nd ed. (Cambridge: Cambridge University Press, 1968), pp. 157, 178.
4. J. W. Cecil Turner, ed., *Kenney's Outlines of Criminal Law*, 19th ed. (Cambridge: Cambridge University Press, 1966), p. 267.
5. Allan Z. Gammage and Charles F. Hemphill, *Basic Criminal Law* (New York: McGraw-Hill, 1974), p. 227.
6. F. L. Attenborough, ed., *The Laws of the Earliest English Kings* (New York: Russell and Russell, 1963), p. 137.
7. Consult Jerome Hall, *Theft, Law, and Society*, rev. ed. (Indianapolis: Bobbs-Merrill, 1952); Theodore F. T. Plucknett, *A Concise History of Common Law* (London: Butterworth, 1948); William Blackstone, *Commentaries on the Laws of England*, vol. IV (Boston: Beacon Press, 1962); also Turner, *Kenney's Outlines of Criminal Law* and Pollack and Maitland, *History of English Law*.
8. Hermann Mannheim, *Criminal Justice and Social Reconstruction* (London: Routledge and Kegan Paul, 1946), pp. 90–93.
9. For a detailed account of the following case see Jerome Hall, *Theft, Law, and Society*.
10. Ibid., p. 33.
11. William J. Chambliss, *Criminal Law in Action* (Santa Barbara, Calif.: Hamilton Publishing Co., 1975), p. 7.
12. Examples are: D. W. Maurer, *The Big Con* (Indianapolis: Bobbs-Merrill, 1940) and Maurer's *Whiz Mob* (New Haven: College and University Press, 1964); Neal Shover, "The Social Organization of Burglary," *Social Problems* 20 (1973), pp. 499–514; and Edwin M. Lemert, "The Behavior of the Systematic Check Forger," *Social Problems* 6 (1958), pp. 141–48.
13. Edwin H. Sutherland, *The Professional Thief* (Chicago: University of Chicago Press, 1937).
14. Ibid., pp. 2–42.
15. Ibid., pp. ix–x.
16. Edwin H. Sutherland and Donald R. Cressey, *Criminology*, 9th ed. (Philadelphia: Lippincott, 1974), p. 285.
17. See Henry Mayhew, *London Labour and the London Poor*, vol. IV (London: Griffin, Bohn, 1862).
18. Harry King, *Box Man: A Professional Thief's Journey*, ed. William Chambliss (New York: Harper and Row, 1972), p. 12.
19. James A. Inciardi, *Careers in Crime* (Chicago: Rand McNally, 1975), p. 52.
20. Ibid., p. 51.
21. Maurer, *Whiz Mob;* see also Inciardi, *Careers in Crime*.

22. Inciardi, *Careers in Crime,* pp. 59–62; Peter Letkemann, *Crime as Work* (Englewood Cliffs, N.J.: Prentice-Hall, 1973), pp. 117–36; and J. B. Martin, *My Life in Crime* (New York: Harper and Row, 1952).
23. Letkemann, *Crime as Work,* p. 124.
24. Harry King, *Box Man,* p. 81.
25. Shover, "The Social Organization of Burglary," p. 502.
26. This path is negotiated not only by professional thieves: See Martin S. Weinberg, "Sexual Modesty, Social Meanings, and the Nudist Camp," *Social Problems* 12 (1965), pp. 311–18.
27. Nicholas Pileggi, "1968 Has Been the Year of the Burglar," *New York Times Magazine,* (November 17, 1968).
28. Julian B. Roebuck and Ronald C. Johnson, "The 'Short Con' Man," *Crime and Delinquency* 10 (1964), p. 242.
29. Martin, *My Life in Crime,* p. 279.
30. Inciardi, *Careers in Crime,* p. 70.
31. Sutherland, *The Professional Thief,* p. 13.
32. Inciardi, *Careers in Crime,* p. 56.
33. See Shover, "The Social Organization of Burglary," pp. 510–11.
34. Ibid., p. 512.
35. Harry King, *Box Man,* p. 89.
36. Inciardi, *Careers in Crime,* p. 70.
37. Letkemann, *Crime as Work,* p. 30.
38. President's Commission on Law Enforcement and the Administration of Justice, *The Challenge of Crime in a Free Society* (Washington, D.C.: U.S. Government Printing Office, 1967), p. 46.
39. Robert Louis Gasser, "The Confidence Game," *Federal Probation* 27 (1963), pp. 47–54.
40. Martin, *My Life in Crime,* p. 171.
41. Inciardi, *Careers in Crime,* p. 67.
42. Duncan Chappell and Marilyn Walsh, "Receiving Stolen Property — The Need for Systematic Inquiry into the Fencing Process," *Criminology* 11 (1974), pp. 484–97.
43. Ibid., p. 494.
44. Plucknett, *A Concise History of Common Law,* p. 427.
45. Gammage and Hemphill, *Basic Criminal Law,* pp. 243–45.
46. See *LEAA Newsletter,* vol. 7 (1978) and vol. 8 (1979).
47. Hall, *Theft, Law, and Society,* p. 291.
48. Shover, "The Social Organization of Burglary," p. 508.
49. Ibid.
50. Michael Pearl, "The Confessions of a Master Fence," reprinted in Duane Denfeld, *Streetwise Criminology* (Cambridge, Mass.: Schenkman, 1974), pp. 97–102.
51. Ibid., p. 102.
52. Martin, *My Life in Crime,* p. 117.
53. Letkemann, *Crime as Work,* p. 33.
54. Ibid., pp. 42–43.
55. *LEAA Newsletter* 9 (1979–1980), p. 5.
56. Arthur L. Hayward, ed., *Lives of the Most Remarkable Criminals* (London: George Routledge and Sons, 1920), p. 375.
57. For a survey of past and current shoplifting techniques, see Loren E. Edwards, *Shoplifting and Shrinkage Protection for Stores* (Springfield, Ill.: Charles C Thomas, 1958), pp. 4–15 and 33–41.
58. Mary Owen Cameron, *The Booster and the Snitch* (New York: Free Press, 1964).
59. Michael J. Hindelang, "Decisions of Shoplifting Victims to Invoke the Criminal Justice Process," *Social Problems* 21 (1974), pp. 580–93.
60. Apart from Cameron, *The Booster and the Snitch,* consult Fourth International Criminological Congress, The Hague, September 5–11, 1960, *Proceedings,* vol. II; Jon R. Waltz, "Shoplifting and the Law of Arrest," *Yale Law Journal* 62 (1953), pp. 788–805; and Gerald Robin, "The American Customer: Shopper or Shoplifter?" *Police* (1964).
61. Cameron, *The Booster and the Snitch,* p. 164.
62. Wolfgang Doleisch, "Theft in Department Stores" (paper presented to the Fourth International Criminological Congress, The Hague, September 5–11, 1960), *Proceedings,* vol. II, sect. 2, p. 4.
63. Waltz, "Shoplifting and the Law of Arrest," p. 794–96.
64. Ibid.; see also Loren Edwards, *Shoplifting and Shrinkage Protection.*
65. Harry C. Bredemeier and Jackson Toby, *Social Problems in America* (New York: Wiley, 1961).
66. Cameron, *The Booster and the Snitch,* p. 171.
67. Samuel A. Stouffer, *Communism, Conformity, and Civil Liberties* (Garden City, N.Y.: Doubleday, 1955), pp. 58–70.
68. Bredemeier and Toby, *Social Problems in America,* p. 62.
69. How often have you felt that stores charge too much or give you a poor exchange for your money?
70. Pileggi, "1968 Has Been the Year of the Burglar."
71. The studies upon which the following summary is based are: Harry A. Scarr, *Patterns of Burglary* 2nd ed. (Washington, D.C.: U.S. Government Printing Office, 1973); John E. Conklin and Egon Bittner, "Burglary in a Suburb," *Criminology* II (1973), pp. 206–32; Thomas A. Reppetto, *Residential Crime* (Cambridge, Mass.: Ballinger, 1974); Peter D. Chimbos, "A Study of Breaking and Entering in 'Northern City,' Ontario," *Canadian Journal of Criminology and Corrections* 15 (1973), pp. 316–25. These and other studies are reviewed in three Analytic Reports by Carl E. Pope published by the U.S. Department of Justice under the following titles: *Crime-Specific Analysis: The Characteristics of Burglary Incidents* (SD-AR-10, 1977); *Crime-Specific Analysis: An Empirical Examination of Burglary Offender Characteristics* (SD-AR-11, 1977); *Crime-Specific*

Analysis: An Empirical Examination of Burglary Offense and Offender Characteristics (SD-AR-12, 1977) (Washington, D.C.: U.S. Government Printing Office, 1977).

72. Conklin and Bittner, "Burglary in a Suburb."
73. Ibid.; see also Shover, "The Social Organization of Burglary"; and Robert Wallace, "Confessions of a Master Jewel Thief," *Life* (March 12, 1956), pp. 121–26.
74. Letkemann, *Crime as Work*, p. 55.
75. Ibid.
76. Ibid., pp. 57–86.
77. Ibid., p. 88.
78. Edward P. Foldessy, "The Paper Hangers," in Michael Gartner, ed., *Crime as Business* (Princeton, N.J.: Dow Jones Books, 1971), pp. 81–88; President's Commission on Law Enforcement and the Administration of Justice, *Crime and Its Impact — An Assessment* (Washington, D.C.: U.S. Government Printing Office, 1967), p. 51.
79. Bloch and Geis, *Man, Crime, and Society*, p. 178.
80. See Edwin M. Lemert, "An Isolation and Closure Theory of Naive Check Forgery," *Journal of Criminal Law, Criminology, and Police Science* 44 (1953), pp. 297–98.
81. Foldessy, "The Paper Hangers."
82. See Don C. Gibbons, *Society, Crime, and Criminal Careers*, 2nd ed. (Englewood Cliffs, N.J.: Prentice-Hall, 1973), p. 250.
83. See Lemert, "An Isolation and Closure Theory," also Maurice Gauthier, "The Psychology of the Compulsive Forger," *Canadian Journal of Cor-* rections 1 (1959), pp. 62–69; Irwin A. Berg, "A Comparative Study of Forgery," *Journal of Applied Psychology* 28 (1944), pp. 232–38; and Norman S. Hayner, "Characteristics of Five Offender Types," *American Sociological Review* 26 (1961), pp. 96–102.
84. Edwin M. Lemert, "The Behavior of the Systematic Check Forger"; Inciardi, *Careers in Crime*, pp. 25–28; and Bruce Jackson, *A Thief's Primer* (New York: Macmillan, 1969).
85. Jackson, *A Thief's Primer*, p. 23; see also Inciardi, *Careers in Crime*.
86. Lemert, "The Behavior of the Systematic Check Forger."
87. Bloch and Geis, *Man, Crime and Society*, pp. 179–80.
88. Inciardi, *Careers in Crime*, p. 27.
89. Ibid., pp. 23–24.
90. Roebuck and Johnson, "The 'Short Con' Man"; see also Gasser, "The Confidence Game."
91. Roebuck and Johnson, "The 'Short Con' Man," p. 236.
92. Sutherland, *The Professional Thief*, p. 3.
93. Inciardi, *Careers in Crime*, p. 24.
94. Gasser, "The Confidence Game," pp. 48–51.
95. Roebuck and Johnson, "The 'Short Con' Man," p. 239.
96. See Maurer, *The Big Con*.
97. Erving Goffman, "On Cooling the Mark Out: Some Aspects of Adaptation to Failure," *Psychiatry* 15 (1952), pp. 451–63.
98. Ibid., p. 456.

Occupational Crime

So far, our attention has focused almost exclusively on what might be called "traditional" crime and criminality. Robbery, murder, assault, burglary, and other street property offenses are traditional crimes in a number of senses. First, they are among the activities that most readily come to mind when we think of crime. Second, they are the conventional targets of official criminalization. Third, they have long been the prime focus of law enforcement efforts. And finally, it is primarily around these kinds of crime that criminologists have framed their theories of criminality.

To say that robbery, burglary, and interpersonal violence are traditional crimes is not to say that they are the most common forms of crime, nor that they have the greatest societal impact in terms of numbers of victims, economic costs, and damage to prevailing social institutions. Having far greater impact are occupational crimes.

What Is Occupational Crime?

As used here, the term *occupational crime* refers to illegal activities that occur in connection with a person's job. Occupational crime is preferred over the more conventional term *white-collar crime* because it makes no reference to the occupational status of the offender. When the late Edwin H. Sutherland coined the expression "white-collar crime" in the late 1930s, he had in mind crimes committed by persons of respectability and high social status in the course of their occupations.[1] He observed that criminologists had virtually ignored the illegal activities of those in business, politics, and the professions, concentrating instead on the world of lower-class criminality pictured in official statistics and emphasized in the normal routine of the administration of criminal justice. Lawbreaking, he argued, goes on in all social strata, and a vital criminology will focus on the full range of criminal activities. Among the illegal activities generally ignored, Sutherland believed, were those engaged in by middle- and upper-class individuals while performing their occupational roles. Such things as restraint of trade, misrepresentation in advertising, violations of labor laws, violations of copyright and patent laws, and financial manipulations were a part of what Sutherland called white-collar crime.

But as some authors have noted, Sutherland's emphasis on high social status results in the exclusion of a host of other occupation-related crimes that are similar to his white-collar offenses, in that (1) a person's legitimate occupation provides the context, and sometimes the motivation, for the offense; and (2) the offense (and offender) largely escapes official processing at the hands of legal authorities.[2] The broader notion of occupational crime thus includes criminal activities committed by anyone in connection with his or her job. (We do exclude, however, crimes that happen to occur during the course of a person's job but are not in themselves specifically job-related. In other words, a businessman who assaults his secretary commits a crime, but not an occupational crime; likewise, a dentist who murders a patient commits a crime, but not an occupational crime).

Types of Occupational Crime and Types of Offenders

Many different examples of occupational crime readily come to mind. Apart from the illegal activities already mentioned (restraint of trade, unfair labor practices, and so on), there is embezzlement, a variety of consumer frauds, thefts using a computer, music and record pirating, prescription law violations by physicians and pharmacists, employee pilfering at work, food and drug law violations, corporate tax violations, housing code violations, bribery and other forms of corruption by public officials, kickbacks, bid rigging, and real estate frauds — the list could go on.

While we bring these diverse crimes together under the umbrella of occupational crime, there are some important differences between them and between the persons who commit them. This has led some scholars to construct typologies of occupational crime (usually called white-collar crime in deference to Sutherland) in which similarities and differences are stressed. One typology was recently offered by Herbert Edelhertz, a former Justice Department official. Extending the notion of white-collar crime to include such nonoccupational offenses as personal violations of income tax laws, credit card frauds, and personal bankruptcy frauds, Edelhertz suggested the following typology:

1. *Crimes committed by persons on an individual, ad hoc basis* [individual income tax evasions; bankruptcy frauds; credit card frauds; social security frauds, credit purchases with no intent to pay]
2. *Crimes committed in the course of their occupations by those operating inside business, government, or other establishments, in violation of their duty of loyalty and fidelity to the employer or client* [bribery and kick-backs; embezzlement; employee pilfering; payroll padding].
3. *Crimes incidental to, and in furtherance of, business operations, but not the central purpose of the business* [antitrust violations; food and drug violations; misrepresentation in advertising; prescription fraud].
4. *Crime as a business or as the central activity of a business* [medical or health fraud schemes; land and real estate frauds; securities and commodities fraud; home improvement fraud schemes; charity and religious frauds; music pirating].[3]

While Edelhertz used what he called "general environment and motivation of the perpetrator" as the basis for his classification, there are other possibilities. One is to differentiate between occupational crimes on the basis of the victim constituency. One might, for example, distinguish among crimes that involve employers as victims and those that involve fellow employees, the public, or the government as victims. Or we might follow Bloch and Geis and distinguish among different offenders: persons acting as individuals against other individuals (lawyers, doctors, dentists, self-employed accountants), those committing crimes against the businesses that employ them (embezzlers), those in policy-making positions who commit crimes for the corporation (antitrust violators), agents of a corporation who victimize the general public (as in advertising fraud), and merchants victimizing their customers (as in shortchanging).[4]

Most of this chapter will be concerned with those types of occupational crime thought to be most prevalent and to have the greatest impact on the nature of social life in America. In organizing the material I have fashioned the discussion around categories 2, 3, and 4 of the Edelhertz typology. His category 1 is not included here, mainly because this category bears no clear connection with work, the essential criterion for separating occupational crime from other types of crime.

Work and the Historical Development of Legal Controls

Because of its intimate connection with the world of work, occupational crime cannot be divorced from technological advances and social change in general. While some crimes require no special technology or social arrangements in order to exist as a form of human conduct — rape and murder are examples — such is not the case with many occupational crimes. Thus if the phonograph had never been invented, there would be no record industry and no possibility for people to engage in record pirating.

Of course, some forms of occupational crime require less sophisticated and complex technologies and occupational arrangements than others. Certain forms of commercial fraud are possible with only a simple division of labor and a rudimentary system of economic exchange. In the simplest of cases it may merely be a matter of merchants shortchanging their customers via the manipulation of weights and measures — actions that have been possible since the time people first became dependent on others for particular goods and services and the complementary roles of buyer and seller were established.

In early legal codes we find evidence of attempts to regulate occupations and the practices possible in connection with them. The Code of Hammurapi, for example, lists a variety of work-related activities for which penalties and victim compensations of one kind or another were to be assessed. Here is a sampling:

> [Laws 53–54, dealing with the obligations of farmers:] If a man has neglected to maintain the dike of his field, and has not kept his dike strong enough so that a break has been found in the dike and he has let the water ravage the farmland, the man in whose dike the breach was opened shall make good the grain that he caused to be lost. If he cannot make good the grain, they shall sell him and his goods for silver, and the farmers whose grain the water carried off shall divide the proceeds.
>
> [Law 90 deals with loans and interest rates, and sets down that those lending grain or silver will forfeit the principal lent if they charge more than 20 percent interest.
>
> Laws 94–107 regulate commerce and the relations between business partners and the activities of salesmen. Apart from setting penalties for shortchanging customers (law 94), these laws establish what might be called the ethics of business.
>
> Laws 218–225 deal with physicians and veterinarians. For example, Law 218 specifies:] If a physician has performed a major operation on a patrician with a bronze knife and has caused the patrician to die, or opened up the eye-socket of a patrician with a bronzed knife and caused the destruction of the patrician's eye, they shall cut off his hand.
>
> [Law 229 covers shoddy work in the building trade:] If a builder has constructed a house for a man, but did not make his work strong, so that the house which he built collapsed and caused the death of the owner of the house, that builder shall be put to death. [Law 230 states that if a son of the owner is so killed, the builder's son shall be put to death.
>
> And finally, Law 253 deals with violation of trust and employee theft:] If a man has hired someone to oversee his field, and entrusted him with feed-grain, and entrusted cattle to him, and has contracted with him to cultivate the field, if that person has stolen the seed or fodder and it has been found in his possession, they shall cut off his hand.[5]

Though by no means as extensive as Hammurapi's regulations, the laws of various Anglo-Saxon kings also assessed monetary compensation or punitive sanctions against those violating work-related regulations. Among the activities brought under legal control were withholding of taxes, failure to carry out official duties, buying and selling outside designated market areas, minting of coins of base metals or of insufficient purity, and bribery of or by the kings' appointed officials.[6]

Some of these early laws were clearly designed to encourage orderly, predictable, and honest relations among persons dependent on others for their livelihoods. In this sense, laws governing work in general and certain occupations in particular can be seen as efforts to stabilize and cement some of the relations binding people to each other. It requires little imagination to see how important this must have been in a time when group survival was at best a questionable proposition.

INTERESTS AND OCCUPATIONAL CRIME

However, the full flavor of legal inroads into the realm of occupations is lost unless we also consider the role of special interests. Besides the fact that many past laws were weighted in favor of higher-status individuals, such that penalties for violation were less the higher one's social status, few laws formalized the obligations of masters and employers toward their servants, slaves, and employees. In addition, some laws were clearly designed to consolidate ruling-class control over economic and political activities and thus over the production and distribution of wealth and material advantages.

If we move to more recent periods in the history of laws dealing with the world of work, we have an opportunity to look more closely at the operation of special interests. Consider, for example, laws against embezzlement and criminal fraud.

Embezzlement   As we observed in the preceding chapter (see page 172), embezzlement first found its way into the statute books as a modification designed to plug gaps in the existing common law that were proving an annoyance to merchants and employers. Until 1529, the criminal liability of servants did not extend to instances in which they kept for themselves valuable goods that were in their legal possession by virtue of their role as bailees for their masters. This meant that a servant committed no crime if he subsequently converted to his own use things delivered into his possession in the course of his role as a servant. Responding to the obvious risk posed for employers by this gap in the common law, Henry VIII made the "imbezilment" of such goods a felony.

Still, the new law did not cover cases in which a third party gave servants or employees cash or goods for delivery to their masters, only to have them pocketed by the servant. In cases such as these the only recourse for the employer was to institute civil proceedings against his servant, employee, or agent. And things might well have remained this way had it not been for the expansion of commerce and trade and the subsequent rise of banking, accounting, and related business pursuits. The financial interests of the business community, coupled with its growing reliance on the trusted employee and business agent roles in commerce, moved members to look for additional protection under the criminal law. Once identified as crimes, embezzlement and other types of fraudulent conversions would become the targets of coercive repression, and the offenders the objects of punitive sanctions not available in civil dispositions. Their special interests at stake, businessmen thus sought modifications in the existing legal situation that would further entrench the weapons of criminal law in their corner. So in 1799 Parliament once again extended the embezzlement provisions, and later added the crimes of "false accounting" and "fraudulent conversion" to cover other features of the business relationship between employers and those working for them in positions of financial trust.[7]

Frauds When you induce someone to part with money or valuables through the use of deceit, lies, or misrepresentation you commit *fraud,* or what was called a "cheat" in earlier times. Under English common law the possibility of fraud had long been recognized; however, criminal liability was for centuries extended only to situations in which (1) some false token or tangible device of trickery was involved; and (2) the activity was such that reasonable prudence could not guard against it, and any member of the general public was its potential victim.[8] Under the common law, a personal fraud directed against a private individual was no crime, since it was customary to assume that individuals would exercise due caution in their financial dealings with others, and because if an individual were deceived, civil remedies were available.

With the extension of business and the growing complexities in commercial and industrial transactions associated with the rise of capitalism, entrepreneurs throughout the business community urged Parliament to broaden the range of criminal liability associated with fraudulent practices. In 1757 a statute was passed establishing the crime of "obtaining property by false pretenses." Subsequently adopted in the American colonies, this law has remained one of the few specifically criminal statutes dealing with fraud.

In fact, frauds can be perpetrated in many ways; the mechanics of fraud are limited only by one's imagination and ability. Sutherland and Cressey contend that fraud is probably "the most prevalent crime in America."[9] The victim of fraud can be anyone, but it is likely the most commonly deceived persons are consumers — those who buy goods and services from people in the business of selling — acting on their own behalf as private individuals. This so-called consumer fraud reaches all the way from the one-man small business to the immense and wealthy insurance companies, retail chains, and manufacturers of consumer goods. It costs the United States more than $25 billion a year.

Despite the extensive victimization associated with consumer fraud, the courts had until recently operated on the principle of *caveat emptor* — buyer beware. The idea was simply that in making a purchase, the consumer must protect himself against deception, and since he can presumably refuse to complete the transaction, he has only himself to blame if he gets "taken." Reasonable as this may sound, it actually encourages victimization in the modern marketplace, where the complex nature of many products and services and the techniques and organization of consumer transactions are such that even a prudent purchaser finds it well-nigh impossible to protect himself against fraud. For example, given modern supermarket packaging practices, shoppers can rarely inspect the products they want to buy in anything more than a superficial way. And if they want to make that inspection, they are forced to pay for the privilege, since the supermarkets generally undersell the small grocery stores where many products are still displayed without plastic wrapping and other "sanitary" devices.

Protection against consumer fraud has been slow to gain momentum largely because such efforts are not in the best interests of those in the business of selling and those in the various support industries of banking, financing, and advertising. Their interests lie in profits and dividends, and anything threatening these is heartily resisted. Despite these interests, events over the past few years have demonstrated that the interests of public health and safety — if not financial well-being — may at last be receiving some of the attention they deserve. This is best evidenced in the area of food, drugs, and cosmetics.

PURE FOOD AND DRUG LAWS

The production, distribution, and sale of food and drug products are now regulated by a variety of laws aimed at the protection of public health and safety. Interest in the regulation of the food and drug businesses first gained prominence during the latter part of the nineteenth century, as the consumer found himself further and further removed from agricultural producers and marketers, and the possibilities for adulteration, spoilage, exploitation, and fraud increased. Public awareness of the threats posed to their interests was enhanced partly through the changing experience of buying itself, but mostly by newspaper editorials, magazines, novels, and research findings in which the dangers of existing business practices were stressed, sometimes in lurid and frightening detail.

The first major federal legislation aimed at regulating the food and drug businesses was introduced in 1880 and soundly defeated, as were many subsequent bills. In his book, *The Therapeutic Nightmare,* Morton Mintz observes: "It and other efforts like it were defeated by a durable alliance of quacks, ruthless crooks, pious frauds, scoundrels, high-priced lawyer-lobbyists, vested interests, liars, corrupt members of Congress, venal publishers, cowards in high office, the stupid, the apathetic, and the duped.''[10] When Congress did finally pass the Federal Food and Drug Act of 1906, it was only the first step in what has turned out to be a long and hard battle between public interests and the food and drug industries.

The 1906 law declared it illegal to manufacture or introduce into an American state any adulterated or misbranded food or drug. Offenders could have their products seized, and those convicted of violating the law would be subject to criminal penalties. Thus a new area of occupational crime was born. But as Richard Quinney has observed:

> The need for revision of the act . . . became apparent shortly after its passage. The absence of adequate control over advertising provided an especially serious loophole for evasion of the spirit of the law, and labeling requirements of the law were such as to permit extravagant and unwarranted therapeutic claims for a product. Also, the 1906 act contained no provisions applying to cosmetics and failed to provide measures for safe and effective health devices.[11]

Some of these inadequacies were corrected by the 1938 Food, Drug, and Cosmetic Act, passed by both houses of Congress despite heavy resistance from the industries involved. Still, by the 1960s, nearly 100 years after public interest was first mobilized, Americans could count on one hand the number of truly significant bills designed to regulate the immense and powerful industries supplying our food, pharmaceutical products, and cosmetics. As Stuart Hills points out, "it has usually required a well-publicized major crisis to shock" legislatures into the passage of significant laws.[12] Such was the case when the Kefauver-Harris Drug Act of 1962 was passed: had it not been for the thousands of deformed babies born to mothers who had taken thalidomide during pregnancy, the bill would probably have failed.

If it were not for the efforts of Ralph Nader, the American public might still be buying meat products largely unregulated by legal controls. As long ago as 1906, Upton Sinclair had described the disgusting conditions of meat slaughterhouses in his highly popular novel, *The Jungle*. Writing in 1967, Ralph Nader pointed out that "we're still in the Jungle."[13] Following his own exhaustive investigation of the meat industry, Nader concluded that Americans were still buying meat products that were not only adulterated with substances ranging from water and cereals to toxic chemicals, but also were prepared under unsanitary conditions, contaminated with diseased and spoiled carcass pieces — even manure and pus — and often sold in a deceptive and fraudulent manner.

The reason, in Nader's view, was partly the substantial inadequacy of existing federal and state laws and partly the pitiful efforts to enforce them. Both the inadequacy of legal controls and their ineffective enforcement were blamed on the cozy relationship among the United States Department of Agriculture, state agriculture agencies, and the meat production and processing interests. Rather than ensure the safety of meat products and promote honesty in their packaging and sale, the interest shared by all concerned was to promote the sale of meat products. When Congress eventually passed the Wholesale Meat Act of 1968 — bringing intrastate meat processing under federal jurisdiction and establishing stricter controls — another small victory for public welfare was achieved and the range of legal penalties extended.

Violations of Loyalty and Fidelity to Employer or Client

Violations of loyalty and fidelity to employer or client, Edelhertz's second category of occupational crime, deals primarily with crimes committed by individuals acting in their own interest and against the interests of those who employ them or who are their clients. Embezzlement, other forms of employee theft, and political corruption are included in this category.

EMBEZZLEMENT

As we have already seen, embezzlement involves the conversion to his own use of funds or property entrusted to an employee or agent by another. Embezzlement is thus both theft and a violation of financial trust. It has, since its statutory origins in 1529, been regarded as a serious offense, and is a felony regardless of the amount embezzled. We might note, however, that the language of embezzlement statutes has not been easy to apply in the real world, and there is considerable variation from jurisdiction to jurisdiction, and from court to court. Donald Cressey observes that "persons whose behavior was not adequately described by the definition of embezzlement were found to have been imprisoned for that offense, and persons whose behavior was adequately described by the definition were confined for some other offense."[14] Cressey offered as his definition of embezzlement *the criminal violation of financial trust*. He further stipulated that to be called an embezzler a person must have accepted a position of trust in good faith and have violated that position by the commission of a crime.

When arrests for embezzlement are made, which is rare compared to the frequency of arrests for most other felony crimes, the suspect is usually a white middle-class middle-aged male, quite unlike the prevailing stereotype of the criminal. The embezzler has been called "the respectable criminal."[15] Respectable or not, estimates of the frequency and costs of embezzlement are staggering. In 1967, the President's Commission on Law Enforcement and the Administration of Justice put the annual cost at more than $200 million; that figure is dwarfed by a 1974 estimate of $4 billion.[16] Recent estimates of embezzlement through use of computers place the annual losses at $100 million, and a study of twelve cases put the average loss per offense at $1,090,000.[17]

The respectability of embezzlers mentioned by many authors acknowledges not only the relatively high occupational status of most offenders, but also the fact that they rarely have a delinquent or criminal record prior to their embezzling activities, and rarely think of themselves as real criminals. According to a study of 1,001 embezzlers conducted some years ago, the typical male embezzler is the epitome of the moderately successful family man. He is ". . . thirty-five, married, has one or two children. He lives in a respectable neighborhood and is probably buying his own home. He drives a low or medium priced car and his yearly income is in the top forty percent of the nation's personal income distribution."[18] The female embezzler also fits the picture of a respectable American, though her income was found to be in the bottom third of the nation's income distribution — a reflection of sex discrimination in jobs and salaries more than anything else.

Donald Cressey has conducted an in-depth study of embezzlement. In *Other People's Money,* Cressey bases his analysis on interviews with 133 persons in penitentiaries in Illinois, Indiana, and California. His findings regarding the etiology of embezzlement — the factors leading up to it — lead him to generalize that the embezzler commits his offense after (1) he comes up against a financial problem Cressey defines as "nonshareable"; (2) he recognizes that he can secretly resolve the problem by taking advantage of his position as one in whom financial trust is invested; and (3) he arms himself with an assortment of rationalizations and justifications, so that he can think of his subsequent actions as noncriminal and justified, and can retain a conception of self emphasizing that he is, in fact, still worthy of financial trust.

It is clear that without the possibility of violating financial trust that comes with the embezzler's occupational position one important part of the etiological chain would be missing. But it is the presence of a nonshareable problem and the adoption of justifiable rationalizations that lie at the heart of Cressey's explanation. By a *nonshareable* problem Cressey has in mind almost any kind of financial difficulty the individual feels cannot be resolved by enlisting the help of another. It could be some unusual family expense or gambling debts, once thought the major cause of embezzlement.[19] It could even be linked to his attempts to keep up a particular standard of living. As for the role of rationalization, this process occurs before, or at least during, *but not after,* the act of embezzling. Many of Cressey's subjects, and especially those who had been independent business men, reasoned that they would be merely "borrowing" the money, or that it really belonged to them anyway. The embezzler-to-be would often argue that he was merely adhering to a standard business practice, borrowing against future earnings. Looked at sequentially, then, the nonshareable problem leads to the search for a personal and secret solution; the position of financial trust provides the means to solve the problem; and the rationalization provides the final push.

Cressey's explanation of embezzlement has not been without its critics. One of the most damaging criticisms was put forward by Karl Schuessler in a review published by the *American Journal of Sociology*. Schuessler noted that Cressey's generalization, based as it is on an *ex post facto* (after the fact) inductive analysis using only actual offenders, sits upon a weak methodological foundation and cannot be verified:

> The finding that all cases in the sample had a single set of circumstances in common does not, unhappily, prove that all persons in such circumstances will embezzle. The empirical validation would require an unselected group of persons having in common the hypothesized circumstances who then should all subsequently display the expected behavior. Needless to say, Cressey's proposition is impossible to test.[20]

A different criticism comes from Gwynn Nettler, whose own study could not substantiate Cressey's emphasis on the nonshareable financial problem as a precondition for embezzlement. Nettler's embezzlers were apparently driven to their crimes by temptation and avarice, and their jobs provided the opportunity and the means.[21] It does not look as if the explanation of embezzlement is a matter of consensus as yet.

EMPLOYEE PILFERING

Cressey's study, despite the criticisms, remains a competitive theory. Indeed, one element of Cressey's argument has proved most productive in the study of criminal behavior, his emphasis on the role of verbalized rationalizations prior to illegal behavior. We have already noted the importance of this idea in the work of Gresham Sykes and David Matza on delinquency (see pages 44–45), and we find it surfacing again in attempts to explain employee pilfering.

It is virtually impossible to assess with accuracy the losses to employee pilferage. Estimates, however, usually place them in the billions of dollars annually, and it is probable that employee theft is far more prevalent than shoplifting, the other major cause of what companies call "inventory shrinkage." The retail industry alone estimates that 75 to 80 percent of all shrinkage is the result of some kind of dishonesty. In 1967, that represented more than $1.3 billion;[22] today it is probably closer to $10 billion. In nonretail businesses, the losses to employee pilferage are even harder to estimate, for there is little reliable information and many companies find it impossible to keep track of all the property and valuables within a plant, office building, or warehouse.

Employee pilferage takes numerous forms and is by no means an exclusive activity of the lower-level employee. Indeed, Norman Jaspan has reported that 62 percent of the $60 million lost by selected retail stores in one year alone was stolen by employees at the executive or supervisory levels.[23] Further, in his investigation of three department store companies, Gerald Robin found that when executives were known to have stolen from the company, their thefts averaged larger amounts than those of lower-level employees.[24] There are different kinds of employee pilferage: casual thievery and systematic, repetitive thievery; thievery by individuals and thievery by groups of employees working together; thievery that victimizes the company and thievery that victimizes clients or other employees; the theft of cash and securities and the theft of tools, merchandise, parts, finished products, and materials; there is even the theft of wages, when employees ensure themselves overtime pay for work that could have been completed during regular working hours.

An informative study of employee pilferage was conducted recently by Donald Horning. The author conducted his investigation at a midwestern electronics assembly plant and focused on what he calls "blue-collar theft," defined for the purposes of his study as "the illegal or unauthorized utilization of facilities or removal and conversion to one's own use of company property or personal property located on the plant premises by nonsalaried personnel employed in the plant."[25] He interviewed eighty-eight operatives and found that 91 percent admitted having pilfered at least once. Horning discovered that the workers conceived of three types of property: (1) company property; (2) personal property; and (3) property of uncertain ownership. The hard core of company property consisted of buildings, fixtures, heavy machinery, power tools, and expensive components, such as TV picture tubes and transformers. Personal property was visualized as anything known to belong to fellow workers or marked with someone's name: wallets, lunch boxes, modified tools, and clothing.

The property category identified as the central object of theft activities was property of uncertain ownership. This consisted of unmarked clothing, screws, nuts, bolts, scraps, waste, small tools, and loose money. These items were considered fair game by the employees. For one thing, there was no clearly identified victim. For another, the workers saw themselves as having legitimate possession of many such items, the company having placed them at their disposal. Interestingly, this harkens back to the old common law notion that you cannot steal what has been lawfully placed in your possession.

Horning found that the employees had armed themselves with a set of verbalized motives or justifiable rationalizations for their behavior: "It's a corporation. . . . It's not like taking from one person"; "The company doesn't mind"; "They've got plenty . . . they're not losing anything on what I take"; "Everyone is doing it." While it is not clear that these rationalizations are invoked prior to the illicit conduct, as Cressey argued in the case of embezzlement, a number of things point to this conclusion. First, the existence of an attitudinal milieu in support of the pilferage of certain items and yet *against the pilferage of others* provides workers with a normative framework within which to shape their own subsequent conduct. The fact that pilferage of personal items was rare while the pilferage of items of uncertain ownership was found to be pervasive suggests the adoption of appropriate rationalizations *before* theft is committed. In other words, rather than rationalization merely excusing conduct after it has occurred, the discrimination in the choice of theft items suggests action guided by these rationalizations.

POLITICAL CORRUPTION

This section would certainly be incomplete if we ignored occupational crime in government and politics. While it would be comforting to believe that those we entrust with running our local, state, and federal governments are free of job-related criminality, the realities are such that there would be little substance to our comfort.

We speak of political corruption when office-holders in government and politics violate the laws regulating their official conduct so as to benefit themselves or specific others, or use the power and influence associated with their office to induce others to commit crimes. We may encounter political corruption at the city, county, state, and federal levels of the political process.

Forms of Political Corruption It is generally argued that political corruption manifests itself in two different, though often related, forms: (1) activities designed to bring about economic gain; and (2) activities designed to perpetuate or increase political power.[26] The government official who accepts or demands a monetary kickback in return for legislation favorable to some individual or special group is engaged in corrupt activities that promise economic gains. The politician who arranges to have cronies stuff ballot boxes with the names of nonexistent voters is engaged in a corrupt practice designed to keep him in office, or put him there. Needless to say, those who gain economically from corrupt activities may also gain political power; and, conversely, those who gain political power may also gain financially. Thus it is sometimes difficult to separate the economic from the power dimension of political corruption.

It is pointless to speculate on the prevalence of corrupt practices among those in government. We simply have no way of knowing how extensive political corruption is, and we are unlikely ever to find out with any certainty. In fact, it could be that the more corruption we know about, the less there actually is, for it is in the nature of corrupt practices that they thrive under a cloak of secrecy and third-party indifference. Reading today's newspapers might lead one to argue that corruption is more prevalent now than in the past; but that is speculation based on the flimsiest of evidence. What we can say with reasonable assurance is that the opportunities for corruption are probably greater today than they have ever been. As governments have come to dominate more and more areas of social life, and have expanded their roles as employers, producers, consumers, taxers, and spenders, those in political jobs have found an expanding number of opportunities to reap illicit benefits from their position in the occupational structure.[27]

Finding out about political corruption is no easy task, and this is as true for the criminologist and political scientist as it is for the general public. One reason is the insider-outsider barrier that politicians tend to erect in their dealings with others who are not part of the political establishment. Another is the cronyism characterizing relations among politicians and their friends in business and government; this leads to a kind of "mutual protection and aid society" and encourages a "politics is politics" attitude among insiders, who would rather look the other way than make public trouble for a colleague. It is instructive to note in this regard that during the entire history of the United States Congress, only seven senators and eighteen representatives were censured by their colleagues as of June 1976.[28]

A third reason is that the agencies responsible for policing the politicians are themselves run by politicians. If an investigation of a particular official or agency is called for, it is usually pursued without fanfare and rarely results in the pressing of formal charges. Even when an investigation is reliably known to be under way, heads of the responsible agencies will often deny it. Fourth, it should come as no surprise that there are no national (or regional) statistics on the kinds of occupational crime committed by those in politics and government. One looks in vain for "official misconduct," "high crimes and misdemeanors," "bribery," "influence peddling," and so forth, in either the Part I or Part II offense lists published by the FBI in their annual *Uniform Crime Reports*. In fact, the only specifically occupational crime listed at all is embezzlement, which victimizes the establishment.

We become aware of political corruption primarily through the efforts of journalists and those who keep a constant watch on government in the public interest; for example, "Nader's Raiders" and Common Cause. Sometimes corruption comes to light because persons involved in it turn informer. Such was the case with the 1976 scandal involving Representative Wayne Hays and his former secretary Elizabeth Ray. The latter made public charges asserting that Hays had, among other things, put her on his office payroll because she furnished sex — not secretarial work, as her official job would lead one to believe.

Crimes for Money The political occupational crimes that come to light are usually notable because they have been committed by high officials, have involved substantial losses to the taxpayer, or have represented a systematic and extensive violation of public trust or civil rights. During the last few years, political corruption at the national and international levels has so dominated the headlines that more local scandals seem mild by comparison. Actually, the victimization brought about by local corruption may have a more far-reaching and harmful effect on the lives of Americans. When, as happened recently in a midsized Illinois city, school board officials misappropriate thousands of dollars in school funds, it may take years to overcome the damage to education, not to mention public trust.

In the course of their political careers, government officials sometimes find their past catching up with them after they have moved up from local and regional to national prominence. Such was the case with ex-Vice-President Spiro Agnew. It was revealed that while he had been governor of Maryland, and earlier while a county official, Agnew had received kickbacks from contractors doing business with the county and state governments. Upon these disclosures, Agnew resigned the vice-presidency and subsequently pleaded "no contest" to an income tax violation charge ("no contest" is not a plea of guilty, but subjects the defendant to conviction). Another case of corruption that came to light after the offender had become an official of the federal government involved Judge Otto Kerner, formerly the governor of Illinois. Kerner was tied to an Illinois scandal involving offers of racetrack stock to politicians. Subsequently he was convicted of numerous criminal offenses, including perjury, and became the first federal judge ever to spend time in prison. Kerner died in 1976, shortly after his early release from federal prison because of illness. These cases, in which bribery and kickbacks were prominent, clearly involve corruption for economic gain. To them can be added other cases that have tarnished the image of officials in government.[29]

Political corruption for economic gain is made possible, and probable, primarily because of the tight links between politics and business. Aside from the fact that for years businesses provided financial support for political campaigns, and that governments dispense billions of dollars worth of contracts to industry, there is also the fact that many government officials retain, while in office, a financial interest in business pursuits. Members of Congress, from newcomers to those in such powerful positions as minority leader, party whip, or committee chairman, remain active in businesses ranging from real estate and insurance to construction, law, oil, and gas. Temptations for abuse of their political connections abound, particularly when proposed legislation or government contracts bear upon personal finances and those of business colleagues.

The extensiveness of the connection between business and politics is best illustrated by the 1976 international scandal involving payoffs to foreign government officials by multinational corporations based in the

United States. Uncovered in the post-Watergate period of government and press investigations of political corruption, the scandal brought charges of payoffs to politicians and government officials around the world for their aid in granting lucrative government contracts to U.S. corporations. By early 1976, forty corporations had been accused of such bribes and other questionable payoff practices, and some of the United States' largest corporate concerns were admitting their involvement. For example, Gulf Oil admitted paying $4 million to the South Korean ruling party and $460,000 to Bolivian officials; Burroughs Corporation admitted $1.5 million in improper payments to foreign officials. Aircraft companies such as Lockheed, Northrop, and McDonnell Douglas admitted by far the largest bribes, payoffs, and questionable commissions. As sellers of military and civilian aircraft, these companies stood to gain or lose billions of dollars in government contracts, and they aggressively pursued any avenue to acquisition of those contracts. Lockheed was charged by Senator Frank Church's Subcommittee on Multinational Corporations with paying an incredible $202 million to foreign officials in Japan, the Netherlands, Turkey, Italy, and elsewhere. Even more recently McDonnell Douglas was indicted in federal court for paying $1 million in bribes to Pakistani International Airlines officials.[30] These schemes will not work, of course, unless some politicians and government officials are willing to accept the bribes, and so violate public trust, not to mention the criminal laws of their country.

Crimes for Power   Where corruption for purposes of acquiring, retaining, or increasing one's political power is concerned, the Watergate scandal immediately comes to mind. Brought to light following the uncovering of a June 1972 burglary attempt at the Democratic National Committee headquarters in the Watergate hotel and apartment complex in Washington, D.C., the Watergate affair resulted in the first resignation of a U.S. president and touched people in all areas of national politics. Due in part to vigorous investigative journalism by *Washington Post* reporters Carl Bernstein and Bob Woodward, the American public was given a two-year in-depth look at political corruption at its worst. Not only had the White House been deeply involved in the scandals, but also included were a former secretary of the treasury, the attorney general of the United States, officials of the FBI, CIA, and Internal Revenue Service, persons connected with organized crime, international terrorists, and even some whose records looked little different from the street criminals who are the routine business of local police departments.

The central theme around which the Watergate affair revolved was clearly one of political power. The involvement of the Committee to Re-Elect the President, the activities of White House staffers, and the routine subversive manipulation of government agencies by Richard Nixon and his allies bear this out. Here was an incident, or rather a combination of incidents, in which maintaining and extending power stood as the central goal. The string of events began in early 1972, when the office of Daniel Ellsberg's psychiatrist was burglarized so that evidence from the files could be used to political advantage. During the presidential campaign of that year, Nixon supporters and staffers committed various illegal actions: the United States Postal Service was used for fraudulent and libelous purposes, an aspect of the so-called dirty tricks used to discredit Democratic opponents; the Watergate break-in itself was for the purpose of "bugging" the Democratic National Committee headquarters and scrutinizing its files; the Internal Revenue Service was pressured to harass political opponents and Nixon's so-called enemies; the FBI and CIA were encouraged to obstruct justice so that these and other criminal activities would not come to light, and if they did come to light, would not be linked with the White House; "hush money" was paid to the Watergate burglars; public funds were misused and campaign contributions solicited in violation of federal laws. Eventually, White House staffers were fired and government officials forced to resign in a last-ditch effort to plug the ever-widening holes in the defenses around the Oval Office.

In the summer of 1974 the House of Representatives' Judiciary Committee voted to impeach President Nixon. He was charged with obstruction of justice and failure to carry out his constitutional oath and duty to uphold the laws of the United States. He resigned on August 9, 1974. Much still remains unknown about the political corruption in Richard Nixon's administration. Nixon himself was pardoned by President Gerald Ford, thus making it unlikely that the true nature of his offenses will ever come to light. One is certainly left wondering whether anything would have come to light had it not been for the ill-fated break-in of the Watergate and the tenacity of two young reporters in search of news.

Writing in 1970, before Watergate, James Boyd noted that in American public life "there is no sense of honor, no concept of it, no expectation of it, no reward for it." This, Boyd contended, was a basic premise underlying what he called the "ritual of wiggle." The ritual is an enduring feature of political folk wisdom among public officials and consists of a series of steps or rules to follow if those in public life are confronted with charges of misconduct and expect to weather whatever storm develops. It is instructive to consider Boyd's comments here, for they give us some clues as to why political corruption persists and will continue to persist even in the face of scandals such as Watergate, which have sharpened public scrutiny and distrust of politics and politicians. Corruption persists because even when confronted with exposure and the possibility of ruin, the "ritual of wiggle" helps to redefine the wrong as right, or at least acceptable, and guards against discovery of the "whole truth," against loss of political career, and against punishment commensurate with the gravity of the offenses. Here are the steps of the wiggle:

1. Admit nothing until you know the worst; if it looks like a one-shot affair, hide till it blows over.
2. If you must speak out — confess to what is known, evade what is unknown, and cry.
3. If at all possible, give the money (if money is involved) back — or at least give it to someone else.
4. If partial confession and restitution fail to stem the headlines, arrange a quickie exoneration from a semirespected source (e.g., the House Speaker, the respective chairmen of the Senate and House Ethics Committees, the attorney general).
5. If the unpleasantness persists, use the "stranger in paradise" routine: You can't help it if goodhearted friends have an urge to shower you with gifts or if lucky fate strews your path with roses.
6. Insist that you would have done the same favor for any constituent.
7. At the moment of deepest personal disgrace, announce for reelection.
8. Set up a series of endorsements by prominent churchmen.
9. It's time to pick a scapegoat.
10. If the newsmen persist, bolder moves are advisable: issue a statement requesting an official investigation.
11. Threaten a multimillion-dollar libel suit against your accusers but don't file it; if you must file it for tactical reasons, withdraw it before it gets to trial.
12. When judicial proceedings become inevitable, claim constitutional immunity.
13. During trial or impeachment proceedings, observe the traditional formalities [some of which are listed below]:
    a. Never appear in public without your wife; be sure that your entire family, including preschool children, attend every court session.
    b. Feign illness and a sort of stunned vacuity, as if the indignity of it all is too much for your sensitive nature.
    c. When questioned by the press in the hallways, emphasize how you welcome the chance to clear your name, how you asked for this trial, how the only thing that bothers you is the suffering it's inflicting on your family.
    d. If convicted, abandon all dignity and beg for mercy.[31]

Crimes Incidental to, and in Furtherance of, Business Operations

This section deals with occupational crimes arising in connection with business pursuits that are not the central purpose of the business. They are committed *on behalf of* business interests, sometimes by individuals, sometimes by groups; they surface among the self-employed and among executives of companies large and small. We shall concentrate on corporate activities that violate laws governing commerce and trade.

Business and politics go hand in hand, especially where government contracts are concerned. Aircraft manufacturers have been implicated time and again in scandals involving payoffs to government functionaries and other illegal practices.

RESTRAINT OF TRADE

Among the occupational crimes committed by corporate decision makers on behalf of their organizations are those violating state and federal laws dealing with restraint of trade. The major federal statute involved is the Sherman Antitrust Act of 1890. Designed to curb the threat to a competitive, free-enterprise economy posed by the nineteenth-century spread of trusts and monopolies, this act made it a criminal misdemeanor for individuals or organizations to engage in restraint of trade by combining or forming monopolies to that end.

There are three principal methods of restraint of trade: (1) consolidation, so as to obtain a monopoly position; (2) price fixing to achieve price uniformity; and (3) price discriminations, in which higher prices are charged to some customers and lower ones to others.[32] From the standpoint of those engaging in these practices, they make admirable sense:

the less the competition and the greater the control over prices, the larger the profits. But the small and independent businesses will lose business and the public at large will face higher prices and loss of discretionary buying power.

The most common violations of restraint of trade laws involve price fixing and price discrimination. In Sutherland's investigation of seventy of the largest American corporations over a fifty-year period, violations of this sort (including the illegal use of rebates) were the most prevalent restraint of trade activities. Interestingly, many of the suits charging restraint of trade through price fixing and discrimination were brought by private interests rather than by the Federal Trade Commission or the Department of Justice, the two agencies given primary responsibility for the enforcement of restraint of trade provisions. In this as well as in other areas of occupational crime, where corporate decision makers break the law on behalf of their organizations, officialdom has not been at its most aggressive in ferreting out violations and bringing charges. But this should hardly come as a surprise, given the intimate relationship between business and politics.

The Sears-Goodyear Case The following account given by Sutherland describes a case of price discrimination that, while typical of the pattern followed in other cases, ended in a dismissal of the suit brought against the companies involved:

> The discrimination favoring the large purchaser is shown in the suit against Goodyear Tire and Rubber Co., and Sears, Roebuck and Co., which was finally dismissed on a technicality although the facts of discrimination seemed to be adequately proved. Goodyear made a contract with Sears Roebuck to furnish tires under a special brand at cost plus six percent; these tires, except in the brand name, were identical with the tires sold under Goodyear's name. From 1926 to 1933 Sears Roebuck bought approximately 200,000,000 casings and 17,500,000 tubes at a price $42,000,000 lower than the figure at which the same tires would have been sold to independent tire dealers. . . . Goodyear sold 18 percent of its entire output of tires to Sears Roebuck under these contracts and received in payment only 11 percent of its income from the sale of tires. Because of this preferential price, Sears Roebuck cut the retail price of tires by approximately 25 percent and still had a profit of approximately 40 percent. The independent tire dealers appealed to Goodyear for assistance in meeting the competition of Sears Roebuck, since the contracts between Goodyear and Sears Roebuck were not known to outsiders [i.e., the dealers were unaware of Sears' preferential position]. Goodyear produced a new tire to meet the competition but it was inferior in quality and proved inadequate. The consequence was that approximately half of the independent tire dealers in the United States in 1926 had abandoned this business by 1931. . . .
>
> The price discrimination not only gave Sears Roebuck a monopolistic position in the sale of tires but also gave it a great control over Goodyear. Sears

Roebuck exercised its right to inspect the Goodyear books as to costs, and during the life of these contracts disallowed from half a million to one million dollars a year claimed by Goodyear as costs. When the first contract terminated in 1928, Sears Roebuck claimed that other tire manufacturers were prepared to make better offers than Goodyear had made, and insisted that Goodyear build a new plant in the South in order to reduce the freight charges for the southern trade of Sears Roebuck. Although the president of Goodyear asserted that this additional capacity was not needed, he was forced, in order to secure a renewal of the contract, to build a plant at Gadsden, Alabama, at a cost of $9,000,000. While the renewal of that contract was under consideration, Sears Roebuck forced additional concessions in the form of a gift by Goodyear of 18,000 shares of common stock of the Goodyear corporation plus $800,000 cash with which to purchase 32,000 additional shares, making a total of 50,000 shares with an approximate market value of $2,250,000.[33]

Reading this, one might imagine that Goodyear suffered. Sears, Roebuck got rich, and the public was blessed with an opportunity to buy good tires at lower prices. While Sears certainly benefited financially from the deal, Goodyear did not suffer, for 18 percent was a healthy chunk of its business. But the public would not really benefit from the arrangement, at least in the long run. Unchecked, practices such as these inevitably lead to higher, not lower, prices for the consumer, not to mention a decline in purchasing discretion.

"The Great Electrical Conspiracy"　In 1961, twenty-one corporations and forty-five high-ranking executives in the heavy electrical equipment industry were successfully prosecuted for criminal violations of the Sherman Antitrust Act. They had been involved in a price fixing and bid rigging scheme that, over nearly a decade, had bilked local, state, and federal governments (and the taxpayer) out of millions of dollars on purchases averaging nearly $2 *billion* a year.[34]

In carrying out their scheme — called by the trial judge, "the most serious violations of the antitrust laws since the time of their passage at the turn of the century" — executives of the conspiring companies would meet secretly under fictitious names in hotel rooms around the country. Referring to those in attendance as "the Christmas card list," and to the meetings as "choir practice," the conspirators arranged prices for equipment, allocated markets and territories, and agreed on which companies would supply the low bids on pending government contracts. The participants covered their tracks well, and were only discovered because officials of the Tennessee Valley Authority had received identical sealed bids on highly technical equipment. The companies involved in the conspiracy ranged from such giants in the electrical equipment business as General Electric, Westinghouse, and Allis-Chalmers, to such smaller firms as the Carrier Corporation, the I.T.E. Circuit Breaker Company, and Federal Pacific.

Some Recent Price Conspiracies   At least three other large-scale price-fixing conspiracies have come to light in the years since the electrical equipment conspiracy.[35] Though significant primarily because of their overall economic impact and the extensiveness of the conspiracies, they doubtless represent but a small portion of all price-fixing activity.

In 1967, the Senate Antitrust Subcommittee found evidence of an international scheme to corner the market and inflate the price of a chemical derivative of quinine. Directly involved were British, American, and Dutch companies, and complicity was discovered on the part of officials in the State Department and General Services Administration of the United States. As far as the financial aspects of the conspiracy were concerned, the international cartel was able to sell for three dollars an ounce what cost them twenty-one cents to produce. The public, of course, paid more; among those relying on the drug are elderly persons with heart problems.

In another case involving drugs, American Cyanamid, Charles Pfizer, Bristol Myers, and other major pharmaceutical companies were convicted of price fixing and monopolistic practices in their distribution and sale of certain antibiotics. In the case of one drug, tetracycline, it was discovered that the conspirators guaranteed a markup of 3,350 percent! For example, one hundred 250-milligram capsules were produced for $1.52, sold to druggists for $20.60, and then to customers for $51. In 1971, after the conspiracy ended, these same hundred capsules sold for $5 at the retail level. Once again, the victims of this conspiracy included non-involved competitors and the general public, especially those in need of the particular antibiotics.

The third major price conspiracy involved a four-year period of price fixing and illegal market manipulation by fifteen plumbing fixture manufacturers and eight executives. With total sales over $1 billion a year, American Standard and its fourteen coconspirators cheated wholesale and retail customers by setting artificially high prices and by stifling competition — together they controlled nearly 100 percent of total American sales of enameled cast-iron plumbing fixtures and 80 percent of vitreous china fixture sales.[36] All conspirators pleaded guilty or "no contest" in 1969.

CONSUMER FRAUD: MISREPRESENTATION IN ADVERTISING AND SALES PROMOTION

Consumers become the victims of fraud in many different ways. In this section we shall focus on misrepresentation in advertising and sales. Misrepresentation in advertising means that what prospective buyers are told about a product is untrue, deceptive, or misleading. Sometimes the misrepresentation is in regard to the quantity of a product or the actual contents of a package or container; sometimes it concerns the effectiveness of a product; and sometimes it is a lack of information or insufficient information regarding a product or service such that buyers are misled.

The fact that a fine line divides fraudulent and nonfraudulent sales promotion will become evident as we consider a problem faced by nearly all businesses: creating a need for their products and services.[37] Many of the things we consider necessities today — canned foods, refrigerators, automobiles, insurance polices — either did not exist a few decades ago or were thought of as luxuries, certainly not necessities. We have come to think of them as necessities largely because the companies selling them have convinced us to do so. When things are necessities, people want to purchase them.

In their efforts to convince us that we need their goods and services, businesses use a variety of different ploys. To use a *fraudulent* ploy is to make false claims as to the effectiveness of a product in doing what it is supposed to do. Those who believe the claims will see a need for the product. An example is the advertising plan followed some time ago by the makers of Listerine. In their campaign, the makers sought to create a need for Listerine as a mouthwash, a fairly new idea at the time, and to establish that need they presented fake claims as to the germ-killing powers of the mixture.[38]

Less clearly fraudulent, though possibly more dangerous to health, are the recent sales promotions of vaginal deodorants, discussed here by Burton Leiser:

> The creation of a need is best exemplified by a new line of products that is just emerging. The advertisers have been going all out to convince women of the need for vaginal deodorants. Full-page advertisements have appeared in women's magazines recently, and on television as well, designed to convince women of the need for these deodorants and of the effectiveness of particular brands. A typical ad says:
>
> "Some sprays hide it. Some sprays mask it. But Vespre actually prevents intimate odor.
> "*Made especially for the external vaginal area.* Unlike sprays that only hide odor, Vespre feminine hygiene deodorant stops odor-causing bacteria. Contains twice the active odor-fighter of other leading sprays.
> "*Tested by gynecologists.* Vespre was tested in leading hospitals. It's so effective it works all day, every day of the month. . . ."[39]

What makes these sprays potentially dangerous is that when used regularly they may mask vaginal odor, which can be a sign of infection or disease. Also, they can themselves contribute to skin irritations and other troublesome reactions. Leiser goes on:

> Vespre, Easy Day, and similar preparations are totally unnecessary and may be harmful. But a demand is being created for them by extensive advertising campaigns designed to market products that would never have been missed if they had not been produced. . . .

We may suppose that nothing false has been stated in these advertisements. But lying behind each of them there is a suppressed premise — one that the reader is expected to supply for herself — namely, the assumption that women need vaginal deodorants. But this suppressed premise is false. To be sure, every woman can consult her physician to find out whether she really needs these products, but few will ever do so. Many, worried about their attractiveness, and insecure, perhaps, over a fear that they may have an unappealing odor that they themselves cannot perceive, will accept the suppressed premise uncritically and, in the process, make the marketers of Vespre and Easy Day and similar products rich.[40]

As noted, sales promotion strategies such as that just described may not be fraudulent — in the criminal sense. But it is only a short step from these strategies to those the common swindler uses. As an example of clearly fraudulent attempts to create needs, consider the activities of the Holland Furnace Company. This company was in the business of selling home heating furnaces. With some five hundred offices and a sales force in the thousands, the company put its resources to work on a fraudulent sales promotion involving misrepresentation, destruction of property, and, in some cases, what amounted to extortion:

> Salesmen, misrepresenting themselves as "furnace engineers" and "safety inspectors," gained entry into their victims' homes, dismantled their furnaces, and condemned them as hazardous. They then refused to reassemble them, on the ground that they did not want to be "acessories to murder." Using scare tactics, claiming that the furnaces they "inspected" were emitting carbon monoxide and other dangerous gases, they created, in the homeowners' minds, a need for a new furnace — and proceeded to sell their own product at a handsome profit. They were so ruthless that they sold one elderly woman nine new furnaces in six years for a total of $18,000. The FTC finally forced the company to close in 1965, but in the meantime, it had done some $30 million worth of business per year for many years.[41]

Though blatant and outright swindles, the activities of Holland Furnace Company salesmen and other purveyors of consumer fraud differ, in Leiser's view, only marginally from those of the sellers of mouthwash, vaginal deodorants, and a host of other "necessary" products:

> The difference between the cosmetic manufacturer who is trying to persuade women that they need vaginal deodorants and the exterminator who brings his own termites to display to customers whose homes he has inspected, claiming that he found them in the foundation of the home, is one of degree only. To be sure, the advertiser does not victimize any one person to the same degree. He gets rich by extracting a little money from multitudes of women, rather than by taking a lot from a very few gullible people. He has not pulled bricks from his victim's home or dismantled her furnace. But he has produced a pocketful of termites that weren't there when he arrived.[42]

With more than $20 billion spent annually on advertising, businesses are making an enormous investment in the art of persuasion. Given such an investment it should come as no surprise that those making it seek all possible avenues to a healthy payoff. If it were simply a matter of meeting their investment, they would have no reason to spend the money in the first place; but companies expect to make a considerable profit out of the enterprise. To make that expectation a reality the emphasis inevitably comes down on the side of persuasion, rather than honesty and concern that prospective consumers be told all that would be beneficial to them. It hardly bodes well for the future when young business students hold the opinion that forms of deception in advertising can be acceptable business practice and are not immoral.[43]

Misrepresentation, deception, and falsehood in sales promotion surface in all advertising media, and it is not just the large corporations, with their immense advertising budgets, that find themselves charged with this kind of occupational crime. Small concerns advertising in local newspapers and on billboards are just as prone to the practice as their wealthier business colleagues. A sense of the range and extensiveness of misrepresentation in advertising is provided by Edwin Sutherland in this list of products found in the typical home that have been advertised in violation of legal regulations:

> In the kitchen: Kelvinator, Quaker Oats, Wheaties, Cream of Wheat, Swans Down Cake Flour, Fleishmann's Yeast, Knox Gelatin, Kraft-Phoenix Cheese, Carnation Milk, Horlick's Malted Milk, Diamond Crystal Salt, Morton's Salt, Welch's Grape Juice, Nehi.
>
> In the laundry: Ivory Soap, P & G Naphtha Soap, Chipso, Palmolive Soap.
>
> In the bathroom: Scott's Tissue Toilet Paper, Dr. Lyon's tooth powder (or almost any other tooth powder or tooth paste), Schick Dry Shaver, Wildroot Hair Tonic, Ingram's Shaving Cream, Marlin razor blades, Drene, Herpicide.
>
> In the medicine chest: Phillip's Milk of Magnesia, Piso, Zonite, Absorbine Jr., Pond's Extract, Retongo, Smith Brothers Cough Drops, Bayer's Aspirin.
>
> On the dressing table: Cutex, Peroxide, Ingram's Milkweed Cream, Coty's cosmetics, Vivadou, Djer Kiss Talc, Mavis Talcum Powder, Elizabeth Arden cosmetics, Murine Eye Wash.
>
> In the man's wardrobe: Hart, Schaffner & Marx suits, and Cluett Peabody shirts.
>
> In other parts of the house: Fanny Farmer candy, Life Savers, Wurlitzer piano, Philco radio (or almost any other radio), Hoover Sweeper, Remington Typewriter (or almost any other typewriter), and the Encyclopaedia Britannica.
>
> In the garage: Buick automobile (or almost any other standard automobile), equipped with Goodyear or almost any other standard tires, with Perfect Circle Piston Rings, and lubricated with Quaker State Oil.[44]

Sutherland wrote this in the 1940s, but there is little reason to presume that things have changed since then, that companies are now providing honest, clear, and full information in their promotional campaigns. The truth is quite to the contrary. Advertising deception and fraud continues

1974

Airlines: Jan. 6: Air France agrees to terminate deceptive practices in connection with promotion of its flights and tours to Europe. May 4: TWA charged in suit with failure to live up to advertised quality and warranty specifications on its first class tours to Spain and Portugal.

Automobiles: Feb. 14: Fram oil filter ads ruled misleading. June 18: Ford Motor Co. and J. Walter Thompson, Inc. agree to end deceptive ads regarding steel reinforcements and the level of noise in Ford cars. Aug. 1: FTC moves against ads dealing with fuel economy claims by GM, Ford, and Chrysler during energy crisis.

Birth Control: American Cyanamid charged with misleading promotion of its Zorane birth control pills.

Cleansers: March 12: Clorox and Calgon agree to change labels and ads on two products after charges that they were misleading. Oct. 11: Sterling Drug agrees to change or stop certain ads for Lysol Deodorizing Cleaner.

Cold Remedies: April 11: Warner-Lambert is ordered to state in its advertisements that Listerine will not prevent or cure colds.

Disinfectant: June 15: Sterling Drug agrees to stop deceptive advertisements claiming that Lysol disinfectant kills germs associated with colds, flu, sore throats.

Divorce: July 26: Latinamerica Co. charged with violating the Consumer Protection Law by misleading Spanish-speaking persons into thinking that they can get divorces in 24 hours.

Drugs: June 4: FTC charges that TV ads aimed at children and promoting vitamins and various over-the-counter drugs are not informing customers of the potential dangers. Oct. 6: Texas Supreme Court rules that Winthrop Labs, a division of Sterling Drug, is liable for the death of an individual who died as a result of taking Talwin, a drug advertised by the company as "harmless as aspirin."

Education: Dec. 4, 5: Public hearings by the FTC indicate that there is rampant deception and misrepresentation in ads promoting private schools, especially trade schools.

Food: Aug. 20: FTC moves against A & P and other food retail chains for mispricing and advertising unavailable products. A & P files suit to stop further prosecutions.

Hair: Feb. 12: FTC charges two Boston hair replacement firms with failure to notify potential customers in their ads that surgically implanted hairpieces can cause infections and permanent scarring.

---

apace, as can be seen from accounts published by the *New York Times* during 1974 and 1978 (see box on pages above).

FRAUD IN THE MAINTENANCE AND REPAIR BUSINESS

When it comes to the maintenance and repair of his property, the consumer is inevitably dependent upon the services of others. Those in the business of providing maintenance and repair services thrive on this consumer dependence, and some, if not many, are quick to take advantage of the many opportunities for fraud that that dependence generates.

Maintenance and repair attracts swindlers and opens up avenues for consumer fraud precisely because the typical consumer finds it necessary to maintain or repair things that he owns but does not usually have the time, resources, or know-how to do it himself. But even if we could fix or service our property, we are induced not to. Inducements may take the form of warranty specifications threatening us with lapse of the product guarantee if we do not make use of manufacturer-approved personnel or parts. Or they may be less blatant, such as the purposive withholding by

Hearing aids: May 8: FTC files against six manufacturers of hearing aids charging deceptive ads. (The *Times* also notes that in 1972, five of the six companies were prosecuted for restraint of trade practices.) May 23: FTC to investigate fraudulent advertising practices by hearing aid manufacturers and marketers.

Hosiery: Oct. 25: Hanes files $20 million suit against Kayser-Roth alleging that Kayser pantyhose ads are false and deceptive.

Hotels: July 1: Hardees Food Systems agrees not to advertise their hamburgers as "charco-broiled" since in fact they are cooked over "gas-fired ceramic briquets," not charcoal. July 17: Carte Blanche asked to substantiate its claim that more U.S. hotels honor Carte Blanche than American Express since data from a hotel survey shows that only 5 percent took Carte Blanche.

Milk: April 11: FTC charges California Milk Producers Advisory Board ads are misleading since no evidence that milk can reduce the frequency of colds. Aug. 26: FTC to act against California Milk Producers Advisory Board on grounds that its ads claiming that milk is healthy for everyone are misleading and potentially dangerous.

Oil: Aug. 1: FTC administrative law judge rules that Sun Oil's TV ad campaign on the superiority of its blended gasoline is deceptive.

Peanut Butter: Sept. 11: Best Foods halts allegedly deceptive ads for Skippy peanut butter.

Real Estate: May 17, Sept. 4: FTC charges deception and falsehoods in ads by GAC Corp. for its lots in Arizona and Florida; contrary to ads, some lots had no sewage and water connections and some were under water.

Recordings: Feb. 12: FTC accepts consent order from Talent Inc., charged with misleading advertising; the company had been soliciting lyrics from the public and then charging the lyricist for the production of records which had no commercial value.

Ships' Cruises: March 17: New York State probes cruise companies that do not inform their customers of itinerary changes in conflict with their advertisements.

Stocks and Securities: Jan. 17: Misleading ad charge filed against Reynolds Securities for a Florida newspaper ad claiming that the company has expertise in law.

Sugar: Feb. 8: The National Advertising Review Board finds that a Sugar Assoc. ad claiming that sugar is "good food" is without substantiation.

(*Continued on pages 232–233*)

the manufacturer of important information about the product and its repair, lengthy delays in the supply of replacement parts, or the use of special techniques and devices that are meant to guard against work by "amateurs" and may even cause further damage when not handled by those "in the know."

The best opportunities for fraud arise in the maintenance and repair of expensive products and those so sophisticated or specialized as to be beyond the technical expertise of most consumers. Automobiles, electrical appliances of every sort, heating and air-conditioning systems, motorized garden equipment, and a multitude of home maintenance items can be included here. Fraud in home maintenance is especially common in the area of home improvements. Home-improvement plans may be considered by owners in order to improve their investment, but often the intent is merely to maintain the condition of the property. In either case, because a home is usually a family's largest investment, improvement is generally far less costly than replacement, and this is one of the major reasons for its attractiveness to consumers. The area of home improve-

Swimming Pools: July 8: Citizen complaints are filed in the hundreds against pool dealers who advertise low cost pools but subsequently claim they cannot be installed until the end of the summer, while more expensive pools are installed within two or three weeks.

Tobacco: Sept. 11: Brown & Williamson agrees to halt ads allegedly presenting false claims for Viceroy cigarettes.

Toys: Feb. 18: FTC action continues against toy manufacturers who continue to mislead and deceive in their labeling and packaging practices.

Training Schools: May 22: Ryder Technical School charged with deceit and misrepresentation in its ads promoting their tractor-trailer training programs.

Weight-Reducing July 17: FTC accuses Jack LaLanne Health Spas in the New York area with deceptive or misleading advertising practices; the chain agrees to cease and desist. Aug. 14: Elaine Powers figure salons agree to modify or withdraw an ad challenged as deceptive. Dec. 12: The U.S. Postal Service refuses the mailing of Slimmer Shake or Joe Weider's Weight Loss Formula XR-7 on grounds that the ads promoting these products are false.

1978

Acne: July 17: Better Business Bureau (BBB) ad division halts probe of alleged misleading ad for Oxy-10 acne medication, after Norcliff Thayer cancels ads.

Antacids: July 17: BBB ad division halts probe of alleged misleading ad for Gaviscon antacid tablets after Marion Laboratories cancels ad.

Beer: July 23: FTC probes whether ads for Löwenbrau mislead consumers into thinking beer is brewed according to original formula.

Blood Pressure: July 27: FDA charges Searle with misleading ad for antihypertensive drugs Aldactone and Aldactazide; charges hazard warnings are not adequately represented.

Cereals: April 18: Ralston-Purina drops ad for Moonstones cereal following probe by BBB national advertising division.

Comic Books: April 23: FTC announces its plans to investigate comic book industry to determine whether the ad it carries is deceptive or unfair.

Education: July 16: Education Commission of the U.S. and U.S. Education Office recommends that HEW suspend or terminate federal assistance to institutions that misrepresent their academic programs.

ments bristles with opportunities for fraud: first, because of its attractiveness to consumers — there is a ready-made, or easily encouraged, demand for improvement services; second, because consumers expect that costs will be relatively high — meaning the swindler can pad the costs of his work or, alternatively, offer a deal that is hard to refuse because it costs far less than the victim had expected; and third, because even costly home improvements are readily financed through second mortgages and are tax deductible — customers feel that they can afford them.

Fraudulent activities in the maintenance and repair business have been found not only among fly-by-night operators who descend on a town and swindle as many customers as they can before disappearing, but also among businesses with an established clientele, a permanent address, and even a respectable name in the repair field. The fly-by-nighters use a variety of techniques ranging from the offer of special discounts, prizes, and free services to tricky financial plans, the use of inferior products and parts, and promises of work that is never done.[45] By the time the cus-

Electrical Appliances: April 18: GE drops ad for major appliances that was challenged before national ad division of the council of BBB.

Encyclopedia: April 5: FTC rules that Grolier, publisher of Encyclopedia Americana, made deceptive pricing claims and used unfair sales practices.

Eyeglasses: May 26: NYC commissioners have received numerous consumer complaints of misleading ads.

Floor Covering: July 17: Earl Grissmer Co., division of Liggett Group, drops ad campaign for Rins-N-Vac carpet cleaning system; BBB had been investigating the ad.

Food: Sept. 30: Feingold Assn. spokeswoman calls for more complete listing of additives on labels.

Food Prices: Mar. 27: NYC Consumer Affairs Commission says A & P chain continues to sell items at prices higher than ads despite previous fines and warnings.

Mail Order Companies: Nov. 24: Famous Cosmetics, offering "famous brand-name cosmetics" and "fine and unique jewelry" at reduced prices, is barred by New York State attorney general from making unsubstantiated ad claims and ordered to make restitution to dissatisfied customers.

Mouthwashes: April 4: U.S. Supreme Court declines to reverse lower court ruling that Warner-Lambert must include in future ads disclaimer of past claims that product can prevent ailments or lessen their severity.

Oil: Feb. 10: STP agrees to stop making some ad claims for its motor oil, gasoline additives, and oil filters.

Pain Relieving Drugs: Sept. 17: FTC administrative judge rules American Home Products falsely advertised Anacin as a tension reliever and should correct impression.

Retail Stores: June 22: Many stores offering close-out sales in NYC midtown area have been issued summonses for misleading sales ad.

TV Programs: Nov. 15: Coalition of forty-six national consumer, professional, and labor organizations contend that most TV ads aimed at children are deceptive.

Toiletries: August 5: Helene Curtis is sued by S. C. Johnson & Son on charges of false and misleading advertising.

Wines: Nov. 18: Taylor denies that its ads for new wines are misleading, urges Bureau of Alcohol, Tobacco and Firearms to establish guidelines for taste-test ad.

SOURCE: *New York Times*, dates as given, 1974 and 1978.

---

tomer realizes that he or she has been duped, the repairmen have long since disappeared.

One study demonstrates the widespread occurrence of fraudulent repair practices even among supposedly reputable businesses. In 1941, investigators working for *Reader's Digest* disconnected a coil wire in the engine compartment of an automobile and then took the car to a garage for repair. In all, 347 garages in forty-eight states were contacted; of these 63 percent (218) either overcharged, did unnecessary work, charged for work not done or for unneeded parts, or perpetrated similar swindles. In a similar study, investigators took a radio in which a tube had been loosened to 304 repair shops. Once again, nearly two-thirds of the shops visited swindled the customer. In another study, a watch was taken to jewelry stores throughout the country. The investigators had simply loosened the small screw that holds the winding wheel to the internal spring of the watch. Nearly half of the repair shops visited deliberately cheated the investigators.[46]

Though the *Reader's Digest* study was completed forty years ago, there is no good reason to believe that the situation has changed significantly since then. While the extent of fradulent activities among maintenance and repair businesses is unknown and unknowable — just as is the true rate of most other forms of crime — the meager data that do surface from time to time suggest the problem is pervasive.[47] One estimate places the costs of home improvement rackets at more than $1 billion a year.[48]

While no one kind of repair business has a monopoly on fraud, the ease with which the typical motorist can be duped into paying for unnecessary repairs and services makes fraud an attractive option for auto dealers and service stations. As Leonard and Weber have shown, the major auto dealers are financially dependent upon the auto manufacturers, who control the purse strings and determine the framework within which dealers will operate. The dealer is expected to meet sales quotas, to push the sale of service parts, and to minimize expenses incurred by the manufacturer under new-car warranties. The "big brother" position of the manufacturers is strengthened by the fact that most dealers are in debt to the manufacturer for the physical plant, equipment, and facilities of the dealership. The dealer is thus under considerable pressure to make profits any way he can.[49] The situation is similar for those service station owners who sell name-brand gasoline under lease arrangements with the major oil companies.

An American unfortunate enough to take his car to a really disreputable dealer or service station could find himself the victim of tire "honking" (puncturing the tire in order to sell new ones), the "white smoke trick" (spraying chemicals into a hot engine to produce a cloud of smoke), "short sticking" (not putting the oil dip stick all the way down, so that it looks as if more oil is needed), and a host of other practices designed to sell unneeded parts and services.[50]

An effort to collect systematic data on consumer fraud was recently initiated by the George Washington University National Law Center. Though focusing only on complaints received from persons in the Washington, D.C., area, a data-gathering computer center was established in 1974, and since that time many thousands of complaints have been processed. While some complaints prove minor and without legal import, many illustrate just the kinds of fraud we have been discussing. Here are a few examples of complaints about maintenance, repair, and home improvements:

> Consumer purchased a used car with "25% discount on repairs" as a warranty. The auto failed inspection shortly thereafter, was returned to the dealer who sent it on to a repair shop retained by the dealer for repairing its cars. After unspecified repairs were completed at this shop, the dealer removed the car to the shop of his dealership, where two new tires were installed at a cost of $38, also under the 25% warranty described above. The consumer refused to pay, since he had not authorized and did not want the

tires, but eventually capitulated in order to get his car back, paying 75% of the total repair bill on his car. . . .

Consumer, new owner of an American-made subcompact, received a recall letter from the manufacturer indicating a serious problem and representing that the manufacturer would cover the cost of any defect-related repairs at its authorized dealer. The dealer reaffirmed this representation and took the car for repair, estimating that the cost would be $200, but that the consumer would not be charged. The actual cost of repairs turned out to be $564 and the dealer refused to honor the prior representation as to the manufacturer absorbing the cost because "the engine had been tampered with." The consumer denied this, claiming that only the dealer himself had ever worked on the car, but to no avail. The consumer paid for the repair. . . .

Consumer took a piece of furniture to be reupholstered at a shop specializing in such work. The shop was unable to get the material ordered, for which the consumer had paid $150, and refused return of the furniture or the money. . . .

Consumer ordered patio awnings on 5/10/74, giving $200 deposit. Nothing was ever delivered or installed and vendor does not answer phone. . . .

Complainant took sewing machine in to shop in response to advertisement offering "free estimate" of work needed. Repairman took machine apart in course of examination, even though no work was authorized. He then refused to release machine back to consumer until paid for $12.50 charge for reassembly of machine. No repairs were made. Repairman then threatened to sell machine and charge for storage in the meantime if not picked up and paid for. Repairman was willing to drop all outstanding charges for reassembly and storage if repair work was authorized.[51]

CRIMES IN THE HEALTH FIELDS

Physicians, lawyers, accountants, architects, dentists, pharmacists, and others in respected professions are not above illegal activities. Opportunities for fraud and other illegal activities are especially abundant in the various health fields. Because our culture strongly emphasizes health and physical well-being, and because most Americans learn to rely on experts when confronted with health problems, those in the business of health find a vast clientele for their services, and the unscrupulous among them have little difficulty taking advantage of this favorable position. Medical quackery thrives upon customer fears, lack of medical knowledge, and promises of expert help. A good example of quackery is Harry M. Hoxsey, a midwesterner who claimed to have found a cure for cancer. Hoxsey, who was not a physician, got himself listed with an Illinois chamber of commerce and set up "cancer clinics" around the Midwest to which the ill could come for his miracle cure. Though more than once convicted for practicing medicine without a license. Hoxsey pursued his quackery for nearly forty years, and in one year alone is estimated to have seen 8,000 patients and grossed in excess of $1.5 million! Needless to say, his cure was no cure at all; but it was not until the 1960s that the Food and Drug Administration and the American Medical Association finally succeeded in putting him out of business.[52]

Some unscrupulous practices take special advantage of the organization of legitimate medicine and the bureaucratic context within which most health care services are administered throughout the country. As C. Wright Mills observed some years ago:

> Medical technology has of necessity been centralized in hospital and clinic; the private practitioner must depend upon expensive equipment as well as upon specialists and technicians for diagnosis and treatment. He must also depend upon good relations with other doctors, variously located in the medical hierarchy, to get started in practice and to keep up his clientele. For as medicine has become technically specialized, some way of getting those who are ill in contact with those who can help them is needed. In the absence of a formal means of referral, informal cliques of doctors, in and out of hospitals, have come to perform this function.[53]

The informal organization of medical referrals and the clique system provide a means by which less scrupulous physicians and dentists can take advantage of their patients. One well-known scheme is called "ghost surgery." A patient is led to believe that the surgeon he has been dealing with will perform a needed operation. In fact, another surgeon (the ghost) whom he has never seen performs the operation. The patient ends up paying an inflated price for the surgery because the original surgeon has to pay his accomplice. Another practice made easier by the informal networks among physicians and dentists is fee splitting. Though illegal in most states, fee splitting is reckoned to be a fairly common practice. It involves kickbacks from specialists to the general practitioner who refers patients to them. Again, the patient is overcharged to accommodate the payoff.

With the extension of government involvement in medicine that has emerged along with the Medicare and Medicaid programs, many health services now operate in a complicated bureaucratic atmosphere that makes control of these services extremely difficult. Physicians, dentists, and those in such support services as lab testing and retail pharmacy sometimes take advantage of the unwieldy bureaucracy by claiming payment for services and products that were never provided, by issuing prescriptions in violation of federal regulations, and by performing unnecessary services, such as surgery, hospitalization, and lab tests. Haskell and Yablonsky report a case involving a physician who had claimed as much as $70,000 a year from the government for visits to Medicare patients, most of which never took place.[54]

One of the most alarming facets of medical fraud is the performance of unnecessary surgery. While we have no accurate way of knowing how much surgery is unnecessary — even the most qualified physicians may not agree as to the need for a particular operation — evidence compiled over the past few years suggests that many physicians are quick with the knife, and not always for the most professional of reasons. In one study of 6,248 hysterectomies performed in West Coast hospitals, the author found that 40 percent of the operations could be questioned for one reason or another, and 13 percent could not be supported by any available evidence.[55] Similar findings have been recorded for appendectomies, gall bladder operations, tonsillectomies, and other common surgical treatments.

Unnecessary surgery is sometimes linked to declining occupancy levels in the hospitals and clinics to which offending doctors are attached. When the occupancy level in a hospital declines there is considerable pressure to reverse the situation, otherwise income declines while operating costs remain the same or increase. Economic decline is viewed with alarm not only because jobs are at stake but also because important support services may have to be curtailed or dropped, thus damaging health care delivery, not to mention public trust. From the standpoint of modern medical organization, anything threatening the hospital threatens the entire field of professional health care; from the standpoint of some doctors there is also the threat of personal financial troubles as their hospital investments turn sour.

In his study of prescription violations by retail pharmacists, Richard Quinney showed how the existence of conflicting occupational roles can result in job-related crime.[56] The organization of retail pharmacy is such that the pharmacist must fill two occupational roles: the business role and the professional role. The values and expectations embodied in the business role emphasize profit making; those embodied in the professional role emphasize the correct procedures for such things as compounding and dispensing prescriptions and the proper relationship between pharmacist and doctor and pharmacist and customer. Quinney found that pharmacists tended to overcome the strains posed by these different roles by orienting themselves toward one role more than the other. Those who had adopted an "occupational role organization" stressing the business role were more likely to violate prescription laws than those with a professional role orientation.

It appears that occupational crime in the professions is inadequately accounted for by economic factors alone. Certainly, economic pressures can and do enter into the picture; yet economic pressures may just as well lead other professionals to pursue legitimate avenues of gain — working longer hours, improving one's skills, or writing books.[57] It seems that a more adequate explanation of occupational crimes among professionals is one that takes account of social structure; for example, the way occupations are organized, the interrelationships among them and those who work in them, and the normative contexts of work.

Crime as the Central Activity of a Business

The fly-by-night operators who defraud the American consumer by promising work they have no intention of doing, by charging exorbitant prices for shoddy and inferior services, by creating needs for a new furnace, a new roof, pest control, or aluminum siding where no need existed, or by selling products that don't exist are little different from the short-con operators we encountered in chapter 6. They are in the business of fraud as their business. It is their work.

It is not, however, only the fly-by-nighter who makes fraud and deception his business. Over the years some businesses have made fraud their major purpose and yet retain all the trappings of established respectability. They have permanent addresses, they are listed with chambers of commerce, they have boards of directors, they provide annual financial statements, and they may even issue stock available for public purchase. The products and services these companies offer range from vacuum cleaners to swimming pools, from real estate to insurance.

THE EQUITY FUNDING CORPORATION OF AMERICA

One of America's most incredible corporate frauds came to light in 1973. It involved the Equity Funding Corporation of America (EFCA) and centered around life insurance dealings, the major business of the company and its subsidiaries.[58]

Established in the early 1960s, EFCA began life as a new member of the legitimate life insurance business. For a while its business dealings appear to have remained on the right side of the law, though some of its operations would be illegal today. Yet by the mid-1960s, the company's top executives were not content to stay within the law. Instead they embarked on an ambitious program of fraudulent financial manipulations. On the surface EFCA remained, until its fall in 1973, a respectable company with growing assets and growing prestige within the world of high finance. In reality, however, the company's major business turned out to be fraud.

In November 1973, a federal grand jury in Los Angeles handed down criminal indictments charging twenty-two of the company's executives, including a number of its original founders, with 105 counts of criminal conspiracy for such illegal activities as "securities fraud, mail fraud, bank fraud, interstate transportation of counterfeit securities and other securities obtained by fraud, electronic eavesdropping, and the filing of false documents with the Securities and Exchange Commission.[59]

At the heart of EFCA's fraudulent activities was a scheme involving the creation of fictitious insurance policies for the purposes of resale, in order to make the company seem worth far more than it actually was. Using the information contained in the files of their real policyholders,

	CLAIMED IN ITS 1971 REPORTS TO STOCK EXCHANGES	REPORTED BY THE FEDERAL GRAND JURY IN LOS ANGELES ("AT MOST" FIGURES)
Earnings before taxes	$ 26,636,000	$ −400,000
Funded loans and accounts receivable	88,616,000	45,000,000
Total assets	496,695,000	424,000,000
Tangible net worth	141,200,000	104,000,000
Life insurance sales, face amount	1,780,270,704	1,100,000,000

the company issued 64,000 phony policies, which were then sold to other insurance companies for cash. The companies that purchased the phony policies thought they were reinsuring bona fide policies with a total face value of $5 billion. In fact, they were buying nothing. In addition to this scheme, EFCA routinely faked its assets and earnings in its annual reports, and in 1972 began the printing of counterfeit bonds with a face value of more than $100 million. The executives behind this last operation even established a "mail drop" in Chicago for their counterfeit bank bonds.

The full extent of EFCA's fraudulent operations is perhaps best grasped by a comparison of its claimed income and assets with its real income and assets, as reported by the grand jury. Here are a few of the relevant figures:[60]

THE SHADY LAND-DEVELOPMENT BUSINESS

Land, it is said, is the best investment. Many Americans have found quite the opposite, however. They have found that far from being a good investment, land they have purchased has turned out to be worthless, nonexistent, under water, or already owned by someone else. Even when the land has been worth something, purchasers have found that worth to be far less than its price, and that the purposes for which it was brought (as a nest egg, for a vacation home, as a place for retirement) cannot be realized without extraordinary expense and inconvenience.

Disclosures in the popular press have left little doubt that fraud has been booming in the land development and investment business over recent years. Shady land sale and development schemes have cashed in on the supposed value of land as an investment and on the dreams of many Americans to own a vacation or retirement home away from urban areas. The picture that emerges from the popular press and the few government investigations suggests that land fraud may well be tied to organized crime. The initial purchase of large slices of land, the national advertising and promotion campaigns, the construction or rental of sales facilities, and the appearance of respectability and financial success require the kind of funding and organization that organized crime has.

Rich and poor alike can be the victims of land fraud schemes. For the poor victims, it often means the loss of life savings or a future of substantial indebtedness; for the rich, it means a bad investment that could reduce not only financial worth but also respect in the eyes of the financial community, and hence access to investment credit and services in the future.

Land fraud businesses look just like their legitimate counterparts. They employ advertising agencies, maintain a sales force, keep up offices around the country (often in tourist and resort towns), and are listed in business directories and with chambers of commerce. They put together impressive brochures and they advertise in respectable newspapers and magazines such as *The Wall Street Journal, Newsweek,* and *Parade*. For the investor who thinks himself knowledgeable and cautious the sales people have ready answers for critical questions, and can show financial statements, company investment portfolios, and other official-looking documents to underscore their legitimacy and the sound financial status of the operation. The investors discover too late that they have thrown their money down the drain and like the victim of the con artist (see chapter 6) vow never to be taken again. But things are heavily weighted in favor of the shady land dealers.

In 1969 Congress passed the Interstate Land Sales Act, a law designed to protect prospective purchasers. It required land developers operating on an interstate basis to register their subdivisions with the Office of Interstate Land Sales and to make a property report disclosing certain features of the land offered for sale or development. While the new regulations may help the prospective land purchaser avoid a bad investment, developers can take advantage of numerous loopholes. The major responsibility for seeing that things are in order still rests with the buyer himself. The government does not endorse or recommend what is offered for sale, it does not substantiate the accuracy of the registration or the company's disclosures, and it does not protect the customer against developers who sell only within the boundaries of one state or who take advantage of legal loopholes. As Rosefsky points out, it is possible "for an unscrupulous developer to fit his program within one of the legal exemptions, such as limiting the size of an interstate subdivision to 49 parcels [lots of land], then when that's all sold out open up another one nearby of 49 parcels."[61] The law exempts subdivisions under fifty lots.

The Costs of Occupational Crime

Let us return to a matter raised in the opening paragraphs of this chapter: the costs to individuals and to society associated with this broad category of crime. A brief look at some of these costs should help us maintain a balanced view of the impact of crime in America, and will serve to remind us that societal reactions to a particular form of crime are not necessarily an accurate reflection of its impact on people's lives, their communities, and their institutions.

FINANCIAL COSTS

It is widely agreed that the financial costs of occupational crime far exceed those resulting from traditional crimes. The reason is partly the greater frequency with which occupational crimes are committed, but more important, the fact that a single offense can result in losses running into the millions of dollars. In 1967, the President's Commission on Law Enforcement and the Administration of Justice estimated that while about $600 million was annually lost to traditional crimes such as burglary and robbery, $1.4 billion was lost to various kinds of fraud and $1.3 billion to unreported commercial theft, mainly employee pilfering. Some $200 million was estimated to be the yearly loss to embezzlement alone.[62]

More recent estimates of the financial impact of occupational crime place the annual costs at over $40 billion a year, a figure that does not include the financial costs of price fixing and other restraint of trade practices, industrial espionage, or corporate violations of health and safety regulations. Here are some 1974 estimates of the annual economic cost associated with selected occupational crimes.[63]

Bribery, kickbacks, and payoffs	$ 3 billion
Computer-related crime	10 million
Consumer fraud and deceptive practices	21 billion
Embezzlement	3 billion
Employee pilferage	4 billion
Securities theft and frauds	4 billion
Insurance fraud	2 billion

DAMAGE TO INSTITUTIONS AND MORAL CLIMATE

Deception, fraud, price fixing and other monopoly practices, bribery, kickbacks, payoffs, and violations of trust not only undermine the basic principles upon which the American economy and policy have long been ostensibly based, but also foster a moral climate in which lawlessness provokes little indignation — especially when its victims are vague entities such as "the public," "the consumer," "the corporation," and "the government" — and occurs largely free from any sense of guilt on the part of offenders. In particular, when those in positions of wealth, power, and prestige violate the law with relative impunity, their activities serve as a model for the rest of us, for they are the people to whom we look for leadership in our own efforts to get ahead. Looking out for number one, beating the system, getting something for nothing, or doing a favor for a price, have become not disreputable approaches to life but, rather, the accepted and expected approaches for all social strata. "The businessman may pad his expense account, inflate his deductions on his income-tax return, exaggerate insurance claims, and overcharge when he can. The worker may goldbrick on his job, take as many breaks as possible, feign illness, and use other methods available to him to cheat his employer."[64] Armed with the knowledge of pervasive and unpunished thievery and corruption among those we have been brought up to respect or, at least, emulate — the businessman, the physician, the government official — those who commit traditional crimes find handy and powerful rationalizations for their own illegal conduct. Their betters turn out to be surprisingly like themselves when it comes to lawbreaking.

PERSONAL HEALTH AND SAFETY

Finally, there are the costs to personal health and safety. Occupational crimes of various sorts pose health and safety hazards in numerous ways. Landlords and builders who violate building code regulations may expose their tenants to the threat of fire, building collapse, and serious disease; companies violating safety standards for their products (cars, tires, electrical appliances, toys, nightclothes, Christmas tree lights, or whatever) expose their customers to possible injury or death; physicians who do unnecessary surgery expose their patients to the risk of surgical complications; pharmaceutical companies conspiring to fix high prices threaten the well-being of those who need, but cannot afford, their products; mine and factory bosses who violate health and safety regulations expose their workers to injury, disease, and death; and companies manufacturing or selling contaminated food products or mislabeled drugs expose their customers to unnecessary health hazards. All of these activities may, of course, result in severe psychological stresses and strains for the victims.

There can be little doubt that when the health and safety of the population as a whole are considered, the threat posed by occupational crime far exceeds that posed by traditional crimes. This is not to minimize the physical dangers associated with violence, rape, robbery, and the like but, rather, to place the two broad categories of crime in proper perspective vis-à-vis these particular costs. It is easy to overlook the physical dangers posed by occupational crime precisely because these are often less visible, less direct, and appear less concrete than those of, say, robbery and interpersonal assault. Yet they exist and are extensive. Take, for instance, the physical dangers associated with environmental pollution in the air, water, soil, workplace, and home. Millions of Americans are exposed every day to known carcinogens and other potentially lethal substances, often because corporations and businesses fail to meet environmental standards or find legal ways to circumvent them. Among industrial workers alone, many thousands will become diseased or die because they must work under conditions that needlessly expose them to the very real threat of cancer and severe respiratory ailments. Those in the rubber, steel, asbestos, coal, and chemical industries are especially vulnerable to such diseases.[65] If we are really concerned with the physical suffering linked to crime then we should point not so much at the traditional criminal but at those in executive suites who permit environmental pollution or condone other injurious or fatal business practices, and at those in congressional offices who drag their feet and pass the buck when faced with the opportunity to reduce these dangers.

Reactions to Occupational Crime

One of Sutherland's major contentions regarding white-collar crime was that offenders generally escape the punitive action and criminal stigmatization evoked by other forms of crime. In the unlikely event that corporate crooks are brought before a judge, they rarely receive a prison term upon conviction.[66] This situation has not changed much over the years. The period from 1940 to 1970 actually saw a decline in the proportion of antitrust cases resulting in criminal prosecution: from 59 percent between 1940 and 1949 to only 9 percent in 1970.[67] From 1940 to 1961 only twenty executives and businessmen actually served jail sentences for antitrust violations.[68] More recently, the Joseph Schlitz Brewing Company was convicted of bribery to the tune of more than $3 million; its criminal punishment was $11,000 following a reduction of charges to two misdemeanors.[69] Marshall Clinard has estimated that when convicted the corporate crook spends an average of 2.8 *days* in prison.[70]

Any demonstration of the leniency with which corporate offenders are often handled by the courts would have to include the following case, reported in a recent *Newsweek* article:

> In 1975, chairman William E. Grace and president Robert D. Rowan [of Detroit's Fruehauf Corporation] were both found guilty of masterminding a decade-long scheme to cheat the Federal government out of $12.3 million in excise taxes. One method involved selling truck-trailers to distributors at a "discount," thus reducing the excise tax Fruehauf collected and then passed on to the government. But the company still got its full price: it recovered the "discounts" by billing the distributors for services it never performed.
>
> Following conviction, the two executives continued to run the company — they did not resign until [1978], when their legal appeals ran out. Originally, Grace and Rowan were sentenced to six months in jail — but, last January [1979], the judge relented and reduced their sentences to supervised probation while they performed community service. In June, Fruehauf restored both executives to full rank. In their absence, the company had elected to install only an "acting" chairman and an "acting" president.[71]

There are signs that things might be changing. *Newsweek* reports that during 1978 twenty-nine executives were imprisoned compared with only six during 1976; fines for the two years totaled $12 million (1978) versus $3.7 million (1976).[72] John Conklin notes that substantial fines have recently been levied by the Environmental Protection Agency against automobile manufacturers who falsified pollution control data. Thus in 1973 Ford Motor Company was fined $7 million, and in 1976 American Motors Corporation was fined $4.2 million.[73]

Although lenient sentences for occupational crimes of all sorts appear to be the rule, the offender's social status clearly has a bearing on punishment. It is fashionable to refer to the pardon of ex-President Nixon and the prison terms given his aides following Watergate as an illustration of the link between status and punishment. It is also true that the twenty antitrust offenders mentioned earlier who received jail terms were not giants of the corporate world, but small timers and lower-level executives. In fact, of the 48 jail terms handed down in antitrust cases from 1890 to 1959, few involved higher-level executives of large corporations.[74]

We also find a link between status and punishment in the case of employee theft. Consider the findings of a study of the corporate and judicial disposition of 1,631 employee-thieves.[75] In that study, Gerald Robin found that whereas most of the thieves were fired by their employers (99.5 percent), only 17 percent were dismissed and prosecuted. However, regardless of length of service and size of theft, a significantly larger proportion of lower-level employees than higher-level employees were prosecuted. Since 99 percent of those prosecuted were convicted, the act of prosecution virtually ensured conviction and a criminal record for the offender.

REASONS FOR LENIENCY FOR OCCUPATIONAL CRIMINALS

The relatively low probability of criminal sanctions being imposed, and the relatively high probability that they will be mild when they are imposed, is enjoyed not only by corporate offenders who violate regulatory laws, but also by those who steal from their employers, by those who defraud the public, and by those who violate public trust while holding political office. Compared to the "traditional" criminal — the robber, burglar, heroin pusher, rapist — the occupational criminal generally faces little in the way of organized efforts to enforce the law. When exposed he is ignored, handled informally and unofficially, ordered to "cease and desist," forced to pay a nominal fine, or placed on probation.

A number of reasons can be advanced for the general absence of a rigorous and punitive reaction to occupational crimes and those who commit them. In the first place, many of those who violate the law in connection with their work are simply not thought of as criminals. Not only are their crimes not the kinds of activities to which that label is culturally, or even legally, applied; they also do not often look like real criminals. They are not poor, transient, unemployed, black, inner-city, uneducated, lower-class people with a history of involvement in delinquency and street crimes. They are, instead, people with all the trappings of respectability, and some are wealthy and powerful to boot. Haskell and Yablonsky ask, "How can jurors send that well-dressed, white, wealthy father of three to jail with unkempt, nonwhite, poor, uneducated criminals?"[76] The same question can be asked of judges:

On January 15, 1973, two cases were called for sentencing before a United States District judge in Manhattan's Federal Court. The first was *United States v. Velasquez*. A twenty-two-year-old Puerto Rican woman with two children, five and four years old, pleaded guilty to aiding in the theft of part of a group of welfare checks amounting to a total of $2,086. The woman had come to New York only a few years before, could not speak English and was on welfare herself. She was living with her husband in Brownsville, a poverty-stricken section of Brooklyn. Her husband was a diabetic and she provided insulin for him. She had no prior criminal record. The judgment of the court: imprisonment for eighteen months.

The next case was *United States v. Delatorre*. An educated white-collar defendant pleaded guilty to commercial bribery and extortion in the amount of $23,000, as well as perjury. . . . The judge went out of his way to point out, along with other considerations, that the defendant had two young children and no prior criminal record. The judgment of the court: a suspended sentence.[77]

Those occupational offenders with relatively high social status avoid criminal stigmatization not only because they do not look like real criminals, but also because their wealth, prestige, and power — and the interests they hold in common with those who create our laws and pass out sentences — help defend against organized repression and the legal identification of their activities as criminal. The history of legislation and resource allocation for the enforcement of legal controls in the realm of business, politics, and the professions attests to the success of these defenses. Whenever new or more repressive legislation is under consideration in state or federal legislatures, it is remarkable how quickly it dies in committee, how easily it is held over to the next session, or how often it is amended into a completely different animal with plenty of loopholes.

Another reason for the absence of a rigorous and punitive reaction to occupational crime in general is the "relatively unorganized resentment of the public toward" occupational crime.[78] It is difficult to generate organized public resentment toward occupational crime when the effects of much of this crime are diffused rather than simple and direct, and when the acts themselves occur within a complex, often technically sophisticated economic or political context. As members of a Ralph Nader study group put it: "When one person is robbed face to face, the injustice and indignity are obvious. But when millions are deceived in a complex economic structure, when pinpointing the blame is difficult if not impossible, when crime grows so impersonal that it becomes 'technical' — then we lose our perception of the criminal act.''[79]

Then again, organized public resentment is unlikely when value priorities strongly support self-reliance, free enterprise, individual initiative, and the drive for profits and power. When the public learns that someone's financial achievements or political successes were the result, in whole or in part, of deceit, fraud, bribery, influence peddling, embezzlement, and the like, the inclination is to applaud his obvious commitment to American success values and to play down the fact that he has been dishonest in his pursuits.

When large, impersonal organizations are the victims of crime, public sentiments expressing disapproval and indignation are well hidden, if they exist at all. Employee theft, embezzlement, tax evasion, and other activities victimizing corporations and government bureaucracies are considered excusable, if they are not actively condoned, in part because the victims are themselves unpopular, and in part because history has not provided strong ethical guidelines for relationships between large organizations and individuals who work in them or have dealings with them.[80] Different individuals may have different reasons for disliking large organizations, but on the whole it seems that their unpopularity results from their impersonality, their power and influence over people and social life generally, their wealth, and their emphasis on rule-following as opposed to the personal attributes of initiative and creativity.[81] The unpopularity of organizations and lack of strong ethics governing the relationship between individuals and organizations not only make it unlikely that public reactions to crimes such as employee theft will be hostile, but also serve as powerful justifications in the event crimes against them are under consideration (see the discussion of shoplifting and naive check forging on pages 187–193 and 196–199). Erwin O. Smigel found that when a sample of 212 adults in Indiana were asked what type of organization they would steal from if forced by necessity to do so, 155 respondents indicated they would prefer to steal from large business (102) or government (53) than from small business.[82]

Occupational crime is likely to flourish for a long time to come. Even if organized public resentment were to appear, there are major obstacles to successful prevention of occupational crime. One concerns the nature of work itself. Constant changes in the organization and technology of work provide new opportunities for crime. The inventive mind is able to take advantage of these opportunities, and can often stay ahead of the law and its enforcement. This has happened with computer technology, and now threatens to occur — with greater potential for injury — in the area of nuclear power.[83]

Prevention efforts are also frustrated by the close ties between business and politics mentioned earlier. The crimes likely to victimize most people, at greatest cost, are those dreamed up in corporate suites, in the offices of highly skilled professionals, and in the back rooms where political deals are often made. These high-status criminals are the people best able to capitalize on their occupational position. If they are caught they can hire the best lawyers, arrange the longest court delays, and manufacture the most compelling justifications for their actions. But usually it doesn't come to that; mutual protection serves mutual interests, and all parties (except the public at large) benefit when things are kept quiet and policing takes place from within.

Uncertain and diffused as it is, public sentiment regarding occupational crime, especially crime in business and politics, seems to favor more severe penalties than are currently the norm.[84] This may give reason to hope that the public's conscience is uneasy and its patience strained. It remains to be seen whether it means much more.

References

1. See Edwin H. Sutherland, *White Collar Crime* (New York: Dryden Press, 1949), p. 9. Also see his "White Collar Criminality," *American Sociological Review* 5 (1940), pp. 1–12.
2. Donald J. Newman, "White Collar Crime," *Law and Contemporary Problems* 283 (1958), pp. 735–53; and Earl R. Quinney, "The Study of White Collar Crime: Toward a Reorientation in Theory and Research," *Journal of Criminal Law, Criminology, and Police Science* 55 (1964), pp. 208–14.
3. Herbert Edelhertz, *The Nature, Impact, and Prosecution of White-Collar Crime* (Washington, D.C.: U.S. Government Printing Office, 1970), pp. 19–20 and 73–75.
4. Herbert A. Bloch and Gilbert Geis, *Man, Crime, and Society,* 2nd ed. (New York: Random House, 1970), p. 307.
5. From Cyrus H. Gordon, *Hammurapi's Code: Quaint or Forward Looking?* (New York: Holt, Rinehart and Winston, 1957), pp. 7–9 and 22–24.
6. See F. L. Attenborough, ed., *The Laws of the Earliest English Kings* (New York: Russell and Russell, 1963), pp. 105, 119, 125, 135, 155.
7. For more detailed discussions of the crime of embezzlement and related offenses see J. W. Cecil Turner, ed., *Kenney's Outlines of Criminal Law,* 19th ed. (Cambridge: Cambridge University Press, 1966); and Allen Z. Gammage and Charles F. Hemphill, Jr., *Basic Criminal Law* (New York: McGraw-Hill, 1974), pp. 229–33.
8. Turner, *Kenney's Outlines of Criminal Law,* pp. 351–52.
9. Edwin H. Sutherland and Donald R. Cressey, *Criminology,* 9th ed. (Philadelphia: Lippincott, 1974), p. 42.
10. Morton Mintz, *The Therapeutic Nightmare,*

quoted in Richard Quinney, *The Social Reality of Crime* (Boston: Little, Brown, 1970), pp. 78–79.
11. Quinney, *The Social Reality of Crime,* p. 79.
12. Stuart L. Hills, *Crime, Power, and Morality* (Scranton, Penn.: Chandler Publishing Co., 1971), p. 151.
13. Ralph Nader, "We're Still in the Jungle," *The New Republic* (July 15, 1967), pp. 11–12.
14. Donald R. Cressey, *Other People's Money: A Study in the Social Psychology of Embezzlement* (New York: Free Press, 1953), p. 19.
15. Donald R. Cressey, "The Respectable Criminal," *Transaction* 3 (1965), pp. 12–15.
16. The President's Commission on Law Enforcement and the Administration of Justice, *Task Force Report: Crime and Its Impact* (Washington, D.C.: U.S. Government Printing Office, 1967), p. 44; Chamber of Commerce of the United States, *A Handbook on White Collar Crime* (Washington, D.C.: National District Attorney's Association, 1974), p. 6.
17. *Newsweek,* December 3, 1979; W. Thomas Porter, Jr., "Computer Raped by Telephone," *New York Times Magazine,* September 8, 1974, p. 40. Cited in John E. Conklin, *Illegal but Not Criminal* (Englewood Cliffs, N.J.: Prentice-Hall, 1977), p. 4.
18. Norman Jaspan and Hillel Black, *The Thief in the White Collar* (New York: Lippincott, 1960), pp. 24–25.
19. See Virgil W. Peterson, "Why Honest People Steal," *Journal of Criminal Law, Criminology, and Police Science* 38 (1947), pp. 94–103.
20. "Review," *American Journal of Sociology* 49 (1954), p. 604.
21. Gwynn Nettler, "Embezzlement Without Prob-

lems," *British Journal of Criminology* 14 (1974), pp. 70–77.

22. President's Commission, *Crime and Its Impact,* p. 48.

23. Norman Jaspan, "Wholesale Theft on the Retail Level," *Stores* (1964), p. 34.

24. Gerald D. Robin, "Employees as Offenders," *Journal of Research in Crime and Delinquency* 6 (1969), pp. 26–27.

25. Donald N. M. Horning, "Blue-Collar Theft: Conceptions of Property, Attitudes toward Pilfering, and Work Group Norms in a Modern Industrial Plant," in *Crimes Against Bureacracy,* eds. Erwin O. Smigel and H. Lawrence Ross (New York: Van Nostrand, 1970), p. 48.

26. See Charles H. McCaghy, *Deviant Behavior: Crime, Conflict, and Interest Groups* (New York: Macmillan, 1976), p. 195.

27. See James C. Scott, *Comparative Political Corruption* (Englewood Cliffs, N.J.: Prentice-Hall, 1972), pp. 14–18.

28. *Newsweek,* June 14, 1976, p. 22.

29. Ibid., p. 21.

30. See *Newsweek,* February 23, 1976, p. 30; see also *Newsweek,* December, 3, 1979, p. 114.

31. James Boyd, "The Ritual of Wiggle: From Ruin to Reelection," *The Washington Monthly* 2 (1970), pp. 28–43.

32. Sutherland, *White Collar Crime,* pp. 62–83.

33. Ibid., pp. 81–82.

34. For more detailed descriptions of this case, see Richard Austin Smith, "The Incredible Electrical Conspiracy," *Fortune* (April 1961), pp. 132–80, and (May 1961), pp. 161–224; Gilbert Geis, "The Heavy Electrical Equipment Antitrust Cases of 1961," in *Criminal Behavior Systems: A Typology,* eds. Marshall B. Clinard and Richard Quinney (New York: Holt, Rinehart, and Winston, 1967), pp. 139–51; and John G. Fuller, *The Gentlemen Conspirators* (New York: Grove Press, 1962).

35. These are discussed in Mark J. Green, Beverly C. Moore, and Bruce Wasserstein, *The Closed Enterprise System: Ralph Nader's Study Group Report on Antitrust Enforcement* (New York: Grossman, 1972).

36. Figures cited in Hills, *Crime, Power, and Morality,* p. 159.

37. The following discussion follows closely that of Burton M. Leiser in *Liberty, Justice, and Morals* (New York: Macmillan, 1973).

38. Ibid., p. 264.

39. Ibid., p. 268.

40. Ibid., pp. 269–270.

41. Ibid., p. 270.

42. Ibid., p. 271.

43. See Bertrand N. Bauer, "Truth in Lending: College Business Students' Opinions of *Caveat Emptor,* Fraud and Deception," *American Business Law Journal* 4 (1966), pp. 156–61.

44. Sutherland, *White Collar Crime,* p. 116.

45. See William Mathewson, "The Terrible Williamsons," in *Crime and Business,* ed. Michael Gartner (Princeton, N.J.: Dow Jones Books, 1971), pp. 139–42.

46. See Roger Riis and John Patric, *The Repairman Will Get You If You Don't Watch Out* (New York: Doubleday, 1942), pp. 53–184.

47. For comments on home improvement frauds in just one state, see Clifford W. Youngblood, "Home Improvement Frauds and the Texas Consumer Credit Code," *Texas Law Review* 47 (1969), pp. 463–77.

48. Robert S. Rosefsky, *Frauds, Swindles, and Rackets* (Chicago: Follett, 1973), p. 73.

49. See William N. Leonard and Marvin Glenn Weber, "Automakers and Dealers: A Study of Crimogenic Market Forces," *Law and Society Review* 4 (1970), pp. 408–22. See also Harvey A. Farberman, "A Crimogenic Market Structure: The Automobile Industry," *Sociological Quarterly* 16 (1975), pp. 438–57.

50. Rosefsky, *Frauds, Swindles, and Rackets,* pp. 237–38.

51. Cited in testimony by John Sears before the United States Senate Committee on Commerce. See *Consumer Fraud Act: Hearings Before the Committee on Commerce, United States Senate, April 15 and 23, 1975,* Serial No. 94-15 (Washington, D.C.: U.S. Government Printing Office, 1975), pp. 45–46.

52. See James H. Young, *The Medical Messiahs* (Princeton, N.J.: Princeton University Press, 1967), chapter 17.

53. C. Wright Mills, *White Collar* (New York: Galaxie Books, 1956), pp. 115–16.

54. Martin R. Haskell and Lewis Yablonsky, *Crime and Delinquency,* 2nd ed. (Chicago: Rand McNally, 1974), pp. 146–47.

55. James C. Doyle, "Unnecessary Hysterectomies," *American Medical Association Journal* 151 (1953), pp. 360–65.

56. Richard Quinney, "Occupational Structure and Criminal Behavior: Prescription Violations by Retail Pharmacists," *Social Problems* 11 (1963), pp. 179–83.

57. This point is made by Bloch and Geis, *Man, Crime, and Society,* p. 309.

58. The following is based on Raymond L. Dirks and Leonard Gross, *The Great Wall Street Scandal* (New York: McGraw-Hill, 1974).

59. Ibid., p. 229.

60. Ibid., pp. 237–38.

61. Rosefsky, *Frauds, Swindles, and Rackets,* p. 155.

62. President's Commission, *Crime and Its Impact,* chapter 3.

63. Chamber of Commerce, *Handbook on White Collar Crime,* p. 6.

64. Haskell and Yablonsky, *Crime and Delinquency,* p. 149.

65. See Larry Agnon, "Getting Cancer on the Job," *Nation,* April 12, 1975.
66. Sutherland, *White Collar Crime,* pp. 8–9.
67. Ralph Nader and Mark Green, "Coddling the Corporations: Crime in the Suites," *The New Republic* 166 (1972), p. 18, cited in Conklin, *Illegal but Not Criminal,* pp. 104–105.
68. Allen M. Dershowitz, "Increasing Control Over Corporate Crime: A Problem in the Law of Sanctions," *Yale Law Journal* 71 (1961), p. 291.
69. *Newsweek,* December 3, 1979, p. 119.
70. Ibid.
71. Ibid.
72. Ibid., p. 120.
73. Conklin, *Illegal but Not Criminal,* p. 107.
74. Ibid., p. 104.
75. Gerald D. Robin, "The Corporate and Judicial Disposition of Employee Thieves," *Wisconsin Law Review* (1967), pp. 635–702.
76. Haskell and Yablonsky, *Crime and Delinquency,* p. 125.
77. Whitney North Seymour, Jr., *Why Justice Fails* (New York: William Morrow, 1973), p. 43.
78. Sutherland, *White Collar Crime,* p. 49.
79. Green, et al., *The Closed Enterprise System,* quoted in *Crisis in American Institutions,* 3rd ed., ed. Jerome Skolnick and Elliott Currie (Boston: Little, Brown, 1976), p. 554.
80. Smigel and Ross, *Crimes Against Bureaucracy,* pp. 7–8.
81. Ibid., p. 8. See also Erwin O. Smigel, "Public Attitudes toward Stealing as Related to the Size of the Victim Organization," *American Sociological Review* 21 (1956), pp. 320–27.
82. Smigel, "Public Attitudes toward Stealing," pp. 325–26.
83. See August Bequai, *White-Collar Crime: A Twentieth Century Crisis* (Lexington, Mass.: Lexington Books, 1978), especially chapter 12. On crimes involving nuclear power see Herbert Edelhertz and Marilyn Walsh, *The White-Collar Challenge to Nuclear Safeguards* (Lexington, Mass.: Lexington Books, 1978).
84. See, for example, Donald J. Newman, "Public Attitudes toward a Form of White Collar Crime," *Social Problems* 4 (1957), pp. 228–32; Arnold M. Rose and Arthur E. Prell, "Does the Punishment Fit the Crime," *American Journal of Sociology* 61 (1955), pp. 247–59; and Don C. Gibbons, "Crime and Punishment: A Study in Social Attitudes," *Social Forces* 47 (1969), pp. 391–97.

8

Organized Crime

Few Americans are unfamiliar with the term *organized crime*. However, it is unlikely that many of us know much about the phenomenon. Certainly we have heard of Al Capone, Frank Nitti, Vito Genovese, Joe Bonnano, Joe Valachi, and Charlie "Lucky" Luciano. We have also heard of Eliot Ness, the Justice Department agent assigned to break up Capone's bootlegging operations during Prohibition. And it is common knowledge that Chicago and the New York–New Jersey area are two of the major centers of organized crime activities. But what most of us have learned about organized crime has come from the more sensational portrayals presented by the mass media. Apart from periodic news items, which are usually colorful and designed to demonstrate some special kind of inside knowledge, the entertainment industry has been our major window on organized crime.[1] The success of "The Untouchables" and *The Godfather,* among other television and film dramas, shows that we have enjoyed looking through that window.

At best, the information available to the public via the mass media is fragmentary, superficial, and of questionable accuracy; at worst, it is patently false and purely titillating. And yet over the years many of us have come to believe that there is in America a national alliance or cartel composed of organized groups of criminals, dominated by Sicilian- and Italian-Americans, and involved in an extensive range of illicit, often violent activities. Whether called the Mafia, the Mob, the Syndicate, the Organization, or the Cosa Nostra, we simply know that it exists. But does it really? Is there, in fact, a national alliance or structure linking local crime groups, "families," or syndicates? Equally important, just how organized is organized crime?

The Case for a National Cartel of Corporatelike Crime Groups

In 1951, and then again in 1969, highly credible sources provided what appeared to be confirmation that a national crime cartel does exist in America. First, the so-called Kefauver Committee of the Senate reported that

1. There is a Nation-wide crime syndicate known as the Mafia, whose tentacles are found in many large cities. . . .
2. Its leaders are usually found in control of the most lucrative rackets in their cities.
3. There are indications of a centralized direction and control of these rackets, but leadership appears to be in a group rather than in a single individual.
4. The Mafia is the cement that helps bind the Costello-Adonis-Lansky syndicate of New York and the Accardo-Guzik-Fischetti syndicate of Chicago as well as smaller criminal gangs and individual criminals throughout the country. . . .
5. The domination of the Mafia is based fundamentally on "muscle" and "murder." The Mafia is a secret conspiracy against law and order which will ruthlessly eliminate anyone who stands in the way of its success in any criminal enterprise in which it is interested. It will destroy anyone who betrays its secrets. It will use any means available — political influence, bribery, intimidation, etc., to defeat any attempt on the part of law-enforcement to touch its top figures or to interfere with its operations.[2]

The findings of the Kefauver Committee were based on information supplied mainly by police officials and informants. Using basically the same kinds of information, Donald Cressey summarized the discoveries he made while working on behalf of the President's Commission on Law Enforcement and the Administration of Justice:

1. A nationwide alliance of at least twenty-four tightly knit "families" of criminals exists in the United States (because the "families" are fictive, in the sense that the members are not all relatives, it is necessary to refer to them in quotation marks).
2. The members of these "families" are all Italians and Sicilians, or of Italian or Sicilian descent, and those on the Eastern seaboard, especially, call the

entire system "Cosa Nostra." Each member thinks of himself as a "member" of a specific "family" and of Cosa Nostra (or some equivalent term).

3. The names, criminal records, and principal criminal activities of about five thousand of the participants have been assembled.

4. The persons occupying key positions in the skeletal structure of each "family" — consisting of positions for boss, underboss, lieutenants (also called "captains"), counselor, and for low-ranking members called "soldiers" or "button men" — are well known to law-enforcement officials having access to informants. Names of persons who permanently or temporarily occupy other positions, such as "buffer," "money mover," "enforcer," and "executioner," also are well known.

5. The "families" are linked to each other, and to non–Cosa Nostra syndicates, by understandings, agreements, and "treaties," and by mutual deference to a "Commission" made up of the leaders of the most powerful of the "families."

6. The boss of each "family" directs the activities, especially the illegal activities, of the members of his "family."

7. The members of this organization control all but a tiny part of the illegal gambling in the United States. They are the principal loan sharks. They are the principal importers and wholesalers of narcotics. They have infiltrated certain labor unions, where they extort money from employers and, at the same time, cheat the members of the union. The members have a virtual monopoly on some legitimate enterprises. . . . Until recently, they owned a large proportion of Las Vegas. They own several state legislators and federal congressmen and other officials in the legislative, executive, and judicial branches of government at the local state, and federal levels. Some government officials (including judges) are considered, and consider themselves, members.

8. The information about the Commissions, the "families," and the activities of members has come from detailed reports made by a wide variety of police observers, informants, wire taps, and electronic bugs.[3]

In Cressey's view, these crime families are organized along the lines of what sociologists have called "formal organization." In this structure labor is divided such that tasks and responsibilities are assigned primarily on the basis of special skills and abilities; there is a strict hierarchy of authority; rules and regulations govern the activities of members and the relationships among them and with the outside world; and recruitment and entrance are carefully regulated. In short, the crime families are, like other formal organizations, rationally designed for the purposes of achieving specified objectives.[4]

An Alternative View

Not all authorities on organized crime agree entirely with the above picture. Some, for example, deny the existence of any national organization or structure linking and coordinating the activities of organized crime groups. The alternative view, suggested by Daniel Bell, John Conklin, and Francis Ianni, among others, emphasizes more or less organized local criminal gangs, some of whose activities inevitably bring them into working contact with groups operating elsewhere. These authors see no real evidence of any centralized direction or domination of these localized syndicates.[5]

Another point of contention concerns the degree and nature of organization. Contrary to the position advocated by Cressey and others, some authors reject the idea that organized crime groups fit the formal organization model. Basing his argument on his own in-depth study of one Italian-American crime family, Francis Ianni notes:

> Secret criminal organizations like the Italian-American or Sicilian *Mafia* families are not formal organizations like governments or business corporations. They are not rationally structured into statuses and functions in order to "maximize profits" and carry out tasks efficiently. Rather, they are traditional social systems, organized by action and by cultural values which have nothing to do with modern bureaucratic virtues. Like all social systems, they have no structure apart from their functioning; nor . . . do they have structure independent of their current "personnel." . . . Describing the various positions in Italian-American syndicates as "like" those in bureaucracies gives the impression that they are, in fact, formal organizations. But they are not.[6]

Perhaps the best way to approach the issue of organization is to recognize that there are degrees of organization. While some crime families or syndicates exhibit many of the elements found in highly rationalized bureaucratic structures, as Cressey has shown, others do not. This distinction is important when we consider the growing organized crime involvement of blacks, Puerto Ricans, and Cubans. According to studies focusing on these ethnic groups, while they clearly participate in organized crime, the level of organization remains rudimentary for some gangs compared to others. To exclude these loosely organized groups from discussions of organized crime is to ignore an important facet of organized crime in America today.

Distinguishing Characteristics of Organized Crime

It is unlikely that criminologists will soon reach a consensus on the issues we have been discussing. Even if detailed and dependable information were forthcoming, how complete a picture could be drawn from it? When we deal with organizations that place a premium on secrecy and engage in criminal activities, we are rarely able to learn everything we need to know. And even those in a position to know more than most — a participant who turns informant, such as Joe Valachi — may only know the facts about some aspects of their own organization, and thus cannot be considered authoritative sources of information on other aspects or other organizations.[7] Even so, criminologists generally agree on some important features of organized crime, which, when taken together, set the phenomenon apart from other kinds of participation in the American crime scene.

First is *organization for the explicit purpose of making money* by whatever means present themselves or can be devised, legal or otherwise. Because the bulk of the money-making activities are criminal, we speak of these activities as organized crime. Second, the core objective of these criminal activities is to *provide illegal goods and services to those who want them or can be induced to want them*. This does not mean, however, that those in organized crime have nothing to do with "traditional" crimes such as burglary or robbery. As Stuart Hills points out:

> The belief . . . that organized crime is a phenomenon unrelated to conventional "street crimes" — which generate most of the alarm and anxiety in the general public — helps to obscure our understanding of the larger impact of organized crime. It is the syndicate that has mostly controlled the importation and wholesale distribution of narcotics that, together with prohibitionist laws and police activity, compel most addicts to engage in burglary, robbery, and larceny to pay the exorbitant black-market prices. And it is the "fences," aligned with organized criminal groups, who allow thieves to convert their booty into cash. Organized crime has also been known to promote bank robbery, cargo hijacking, arson, and burglaries, sometimes in cooperation with individual professional thieves.[8]

Remember, however, that in their pursuit of money those in organized crime have found gambling, prostitution, loan sharking, narcotics, and racketeering the big money-makers, hence their major interests.

A third important characteristic of organized crime is its connections with the world of government and politics. *Organized crime makes political corruption an integral part of its business.* Indeed, political corruption is not merely a distinguishing feature of organized crime; it is critical to its survival.

The fifth feature of organized crime worthy of note is its *generational persistence*. Unlike most other types of participation in crime, the syndicates or families comprising organized crime continue to operate despite the comings and goings of members. While the death or retirement of persons in leadership positions can sometimes result in significant changes of one sort or another, organized crime does not disappear and individual organizations usually do not cease to exist. The persistence of organized crime despite the inevitable disappearance of its human participants can be explained in part by a final important feature of the phenomenon: *sanctioned rules of conduct for membership* (sometimes called "the code"). The survival of any group or organization is problematic if the behavior of members is neither predictable nor conforms to the evaluations of at least some other members of the group. Rules of conduct help to establish conformity and predictability; sanctions for violations of the rules help to ensure the persistence of conformity and predictability, hence the persistence of the group.

RULES OF CONDUCT

It should be stressed that there is no conclusive evidence of one particular code being shared by the various criminal organizations making up organized crime. Investigators have found numerous obstacles to a definitive statement of what the code (or codes) might be. Noting some of the difficulties, Cressey observed:

> We have been unable to locate even a summary statement of the code of conduct used in governing the lives of Cosa Nostra members. . . .[T]here are no hard data at all on "the law" of the organization. Because the code of conduct for Cosa Nostra members is unwritten, the files of law enforcement and investigative agencies, even those whose principal function is assembling intelligence information on organized crime, cannot contain information even remotely comparable to the information available to . . . the student of the American criminal law. There are no statutes to memorize, no Supreme Court decisions to analyze, no law-review analyses to ponder, and no textbooks to provide answers for examination questions. Further, informants are only rarely available for interview, so one cannot locate the organization's "criminal law" in oral codes, as anthropologists do when studying "primitive law." Merely observing the everyday interactions of Cosa Nostra members with each other, with other criminals, or even with noncriminals would provide clues about any special code of conduct they have formulated, but there is no way to observe such interactions in detail. Cosa Nostra cannot be infiltrated.[9]

Notwithstanding the difficulties, Cressey combined snippets of information from informants with clues deduced from an analysis of the social structure of Cosa Nostra, and was able to suggest the following as the code or organized crime:

1. *Be loyal to members of the organization. Do not interfere with each other's interests. Do not be an informer.* This directive, with its correlated admonitions, is basic to the internal operations of the Cosa Nostra confederation. It is a call for unity, for peace, for maintenance of the *status quo. . . .*
2. *Be rational. Be a member of the team. Don't engage in battle if you can't win.* What is demanded here is a corporate rationality necessary to conducting illicit businesses in a quiet, safe, profitable manner. . . .
3. *Be a man of honor. Always do right. Respect womanhood and your elders. Don't rock the boat.* This emphasis on "honor" and "respect" helps determine who obeys whom, who attends what funerals and weddings,

who opens the door for whom, . . . and functions to enable despots to exploit their underlings. . . .

4. *Be a stand-up guy. Keep your eyes and ears open and your mouth shut. Don't sell out.* A "family" member, like a prisoner, must be able to withstand frustrating and threatening situations without complaining or resorting to subservience. The "stand-up guy" shows courage and "heart." . . .

5. *Have class.* Be independent. Know your way around the world. . . . A man who is committed to regular work and submission to duly constituted authority is a sucker. . . . Second, the world seen by organized criminals is a world of graft, fraud, and corruption, and they are concerned with their own honesty and manliness as compared with the hypocrisy of corrupt policemen and corrupt political figures.[10]

In discussing the code, Cressey points out that it is similar to codes adopted by professional thieves, prisoners, and other groups whose activities and conditions of existence bring them into confrontation with official authority and generate the need for "private" government as a means of controlling the conduct of the membership. Other authors have made similar observations.[11]

Ralph Salerno and John Tompkins present a more detailed code as the "law" governing what they call "the crime confederation." Among the unwritten rules and directives are: maintain secrecy; keep the organization before the individual; keep other members' families sacred; reveal nothing to your wife; do not kidnap; do not strike another member; do not disobey orders; and always be a stand-up guy.[12] Again, the authors' information came mainly from police intelligence and organized crime informants. Also like Cressey, Salerno and Tompkins imply that all organized crime groups subscribe to their code.

Taking exception to this position, Ianni proposes that different syndicates may well follow different codes, and that the presumption of a shared code is based on the shaky grounds that there is a single national organization, and that each individual organized crime group has achieved similar levels of organizational sophistication and shares similar cultural and experiential backgrounds.[13] In Ianni's view, clues to organized crime codes are best discovered by the direct observation of members' behavior. His method "was to observe and record behavior and then seek regularities that had enough frequency to suggest that the behavior resulted from the pressures of the shared social system rather than from idiosyncratic behavior."[14] In addition, family members were asked why they and other participants behaved in a certain way.

From his two-year participant observation of one Italian-American crime family operating in New York (the "Lupollo" family) and his later research on black and Hispanic groups in organized crime, Ianno was able to construct a picture of the various rules of conduct his different subject groups subscribed to. As he anticipated, he found evidence of different codes for different groups. More important still, he was able to provide reasons for the disparities in the codes.

In the case of the Lupollo family, Ianni found evidence of three basic rules for behavior:

> . . . (1) primary loyalty is vested in "family" rather than in individual lineages or nuclear families, (2) each member of the family must "act like a man" and do nothing which brings disgrace on the family, and (3) family business is privileged matter and must not be reported or discussed outside the group.[15]

Ianni found that in some respects black and Hispanic organized crime codes differed from the Lupollo rules, as well as from each other. For example, while the black and Hispanic groups placed special emphasis on loyalty and secrecy (as did the Lupollo family), some of these organized crime networks also stressed the rules "Don't be a coward" and "Don't be a creep" (in other words, the member's attitudes and actions must "fit in" with the group). Some stressed the rule "Be smart" (know when to obey, but also when to beat the system). And some stressed the rules "Don't tell the police," "Don't cheat your partner or other people in the network," and "Don't be incompetent."[16]

Ianni discovered that which rules were stressed depended in large part on how the gangs came together in the first place. Those gangs with shared family roots placed a premium on rules supporting kinship ties. On the other hand, gangs with origins in youthful street associations and partnerships tended to stress rules underscoring personal qualities ("Don't be a coward"). Those originating in strictly business or entrepreneurial associations tended to stress rules emphasizing more impersonal, activity-oriented obligations ("Don't be incompetent").[17] The code adopted by any one criminal organization reflects far more than the mere fact that it is a secret association engaged in regular criminal activities. How and why the participants came together in the first place (*bonding relationships* or *linkages*), how long the organization has been operating, the cultural heritage of its major participants, and the nature and range of its activities, legal as well as illegal, all are likely to influence the rules of conduct adopted and maintained.

The History of Organized Crime in America

One of the most important factors likely to influence the activities, structure, and code of an organized crime syndicate is the length of time it has been in the business of crime. The crime syndicates we read about most often — those identified as Italian-American and operating primarily in the Midwest and East — have been around for half a century; others are relative newcomers, with some just emerging. To understand organized crime today we must understand how it was in the past. When did organized crime first emerge? When and how did it achieve prominence and power in social life? What changes have occurred over the years, of what significance? In short, what has been the history of organized crime in America?

Most authors trace the origins of organized crime to the gangs of thugs that roamed the streets of New York and other cities and followed the frontier west during the nineteenth century. In New York City the earliest gangs were made up of the sons of immigrant Irish families. During the first half of the century it was the Irish who filled the slum areas of New York City. They not only constituted the core of poor people, but were also deprived of political power and were the routine object of discrimination. In the eyes of many of the youths growing up during the period, their survival, and their path out of the ghetto, lay not in meek submission, but in muscle and the willingness to use it. As Gus Tyler has observed, "the story of the early gangs — whether in New York, San Francisco, or the frontier — is told against a background of conflict; ethnic, economic, and political. It is the tale of men making their own law, legislating with their fists, striking out against real or imagined enemies."[18]

From loafing and brawling the New York gangs moved into extortion and the instrumental use of force. They soon discovered that money was easily made through the intimidation of brothel owners, gambling proprietors, and others in the business of providing illicit services. More money came, and with it power, when it was discovered that politicians and businessmen would pay for their muscle. Gangs were hired to break up picket lines, to intimidate voters, to stuff ballot boxes, and to protect establishments from harassment by other gangs, not to mention the authorities. By the 1850s the gangs were the muscle behind Tammany Hall, the Democratic headquarters and the political heart of the city. With this new power, the gangs were able to open doors that formerly had been closed to their fellow Irish. The docks were under their control, and this meant work for Irishmen; city hall felt their power, and this meant city jobs for their fathers, brothers, and cousins.

RAGS TO RICHES AND THE QUEST FOR RESPECTABILITY

What had happened in New York City happened elsewhere, with shades of difference. The history of organized crime in America is in large part the history of people seeking riches and respectability, and of the social, legal, and political conditions providing both the incentive and means to attain them. Whether we look at the nineteenth-century Irish gang, the Italian-American crime family, or the emergent black and Puerto Rican crime networks, the picture is essentially the same. We see migration and the herding of newcomers into ghettos, with few legitimate avenues of escape; we see poverty, discrimination, and degradation; we see corruption in politics and government; we see laws rendering criminal many goods and services in public demand; and we see material things held up as the legitimate symbols of success and respectability but the means to them denied the newcomers. Identifying the ghetto as the social setting in which organized crime is spawned, one author has written:

> The social history of American urban ghettos documents how ghetto dwellers were forced to seek escape from underclass status into the dominant society through the interrelated and interdependent routes of crime and politics. The corrupt political structures of major American cities and organized crime have always enjoyed a symbiotic relationship in which success in one is dependent on the right connections in the other. In this relationship, the aspiring ethnic, blocked from legitimate access to wealth and power, is permitted to produce and provide those illicit goods and services that society publicly condemns but privately demands — gambling, stolen goods, illegal alcohol, sex and drugs — but not without paying tribute to the political establishment. The gangsters and racketeers paid heavily into the coffers of political machines and in return received immunity from prosecution. The ghetto became a safe haven in which crime syndicates could grow and prosper. Two factors — immigrant slum dwellers' alienation from the political process and society's characteristic attitude that so long as "they" do it to each other, crime in the ghetto is not an American problem — kept the police indifferent and absent and added to that prosperity. The immigrant and his children found organized crime a quick means of escaping the poverty and powerlessness of the slums. The successful gangster like the successful politician was seen as a model who demonstrated to the masses of lower-class co-ethnics that anyone could achieve success and power in the greater society. And if they did this while defying the police and other oppressors, so much the better. Then, when political power came to the group, partly as a result of these same illegal activities, access to legitimate opportunities became enlarged and assimilation was facilitated. The tradition became one of up and out.[19]

ITALIAN-AMERICANS IN ORGANIZED CRIME

Over the years virtually all ethnic groups have been involved in organized crime. The Irish were followed by Eastern European Jews, the Jews by Italian and Sicilian immigrants, and in recent years this ethnic succession has encompassed Cuban immigrants, Puerto Rican immigrants, and blacks. Even the Chinese immigrants who settled on the West Coast made a place for themselves in organized crime.

Of all these groups, the Italian-American immigrants made the most lasting impression on the organized crime scene and achieved, over the years, a dominating role in it. Let us, then, examine the involvement of Italian-Americans in organized crime.

Immigration and Ghetto Residency   Between 1820 and 1930 an estimated 4.7 million Italians arrived in the United States. Many of the early immigrants traveled to the West and South and became farmers, fishermen, tradesmen, and craftsmen. Over 2 million Italians arrived between 1900 and 1910, 80 percent coming from southern Italy and Sicily.[20] Poor, illiterate, and lacking in occupational skills, many soon returned to Italy, but the majority remained in the East and congregated in the "Little Italy" ghettos found in most urban centers, especially New York City. Like the Irish before them, they were desperate for the chance to improve their lot and achieve success and respectability in their new country. Also like the Irish, many found crime the easiest and quickest way up and out.

Unable to speak English, unfamiliar with American ways and big city life, and dependent upon each other for guidance and help, many Italian immigrants fell prey to those among them who were ready and willing to exploit their neighbors. Apparently, crime among the Little Italy residents was first of all crime against Italians: extortion, vendettas, and the kidnapping of brides.[21] It was not, at first, organized crime, nor did the Italian criminal often venture beyond the boundaries of the ghetto. As a member of the "Lupollo" family related to Ianni:

> Can you imagine my father going uptown to commit a robbery or a mugging? He would have had to take an interpreter with him to read the street signs and say "stick 'em up" for him. The only time he ever committed a crime outside Mulberry Street was when he went over to the Irish section to steal some milk so that my mother could heat it up and put in my kid brother's ear to stop an earache.[22]

Yet this was the beginning of Italian involvement in organized crime. By using muscle and by cashing in on ghetto conditions and police indifference to what went on in Little Italy, some immigrants became rich and powerful. They began to extend their illicit activities and hired other men to help them.

One key to wealth and power was extortion. Acting alone or in the company of others, the extortionist would select his victims from among his newly arrived neighbors. Some extortionists associated themselves with the infamous "Black Hand," a loosely connected band that terrorized the vulnerable immigrant. A favorite tactic was to send a letter demanding money, the letter being signed with a drawing of a black hand. Other letters would follow, each successively more blatant in its threats of physical violence if the money was not paid. The fearful victim would search for help, which often came in the form of a man who was himself associated with the Black Hand. Sometimes the victim was able to secure a loan from a local source, thus helping to enrich not only the extortionist but also his creditor. In this way, "respectable" members of the community grew wealthy from the activities of criminals. In either case, the victim found himself in debt, hence more dependent and more vulnerable.

The Mafia Connection   The Italian immigrants brought with them their traditional attitudes and ways. During the years of adjustment following the move to unfamiliar surroundings, many naturally came to rely on their social and cultural heritage to help them, and the tendency to cling to old ways was heightened by the ethnic homogeneity of Little Italy. To understand Italian involvement in organized crime, and the form it has taken, we must recognize the role played by the immigrant heritage itself.[23]

Important in that heritage were the secret organizations that had flourished for years in southern Italy — among them, the Mafia and the Camorra. The origins of the Mafia and the Camorra are generally traced to the early nineteenth century; the Camorra was centered in Naples, the Mafia in Sicily. Though their actual beginnings are unknown, they both flourished in large part because of the widespread political and social unrest characterizing the southern Italian and Sicilian societies during the nineteenth century.[24]

The concept of *mafia* was also important in the heritage. It refers not to the organization but, rather, to "a state of mind, a sense of pride, a philosophy of life, and a style of behavior which Sicilians recognize immediately."[25] To describe someone as a *mafioso* does not necessarily mean that he is a member of the Mafia; it may simply mean that he is a man who is respected and held in awe. He is a man who seeks protection not from the law but by his own devices; he is a man who commands fear; he is a man who has dignity and bearing; he is a man who gets things done; he is a man to whom people come when in need; he is a man with "friends."

While not all Italian immigrants were familiar with either the organization or the concept, those from southern Italy, especially western Sicily, undoubtedly were. Some of the immigrants may themselves have been mafiosi, in either meaning. In short, there is good reason to believe that familiarity with Mafia ways and the spirit of mafia did exist among Little Italy residents and that behavior was affected by it. For example, Ianni notes that in the Italian ghettos people went for protection or a redress of grievances to informal "courts" held by real or reputed mafiosi.[26] In addition, Luigi Barzini suggests that in their efforts to beat rival gangs, immigrant criminals of Sicilian origin fashioned their organizations after the southern Italian models of Mafia and Camorra. In his testimony before the 1963 McClellan Committee of the Senate, Joe Valachi made much of the ties between the American Cosa Nostra and the secret organizations of southern Italy. One clear tie is the oath-taking ritual that changed little from that used in the early nineteenth century by both the Camorra and Mafia organizations:[27]

Flanked by the boss and his lieutenants, the initiate and his sponsor may stand in front of a table on which are placed a gun and, on occasion, a knife. The boss picks up the gun and intones in the Sicilian dialect: "Niatri reprentam La Costa Nostra. Sta famigghia è La Cosa Nostra. (We represent La Cosa Nostra. This family is Our Thing.)" The sponsor then pricks his trigger finger and the trigger finger of the new member, holding both together to symbolize the mixing of blood. After swearing to hold the family above his religion, his country, and his wife and children, the inductee finished the ritual. A picture of a saint or a religious card is placed in his cupped hands and ignited. As the paper burns, the inductee, together with his sponsor, proclaims: "If I ever violate this oath, may I burn as this paper."[28]

This is not to say that Italian immigrants imported wholesale the Mafia or the Camorra. Rather, they imported a knowledge of the ways of secret societies and the spirit of mafia. This spirit seems to have been particularly important during early ghetto life, for those who grew rich — whether through crime or by essentially legal means such as loaning money in exchange for a part interest in a business — were able to cash in on the mafia idea. These men became the mafiosi, and like those back home were feared while at the same time were respected and upheld as models for emulation by the young. Ianni suggests that it was in the role of mafioso that Giuseppe Lupollo, grandfather of the crime family he studied, gained much of his strength.[29]

The Impact of Prohibition Lupollo and other Little Italy residents grew rich and powerful through a combination of criminal and legal activities. Usually they worked alone or with other members of their families. No secret organization tied them together, and the immigrants did not form a new Mafia or Camorra on American soil. Ianni suggests three reasons why, until the 1920s at least, a Mafia-style organization did not emerge. First, they had not had enough time. The southern Italian immigrants were newcomers, and twenty years was hardly enough time to establish what had taken decades at home. Second, the Italian immigrants had come mostly as individuals; hence they had to establish new patterns of organization and new sources of power and profit. Third, the traditional pattern of father-son respect and obedience was not reinforced in American schools and in church; especially in school, the lessons stressed individualism, not family loyalty.[30]

The onset of Prohibition, however, added two of the missing ingredients. Prohibition provided the incentive and means to move outside the ghetto and offered substantial rewards to those who ventured into bootlegging and other liquor-related activities. The illegal market for alcohol provided the incentive for mafiosi to work together and establish contacts outside the ghetto. Prohibition also supplied new organizational models that replaced the traditional family model the older immigrants stressed but their American-born sons tended to reject. The organizational model was that of the American crime gang of Irish and Jewish thugs, which offered lower-echelon positions to Italian youths who had gained criminal experience in ghetto street gangs. Working relationship with non-Italians, frowned upon by the older generation immigrants — called "Old Moustaches'' or ''Moustache Petes'' by the youngsters — became an important feature of the new Italian-American involvement in organized crime.

What emerged was an Italian-American participation in organized crime that combined aspects of the old Mafia and the mafia spirit with strictly American contributions. Unlike the Italian Mafia, however, the new crime syndicates operated beyond the boundaries of the local community and employed non-Italians. Yet strong ethnic bonds persisted and became especially important as Italians began to secure positions within legitimate government as councilmen, judges, and policemen. By the same token, the domination of the older mafiosi was weakened as ambitious second-generation Italian-Americans sought leadership roles and endeavored to seek out lucrative fields of operation (drugs, for example) over the objections of their elders.

Toward the end of Prohibition, internal dissension threatened the power and profits of the Italian-American crime syndicates, as the Old Moustaches fought for authority with their younger Americanized counterparts. The so-called Castellammarese War of 1930–1931 marked the height of the conflict. Originating in New York between the older Salvatore Maranzano faction and the second-generation gangs under Giuseppe Masseria, the feud spread to Chicago and other cities. Although Maranzano was the victor, many of the Old Moustaches were killed, and it was the Americanized gangsters such as Joe Adonis, Vito Genovese, Charlie Luciano, and Frank Costello who subsequently emerged as the powerful figures in the Italian-American syndicates. Some authors have pointed out that if the Mafia ever really existed in America, it did not survive the Castellammarese War as a force behind organized crime, nor as an organization to which Italian-American syndicates belonged or with which they identified themselves.

Since Prohibition, however, Italian-American crime families have continued to flourish and have achieved a dominant place in organized crime. This was due to a number of events and conditions: the massive influx of Italian immigrants during the early decades of this century; the conditions of ghetto life to which they were subject; the indifference of the authorities to what went on inside the ghettos; the immigrants' familiarity with, and fear of, the Mafia and mafiosi; the attempt by Mussolini to crush the Mafia and other secret societies, thus forcing mafiosi to seek shelter in America; the existence and successes of the semiorganized American crime gangs; and the widespread political corruption in urban areas. But most of all, it was due to Prohibition itself. It was Prohibition that promised a quick and easy path to riches and provided the impetus for mafiosi and other Italian-Americans to organize and venture outside the ghetto. It was Prohibition that showed the criminal gangs in the ghetto how to turn their thousands into millions, and their limited power into considerable power. It was, in short, Prohibition that helped organized crime come of age.

The Money-Making Enterprises of Organized Crime

During Prohibition, crime syndicates made the manufacture, distribution, and sale of alcoholic beverages their major business. While extortion, blackmail, robbery, prostitution, gambling, and the sale of protection had been lucrative enterprises, bootlegging outweighed them all. Suddenly the law had made illegal what was much in demand by all segments of the population. Fortunes could be made by those who cared to break the law and could organize to do it.

When Prohibition came to an end in 1933 the black market quickly fell apart. This did not mean, however, that no money was to be made by dealing in booze; only that much less was to be made from it. Actually, organized crime continues to dabble in the liquor business. Some jurisdictions are still "dry," and others permit only beer or only certain labels to be sold. But even where liquor of any sort is legal, money can still be made. With the right connections, profitable liquor licenses can be bought on behalf of the syndicate; through control of bottling, warehousing, and distributing, syndicate liquor finds its way into legitimate outlets, sometimes hiding behind the label of a legal competitor.[31]

As Stuart Hills points out, organized crime is not restricted to any one kind of activity, legal or otherwise, and like any entrepreneur must keep up with changing times or go out of business.[32] To fill the void created by the repeal of Prohibition, organized crime turned its attention to new avenues of profit, and has continued to branch out ever since.

CRIMINAL ENTERPRISES

The major enterprises providing illicit profits have been gambling, usury (loan sharking), drug trafficking, theft, and racketeering. In all these areas the money to be made is enormous. While we can only guess, it is generally held that profits from each one of these areas run into billions of dollars every year. Estimates of the annual gross from gambling enterprises go as high as $50 billion; drug trafficking is estimated to be a $75 billion business; and a conservative estimate of the gross from loan sharking is $10 billion. Even the sale of sex, not one of the big money-makers, is estimated to gross $2 billion a year.[33] When we remember that organized crime avoids most, if not all, of the overhead and taxes legitimate businesses have to absorb, these gross figures indicate tremendous incomes for organized crime — a conservative estimate of the net profits would be 30 percent of the gross.

Gambling   Though some speculate that the money-making possibilities of illegal gambling may be on the decline following the spread of state lotteries, gambling remains one of the principal sources of income for organized crime. Most of the money is made from the policy, or numbers,

Organized crime controls most of the nation's illegal gambling, from numbers to off-track betting to casino style games played in opulent surroundings.

racket. Legend has it that the term *policy* originated from the nineteenth-century practice among the poor of gambling with money set aside for insurance policy premiums; Cressey, however, suggests that the term came from the Italian word for lottery ticket, *polizza*.[34] Whatever the truth, one fact is clear: policy, or numbers, betting is predominantly a feature of urban slum life. Citing a *New York Times* article, Charles McCaghy notes that in 1968, 75 percent of all adults and older teenagers residing in New York City's slum areas spent an average of four dollars a week on numbers.[35] Combined with the money spent on illegal drugs, the total for the central Harlem, Bedford-Stuyvesant, and South Bronx slum areas almost equals the total amount of welfare funds pumped into these same areas![36]

Numbers betting is a simple concept and easy to do. The gambler simply picks any three-digit number and bets that this number will correspond to the winning number, selected in accordance with some predetermined procedure. Over the years the winning numbers have been computed from the number of shares traded on the Stock Exchange, the daily cash balance in the United States Treasury, and the payoffs at local parimutuel racetracks. At one time, the number was simply drawn from a revolving drum. The odds are 1,000 to 1 against the bettor, while the payoff never exceeds 600 to 1.

The numbers racket attracted organized crime not only because of the immense profits to be made from it, but also because the game requires organization, money, and a good deal of corruption in the right places — things only organized crime had. While small-scale games, involving small bets and a small betting clientele, have existed in the past, they were neither very profitable nor very secure for those who ran them. To work, the numbers racket needs organized crime. The boss of a New Jersey crime network explains why:

> Everybody needs the organization — the banker, the controllers, the runners, even the customers. Here's why. Only a big organization can pay up when the bank gets hit very hard. Suppose a lot of people play the same number one day. For example, when Willie Mays hit his 599th home run, a lot of black people played "600" the next day, figuring Willie was going to make it and so were they. If that number had come up, the banker would have been wiped out, and not only that, a lot of customers would have gone without their payoffs. The whole system would have collapsed. . . .
>
> There was another reason why they needed the organization. Only the organization had the money and the muscle to keep the cops and politicians from breaking up the game and shaking down the players and operators.[37]

Though the specifics vary from place to place and from syndicate to syndicate, the numbers operation is organized along the following lines. The bets are picked up by "runners" from "numbers drops" in shops, factories, office buildings, and bars, or simply on the street. The runners pass the money and betting slips on to local "collectors," or "route men," in charge of their neighborhoods. The collectors pass the money and numbers tickets on to the "controller," who sends it on to the "district controller," who works for the "policy operator." The policy operator actually runs the enterprise, and sometimes is known as the "banker" or "owner." He is usually one of a number of operators, all of whom pay a commission to the crime syndicate under whose overall supervision and control and in whose territory the racket operates. These policy operators may or may not be actual members of the crime family. At payoff time, the money simply follows the reverse route, usually starting at the "branch" or "district bank" run by the policy operator.

Loan Sharking   Loan sharking thrives because some people who need loans are unable or unwilling to secure them through legitimate lending institutions. Loan sharks will lend them the money, for a price. To make loans you need money; organized crime has it. To ensure that the money is repaid, with interest, you need organization and the ability to make collections; organized crime has them. Because usury is illegal, you must be able to collect without resorting to legal channels, and without the interference of the law; organized crime accomplishes this through muscle and corruption.

The borrower who comes to the loan shark usually wants a quick loan with no questions asked. He may be a gambler in need of money to pay off debts or finance further play; he may be a businessman faced with bankruptcy or wanting to invest in a risky, perhaps illegal, venture; he may simply be poor and in need of a small loan, but lacking the credit or collateral required by licensed lending institutions. The interest he will pay depends on how much he borrows, the intended use of the loan, his repayment potential, and what he is worth to the mob if he cannot make his payments. Generally, the interest runs anywhere from 1 to 150 percent per week, with most smaller loans at 20 percent per week — the "six for five" loan, where each five dollars borrowed requires six to be paid back at the end of a week. Usually a set time is established for payments, and if the required payment is not made on or before that exact time the borrower owes another week's interest, computed from the principal plus the interest already accrued.[38]

When payments cannot be made, intimidation and physical violence are sometimes awaiting the borrower. Collectors employed by the loan shark use a variety of techniques, from thinly veiled threats to outright violence, to stir the borrower into meeting the terms of the loan. It is unusual for a borrower to be killed, however, for his death means the money is lost forever. While a killing may be committed occasionally to make the victim an example to others, the loan shark wants his money first and foremost, and if this cannot be secured with threats he will look for other ways to get it. Indeed, loans are sometimes made — at very high interest rates — not in the expectation that they will be repaid but for the purpose of making the borrower a pawn in the hands of the syndicate. The mob may be looking to garner a controlling interest in a borrower's business, and when loan payments falter this provides the leverage necessary to bring this goal about. The borrower simply turns over all or a part of his business in exchange for a temporary (rarely a permanent) delay of his payments. This is one of the ways that organized crime secures a footing in legitimate business enterprises.

Drug Trafficking   Organized crime is involved in drug trafficking at all levels, but especially in importation and whlesale distribution. The need for organization, contacts, and large sums of money puts the business outside the reach of most individuals and small criminal groups. This does not mean, however, that organized crime is not interested in what goes on at the neighborhood and street levels of the drug scene. Since its own profits depend on a healthy drug traffic, it observes the street closely and helps keep open the channels through which the drugs will flow. The syndicate will also supply loans to dealers — at least the bigger, more successful ones — and through loan sharking and fencing on the street endeavor to ensure that money circulates so that buys can be made. Today much of the local heroin trade is controlled by black and Hispanic criminal groups, and this has been one of the avenues providing these groups with access into the world of organized crime.

Theft Organized crime has been interested in theft since its earliest days. Today most organized crime efforts are directed at the kinds of thievery that promise high returns while avoiding high risks, such as truck hijacking, car-theft rings, thefts from warehouses and docks, securities theft, and fencing. Once again the organization, money, muscle, and contacts of organized crime are major factors in explaining syndicate activity in these areas.

Much has recently been made of syndicate involvement in securities theft and manipulation. Millions of dollars in securities have been disappearing every year from the vaults of major brokerage houses. The lost bonds are not always stolen, but theft seems to be the major reason for their disappearance. Recent testimony before the Senate Committee on Banking, Housing, and Urban Affairs indicates that securities theft is a major problem these days, and that behind much of the thievery lie organized crime syndicates. While estimates of the actual amounts stolen are difficult to make, the yearly totals are generally thought to exceed $2 billion, and may be much higher when we include thefts from the mails and manipulations during securities transfers.[39]

To accomplish the theft and manipulation of stocks and bonds, organized crime needs insiders, persons employed by brokerage firms who have access to vaults or routinely handle securities. Sometimes these important contacts are indebted to loan sharks, and steal securities in exchange for a respite from their payments; sometimes extortion and intimidation are used to frighten employees into working with the underworld; and sometimes the mob manages to place one of its own into a position of trust within a brokerage firm. Once in syndicate hands, the stocks and bonds are often converted into cash. This can be accomplished by using the stolen securities as collateral for loans, as part of a company's portfolio of assets, or merely by reselling them through brokers either here or abroad.

LABOR RACKETEERING

During the nineteenth century, organized criminal groups learned that money could be made in the fields of industrial organization and management-worker relations. Faced with the prospects of strikes and unionization, companies were calling upon criminal gangs to help them combat these threats to their power and profits. The companies paid well for the gangs' muscle, and the gangs, in turn, were happy to oblige. The infiltration of the union movement by organized crime soon followed, and with it came money and power for leaders of the fledgling unions. First the building trades and then service industries fell under the influence and domination of corrupt officials backed by gangsters with their connections and muscle. Money was collected from both employers and employees, organized crime playing off each side against the other.[40]

Racketeering is explained not merely by the corruption of union and company officials nor by the fact that organized crime is in the business of making money any way it can. Rather, the spread of racketeering stems from a combination of social, political, economic, and cultural conditions. Important among the economic conditions are excessive entrepreneurial competition and an excess supply of labor. As Walter Lippmann observed many years ago:

> Given an oversupply of labor and an industry in which no considerable amount of capital or skill is required to enter it, the conditions exist under which racketeering can flourish. The effort to unionize in the face of a surplus of labor invites the use of violence and terror to maintain a monopoly of labor and thus to preserve the workers' standard of living. Labor unionism in such trades tends to fall into the control of dictators who are often corrupt and not often finical about enlisting gangsters to enforce the closed shop. The employers, on the other hand, faced with the constant threat of cutthroat competition, are subject to the easy temptation to pay gangsters for protection against competitors. The protection consists in driving the competition from the field.[41]

Identifying additional conditions that support organized crime infiltration into unions, John Hutchinson includes the traditions of frontier violence, cultural values stressing individualism, an entrenched philosophy of acquisition, an admiration for sharp practices, a tolerance of the fix, and a legacy stressing politics as a source of personal profit.[42] Companies and unions went along with the spread of racketeering because both saw the benefits outweighing the costs, and because the conditions and temperament of the times presented no great obstacles. Actually, of course, both company officials and union leaders risk becoming pawns in the hands of organized crime syndicates. This is precisely what has happened over the years, with the costs borne not only by the rank-and-file union membership but also by members of the general public who hold company stock, or who are simply consumers of the companies' goods and services.

In the view of Gordon Hostetter and Thomas Beesley, who wrote during the racketeering days of the Capone gang and of Willie Bioff and George Browne (gangsters in control of the 12,000 member International Alliance of Theatrical and Stage Employees, IATSE), racketeering depends for its persistence and success on five distinct but interdependent components: (1) businessmen in search of a monopoly and artificially high prices for their products and services; (2) union officials seeking a monopoly of control over workers in a given trade, hence the power to extract substantial dues and to dispense the right to work; (3) politicians willing to manipulate the law in exchange for campaign contributions or votes; (4) criminal gangs willing to use muscle and organization to control the racketeering; and (5) lawyers willing to create the legal ''charters of corruption,'' to twist the law to suit their criminal clients, and to present a public façade of respectability behind which the racket can operate.[43]

Nobody knows for sure how much organized crime syndicates make from labor racketeering. Suffice it to say that Bioff and Browne alone are reputed to have pocketed more than $2 million in IATSE funds in less than two years.[44] In 1958, the Senate Select Committee on Improper Activities in the Labor or Management Field found that $10 million in Teamsters Union funds had been siphoned off into the pockets of union officials and their gangster friends.[45] Today, the Teamsters Coastal States Pension Fund is widely acknowledged to have been under the control of syndicate figures. The fund is worth billions of dollars, and millions have apparently been spent without knowledge of the rank-and-file membership, whose money it really is.

PSEUDO-LEGITIMATE ENTERPRISES

Apart from their patently illegal enterprises, organized crime groups have infiltrated the world of legitimate business. While any complete list of the different businesses in which organized crime is involved would be impossible to compile, the following have been specifically identified: banking, hotels and motels, real estate, garbage collection, vending machines, construction, delivery and long-distance hauling, garment manufacture, insurance, stocks and bonds, vacation resorts, funeral parlors, bakeries, sausage manufacture and processing of other meat products, paving, tobacco, dairy products, demolition, warehousing, auto sales and leasing, meat packing, janitorial services, beauty and health salons, lumber, horse breeding, nightclubs, bars, restaurants, linen supply, laundries, and dry cleaning.[46] There may well be no legitimate business enterprise in which organized crime does not have a direct financial interest.

Organized crime has sought involvement in legitimate businesses for a number of reasons. First is the obvious economic incentive: legitimate businesses can and do make profits, hence are additional sources of income. Second, legitimate businesses can provide a front for illegal activities; owning a trucking firm, for example, provides a crime syndicate with the means of transporting stolen property or with a cover for bootlegging. Third, legitimate businesses can serve as an important outlet for monies earned through criminal activities. Profits from the latter invested in businesses under syndicate control appear to be "clean"; also, syndicate members can receive legitimate-looking salary payments from those companies with which they are associated. These salaries constitute the members' visible sources of income, and they declare this income on tax returns in the continuing effort to keep federal agencies off their backs. Needless to say, those receiving such salaries may have contributed little or nothing to the actual day-to-day operations of the companies concerned.

A final, but no less important, reason organized crime has sought holdings in legitimate enterprises is respectability. Crime is not respectable work and the profits from it are dirty money. A long-standing interest among higher-echelon mobsters, especially Italian-Americans with their traditions of family honor, has been the acquisition of respectability for their children and grandchildren, if not for themselves.[47] Legitimate businesses provide a route to just this respectability. Instead of following in the footsteps of their elders, the younger generation is able to acquire the trappings of respectability by working in enterprises with no apparent connection to crime. Even so, the legitimate enterprises are rarely, if ever, completely divorced from a syndicate's illegal enterprises, and for this reason it seems more appropriate to call them "pseudo-legitimate" enterprises. A certain real estate company may appear quite legal and aboveboard; if organized crime has anything to do with it, however, we can anticipate that all is not entirely what it appears to be.

Organized crime moves into its pseudo-legitimate enterprises in various ways. Some involve intimidation and force, others seem more like the normal avenues of business acquisition. When interested in a particular business, it is not rare for the syndicate to use the carrot-and-stick approach — in Don Corleone's words, "I'll make him an offer he can't refuse." Such a case was reported in the New York Court of Appeals a few years ago. An executive of several successful vending machine companies was simply told that he was to pass over to a certain family of interested persons a 25 percent share of his business interests. The request was backed up by assaults on his wife and various other forms of intimidation.[48] Another way to infiltrate businesses is to arrange, through extortion or bribes, to have syndicate associates placed in executive positions, so that eventually the company is controlled by the syndicate. Yet another way is to purchase large blocks of company stock through legitimate trading channels, though under the cover of fictitious names and companies.

One of the most common ways to acquire part or all of a business is to take advantage of a borrower's indebtedness to the syndicate loan shark and his inability to repay as agreed. Sometimes the indebtedness and the inability to pay are merely fortuitous, in the sense that a businessman finds himself in that position because of factors unconnected with any particular design on the part of syndicate loan sharks. He may have asked for the loan and was simply unable to meet his payments; had he met the terms of the loan things would have turned out differently. At other times, however, the syndicate has an interest in the business in mind all along. On such occasions the syndicate creates both indebtedness and inability to pay, thus placing the borrower in a position from which he can escape only by turning over part or all of his business.[49] To create indebtedness and inability to pay the syndicate actively solicits use of its loan-sharking services — it may begin by forcing a company into bad financial straits through any number of underhanded means — and then sets ridiculously high interest rates or arranges things so that the borrower conveniently misses one or more of his payment deadlines. No matter how the two important conditions arise, the end result is almost the same: the mob secures an interest in the business in lieu of loan repayment.

Organized crime will sometimes take over a business not to keep it alive and healthy but to force the company into bankruptcy after a quick cash profit is made. This is the "bust out" or "scam" operation. Salerno and Tompkins describe a scam case uncovered in the early 1960s:

> Murray Packing Co., Inc. in New York City was a supplier of meat, poultry, and eggs to wholesale houses and markets. It was operated by Joseph Weinberg, his son Stanley, and David Newman. One of Murray Packing's many customers was Pride Wholesale Meat and Poultry Corp., headed by a man named Peter Castellana. He was a member of the Carlo Gambino family of Cosa Nostra and a second cousin of the Boss.
>
> In December 1960 Murray Packing was short of working capital and a salesman for the firm, Joseph Pagano, told his employers that he could arrange a convenient loan for them. Pagano was a member of the Vito Genovese family. He arranged with Jo-Ran Trading Corp. — half-owned by Castellana — that Murray Packing be advanced $8500 at an interest charge of 1 percent a week. The other partner in Jo-Ran was Carmine Lombardozzi, a capo in the Gambino family.
>
> In January 1961 the Weinbergs and Newman were required to help "protect the investment" by selling a one-third interest in Murray Packing to Pagano. He was made president of the company and became co-signer of every check issued.
>
> At this point, Pride Wholesale Meat, Castellana's company, which normally bought about $1,000 a month in provisions from Murray Packing, began to buy huge quantities. In January it bought $241,000 worth, in February, $298,000 worth, and in March $922,000. These purchases were at prices below Murray Packing's own costs.
>
> Castellana got Pagano to transfer Murray Packing's bank account to the bank where he did business. Pride Wholesale Meat checks payable to Murray Packing would be taken to the bank and presented by Pagano together with Murray Packing checks made out to him in the same amount. In this way, Murray Packing was milked of $745,000 in three months and forced into bankruptcy. Murray Packing's suppliers all over the country were left holding the bag and $112,000 more was siphoned out of the company during the bankruptcy proceedings.[50]

In a federal trial on bankruptcy fraud charges, rare for organized crime, Pagano, Castellana, Newman, the Weinbergs, and others were convicted in December 1964.

The Survival of Organized Crime

How can organized crime persist and show no signs of decline? The answer to this important question lies beyond the more obvious defenses that secret societies and groups erect against outsiders — secrecy, codes of conduct, mutual proctection among members, and the like. We must look within the organization of crime syndicates at survival mechanisms that come into play whenever the more obvious defenses are threatened, as they will be from time to time. We must look at survival mechanisms brought into play in interactions between organized crime and the larger society. We must also look at the roles played by public attitudes and behavior, and at the attitudes and behavior of those ostensibly responsible for combating organized crime. We must look at the nature of criminal law itself, especially as it focuses on moral choices and private behavior. The search inevitably brings us into the realms of culture, law, politics, and economics.

ROLE IMPERATIVES WITHIN ORGANIZED CRIME

Two of the most important internal survival mechanisms appear to be the roles of "enforcer" and "buffer." These roles, assumed by select individuals within crime organizations, might well be called *role imperatives,* for without them (or something very similar) the survival of any crime organization is seriously called into question.

Donald Cressey goes so far as to argue that unless the division of labor provides for at least one enforcer, the organization in question is not a part of true organized crime.[51] Yet Ianni found only weak evidence of enforcer positions in the established division of labor and authority structure of the crime family he intensively studied.[52] Even so, internal discipline and security must be maintained if the crime organization is to survive and prosper, and even if it has no specifically identified position for an enforcer, the organization will provide for the enforcement of its rules and the directives of those in authority. It is imperative that enforcement activities are undertaken by at least one member when necessary. The methods of enforcement range from verbal warnings all the way to maiming or murder. A set of rules is not enough; from time to time they have to be enforced, and organized crime sees to it that they are. Organized crime has been likened to government in this sense: not only do syndicates create their own rules, but like states, have their own machinery for enforcing them and their own methods of doing it.

The "buffer" role identified by Cressey and others also enhances the organization's survival possibilities. The buffer is akin to the corporate "assistant to the president," his tasks being primarily centered on internal communications and the flow of decisions in the hierarchy of authority. The buffer may also be likened to a spy, for he keeps tabs on what lower-level members do and say, and reports back to his superiors. Without the buffer role, the smooth functioning of the organization would be impaired, and the decision-making process undermined. It is the buffer who keeps lines of communication between leaders and followers open, who passes down important messages from the top, who forewarns of internal dissensions and problems with operations at the street level, and who helps smooth out disagreements and conflicts.

Another role imperative is the "corrupter." Since organized crime syndicates are in the business of crime, survival greatly depends upon the fix. To put the fix in, and maintain important connections with those in government and law, organized crime groups typically have one or more members assigned to corrupt officials in order to preserve good relations with them.[53] The corrupter may be found anywhere in the organizational hierarchy, and his job is to bribe, buy, intimidate, negotiate, persuade, and sweet-talk "himself into a relationship with police, public officials, and anyone else who might help 'family' members maintain immunity from arrest, prosecution, and punishment."[54]

Cressey calls the political objective the "nullification of government," and it is sought at two different levels:

> At the lower level are the agencies for law enforcement and the administration of justice. When a Cosa Nostra soldier bribes a policeman, a police chief, a prosecutor, a judge, or a license administrator, he does so in an attempt to nullify the law-enforcement process. At the upper level are legislative agencies, including federal and state legislatures as well as city councils and county boards of supervisors. When a "family" boss supports a candidate for political office, he does so in an attempt to deprive honest citizens of their democratic voice, thus nullifying the democratic process.[55]

It should be obvious why nullification of government is an important survival mechanism in organized crime. For nullification to work there must be officials willing or able to be corrupted. We already know that some persons are willing to be corrupted, but even if there were no willing corruptees, organized crime's muscle and its willingness to use it would probably ensure viable corrupter-corruptee relationships.

The truth of the matter is, however, that organized crime rarely has to use muscle in order to nullify government, no matter at which level. The nature of politics and government is such that those acting in violation of the law and those ostensibly responsible for its creation and enforcement readily enter into mutually beneficial relationships. An associate of Louisiana mobster Carlos Marcello explains how easy and inevitable it was that those on the legitimate side of the fence would join in working relationships with those on the illegitimate side:

> You have to remember that when Carlos and I were starting out in the rackets, just about the only money available for political campaigns in Louisiana and other Southern states was rackets money. These were poor states. There were no "fat cats" around to finance political campaigns. If a guy wanted to run for any important office, the only place he could get enough money was from us. So we got control of the political machinery. We picked the candidates; we paid for their campaigns; we paid them off; we told them what to do.[56]

Just how successful and important these connections are is evidenced by the fact that since its very beginning organized crime has made one of its first tasks the establishment of working relationships with those in politics, government, and law enforcement. Because it pays off in security, organized crime will continue to pursue the nullification of government.[57]

THE LEGISLATION OF MORALITY

Organized crime will continue to persist and flourish if lawmakers continue to enact legislation rendering illegal any activities, products, and services demanded by significant numbers of the population. Organized crime makes the bulk of its profits in supplying illegal commodities and services. Drugs, gambling, sex, and other so-called vices are profitable precisely because there are criminal laws, which have the effect of driving the activities underground and into the hands of those willing and able to carry out illicit business. In this way, criminal laws create the very conditions conducive to the emergence and spread of organized criminal activities.

The legislation of morality is, then, yet another factor in the survival of organized crime. But apart from encouraging the emergence of black marketeering, laws designed to repress what some people think of as vices also help to give "a kind of franchise to those who are willing to break the law."[58] This is what Herbert Packer has called "the crime tariff"; it serves to protect those among us who will break the law by supplying drugs or gambling opportunities from those who are unwilling to do so but who will take advantage of their availability.[59] Journalist and social commentator Walter Lippmann first drew attention to this unintended consequence of moral legislation when he noted more than forty years ago that

> . . . we have a code of laws which prohibit all the weaknesses of the flesh. This code of laws is effective up to a point. That point is the unwillingness of respectable people to engage in the prohibited services as seller of prohibited commodities. . . . The high level of lawlessness is maintained by the fact that Americans desire to do so many things which they also desire to prohibit. . . . [They] have made laws which act like a protective tariff — to encourage

the business of the underworld. Their prohibitions have turned over to the underworld the services from which it profits. Their prejudice in favor of weak governments has deprived them of the power to cope with the vast lawbreaking industries which their laws have called into question.[60]

THE ATTITUDES AND BEHAVIOR OF THE PUBLIC

If few among us took advantage of the illegal goods and services provided by organized crime, an important ingredient in its survival would be missing: organized crime depends for its profits and power on widespread demand for its services. By demanding its products and services, the public helps organized crime survive.

In addition to public behavior, public attitudes and perceptions also help organized crime survive. How Americans view crime and criminals helps shape the crime scene itself. In the case of organized crime, public perceptions and attitudes are probably more fuzzy and mixed than anything else, but so far no evidence has been presented to indicate that the public perceives organized crime as a real problem deserving stringent control.

The lack of attitudinal opposition to organized crime reflects in part the fact that some of us have made use of its services and that many of those who have not are unconvinced of the harmfulness of the services it provides. Moreover, many of us probably have only a vague idea of what organized crime is really all about, and, when we go into droves to films like *The Godfather,* the picture we see hardly fits in with our day-to-day experiences or our images of the world. Indeed, the mystery surrounding organized crime provides it with a certain charm and appeal. Then again, even when we consume the products and services supplied by organized crime, we rarely come in contact with persons who represent themselves as members of a crime family or syndicate, and those we do encounter have no distinguishing marks about them to suggest that they are part of organized crime. Stuart Hills points out: "Many of the customers who place a friendly bet with that nice old man in the corner bar do not perceive, in fact, that this criminal bookmaker is a businessman — not an unorganized individual gambler."[61]

Perhaps the most important reason public perceptions and attitudes are sketchy, stereotypical, and ambivalent is that those to whom we customarily look for clues and guidance in our thinking about crime have themselves presented a fragmented and warped picture. Government officials and law enforcement agencies have tended to stress the individual character of crime and criminality, and have downplayed its organizational features.[62] Beyond this, the stereotype of the dangerous criminal fostered by the authorities fits the mugger, rapist, burglar, and dope pusher, not Vito Genovese, Carlo Gambino, or Sam Giancana. Whether government officials purposely play down organized crime and systematically keep information about it from the public is hard to say. Salerno and Tompkins think that might be the case: "Too much effort spent exposing organized crime could be damaging in future elections."[63]

Future Trends

Organized crime is undoubtedly here to stay, at least for the foreseeable future. But changes are afoot, just as changes occurred in the past. Today there is evidence of further ethnic succession. Blacks, Chicanos, Puerto Ricans, and Cuban-Americans have established a footing in organized crime, especially in the highly populated Northeast and in Chicago and Miami.

Ianni has studied these recent entrants in the field.[64] As yet they are neither as well organized nor as far-reaching in their activities as Italian-American crime syndicates. They also differ among themselves in a variety of respects. But the die seems to be cast: in the next decade or so members of these groups should increase their participation in organized crime, and the Italian-American domination of vice should decline in the urban centers where large populations of blacks and Hispanics are concentrated.

According to Ianni, the same ghetto conditions that spawned early organized crime helped produced the contemporary ethnic succession. In addition, the Italian-American crime syndicates themselves may have helped bring about change. For one thing, established organized crime groups inevitably came to employ ghetto residents as soldiers, lower-echelon pushers, and numbers runners in their own neighborhoods. Street-wise blacks, Chicanos, Puerto Ricans, and Cubans became the vital link between the organization and the street-level buyers of commodities and services. With involvement came knowledge, contacts, and, for some, wealth. With involvement also came efforts to control the business in one's territory. An added incentive for Cuban involvement came with the establishment of a cocaine and heroin connection from South America through Cuba and Miami. Ianni points out the significance of this connection for the future:

> If our information is accurate, and I am confidant that it is, this new route for drugs from South America should have some important effects on the drug scene in the United States. The most important effect will be the continued displacement of Italian-American syndicates from the international drug traffic as this new connection replaces the older one that came through Europe. The "street" implications of this are enormous. It not only means that new patterns of wholesaling will be established, changing the ethnic balance of power in organized crime, but it also means that cocaine may very well displace heroin as *the* street drug.[65]

Although mainly restricted to their own ethnic neighborhoods, the crime networks of blacks and Hispanics are emerging as the new forces in the organized delivery of drugs and sex, and are gaining more control over the numbers racket and loan sharking in the ghetto. Yet in order to really extend and expand, these newcomers will have to accomplish what the Italian-Americans did before them: "(1) greater control over sectors of organized crime outside as well as inside the ghetto; (2) some organizing principle which will serve as kinship did among the Italians to bring the disparate networks together into larger criminally monopolistic organizations; and (3) better access to political power and the ability to corrupt it."[66] While the first requirement may well be the easiest to meet because of their growing control over the drug traffic, the newcomers may yet be some way away from meeting the other two requirements, and much will depend upon the willingness of established crime syndicates to allow a blossoming competition.

We can expect to continue hearing about organized crime. It should be apparent that organized crime is a consequence of numerous social, cultural, political, legal, and economic conditions, some of which seem destined to remain with us. Stuart Hills suggests why organized crime will continue to flourish:

> As long as we attempt to blame organized crime on individually maladjusted "foreigners"; as long as we persist in equating "sinful" behavior with crime and thereby make illegal the activity in which significant segments of the American public wish to indulge; as long as businessmen show little interest in persons with whom they do business and are willing to purchase "labor harmony"; as long as we accord a higher value to the rewards of individual success than to the means of their attainment, and invite all comers to compete for these rewards but restrict the opportunities for their realization from various segments of the population; as long as we insist on a fragmented, decentralized, and locally autonomous police system in the name of grass-roots democracy — in short, as long as we cling to various myths and cherish certain cultural values, legal policies, and institutional practices — large-scale syndicated crime is likely to continue to flourish in America.[67]

References

1. See Donald R. Cressey, "Methodological Problems in the Study of Organized Crime as a Social Problem," *The Annals* 374 (1967), pp. 104–5.
2. U.S., Congress, Senate, Special Committee to Investigate Organized Crime in Interstate Commerce, *Third Interim Report,* 82nd Cong., 1st Sess., cited in Gus Tyler, ed., *Organized Crime in America* (Ann Arbor: University of Michigan Press, 1962), pp. 343–44.
3. Donald R. Cressey, *Theft of the Nation: The Structure and Operations of Organized Crime in America* (New York: Harper and Row, 1969), pp. x–xi.
4. Cressey, *Theft of the Nation,* pp. 29–35, and chapter VI.
5. See Daniel Bell, "Crime as an American Way of Life: A Queer Ladder of Social Mobility" in Daniel Bell, *The End of Ideology* (New York: Free Press, 1965), pp. 138–41; John E. Conklin, ed., *The Crime Establishment: Organized Crime and American Society* (Englewood Cliffs, N.J.: Prentice-Hall 1973), pp. 8–13; and Francis A. J.

Ianni with Elizabeth Reuss-Ianni, *A Family Business: Kinship and Control in Organized Crime* (New York: Russell Sage Foundation, 1973), pp. 6–16 and 119–24. For the historical picture, see Alan Block's recent analysis of the early cocaine trade, "The Snowman Cometh: Coke in Progressive New York," *Criminology* 17 (1979), pp. 75–99.

6. Ianni and Reuss-Ianni, *A Family Business*, pp. 120–24.

7. For more on Valachi and his testimony before the McClellan Committee, see Peter Maas, *The Valachi Papers* (New York: Putnam, 1968).

8. Stuart L. Hills, *Crime, Power, and Morality* (Scranton, Pa.: Chandler Publishing Co., 1971), pp. 138–39.

9. Cressey, *Theft of the Nation*, pp. 163–64.

10. Ibid., pp. 175–78.

11. For example, Ralph Salerno and John S. Tompkins, *The Crime Confederation: Cosa Nostra and Allied Operations in Organized Crime* (Garden City, N.Y.: Doubleday, 1969), pp. 105–48.

12. Ibid.

13. Ianni and Reuss-Ianni, *A Family Business*, pp. 150–55.

14. Ibid., pp. 154–55.

15. Ibid., p. 155.

16. See Francis A. J. Ianni, *Black Mafia: Ethnic Succession in Organized Crime* (New York: Pocket Books, 1975), pp. 301–5; also his "New Mafia: Black, Hispanic, and Italian Styles," *Society* 11 (1974), pp. 30–35.

17. Ibid.

18. Gus Tyler, "The Forerunner of the Syndicate," in *Organized Crime in America*, ed. Gus Tyler, p. 92.

19. Ianni, *Black Mafia*, pp. 89–90.

20. Figures cited in Ianni and Reuss-Ianni, *A Family Business*, pp. 48–49.

21. Ibid., p. 55.

22. Ibid.

23. This section borrows heavily from Ianni and Reuss-Ianni, *A Family Business*, chapters 2 and 3; also, Anton Block, *The Mafia of a Sicilian Village* (New York: Harper Torchbooks, 1974) chapter V.

24. See, especially, Ianni and Reuss-Ianni, *A Family Business*, pp. 30–40.

25. Ibid., p. 26.

26. Ibid., pp. 59–60.

27. See ibid., pp. 27–28, for another account of the ritual.

28. Based on Valachi's testimony, cited in *Time* (August 22, 1969), p. 19.

29. Ianni and Reuss-Ianni, *A Family Business*, p. 74.

30. Ibid., p. 61.

31. Michael Dorman, *Payoff: The Role of Organized Crime in American Politics* (New York: David McKay, 1972), p. 129.

32. Hills, *Crime, Power, and Morality*, pp. 106–7.

33. The various estimates come from Ianni, *Black Mafia*, pp. xi–xii; and Salerno and Tompkins, *The Crime Confederation*, pp. 128–29.

34. Cressey, *Theft of the Nation*, p. 134.

35. Charles H. McCaghy, *Deviant Behavior: Crime, Conflict and Interest Groups* (New York: Macmillan, 1976), p. 241.

36. Salerno and Tompkins, *The Crime Confederation*, p. 272.

37. Ianni, *Black Mafia*, pp. 59–60. See also, The President's Commission on Law Enforcement and the Administration of Justice, *Task Force Report: Organized Crime* (Washington, D.C.: U.S. Government Printing Office, 1967), p. 189.

38. Cressey, *Theft of the Nation*, p. 81.

39. See Senator Charles H. Percy, "Organized Crime in the Securities Market," in *The Crime Establishment*, ed. John Conklin, pp. 121–27; also McCaghy, *Deviant Behavior*, p. 242; and Tim Metz, "Hot Stocks," in *Crime as Business*, ed. Michael Gartner (Princeton, N.J.: Dow Jones Books, 1971), pp. 90–96.

40. See John Hutchinson, "The Anatomy of Corruption in the Trade Unions," *Industrial Relations* 8 (1969), pp. 135–37.

41. Walter Lippmann, "The Underworld as Servant," *Forum* (January-February, 1931), reprinted in *Organized Crime in America*, ed. Tyler, p. 61.

42. Hutchinson, "The Anatomy of Corruption," p. 143.

43. Gordon Hostetter and Thomas A. Beesley, "Twentieth Century Crime," *The Political Quarterly* 14 (1933); reprinted in *Organized Crime in America*, ed. Tyler pp. 51–53.

44. *New Republic* (October 27, 1941).

45. Salerno and Tompkins, *The Crime Confederation*, p. 295.

46. National Council on Crime and Delinquency, "The Infiltration into Legitimate Business by Organized Crime," pamphlet issued by the National Emergency Committee (New York, 1968); Hostetter and Beesley, "Twentieth Century Crime"; and Dorman, *Payoff*, p. 277.

47. See Ianni and Reuss-Ianni, *A Family Business*, pp. 97–98.

48. Cited in Cressey, *Theft of the Nation*, pp. 103–4.

49. Charles Grutzner, "How to Lock out the Mafia," *Harvard Business Review* 48 (1970), p. 50.

50. Salerno and Tompkins, *The Crime Confederation*, pp. 235–36.

51. See Cressey, *Theft of the Nation*, pp. 313–22.

52. Ianni and Reuss-Ianni, *A Family Business*, p. 128.

53. Cressey, *Theft of the Nation*, pp. 251–52.

54. Ibid., p. 250.

55. Ibid., p. 248.

56. Dorman, *Payoff*, p. 11.

57. For more details of the connection between organized crime and politics, as well as abundant examples of the payoff to organized crime, see

Cressey, *Theft of the Nation,* pp. 248–89; Dorman, *Payoff;* also John A. Gardiner, *The Politics of Corruption; Organized Crime in an American City* (New York: Russell Sage Foundation, 1970); Clark R. Mollenhoff, *Despoilers of Democracy* (Garden City, N.Y.: Doubleday, 1965); Walter Goodman, *A Percentage of the Take* (New York: Farrar, Straus, and Giroux, 1971); and Frederic D. Homer, *Guns and Garlic* (West Lafayette, Ind.: Indiana University Press, 1974).

58. Thomas C. Schelling, "Economic Analysis of Organized Crime," in President's Commission on Law Enforcement and the Administration of Justice, *Task Force Report: Organized Crime,* p. 117.

59. See Herbert L. Packer, "The Crime Tariff," *American Scholar* 33 (1964), pp. 551–57; also his *Limits of the Criminal Sanction* (Stanford, Calif.: Stanford University Press, 1968).

60. Walter Lippmann, "The Underworld as Servant," pp. 65, 67, 68.

61. Hills, *Crime, Power, and Morality,* p. 130.

62. See Cressey, *Theft of the Nation,* chapter XII; also his "Methodological Problems in the Study of Organized Crime as a Social Problem."

63. Salerno and Tompkins, *The Crime Confederation,* p. 271.

64. See Ianni, *Black Mafia;* also his "New Mafia."

65. Ianni, *Black Mafia,* p. 235.

66. Ianni, "New Mafia," p. 36.

67. Hills, *Crime, Power, and Morality,* p. 144.

The Drug Scene

We have argued that nothing inherent in any activity makes it a crime. Rather, activities and those who engage in them become criminal when they are so labeled by persons with the authority to do so. Sometimes acts similar in substance turn out to be labeled differently — some are called crimes, others are not. This is especially the case with drugs. Most Americans are consumers of drugs, but some of us are doing nothing illegal while others are. The world of drugs, then, has two sides, the legal and criminal. Although this is a criminology text, and as such focuses on crime, we cannot hope to grasp the realities of the criminal side of drugs and their use if we do not at the same time consider the legal side. Indeed, it is through understanding the legal use of legal drugs that we find insights into the illegal use of drugs and into drug-related crime.

Some Definitional Problems

Published works on drugs frequently contain terms that may be unfamiliar to many readers. Even familiar terms are sometimes defined in unexpected ways. While scholars have been wrestling with definitions for a long time, their efforts have produced little concrete agreement. Even the word *drug* has taken on a variety of meanings.

From the standpoint of a physician, for example, a drug can be any substance with medicinal or therapeutic properties. A research chemist, in contrast, may be interested in a definition that goes beyond medicinal effects. He would probably adopt a pharmacological definition, one incorporating both the chemical nature of a substance and its related effects on the human organism. The lawyer is likely to focus attention on the legal conception of substances as drugs. Legal definitions may or may not take into account the pharmacological or medicinal properties of a substance. For lawyers, policemen, judges, and others working in the field of law, substances are drugs when defined as such in the law.

Not surprisingly, substances are inconsistently identified as drugs. Alcohol, for example, is usually not considered a drug by the layman or by the medical profession. Nor, in most jurisdictions, is it legally classified as a drug. In the pharmacological literature, however, alcohol is identified as a drug.

We will use the word *drug* to refer to any psychoactive substance. A *psychoactive substance* is one having the capacity to alter mental states and hence influence human activity. Identifying an "altered mental state" involves a subjective assessment by the drug user, which sometimes complicates the identification of a substance as a drug. However, the evidence consistently indicates that some of the major examples of currently available drugs are alcohol, nicotine, caffeine, opiates, hallucinogens (LSD, DMT), cocaine, barbiturates ("downers"), amphetamines ("speed"), marijuana, tranquilizers, and even aspirin.

While on the subject of terms and their definitions, we might as well confront one of the most confusing of all: addiction. Since this term will crop up from time to time throughout our discussion, it will help if we can agree on what we mean by it. In popular use, the word *addiction* immediately conjures up negative images. It is something to be feared, resisted, and condemned. Addiction suggests being unable to do without something, and this is a condition of the weak, the depraved, and the deviant. Among scientists, the term has been treated a little more rigorously, but this does not mean that they agree on its definition.

To define addiction we must really confront two issues. One is the direct physical effects of a drug on the biochemical structure of the human body, and the other is the mental and physical reactions to it by those using it. When a person habitually takes a drug we might be inclined to say that he is addicted to its effects — he cannot do without them. But the problem is that some drugs create a bodily craving while others do not. That is, some drugs have specific effects on the cells of the body such that the cells in question "adjust" to the drug's presence and assume stable functions only when the effects of the drugs are working. The body needs the drug. Other drugs have no such effects, yet people habitually use them.

The term *addiction* is best reserved for situations in which a particular drug produces bodily dependence. The term *habituation* can then be used to describe those situations in which a person regularly uses a drug even though his body exhibits no physical dependence. Habituation has much to do with personality and situational factors, while addiction has much to do with the substance itself.[1]

A corollary of addiction is *withdrawal*. When an individual either ceases to take a drug to which he is addicted. or reduces the dosage, his body cells respond to its withdrawal. The resulting adjustment can take several hours or several days. In most cases the withdrawal process is extremely distressing and in some situations it can be fatal; alcohol, heroin, and barbiturate withdrawal are extremely dangerous. It is this feature more than any other that makes drug addiction a real problem for the individual involved, and which may lead him to take extraordinary measures to support his dependence.

Those drugs that are potentially addicting are alcohol, nicotine, opiates, and barbiturates. Marijuana, the psychedelics such as LSD, amphetamines, and cocaine are not addicting, though users of amphetamines and psychedelics may find that increasing doses are required in order to produce desired physical and mental reactions.[2] Though not addicted to such drugs, some users are habituated to them in that they use them on a regular, frequent basis.

Drugs in American History

Psychoactive substances of one sort or another have been a part of American life since the founding of the country. Alcohol, perhaps the oldest known drug, was widely used in Europe at the time New England was settled. Immigrants had a variety of uses for alcohol. Following the customs of their home countries, alcohol was used "as a social beverage, a before-meals aperitif, a thirst-quenching beverage during meals, an after-dinner drink, an evening drink, a nightcap, a tranquilizer, an anesthetic, a deliriant, and a means of getting drunk."[3]

Substances capable of producing hallucinations in humans (hallucinogens, or, more popularly, psychedelics) were also used during the early history of America. It is quite likely that some drug use — particularly the hallucinogens psilocybin and psilocin, found in certain mushrooms — became popular after the period of early settlement, and we know that in the Southwest mescal "buttons" from the peyote cactus were widely used by some Indian tribes.[4] Unfortunately, we know very little about the extent of early hallucinogen use.

Much more is known about the use of opium and marijuana. The extensive study of opium use by C. E. Terry and Mildred Pellens attests to the early use of this drug.[5] Reviewing the available literature on the "opium problem," these authors conclude that opium use is by no means a recent

American phenomenon but is "the result . . . of a continuous growth [in use], probably from Colonial days."[6] Personal accounts by opium users indicate that by the late 1800s the practice had gained considerable ground throughout the United States.

Indeed, nineteenth-century America has been characterized by one author as a "dope fiend's paradise."[7] Opium and its alkaloid extract, morphine, were readily available and could be legally purchased by almost anyone. By midcentury, morphine had become a standard medical drug. It was so widely prescribed in the treatment of the Civil War wounded that morphine addiction became known as the "soldier's disease." In addition, opium was adopted as a household remedy for a variety of ills. The household medicinal uses of opium ranged from remedies for coughs, diarrhea, and dysentery to the relief of childhood teething problems. The medical profession also used opium and its newly discovered derivatives for conditions ranging from angina pectoris, diabetes, and tetanus to insanity and nymphomania!

Opiate use was actively encouraged by some segments of society, most notably by those who stood to gain financially from it. The sale of opiates and opiate-containing preparations was big business. Edward Brecher has identified five major channels of opiate distribution: (1) dispensing or prescribing by physicians; (2) nonprescription sale by drugstores; (3) sales in grocery and general stores; (4) mail-order sales; and (5) widespread sale of patent medicines containing opiates — for example, Ayers Cherry Pectoral, Mrs. Winslow's Soothing Syrup, and Godfrey's Cordial.[8] Whether the general public realized it or not, opiates were everywhere at hand, and many thousands became addicted to them. By the last quarter of the nineteenth century, somewhere between 1 percent (more than 250,000 and 4 percent (1,250,000) of our population were regularly using opiates in one form or another.[9] While it is impossible to ascertain what proportion of users were in fact addicts, there would need to be from 2 to 8 million opiate users today for an equivalent usage rate. Most estimates place the current addict population at between 250,000 and 400,000.

MARIJUANA

Like opium, Indian hemp (*Cannabis sativa*) has been used for centuries. It is the female plant that produces the psychoactive resin in its flowering tops. The resin, called *charas* by the Hindus, and known as hashish today, was long used by the inhabitants of India for spiritual and ritualistic purposes. The Chinese before them had found a variety of medicinal uses for the drug.[10] When the top leaves of the hemp plant are cut, dried, and eaten or smoked, a much less potent concoction is consumed. The Indians called it bhang, and we call it marijuana (or, popularly, grass or pot).

It is difficult to pinpoint when marijuana was first consumed in America. We do know that the early settlers cultivated hemp for its fibers, used in the manufacture of rope, and a number of authors have suggested that hemp was grown for its psychoactive resin as well.[11] By the mid-nineteenth century, marijuana was being used quite freely as a medicinal preparation. Major pharmaceutical companies and the nation's physicians were distributing it, and it was a favored remedy for respiratory ailments, headaches and other pains, and a variety of other ills.

In the same period, marijuana and hashish gained ground as a divertissement for pleasure seekers. Colorful accounts from that time indicate an expanded recreational use.[12] A number of major American cities had "hashish houses" where customers could indulge in privacy. Compared to opiate use, however, all evidence indicates that marijuana and hashish were used less widely for either medicinal or recreational purposes.

OPIUM AND THE LAW

Even as the legal use of opiates, marijuana, and other drugs was escalating, forces were gathering that would ultimately lead to severe legal repression. Sanctions against the opiate user first appeared in local ordinances forbidding the smoking of opium in so-called opium dens. San Francisco adopted the prohibition in 1875 and other cities soon followed suit. Opium smoking was designated criminal not so much because of the effects of the drug itself but, rather, because of the circumstances surrounding its use. In the main, the decision to outlaw opium dens was rooted in prejudice, discrimination, and misinformation.

In San Francisco and other cities, opium smoking was tied directly to the Chinese immigrants who entered the United States as cheap labor to be used in the construction of mines and railroads. Being both nonwhite and non-English-speaking, the Chinese immigrants were treated differently almost as a matter of course. When they settled in San Francisco their visibility increased. The marked difference between native and Chinese life-styles and the willingness of the Chinese to work for a pittance both helped foster an attitude of hostility among the townsfolk. Attitudes and prejudices were brought to a focus on the issue of opium dens, a unique Chinese contribution to the San Francisco scene.[13] When white Americans, especially women and those of "respectable" background, began visiting the dens, strong official reactions were forthcoming, and these served to outlaw opiate use for pleasure.

The laws aimed at prohibiting opium smoking had little effect on opium's availability or use. When Congress later moved to control the legal importation of opium used in smoking mixtures, smuggling merely took its place. Citing Treasury Department figures, Brecher notes that even the legal importation of opium increased. From 1860 to 1869, 21,176 pounds of smoking opium were legally imported. For the first decade of the twentieth century the amount imported had grown to 148,168 pounds.[14] By this time the opium problem had taken on an important political dimension, setting the scene for the broadest controls yet, those of the 1914 Harrison "Narcotics" Act.

Considerable pressures were placed on Congress to treat the opium question as an international problem. The United States was becoming increasingly involved in the arena of international trade and political maneuvering, a major incentive for American participation in the debate over opium. Various international conferences were held, culminating in the Hague Convention of 1912, which produced the first international opium agreement.[15] When Congress took up the Harrison bill, advocating strong controls on opiates and other narcotics, the question of international politics was a central issue:

> The supporters of the Harrison bill said little in the Congressional debates (which lasted several days) about the evils of narcotics addiction in the United States. They talked more about the need to implement the Hague Convention of 1912. Even Senator Mann of Mann Act fame, spokesman for the bill in the Senate, talked about international obligations rather than domestic morality.[16]

ALCOHOL

Although throughout the history of Anglo-American criminal law alcohol use had been subjected to controls of one sort or another, it was not until the twentieth century that efforts at stringent legal control saw fruition. For many years, various segments of American society had viewed the consumption of alcohol as a problem about which something should be done. Rooted primarily in the teachings of Quakers, Methodists, and other Protestant groups, the ideas expressed by those opposing the consumption of alcoholic beverages gained national prominence during the nineteenth century. The temperance movement was born, and by 1869 its offshoot, the Prohibition party, became a major force in American politics.[17]

Apart from their concern with moral and religious issues, those waging war against alcohol were also concerned for some very practical reasons. They felt that social life itself was threatened by the relatively free consumption of alcohol. Drinking was seen as a threat to family life, to the economy, to the quality of both urban and rural life, and to harmonious interpersonal relations. Alcohol was linked to crime, broken homes, poor workmanship, unemployment, and a host of other social and moral evils.

By the 1900s scientific and medical research underscored the harmful effects of alcohol, particularly on the physical and mental state of regular imbibers. Findings showed damage to nerve cells, impairment of mental functioning, weakening of blood vessels and the heart, lowered resistance to disease and illness, impairment of reaction time and judgment, and adverse effects on digestion. The most recent research on the physical and mental effects of alcohol confirms these earlier observations.[18] Armed with religious, social, economic, and medical arguments, the temperance movement quickly achieved its legislative victory in the 1919 ratification of the Volstead Act. National Prohibition, the "great experiment," had begun.

Early Effects of Criminal Legislation

The immediate consequence of the Harrison and Volstead acts was to label the use of opiates and alcohol as criminal behavior.* Even though neither law specifically criminalized the act of consuming these drugs, both in effect made their use a crime and the user a criminal. The production, manufacture, and distribution of the drugs were regulated such that systematic lawbreaking was typically involved for anyone to obtain them. In short, people who had previously been acting legally now found themselves tagged and reacted to as criminals.

Use of the drugs apparently decreased after passage of these laws.[19] At first there was a period of adjustment, as customary sources of supply dried up. But then some people stopped altogether, as their desire not to be labeled criminal outweighed their desire for the drug. More important, however, were the effects of these new laws on the social context of drug use, the characteristics of the typical user, and the attitudes of different segments of the population toward the drugs in question. In the case of alcohol, these effects culminated in the repeal of Prohibition in 1933. In the case of narcotics, however, these effects were instrumental in creating new problems associated with their use. These new problems, in turn, led to more repressive measures, resulting in harsher punishments for the criminal and more systematic efforts to detect and arrest him.

With legal access to alcohol and opiates closed off, customary users sought alternative avenues to their acquisition. Use became marked by secrecy and risk taking. Underworld networks of communication, production, distribution, and sale sprang up. People still wanted or needed the drugs and profiteers were quick to respond to the continuing demand.

Black market supplies posed special hazards for the user, apart from the risks of arrest and conviction on a criminal charge. Since the production and distribution of the drugs were free from government regulation, the consumer was no longer guaranteed that the product was safe from contamination, or even that it was what it was supposed to be. To the risks of being caught were added the risks of illness, even death. As one commentator of the period noted: "The liquor that law violators are drinking today is perhaps the most deadly stuff that was ever put into the

---

*The Harrison Act erroneously labeled cocaine, which comes from coca leaves, as a narcotic, and included this drug along with opium and its derivatives and synthetic cousins, morphine and heroin.

human stomach as a beverage. . . . It is harsh, raw, laden with poison, and utterly unfit to drink."[20] Similarly, black market opiates were of questionable quality and purity. The buyer usually had no knowledge of just how much he was taking in a single dose, or with what other substances the drug had been "cut." So it is today: the addict "literally stakes his life everytime he takes a dose; death, both of the quick and relatively slow varieties, is tragically common."[21]

The demand for alcohol was far greater than that for opiates, and every effort was directed at meeting it. Crime syndicates flourished in the larger cities, and the organizational sophistication they attained during Prohibition has remained a major feature of contemporary organized crime. The success of organized crime after Prohibition depended on the skills learned in handling the illicit liquor trade. With the repeal of Prohibition, organized crime turned to other avenues of lush profit, one of which turned out to be the narcotics market.

CHANGING CHARACTERISTICS OF OPIATE USERS

During Prohibition, members of all social classes continued to drink. In addition, drinking habits cut across lines of age, sex, and race. Despite the difficulties associated with securing a ready supply of booze, those who wanted it could get it. One of the consequences of legal control of opiate use, on the other hand, was a change in the social characteristics of the typical user. Prior to the Harrison Act, opiate use had been widespread but especially prevalent among white, female, middle-class persons between 35 and 50. Following the Harrison Act, the known population of users shifted largely to lower-class males under 30 years old, who lived primarily in inner-city areas of the larger towns. Many were black, or of Puerto Rican or Mexican descent.[22]

A variety of reasons explain the change in social characteristics of the opiate-using population. Some previous users were undoubtedly intimidated by their new status as criminals and were able to discontinue use. In all likelihood the level of use for some of these people had not attained addicting proportions. Erich Goode has suggested that some previous users switched from illegal opiates to sedatives, more readily obtained through prescription:

> Exactly the same types of people who used narcotics in 1900 are now using barbiturates — middle-aged, middle-class, white women with various quasi-medical, largely emotional problems that (they feel) can be solved by taking a drug. The laws did absolutely nothing to terminate this class of addicts, who certainly were in the majority in 1900 — they simply changed the drug to which people were addicted.[23]

Special interest groups also played a role in the status changes following criminalization of narcotics use. Both pharmaceutical concerns and physicians were served by the switching of drugs. Pharmaceutical companies were able to sell more drugs. Doctors were able to avoid the harassment, as well as the stigma, associated with energetic law enforcement efforts to stamp out narcotics use, and yet still keep their patients happy. Indeed, the medical profession was subjected to continued harassment in their efforts to serve the needs of patients, particularly addicts. Goode estimates that between 1914 and 1938 as many as 25,000 physicians were charged with violations of drug laws. If anything, this helped foster a negative attitude among physicians toward narcotics use in particular, and the use of illegal drugs in general.

The Harrison Act and subsequent tightening-up measures, coupled with the refusal of physicians to dispense opiates to addicts, forced the acquisition and sale of opiates into places where secrecy, anonymity, ease of distribution, and a concentrated consumer population could be found or fostered. In other words, opiates went to the urban areas and the inner city. A subculture of inner-city heroin use slowly emerged, with intravenous injection ("mainlining") the preferred mode of ingestion. Street crime became the major means of financing a drug need that was constant among the addict population. Police surveillance and harassment, illness, death, and a life-style of secrecy and fear became features of inner-city heroin use. Meanwhile, the middle-class American felt far removed from all this, and with a clear conscience could sit back with his cigar or cigarette, his now-legal glass of beer, and his tranquilized wife, and applaud the just and untiring efforts of the law to stamp out this new menace.

THE ROLE OF INTERESTS IN THE REPEAL OF PROHIBITION

While opiates and cocaine have remained the targets of legal repression, the consumption of beer, wine, and liquor became legal in most states with the repeal of Prohibition in 1933. This move may seem surprising in view of the known adverse effects of the drug. In fact, the repeal of Prohibition provides a good illustration of the role of interests in the decriminalization of behavior. If we consider the power of those interests, we find that repeal of Prohibition is not at all surprising.

Consider, first, the public demand for alcohol. While it is impossible to measure that demand, we know that despite Prohibition vast numbers of Americans continued to imbibe, and illegal manufacturing operations were set up across the country to keep supplies available. To enforce Prohibition meant to subject suppliers and willing users to police action and the stigma of criminalization. Also, the law sought to deprive them of a valued thing. Those in the upper echelons of society did not take kindly to this, and much pressure to repeal Prohibition resulted from upper-class resentment.[24]

The liquor interests were also formidable. One author reports that prior to Prohibition, 268 million gallons of distilled spirits were legally produced each year, while over 1,300 breweries produced 2 billion gallons of beer. With the Volstead Act, breweries and distilleries were put out of business. Across the United States some 178,000 saloons closed down.[25] For the liquor interests, even a month of Prohibition was a month too long.

Other factors operating in the case of alcohol, but not the opiates, included demands for states' rights and freedom from federal control of local affairs and a growing concern in many quarters that organized crime would constantly spread unless alcohol could once more be produced and sold legally. Finally, the feeling was widespread that enforcement of the Volstead Act had failed. Not only were people still drinking, but the police themselves were manifestly inefficient, and corruption was rampant.

Prohibition actually helped foster a redefinition of alcohol use as acceptable behavior that should largely be free from legal controls, particularly those aimed at making suppliers and users criminals. Public opinion placed alcohol on a different plane from other drugs. It was not thought of as a drug, and the terms *drug abuse* and *drug problem* were reserved for the vague "narcotic" group of substances and those who used them. Pressures to legalize narcotics use, even by those with medical and quasi-medical problems, were notable by their absence. Those who would use them if they were legal had alternatives. Pharmaceutical companies and the manufacturers of patent medicines were not dependent on opiates for their livelihood. The medical profession turned its back on the opium and heroin addict, while lawmakers used the failures of enforcement as a justification for harsher, more punitive measures. The illicit use of "hard drugs" was seen as a problem by the same people who had urged the repeal of Prohibition.

In Search of Pleasure: Marijuana Use in America

The use of marijuana for recreational purposes received a major boost during Prohibition. Though previously used largely for medicinal and quasi-medicinal purposes, some recreational use had emerged among jazz musicians, sailors, and artists. By the 1930s, the price of alcohol had increased considerably, and marijuana emerged as one substitute. A growing commercial trade in marijuana developed, with increasing use reported in many of the nation's larger cities. The Mayor of New York's Committee on Marijuana in 1944 concluded that there were 500 known marijuana peddlers in the city, and in Harlem alone an estimated 500 "tea-pads" were operating.[26] Tea-pads were places where people gathered to smoke marijuana, rather like opium dens.

Many accounts of marijuana use linked the drug to those segments of the population already viewed as deviant. Minority groups, criminals, juvenile delinquents, prostitutes, and transients were marked as those most likely to use marijuana. The "new menace" was reported among these groups in most large cities, and the newspapers carried story after story emphasizing the evils of marijuana.[27] In short order, state and local governments began passing legislation aimed at wiping out this threat to middle-class order and values.

In the early 1930s, the newly established Federal Bureau of Narcotics took on a crucial role in the fight against marijuana. Under the directorship of Harry J. Anslinger, a rigorous campaign was waged against the drug and those using it. By 1937 many states had adopted a standard bill making marijuana illegal. In that same year, the federal government stepped in with the Marihuana Tax Act, a bill modeled after the Harrison "Narcotics" Act. Repressive legislation continued, and by the 1950s severe penalties were imposed on those convicted of possessing, buying, selling, or cultivating the drug.

It was largely as a result of Anslinger's campaign against marijuana that the drug came to be viewed with horror by most Americans. People spoke of marijuana addicts, crime under the influence of marijuana, and marijuana-induced violence. A host of other disreputable actions and attitudes were also linked with the drug, and marijuana became "America's new drug problem."[28]

Notwithstanding all of this, marijuana has emerged as one of the most popular drugs of all time. How did this come about? It was in part a result of the emergence of "hip culture" in America, and the "turning on" of American youth. No doubt also important was the continued public exposure to the drug through the media, and the growing awareness that marijuana use was not monopolized by society's misfits. But more important, perhaps, than either of these factors was the impact of what might be called "drug mania" among Americans as a whole and particularly the adult population.

THE HIP CULTURE AND DRUGS

During the 1950s America came to know the beats and beat generation.[29] Localized in such favorite places as San Francisco and New York's Greenwich Village, the beats received media exposure that brought them to the attention of many Americans. The beats produced their own literature (Jack Kerouac's On the Road), their own poets (Allen Ginsberg and Lawrence Ferlinghetti), and other trappings symbolic of an alternative life-style. According to sociologist Ned Polsky, the beats were characterized by (1) a liking for drugs, particularly marijuana; (2) a liking for jazz; (3) a scorn for bourgeois careers; (4) a desire to withdraw from society; (5) an antipathy toward regular employment; (6) a belief that society exerts too much influence over its members; (7) an antipolitical orientation; (8) a tolerance of a wide variety of sexual behaviors; and (9) a disregard for the illegality of the drugs they used.[30]

In the 1960s the beats were succeeded by the hippies, the renowned inhabitants of the Haight-Ashbury district in San Francisco. Though similar in many ways to the beats, the hippies replaced jazz with acid- or folk-rock, and took pains to show off their alternative life-style. A favorite hippie game was "putting on straights," especially tourists, and trying to "blow their minds" by broadcasting their rejection of societal values and norms. As their activities and ideas gained wider attention, some aspects of their life-style attracted others, particularly those attending colleges and universities. By the end of the 1960s, hippie culture had spread to all parts of the country, and many young people became involved in some of the behavior, though rarely the ideology, emphasized by the hippies. Rock music appears to have been a major vehicle in the spread of hip culture.

But why were drugs important? And why illegal drugs? Why the emphasis on marijuana, and later the psychedelics, and not alcohol? What, if any, is the connection between drugs other than alcohol and the experiences, viewpoints, and behaviors supported by hip culture?

Adherents of hip culture felt that certain drugs matched their perspectives on life. The drugs were those perceived as helping one make the most of the present. The hip culture was for the "now" generation, and the drugs were thought to provide a means of grasping and apprehending the present. Those who smoked marijuana claimed that it relaxed them, calmed them, and heightened their sensitivity to themselves and their immediate environment. These claims are still made, and the sense that time is passing slowly is often mentioned as a key effect of marijuana.[31]

Objections to conspicuous consumption and a perceived lack of expressivity in American culture were also answered by drugs.[32] Rather than emphasize the superficial symbols of success, hip culture placed emphasis on the use of drugs as a means to develop one's "internal self." Self-reflection, "mind expansion," and finding the self became keynotes of hip culture. A "trip" on drugs, especially marijuana and the hallucinogens, was a means to "get your head right."

Being illegal, the use of marijuana and psychedelics also underscored the opposition of hip culture to dominant American values. Use of these drugs was a demonstration of unwillingness to play the game that society dictates through its laws, especially those circumscribing personal conduct. In short, the use of illegal drugs was a demonstration that major values of society have been rejected, that the self is independent of them, and that these values are invalid as guides to personal conduct.

Use of illegal drugs may lead to further reexamination, and rejection, of societal values when it is discovered that many of the supposed ills associated with their use prove not to be caused by the drugs themselves. For example, officialdom repeatedly informed the public during the 1950s and 1960s that marijuana is addicting, that it leads to violence, degradation, mental illness, and addiction to harder drugs such as heroin. These claims were (and still are, in some quarters) bandied about by the media, by school officials, so-called experts, and, most consistently, by government agencies.[33] When marijuana users found out otherwise, they perceived that they had been lied to, and rejection of the Establishment was reinforced.

While marijuana use has escalated during the past few years, LSD and other psychedelics have remained primarily a feature of hip culture. Discovered in 1943, LSD was virtually unknown until the early 1960s. Much of its early use was among physicians, psychiatrists, and other mental health officials who were aware of its mind altering qualities, and who experimented with the drug in therapeutic and quasi-therapeutic situations.[34]

During the early 1960s LSD was outlawed. However, a clandestine supply soon developed, and this drug joined other illegal substances on the street. The drug orientation of hip culture, coupled with the touted mind expanding characteristics of LSD, were in large part responsible for its adoption by Haight-Ashbury residents in the mid-1960s. The spread of LSD use beyond the localized hippie enclaves seems to have been due to additional factors. First, the drug received enormous publicity through the media and entertainment world. A second factor was the considerable ignorance concerning the drug's hallucinogenic effects. When government officials linked LSD with marijuana, the uninitiated saw the two drugs as similar and hence appropriate for experimentation and substitution. Finally, as an illegal drug, LSD became a profitable addition to the black marketeers dealing in drugs, and it soon became available wherever dealers and pushers sold their wares.

AMERICA: A DRUGGED SOCIETY?

One factor thought to have helped foster criminal drug involvement is a drug mania among Americans. Actually, the term *mania* may be rather strong. Nevertheless, drug use has certainly become a notable feature of American society, and our involvement with drugs is probably unsurpassed in the world. Whatever else we are, we are a people for whom drug use has become a way of life. Quite apart from the use of drugs for medicinal purposes, Americans routinely consume drugs in nonmedicinal contexts: beer, wine, liquor, cigarettes, coffee, tea, and an assortment of pills and potions are our daily fare.

Marijuana is America's most popular illegal drug. In most jurisdictions, merely possessing the drug is a criminal act, for the drug itself is outlawed. Yet estimates by the National Commission on Marihuana and Drug Abuse suggest that nearly 25 million Americans over the age of 11 have tried marijuana at least once. Those most likely to have tried the drug are white college educated males under 30. However, marijuana use cuts across social class, age, sex, and racial boundaries.[35]

Drugs hold an important place in the lifestyles of most Americans. It is unlikely that illegal drug use will decline while the use of legal drugs continues to increase.

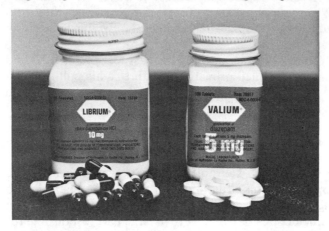

A recent national survey shows that 55 percent of American males from 20 to 30 years of age claim to have used marijuana for pleasure, and 38 percent claimed to be doing so at the time of the interviews (in 1975).[36] This same study found that psychedelics, heroin, other opiates, and cocaine were less widely used than marijuana. Even so, of those males surveyed, 22 percent claimed to have used psychedelics at some time, 6 percent heroin, 31 percent other opiates, and 14 percent cocaine. A third of those who had used a nonheroin opiate did so for quasi-medical purposes (self-prescribed medication for some real or imagined ailment).[37] In recent years cocaine has emerged as an increasingly popular drug. Estimates put the amount smuggled into the United States each year at more than 25 tons.[38]

One of the most interesting findings of these recent surveys is that the single most significant behavior correlate of illegal drug use is the consumption of legal drugs for nonmedicinal purposes. By far the most commonly used drugs today are alcohol, caffeine, and nicotine. These are the most popular drugs in terms of the "number of people who have ever used, number of regular users, number of daily users, number of man-hours spent under the influence of the drug, and money spent for the drug."[39]

A study supported by the National Institute of Mental Health (NIMH) found that of those surveyed in 1970 and 1972, 82 percent regularly drank coffee during the previous year and 52 percent drank tea. Twenty-five percent drank six or more cups of tea or coffee daily. All told, about 180 billion doses of caffeine were sold in 1970, and this excludes hot chocolate, cocoa, cola beverages, and over-the-counter preparations containing caffeine, such as NoDoz. This same NIMH study found that of those surveyed, 75 percent of the males and 49 percent of the females said they had been cigarette smokers or currently smoked. Over 600 billion cigarettes are annually purchased in the United States. Over the last few years, the proportion of smokers who are female has increased slightly, though approximate figures place regular cigarette smokers at about 42 percent of all males and 34 percent of all females.[40] Males between 20 and 30 seem to be the largest group of smokers, with one study reporting 60 percent of those interviewed as current users.[41]

Caffeine (and possibly aspirin) use surpasses use of alcohol. The NIMH study reports 78 percent of males and 63 percent of females as current users. The National Commission on Marihuana and Drug Abuse reported that 65 percent of males and 42 percent of females had consumed alcohol during the seven days prior to the survey.[42] Again, however, greatest use seems to be concentrated in the under-30 age bracket, especially among males. In a National Institute of Drug Abuse survey, 92 percent of males between 20 and 30 said they were current consumers of alcohol.[43]

Legal consumption of drugs for health purposes is vast, and has been growing over the past decade or so. In 1964, 149 million prescriptions for psychoactive substances were filled. In 1970, the amount had grown to 214 million, an increase far exceeding the population growth during the period.[44] The bulk of the increase is due to the rise in the number of prescriptions for "minor" tranquilizers such as Equanil, Valium, and Librium, and for hypnosedatives (sleeping pills) such as Somnos and Doriden. Other widely used prescription drugs include stimulants (mostly amphetamines) such as Dexamyl, Tepanil, and Ritalin, and "major" tranquilizers (barbiturates) such as Nembutal and Seconal.

The uses to which these prescription drugs are put varies from individual to individual, but in many cases they are not used for medicinal purposes. The Drug Abuse Commission concluded:

> The data show that the preponderant use of sedatives is for experimentation and enjoyment, that tranquilizers are used more often as coping mechanisms, and that the primary uses of stimulants are for the more specific purpose of accomplishing something or just to see how they work.[45]

Although use of prescription drugs for nonmedical purposes by no means equals the consumption of alcohol, tobacco, or caffeine, indications are that it is widespread. A study of New York State households found that 20 percent of the sample admitted using barbiturates, 20 percent minor tranquilizers, 12 percent amphetamines, and 9 percent major tranquilizers. Of those who used these drugs, over 70 percent obtained them by prescription. In terms of absolute numbers, this study estimated that 361,000 people used barbiturates, 330,000 used amphetamines, and 525,000 used minor tranquilizers at least six times during the month prior to the survey.[46] The typical user appears to be a white middle-class female between 25 and 45 — precisely the same class of people who regularly used heroin prior to 1914!

Over-the-counter nonprescription drugs are also readily available and widely used in the United States. According to the Drug Abuse Commission report, 1970 sales of nonprescription drugs included $28,320,000 for sleeping agents (such as Sominex and Sleep-eze) and $4,401,000 for calming agents (such as Compoz).[47] Richard Blum has estimated that a total of $25 billion is spent annually on over-the-counter drugs, including aspirin, tobacco, and alcohol.[48]

Clearly, drugs are big business, and little effort is spared to encourage us to consume them. We learn to think of drugs as a natural and normal part of our existence from an early age. From our orange-flavored aspirins and vitamins for children, we grow up seeing drugstores on almost every corner and associating drugs with health and a better life. Commercial advertising constantly bombards our senses with the message: Drugs are good for you. The public is asked to use drugs to handle situations in which it has already found itself, or is likely to find itself. Often the product is shown as making problems and difficulties go away. Some advertisements stress that drugs bring the "good things in life." Alcohol and tobacco have long been portrayed in this light, but in recent years vitamins, painkillers, sleeping pills, and other drugs have also.

The typical drug advertisement emphasizes the respectability and acceptability of using drugs to enhance the moment. The usual ploy is to frame the sales pitch around the benefits of a particular drug, even though these benefits are often unrelated to the specific ailment for which the drug is supposedly intended.[49] A wide variety of claims are made, and assertions that the drugs in question will soothe you, help you relax, and protect you are not uncommon. Sometimes drugs are touted as making you feel younger and look better. In short, many drugs are pushed as both necessary and sufficient ways to solve some of the problems of life.

But just as the business world encourages us to consume legal drugs, those with an economic interest in drugs also encourage the illegal consumption of drugs:

> The legitimate drug industry is, both directly and indirectly, responsible for much of the illegal drug use taking place today. The "pusher" should be sought not only on the street but in the physician's office, the pharmacy, the tavern — and the home. Schenley's and drug companies such as Smith, Kline, and French are as implicated in drug peddling as any illicit dealer. When parents ask why their children smoke grass — or shoot heroin — they cannot imagine that they themselves are in part responsible. When the local doctor speaks to high school students on the medical pathologies of marijuana, methedrine, or heroin, he never stops for a moment to consider his own role in what he condemns. . . .
>
> It is ironic that physicians, who lead the attack in declaring all nonmedical drug use as harmful and pathological, are probably society's most avid consumers and peddlers of legal drugs. . . . The trend in medicine has been to prescribe chemicals to deal with emotional problems. Thorazine is used to

turn troublesome mental patients into vegetables. Ritalin and amphetamines are prescribed to pacify overactive schoolchildren. Librium is indicated for the anxious and the nervous; Thorazine for the elderly; methadone for the addict.[50]

With so many drugs around, and with the constant encouragement to use them, the youth of our society grow up anticipating a place for drugs in their lives. That first cigarette, puffed courageously in some secluded spot, that first can of beer, downed with much bravado in a friend's car, are milestones along the road to adulthood. Most youthful drug experimenters know the activity breaks the law, but that merely adds flavor to the enterprise. It is all part of the challenge: What is "cool" about doing the things children are supposed to do? Anyway, there must be something to smoking, drinking, and popping pills, for why else would parents and other adults spend so much time doing it, and why would all those advertisements encourage it?

Those most likely to "turn on" to illegal drugs are precisely those who have grown up in a social environment where legal drugs are commonly used, and who have themselves joined the ranks of users. No matter what the illegal drug may be — cocaine, heroin, marijuana, psychedelics — studies have consistently shown both generational continuity in drug use (when parents use drugs, children are likely to use them) and a progression from legal to illegal substances.[51] Here, then, are clear grounds for asserting a link between noncriminal drug use and criminal use.

Of course, it would be facile to argue that parental use of drugs, or the individual's own use of drugs, causes him to take up illegal drug use. Thousands of Americans have not turned to illegal drugs even though drug use has been a feature of their own or their family's life. And many of those who do try marijuana and other outlawed drugs are experimental users who discontinue use after one or two episodes, though they usually remain consumers of legal drugs such as alcohol.[52] The important point is simply that *we are more likely to find illegal drug use where the climate is favorable to drug use in general than where no such climate exists.*

Suppliers, Pushers, and the Heroin Addict

The millions of Americans who routinely consume psychoactive substances with little thought that they are drug users or drug addicts contrast with the relative few who are addicted to heroin. The heroin addict bears the brunt of social and legal intolerance, and his world is quite different from that of the typical drug user in America. It is a world of enforced secrecy, of fear, hustling, and pain; of danger, ill health, malnutrition, and exploitation. It is a world in which getting the "shit" (or "horse," "smack," "H," "junk") and staying out of trouble consume most of every waking day.

What makes this world different is not so much the substance itself but the circumstances surrounding its acquisition and use. Of course, the drug's addicting quality makes its own incessant demands: without heroin, life for the addict is miserable, if not unbearable. But the fact of the drug's illegality and the continuous efforts to suppress its use are what makes the life of the typical heroin addict so brutal.

Simply to obtain the drug the addict must submit to exploitation at the hands of racketeers and parasites. The black market is his primary source, and thus the addict finds himself dependent on those who would squeeze his last dime from him, and do. A criminal by virtue of his use of an illegal drug, the addict must consort with those in a position to exploit him, mainly as a result of that status. Caring nothing about his personal plight, the importers, wholesalers, and dealers in fact feed off it. Submerged as he is in crime, the addict can rarely look for support outside his small circle of dope using friends and acquaintances. He is locked in a world of social outsiders and is, to boot, an easy target for the deprivations respectable society seems intent on imposing.

The importers, wholesalers, and larger dealers are the heroin addict's lifeline. While society understandably looks upon these suppliers with horror and revulsion, to the addict no person is more important, which is not to say liked and respected.[53] In the heroin trade, the higher-echelon suppliers and dealers are akin to the professional fence (see pages 182–185). They straddle the boundary between legitimate and illegitimate society, using their experience and connections with the former to aid them in their efforts to maximize the profits reaped from the heroin trade. Since heroin is imported from abroad, the availability of street supplies is keyed to the success of smuggling operations. This success, in turn, depends upon four key aspects of the heroin business — secrecy, organization, financial resources, and ingenuity. If for some reason smuggling operations falter, the impact is soon felt on the street.

HEROIN SUPPLY AND DISTRIBUTION

Before the addict gets his hands on heroin it has often traveled thousands of miles and passed across numerous links in a complex underground chain of importation and distribution. Over the past decades, the primary foreign sources of heroin have been the Middle East, India, the Far East, and Mexico. In recent years Mexico has emerged as the major foreign source, with an estimated 80 percent (10 tons) of the 1975 domestic supply originating there. In that year, the production and importation of Mexican heroin worked roughly as follows.[54]

Peasant farmers cultivated small plots of opium poppies in the dusty, impoverished, northern provinces of Mexico. An annual harvest of six or seven acres would be sold to an unknown middleman by the peasant grower for around $3,000, a sizeable sum there. Opium gum would then be extracted and turned into heroin in secret laboratories in various towns and villages. After processing, the heroin was cut (diluted) to less than 20 percent of its original purity. The cut heroin would then be smuggled into the United States, often by so-called burros, who brought it across the border in backpacks, cars, and light trucks. Sometimes the heroin would be brought in by light plane or fishing boats. Once in the United States, most of the heroin found its way to Chicago, America's major center for domestic distribution. Now in the hands of wholesalers, the heroin would be distributed to cities and states with the largest addict populations. Then the heroin would be bought by local dealers, who in turn would supply the street vendors and pushers.

The mechanics of importation vary according to the location and availability of raw opium — Mexico became an important source only after America withdrew from Vietnam and the Turkish government cracked down on opium production. But the local dealers and vendors always remain the important final links in the chain and effectively control matters at the street level. It is the pusher, the small-time vendor, who provides the addict and user with heroin. The pusher is usually an addict himself; he finances his own drug purchases through sales to others.[55] In a way, the addict-pusher is akin to the foreman in a factory. He has come from the ranks of users (the rank-and-file workers), can identify with them, and may even think of them as friends. Certainly they have common backgrounds, interests, and past experiences. Yet the addict-pusher is also a supplier (manager) who must shape his behavior according to the demands of dealers (higher-echelon managers) who generally have nothing in common with the addict. Their only interest is maximization of profits. Accordingly, the pusher finds himself in a delicate position. He must play on both teams for his survival in the business — not to mention his physical survival — and is dependent on good relations with both dealers and users. If he offends the dealer he finds his supplies cut off; if he mistreats his customers they may turn elsewhere, or even worse, expose him to unfriendly competitors or the police.

The heroin pusher is in an especially precarious position when it comes to staying out of trouble with the law. He is the weakest link in the drug supply chain and the prime target of police operations. Since he sells directly to users, his role is known to them and he can be identified. In addition, the pusher can put the finger on local dealers. He is thus of added interest to the police. If the pusher expects to stay in business and out of trouble, he will soon learn to avoid strangers. He will sell only to those with whom he is acquainted, or who have been referred to him by a very trusted friend. And he will immediately be suspicious of a prospective customer who is buying "for a friend," or who asks him questions about where he got the stuff. These "rules" help maintain a defense against the police threat, and they can be found in all corners of the illegal drug scene, not simply the heroin trade.[56]

THE MONEY ANGLE

Big money can be made in every corner of the drug world, including the world of legitimate drug use. In the criminal drug scene, a drug's illegality increases its potential for profits and its costs to the user. If the substance is also addicting, profit possibilities increase even more. Addicts need the drug, they do not merely desire it as a person might desire a new car or a color TV.[57]

The price a user pays reflects, of course, the availability of his drug. When supplies dry up the price goes up. But the bulk of drug profits is explained by the fact that this demanded item can be manufactured, distributed, and sold free from many of the constraints that operate in the legitimate business world, and free from the merchandising costs that must be met by retailers. Most businesses would be proud to list sales in the hundreds of millions of dollars. Most of this, however, would not be profits. Yet with heroin, to take just one illegal drug, sales are mostly profits. And the sales figures are staggering: Donald Cressey estimated 1963 heroin sales in the United States at $350 million; Richard Blum and his colleagues cite a 1970 figure of $463 million for New York City alone, meaning that the total United States sales of this drug probably run close to $1 billion a year.[58] An estimated $20 billion a year is spent on cocaine alone.[59]

Those who have studied the economics of black market drug operations point out that the rate of return on investment far exceeds that found in legitimate business. For instance, the heroin that costs roughly twenty-five cents to manufacture sells for $5 (the "nickel bag") on the street. In one study, the authors found that importers often secure a 300 percent return on their investment, while wholesalers, local dealers, and pushers each garner over a 100 percent return.[60] A pusher can often make over $1,000 a week by selling small amounts of heroin to a small circle of buyers. And he pays no income taxes.

INSTRUMENTAL CRIME:
THE USER'S ANSWER TO HIS FINANCIAL PROBLEMS

Heroin can cost the addict $100 a day. That's $36,500 a year, and doesn't include food, rent, clothing, utilities, and other essential living expenses. Where does the addict get the money?

To meet their financial needs most heroin addicts and many other users of illegal drugs must turn to activities that further isolate them from mainstream society, and sink them deeper into criminal involvement. Studies in New York and Florida indicate that selling drugs ranks first among the money-making crimes committed by heroin addicts.[61] In the Florida study, Inciardi compared male and female addicts and found that for males the next most likely offense was burglary (69 percent of the addicts), followed by shoplifting (59.4 percent), and robbery (46.9 percent);

for women, prostitution (72.6 percent) was followed by shoplifting (70.1 percent), and prostitute theft from clients (51.3 percent). Using official records as well as self-reports, Inciardi estimated that in one year his sample of 356 heroin addicts committed a total of 118,134 offenses.[62]

Addict involvement in crimes other than their drug use tends to begin early in life, even before they reach the point of heavy drug use. The use of illicit drugs merely escalates that criminal involvement, and the addict must work hard at crime to finance his habit. Almost half of the Florida addicts held legitimate jobs in addition to their regular criminal activities. One econometric study showed that when the price of heroin goes up there is a corresponding increase in burglary, robbery, larceny, and auto theft.[63] An addict must steal merchandise worth three to four times the cost of his drugs, for he will rarely receive more than 30 percent of the value of the stolen items he fences. The addicts' crimes are *instrumental crimes,* pursued not as an end in themselves, but as a means of supporting their habit. Like other nondrug addicts who engage in street crime, the heroin users face many risks and dangers, but in their case these risks are compounded: there is the constant need for the drug and the inevitable involvement in a deviant subculture continually monitored by the police.

Criminal Drug Use and the Police

The existence of drug laws calls for a police response to people who violate them. A number of things, however, work to make the enforcement of drug laws extremely difficult. For one thing, the possession, sale, and use of illegal drugs are in essence *victimless crimes,* that is, they usually involve willing participants.[64]

Some, needless to say, reject the idea that violations of drug laws are victimless crimes. After all, the user is a victim of his own behavior; he is also a victim of the pusher and others who directly or indirectly supply him with drugs. Then there is the drug victim whose property is ripped off by an addict seeking money for drug purchases. Finally, there is society as a whole, which must spend millions of dollars and man-hours dealing with the drug problem.

The point, however, is not that we cannot conceive of victims when speaking of the criminal drug scene. Rather, it is that drug crimes such as possession and sale are usually consummated without depriving or coercing innocent or unwilling third parties. The police, then, will usually not have an aggrieved person who will complain that he or she has been the victim of a crime. The police must typically discover drug law violations on their own.

To make enforcement more difficult, drug offenses are rarely witnessed by noninvolved observers, nor is there usually much in the way of telltale evidence to indicate that a crime has in fact been committed. An individual can violate a drug law with no one any the wiser. Who is to know that in his pocket he carries two or three joints, some illegal pills, or a day's supply of heroin?

These and other features of the illegal drug scene offer a stiff challenge to the police. To meet that challenge, law enforcement agencies, backed by local, state, and federal governments, have devised strategies and techniques that depart in many ways from those employed in the bulk of other police matters. Over the past few years these agencies have also acquired substantial funding and manpower allotments for the specific purpose of enforcing drug laws. Consider, for instance, the federal government's own drug enforcement agency, the Drug Enforcement Administration (DEA). According to an American Bar Association special report, this agency's budget rose from $6 million in 1966 to $74 million in 1973, while the number of its narcotics agents went from 267 to 1,600 during the same period. Some states have established special police agencies whose primary responsibility is drug law enforcement, and most larger cities and counties have special police units and squads to deal solely with drug-related matters.

THE "NARC" AND THE INFORMANT

Because illicit drug offenses are mostly consensual crimes and because they are not readily observed, police enforcement strategies place a premium on infiltration and the cultivation of police informants. Through infiltration into the ranks of users, the undercover drug agent is able to develop important trusting relationships with users, addicts, and pushers, and thus keep tabs on the people, events, and places having to do with illegal drugs. To maintain his cover and keep on top of things, the "narc" must learn and adopt street ways — the rules, language, and nuances of the criminal drug scene. He must virtually live among those he is charged with catching. Following his recent investigation of the junkie's world in New York, Houston, Austin, and Los Angeles, Bruce Jackson concluded that the narc cannot separate himself from that world even though he may despise it and his purpose is to destroy it.[65]

Helping the police are the informants. Called a "classic enforcement tool" by a past administrator of the DEA, the informant is one who will "be induced for one reason or another to disclose his knowledge of [illegal drug] activities."[66] Usually an active participant in criminal drug activities, the informant is cultivated by the police, who rely heavily on the information he passes and on the contribution he can make to "good busts," arrests that hold up in court. The informant's own crimes are often used as the means to induce him to work for the police. Under the threat of arrest and a jail sentence, the prospective informant finds his options limited and unattractive. Besides, the police can always threaten to let the word get around that he is an informant (whether true or not). If the threat of jail is not enough, this will be an added inducement to go along with the police.

In his discussion of police tactics, Jerome Skolnick points out that it is not uncommon for the police to break the law themselves as they seek to nail users so that they can pressure them into being informants. For example, an unlawful search of a suspect's person or rooms may be undertaken; if drugs or drug paraphernalia such as hypodermic needles are found, the addict is in a highly vulnerable position. Skolnick explains how the police justify such illegal activities:

> The process by which the policeman justifies his unlawful exploratory search is similar to that by which many criminals justify their [illegal activities]. Thus, the policeman distinguishes between *legality* and *morality,* just as the criminal does, and as we all do to a certain extent. The prostitute, for example, justifies her activity by asserting that she engages in an enterprise her "trick" desires. The confidence man rationalizes his deceptions with the belief that "there is a little bit of larceny in the soul of every man" and that his motives are no different from his victims'. . . . Similarly, the policeman justifies *his* unlawful exploration by pointing to the difficulties of his job and asserting that his activity has no adverse effect upon the person whose property is unlawfully searched, *provided* that person is not a criminal. Thus, the policeman typically alleges that unless he conducts unlawful searches, for example, dangerous addicts will escape capture; furthermore, he maintains that innocent persons have no cause for complaint.[67]

A common feature of the drug enforcement strategy is for undercover agents to spend weeks, if not months, developing information on drug use and traffic so that when they are ready the police can pounce on a large number of suspects at the same time. These dragnet raids usually take place in the early morning hours, and not uncommonly produce upward of fifty arrests. For the police, such raids have the flavor of an adventurous night out. Usually out of uniform, police from federal, state, and local agencies get together for the raid and systematically root out those on the list of suspects. Sometimes these raids have had their bizarre sides, as in the notorious "Collinsville Raid," when officers barged in on the wrong houses, causing havoc and terror for the families involved.[68] Apart from producing relatively large numbers of simultaneous arrests, there is no real evidence that raids of this kind accomplish much of a reduction in the availability, sale, and use of illegal drugs. They do, however, result in much local publicity, and the public is reassured that the police are working hard in their fight against the drug criminal.

In their efforts to reduce the availability of drugs such as heroin, marijuana, and cocaine, the police have met with little success. The drug pipeline is not easily breached, not only because the major importers, wholesalers, and distributors are well organized and equipped, but also because the profitability of small quantities of these drugs make large shipments unnecessary. It is like looking for the proverbial needle in the haystack.

The failure of attempts to curb the flow of drugs is amply illustrated by the ill-fated "Operation Intercept." Initiated on September 21, 1969, this federal program employed thousands of police agents and cost millions of dollars. Its essential purpose was to stem the flow of drugs across the Mexico–United States border. It proved to be an utter disaster:

> Within a few days it had an immediate impact: it tied up border traffic for miles, irritated hundreds of individuals who were forced to strip nude, and aggravated the Mexican government, at whose request the operation was terminated in twenty days. The more long-term effect was to encourage the importation of stronger marihuana than the Mexican variety from other parts of the world such as North Africa and Vietnam. Operation Intercept also encouraged more serious efforts to grow and harvest the domestic product. The operation did create a marihuana shortage in the United States, but the shortage was only temporary because the higher prices attracted more sellers into the market. Operation Intercept was a failure by any measure, and an expensive one at that.[69]

A new line of attack against the illicit drug scene is the recent crack-down on "head shops," places where drug paraphernalia are sold. The drug paraphernalia industry is big business, estimated at several hundred million dollars annually.[70] The law enforcement effort may help reduce the chances of any respectability rubbing off on illicit drug use, but it is doubtful it will accomplish much in the way of curbing it. In fact, it will probably add to the social problem of drug use, for business will once again move underground, bolstering the black market as well as the profits to organized crime.

DRUG ARRESTS

Notwithstanding the overall failure of drug enforcement efforts, the police do make a lot of drug arrests. In fact, if we combine all such arrests, in any given year more arrests are made for drug-related offenses than for any other broad type of criminal offense, major or minor. Table 9.1 shows that in 1972 and 1973, 38 percent of all criminal arrests were drug-related. In 1977 and 1978 the percentages had decreased slightly, to nearly 35 percent, but drug arrests still accounted for more arrests than any other criminal offense.

The figures in table 9.1 include arrests on charges relating to alcohol. In fact, alcohol-related arrests far outnumber other drug arrests. Around 80 percent of all drug arrests can be linked to alcohol, whether the offense involves public drunkenness (the number-one drug offense), the violation of liquor laws governing sale and consumption, or driving while intoxicated. In terms of police arrests, alcohol-related offenses are clearly America's number-one crime problem.

Headshops are increasingly under attack in new attempts to undermine illicit drug trade. It is doubtful, however, that this tactic will significantly affect the drug business.

Most drug-related arrests occur among the larger urban populations. Easy accessibility to drugs, concentrated user populations, and more extensive and sophisticated police surveillance all contribute to the higher arrest rates found in larger cities and their suburbs. In the case of alcohol-related arrests, especially those for drunkenness, the typical arrestee is an adult over 30 years of age. Where heroin, marijuana, and other illegal drugs are concerned, on the other hand, the typical arrestee is under age

Table 9.1 Drug-related arrests as a percentage of all arrests

	1972	1973	1977	1978
Total arrests	8,712,400	9,027,700	10,189,900	10,271,000
Drug-related arrests				
Number	3,280,300	3,446,700	3,632,100	3,450,400
As percentage of all				
arrests	$38%	38%	35%	34%

SOURCE: FBI, *Uniform Crime Reports, 1972, 1973, 1977, 1978* (Washington, D.C.: U.S. Government Printing Office, 1973, 1974, 1978, 1979).

30. Over the past few years the number of young people arrested on illegal drug charges has risen considerably. According to available FBI figures, in 1960 there were 1,458 nonalcohol-related drug arrests of persons under age 18. By 1975 the number had increased by 4,417.4 percent to 65,864 — an increase far exceeding the corresponding increase in the proportion of persons under 18. (These figures, it should be noted, are considerably lower than the actual number of arrests, for they are based on the records of only those police departments reporting such arrests in both years.)

Arrests for nonalcohol offenses most likely involve marijuana. In 1973, for example, of the 715,000 "narcotic" and "dangerous drug" arrests, nearly 60 percent were marijuana-related. Interestingly, those 420,700 marijuana arrests are almost twice the number reported in 1971, despite the trend toward the liberalization of marijuana laws that surfaced in the early 1970s. More recently, in 1977, the FBI reported again that marijuana arrests were high in relation to other drugs; 457,600 such arrests took place.[71] Keeping track of arrest data is never easy, but so far there is little indication that the relaxed marijuana laws found in many states are translating into more relaxed police arrest practices.

Alcohol and Crime

Alcohol figures prominently in criminal arrests. Alcohol-related arrests occur more frequently than arrests for any other type of crime, including the broad "property offense" class. In 1978, for example, there were nearly 3 million alcohol-related arrests.

Alcohol surfaces in discussions of crime in two different ways. On the one hand are those activities that are criminal precisely because they violate laws pertaining to the manufacture, sale, and use of alcohol. The most common criminal offense belonging to this class of acts is public drunkenness. In terms of arrests, this is America's most frequent crime. On the other hand, however, are those criminal activities in which alcohol played a part but which are not crimes because alcohol was involved. The interest here is with the role alcohol might have played as one of the situational factors present in, or surrounding, the commission of a crime.

ALCOHOL USE AS CRIME: THE CASE OF PUBLIC DRUNKENNESS

The law's interest in alcohol is not really with the drug itself. It is not an illegal drug as is heroin. Rather, the law deals with the circumstances under which alcohol is made, sold, and used. It is a crime, for example, to sell alcohol to minors. It is also a crime to drink alcohol in a public place not officially designated as one where alcohol may be consumed.

While in most jurisdictions adults are allowed to purchase and consume alcohol, it has long been an offense to appear in public in a state of inebriation. From earliest common-law times, the drunk has been regarded as a public nuisance. One of the duties of the early constables and watchmen was to keep drunks off the street. Though a criminal offense, public drunkenness has always been viewed as a minor infraction of the law. In earlier days the offender might be fined a small sum or whipped or pilloried. The major concern seems to have been to remove the drunk from the presence or sight of the sober, respectable citizenry.

Today, the drunk continues to be treated as a minor offender, and most of us would not think of him as a criminal. Even so, he is labeled criminal by the police more than any other law violator. And it is not hard to explain why the public drunk is arrested with such relatively high frequency. For one thing, the drunk is one of our most visible criminal offenders. He commits his offense in public, and the nature of the drug is such that intoxication is difficult to hide. Drunkenness manifests itself in lowered inhibitions, uncoordinated movements, impaired reactions to external stimuli, and, at times, somewhat bizarre behavior. In addition, public drunkenness is one of the few offenses patrolling police can witness themselves. As we have noted before, the police become aware of most criminal offenses only after someone has complained to them or requested their assistance. Not so with public drunkenness. Hang around any bar, or ride to those sections of town where clubs, liquor stores, or bars abound and you will have little difficulty spotting a drunk or two. And, of course, the police come across drunks not only in those sections but on any public street in any part of town.

Though hard evidence is difficult to secure, some indicates that those most often arrested for public drunkenness have certain characteristics in common. They are usually older males from lower-class backgrounds living in the poorer, worker-class sections of town.[72] From this class of people come those who frequent local bars and taverns, who come and go on foot, and for whom an evening of drinking is a favorite pastime. Many offenders are arrested more than once, and while only a very small minority conform to the classic skid-row image — unemployed, poor, ragged, alcoholic bums living in flophouses and sleeping in alleys — those who are booked by the police get a taste of American justice at its worst. Matching the scorn we tend to heap on those who cannot hold their liquor, the arrested drunk is often treated to a degrading and disgusting journey through the judicial process.

Those whom the police choose to arrest — certainly not all drunks who come to their attention — are invariably thrown into a cell to "sleep it off."[73] Often they find themselves in the drunk tank, a cell set aside for such offenders that sometimes holds up to a hundred prisoners. Just under half of the nation's 3,921 jails have such tanks, and many hundreds of them have no operating toilets, no seating space, no bedding or mattresses, no heat, and no light. Most have no showers or air-conditioning.[74] When the drunks get to court, usually the next morning or the following Monday if arrested on Friday or Saturday, they are paraded through the lower courts as fast as the bailiffs can work, usually with little sign of due process, such as the right to be confronted by the accuser and the opportunity for cross-examination.[75] In her investigation of the courtroom process, Jacqueline Wiseman found that about the only judicial decision made was a sentencing one, and this was geared to the evaluations of nonlawyer helpers and "friends of the court." Though not necessarily typical of courtroom procedures and conditions (Wiseman's study was of an urban court servicing a large population), the whole process reeked of conveyor-belt justice and a total disregard for the offenders' rights and well-being.[76] In a way, the picture painted by Wiseman and others is not surprising. We do not, in this society, treat alcohol use very seriously, and we do not think of the alcohol abuser as any more than a rather weak, overindulgent fool. Perhaps the courts, faced with a morning deluge of drunkenness cases, see their duty as a chore, and a time-consuming one at that, which deserves cursory attention and speedy disposition so that more serious, criminal matters can be attended to. Still, the chronic drunkenness offender may find himself locked up for three months or more, hardly the kind of punishment to be handed down lightly.

ALCOHOL USE WITH CRIME: THE QUESTION OF CAUSALITY

One concern voiced by opponents of legalization of marijuana and softening of other drug laws is that drug use leads to or causes crime. We have seen, indeed, that drug addicts and habitual users may commit crimes to finance their drug use. But this kind of instrumental crime is not all people have in mind when they speak of drug use causing crime. They also have in mind that something about the substances themselves provokes criminal actions — rape, robbery, violence, or whatever.

This issue is important to criminology not only for what it might mean to those seeking to understand the etiology of crime as behavior that is different from other behavior, but also for its impact on criminal labeling and the societal reaction to drug use and drug users. If, indeed, the effects of a particular substance are causally linked to antisocial behavior, we need to know what that link is and under what conditions it may arise. However, we are still far from establishing with certainty that any such link in fact exists for any of the drugs discussed in this chapter. In one of the recent investigations of this question the authors concluded:

> [While] the data . . . show that there is a strong statistical association between the extent of drug use, whether measured in terms of use of alcohol or marihuana, and the extent of self-reported criminal acts, . . . the preliminary analyses . . . do not provide clear support . . . for the idea that drug use leads to crime. . . .[77]

At the heart of the "drugs lead to crime" controversy lies the problem of causality. The issue can be stated as a question: does a particular substance cause a particular behavior? Does heroin, marijuana, or alcohol have an effect on the user such that it directly induces a criminal action? To answer this question a number of other questions must be answered. Is the behavior in question peculiar to those using the drug in question? Does the same person, when not under the influence of the drug, engage in the same behavior? Does the behavior follow after the drug has been taken, but before its physiological effects have disappeared? Have additional nondrug factors operating along with the drug (or prior to it) been taken into account? For instance, a relationship between alcohol and aggression could be spurious if it disappears when some other factors are controlled. These questions and others must be answered by those seeking to establish or disprove a causal relationship between a drug and crime. Unfortunately, researchers have generally been unsuccessful in the endeavor. Definitive answers are still wanting; few scholars are willing to assert categorically that a particular drug causes behavior officials have labeled crime.

Nevertheless, some evidence suggests that of all the popular drugs now taken for nonmedicinal purposes, *alcohol is most consistently and strongly linked with crime,* especially assaultive crimes such as homicide, aggravated assault, rape, and child beating. Alcohol turns up again and again as a situational factor in these crimes. It is commonly found to have been consumed before, during, or after the commission of a violent act. Of course, there is also the criminal negligence of the drunk driver. A majority of auto fatalities and accidents might not have occurred had the drivers refrained from drinking prior to or while driving. In this situation, the lowering of reaction time and inhibitions and the impairment of motor coordination produced by alcohol's effect on the central nervous system are generally regarded as important contributing factors. In short, alcohol, more than any other single drug, plays a major role in crime, especially those types of crime resulting in physical injury.[78]

We need to remember, though, that the physiological effect of any substance depends on more than simply the type and amount of the substance consumed. Such things as the user's general health, body weight, and experience with the substance, all can influence how that substance affects him. Accordingly, no simple relationship exists between the consumption of a particular drug and physical or mental reactions to it. Then, too, an individual's overt behavior may be determined by considerations quite apart from the drug he has consumed. No drug directly causes an individual to pick up a gun and rob a liquor store, for no drug can make the decision. This the individual himself must do, and while the effects of a drug may heighten his confidence in making decisions, or strengthen his resolve and give him more energy (or, on the other hand, slow him up and blur his powers of discrimination), this is a far thing from causing his actions.

Even so, many people still cling to the idea that a causal connection exists between certain drugs and antisocial behavior. One reason is that the belief that a person's criminal behavior is caused by a drug accounts for the behavior without imputing criminal intent to the person himself. If it weren't for the fact that he was "under the influence" he would not have behaved criminally. Under law, this is usually no defense; yet for the offender and those who would like to think the best of him, being on drugs provides an avenue of rationalization and explanation. But the idea that certain drugs cause crime also helps us to support the repressive measures directed at the sale and use of those drugs. Were it not for the belief that such drugs as heroin, cocaine, speed, and LSD caused their users to commit crimes, we would find it more difficult to accept the severe penalties and deceitful enforcement practices currently adopted in our name. We might still want to discourage their use, as we would any drug that could harm its user, but not in the same way. Who ever heard of putting a cigarette smoker in prison?

Public Opinion and the Punitive Reaction to Illegal Drug Use

When we learn, correctly or incorrectly, that a certain substance is linked with crime, we are encouraged in our condemnation of it. However, if that substance happens to be widely used and is considered legal and socially acceptable, our fears and condemnation are appropriately toned down. Thus while alcohol shows the strongest links with crime, we remain less concerned about its availability and use than we are about illegal and socially unacceptable drugs such as heroin and LSD. We do not want to believe that alcohol is as bad as these drugs, no matter what the evidence.

Not surprisingly, then, recent national surveys show Americans to be most concerned about illegal drugs and much less concerned about alcohol. In one survey, far more of those interviewed (more than 90 percent) thought that heroin and the psychedelics were "harmful even in small amounts," than thought the same thing about alcohol (60 percent).[79] As befits such dangerous (and, it is believed, illegal, crime-causing, addicting) drugs, the public supports punitive reactions to their sale and use. Thus in one survey, 80 percent of those interviewed thought that heroin vendors should receive prison terms, and nearly 70 percent felt the same way about users.[80] Backing up drug enforcement practices, 70 percent of the respondents to a 1973 survey thought that police informants should be rewarded for turning in sellers of hard drugs.[81]

Given this climate of opinion, we are likely to see a continuation of repressive drug enforcement and severe penalties for illegal drug sale and use. In our federal prisons, violators of laws dealing with narcotics, primarily heroin, currently serve more time than almost any other type of offender, an average of 37.9 months in 1972.[82] In some states, the penalties for possession and sale of illegal drugs, including marijuana, are equaled or surpassed only by those for murder, rape, and kidnapping.

So long as we continue to view the use of heroin, psychedelics, marijuana, cocaine, and other such drugs as the proper object of legal repression, our reactions will continue to be punitive, as they are with street crime generally.[83] Those features of drug use linked with criminalization will therefore persist. The user will be labeled and treated as a criminal; black market supplies and high prices will flourish; fear, illness, suspicion, and instrumental crime will fill the user's life; and he will be an outcast in a society of drug users.

References

1. For more on the terms *addiction* and *habituation*, see Edwin M. Brecher, *Licit and Illicit Drugs* (Boston: Little, Brown, 1972); Erich Goode, *Drugs in American Society* (New York: Knopf, 1972); and William Bates and Betty Crowther, "Drugs: Causes, Circumstances and Effects of Their Use," *General Learning Press Monograph* (Morristown, N.J.: General Learning Press).

2. Other than sources cited above, see National Commission on Marihuana and Drug Abuse (hereafter, Drug Abuse Commission), *Patterns and Consequences of Drug Use*, vol. I, appendix (Washington, D.C.: U.S. Government Printing Office, 1973).

3. Brecher, *Licit and Illicit Drugs*, p. 195.

4. For a modern study of peyote use among southwestern Indians, see Carlos Casteneda, *The Teachings of Don Juan: A Yaqui Way of Knowledge* (New York: Ballantine Books, 1968).

5. C. E. Terry and Mildred Pellens, *The Opium Problem* (1928; repr. Montclair, N.J.: Patterson Smith, 1970).

6. Quoted in John C. Ball and Carl D. Chambers, *The Epidemiology of Opiate Addiction in the United States* (Springfield, Ill.: Charles C Thomas, 1970), p. 39.

7. Brecher, *Licit and Illicit Drugs*.

8. Ibid.

9. Terry and Pellens, *The Opium Problem*; S. Cohen, *The Drug Dilemma* (New York: McGraw-Hill, 1969).

10. See Norman Taylor, *Narcotics: Nature's Dangerous Gift to Man* (New York: Dell, 1963).

11. See, George Andrews, ed., *The Book of Grass: An Anthology of Indian Hemp* (New York: Grove Press, 1967).

12. The most well known is Fitz Hugh Ludlow's *The Hasheesh Eater,* published in 1857.

13. But it was the British who first introduced opium smoking to the Chinese!

14. Brecher, *Licit and Illicit Drugs*, p. 45.

15. See Alfred R. Lindesmith, *The Addict and the Law* (New York: Random House, 1967).

16. Brecher, *Licit and Illicit Drugs*, p. 49.

17. See Andrew Sinclair, *Era of Excess: A Social History of the Prohibition Movement* (New York: Harper and Row, 1964).

18. For a comparison of early and more recent research on the medical effects of alcohol, see John H. Kellog, "Alcohol: A Discredited Drug," *Prohibition: Modification of the Volstead Law,* ed. Lamar T. Beman (New York: H. W. Wilson, 1927), pp. 49–64; and H. Keith H. Brodie, "The Effects of Ethyl Alcohol in Man," in National Commission, *Patterns and Consequences of Drug Use,* pp. 6–59.

19. There is some debate on the extent to which use fell off. For differing views see Beman, ed., *Prohibition;* Terry and Pellens, *The Opium Problem;* and Lindesmith, *The Addict and the Law.*

20. Allen L. Benson, "The Propaganda against Prohibition," in *Prohibition,* ed. Beman, pp. 133–47.

21. Isidore Chein, Donald L. Gerard, Robert S. Lee, and Eva Rosenfeld, *The Road to H* (New York: Basic Books, 1964), p. 350.

22. See Terry and Pellens, *The Opium Problem;* and Goode, *Drugs in American Society.*

23. Goode, *Drugs in American Society,* p. 193.

24. See John Dollard, "Drinking Mores of the Social Classes," in Journal of Studies on Alcohol, *Alcohol, Science, and Society* (New Haven: Yale University Press, 1945), pp. 95–101.

25. Benson, "The Propaganda against Prohibition."

26. Mayor of New York's Committee on Marihuana, *The Marihuana Problem in the City of New York* (New York: Cattell, 1944).

27. See Robert P. Walton, *America's New Drug Problem* (Philadelphia: Lippincott, 1938).

28. Ibid.

29. This section is a revised version of that appearing in an unpublished paper coauthored by James M. Henslin and myself.

30. Ned Polsky, *Hustlers, Beats, and Others* (Chicago: Aldine, 1967), pp. 151–66.

31. Goode, *Drugs in American Society.* See also his *The Marihuana Smokers* (New York: Basic Books, 1970).

32. See James T. Carey, *The College Drug Scene* (Englewood Cliffs, N.J.: Prentice-Hall, 1968); and Mark Messer, "Running out of Era: Nonpharmacological Notes on the Psychedelic Revolution," *Journal of Psychedelic Drugs* 2 (1968), pp. 157–66.

33. See Brecher, *Licit and Illicit Drugs,* chapters 44, 50, 51.

34. Ibid., pp. 346–60.

35. For the best summary of data on marijuana use, see Drug Abuse Commission, *Marihuana: A Signal of Misunderstanding* (Washington, D.C.: U.S. Government Printing Office, 1972), pp. 251–60.

36. National Institute on Drug Abuse, *Young Men and Drugs — A Nationwide Survey,* Research Monograph Series 5 (Rockville, Md.: National Institute on Drug Abuse, 1976), pp. vii–viii and 42–47.

37. Ibid. pp. ix–x.

38. Associated Press, October 13, 1979.

39. Brecher, *Licit and Illicit Drugs,* p. 475; see also Erich Goode, "Multiple Drug Use Among Marihuana Smokers," *Social Problems* 17 (1969), pp. 48–64.

40. Ibid., p. 476; see also Drug Abuse Commission, *Drug Use in America: Problems in Perspective* (Washington, D.C.: U.S. Government Printing Office, 1973).

41. National Institute on Drug Abuse, *Young Men and Drugs,* p. vii.

42. In Brecher, *Licit and Illicit Drugs,* p. 477.

43. National Institute on Drug Abuse, *Young Men and Drugs,* p. vii.

44. Cited in Brecher, *Licit and Illicit Drugs,* p. 482.

45. Drug Abuse Commission, *Drug Use in America,* p. 57.

46. Carl D. Chambers, *An Assessment of Drug Use in the General Population* (New York: Narcotics Addiction Control Commission, 1971).

47. National Commission, *Drug Use in America,* p. 43.

48. Richard Blum and Associates, *The Dream Sellers* (San Francisco: Jossey-Bass, 1972), p. 6.

49. See F. Earle Barcus, James M. Goldstein, and Stephen K. Pinto, "Drug Advertising on Television," pp. 623–68, and Heffner Associates, Inc., "Over-the-Counter Drug Commercials: Network Television, Spring 1971," pp. 669–97, in Drug Abuse Commission, *Social Responses to Drug Use,* vol. II, appendix.

50. Goode, *Drugs in American Society,* pp. 126–28.

51. Ibid., pp. 34–35.

52. Drug Abuse Commission, *Marihuana: A Signal of Misunderstanding,* pp. 34–35.

53. Goode, *Drugs in American Society,* p. 176.

54. "The Mexican Connection," *Newsweek* (March 15, 1976), pp. 28–30.

55. See Edward A. Preble and John J. Casey, Jr., "Taking Care of Business — The Heroin User's Life on the Street," *International Journal of the Addictions* 4 (1969), pp. 8–12.

56. See James T. Carey, *The College Drug Scene;* also Alan G. Sutter, "The World of the Righteous Dope Fiend," *Issues in Criminology* 1 (1966), pp. 177–222.

57. For an excellent discussion of black market economics see Preble and Casey, "Taking Care of Business"; and Brecher, *Licit and Illicit Drugs,* chapter 11.

58. Donald R. Cressey, *Theft of a Nation* (New York: Harper and Row, 1969), p. 91; Richard Blum and Associates, *The Dream Sellers,* p. 5.

59. Associated Press, October 13, 1979.

60. Preble and Casey, "Taking Care of Business," p. 12.

61. See Richard C. Stephens and Rosalind D. Ellis,

"Narcotics Addiction and Crime: An Analysis of Recent Trends," *Criminology* 12 (1975), pp. 474–87; John F. Halahan and Paul A. Herningsen, "The Economics of Heroin," in *Dealing with Drug Abuse: A Report to the Ford Foundation,* ed. Patricia M. Wald, Peter Barton Hutt et al. (New York: Praeger, 1972); James A. Inciardi, "Heroin Use and Street Crime," *Crime and Delinquency* 25 (1979), pp. 335–46.

62. Inciardi, "Heroin Use and Street Crime," pp. 341–43.

63. *LEAA Newsletter* 8 (October 1979), p. 16.

64. For a now-classic statement on victimless crimes, see Edwin M. Schur, *Crimes without Victims* (Englewood Cliffs, N.J.: Prentice-Hall, 1965).

65. Bruce Jackson, "Exile From the American Dream: The Junkie and the Cop," *The Atlantic Monthly* 219 (1969), pp. 44–51.

66. Henry Dobin, "Narcotics and Organized Crime," *Drug Enforcement* 3 (1975–1976), p. 1.

67. Jerome H. Skolnick, *Justice without Trial* (New York: Wiley, 1969), p. 145.

68. For an account on this and other similar raids see Senator Charles H. Percy, "The Legacy of No-knock: Drug Law Enforcement Abuse," *Contemporary Drug Problems* 3 (1974), pp. 5–8.

69. McCaghy, *Deviant Behavior,* p. 301.

70. *Newsweek,* November 26, 1979.

71. FBI, *Uniform Crime Reports, 1977* (Washington, D.C.: U.S. Government Printing Office, 1978), p. 172.

72. See Joel Fort, *Alcohol: Our Biggest Drug Problem* (New York: McGraw-Hill, 1973); and David J. Pittman, "Public Intoxication and the Alcoholic Offender in American Society," in the President's Commission on Law Enforcement and the Administration of Justice, *Task Force Report: Drunkenness* (Washington, D.C.: U.S. Government Printing Office, 1967).

73. For a discussion of police practices, see David J. Pittman and C. Wayne Gordon, *Revolving Door: A Study of the Chronic Police Case Inebriate* (New York: Free Press, 1958); and Egon Bittner,

"The Police on Skid Row: A Study of Peacekeeping," *American Sociological Review* 32 (1967), pp. 699–715.

74. Data are from U.S. Department of Justice, *The Nation's Jails: A Report on the Census of Jails from the 1972 Survey of Inmates of Local Jails* (Washington, D.C.: U.S. Government Printing Office, 1975). For an excellent recent review of the American jail system, see Ronald Goldfarb, *Jails: The Ultimate Ghetto* (Garden City, N.Y.: Doubleday, 1975), chapters 4 and 5.

75. For more on the problems of due process and the drug offender see Nicholas N. Kittrie, *The Right to Be Different: Deviance and Enforced Therapy* (Baltimore: Penguin Books, 1974).

76. Jacqueline P. Wiseman, *Stations of the Lost: The Treatment of Skid Row Alcoholics* (Englewood Cliffs, N.J.: Prentice-Hall, 1970), pp. 86–103.

77. National Institute on Drug Abuse, *Young Men and Drugs,* p. 97.

78. For a recent review of the evidence, see Jared Tinklenburg, "Drugs and Crime," in Drug Abuse Commission, *Patterns and Consequences of Drug Use,* pp 242–95.

79. Drug Abuse Commission, *Social Responses to Drug Use,* p. 879.

80. American Institute of Public Opinion, Gallup Survey, May 1970.

81. Gallup Survey, January 1973. For further opinion poll findings see Michael J. Hindelang, Christopher S. Dunn, L. Paul Sutton, and Alison L. Aumick, *Sourcebook of Criminal Justice Statistics* (Washington, D.C.: U.S. Government Printing Office, 1976), pp. 316–22.

82. U.S. Department of Justice, Bureau of Prisons, "Statistical Report: Fiscal Years 1971 and 1972" (Washington, D.C.: U.S. Government Printing Office, 1973), pp. 152–53.

83. The indications are that we will continue to view drugs in this punitive way . See Charles E. Reasons, "The Addict as a Criminal: Perpetuation of a Legend," *"Crime and Delinquency* 21 (1975), pp. 19–27.

10

Criminal Sexuality

Sexual behavior has not escaped the application of criminal labels. Over the centuries, lawmakers have brought numerous sexual activities and situations under legal control. Today the number of sex crimes is as great as it has ever been, despite the more permissive attitudes toward sex that have surfaced over the last decade or so.

Needless to say, sex can be experienced in many different ways. Indeed, such terms as *sex crimes* and *sex offenders* obscure the heterogeneous character of the actions, circumstances, and people to which these labels are customarily applied. Consider the following sex offenses: rape, homosexuality, fellatio, consensual sexual intercourse between an adult and a legal minor, exhibitionism, anal intercourse, prostitution, child molesting, and group sex among married couples. In most American states all these sexual acts are regarded as sex crimes. Yet consider also a few of the differences among these sexual encounters. Some involve consenting persons, others unwilling individuals coerced into participating; some involve persons of the same sex, others do not; some involve strangers, others acquaintances, friends, and relatives; some involve children, others only adults; and finally, some involve sexual intercourse, while others revolve around quite different forms of sexual expression. Clearly, then, the rubric *sex crimes* includes a multiplicity of acts and circumstances.

Sex and the Criminal Law

Lawmakers have acknowledged some of the many differences in sexual situations by using different legal terms and by identifying a variety of grounds upon which to base the application of criminal labels to sex. Four grounds for applying crime labels can be identified: (1) the nature of the sex act; (2) the nature of the sex object; (3) the social setting in which sex occurs; and (4) the absence of consent.[1] Quite often, more than one of these grounds have been taken into account by lawmakers.

When the sex act itself is taken as the sole grounds for the application of criminal labels, the act in question is deemed illegal regardless of the people and circumstances involved. Examples of illegal sex acts are anal intercourse, fellatio (oral stimulation of the penis), cunnilingus (oral stimulation of the female genitalia), and analingus (oral stimulation of the anus). Often, however, the nature of the sex act is coupled with some other facet of a sexual event in the designation of that event as criminal.

One of these other grounds is the nature of the sex object. Most criminal codes have limited what is considered legally acceptable sexual conduct to those situations in which the object of sexual interest is human, an adult, and not biologically related to the sex partner. In all states, sexual behavior is criminal when the sex object is an animal (bestiality), a legal minor, or a brother, sister, son, or daughter (incest). Sexual intercourse is usually defined as criminal when those engaging in it are not married (fornication) or, if so, not to each other (adultery).

Even when both the sex act and the sex object are legal, a sexual event may still be classified as criminal. Those sexual activities that occur in public or that can be witnessed by members of the public are generally regarded as crimes regardless of who is doing what with, or to, whom. Sex in parks, restaurants, theaters, automobiles, trains, or anywhere else it might be witnessed is usually an offense.

Last, but by no means least, is the important question of consent. Not all sexual encounters involve willing participants, and some involve persons who are considered by law incapable of giving consent. No matter what the sex act or social setting, when consent has been withheld or when it cannot legally be given, the sexual situation is generally defined as criminal. Note, however, that the application of criminal labels to situations in which compliance has been gained through the use or threat of force is not automatic. As we shall see when we investigate rape, in many jurisdictions it is not a crime for a husband to force himself upon a nonconsenting wife.

Those situations the law treats as nonconsensual because a participant is incapable of giving consent usually revolve around the condition or status of the sex object. If the sex object is a child, is deemed mentally incompetent, or is drugged or unconsciious, sex with that person is illegal (provided he or she is not married to the other party). While force or threats may not have been used to secure compliance to a sexual demand, the fact that consent cannot legally be given renders the situation similar to one in which consent has been withheld.

THE SHAPING OF MODERN SEX LAWS

In the earliest legal codes, relatively few sexual activities were singled out for legal repression. Concern seems to have focused on those sexual activities and relations that violated prevailing mores. Incest, adultery, fornication, and the defilement of virgins through rape were favored targets of those who made the law.

With the spread of Christianity, an ever-increasing collection of sexual prohibitions emerged in law. As the church gained momentum in spreading its gospel and increasing its power in law and public policy, the foundations of modern sex laws were set in place. In England, for example, the church was quick to impose severe restrictions on the sexual freedoms of those who came under its power and influence. As self-appointed guardians of morality, religious leaders saw in sexual freedom a basic threat to the tenets of Judeo-Christian teachings, hence to the moral underpinnings of society. At the heart of the church's stand was "a definite and detailed code of behavior regarded as obligatory [for] all Christian believers. At the center of the code was the fixed principle that pleasure in sex was evil and damnable. It was not the sex act itself which was condemned, but the pleasure which was connected with it."[2]

The church viewed sex in extremely narrow terms. Heterosexual copulation for the strict purposes of procreation was the rule, and then only within the framework of marriage. Any sexual activity or relationship not meeting these criteria was viewed as inherently wrong and evil. If the sex act was not "straight" intercourse, furthermore, it was considered "unnatural," "perverted" behavior with no redeeming qualities.

This is not to say that the church was successful in suppressing sexual expression. On the contrary, by all accounts it was a dismal failure. Even priests themselves found it hard to abide by church rulings on sexual matters, and there are accounts of monks murdering their superiors when the latter sought to deprive them of heterosexual or homosexual outlets for their desires.[3] Even as late as the sixteenth century, the papal heads of the Roman Catholic church were notorious for their debauchery, incestuous conduct, and sexual adventures.

In England, the developing common law left sexual matters pretty much in the hands of the church. Despite certain exceptions — for example, rape, sexual assault on children, and sexual acts in public — sex was not a concern of criminal law. Morris Ploscowe describes the pre-sixteenth century situation:

> The common law of crimes took a comparatively liberal attitude toward sex expression. A great deal of illicit sexual activity, both non-marital and extra-

marital, was outside the domain of the common law and common-law courts. Fornication was no crime. Single men and women could copulate in secret without violating any penal provisions of the common law. Adultery was not a punishable offense. A man could two-time his wife or a wife cuckold her husband without having to fear the jailor or hangman. Men could masturbate each other in secret without running the risk of landing in jail.[4]

Two things, however, seem to have spurred eventual civil interest in sexual matters. First, the church and its ecclesiastical courts had failed to control sexual expression, and this failure left religious leaders searching for alternative ways to control sex. They turned to the state for help, reasoning, perhaps, that the criminal law and its enforcement machinery would succeed where they had failed. Second, civil leaders grew less content to leave the church with sanctioning power over any area of human conduct, including sex. They saw punishment as the proper domain of the state, and besides, why allow the church to levy fines when these could be paid into the royal treasury?

Henry VIII was one of the first English kings to enact specific sexual legislation. His buggery statute of 1533 made it a felony for a male to have anal intercourse with another male, or for a female to have intercourse with an animal. Urged on by Protestant and later by Puritan leaders — and quite in keeping with their statutory expansion of the criminal law — Henry's successors continued to enact sex laws, such that by the eighteenth century almost every conceivable sexual activity and relationship could be made to fit common law or statutory provisions.

VAGUENESS IN SEX LAWS

Henry VIII's buggery statute was vague, leaving unclear whether anal intercourse with a female was included or whether male sex relations with an animal was a crime. Unfortunately, we still find today that many of our sex laws are unclear regarding what exactly constitutes a crime. Unlike most other areas of criminal law and procedure, sex laws are steeped in confusion.

Part of the problem unquestionably derives from the long-standing reluctance of legal authorities to deal in plain language with what have always been sensitive matters. Writing in the late sixteenth century, Sir Edward Coke, a famed legal expert, found it hard to break with that tradition, and may himself have contributed to its perpetuation. His attitude is well summed up in his now famous reference to buggery as that "detestable and abominable sin, among Christians not to be named." And when it came to a description of the penetration of the vagina or anus during intercourse — an essential element in legal conceptions of carnal knowledge — he could only bring himself to say, in Latin, "the thing in the thing."[5]

While some states have moved toward the much needed clarification of their sexual proscriptions, sex statutes still use vague language and other states still have made no real effort to specify exactly what act or relationship is criminal. Much discretion, therefore, is left in the hands of the law enforcement agencies that must identify crimes, and in the hands of the courts that must interpret statute and precedent. Many defendants are not notified as to the exact particulars of their offenses, a normal requirement of due process. Because the wording of sex laws is often vague, some quite amazing applications of the criminal label are made. Ploscowe recounts a case in which a farmer was charged under a vague "open lewdness" statute for permitting a bull to copulate with a cow close to a public road, and thus in the view of passersby![6]

Perhaps the best illustration of terminological confusion and the ambiguity of sex laws is found in the so-called sodomy statutes most states have on their books. Though the term *sodomy* has been bandied about in legal circles since at least the eighteenth century, there is still little agreement on what it means. Thus some states apply the term only to anal intercourse between males; others, however, apply the term to anal intercourse with females; some include any kind of sexual activity with an animal; and yet others permit charges of sodomy when the act is fellatio or cunnilingus.[7]

The U.S. Supreme Court has not improved matters much, despite its mandate to clarify and interpret the meanings and intent of the Constitution. Consider on the one hand its 1973 ruling in *Wainwright* v. *Stone*.[8] In this case the Court supported the continued enforcement of a Florida statute outlawing sodomy, defined only as "an abominable and detestable crime against nature." On the other hand, there is the matter of obscenity. Here the Court appears to have washed its hands of the matter, leaving things largely up to "the average person," applying "contemporary community standards."[9] From one perspective this might be hailed as progressive, since it allows for variations in community standards. From another it places considerable enforcement discretion in the hands of local authorities, does not reduce the likelihood of breaches of First Amendment freedoms, and encourages the activities of so-called moral entrepreneurs, those who work for the enactment and enforcement of moral prohibitions. Anita Bryant is a good example of a moral entrepreneur.[10]

Just what violates community standards depends, of course, on the standards themselves — and this is by and large a matter of conjecture, not to mention disagreement. Certainly, one sees few attempts made to poll the moral views of the electorate, especially those pertaining to sex. Generally, all that is needed for a public morality law to appear on the books is pressure on legislators from those segments of the population officialdom feels obliged to woo. Whether it is prostitution, homosexuality, massage parlors, or pornography matters little; the important point is that legal officials can generally accommodate moral entrepreneurs with ease. The reason: laws exist that are so worded (or interpreted) that almost anything can be brought under them. The best examples are vagrancy laws and those dealing with "disorderly conduct," and "public nuisances." Though often invoked in situations that have nothing remotely sexual about them, they are also used in cases where conduct is, or appears to be, of a sexual nature. X-rated movies and movie theaters, strip joints, public nudity, homosexual encounters of one sort or another, and massage parlors have all been the object of criminalization under such laws. Today even zoning ordinances are being used in some jurisdictions as a means to suppress "undesirable" sexual activities. One example is Boston's Combat Zone, where pornography, x-rated movies, massage parlors, and other sex-oriented commercial activities have been allowed to flourish in one small downtown area but are illegal elsewhere. More commonly, zoning laws are being used in the attempt to force all commercialized sex out of town.

Sex Without Consent

Some sexual encounters stand out in that they involve unwilling and nonconsenting victims who are forced to participate in some sexual intimacy. Rape, sexual assaults on children, and homosexual assaults in prisons are examples of such encounters. We will confine our attention to those sex offenses that involve force, but which are not linked to any specialized social structure (as is the case with prison rape).[11]

RAPE: VIOLENCE WITH SEX

Not long ago rape was something you read about in sensational news stories and discussed, if at all, in secretive whispers. Even the scientific community kept the subject at arm's length. This collective avoidance was not simply due to the sensitive character of the subject. As some of the recent feminist literature points out, it is women, not men, who are the victims of rape, and so the problem of rape has not been viewed with urgency in male-dominated societies such as our own.[12] In addition, some branches of science have tended to ignore rape, thinking it the proper domain of those disciplines that study behavioral disorders and mental pathologies. It has been left largely to psychiatrists and psychologists to investigate rape. Finally, it has long been commonly believed that rape is a rare thing that crops up from time to time but not often enough to merit general concern, or even concern among women.

   In recent years, however, rape has emerged as a topic of growing interest among scholars and laymen alike. To a large extent, we owe this development to the efforts of women who have sought to remove the mystique and myths surrounding rape, and to help those who may be its victims.

WISCONSIN RAPE AND SEXUAL ASSAULT STATUTES FROM 1858 to 1976

1858

If any person shall ravish and carnally know any female of the age of ten or more, by force and against her will, he shall be punished by imprisonment in the state prison, not more than thirty years nor less than ten years; but if the female shall be proven on the trial to have been, at the time of the offense, a common prostitute, he shall be imprisoned not more than seven years nor less than one year.

1955

(1) Any male who has sexual intercourse with a female he knows is not his wife, by force and against her will, may be imprisoned not more than 30 years.

(2) In this section the phrase "by force and against her will" means either that her utmost resistance is overcome or prevented by physical violence or that her will to resist is overcome by threats of imminent physical violence likely to cause great bodily harm.

1976

(1) FIRST DEGREE SEXUAL ASSAULT.
Whoever does any of the following shall be fined not more than $15,000 or imprisoned not more than 15 years or both:

(a) Has sexual contact or sexual intercourse with another person without consent of that person and causes pregnancy or great bodily harm to that person.

(b) Has sexual contact or sexual intercourse with another person without consent of that person by use or threat of use of a dangerous weapon or any article used or fashioned in a manner to lead the victim reasonably to believe it to be a dangerous weapon.

(c) Is aided or abetted by one or more other persons and has sexual contact or sexual intercourse with another person without consent of that person by use or threat of force or violence.

(d) Has sexual contact or sexual intercourse with a person 12 years or younger.

(2) SECOND DEGREE SEXUAL ASSAULT.
Whoever does any of the following shall be fined not more than $10,000 or imprisoned not more than 10 years or both:

(a) Has sexual contact or sexual intercourse with another person without consent of

---

The Popular Image of Rape   A major contention of some feminists is that a popular image of rape has been fostered by males and sustains certain myths about rape and the rapist. This popular image, portrayed in such films as *Straw Dogs, A Clockwork Orange,* and Alfred Hitchcock's *Frenzy,* emphasizes the violence of male attackers who pop up from nowhere and vent their repressed sexual desires in the rape of unsuspecting females, who in turn do everything humanly possible to prevent their attackers from "taking" them. This image reflects and perpetuates cultural definitions emphasizing: (1) male dominance and female vulnerability; (2) the idea that a woman's body, especially her vagina, is man's property, and, like any other property, can be stolen by those to whom it does not belong; (3) the view that "good" women must defend that property at almost any cost; and (4) the idea that normal males will not need to resort to force in order to acquire the sexual property represented by a woman — they learn to do it in other ways.[13]

The Legal Conception of Rape   Though laws dealing with the subject begin to show signs of change (see box above), the popular image of

that person by use or threat of force or violence.

(b) Has sexual contact or sexual intercourse with another person without consent of that person and causes injury, illness, disease or loss or impairment of a sexual or reproductive organ, or mental anguish requiring psychiatric care for the victim.

(c) Has sexual contact or sexual intercourse with a person who suffers from a mental illness or deficiency which renders that person temporarily or permanently incapable of appraising the person's conduct, and the defendant knows of such condition.

(d) Has sexual contact or sexual intercourse with a person who the defendant knows is unconscious.

(e) Has sexual contact or sexual intercourse with a person who is over the age of 12 years and under the age of 18 years without consent of that person.

(3) THIRD DEGREE SEXUAL ASSAULT.
Whoever has sexual intercourse with a person without the consent of that person shall be fined not more than $5,000 or imprisoned not more than 5 years or both.

(3m) FOURTH DEGREE SEXUAL ASSAULT.
Whoever has sexual contact with a person without the consent of that person shall be fined not more than $500 or imprisoned not more than one year in the county jail or both.

(4) CONSENT.
"Consent" means words or overt actions by a person who is competent to give informed consent indicating a freely given agreement to have sexual intercourse or sexual contact. A person under 15 years of age is incapable of consent as matter of law. The following persons are presumed incapable of consent but the presumption may be rebutted by competent evidence, subject to the provisions of s.972.11(2):

(a) a person who is 15 to 17 years of age.

(b) a person suffering from a mental illness or defect which impairs capacity to appraise personal conduct.

(c) a person who is unconscious or for any other reason is physically unable to communicate unwillingness to an act."

SOURCE: *Wisconsin Statute Book*, 1858, 1955, 1976. Compiled by Ms. Laurel Stepp.

---

rape is mirrored in legal conceptions of it.[14] Common law traditions have long emphasized lack of victim consent, physical resistance, the use of force, actual penetration of the vagina, and offender-victim sexual unfamiliarity.

Force and victim resistance are fundamental. Rape convictions are most likely to be secured when there is evidence of force on the part of the accused and physical resistance on the part of the victim. Physical injuries, torn clothing, and disarray at the scene of the alleged rape are just some of the things courts look for in establishing that force occurred and was met by active resistance. Under common law, the victim was expected to resist vigorously and repeatedly; modern courts, while recognizing that resistance is not a black-and-white issue, are inclined nevertheless to treat active physical resistance as an important factor in establishing that rape actually occurred. Prosecutors across the country tend to screen out cases where evidence of force and resistance is considered weak.[15]

Offender-victim relationships are important also. Legal traditions are such that rape accusations are looked upon with some suspicion in cases where there is anything more than passing acquaintanceship. In some states, a man who lives with a woman, even though they are not married, cannot be accused of raping her.[16] As a general rule, a rape defendant who can show that he has had prior sexual intimacies with his accuser will have a strong point in his favor if the case gets to court.

From the time of the earliest legal codes, the true rape victim has been pictured as a sexually naive woman, usually a virgin. Indeed, the Code of Hammurapi and the ancient Jewish laws specifically distinguished between virgins and nonvirgins in their treatment of rape. According to these early codes, a married woman could not be raped, but if sexually assaulted by someone other than her husband, both parties would be charged with adultery, a capital offense. Furthermore, the ancient Jewish laws did not rely solely on the distinction between virgins and nonvirgins, for they ignored the virginity of those women raped within city walls. In such cases, complicity was assumed, "for the elders reasoned that if the girl had screamed she would have been rescued."[17]

While most jurisdictions no longer emphasize virginity as a legal issue in the determination of rape, much can still be made of the victim's character. A woman who has had premarital or extramarital sex relations, or one who is or has been a prostitute, does not fit the image of the rape victim as a chaste, morally upstanding female who reserves her body for the "rightful owner" — her present or future husband. Some rape statutes even specify that "sexually active" females cannot be raped.[18] The tide is turning, however, and, in the view of some, none too soon. The following states are among those restricting admission in court of a rape victim's prior sexual conduct: Alabama, Arkansas, Kentucky, Maryland, Mississippi, New Jersey, North Carolina, Pennsylvania, Vermont, West Virginia, and Wisconsin.

Rape In Marriage Recent developments in some jurisdictions have led to a significant change in the scope of their rape laws: a husband may be held liable for rape if he forces sexual intercourse on his resisting wife. This possibility has existed for some years in Norway, Sweden, and Denmark, and in many communist countries, but only recently has Anglo-Saxon jurisprudence seriously entertained the idea.[19] Now South Australia and a handful of American states (including Delaware, Wisconsin, and Oregon) allow for the possibility of rape in marriage.

The issue bears comment for two major reasons. First, it represents a significant departure from legal tradition and precedent going back hundreds of years. These traditions were clearly steeped in sexism, with the wife always the loser. Matthew Hale, the seventeenth-century English jurist whose caution on rape (that it is easy to charge and difficult to defend) has guided judges and legislators, was unquestionably a misogynist, as Gilbert Geis amply documents.[20]

Second, the new changes reflect the influence of the feminist movement, showing yet again how important the pressure of organized interest groups has become in the realm of law. The actual extent to which women's interests are met by the rape-in-marriage developments will depend on two factors: how widespread the change becomes, and whether the courts support the change in their rulings on individual cases. A test for Oregon was the much-publicized 1978 Rideout case. Greta Rideout charged her husband, John, with rape; he was subsequently acquitted. A similar case in Belgium also resulted in acquittal, though the husband was given a three-month suspended sentence for assault and battery.[21] We are reminded once more that there can be a marked difference between laws on the books and law in action.

THE OFFICIAL RECORD ON RAPE

According to official police records, around 50 out of every 100,000 American women annually are the victims of rape. Most experts agree, however, that the true rate of victimization is far greater than this. Estimates have placed the figure at from two to ten times the official rate.[22] This difference can be explained in large part by two things: victim reluctance to report offenses, and police labeling practices.

Among the major reasons victims fail to report their rape to the authorities are the embarrassment and humiliation associated with bringing their predicament into the open. Given prevailing views on the subject, and considering that family and friends may be more embarrassed by the incident than the victim herself, the victim is under strong pressures to keep silent. In addition, some women do not report their experience because they would rather avoid what quite often turns out to be a harrowing time at the hands of police and courts. Some victims believe that it would do no good to report their suffering to the authorities for the simple reason that the circumstances of their rape did not fit the popular image. One rape victim recently recounted to the author her own experience, and explained that she "just knew" nothing would come of her accusation. As she described things, not only had she had prior dates with her attacker; she had invited him into her apartment on that particular night. She offered no physical resistance when he ripped off her dress and made his intentions known, and she did not scream, even though her consent to sexual intercourse was vehemently and repeatedly withheld. It may be that it is in situations like these that victims come to view the event as a "personal" or "private" matter. A recent survey of rape victims in twenty-six cities indicates this characterization as another major reason for nonreporting.[23]

As women have begun to talk more freely of rape, the manner in which rape complaints have been received by officialdom has surfaced time and again as a factor in nonreporting. In their dealings with the police, rape victims are often subjected to intense and sometimes hostile questioning quite unlike that typically experienced by the victims of burglaries, robberies, and other crimes. One victim gives this account of her experience at the hands of police interrogators:

> They rushed me down to the housing cops who asked me questions like "Was he your boy-friend?" "Did you know him?" Here I am, hysterical, I'm 12 years old, and I don't know these things even happen to people. Anyway, they took me to the precinct after that, and there, about four detectives got me in the room and asked how long was his penis — like I was supposed to measure it. Actually, they said, "How long was the *instrument?*" I thought they were referring to the knife — how was I supposed to know? *That* I could have told them 'cause I was sure enough lookin' at the knife.[24]

In court rape victims are subject to the rigors of a cross-examination in which they are required to recall, in explicit detail, the humiliating and frightening encounter with the alleged rapist. Of course, rape is a serious offense in all jurisdictions, and defense attorneys quite naturally seek to discredit the testimony of victims and demonstrate that a real rape did not occur. But even so, from the standpoint of the victim who wonders whether to report her rape to the authorities and thus subject herself to this sort of humiliation, the problem is a very real one, and may only be resolved by a decision to keep silent. Here are the comments of two rape victims:

> I had heard other women say that the trial is the rape. It's no exaggeration. My trial was one of the dirtiest transcripts you could read. Even though I had been warned about the defense attorney you wouldn't believe the things he asked me to describe. It was very humiliating.[25]

> I don't understand it. It was like I was the defendant and *he* was the plaintiff. I wasn't on trial. I don't see where I did anything wrong. I screamed, I struggled. . . .[26]

Important in the generation of police records on any crime is the decision to formally acknowledge that an offense has taken place. Where rape is concerned, police reporting behavior has been congruent with the popular image of the offense. The police have generally been more likely to view rape allegations as "founded" when offender and victim are strangers, when there is physical injury, when the offense takes place in the open, when weapons have been used, when the rape did not occur on a date, when there was no prior sexual intimacy between offender and victim, and when sexual acts other than intercourse were also inflicted on the victim.[27]

It would appear that rape charges are now being recorded with greater accuracy by the police. FBI data gathered over the past few years show that forcible rape has been rising faster than any other violent crime. From 1974 to 1978 a rate increase of 21 percent was recorded.[28] It could be that this increase reflects a corresponding change in the true incidence of rape. Conversely, it could be due to more rigorous handling of rape allegations; many large police departments now have special units trained in the handling of such cases. More compassionate treatment of victims may be encouraging more women to come forward, especially blacks and other minority women. In its victimization survey of twenty-six American cities, the Department of Justice reports that 76 percent of minority victims reported to the police compared with only 62 percent of white victims.[29] Nevertheless, the facts remain cloudy, and one can do little more than speculate on how much of the rate increase is due to these factors and how much to changes in the incidence of the offense.

RAPE: PEOPLE AND CIRCUMSTANCES

In the first edition of this text I noted that recent investigations have shed much needed light on the subject of rape. On the basis of information collected independently in Philadelphia, Denver, and Memphis, and by the National Commission on the Causes and Prevention of Violence, I concluded that the popular image of rape accurately depicts only a small portion of all rape incidents.[30] I have not changed my mind in the interim, but the publication of yet more recent research has left some of the earlier findings in doubt.[31] Since these later studies are primarily based on victim reports, I am tempted to favor the newer evidence over that based on official police reports (so-called police-blotter rape). It would be premature, however, to discard the earlier findings as no longer tenable, and we should remember that rape characteristics may well vary from area to area.

Before turning to the conflicting evidence, let us review the points of agreement found in most of the research. First, rape offenders and victims tend to be young, usually under 25. Second, offenders and victims tend to be of the same race and socioeconomic status. Though McDonald's Denver study found otherwise, the bulk of the evidence shows that rape, like homicide, is intraracial. Also like homicide, blacks are disproportionately identified as assailants and victims. As for socioeconomic status, offenders and victims are more often drawn from the less wealthy, less educated, and less stable segments of the population. They tend to reside in the slum and inner-city areas of our large urban centers, where rape rates are the highest.

Third, most rapes are likely to occur in private or semiprivate locations such as homes, apartments, or automobiles. While initial contact between rapist and victim often occurs outdoors or in public places like bars and theaters, the single most common location for the actual assault is inside a home, usually the victim's. Fourth, those intent on rape are more often unarmed than armed with a weapon. When they are armed, rapists tend to carry knives. The presence of a weapon significantly increases the probability that the rape attack will be completed.

Now for the points on which the evidence is conflicting or unclear.

First, the earlier studies put the chances of being raped by someone known to the victim at around fifty-fifty. However, more recent victimization surveys show a different pattern. McIntyre and Myint refer to three mid-1970 studies in which rape by a stranger was more prevalent than rape by an acquaintance.[32] The national survey of victimization in twenty-six cities found that 82 percent of rapes and attempted rapes were by strangers. Thus there appears to be substantial support for the popular view that rape is committed by strangers. A word of caution, however, is necessary. Many victims consider the rape incident a private matter, and it could be that considerable numbers of nonstranger rapes are not reported to survey interviewers. Even taking this possibility into account, it was still estimated that approximately 75 percent of the rapes and attempted rapes were committed by strangers.

Second, there seems to be some question about the extent of injury associated with rape. There is no question that the psychological trauma associated with rape victimization is severe and potentially devastating, but what about physical injuries? Amir and MacDonald found that very few women suffer severe injury, and the bulk of injuries are a result of the rape act itself. The national victimization survey looked in detail at the injury question, and McDermott concludes:

> Briefly, most rape and most attempted rape victims who were attacked were injured. Injuries included rape and attempted rape injuries, as well as additional injuries. . . . [M]ost often the additional injury was in the form of bruises, cuts, scratches, and black eyes. These survey data on injury suggest that the element of violence in rape is the physical force used to attempt and/ or achieve sexual intercourse with a woman against her will. Generally, it does not appear to be violence in the form of additional, capricious beatings, stabbings, and so forth.[33]

The popular image of rape and its legal counterpart has placed considerable emphasis on the violence of rape and on the physical resistance of the victim. The impression gained from Amir's Philadelphia study was that rape victims put up token verbal resistance. The national victimization survey, using a different categorization of resistance, established a rather different picture. Most victims took measures to protect themselves by screaming, trying to use some form of physical force against the attacker, or attempting to flee.

It is important to note that when potential victims resist a rape attack they increase the chances that the rape will not be completed, while at the same time, they increase the chances that they will be seriously injured. Note, too, that the resistance-injury connection points to "an important danger in the popular notion (and some statutory requirements) that a victim of an attack should resist to her utmost."[34]

Third, what of the contention that rapes are not spur-of-the-moment events but are instead planned attacks? We are faced here with an awesome evidentiary problem, for the only way to be certain in any given case is to hear the truth from the offender himself. Failing this, we are left with informed speculation.

Speculation has generally held that rapes are usually not spontaneous. Some sort of planning is involved, and this seems most likely in situations involving multiple attackers. Amir found evidence of planning in 58 percent of single-offender rapes, in 83 percent of two-offender rapes, and in 90 percent of group rapes.[35] The National Commission on the Observance of International Women's Year estimated that 71 percent of all rapes are planned.[36] On the other hand, a national survey of prosecutors found that only 25 percent of the cases presented to them by police showed any evidence of premeditation.[37]

This difference may be due to the fact that few of the rapes in this latter study were committed by multiple offenders. The data here, and in the national victimization survey, show that rapists generally act alone. Still, group rapes do account for a significant minority of reported rapes, a fact that should be kept in mind in assessing the "modern" view that rape is not so much sexual as an aggressive display of male power and domination over women.[38]

UNDERSTANDING RAPE

Some dimensions of police-blotter rape bring to mind other forms of interpersonal violence, most notably, homicide. For example, both rape and homicide are intraracial offenses of violence usually involving lower-class urban youths, many of whom are black, who assault victims of similar status and age. Noting this, some authors have followed Amir's lead in designating rape as yet another manifestation of a lower-class subculture of violence.[39]

The idea is that lower-class urban youths learn to adopt violence as a legitimate means to settle disputes, acquire status and recognition, and bolster self-esteem. Further, the use of force is seen as an acceptable alternative to which one can turn when his goals cannot be reached by other means. If it so happens that the goal he seeks is identified as a challenge to his very identity as a male — to achieve it is to be a "real man" — pressures to secure that goal are considerable, and the likelihood greater that force will be employed when obstacles are met. Women are perceived as a challenge to manliness not only because to "have" a woman is to be a real man, but also because it is expected that sexual advances will be met by at least some resistance, and this must be overcome. A man who cannot overcome that resistance is open to the derision of his peers, especially since prevailing definitions of womanhood include the idea that females are weak and vulnerable and should be submissive to the demands of men.

Among lower-class males, some authors have argued, sex is treated combatively: women are perceived as beings to be conquered and dominated, and sex is one of the prizes.[40] However, the important element in lower-class male-female relationships is not so much the sexual aspect, it seems, but rather the demonstration that the male is indeed dominant and superior. A man gets what he wants from a woman precisely because he is a man. And so, as W. H. Blanchard has shown in his study of gang rape, the pressures to live up to lower-class conceptions of masculinity, superiority, and toughness may find themselves resolved in the violent "taking" of a woman.[41]

The emphasis on rape as a behavioral manifestation of a lower-class subculture of violence has been criticized by some writers who remind us that rape statistics showing a preponderance of black lower-class offenders may not be an accurate reflection of the true rape picture. Furthermore, they remind us that male aggressiveness toward females is by no means limited to one particular category of Americans. Thus, Charles McCaghy writes:

> . . .[I]t is tempting simply to classify sexual assault as another instance of a subculture of interpersonal violence. But it is important to remember that the values supporting interpersonal violence have their roots in more general cultural values supporting violence as a means of solving problems. Despite the statistics, the case for assigning responsibility for sexual violence primarily to lower class, black males is not that convincing. Aggressiveness, if not open violence, by males toward females is pervasive in American society. Indeed, it may be argued that male sexual aggression in the United States has been the rule not the exception.[42]

In virtually all areas of American life — the family, work, politics, sports, education, and so on — males have traditionally found themselves in positions of power, domination, independence, and self-determination. Women, on the other hand, are expected to take subordinate positions and to acquiesce to the decisions and demands made by men. The world of sexuality is no different. The prevailing cultural image of maleness supports the idea of men as dominating, powerful, and active, and as the instigators of sexual interaction; the female is weak, passive, and submissive. The so-called missionary position in sexual intercourse accentuates this asymmetrical relationship.

Dating and Rape   A major way in which the American male is encouraged to adopt and act out the expectations associated with being a man is the institution of dating. Dating is an important social institution for both males and females. For the female it marks the conventional road to courtship and marriage and provides the opportunity to practice her "proper" role as the deferential, acquiescent, admiring, passive partner. For the male, dating also provides the conventional road to marriage, but in addition gives him the chance to demonstrate independence, masculinity, and action in this one-to-one relationship with a woman. As the expected initiator of sexual play, the male is encouraged to view his female companion as a sexual object to be won. His success is measured by how far he gets. (I remember that in high school we had a numerical code from one to ten indicating the extent of success!)

Of course the idea that the male will succeed in this particular demonstration of his manliness — "go all the way" — may not be shared by his female friend. When this happens, the interaction often turns sour, and may result in a physical confrontation with the male attempting to bring about precisely what is being denied him. Influenced, perhaps, by the effects of a few drinks or by what he has wrongly interpreted as sexual acquiescence on the part of his female companion, the rejected male finds it hard to back off once he has reached that point where, in his own mind (and, he presumes, in the minds of other males), his masculinity is put to the test.[43]

Certainly, most dates do not end in physical confrontations and sexual assault. However, studies indicate that rape and attempted rape during a date is by no means rare, and its occurrence is not confined to dating situations involving lower-class males. Studies on college campuses, for example, have discovered that both male and female students — in some cases as many as 25 percent of those interviewed — could recall instances where they had committed or been the victims of sexual assault during a date.[44]

Some males are quick to point out that rape can be justified. A number of convenient myths and falsehoods in our culture mark the female as a legitimate target of male sexual aggression, even violence. Some women, it is said, need to be raped; such women are "uppity," they have stepped out of line, they are not passive or submissive, and thus must be reminded of their place vis-à-vis the male. According to others, some women deserve to be raped; they have been too submissive, and thus any man can have them, or they have (heaven forbid) rejected the male as a sex partner altogether. Then again, some men say, "When a woman says no, she really means "yes" or "In their hearts all women want to be raped." A recent survey of Minnesota men provides evidence of the prevalence of such views. Seventy-one percent of the respondents believed that women have an unconscious desire to be raped, and 48 percent felt that going braless and wearing short skirts was an invitation to rape.[45] Even those who must deal with rape professionally share in many of the myths and help perpetuate them. Physicians and judges, it seems, are no less influenced by these misconceptions.[46] With this assortment of rationalizations and justifications to fall back on, it is not surprising that convicted rapists rarely think of themselves as criminals, and usually lay the blame for their actions — if, indeed, someone is to blame — at the feet of their victims.

The conception of women as legitimate targets for rape fits nicely with prevailing views that prevention of rape depends on women changing their behavior. "Don't hitchhike"; "Don't accept when a stranger or short-time acquaintance invites you to his apartment for drinks''; ''Don't go out at night on your own''; ''Don't wear sexy clothes''; ''Don't initiate sexual play''; and, above all, ''Don't promise what you won't deliver!'' If you are a woman, be what you are supposed to be: vulnerable, demure, passive, dependent, and proper. And so the wheel comes full circle. Men will be men, and women should be women.

The reasoning just presented argues that rape is best viewed not as a manifestation of lower-class values and expectations, but rather as a behavioral consequence of general cultural values and images. According to these values and images, the male is dominating, sexually active, and independent; the female is dependent, passive, and submissive, and a legitimate target of male sexual aggression. Further, institutionalized arrangements of our society (e.g., dating) provide males with the opportunity to act out their culturally supported prerogatives, and hence are conducive to rape.[47]

Building upon this view, Chappell and his colleagues have recently argued that more sexually permissive societies may well find themselves experiencing higher rates of rape than less permissive societies.[48] Their reasoning is simple. In a permissive society, where casual sexual relations are more acceptable and presumed to be commonplace, the male will experience even greater threats to his image of self-worth and masculinity when his sexual advances are denied than he would in a less permissive society, where that denial is expected and culturally valued.

Evidence in support of this view was obtained in a comparison of Boston (considered restrictive) and Los Angeles (considered permissive). In 1969 rape rates were 12.8 per 100,000 people in Boston, and 25.4 per 100,000 people in Los Angeles. In a later paper Gilbert and Robley Geis present further evidence in support of their argument, this time from Stockholm, Sweden.[49] The relatively high rates of rape in this city (18.9 in 1970; 22.9 in 1977) suggest support for the theory; however, the authors also found a different kind of support. In Stockholm many rapes occur after a pickup at some dance hall or bar, and often involve a foreign man and a Swedish woman. After some socializing the couple end up at one or the other's residence, the man makes sexual advances, the woman declines, and a rape follows. The more sexually liberated Swedish woman exercises her prerogative of choice in sexual matters, and that decision is an affront to the foreigner, who sees his masculinity severely challenged by the unexpected refusal. The authors conclude: ''the irony is that the Swedish situation, which we think is a good thing, ends up looking bad in terms of rape rates.''[50]

What of the possibility that rapists are not normal people, that they may be suffering from some mental pathology or personality disorder that leads them to commit rape? After all, most males presumably do not commit rape, even though they are products of a society stressing male supremacy. Perhaps the rapist is one of the few who are mentally ill or brain damaged in some way. This idea certainly fits well with the popular image of rape.

The question has not escaped the attention of psychologists and psychiatrists. In general, however, the research that has been done does not support explanations of rape based on mental pathologies, personality disorders, or brain damage. According to fairly recent studies, most of the convicted rapists who were tested for such disorders proved psychiatrically normal, or at most were suffering from neuroses of one kind or another.[51] Some evidence suggests that those suffering from encephalitis may be prone to sexual violence, but here again the indications are that we are dealing with only a minute proportion of rape offenders, and, in any case, the causal link between this illness and rape has not been conclusively demonstrated.[52] In short, while mental or physiological disorders may be a factor in explaining sexual violence in some individual cases, the available evidence does not support the contention that those who commit rape are abnormal in the senses we have been discussing.

CHILD MOLESTATION

While the most likely victims of rape appear to be the older teenager or young adult, children, including the very young, are sometimes the victims of rape and other sexual assaults. Actually, some authors claim that sexual assaults involving the physical abuse of children may even be more prevalent than nonsexual assaults such as child beating.[53] Such claims are difficult to assess, given the paucity of reliable information on either type of assault, but there is undoubtedly far more of both than is generally recognized.

As with the rapist, there is a popular image of the so-called child molester. He is depicted as a stranger who lurks around playgrounds, parks, and other places where children wander, and who lures or drags his victims into his car or home where he then sexually assaults them. This image is no more accurate than the one of rape and the rapist. For example, he is not usually a stranger. In studies both here and abroad, researchers are finding that in most known cases of child molestation the offender and victim are acquainted with each other. In a New York investigation of the Brooklyn and Bronx areas, only 25 percent of the 250 sampled incidents involved strangers; in the remaining 75 percent of the cases, the offenders were either related to the child or were such acquaintances as neighbors, friends of the family, or baby-sitters.[54] Similarly, in a Wisconsin study of 181 convicted child molesters, 65 percent were at least casually acquainted with their victims.[55]

Learning the details surrounding cases of child molestation is not easy. Those incidents in which very young children are victimized present the greatest difficulties for the researcher. Except where brutal physical abuses are involved, and these are a small minority of known cases, even the nature of the sexual encounter itself may be difficult to determine. From the standpoint of the criminal law, the nature and gravity of the offense hinge on the details of the encounter. Especially important when the victim is an older child, 14 or 15 years old, are the related issues of resistance and consent. Did the child resist? Did the child consent to the sexual act, or even encourage it? Was compliance secured by the use or threat of physical force? In dealing with these questions, both courts and researchers are often confronted with conflicting pictures of the events surrounding the incident. For one thing, the official account of the incident commonly departs from the account given by the suspect.[56] Commenting on this discrepancy, Edward Sagarin notes:

> Both [accounts] are suspect. The child is old enough to understand that she will exonerate herself if she claims resistance or lack of encouragement in the courtroom; and since she is a prosecution witness, the prosecution encourages her in that direction in order to obtain a conviction. On the other hand, the defendant is anxious that the court, the researcher, and even himself believe that he was led on. Indeed, some defendants denied their guilt not only to the courts, but to the investigators as well.[57]

Bearing this in mind, scholars who have looked at the questions of coercion and resistance suggest that as a general rule molesters are unlikely to resort to overt physical coercion, and when a child does offer resistance it is most likely overcome by threats of deprivation (loss of love, affection, privileges) or by rewards (candy, money).[58] Victim resistance and offender use of physical coercion tend more to characterize those sexual incidents involving strangers, which is what we would expect: neither the offender nor victim are bound up in affective relations with one another, hence victim compliance is problematic.

One of the important points of agreement among researchers is that child molesters do not represent a homogeneous group of people. They come from all walks of life, are of varied ages, engage in different sorts of sexual acts, choose different types of child victims, and, as Donal MacNamara has noted, range "from senile old men, through drunken aggressors, to psychotic pedophiles, mental defectives, and adventitious offenders."[59] About the only common characteristic is that they are most often males who choose young females (the most likely victim is 11 to 14 years old) as targets of their sexual demands. Relatively few known cases involve female offenders or male victims.

One promising attempt to identify types of molesters and to differentiate between them has been offered by McCaghy. Rather than focus simply on the characteristics of offenders (their age, social background, or psychiatric state) as some scholars have done, McCaghy's work makes use of information on the extent to which child molesters have interacted with children in the past, and on the circumstances surrounding the offense situation.[60] Four offense circumstances were considered important:

(1) the amount of coercion used; (2) familiarity with the child victim; (3) form of sexual activity; and (4) the nature of the interaction between offender and child immediately prior to the offense. Based on his analysis, McCaghy tentatively identified six types of molesters:

1. high interaction molester [described in the next paragraph]; 2. incestuous molester (whose victim is related and living in his residence); 3. asocial molester (whose molesting offense is but one segment of a lawbreaking career); 4. senile molester (whose older age and low educational level distinguish him from other molesters); 5. career molester (whose current offense does not represent his only arrest for molesting); 6. spontaneous-aggressive molester (whose offense characteristics are opposite those of the high interaction molester).[61]

Though representing only 18 of the 181 subjects studied, the *high interaction molester* category is the one McCaghy feels best meets the typological criteria of internal homogeneity and isolation from other categories. As described by the author, molesters in this category have had life patterns involving "many contacts with children outside their own home and immediate neighborhood."[62] They commit their offenses against children with whom they are familiar, they do not use or threaten force, their interaction with the child begins on a nonsexual level, and the subsequent sexual activity is confined primarily to manual manipulation of their own or the child's genitals.

There is good reason to believe that the high interaction molester may be more prevalent than indicated by McCaghy's sample. For one thing, offender-victim familiarity, coupled with the absence of physical coercion and the mildness of the sexual encounter itself, may render this offender less visible to the authorities and those engaged in research, thus less easily discovered by them. In addition, evidence from other studies shows that parents of child victims are less likely to press charges when the offender is a family acquaintance or friend.[63]

In cases where family members or relatives of the molester are victimized, probably the most common situations of all, the offense is often not an isolated incident but has been committed over a period of weeks, months, or even years. Given the ongoing nonsexual interaction between relatives and family members, this is not surprising. In addition, the sexual encounters themselves may have developed in an atmosphere of consensus and mutual affection. As one author has pointed out, incestuous desire on the part of both adult and child can be interpreted as a quite understandable consequence of close, personal, and satisfying relations between family members.[64] What may begin as a loving nonsexual relationship between an adult and a child may, with the passage of time, expand to include repetitive sexual interactions.

Of course, cultural expectations in most societies do not extend to incest or noncoital sex acts between family members. By engaging in sex acts with any child, in fact, an adult departs from acceptable sexual roles. It is hard to imagine that molesters are, as a group, unaware that they have moved beyond culturally acceptable — not to say legal — boundaries of sexual conduct. A few, and the available evidence indicates that it is relatively few, may be mentally deficient or suffering from severe psychiatric disorders and therefore unaware of the normative implications of their actions.[65] Most, however, are clearly aware of their transgressions, and like other persons who recognize that others will label them deviant or criminal, they tend to disavow their actions or to excuse them by appealing to what they view as socially acceptable justifications.

When asked to account for their actions by the courts, researchers, or their friends, child molesters commonly explain away their conduct by either blaming it on a temporary loss of sense or rationality ("I was drunk"; "I didn't know what I was doing"; "everything went blank") or by blaming it on the behavior of the victim ("she wanted me to do it"; "he started it") or on conditions of family life or other personal troubles. In McCaghy's study, the author found that the most common single response to the question "Why?" was to blame the offense on a temporary loss of rationality. The offenders most likely to deny their deviance in this way were those who had used force to obtain compliance and those who had molested female children.

Some molesters are quite candid about their conduct and do not attempt to deny their deviance or to justify it by appealing to external forces. Male offenders who molest boys and young men seem most likely to fall into this category. Explaining this, McCaghy argues:

> It appears that many homosexual molesters have previously accepted a homosexual role, which in itself represents a drastic departure from the sexual norms of conventional society. Being accused of molesting does not constitute a threat to their present self-concept as sexual deviants. Since deviant sexual conduct is already a way of life for them, they do not feel compelled to deny responsibility for their molesting offense. This interpretation was lent support during the author's interviews with these molesters. Many considered themselves to be first of all homosexuals. Their contact with a person under the age of fourteen was, to them, unfortunate and perhaps accidental, but only secondary to their basic sexual behavior patterns. Since they were already at odds with approved sexual norms, the molesting offense did not result in any need for serious self-examination.[66]

We are, needless to say, far from any complete and accurate picture of child molesting and the child molester. Much research still needs to be done, and the greater willingness of people to talk about sensitive sexual issues will aid in that endeavor. We can expect, however, that most incidents of child molestation will remain hidden from research scrutiny, particularly those offenses in which physical force and abuse are not employed and which involve offenders and victims who are familiar with one another and are associated in continuing relationships of a nonsexual kind.

REACTIONS TO RAPE AND CHILD MOLESTATION

Rape and sexual acts with minors have long been placed in the category of heinous crimes. Even when legal codes were in their formative stages, little sympathy was extended to rapists, child molesters, and those committing incest with children. The usual penalties have been death, banishment, and, in recent years, long prison sentences. Notwithstanding this tradition, public and official reactions to offenders have not been clear-cut. Rather, while generally punitive, reactions have depended on such things as who the offender is, who the victim is, and what kind of interaction the two had.

While most state codes have at one time or another identified rape as a capital crime, for instance, those offenders most likely to receive the death penalty have been blacks. Since 1930 there have been 455 executions for rape; of those executed, nearly 90 percent were blacks. To these legal executions we must add the hundreds of blacks who have been lynched for actually or supposedly raping white women.[67] The feeling among some whites, particularly in the South, seems to have been that only the most severe penalty matches the outrage committed when a black man violates the social taboos surrounding white-black relations and has sex with a white woman. Whether rape was actually committed — and in numerous cases this certainly was not established — seems to have been largely beside the point. A black simply did not become "intimate" with a white, especially a white woman. The charge of rape provided a vehicle for the imposition of death, which usually matched the legal punishment for rape, and, also important, exonerated the white female, who, whites could argue, would never have consented to sexual intimacies with a black. The charge and the punishment thus reinforced prevailing prejudices and discriminatory practices.

The general sense of what "true" rape is affects trial and sentencing. Important to this image are the characteristics of the victim and how she has behaved prior to and during the sexual encounter. If she is a virgin, a minor, or very old, and if there is circumstantial evidence that she put up resistance and was overcome by force, the offender is likely to be convicted and receive a severe sentence. In one recent study, for example, judges of the Philadelphia court system admitted giving considerable weight to circumstantial evidence about the alleged victim and her behavior.[68] These judges seemed to believe in only one kind of true rape, that fitting the popular image described earlier: the stranger leaping out of shadows in the dark alley. When perceived as a genuine victim of rape, the woman received a sympathetic hearing and the offender a severe sentence. It was different, however, when judges perceived the case to be one of "consensual intercourse" (described by some judges as "friendly rape," "felonious gallantry," "assault with failure to please," or "breach of contract") or of "female vindictiveness." Though such perceptions may have been based solely on the fact that, say, the woman had met her attacker in a bar and had allowed him to drive her home, the judicial response was typically unsympathetic to the victim and lenient or supportive to the defendant.

A glaring example of judicial bias and possibly of modern misogyny occurred in Dane County, Wisconsin, in 1977. A 15-year-old boy was convicted of assaulting a 16-year-old girl in a high school stairwell. The judge put the boy on probation, later explaining his decision as follows:

> I'm trying to say to women, stop teasing. There should be a restoration of modesty in dress and elimination from the community of sexual gratification business. . . . Whether women like it or not they are sex objects. Are we supposed to take an impressionable person 15 or 16 years of age and punish that person severely because they react to it normally?[69]

The judge was subsequently removed from office through a public referendum. Other judges with similar views are doubtless sitting in some of the nation's courts today.

Another illustration of the emphasis placed on the victim's own behavior is found in two cases reported by D. A. Thomas in a review of sentencing decisions in English rape trials and appeals.[70] In one case, a girl of 16 had been forcibly carried into a van and subsequently raped by two men. In the other case, a girl of 20 accepted a ride from two men (both of whom had previous convictions for criminal offenses), whereupon she was driven to a secluded spot and raped three times, twice by one man and once by the other. The various defendants were found guilty, but those involved in the second incident received lighter sentences than those in the first. According to Thomas, "The difference in sentence between this case and the previous one can be explained by reference to the girl's acceptance of a lift, as opposed to being dragged forcibly into the car."[71] On what grounds, one may ask, does agreement to ride with a man make his subsequent rape of the hitchhiker somehow less serious than if he had forced her into the car?

Sexual offenses involving adults and young children commonly provoke severe reactions compared to most other criminal offenses, but when pubescent children are involved, marked variations in official reactions can arise. Again, much is made of the victims themselves and of their apparent role in bringing the offense about. Two more examples from England will suffice as illustrations. In one case, a young man had numerous episodes of sexual intercourse with a 14-year-old girl he had met at a dancing school. "It was accepted that the girl was a very willing participant." In another case, a married father of four children had repeated acts of sexual intercourse with his 15-year-old sister-in-law. Circumstantial evidence was entered to support the view that the girl "had been the real instigator." In both of these cases an appeals court reduced the sentences imposed by the trial judge on the major grounds of victim interest and participation.[72]

In general, the chances of obtaining a conviction in cases of sexual assault, especially rape, are slim. When the victims are neither very old nor very young females, the chances are reduced yet further. The fact is that rape juries, as a rule, are dominated by males, not the usual situation in other criminal trials. According to a 1972 editorial in the *Yale Law Journal:* "The existing evidence indicates that juries view rape charges with extraordinary suspicion and rarely return convictions in the absence of aggravating circumstances, such as extrinsic violence."[73] Indeed, most states require that witness testimony be corroborated by external evidence of sexual assault (torn clothing, physical injury, weapons, and so forth). The uncorroborated testimony of the victim, no matter how compelling, cannot be the sole basis for a conviction. While these rules are under challenge in many states, and while some reforms have taken place in recent years (New York State modified the corroboration rules in 1972), there remain doubts as to how successful these challenges will be. At least two states (Georgia and Idaho) have recently beefed up the corroboration rules, making prosecution and conviction in rape cases much more difficult.

SEXUAL PSYCHOPATH LAWS

The belief is widespread that some, if not all, sex offenders suffer from a mental deficiency or some kind of personality disorder. This belief gains popularity whenever we hear of an especially brutal or "perverted" sex crime such as the Richard Speck rape-murders in Chicago, or the atrocities of John Gacy. Confronted with bizarre crimes in its midst, the public characteristically reacts with fear and apprehension, and pressures public officials to do something about the dangerous "sex fiend." One consequence of this pressure has been the enactment in many states of sexual psychopath laws.

Primarily a product of the 1940s and 1950s, these laws are statutory provisions for dealing with sex offenders adjudged to be psychopathic. The laws spread, Edwin Sutherland has argued, because of a combination of public fear, community agitation for legislative action, and the timely emergence of claims of psychiatric expertise in treating behavior abnormalities.[74] Though the language of sexual psychopath laws differs from state to state, their major thrust has basically been the same: to provide a legal means for keeping certain sex offenders out of circulation for as long as it takes to cure them of their behavioral disorder. In some states a suspect need not be convicted of an offense for the courts to order him detained for treatment. Furthermore, the end of treatment does not always mean automatic release; in some states, patients must still stand trial for their alleged offense, and may go to prison upon conviction.

As an attempt to do something about the threat posed by sex offenders who cannot control their behavior because they are "sick," the sexual psychopath laws have generally been a failure. For one thing, psychiatrists themselves disagree as to what constitutes a psychopathic disorder, and for another, these same experts who promised so much when the laws were designed have not delivered. Neither the accurate prediction of sex offense recidivism nor the effective treatment of those designated psychopathic has been forthcoming.[75]

The sexual psychopath laws and their application have been criticized for other reasons. As Morris Ploscowe pointed out some years ago, the laws are often vaguely worded, and partly because of this almost any sex offender or suspect may be detained for treatment over an indefinite period:

> The sex-psychopath laws . . . start with vague and elusive criteria of mental abnormality. What is even worse is that they do not clearly define the sexual misbehavior to which the laws are applicable. This is best illustrated by the provision of the Vermont laws, which require incarceration "until such time as their mental condition no longer constitutes a threat to public welfare, of persons who because of psychotic personality violate the criminal laws of the state or are guilty of gross immoral conduct." Any violation of a minor criminal provision or the participation by the defendant in any conduct which is deemed offensive to a prosecutor may bring an individual within this statute.[76]

Over the years, sexual psychopath laws have been applied in cases of child molesting, rape, consensual homosexuality, exhibitionism, and voyeurism, not to mention a host of other transgressions. Often there appears to be no fundamental difference between those detained for psychiatric treatment and those sent to prison or otherwise dealt with by conventional dispositional processes.[77]

This brings us to another criticism. In some states the sexual psychopath laws are treated as civil rather than criminal in nature — because the sex offender is sick rather than simply a criminal, he should be treated differently — so those to whom the laws are applied may be denied the procedural safeguards extended to criminal defendants. Some states do not give offenders the right to appeal a detention order; some states have no provisions for court-appointed attorneys, so poor defendants must do without counsel; and some states do not allow suspects the right to a jury of their peers.

The idea that detention under psychopathy laws is not criminal detention but is instead a means for dealing with the sick leads to a wide latitude permitted hospital and psychiatric authorities in their treatment programs. Apart from the fact that personnel are not held to constitutional prohibitions against cruel and unusual punishment, they are often left free to experiment with the sex offenders placed in their programs, who then become guinea pigs in psychiatric exploration. In addition, the decision to release or detain patients is usually entirely in the hands of those running the institutions into which the offender is placed. Clearly, then, if the experiments do not work or the patient does not behave in the manner desired by those who run the psychopathy programs, the sex offender, unlike most normal criminals, may spend the rest of his life behind walls.[78]

Consensual Sex Offenses: Prostitution

Some sex offenses are victimless in the sense that they involve consenting adults who voluntarily engage in an activity that happens to be illegal. Homosexual encounters, adultery, fornication, the sale and purchase of pornographic literature, and prostitution are examples. This section focuses on prostitution.

One author has estimated that as many as 600,000 full-time and 600,000 part-time prostitutes are working at any given time in the United States.[79] These figures may be high — other estimates have placed the total number of prostitutes at around 250,000.[80] But in terms of sheer numbers the United States undoubtedly has the largest prostitute population of any Western nation. Yet prostitution is in violation of criminal codes in all states except Nevada, which lets its various county governments decide on legality.

Prostitution has not always been illegal in the United States, and in some Western societies it is tolerated today. In Germany, Holland, and Denmark, for instance, female prostitutes are pretty much left alone so long as they ply their trade in designated areas and fulfill other requirements such as licensing and payment of taxes. Describing the situation in Hamburg, Germany, Walter Reckless tells us:

On one enclosed small street (a block in length) of the Reeperbahn, the prostitutes are permitted to display themselves in the nude at every window of the houses on the narrow street. The entrance way at each end of the street has a sort of privacy screen which shields the prostitutes from view of pedestrians not entering the special section. The two privacy screens have posted notices indicating that only males over twenty-one years of age may enter the street. In addition, solicitation by prostitutes is permitted in certain cafes, especially around the central railroad station of Hamburg (the Haupt-bahnhof). On the side wall of each "booth" table is an "in-house" telephone. When male customers are seated in their booth, the phone rings and the woman at the other end asks for an invitation to join the party.[81]

Some American laws have been so designed that they may actually encourage prostitution, even though the prostitute herself breaks the law by selling sexual favors to interested males. In many states today, for example, the male client commits no offense when he agrees to buy sexual intimacies from the prostitute. Thus the risks of arrest are borne solely by the woman, not the client, and those males in search of sexual fun can feel free to pursue their goal without fear of criminalization. Even in those states that have made it a crime to patronize a prostitute, the designated penalties are often greater for the prostitute than her client. In Victorian England, prostitution was actually encouraged even though it received broad social condemnation. It was encouraged because the existing laws left untouched the activities of those who stood to gain financially from prostitution and were in a position to recruit and protect the girls. While appearing on the surface to be a time of moral respectability, the period was one in which prostitution flourished and the exploitation of females continued.[82]

We see, then, that even though prostitution is illegal it may be outlawed in such a way that it is actually encouraged to persist. Why? Most obviously, because those responsible for the creation of laws are usually male and are potential clients. While paying lip service to precepts of moral decency, our lawmakers remember that "men will be men," and women are there to fulfill their every desire. In this sense, prostitution is, as feminists point out, yet another manifestation of male exploitation of females. It should come as no surprise that most inquiries into prostitution have focused not on the male client but on the prostitute herself. She, after all, is the deviant, the criminal.

SELLING SEX: THE PROSTITUTE AT WORK

Prostitutes work in various ways. At one end of the spectrum are the *streetwalkers,* or *street hookers.*[83] These women may be readily encountered on the street, particularly in those sections of cities where cheap hotels, bars, and mass transportation terminals are to be found. The streetwalker is at the bottom of the pecking order among prostitutes. She works where the risks are greatest, she has little or no control over what clients she takes, she must put up with all kinds of weather, she must generally give a good portion of her earnings away for "protection," and she must usually work long hours to make enough from her "tricks" (paying customers, sometimes called "johns") to keep abreast of her financial obligations. Even the classiest streetwalkers — those working office buildings or conventions during the day or early evening hours — rarely gross more than $200 or $300 a day. The streetwalker does well to stay in business for more than a few years, and her earning capacity declines rapidly after she passes her twenty-second or twenty-third birthday.

Next up the social ladder are those prostitutes who work in *brothels*

Prostitution will continue to flourish as long as there are willing customers. Although it is a consensual crime and in this sense victimless, prostitution involves many elements of exploitation, most of which are suffered by the prostitute.

(also called *bordellos, cathouses,* or *whorehouses*). Until World War II, brothels were the major outlet for prostitution in the United States. In major cities, brothels numbered in the hundreds, and they were usually located close together in areas that came to be known as "red light districts." Run (though not necessarily owned) by *madams,* who themselves might have been working prostitutes at one time, these brothels sometimes had a "stable" of twenty or thirty girls working shifts. Since World War II, however, the brothel has declined in importance, mostly as a result of cleanup operations by city councils pressured by local citizen groups. Brothels still operate as the major context of prostitution in Nevada (the state frowns upon the streetwalker), and most large cities in the United States will have brothels that maintain themselves solely through a system of informal referrals. But gone are the days when a visitor could simply appear on the doorstep of any of a string of houses and buy himself sexual pleasure.

Toward the top of the pecking order are the *call girls.* Though operating methods differ, the established call girl will usually secure her clients through individual referrals by customers or trusted friends.[84] She conducts the sexual transaction in her own apartment or in the office, home, or hotel room of her client. Many call girls work independently and exercise considerable discretion in the choice of clients. Topflight call girls are generally from middle-class backgrounds, some have a college education, and most are in their early twenties. The successful call girl is physically attractive, well groomed, and articulate, and she makes a pleasant date for those men who can afford the $300 or $400 it takes to purchase her company for an evening.

With the advent some years ago of publications such as *Screw,* a New York–based national magazine whose subject is sex, some call girls and male prostitutes have taken to advertising. Pick up any edition of *Screw* and you will find scores of ads from men and women offering to sell or buy sexual intimacies. While not all such ads are linked with the prostitute business, many clearly are. Sometimes the ads are so worded that only those familiar with the language of commercialized sex will understand them. Here, for example, are two ads that might well have appeared in *Screw* magazine:

> If your interests run to English, French, or Greek arts, call . . . between 4 p.m. and 11 P.M. for an appointment. Our international staff of experts eagerly await your patronage.

> Hi! I'm Debbie. I'm new in town and am eager to meet a strong, well-endowed man for mutual fun. I am 19, beautifully curved, and have long silky-blonde hair with which to tickle your fancy. My friends never forget me. Please, males only; no S/M.

THE BAR AND MASSAGE PARLOR AS PLACES OF PROSTITUTION

Access to prostitutes comes not only through walking the streets, visiting a brothel, or being referred to a call girl. Bars and, in recent years, massage parlors are frequently places where contacts between prostitutes and prospective clients are made.

Public bars and nightclubs have long been frequented by prostitutes. Sometimes called *bar-girls* (or, simply, *b-girls*), these women often operate along with the bar management. Not all b-girls are prostitutes — some are merely in the game of enticing customers to spend time, and thus money, in the hope of later sex.[85] But those that are prostitutes find the bar a good place for hustling. For one thing, they can work indoors; in addition, they have a constant flow of prospective clients, they can mingle with the crowd and thus not be so obvious, there are people around who can come to their rescue if trouble should arise, and they can exercise some selectivity in the choice of a client. However, during pre-Prohibition years, the b-girl had to make herself a little more obvious, and she had less control over the process:

Before Prohibition, saloons in the large cities of the United States frequently had two sections: the front section, called the bar, which was for men only and a rear section, called the family entrance, where women accompanied by men could sit at tables. Unaccompanied streetwalkers were permitted to frequent the family entrance section and attract customers from the front section, often by standing in the swinging door between the two sections and making themselves visible.[86]

During the last few years, the massage parlor has emerged as a new, lucrative setting for prostitution.[87] Though some establishments only provide therapeutic massages by trained personnel, many of the hundreds of parlors from coast to coast cater to one thing: sex. The range of sexual activities purchased extends from simple "hand-jobs" — which are permissible in some jurisdictions — to "blow-jobs," "straight" sexual intercourse, and anything else the customer may desire and the "masseuse" is willing to do.

The massage parlor is a good front for prostitution because it provides a legal setting for customer contacts. The girls need not solicit business; it comes to them. The typical customer is looking for more than merely a massage. Furthermore, the masseuses are not dependent on customer purchase of sex because they will receive a commission (usually 30 to 35 percent) on any legal massage they give — and these can cost the customer $100 an hour if he wants frills such as nude masseuses, champagne, and special baths. Other advantages to prostitution in this setting include a comfortable work environment, a potentially speedy turnover in customers, and some protection against police arrest and a criminal conviction for prostitution. The massage parlor prostitute is protected from arrest and conviction partly by the semiprivate character of the parlor and partly because by leaving it up to the customer to do the soliciting, she can minimize the chances of a legal arrest. An undercover cop who first solicits sex and then arrests the masseuse may well be acting illegally under the rules of entrapment. These rules generally are interpreted as follows. The police may not entice a person into committing a crime and then use the offense and evidence of it to bring about a criminal conviction if the person would not normally have voluntarily committed the offense in question.

THE PIMP

A key position in the world of prostitution is held by the *pimp*.[88] While we have no way of knowing exactly what proportion of prostitutes work under the control of pimps, it probably runs to over 70 percent. For the pimp, prostitution is the road to considerable financial success; he, not his girls, reaps the real profits from the billion-dollar business. Even so, without the pimp, many prostitutes would quickly fail in business.

The pimp's importance comes partly from the nature of prostitution itself and partly from his own business acumen and ability to manipulate people. Because prostitution is illegal, those in the game are constantly threatened by arrest. A pimp can help protect prostitutes from legal troubles as well as provide financial and other assistance should the law strike. Since big money can be made in meeting the persistent demand for this illegal service, competition is stiff. The pimp helps defend against that competition by establishing and maintaining control over a particular territory. An independent girl does not have that kind of security. Then, too, the pimp offers protection against the physical or financial threat posed by drunks, toughs, and customers who want something for nothing. Most prostitutes have little control over male access to them — indeed, they must make that access as free as possible — and when confronted by a troublemaker it is nice to have someone in the wings who can deal with the problem.

These features of prostitution open up a role for the pimp. Even so, his place in the business also hinges on his own abilities, particularly his adeptness in establishing and maintaining the prostitute's dependence on him and his control over her. Control and dependence are the central features of what is, at its heart, a relationship of exploitation. To establish that relationship the pimp demonstrates that the practicing or would-be prostitute needs him both for material and emotional reasons. He demonstrates his importance in the realm of material things by taking care of his girl's room and board, clothing, medical and other expenses, and by running the business profitably. On the emotional level, the pimp is at once father, brother, lover, and friend. He is there when the girl needs affection, advice, and love; but he also disciplines her when she falters. Once caught up in his grip, the prostitute quickly learns the extent of her dependence upon him and the pitfalls surrounding any attempt to leave the fold. If she does decide to leave she risks not only her financial security but also her physical safety. It is by no means uncommon for a pimp to maim or even kill a defecting or "retiring" girl.[89]

Today pimps are predominantly blacks, at least at the street level. It is not clear just how blacks have come to dominate the pimping business, but the potential for financial success and status in an acquisitive society, as well as a certain perspective on American society and women in particular, suggest two explanations. In terms of money, a successful pimp can earn far more than most of us dream of: $500 a day is by no means the limit. With that kind of money he is tempted to feel that he can do what he wants, when he wants, how he wants. He is successful by the very standards that white society has set. In addition, the pimping role permits the black male the kind of domination normally reserved for those in the white-dominated world of legitimate business and the professions. Instead of a subservient, dependent role, he assumes a role in which he pulls the strings and others dance. Furthermore, he can bolster his own sense of manly pride by virtue of his relationship to his women and the fact that white men must pay him for their sexual pleasure. In the view of some black pimps, American society as a whole reeks of exploitation, where one person pimps another. They are merely cashing in, in the tradition of free enterprise and individual initiative.[90]

ENTERING THE "PROFESSION"

Those who become prostitutes not only risk police arrest and criminal punishment, but also condemnation by society at large and such work-related hazards as disease, injury, theft, and exploitation. Why, then, do some women become prostitutes? A conventional and long-standing explanation is that they are forced into the role of prostitute by unsavory characters who use devices of compulsion ranging from kidnapping, blackmail, and forced heroin addiction, to the powers of love and dependency. One example of recruitment by force and deceit was reported in *Time* magazine some years ago, and is summarized by Walter Reckless:

> The report claimed that the ring of procurers had operated for ten years and that at least 35 murders of recruited girls had taken place. The girls were lured from poor families by the promise of domestic jobs with upper-class families. The girls were first raped and then sent to a training brothel. It was estimated that at least 2,000 girls had passed through the hands of the ring since 1954 (ten years before the report). The "sick" recruits were sent to [a "concentration" camp] at Leon [Mexico] to die, while the rebellious ones were also sent there for taming.[91]

Doubtless some women are forcibly introduced to prostitution. But current thinking on the subject places less emphasis on the role of force and more on the voluntary decision to enter prostitution and the circumstances surrounding that decision. It seems likely that when considered as a whole, only a very small minority of prostitutes are forced into the profession.

Still, the girls themselves may feel they have no real choice in the matter, and some look upon their entrance into prostitution as something forced upon them by circumstances beyond their control. One circumstance often mentioned by prostitutes and researchers alike is financial insecurity. Simply stated, the belief is that some women (perhaps most) enter prostitution because they need the money. They may have a child to support; they may be out of work and unable to find a full-time job; or they may have pressing financial obligations, such as paying medical bills or financing a drug addiction, which they cannot hope to meet through conventional, legal kinds of work. But Ronald Akers warns us not to misinterpret the nature of the financial incentives in prostitution:

> This may sound trite or overly simplistic, but the nature of the monetary incentive in prostitution is often misunderstood. The woman need not be in dire or desperate economic straits; escape from poverty is only one way (and

probably not the most frequent way) in which prostitution is economically inspired.[92]

The choice, Akers argues, is not often between starving or becoming a prostitute, but is more commonly between a low-paying, low-status, but respectable job and a relatively high-paying job that happens to be illegal and unrespectable. The loss of respectability and the risks of arrest and criminal punishment are offset by the economic rewards believed to accrue from prostitution.

Even so, most people for whom prostitution would offer financial attractions do not become prostitutes. For those few who do, it seems that additional considerations act to facilitate their entry into the prostitute role. Based on the evidence, one factor appears to be experience in sex at a relatively early age; and another, a set of verbalized opinions favorable to prostitution.[93] Those girls who have had early sexual experiences will presumably have less difficulty in accepting the idea of sex as a normal facet of male-female relationships, even among strangers. Opinions favorable to prostitution are bound to vary, but some notable ones are: "prostitution is no worse than any other kind of job"; "people don't really look down on the prostitute"; "the prostitute is necessary, for without her marriages would fail, some men would have to commit rape to get laid"; and "the prostitute gives men what their wives and lovers won't."[94]

Actually, it is not at all easy to become a prostitute — at least a successful one. Not only must the novice learn how and where to find customers, she must also learn those tricks of the trade that help to protect her from disease, the police, the competition, and the customer, and that help to ensure she stays in business. In his study of call girls in the Los Angeles area, James Bryan found that most went through a kind of apprenticeship. Their initial entrance into prostitution was facilitated through personal contacts with an established call girl or a pimp, and from then on they learned the ropes under the direction of other call girls, some of whom ran "classes" in their apartments. Though there was apparently little training in sexual techniques as such, the new recruits were taught the "dos and don'ts" of the game and were helped in building an initial set of customer contacts. Among the rules learned were: get the money first; don't enjoy the trick or fall for the customer; don't be pleasant with the customer unless he has paid; don't engage in unnecessary interaction with him; get him "off" as soon as possible; and stay in good physical and mental health.[95]

Surprising though it may seem to some of us, there is almost an art to prostitution. It is the art of the confidence game. The customer is treated to a pretense and he pays through the nose for it. As it was graphically put by one author: "A whore is a woman who fucks for money. If you pay her enough she pretends to come."[96] A good prostitute is also a good actor. But she must be the director as well: she must always stay on top of things and must know how to manipulate the play to her advantage:

> There's some of them lies still as stones, they think it's more ladylike or something, but I say they don't know which side their bread's buttered. Listen, if you lie still the bloke may take half the night sweating away. But if you bash it about a bit he'll come all the quicker and get out and away and leave you in peace. Stupid to spin it out longer than you need, isn't it? I learned that from Margaret. Wonderful actress, that girl.[97]

REACTIONS TO VICTIMLESS SEX OFFENSES

The prostitute is generally looked upon with mild intolerance by society and its legal officials. Unless community pressure to do something about prostitution builds up, the police and courts rarely go out of their way to make life difficult for prostitutes. It seems that when the police do take the trouble to arrest streetwalkers or to raid local brothels and illegal massage parlors, they do so more to harass them and get some "action" than to enforce the law. When prostitutes are hauled up before a judge, they typically pay a small fine and are back on the street within hours.

The public, police, and courts have traditionally displayed much greater intolerance and a more systematic effort to do something about homosexuality. With the exception of Illinois, Connecticut, and a handful of other states, homosexual acts, even in private and between consenting adults, violate state criminal codes, and sometimes carry penalties placing them on a par with felonious assault, armed robbery, burglary, and even rape and murder. Though the only real difference between the victimless homosexual offense and victimless heterosexual offense is that in the former the participants are of the same sex, this difference means much to criminal justice officials. Compared to heterosexual offenses, the consequences of indulging in homosexual conduct are by and large more demeaning, more punitive, and longer lasting. And when there are victims, as in the case of child molesting, the chances are that life will be made more miserable for the offender if his victim is of the same sex. In one follow-up study of convicted child molesters, the most significant difference between the heterosexual and homosexual offenders was that the latter served much longer prison sentences for the same offense.[98]

The extent to which officialdom has gone in doing something about homosexuals is amply illustrated by recent studies in Los Angeles, St. Louis, and elsewhere.[99] The studies show that the police, armed with values and attitudes of intolerance toward homosexuality, often engage in practices ranging from the routine harassment of gays and suspected gays on the street and in bars, nightclubs, and dance halls catering to the gay community, to far more devious, cold-blooded activities. The public restroom in parks, railroad stations, and bus terminals has been the usual setting for these more perverse police practices. They have included the use of male decoys whose job, essentially, is to lure other males into making sexual advances (sometimes accomplished by the decoy making a show of fondling his own penis), the use of peepholes drilled in walls and ceilings, and the use of still and movie cameras hidden behind two-way mirrors or ventilation screens.

In their enlightening study of male homosexuality in the United States, Denmark, and the Netherlands, Martin Weinberg and Colin Williams point out that despite the availability of felony statutes (the so-called sodomy laws) providing for severe penalties upon conviction, the common practice in the United States is to charge homosexual offenders with misdemeanors.[100] At first glance one might think that this practice reflects an attitude of leniency and tolerance. On the contrary, these authors argue, the use of misdemeanor charges is preferred because these laws are easier to apply and give a greater likelihood of conviction.

Many of those arrested for homosexual acts are first offenders, in the legal sense, hence inexperienced in matters of procedural law and the routine workings of the judicial process. This, coupled with their fears regarding the effects of publicity on their family, work, and social life, makes them easy prey for the disreputable and greedy among our legal officials. Sometimes they are blackmailed by corrupt police; sometimes they become patsies in a scheme of kickbacks involving the police, bonding services, and corrupt attorneys; but more often they find themselves in the hands of lawyers who make their living off the fearful and inexperienced who daily get in trouble with the law. Such lawyers, often called "courthouse regulars" (see pages 401–402), get business by referrals from bondsmen, police, or court officials, or by hanging around police stations and misdemeanor courts, and will routinely charge upwards of $500 just to plead their client guilty. Under a hard sell and promises of no publicity, no conviction, and the like (falsehoods, or in any case things not under the lawyer's control), the suspect finds it hard to refuse the "help" offered by a seemingly sympathetic, knowledgeable, and experienced attorney.

There is evidence that public and official attitudes toward homosexuality are moving in a more tolerant and permissive direction.[101] But any major changes in reactions to victimless homosexual offenses are unlikely until certain myths and attendant beliefs about homosexuality are cleared up. Commenting on these myths and the intolerant orientation toward homosexuality, British social psychologist Michael Schofield shows us striking similarities between the world of homosexuality and that of the pot smoker:

Both groups are thought to be something they are not. Both suffer from myths built up over the years. The information about both groups has been obtained from those who were arrested or were attending clinics, whereas the more typical homosexuals or pot smokers manage to avoid trouble. Both are thought to be sick and in need of medical attention. Many young people go through an adolescent phase of homosexuality and then develop an interest in the opposite sex, and many smoke pot on a few occasions and then give it up; but if either group is apprehended at this stage, they become known as perverts or drug addicts. Both groups have been the object of special campaigns by police, press, and public. As this social hostility develops, both groups tend to form their exclusive coteries and lose contact with the dominant majority.[102]

Legal reform, Schofield goes on, is delayed, even in the face of increasingly informed opinions, because decriminalization or simply more lenient reactions are seen as condoning deviance and are felt to be politically inexpedient by officialdom.

The weight of historical evidence leaves little room for doubt that legal repression of human sexuality is doomed to failure. Hard as it is to curb male sexual aggression toward females, it is even harder to control consensual sex. Even so, there seems to be no end to legislative and enforcement efforts to criminalize those who seek sexual pleasures in ways publicly (much less often privately) denounced. While I have not touched on pornography in this chapter, we might bear this area of sex-oriented activity in mind here. In 1976, efforts to enforce sexual morality reached new heights when actor Harry Reems was prosecuted and convicted under federal obscenity statutes for his part in the widely seen x-rated movie *Deep Throat*. Though the conviction was subsequently reversed, the entire affair has extended the scope of legal repression of essentially personal matters of moral choice. If pursued, this attack will produce more criminals, but is unlikely to reduce the incidence of the behavior in question.

References

1. For a similar classification see Stanton Wheeler, "Sex Offenses: A Sociological Critique," in *Sexual Deviance,* ed. John H. Gagnon and William Simon (New York: Harper and Row, 1967), pp. 79–80.
2. Helena Wright, *Sex and Society* (London: Allen and Unwin, 1968), pp. 20–21.
3. See G. Rattray Taylor, *Sex in History* (London: Panther, 1965) for additional comments on the church's efforts to control sexual expression and the reaction to these efforts.
4. Morris Ploscowe, *Sex and the Law* (Englewood Cliffs, N.J.: Prentice-Hall, 1951), p. 138.
5. Quoted in Alex K. Gigeroff, *Sexual Deviation and the Criminal Law* (Toronto: University of Toronto Press, 1968), p. 11.
6. Ploscowe, *Sex and the Law,* p. 158.
7. Ibid., especially chapter VII; see also Allen Z. Gammage and Charles F. Hemphill, Jr., *Basic Criminal Law* (New York: McGraw-Hill) 1974), pp. 263–64.
8. 414 U.S. 21 (1973).
9. See, e.g., Miller v. California, 413 U.S. 15 (1973).
10. For the classic discussion of moral entrepreneurs see Howard S. Becker, *Outsiders: Studies in the Sociology of Deviance* (New York: Free Press, 1963), chapter 8.
11. See John H. Gagnon and William Simon, "Sexual Deviance in Contemporary America," *The Annals* 376 (1968), pp. 106–22.
12. See Susan Griffin, "Rape: The All-American Crime," *Ramparts* 10 (1971), pp. 34–35; Susan Brownmiller, *Against Our Will: Men, Women, and Rape* (New York: Simon and Schuster, 1975).
13. Ibid.
14. Much of the following discussion is based on Gammage and Hemphill, *Basic Criminal Law,* pp. 184–87.

15. See LEAA, *Forcible Rape: A National Survey of the Response by Prosecutors* (Washington, D.C.: U.S. Government Printing Office, 1977), pp. 30–31.

16. Ibid., p. 184.

17. Brownmiller, *Against Our Will*, p. 20.

18. Ploscowe, *Sex and the Law*, pp. 183–84.

19. See Gilbert Geis, "Rape-in-Marriage: Law and Law Reform in England, the United States, and Sweden," *Adelaide Law Review* 6 (1978), pp. 284–303.

20. Gilbert Geis, "Lord Hale, Witches, and Rape," *British Journal of Law and Society* 5 (1978), pp. 26–44.

21. Lloyd Shearer, "Rape in Marriage," *Parade*, April 22, 1979.

22. Griffin, "Rape: The All-American Crime"; also U.S. Department of Justice, *Crime in the Nation's Five Largest Cities: National Crime Panel Surveys of Chicago, Detroit, Los Angeles, New York, and Philadelphia* (Washington, D.C.: U.S. Government Printing Office, 1974); and Donald J. Mulvihill and Melvin M. Tumin, with Lynn Curtis, *Crimes of Violence*, A Staff Report to the National Commission on the Causes and Prevention of Violence, vol. 11 (Washington, D.C.: U.S. Government Printing Office, 1969), especially chapters 3 and 5.

23. M. Joan McDermott, *Rape Victimization in 26 American Cities* (Washington, D.C.: U.S. Government Printing Office, 1979).

24. Brownmiller, *Against Our Will*, p. 365.

25. "Rape Alert," *Newsweek* (Nov. 10, 1975), p. 71.

26. Brownmiller, *Against Our Will*, p. 373.

27. See "Police Discretion and the Judgement That a Crime Has Been Committed — Rape in Philadelphia," *University of Pennsylvania Law Review* 117 (1968), pp. 272–322; also Simon and Gagnon, "Sexual Deviance," p. 120. See also LEAA, *Forcible Rape*.

28. FBI, *Uniform Crime Reports*, 1978 (Washington, D.C.: U.S. Government Printing Office, 1976), p. 15.

29. McDermott, *Rape Victimization*, p. 45.

30. Menachem Amir, *Patterns in Forcible Rape* (Chicago: University of Chicago Press, 1971). See also Amir, "Patterns of Forcible Rape," in *Criminal Behavior Systems: A Typology*, ed. Marshall B. Clinard and Richard Quinney (New York: Holt, Rinehart and Winston, 1967), pp. 60–75. John M. MacDonald, *Rape: Offenders and Their Victims* (Springfield, Ill.: Charles C Thomas, 1971). Brenda A. Brown, "Crime Against Women Alone: A System Analysis of the Memphis Police Department Sex Crime Squad's 1973 Rape Investigations," May 18, 1974, mimeographed.

31. LEAA, *Crime Victims in the United States, 1973*, Advance Report (Washington, D.C.: U.S. Government Printing Office, 1975); McDermott, *Rape Victimization;* William B. Sanders and Nancy Jo Jahnke, "Rape Situations," presented to the annual meeting of the American Sociological Association, Boston, August 27–31, 1979; Jennie J. McIntyre and Thelma Myint, "Sexual Assault Outcomes: Completed and Attempted Rapes," presented to the annual meeting of the American Sociological Association, Boston, August 27–31, 1979.

32. "Sexual Assault Outcomes," table 1.

33. McDermott, *Rape Victimization*, pp. 36–38.

34. LEAA, *Forcible Rape*, pp. 14–15.

35. Amir, *Patterns in Forcible Rape*, p. 143.

36. National Commission on the Observance of International Women's Year, *Rape* (Washington, D.C.: U.S. Government Printing Office, 1978).

37. LEAA, *Forcible Rape*, p. 16.

38. Amir found that almost 50 percent of his rape cases involved more than one offender. See his *Patterns in Forcible Rape*, pp. 185–200. See also MacDonald, *Rape: Offenders and Their Victims*, p. 160.

39. See Amir, *Patterns in Forcible Rape*, pp. 319–26; also Brownmiller, *Against Our Will*, chapter 6.

40. See Theodore N. Ferdinand, "Sex Behavior and the American Class Structure: A Mosaic," *The Annals* 376 (1968), pp. 82–84.

41. W. H. Blanchard, "The Group Process in Gang Rape," *Journal of Social Psychology* 49 (1959), pp. 259–66.

42. Charles H. McCaghy, *Deviant Behavior: Crime, Conflict and Interest Groups* (New York: Macmillan, 1976), p. 133.

43. For more on these issues see Kurt Weis and Sandra S. Borges, "Victimology and Rape: The Case of the Legitimate Victim," *Issues in Criminology* 8 (1973), pp. 85–89.

44. See Clifford Kirkpatrick and Eugene J. Kanin, "Male Sex Aggression on a University Campus," *American Sociological Review* 22 (1957), p. 53; Harold T. Christensen and Christina F. Gregg, "Changing Sex Norms in America and Scandinavia," *Journal of Marriage and the Family* 32 (1970), pp. 625–26; and Eugene J. Kanin, "Reference Groups and Sex Conduct Norm Violation," *Sociological Quarterly* 8 (1967) pp. 495–504.

45. Susan Hotchkiss, "Realities of Rape," *Human Behavior* (December 1978), pp. 18–23.

46. Nancy Gager and Cathleen Schurr, *Sexual Assault: Confronting Rape in America* (New York: Grosset and Dunlap, 1976), p. 105.

47. For a model summarizing the discussion just presented, see McCaghy, *Deviant Behavior*, p. 136.

48. Duncan Chappell, Robley Geis, and Gilbert Geis, eds., *Forcible Rape: The Crime, the Victim, and the Offender*, (New York: Columbia University Press, 1977), pp. 227–44.

49. Gilbert Geis and Robley Geis, "Rape in Stockholm," *Criminology* 17 (1979), pp. 311–22.

50. Ibid., p. 320.

51. See Albert Ellis and Ralph Brancale, *The Psychology of Sex Offenders* (Springfield, Ill.: Charles C Thomas, 1965); and Paul Gebhard, John H. Gagnon, Wardell B. Pomeroy, and Cornelia V. Christensen, *Sex Offenders: An Analysis of Types* (New York: Harper and Row, 1965).

52. See Benjamin Karpman, *The Sexual Offender and His Offenses* (New York: Julian, 1954).

53. Vincent DeFrancis, *Protecting the Child Victims of Sex Crimes Committed by Adults* (Denver: American Humane Society, 1969), pp. vii, 66.

54. Ibid., pp. 66–68.

55. Charles H. McCaghy, "Child Molesters: A Study of Their Careers as Deviants," in *Criminal Behavior Systems*, ed. Clinard and Quinney, p. 80.

56. Gebhard et al., *Sex Offenders*.

57. Edward Sagarin, "Sexual Criminality," pp. 138–64, in *Current Perspectives on Criminal Behavior*, ed. Abraham S. Blumberg (New York: Knopf, 1974), pp. 147–48.

58. DeFrancis, *Protecting the Child Victim*, p. 69.

59. Donal E. J. MacNamara, "Sex Offenses and Sex Offenders," *The Annals* 376 (1968), p. 153.

60. McCaghy, "Child Molesters, pp. 86–88. Some of the other studies are J. W. Mohr, R. E. Turner, and M. B. Jerry, *Pedophilia and Exhibitionism* (Toronto: University of Toronto Press, 1965); and Gebhard et al., *Sex Offenders*.

61. McCaghy, "Child Molesters," p. 87.

62. Ibid., p. 79.

63. DeFrancis, *Protecting the Child Victim*, p. xi.

64. See Leslie A. White, "The Definition and Prohibition of Incest," in *Sex and Society*, ed. John N. Edwards (Chicago: Markham, 1972), pp. 160–71.

65. Ellis and Brancale, *The Psychology of Sex Offenders;* Gebhard et al., *Sex Offenders*.

66. McCaghy, "Child Molesters," pp. 82–83.

67. On capital punishment see Frank E. Hartung, "Trends in the Use of Capital Punishment," *The Annals* 284 (1952), pp. 8–19; on lynching see Brownmiller, *Against Our Will*, chapter 7; see also Alan Valantine, *Vigilante Justice* (New York: Reynal, 1956).

68. Carol Bohm, "Judicial Attitudes toward Rape Victims," *Judicature* (1974), pp. 303–7.

69. *Time*, September 12, 1977, cited in Robert H. Lauer, *Social Problems and the Quality of Life* (Dubuque, Iowa: Wm. C. Brown, 1978), p. 260.

70. D. A. Thomas, "Sentencing: The Basic Principles," *Criminal Law Review* (1967), pp. 514–20.

71. Ibid., p. 515.

72. Ibid., pp. 516–17.

73. *Yale Law Journal*, 81 (1972), p. 1380.

74. Edwin H. Sutherland, "The Diffusion of Sexual Psychopath Laws," *American Journal of Sociology* 56 (1950), pp. 142–48.

75. See Nicholas N. Kittrie, *The Right to Be Different: Deviance and Enforced Therapy* (Baltimore: Penguin Books, 1973), pp. 189–99.

76. Ploscowe, *Sex and the Law*, p. 229.

77. Gebhard et al., *Sex Offenders*, pp. 845–67.

78. Kittrie, *The Right to Be Different*, pp. 199–204.

79. C. Esselzstyn, "Prostitution in the United States," *The Annals* 376 (1968), p. 126.

80. See Gail Sheehy, *Hustling: Prostitution in Our Wide-Open Society* (New York: Delacorte Press, 1973), p. 82; Marshall B. Clinard, *Sociology of Deviant Behavior*, 3rd ed. (New York: Holt, Rinehart and Winston, 1968), p. 372.

81. Walter C. Reckless, *The Crime Problem*, 5th ed. (Englewood Cliffs, N.J.: Prentice-Hall, 1973), p. 175.

82. Wright, *Sex and Society*, p. 29.

83. For good discussions of streetwalkers and their work, see Sheehy, *Hustling;* Charles Winick and Paul M. Kinsie, *The Lively Commerce: Prostitution in the United States* (Chicago: Quadrangle Books, 1971); and C. H. Rolph, *Women of the Streets* (London: Secker and Warburg, 1955).

84. See James H. Bryan, "Apprenticeships in Prostitution," *Social Problems* 12 (1965), pp. 287–97.

85. See Sherri Cavan, *Liquor License: An Ethnography of Bar Behavior* (Chicago: Aldine, 1966).

86. Reckless, *The Crime Problem*, p. 166.

87. See Clifton D. Bryant and C. Eddie Palmer, "Massage Parlors and 'Hand Whores': Some Sociological Observations," *Journal of Sex Research* 11 (1975), pp. 227–41; Albert J. Velarde and Mark Warlick, "Massage Parlors: The Sensuality Business," *Society* 11 (1973), pp. 63–74; Albert J. Velarde, "Becoming Prostituted," *British Journal of Criminal Justice* 15 (1975), pp. 251–63.

88. For more on the pimp and pimping see Christina Milner and Richard Milner, *Black Players: The Secret World of Black Pimps* (Boston: Little, Brown, 1972); and Susan Hill and Bob Adelman, *Gentleman of Leisure* (New York: New American Library, 1972). This latter book sees the pimp through the eyes of his whores.

89. See McCaghy, *Deviant Behavior*, pp. 353–54; also, Hill and Adelman, *Gentleman of Leisure*.

90. Milner and Milner, *Black Players*, pp. 242–44.

91. Reckless, *The Crime Problem*, p. 169–244.

92. Ronald Akers, *Deviant Behavior: A Social Learning Approach* (Belmont, Calif.: Wadsworth, 1973), p. 166.

93. See McCaghy, *Deviant Behavior*, pp. 355–56.

94. See James H. Bryan, "Occupational Ideologies and Individual Attitudes of Call Girls," *Social Problems* 13 (1966), pp. 441–50; and Norman R. Jackman, Richard O'Toole, and Gilbert Geis, "The Self-Image of the Prostitute," *Sociological Quarterly* 4 (1963), pp. 150–61.

95. Bryan, "Apprenticeships in Prostitution."

96. From an excerpt of *Eros Denied: Sex in Western Society* by Wayland Young (New York: Grove Press, 1964), reprinted in *Observations of Deviance*, ed. Jack D. Douglas (New York: Random House, 1970), p. 66.

97. Ibid., p. 66.

98. J. H. Fitch, "Men Convicted of Sex Offenses Against Children: A Follow-Up Study," *British Journal of Sociology* 13 (1962), pp. 18–37.

99. See Jon J. Gallo, "The Consenting Adult Homosexual and the Law: An Empirical Study of Enforcement and Administration in Los Angeles County," *UCLA Law Review* 13 (1966), pp. 647–832; and Laud Humphreys, *Tearoom Trade: Impersonal Sex in Public Places* (Chicago: Aldine, 1970).

100. Martin S. Weinberg and Colin J. Williams, *Male Homosexuals: Their Problems and Adaptations* (Baltimore: Penguin Books, 1975), p. 37.

101. See the discussion in McCaghy, *Deviant Behavior,* p. 366.

102. Michael Schofield, *The Strange Case of Pot* (Baltimore: Penguin Books, 1971), p. 175.

Part III

Doing Something About Crime

11

Policing Society

The modern state places its police force in the front line of the confrontation with those who violate its laws or otherwise threaten the social order. While other agencies of the state create its laws, fashion its legal priorities, and hand down official penalties, the job of uncovering law violations, apprehending violators, and seeing to it that order is maintained rests squarely with the police. As a practical matter, the police must assume the burden of routinely translating law on the books into law in action.

To the man in the street the police officer is the law. Not only are police officers expected to interpret, investigate, and take action in matters of law and order, but they are also the typical citizen's most common and direct contact with the social control aspect of government. Whether or not they are invited into a situation, once an officer is present the situation takes on new meaning — the "long arm of the law" has entered, and attached to that arm is the enforcement machinery of government. Police officers carry symbols of the law and confirm for us in no uncertain terms what it represents. Their uniforms and badges symbolize their authority to take action in the name of the state; their weapons symbolize the availability of coercive force to back up their commands; their handcuffs symbolize the state's power of detention.

What the police do and do not do carries more weight in the legal process than the actions of any other single agency of criminal law — perhaps more than all others put together. It is *whether* and *how* laws are enforced that most directly and completely shapes the working character of the legal process. The police are clearly at the heart of the criminal justice process.

When we consider the police impact on the legal process we must not forget that the police are usually the first officials to confront the crime — or, more important perhaps, the criminal. The police, in their capacity as "first-line enforcers," make the important decision to take official action when confronted by situations in which acts legally defined as criminal have occurred.[1] If they choose not to identify an act as a crime, or if they choose not to label a person as a suspect, or if they choose not to take official action even when they have applied the legally appropriate labels, then for all practical purposes the act or person escapes further processing at the hands of official agencies of criminal law. By their decisions not to invoke the legal process, the police effectively determine the outer boundaries of law in action.[2] As a rule, the police are the first to apply the *official* labels crime and criminal, and in doing so start the wheels of the criminal process turning. Whatever might happen at subsequent stages in the legal process can happen only after that crucial action has been taken.

Police merit serious attention in criminology not only as part of the official machinery of law; *the police also shape the crime scene itself.* In their roles as crime detectors, crime investigators, and crime preventers, the police make crime a part of their work, just as does the professional thief. This is not to say that the police commit crimes (although such acts do occur from time to time), but, rather, to draw attention to their work in dealing with criminal matters, complainants, witnesses, suspects, and victims, and the impact this has on the character of crime within their jurisdictions. It is in how they perceive and do their jobs that we find the unique contribution police make to the overall shape of crime. Aspects of police work such as patrolling practices and techniques, discretion, use of force, training, departmental norms and policies, and the operation of specialty details (vice, traffic, or intelligence) all have a direct impact on the reality of crime as both an aspect and product of social life.

Origins and Growth of Modern Police

While most of us assume police were always present in society, the police force as we know it today is of relatively recent origin. Most students of the police trace its modern origins to the rapid industrial expansion and population growth in the late eighteenth and early nineteenth centuries in western Europe, particularly England.

For centuries, England relied for law enforcement on the services of generally unpaid, though not necessarily unrewarded, volunteers and patronage appointees. Together with the military, these early constables and sheriffs saw to it that the interests of landowner, nobility, and monarchy were protected. Considerable time and energy were spent collecting taxes and making sure that villagers and townspeople ran their personal and community affairs according to the dictates of the wealthy and powerful. Since the tradition of self-help justice was slow to die away, the essential responsibility for doing something about crime was placed on the shoulders of the citizenry. Individual towns and villages were held accountable for the enforcement of laws and prohibitions, and enforcement, such as it was, was largely a collective affair. As towns grew, able-bodied men (especially property owners) were expected to volunteer for nighttime duty as watchmen. These unpaid citizens were to look out for disruptions of public order or threats to property, and were to guard the moral standards of the day, which covered an incredible array of "sins." The constables worked at upholding law and order during the day, the watchmen took their turns at night.

IMPACT OF THE INDUSTRIAL REVOLUTION

Though the constables and watchmen were accorded the powers of arrest and in some towns were armed, little public protection and crime control was apparently expected of them, and little was delivered. The job seems to have been treated as a big chore, and as time passed many property owners who had participated as watchmen found ways to escape the responsibility, while those who stayed on the job made the most of it through a variety of corrupt and unlawful practices.[3] Over the centuries, public and corporate faith in the reliability of the constable and watchman system steadily deteriorated.

Even though the watch system was long held in low esteem, substantial changes were not introduced until the Industrial Revolution was in full swing and cities were beginning to swell with population. The rise of capitalism and attendant Industrial Revolution changed economic and social conditions dramatically, and in many ways extremely painfully. The migration of countless thousands of hopeful workers into already crowded towns and cities added new tensions to the hard times suffered by the masses. Brutal living conditions; small wages and long hours for those lucky enough to have jobs; growing poverty in the midst of growing affluence; and the ideology of laissez-faire all helped contribute to social disorder. Add to this periodic waves of assaultive and property crimes, vagrants and beggars by the thousands, and an extremely punitive system of laws, and the scene was set for a breakdown in the existing police system, which cried for reassessment and innovation.

Matters came to a head with a series of militant demonstrations and riots in which the disadvantaged and disaffected citizenry sought to improve their lot. Those reaping the benefits of industrialization, the property owners and emerging middle class, saw opposition and resistance, and felt that the very foundations of the new industrial era were under attack. It became popular to refer to the poorer classes — the unemployed, the disadvantaged, the menial factory workers — as social scum or the dross of society, and these unfortunates found themselves lumped together with petty criminals under the title "dangerous classes." It was to contain and suppress these dangerous classes that many advocated police reforms and innovations.[4]

The English were reluctant to accept the notion of an organized, professional, paramilitary police force, feeling it would seriously threaten traditionally prized liberties.[5] Despite this opposition, the reform proposals of men such as Patrick Colquhoun eventually gained widespread support. Colquhoun proposed that a well-regulated, full-time, centrally administered police organization be set up to prevent crime by patrolling the streets of London. Its officers would be salaried men under the direction of commissioners accountable directly to the government.[6] In 1829, Parliament, under the leadership of Home Secretary Robert Peel, enacted the Metropolitan Police Act. This act followed the model for police organization and strategy long advocated by Colquhoun. So was born the forerunner of the modern police force.

In America, meanwhile, the larger cities were facing some of the same problems that so alarmed English politicians and businessmen. Though industrialization and modern capitalism were slower to appear on the American scene, by the early 1800s many American cities were experiencing rising rates of poverty, unemployment, migration, and crime, and were feeling signs of growing urban unrest. Riots and demonstrations erupted in Boston, New York, and elsewhere, and the police came under attack for ineffectiveness in controlling the dangerous classes.[7]

During the early colonial period, American towns and cities had relied on the constable and watchman. The protection of life, property, and public order was considered a civic responsibility, as it had been in England, and able-bodied property owners were expected to assume constable and watchman duties on a rotating basis. But these policing methods soon acquired a dubious reputation; as towns grew and abuses of duty became commonplace, city fathers sought to beef up crime control efforts. In 1772, Williamsburg, Virginia, instituted one of the first municipal night patrols, composed of four "sober and discreet people" who were its permanent, paid members. Their job was "to patrol the streets of this city from ten o'clock every night until daylight the next morning, to cry the hours, and use their best endeavors to preserve peace and good order, by apprehending and bringing to justice all disorderly people."[8] Boston and New York soon followed suit, and the new patrols were given authority to enforce all laws and to stop and question anyone suspected of criminal designs.[9]

Yet these moderate reforms failed to satisfy the demands for order and crime control voiced in many quarters. American city officials looked to England for help. The London "New Police," as they were called, seemed to be doing a good job, so why not try the same system in America? In New York, an 1845 ordinance established a police force with around-the-clock patrol and law enforcement duties. The police force was administered by a Board of Police Commissioners (composed of the mayor, the recorder, and a city judge), a model soon after adopted by New Orleans in 1853, Cincinnati and San Francisco in 1859, Detroit, St. Louis, and Kansas City in 1861, and Buffalo and Cleveland in 1866.

It became patently clear, however, that the police commissions were little more then political tools in the hands of the parties in power. Further, they proved ineffective in managing the administrative affairs of their departments, with the result that they quickly fell into disfavor. By the early 1900s many cities had abandoned them in favor of a single public official acting as police executive.

One marked difference between the organization of the English and American police has been the "home rule" jurisdictional structure in America. While local and regional hierarchies do administer the day-to-day operations of English police forces, the English police nevertheless retain a national character, in that Parliament and the Home Office oversee operations, and the police have jurisdiction in what here would be called federal matters. In America, the Constitution reserves the bulk of criminal law matters for state control and makes a clear distinction between federal and state laws and their enforcement. In states, the county is the political unit having essential jurisdictional control over criminal law matters, and in counties, city governments retain yet further jurisdictional control. In short, law enforcement in America operates under a complicated system of jurisdictional controls, with local, county, state, and federal political units exercising varying degrees of authority and retaining varying amounts of autonomy in police affairs.

One consequence of this division of authority is the *politicization* of law enforcement. Police operations are not divorced from politics in England; but in America, they are firmly entrenched in politics, and day-to-day political interference at all levels is the risk, if not the inevitable consequence. The association between machine politics and police work has been well documented in the case of Chicago. At the turn of the century, when Chicago was experiencing unprecedented growth and industrial development, the law enforcement apparatus was an indispensable part of machine politics. Police promotions as well as judgeships were dependent upon the demonstration of party loyalty. All police employees paid a portion of their salaries into the party treasury and were required to do its bidding, even if this meant occasionally breaking the law. Today the connection between politics and police may no longer be so blatant, but it is there nonetheless.[10]

EXPANSION OF POLICE SERVICES
UNDER THE FEDERAL GOVERNMENT

Over the past few decades, American crime control agencies have mushroomed in number, personnel, and budgets. Today more than 40,000 federal, state, and local police agencies employ nearly half a million officers and operate with a combined budget in excess of $8 billion.[11] These figures do not include the many thousands of people and millions of dollars working in private police agencies (e.g., Pinkerton's) and in the various inspection services employed by public authorities (e.g., game wardens or bank examiners). If past trends indicate what the future holds, we can expect a continuing rise in the proportion of government expenditures on police operations, as well as in the ratio of law enforcement personnel (including civilians employed by police agencies) to total population.[12]

One of the most noteworthy aspects of the growth in American police services has been the expansion of federal involvement in crime control. Although the Constitution reserves the bulk of general criminal law matters for the states, congressional action over the past seventy-five years or so has made extensive federal participation in law enforcement inevitable.

The first federal inroads into crime control came with the establishment of the Revenue Cutter Service (later the Coast Guard) under the Treasury Department in 1790. This agency was mainly concerned with smuggling and the collection of maritime revenues. It was quickly followed by creation of the Customs Service, also under the Treasury, in 1799. The establishment of regular land patrols at the borders followed, and national Prohibition in 1920 brought two special enforcement agencies for border surveillance and enforcement of federal laws, the Border Patrol and the Customs Patrol.

Other early federal enforcement agencies included the Postal Inspection Unit under the Post Office, whose agents were in 1880 given responsibility for the detection and arrest of postal law violators. The Bureau of Internal Revenue (now known as the IRS) was put in charge of enforcing general revenue laws, and in 1868 received authority to employ special agents to uncover and pursue arrest and prosecution of tax evasions and frauds. With Prohibition, the Internal Revenue Intelligence Unit was established, and the bureau was placed in charge of enforcement of the new alcohol laws. The Harrison "Narcotics" Act of 1914 and the Volstead Act of 1919 created new federal crimes, requiring more federal enforcement services, and "federal functions . . . now involved a vastly increased amount of pure police work — patrolling, detection, searches and seizures, pursuit and arrest.''[13]

Though the Department of Justice was formally established in 1879, it did not become actively involved in crime control until 1908. In the interim one of its primary tasks was the collection of information on federal crimes and criminals, and heavy use was made of agents attached to other federal agencies. In 1908, however, the Justice Department received authorization from Congress to establish its own enforcement agency; first called the Bureau of Investigation, its name was changed to the FBI in 1935.

Originally sold to Congress as an agency mainly concerned with interstate commerce and the enforcement of the Sherman Antitrust Act, the bureau soon acquired jurisdiction over a whole range of federal laws, from vice (under the Mann Act of 1910), to violations of copyright, espionage, and radical political activism. A continued expansion of responsibilities and the leadership of J. Edgar Hoover (appointed director in 1924) provide some clues to understanding the phenomenal role this police agency has come to play in crime control and law enforcement.

From 1910 on, federal legislation added crime after crime to the enforcement responsibilities assumed by the bureau. Following the Mann Act — outlawing transportation of females across state lines for immoral purposes, but long used as a basis for investigation and arrest in sundry other vice matters — the new legislation covered, among other activities, the interstate transportation of motor vehicles (the Dyer Act of 1919), kidnapping and the use of mails to send threatening letters (the so-called Lindbergh Act of 1932), escape across state lines to avoid prosecution for felony crimes (the Fugitive Act of 1934), and bank robbery. Throughout this period, Hoover fashioned the bureau into one of the best equipped, best trained, and best financed police bureaucracies in the world. Under his leadership, the FBI sponsored numerous innovations in law enforcement techniques, developed a training academy unsurpassed anywhere for its instructional sophistication and depth, and garnered considerable acclaim for programs such as its uniform crime reporting, its "ten most wanted" list of fugitives, and its comprehensive crime information gathering.

The bureau also received considerable criticism over the years. Whatever Hoover's motives — and as with many a controversial figure, people have always hotly debated what his motives might have been — he guided the agency into activities and policies that upset members of congress, union leaders, journalists, fellow police officers, and even some of his own agents (whom the director could dismiss at will). Some of the strongest criticisms have concerned the bureau's involvement in the suppression of political activists, especially those of the left; its interference in management-worker conflicts; its extensive files on thousands of citizens, many of whom have never been convicted of a crime; and its participation in activities that were clearly criminal. The extent of the FBI's fall from grace in recent years is evidenced by public opinion polls showing a considerable decline in the proportion of respondents holding "highly favorable" attitudes toward the agency. In 1965, 84 percent of those polled held highly favorable attitudes toward the FBI; by 1975, that figure had dropped to 37 percent.[14]

The Police at Work

Before investigating the police at work, a number of observations are in order. First, *not all police agencies are alike*. They differ in the scope of their routine enforcement responsibilities; in the territorial and population size of their jurisdictions; in the composition of the populations they serve; in their size, training, and salaries; and in their internal organization. Second, *not all police officers are alike*. They differ in background, personality, experience, attitudes, behavior on the job, qualifications, and interests. Third, though collectively referred to as the police, the occupational demands placed on any one officer differ from those placed on another. *There is no one type of police work.* A division of labor, or occupational specialization, exists in police work just as it does in most other work organizations. For at least these three reasons, then, we should remember that when speaking of the police we are not dealing with a collection of homogeneous organizations, people, or activities. We are dealing with people and agencies that share a common occupational responsibility, the enforcement of laws and the preservation of domestic order.

JOINING THE FORCE

Much police work is "dirty work."[15] Dirty work is work that respectable or good people shun, prefer not to have to think about, and leave for others to perform. It is work that is at once demanded and rejected; it is work that is both disgusting and indispensable; it is work that garners relatively little prestige and recognition for its practioners, while at the same time it is touted as essential for maintaining the "proper" moral and social standards of the community; it is work that protects the in-group from the out-group, but those who consider themselves "in" hire outsiders to perform it.

The dirty aspects of police work — handling drunks, dead bodies, accident victims; dealing with family squabbles, prostitutes, homosexuals, muggers, and other "deviants"; and sometimes using violence to achieve control — merely reinforce the view that such work is not for us.[16] To most respectable citizens it is precisely this facet of police work that identifies the real job of the police. How often do policemen hear: "In-

While most police work is not like this, the threat of danger is always present and guides the officer's behavior while on patrol.

stead of bothering me, why don't you go and arrest real criminals like we're paying you to?'' or ''Why don't you clean up the streets so that respectable people like me can walk safely at night?''

In view of the dirty work of the job it is reasonable to wonder whether there is anything particularly striking about those who enter the occupation. Is there a pool or supply of individuals who are ready candidates for police work? Do they share social and personality characteristics that make them somehow different from other citizens? Are only certain types of people actively recruited by police agencies?

There are few indications that police recruits share background and personality characteristics that identify them as different from those who enter myriad other occupations. It is true that they show a fair degree of homogeneity in their educational, occupational, and family backgrounds. The recruit typically comes from a lower-middle- or working-class background, has no more than a high school education, and has previously worked in clerical, sales, or manual jobs.[17] For many, police work represents a step up the occupational status ladder. But this is true for millions of other American workers.

The evidence on personality traits again offers no sound basis for distinguishing the recruit from his peers. Some have argued that the police recruit exhibits traits associated with the ''authoritarian personality.'' Among these traits are conventionalism (rigid adherence to middle-class values), cynicism (a view that ''things are going to pot''), aggression, and stereotypical thinking. Administering the F-scale (designed to measure authoritarianism) to 116 New York City police recruits, Arthur Nieder-hoffer and John H. McNamara found a relatively high mean score of 4.15 (the highest possible score is 7.0). But this score was *almost identical* to previous scores for general working-class samples, indicating nothing exceptional about the recruits, considering their predominantly working-class backgrounds. In summarizing his discussion of the issue, Nieder-hoffer concluded that while police officers may well develop strong authoritarian personalities once they have been exposed to training and the demands of the job, nothing suggests "self-selection among authoritarian personalities prior to appointment."[18]

Why, then, do people enter police work? Niederhoffer suggests they do so for reasons such as security, decent working conditions, adventure, and relatively good pay, which make the job attractive for those with little formal education, few marketable skills, and lower-class backgrounds.[19] David Bayley and Harold Mendelsohn, investigating Denver police entrants, echo this interpretation:

> One does not need a special theory to explain why men go into police work. . . . One explains recruitment to the police force as one explains recruitment to any occupation, namely, in terms of its status, rewards, minimal educational requirements, and conditions of service. . . . Recruits bring to police work the same kinds of evaluations of the police made by people generally. They are neither more starry-eyed nor more cynical. They choose to be policemen because it fits their potentialities and promises the kinds of rewards considered by them commensurate with their background and training. By and large, it represents an advance over what their parents obtained. One understands police recruitment, then, in terms of a practical upward step in social mobility as well as an improvement in life prospects.[20]

When questioned about their reasons for joining the force, officers voice many of the same reasons that move people to seek nonpolice jobs. Among the most often cited reasons are security and retirement benefits. Few officers speak of excitement, action, or the dirty facets of police work as reasons for joining, and few recruits are drawn to police work for idealistic reasons, such as helping to rid society of criminals or contributing to law and order.[21] These findings reinforce the view that those who enter police work are in no way a special category of people and no different from others with similar backgrounds.

Most police agencies exercise considerable control over who gets accepted for police work. The days when departments were willing to take just about anyone are over. The typical police agency now requires applicants to pass a standard civil service exam, undergo a battery of other tests and examinations (sometimes including lie-detector tests), and pass checks on health, background, and character. Many agencies place considerable weight on these last checks, and a good portion of recruits never make it past one or another of these hurdles.[22]

Besides weeding out applicants whose examinations, test scores, and character investigations fall short of departmental standards, the screening process helps to ensure that only those persons *who are cast in roughly the same mold as officers already on the force* actually see police service.

Interviews are especially important for this purpose. The interview is usually conducted by senior officers and it permits recruiters to reject applicants who might otherwise be acceptable. In this way, recruits who possess undesirable value systems, or whose political attitudes and ethnic backgrounds conflict with those dominant in the force, can also be weeded out. This tends to perpetuate the class, ethnic, and value characteristics of those already employed.[23] Such homogeneity in personnel makes it easier for departments to retain already fashioned policies and practices, to reduce potential internal disruptions, and to maintain more complete control over their policing operations. From the standpoint of the officers themselves, it cements distinctions between the in-group and out-group and aids in the development of predictability, solidarity, and secrecy. These three important dimensions of organization and work are further emphasized as the recruit begins his journey toward becoming a police officer.

TRAINING AND THE ACQUISITION OF POLICE PERSPECTIVES

Most police officers will tell you that the only way to learn about police work is by doing it; experience counts for all. While this view is by no means unique to police officers, many features of police work not found in most other occupations underscore the importance of experience. The police carry guns and other weapons that can be used with deadly results. They are subject to other people's aggressions and hostilities just because they are police officers. They are given the authority to act in situations in which other citizens must stand back. In many jurisdictions, they are expected to be police officers twenty-four hours a day. And if they make mistakes they may be subject to criminal and civil suits.

Because most recruits are ill prepared for the demands of police work, and also because there are insistent pleas for professionalization of the police, many police agencies offer quite extensive training courses for their new recruits.[24] If they have no police academy, they send them to universities and colleges with special law enforcement curricula. These training programs introduce the newcomer to the legal, ethical, organizational, and operational facets of police work. It is while enrolled in the programs that the recruit gets his first taste of what it means to be a police officer. It is also during this period of formal training that an intensive socialization process begins and the "cord binding the rookie to the civilian world is cut."[25]

In his training by police instructors, the rookie sees for the first time something of the ambiguities and conflicts inherent in police work. He learns that he is expected to enforce all criminal laws, but that in practice he must be selective. He learns that the public is something akin to an enemy — he is told to be suspicious, always on the lookout for a setup, and never to rely on any help from citizens — but that he must serve and protect its members. He learns that while the powers that be demand that he combat crime and arrest criminals, they also insist that he follow procedures, even if that sometimes means the escape of a criminal, the commission of a crime, or perhaps his own injury and death. He learns that police work is also public relations work, and that valued attributes such as zeal in job performance and honesty may get him into trouble with his superiors.[26] Most important of all, perhaps, he learns that what he is told in class often differs markedly from what he knows from his experience as a private citizen. Whatever idealism he brought with him is soon forgotten — perhaps temporarily but most likely permanently.[27]

Defensiveness, Professionalization, Depersonalization A recent study of a police training academy suggests that one of the primary goals of formal police training is the development of uniform behavior among officers so that there is less room for personal judgment and individualized behavior. The recruit must be stripped of his identity and taught to assume a police identity; to think, act, and be a police officer. Richard Harris suggests that three themes emerge during training to help generate in recruits a proper police perspective.[28] The first, perhaps most important, is *defensiveness* — be alert to the many dangers of police work and build defenses against them. These dangers are not merely physical. They include the dangers of procedural violations that can lead to criminal charges, civil suits, reprimands, lost cases, and dismissal. They include the dangers of corruption, inefficiency, and emotional involvement in police-citizen encounters as well as the danger of provoking hostile and punitive reactions on the part of members of the public who are in a position to make trouble for the department.

The second theme is *professionalization* — the development of a professional image, techniques, esprit de corps, service ideals, and a sense of "us" as opposed to "them." The third theme is *depersonalization,* which has two sides. On the one hand, the recruit faces the fact that those with whom he comes in contact, the public and his own supervisors, often treat him as faceless, lacking an individual identity; he is less a person than a thing. He also learns that some occupational demands necessitate the denial of personal qualities — a police officer dares not personalize his official relationships with the public and must beware of those who try to personalize their relationship with him. The other side of depersonalization involves the officer's own adoption of stereotypes, black-and-white distinctions, and intolerance toward out-groups, whose members, in turn, become faceless.

In Harris's view, one important product of defensiveness, profession-alization, and depersonalization is the cultivation of solidarity among recruits — "a subjective feeling of belongingness and implication in each other's lives."[29] This solidarity, the we-feeling that comes with group identity and belonging, firms up and helps preserve the police identity fostered during training.

Danger, Authority, Efficiency In a study of city police at work, Jerome Skolnick argued that policemen typically develop a distinctive "working personality."[30] A unique combination of work elements foster in the policeman a particular way of looking at the world and responding to it. The key elements identified by Skolnick are *danger, authority,* and *efficiency.* Together they encourage the development of suspicion, social isolation, and solidarity — central characteristics of the policeman's relations with the world in which he works. He becomes suspicious of events, persons, and things he learns to associate with danger, and the defensive posture caused by this suspicion moves him to erect barriers between himself and the world. Even if he might not wish to erect barriers — as in his relations with neighbors, family acquaintances, civilian friends, and members of the opposite sex — he finds that they may be erected for him, because his work makes him less desirable as a friend.

This social isolation is enhanced by the police role as an enforcer of public order and public morality: "Typically, the policeman is required to enforce laws representing puritanical morality, such as those prohibit-ing drunkenness, and also laws regulating the flow of public activity, such as traffic laws. In these situations, the policeman directs the citizenry, whose typical response denies recognition of his authority and stresses his obligation to respond to danger."[31] Expected to enforce laws that he may not himself support, or which are resented by large segments of the population, the policeman's official authority once again encourages erec-tion of barriers and contributes to social isolation.

Added to the effects of authority and danger is a persistent pressure to be efficient, to produce, to demonstrate that he is living up to the expec-tations of his superiors. Sometimes required to fill quotas for such things as traffic tickets (Skolnick reports that motorcycle patrolmen were re-quired to write two tickets an hour) and vice arrests (a "rigidly enforced" expectation in some cities), the policeman finds himself further alienating the public as he seeks to meet demands for efficiency.[32]

With barriers erected between themselves and the general public the police seek support and reciprocity in their relations with colleagues. To counteract the threat of danger and the effects of public hostility, and to fulfill the persistent demands that they produce, the police are drawn together in relationships of mutual dependence and aid.[33] The solidarity thus encouraged becomes a central facet of police working relationships and officers draw upon their we-feeling as they act out their roles. Sensing that they can rely on neither the public nor their higher-echelon superiors, they turn to each other, further separating themselves from the world around them.

STEREOTYPING AND THE EXERCISE OF POLICE AUTHORITY

The modern policeman must reduce the complexities of a heterogeneous world to manageable proportions. In this respect he is no different from the rest of us. So that we can handle the task of living amidst a vast array of life-styles, living arrangements, value systems, and behavior patterns, we resort to simplification , distortion, and, inevitably, stereotypes.

A stereotypical view of the world means that we treat others not on the basis of complete, impartial knowledge about them but, rather, according to what "box" we can readily place them in. Obviously, the result need not always be injurious to the person so categorized, but often it is. When the police stereotype, the potential for injury is clearly accentuated, for they are in a position to take the kind of actions prohibited to the rest of us. In their official roles they can search, seize, command, arrest, wound, and even kill, often on no firmer ground than suspicion or proba- ble cause. In other words, if events, persons, or things are defined by the police as requiring authoritative and coercive action, then whether or not they deserve it, they are subject to that action.

All this means that authority can be invoked in situations that would not warrant such action if all the facts were known. From the standpoint of the police, however, the possible undesirable consequences of this are outweighed by the benefits of stereotyping. From the first day of training through the rest of his career, the policeman finds little reason to find out all the facts first, nor could he afford to. If anything, he learns that the facts are less important than initial appearances, and that the best way to approach appearances is to have ready a set of categories into which he can quickly place them.

As noted already, suspicion is central to the policeman's approach to his work.[34] It is toward people, objects, places, and events labeled sus- picious that the police direct much of their attention. Perceptual catego- rization and simplification are important devices in defining what is suspicious — police cannot suspect everything and everyone. It has been suggested that the police arrive at their categorization of persons and things as suspicious through *pragmatic induction:*

> Past experience leads them to conclude that more crimes are committed in the poorer sections of town than in the wealthier areas, that Negroes are more likely to cause public disturbances than whites, and that adolescents are a greater source of trouble than other categories of the citizenry. On the basis of these conclusions, the police divide the population and physical territory under surveillance into a variety of categories, make some initial assumptions about the moral character of the people and places in these

categories, and then focus attention on those categories of persons and places felt to have the shadiest moral characteristics.[35]

In this way the police create a self-fulfilling prophecy: the official criminals come from precisely those areas and groups that fit the stereotype. On the other hand, those areas and groups that do not fit the stereotype retain their "clean" look and continue to receive modest police scrutiny.

English sociologist Dennis Chapman provides a number of illustrations of the impact and perpetuation of police stereotypes and their attendant enforcement patterns.[36] Chapman tells of a case in which for six months residents of an upper-middle-class neighborhood removed building materials from a construction site:

> Each evening and every weekend, after the workmen had departed, the site was visited by between five and fifteen men with motor-cars or wheelbarrows. They removed bricks, tiles, paving slabs, timber, mortar, and other building materials systematically, and often in large quantities.[37]

When asked by an observer why he did not intervene, a police officer who happened to witness one evening's thievery replied that he assumed they all had had permission! Neither the thieves nor the circumstances fit the prevailing stereotypes of suspicious persons and activities. Had they done so, Chapman does not doubt that police action would have been taken.

Contrast this case with an incident Alan Bent observed during his investigation of Memphis police at work. Some police officers were under pressure to produce following an uneventful evening. Their categorization of adolescents as suspicious persons directed their subsequent activity and paid off in a pinch. Officers in four cars descended on an area adjoining a converted warehouse in which a dance was being held. The officers made numerous attempts to uncover evidence of illegal activity by teenagers moving around the area or parked in their cars. Eventually four adolescents were discovered with a couple of joints and a bust was made. The stereotype linking young people, play, and crime (in this case illegal drugs) had worked, thus providing fuel for its further use.[38]

The fact that considerable energy and resources are spent dealing with members of selected segments of the population — usually the poor, the inner-city residents, the young, and the black — should not be taken to mean that police enforcement practices reflect only *police* prejudice, stereotypes, and decisions. It can be forcefully argued that the police are conforming to dominant American stereotypes, prejudices, and policies rather than deviating from them, and as such we must look beyond the police for an explanation of resource and energy allocation and police enforcement patterns. The police operate in a sociopolitical climate that generally rewards those who conform to dominant cultural values, predispositions, and behavior patterns. In America the white middle class looks not to itself for the criminal and the disorderly but, rather, to those believed to pose threats to order, stability, and the preservation of traditional values.

Some recent evidence of police conformity with prevailing middle-class standards comes from Bent's study in Memphis. Bent found much agreement in self-appraisals and attitudes toward others between the police and white middle-class samples, despite disparate backgrounds of the two groups. Though police views of some subjects differed from those of the white middle-class sample, their views differed most consistently from those held by blacks and students. Both the police and the typical white middle-class respondents held to an "order-stability" value structure, stressing crime control, improved police efficiency and production, and enforcement patterns aimed at preserving order and stability. This value system is contrasted with the "democratic-active," which emphasizes service responsibilities, social needs, due process, justice, human dignity, and respect for human differences. The order-stability group — represented by the white, middle-aged person with at least a high school education who earns over $15,000 a year — held "warm feelings" toward the military, conservatives, Republicans, policemen, whites, and the National Guard. So did the police sample. The group held "cold feelings" toward liberals, blacks, women's liberation, and other persons and groups most closely associated with social innovation. So did the police. Since white, middle-class individuals typically are in the best position to influence the activities of governments and their agencies, it should come as no surprise that the police share a similar set of values and engage in behavior in support of them.[39]

It is interesting to note that programs of higher education have been advocated as a means of broadening police attitudes, of reducing prejudice, authoritarianism, stereotyping, and hostility toward those with whom they come into contact as enforcers. In 1966, 184 colleges and universities offered degree programs in criminal justice; in 1978, there were 816 such programs.[40] Yet it appears far from conclusive that higher education for police produces change in their attitudes and behavior. Indeed, "there is strong evidence that the value of police education may be nullified by the realities of the police role as it is now constituted."[41] The nature of police work, especially the need to be suspicious and to pattern enforcement in terms of arrest-productive stereotypes, coupled with pressure from middle-class law-and-order interests, seem to be blocking any real liberalization of police attitudes and behavior.

Police Exercise of Discretion

In their daily work, the police are faced with two related decisions whenever they enter a situation. The first is whether or not to take any action at all; the second is what kind of action to take. It is in making these decisions that the police invoke their awesome discretionary powers. The exercise of discretion lies at the heart of real police work, and its ramifications touch the entire legal process, not to mention the people immediately involved.

Discretion is, of course, exercised at all levels of the legal process:

> Police officers decide what "suspicious" persons to "stop and frisk," to round up in a "dragnet raid," to warn, or to arrest. Judges pass on the guilt of suspected offenders, make decisions on whom to release and whom to hold for further hearings (in jail or on bail), and determine the kind and length of sentence. Prosecuting attorneys exercise considerable latitude in what cases to prosecute and when to negotiate with the defense attorney over pleas, charges, and dispositions. A sifting and sorting operation occurs in which certain persons are processed through the legal machinery, with a steadily increasing attrition as suspected offenders move through the various procedural stages of the criminal justice system. At each of these stages, decisions made by certain legal officials will limit the alternatives for those operating in subsequent stages.[42]

Since the police are typically the first legal reactors to exercise discretion, their decisions are crucial in determining law in action and the official character of the crime scene.

SOME REASONS FOR NONENFORCEMENT OF THE LAW

Discretionary decisions are available to the police in all police operations. Some scholars have argued that the most important discretionary decisions are the negative ones, such as not to arrest, not to investigate, or not to bargain. When the police do take action, their decisions are often subject to review and examination; this is seldom the case for decisions not to invoke the legal process, for these decisions are usually of low visibility.[43] Negative decisions, then, can remain largely free from scrutiny by interested nonpolice parties and by other police officers, particularly superiors. This promotes secrecy in police operations while lessening both internal and external control.

Given the low visibility of police decisions not to invoke the criminal process, conclusive evidence regarding such discretionary actions is hard to find. However, both insider and outsider observations provide some clues as to why and when nonenforcement decisions are made. We can frame the discussion around seven observations recently made by Mortimer and Sanford Kadish.[44]

First, the police may believe that the legislative purpose behind a particular law "would not be served by arresting all persons who engage in the prohibited conduct."[45] Examples are gambling laws, various sexual prohibitions (those concerning consenting adults), and laws considered obsolete. Second, some enforcement selectivity is inevitable given the limitations of police resources. These resource limitations involve more than police time, money, personnel, or equipment: if there is not enough jail space, police arrests and bookings may decline. In her study of skid-row alcoholics, Wiseman found a negative relationship between the number of men the police arrest and the level of occupancy of the jail.[46]

Third, the police may be aware that some laws prohibit behavior that is acceptable and expected in some subcultures of society and thus treat violators selectively on that basis. Fourth, in some situations, victims are more interested in restitution than criminal sanctions (recall the discussion of shoplifting on pages 189–190, and the police go along with victim interests. Fifth, the police shape their enforcement patterns to some extent on the basis of community preferences. An excellent illustration of this by Ernest Alix describes police enforcement practices in a run-down river and railroad town.[47] Rather than bust taverns and other commercial violators of liquor and vice laws upon each violation, the police responded to community pressures by rotating their raids, thus keeping the offending businesses open and the revenue flowing into the town's meager bank account. Sixth, the police routinely make use of informants, and many of these informants are known offenders whom the police decide not to arrest or charge in view of their potential usefulness:

> [The policeman's] steadiest source of information is what he collects as rent for allowing people to operate without arresting them. "Prostitutes and faggots are good. If you treat 'em right, they will give you what you want. They don't want to get locked up, and you can trade that off for information. If you rap 'em around," a very skilled patrolman said, "the way some guys used to, or lock 'em up, you don't get nothing." At a lunch counter another officer said, looking at the waitress who was getting his order, "She thinks I don't know she's hustling the truck drivers. She'll find out tomorrow. I don't care if she makes a few bucks on her back, but she is gonna tell me what I want to know."[48]

Finally, there are some occasions when officers do not invoke the criminal process because "the personal harm the offender would suffer on being arrested outweighs the law enforcement gains . . . achieved by arresting." Such decisions probably have much to do with the status of the offender (age, occupation, and community standing) and are most likely to be invoked for nonstreet crimes such as shoplifting. They are unlikely, therefore, to be invoked in dealings with those segments of society stereotypically linked with serious crime, namely, the poor and relatively powerless.

To these seven clues concerning discretionary nonenforcement practices we should add the impact of relationships between the police and other agents of the legal process. What the police do in their daily work cannot be divorced from what goes on among prosecutors, judges, and other legal reactors. If the decision is whether or not to arrest or charge a suspect, a negative decision may well be influenced by police expectations regarding how the case will be handled at subsequent stages in the criminal process: "Whatever their own views of the importance of particular crimes might be, if it is common knowledge that local magistrates take a very different view which is reflected in their sentencing decisions, the police will often not wish to 'waste' time on arresting individuals who may subsequently be given a merely nominal sentence by the court."[49]

CRIME VICTIMS AND POLICE DISCRETION

Most police work is "reactive" rather than "proactive."[50] That is, police enforcement action is usually taken when a member of a public acts as a complainant. In practical terms, this means that *the police are usually not the first to exercise discretion in enforcement matters.* The citizenry has enormous discretionary power, for the citizen's decision whether or not to bring events and people to the attention of the police in most cases determines whether the police will be in a position to exercise their discretionary judgments.[51]

The relationship between citizen complaints and police use of discretion has only recently come under the scrutiny of criminologists, and much work still needs to be done. We have found out, however, that police decision making is influenced not only by the presence of a complaint and the circumstances surrounding it, but also by its absence. Police decisions are influenced by a variety of things that have little or nothing to do with legal issues; for example, the complainant's demeanor, preference, and relational ties with the suspect (see page 70). But another important set of factors concerns victim decisions to appear as prosecution witnesses and to formally sign complaints when these are needed. Those reluctant to follow their complaints with further actions present police with a dilemma, and the police may refuse to pursue a complaint from those they know or believe will back away from these responsibilities. Offenders are rarely arrested or charged in family disturbance calls. Often this is because the police anticipate no further enforcement action from the complainant.[52]

When citizen complaints come in on police switchboards, the responsibility for directing the police reaction rests squarely on the police dispatcher. Because police communication systems lie at the heart of mobilization procedures, operators are in a position of considerable power and responsibility. Their decisions determine whether or not official action will be taken, the initial nature of that action, and the time lag between call and response. Their discretion has a profound effect on enforcement efforts. Because police departments typically take steps to monitor incoming and outgoing communications, dispatchers have less discretionary leeway than their colleagues working the streets. Even so, discretionary decisions are made, and sometimes with results clearly in violation of victim interests. Here is a complainant-dispatcher conversation reported in a recent study:

"Hello, is this the police?"

"Yes, Madame, what is the problem?"

"He is coming up to get me."

"Where are you, Madame?"

"At home."

"Where?"

"230 Sutton Avenue."

"Who's coming to get you?"

"George."

"How do you know?"

"He just telephoned and said he would take the kid."

"Is it his child, Madame?"

"Yes."

"Is he living with you?"

"Yes."

"When is he coming?"

"Now."

"Why would he want to kill you?"

"I don't know."

"Does he have a weapon?"

"I don't know."

Pause by dispatcher. "Madame, if George arrives and causes any trouble, you call the station and we will send a car."

Dispatcher hangs up.[53]

It turned out that the police might have been able to prevent a crime, for the caller was subsequently assaulted by George. Why did the dispatcher decide not to activate an official police response? Apparently, so Brian Grossman tells us, because available cars in the area were tied up, and also because in the dispatcher's opinion the caller sounded as if she came from a particular ethnic group known for its disproportionate use of police resources, and previous experience suggested that a response would probably tie up police resources to no useful end.[54]

The unresponsiveness of police in situations like these is not adequately accounted for by their lack of resources. True, if the police were to respond to every call for assistance — even those coming in on emergency numbers — there would be absolute chaos. There are simply too many calls, and many of these turn out not to be emergencies (see table 11.1). The police are asked to deal with barking dogs, lost cats, personal problems of a noncriminal nature, and a host of other things. These are support services that, while of importance to callers, are often considered by police as a drain on resources and a hindrance to their crime-fighting mission.[55]

Another view held by some police officers is that certain groups do not deserve their attention and continued support. In a paper presented at the 1979 annual meeting of the American Sociological Association, Clifford Shearing reported on a six-month study of the communications center of

Table 11.1 Emergency calls for police assistance, 1968

	NEW YORK	DETROIT	ST. LOUIS
Number of calls on emergency phone numbers	5,200,000	1,027,000	461,000
Number of calls to which police responded by sending patrols	2,080,000	370,000	98,000
As percent of total calls	40%	36%	21%

SOURCE: This table drawn from "Calls for Police Assistance: Consumer Demands for Governmental Service" by Thomas E. Bercal is reprinted from *American Behavioral Scientist* Vol. 13, Nos. 5 & 6 (May/June, July/August 1970) p. 682 by permission of the publisher, Sage Publications, Inc.

a large Canadian police department. After observing and recording thousands of communications between citizens and the police and between police officers themselves, Shearing found that police officers "made a fundamental distinction between 'the public' on the one hand, and 'third- and fourth-class citizens,' 'the dregs,' or more expressively, 'the scum,' on the other. . . . The public were people the police felt duty-bound to serve and protect."[56] The scum, on the other hand, were troublemakers; they needed police control, hence were viewed as an enemy of the police. Armed with this view it is doubtful the police will respond energetically to calls for assistance by persons identified as scum or those who, because of their "stupidity" or "ignorance" about what the police should really be doing, are only marginally part of the "public."[57]

Corruption and Abuses of Police Authority

Police discretionary practices need not result in misuse of police authority, but in many cases they do. Abuse of police authority occurs when decisions are based not on legal considerations or other matters over which the police officer has no real control (e.g., resources or departmental policies), but instead on personal whim or fancy or in consideration of personal gain.

The sensitive and controversial issue of police corruption has followed the police from their earliest origins. An 1816 report to England's House of Commons described corruption among the early constables and sheriffs' deputies:

> [The] deputies in many instances are characters of the worst and lowest descriptions; the fine they receive from the person who appoints them varies from ten shillings to five pounds; having some expense and no salary they live by extortion, by countenancing all species of vice, by an understanding with the keepers of brothels and disorderly ale-houses, by attending courts of justice, and giving there false evidence to ensure conviction when their

expenses are paid, and by all the various means by which artful and designing men can entrap the weak and prey upon the unwary.[58]

The practices referred to in this report — extortion, perjury, protection, and more — are merely a few of the activities included under the rubric of police corruption. To these have been added brutality, neglect of duty, nepotism, racism, and bribery.

Depending on whose opinion we accept, almost any police activity can find its way onto the list of things identified as corrupt police practices. Historically, much of the concern about corruption has focused on blatant abuses of police authority such as misuse of force, extortion, the taking of bribes, and perjury, but some authors now include many common police practices. Examples are "police perks" such as free meals and discounts at certain stores; the use of abusive or profane language; stopping and questioning citizens; and intraorganizational practices such as payoffs for favors granted by police colleagues. In 1972, the Knapp Commission report to the mayor of New York added another dimension of corruption in arguing that "even those who themselves engage in no corrupt activities are involved in corruption *in the sense that they take no steps to prevent what they know or suspect is going on about them*" (italics added).[59]

The following definition of police corruption is not intended to resolve the probably endless debate over what constitutes corruption. It is offered instead as a guide, so that readers can better identify the common threads linking the police activities discussed below. It is, therefore, necessarily broad. Police practices are corrupt, *if they violate either legal or official departmental rules covering police conduct; if they violate any of the criminal laws operative in the jurisdiction in which the police hold authority; or if they result in activities that involve the use of legitimate police authority and organization for personal or collective gain.* The term *practices* means regular patterns of police action rather than idiosyncratic activities on the part of this or that police officer.

One of the most promising typologies of police corruption is that by Roebuck and Barker.[60] These authors attempt to distinguish types of police corruption on the basis of (*1*) *the kinds of norms violated,* (*2*) *the amount of peer group support,* (*3*) *the extent of organization needed to put the practices into effect,* (*4*) *who is involved in the corruption apart from the police,* and (*5*) *departmental reaction.* Eight types of police corruption have been identified.

1. Corruption of authority involves receiving unauthorized, unearned material gains by virtue of status as police officer. This includes free liquor, meals, discounts, and payments by merchants for more police protection. The corrupters are respectable citizens, there is considerable peer group support, little adverse departmental reaction, little organization is required, and the violation involved is primarily that of departmental regulations.

2. Kickbacks involve receipt of goods and services in return for referring business to a variety of patrons (doctors, lawyers, bondsmen, garages, taxicab companies, service stations, and so on). Corrupters are usually respectable persons who stand to gain from the scheme. Departments tend to ignore it, or actually condone it, depending on the respectability of the corrupter, though the practice is usually in violation of formal departmental rules. Peer group support is often substantial, though its degree may depend on the reputation and trustworthiness of the businessman. The organization involved is relatively simple and "inheres in the collusion between businessmen and policemen."[61]

3. Opportunist theft includes illegal taking of goods from arrestees, victims, crime scenes, or unprotected property. It involves no corrupter and is clearly in violation of criminal laws as well as departmental rules. Reaction from departments is usually negative but may depend on value of goods or cash taken, public knowledge, and willingness of the victim to prosecute. Peer group support depends on informal norms governing distinctions between "clean" and "dirty" money. Little organization is involved; the activities result from situational decisions.

4. Shakedowns are opportunistic behavior that occur when the police know about a crime but accept money or services from suspects in exchange for doing nothing. The corrupter may be respectable or known to be habitually involved in criminal activities. Shakedowns violate legal and departmental norms, and, while peer group support is necessary for routinization of shakedown operations, that support is often contingent on what the suspect is known to be engaged in — bribes from narcotics pushers and robbers are apparently frowned upon.[62] Secrecy in peer group relations is a prime element of shakedowns.

5. Protection of illegal activities involves corrupters who seek to continue their illegal operations free from police harassment. The corrupters can be respectable or nonrespectable; in either case they are doing something illegal, which makes protection important. Protection violates criminal and departmental rules and involves considerable collusion, peer group support, and organization to pull it off (for one thing, officers have to know which businesses are protected). While departmental reaction is often severe (suspension, dismissal, or criminal charges), the severity and consistency of negative reactions may depend on the degree of community support of the illegal activities being protected.

6. The fix includes either quashing of legal proceedings or "taking up" traffic tickets. Corrupters are arrestees attempting to avoid police action that would probably embarrass them in one way or another. The fixer is often not a patrolman but someone with access to the investigative aspects of police work. The fix, of course, violates legal and departmental rules, and reaction is usually severe when cases are brought to light. The authors suggest that in departments where the fix occurs frequently and with considerable regularity it is a highly organized activity.[63]

7. Direct criminal activities involve no corrupter, as the police alone are parties to the corruption. Direct criminal activities include crimes by police officers against suspects, victims, pedestrians, or whomever, and against property. Lack of peer group support and severe departmental reactions generally underscore the blatant criminal character of these practices. For these activities to continue some organization is necessary, and therefore they are unlikely to persist as opportunist efforts by individuals or two-man teams.

8. Internal payoffs involve bribes within the police department for such things as assignments, hours, promotions, control of evidence, arrests, and so forth. Some officers are in a particularly advantageous position to take payoffs, as Jonathan Rubinstein's comment on the police dispatcher shows:

> He has numerous little favors he can grant a man that will ease the burdens of the tour. For instance, the patrolman can go to "lunch" (policeman [in Philadelphia, at least] refer to all their meal breaks as lunch, regardless of the hour) only with the dispatcher's permission. If the dispatcher wants a man to remain in service, he simply tells him that he cannot go. The men are not supposed to eat together and the dispatcher is responsible for seeing that they do not gather. A sympathetic dispatcher will allow several men to share their lunchtime by permitting one man to give a location where the dispatcher knows the police do not eat.[64]

The internal payoff system is usually highly organized, particularly in those departments under pressure to produce and in those departments where lucrative and corrupt practices such as shakedowns and protection are regular aspects of police work. Peer group support is usually considerable. Departmental reaction is tolerant if it means a more satisfied work force, and if officers involved in the payoff system are not in violation of high priority regulations or the criminal law.

The value of Roebuck and Barker's typology lies in its applicability across departments, jurisdictions, and cultures, and in its attempt to specify some of the dimensions in terms of which corruption can be analyzed. This brief review of one typology shows that police corruption is hardly to be understood only by reference to what the police do. As William Chambliss recently argued, the roots and supports for corruption lie not in the police per se, but in the larger social, cultural, economic, and political climates in which they operate.[65]

BRUTALITY AND MISUSE OF FORCE

One aspect of police operations continually appears in discussions of corruption and abuse of police authority — the use of coercive force. police are charged from time to time with brutality and abuses of their authority to employ coercive force.

What is meant by brutality and misuse of force when these are applied to police operations? As you might have guessed, there is hardly consensus on their meaning. Albert Reiss suggests that almost any routine police action will be interpreted by someone as an instance of police brutality. He argues, further, that if brutality is the actual use of force, the police themselves have no clear-cut legal or normative statements on the issue.[66] Police training films, such as Motorola's *Shoot, Don't Shoot,* endeavor to instruct the police in the matter of using deadly force, but most officers are rarely, if ever, faced with situations in which such force is authorized or used. At lesser levels of violence, the police rely on the notion of reasonable force, but what constitutes reasonable force? A rule of thumb adopted by most police agencies, and supported by judicial actions, is that *reasonable force* means that force necessary to secure a legal goal without endangering innocent citizens. Any unnecessary force is unreasonable and may be illegal. But these are difficult distinctions to apply in practice, particularly under pressure.

In any police-citizen encounter the actors may hold different conceptions of brutality, depending on their status (policeman or suspect); their ability to use force (handcuffed or free to move); the weapons available (guns, knives, or fists); their sex, age, physical condition, and race; their prior experiences; and their expectations and evaluations of what will happen and what ought to. Some people apply the term *brutality* only to those situations involving force, but others include situations involving psychic manipulations, when there is loss of self-respect and threats to a positive self-concept. While we no longer see the routine use of "third degree" techniques among our police forces, other practices associated with the questioning of suspects may be seen as unnecessarily brutal.[67] Many no doubt would question the claim that "in dealing with criminal offenders, and consequently also with criminal suspects who may actually be innocent, the interrogator must of necessity employ less refined methods than are considered appropriate for the transaction of ordinary, everyday affairs by and between law-abiding citizens."[68] And some might have little trepidation about denouncing as brutality police use of trickery, deceit, and other psychological devices designed to maximize psychic tension and emotional insecurity — procedures quite acceptable to the author of the statement just quoted.[69]

The line between brutality and misuse of force is hazy. While all brutality may well be misuse of authorized force, not all misuse of force is brutality. An officer who fires his revolver at a fleeing felon (a legal action in most jurisdictions) and hits instead an innocent bystander would probably be considered to have used deadly force inappropriately; but is his action also properly identified as an instance of police brutality? To draw the line we need to know something about police motives, experiences, intentions, and knowledge. *Brutality* may perhaps best be used in reference to those situations in which policemen knowingly and intentionally use force in order to satisfy personal or group whims, prejudices, and interests. *Misuse of force,* then, can be applied to those situations in which the police use force in a manner that goes beyond that required for the satisfaction of legal obligations, though the intent is to meet those obligations and not personal whims.

We can reasonably imagine situations in which brutality is more likely to be at issue than misuse of force. We are more likely to be looking at brutality, for instance, if the police assault others who offer no resistance, are in no position to offer any resistance (if they are handcuffed), or if a number of officers join in the assault of a lone citizen who clearly can be subdued with less forceful means.[70] A clear example of brutality is the following account of a recent incident in Philadelphia. A man suspected of sexually molesting a child was treated to the following at the hands of his police captors:

> Any squad member who wished was allowed to beat the suspect from the ankles to the armpits with his stick. Men came in off the street to participate in the beating and then returned to patrol. Before he was taken downtown, the suspect had been severely battered, although he had no broken bones. At no time did he utter a complaint, ask for mercy, or curse the police. Without a murmur he absorbed a brutal beating, which caused him to foul himself and drew the admiring comments of several men who admitted he could "really take it."[71]

A less shocking situation, but nevertheless in line with our definition of brutality, is the following, again reported by Rubinstein. Suspects who are arrested are often transported in wagons. They are handcuffed and sit on benches with no handrails or other devices on which to rely for support during the ride. The driver of the wagon can give prisoners a very uncomfortable ride merely by swerving and braking unpredictably. As Rubinstein describes it: "Rarely is a prisoner injured by any of these methods, but anyone who runs when he is told to halt, swears or spits at a policeman, or threatens him in any way may find himself chastened by these methods."[72]

Police misuse of force is likely to surface if the police are under relatively extreme pressure, if they are acting overzealously, or if they have misinterpreted the events or actions they have witnessed. In addition, poorly trained and inexperienced policemen are probably more apt to use excessive force than the more experienced. Firing warning shots in the air or shooting at fleeing suspects, practices not officially condoned by most police agencies, may have been triggered by one of these factors.

Misuse of force and, on occasion, police brutality can be linked to the policeman's desire, if not his obligation, to gain control in encounters. A number of authors point out that police efforts to gain the upper hand in their dealings with suspects, witnesses, victims, and others are given high priority in police operations, for understandable reasons.[73] But in the effort to gain control, the police may sometimes misuse or abuse their authority to employ coercive force. Also, if police control is threatened it is likely to be perceived by officers as a challenge to their authority, an issue to which the police are particularly sensitive. It is not too surprising, then, that excessive use of force tends to surface if police control of a situation is threatened.[74]

The "Stop" Police authority to use coercive force is most often invoked when an arrest is taking place. But in addition to actual arrests, the police exercise this authority whenever they make a routine "stop," that is, stop a citizen for questioning. Subjects may not know that failure to heed an officer's command to stop makes them liable for arrest on charges or refusing to obey a lawful command by a police officer. Behind the officer's authority to make the stop lies his authority to use force if need be.

Brutality is most likely to erupt when stop situations are contrived events bearing no relationship to legal objectives, but designed instead for purposes of harassment and to satisfy personal whim. Bent identifies a desire for "action" as one factor leading to such stops:

> With some police officers, an unrequited need for activity resulted in prankish behavior that did little to elevate the esteem of law enforcement in the eyes of the public. Occupants of a police car actively looked for "deviants" on their beat to break the monotony of a quiet evening. To these officers, deviants included anyone whose clothes, hair length, mannerisms, or race did not conform with officers' standards of acceptability. Thus, youths with long hair or garish dress — "hippies," as defined by the policemen — transvestites, and blacks were stopped and questioned at the pleasure of the patrolmen. . . .
>
> A typical scenario in a two-man squad car during periods of prolonged inactivity went something like this: Patrolmen Harry and Jack have had an uneventful evening when a car driven by some teenagers goes by. One of the youths stares (or smiles, or grimaces, or sneers, etc.) at the police car. Patrolman Jack turns to his partner and says, "Harry, let's pull that car over. Those kids are guilty of 'contempt of cop'!" Or one of the officers spots a pedestrian who appears likely to provide some "activity" and turns to his partner saying, "Jack, let's stop the fag (or hippie, or whore, or nigger, etc.) and ask him a few questions. That ought to liven things up."[75]

Weapons and Brutality The police are encouraged to misuse and abuse their authority to employ force in a multitude of different ways. Two of the most alarming sources of encouragement come from traditions within police departments that support the use of nonregulation weapons and advertisers who are trying to sell police equipment.

The use of nonregulation weaponry is no longer as widespread as it used to be. According to Rubinstein, for example, large city forces have had some success in outlawing such practices. Nevertheless, Rubinstein goes on, a significant number of officers still carry with them weapons that look as if their sole purpose is the infliction of great pain and suffering. Among these weapons are lead-loaded saps, some of which come in the form of an innocent-looking glove with built-in lead; hollowed-out nightsticks filled with lead; ax handles; and sticks fitted with a metal ball on their knob.[76] Officers have also been known to carry two or even three guns. The so-called dumdum bullets that blow apart on impact are routinely used in many state, local, and federal agencies, although they are outlawed in international warfare. Armed in these various ways, officers are not encouraged to use force defensively, and a clear means, if not an incentive, exists for abuse of police power.

Advertisers' interests lie in making sales, and they will go to some extraordinary lengths to interest the police in their wares. One recent flier, sent out by the manufacturers of Second Chance bulletproof vests and clothing, contains various "comic strips" depicting police officers in life-or-death situations. Many include bizarre references to the policeman's uphill fight against procedural requirements of due process and Supreme Court liberalism. One even depicts a smiling policeman dreaming about two hoodlums who are stabbing the judge who gave them probation for shooting at a cop. The advertisers end their twenty-page flier with the following "editorial":

> Everytime a policeman is killed, public figures will make a big show about how sorry they are. Yet, even if the killer is somehow convicted, they will refuse to enforce Capital Punishment. So-called "life imprisonment" usually means parole in five or ten years. It seems that the majority of cop killers eventually go free, thus giving no deterrent to future killers.
>
> Due to recent court decisions and a prevailing social attitude of permissiveness, there exists only one way to give Capital Punishment to cop killers. You must survive his attack to do it.[77]

The last paragraph leaves little doubt that the makers of Second Chance vests support the view that policemen should be executioners.

How Much Police Corruption and Abuse of Force? The extent of police corruption and abuse of force is unknown and unknowable. To remove the cloak of secrecy surrounding police operations, particularly their unlawful ones, requires powers beyond the control of even congressional committees and those who head up police agencies. Serious investigations into these matters are also hampered because the time and money required for in-depth research are beyond the grasp of most criminologists, assuming they could raise the veil of secrecy. Even police officers themselves find it difficult, if not dangerous, to bring corrupt practices to light. The movie *Serpico,* which dealt with corruption in New York and was based in part on the Knapp Commission investigations, brought some of these difficulties and dangers to wide public attention. Some evidence shows that those who try to remain aloof from corruption are placed under considerable pressure to conform with the practices of their colleagues.[78]

All in all, what meager evidence we do have suggests two things. First, as the Knapp Commission concluded, corruption is widespread and is likely to remain so given prevailing stereotypes of the criminal, long-standing traditions in police work, and the demand that the police enforce laws over which there is considerable disagreement and no little resentment. Second, excessive use of force by police seems to be less prevalent than many appear to think. Albert Reiss found that out of 5,012 police-citizen encounters around 10 percent involved what was considered police misconduct, and in most of these cases abusive language and ridicule constituted the misconduct.[79] He did discover one very alarming fact, however. Around 33 percent of the incidents in which excessive force was used occurred *while the suspect was in police custody, under physical control.*[80] Just how much violence occurs behind closed doors is impossible to ascertain. The fact that it does at all raises the specter of rule by terror rather than by law.

References

1. Austin Turk, *Criminality and Legal Order* (Chicago: Rand McNally, 1971), p. 67.
2. Joseph Goldstein, "Police Discretion Not to Invoke the Criminal Process: Low Visibility Decisions in the Administration of Justice," *Yale Law Journal* 69 (1960), p. 543.
3. See Jonathan Rubinstein, *City Police* (Farrar, Straus and Giroux, 1973), pp. 6–8.
4. See T. A. Critchley, *A History of Police in England and Wales,* 2nd ed. (Montclair, N.J.: Patterson Smith, 1972), pp. 38–42; Allan Silver, "The Demand for Order in Civil Society," in *The Police: Six Sociological Essays,* ed. David Bordua (New York: Wiley, 1967), pp. 1–24; Evelyn L. Parks, "From Constabulary to Police Society: Implications for Social Control," *Catalyst* (1970), pp. 76–97.
5. Michael Banton, *Police Community Relations* (London: William Collins, 1973), p. 18.
6. See Patrick Colquhoun, *A Treatise on the Police of the Metropolis,* 6th ed. (London: Joseph Mawman, 1806). On the early police reform movement, see also Leon Radzinowicz, *A History of English Criminal Law,* vol. 1 (London: Stevens, 1948); and Critchley, *A History of the Police in England and Wales,* pp. 38–50.
7. See espcially Sheldon Bacon, *The Early Development of American Municipal Police* (Ph.D. diss., Yale University, 1935); also Roger Lane, *Policing the City: Boston, 1822–1885* (Cambridge, Mass.: Harvard University Press, 1967).
8. Cited in Paul B. Weston and Kenneth M. Wells, *Law Enforcement and Criminal Justice* (Pacific Palisades, Calif.: Goodyear, 1972), p. 6.
9. See Bacon, *Development of American Police;* Lane, *Policing the City;* and James F. Richardson, *The New York Police — Colonial Times to 1900* (New York: Oxford University Press, 1970).
10. See Mark H. Haller, "Historical Roots of Police Behavior: Chicago 1890–1925," *Law and Society Review* 10 (1976), pp. 303–23.
11. *U.S. News and World Report* December 16, 1974.
12. For some recent trends see Morris Cobern, "Some Manpower Aspects of the Criminal Justice System," *Crime and Delinquency* 19 (1973), pp. 198–99.
13. Arthur G. Millspaugh, *Crime Control by the National Government* (1937; repr. New York: Da Capo Press, 1972), p. 71.
14. Figures by Roper Public Opinion Research Center, Williamstown, Mass.; cited in Michael J. Hindelang, Michael R. Gottfredson, Christopher S. Dunn, and Nicolette Parisi, *Sourcebook of Criminal Justice Statistics, 1976* (Washington, D.C.: U.S. Government Printing Office, 1977), p. 321.
15. For the classic statement on "dirty work" see Everett C. Hughes, "Good People and Dirty Work," in *The Other Side: Perspectives on Deviance,* ed. Howard S. Becker (New York: Free Press, 1964), pp. 23–36.
16. See Richard N. Harris, *The Police Academy: An Inside View* (New York: Wiley, 1973), pp. 5–6; also, William A. Westley, *Violence and the Police* (Cambridge, Mass.: MIT Press, 1970), pp. 18–19.
17. John H. McNamara, "Uncertainties of Police Work: Recruits' Background and Training," in *The Police: Six Sociological Essays,* ed. Bordua,

pp. 191–94. See also Arthur J. Niederhoffer, *Behind the Shield: The Police in Urban Society* (New York: Anchor, 1967); James Q. Wilson, *Varieties of Police Behavior* (Cambridge, Mass.: Harvard University Press, 1968). But see also Harris, *The Police Academy,* pp. 14–15, for indications of upward trends in social class backgrounds.

18. Niederhoffer, *Behind the Shield,* p. 159.
19. Ibid., p. 156.
20. David H. Bayley and Harold Mendelsohn, *Minorities and the Police: Confrontation in America* (New York: Free Press, 1968), pp. 32–33.
21. See James Ahern, *Police in Trouble: Our Frightening Crisis in Law Enforcement* (New York: Hawthorne Books, 1972), pp. 4–5; Harris, *The Police Academy,* pp. 16–17.
22. Harris, *The Police Academy,* pp. 16–17; and Niederhoffer, *Behind the Shield,* pp. 36–38.
23. Alan Edward Bent, *The Politics of Law Enforcement* (Lexington, Mass.: D. C. Heath, 1974), p. 16.
24. See, for example, The President's Commisson on Law Enforcement and the Administration of Justice, *The Challenge of Crime in a Free Society* (Washington, D.C.: U.S. Government Printing Office, 1967), chapter 4; National Advisory Commission on Criminal Justice Standards and Goals, *The Police* (Washington, D.C.: U.S. Government Printing Office, 1973), part III; Egon Bittner, *The Functions of the Police in Modern Society* (Chevy Chase, Md.: National Institute of Mental Health, 1970).
25. Niederhoffer, *Behind the Shield,* p. 43.
26. Harris, *The Police Academy,* p. 37.
27. Niederhoffer, *Behind the Shield,* pp. 47–48.
28. Harris, *The Police Academy.*
29. Ibid., p. 163.
30. Jerome H. Skolnick, *Justice without Trial,* 2nd ed. (New York: Wiley, 1975), pp. 42–70.
31. Ibid., p. 44.
32. Ibid., p. 55; and Rubinstein, *City Police,* p. 50.
33. See Bent, *The Politics of Law Enforcement,* pp. 36–37. See also Peter K. Manning, "The Police: Mandate, Strategies, and Appearances," in Jack D. Douglas, ed., *Crime and Justice in American Society* (New York: Bobbs-Merrill, 1971); also his *Police Work: The Social Organization of Policing* (Cambridge, Mass.: MIT Press, 1977).
34. See Harris, *The Police Academy,* chapter 3, in addition to Skolnick, *Justice without Trial.*
35. Carl Werthman and Irving Piliavin, "Gang Members and the Police," in *The Police: Six Sociological Essays,* ed. Bordua, pp. 68–69.
36. Dennis Chapman, *Sociology and the Stereotype of the Criminal* (London: Tavistock Publications, 1968).
37. Ibid., p. 56.
38. Bent, *The Politics of Law Enforcement,* pp. 26–27.

39. Ibid., chapter 4.
40. Richard W. Kobetz, *Criminal Justice Education Directory, 1978–1980* (Gaithersburg, Md.: International Association of Chiefs of Police, 1978), p. 1.
41. Norman Weiner, "The Effect of Education on Police Attitudes," *Journal of Criminal Justice* 2 (1974), p. 323.
42. Stuart L. Hills, *Crime, Power, and Morality* (Scranton, Pa.: Chandler, 1971), p. 22.
43. Goldstein, "Police Discretion Not to Invoice the Criminal Process."
44. Mortimer R. Kadish and Sanford H. Kadish, *Discretion to Disobey* (Palto Alto, Calif.: Stanford University Press, 1973), pp. 74–75. See also Wayne R. Lafave, *Arrest: The Decision to Take a Suspect into Custody* (Boston: Little Brown, 1965).
45. Ibid., p. 74.
46. Jacqueline P. Wiseman, *Stations of the Lost: The Treatment of Skid Row Alcoholics* (Englewood Cliffs, N.J.: Prentice-Hall, 1970), p. 71.
47. Ernest K. Alix, "The Functional Interdependence of Crime and Community Social Structure," *Journal of Criminal Law, Criminology, and Police Science* 60 (1969), pp. 332–39.
48. Rubinstein, *City Police,* p. 207.
49. A. Keith Bottomley, *Decisions in the Penal Process* (London: Martin Robinson, 1973), p. 41.
50. See Donald J. Black, "Production of Crime Rates," *American Sociological Review* 35 (1970), p. 735.
51. Albert J. Reiss, Jr., *The Police and the Public* (New Haven: Yale University Press, 1971), p. 114.
52. See R. I. Parnas, "The Police Response to Domestic Disturbance," *Wisconsin Law Review* (1967), p. 914.
53. Brian A. Grossman, "The Discretionary Enforcement of Law," in *Politics and Crime,* eds. Sawyer F. Sylvester and Edward Sagarin (New York: Praegar, 1974), p. 67.
54. Ibid.
55. See Clifford D. Shearing, "Subterranean Processes in the Maintenance of Power: An Examination of the Mechanisms Coordinating Police Action," presented to the annual meeting of the American Sociological Association, Boston, August 17–21, 1979. See also Elaine Cumming, Ian Cumming, and Laura Edell, "Policeman as Philosopher, Guide and Friend," *Social Problems* 12 (1965), pp. 276–86.
56. Shearing, "Subterranean Processes," p. 6.
57. See also Harold E. Pepinsky, "Police Patrolmen's Offense–Reporting Behavior," *Journal of Research in Crime and Delinquency* 13 (1976), pp. 33–46.
58. Quoted in Luke Owen Pike, *A History of Crime in England,* vol. II (Montclair, N.J.: Patterson Smith, 1968), p. 464.

59. *Knapp Commission Report on Police Corruption* (New York: George Braziller, 1972), p. 3.

60. Julian Roebuck and Thomas Barker, "A Typology of Police Corruption," in *Crime Prevention and Social Control,* eds. Ronald Akers and Edward Sagarin (New York: Praeger, 1974), pp. 118–27. Another typology is offered by Lawrence Sherman in his recent book, *Police Corruption: A Sociological Perspective* (Garden City, N.Y.: Anchor, 1974), pp. 6–12.

61. Roebuck and Barker, "A Typology of Police Corruption," p. 120.

62. Ibid., p. 122.

63. Ibid., pp. 124–25.

64. Rubinstein, *City Police,* p. 85.

65. William J. Chambliss, "Vice, Corruption, Bureaucracy, and Power," *Wisconsin Law Review* (1971), pp. 1150–73.

66. Albert J. Reiss, Jr., "Police Brutality: Answers to Key Questions," in *Law and Order: Police Encounters,* ed. Michael Lipsky (Chicago: Aldine, 1970), pp. 57–83.

67. For a look at how things were not so long ago, see Zachariah Chafee, Jr., Walter H. Pollack, and Carl S. Stern, *The Third Degree,* originally published as a report to the National Commission on Law Observance and Enforcement, 1931. (New York: Arno Press, 1969).

68. Fred Inbau, "Police Interrogation — A Practical Necessity," in *Police Power and Individual Freedom,* ed. Claude R. Sowle (Chicago: Aldine, 1962), p. 150.

69. For a discussion of the use of psychological coercion in police interrogations, see Edwin D. Driver, "Confessions and the Social Psychology of Coercion," *Harvard Law Review* 82 (1968), pp. 42–56.

70. See Reiss, "Police Brutality," p. 648.

71. Rubinstein, *City Police,* p. 183.

72. Ibid., p. 329.

73. Bottomley, *Decisions in the Penal Process,* p. 51; also Rubinstein, *City Police,* chapter 7.

74. Reiss, *The Police and the Public,* pp. 144–48.

75. Bent, *The Politics of Law Enforcement,* pp. 17–18.

76. Rubinstein, *City Police,* pp. 288–89.

77. Advertising flier, "Second Chance" (September 1973), Central Lake, Michigan.

78. See Ellwyn R. Stoddard, "The Informal 'Code' of Police Deviancy: A Group Approach to 'Blue Coat Crime,'" *Journal of Criminal Law, Criminology and Police Science* 59 (1968), pp. 201–13.

79. Reiss, *The Police and the Public,* p. 142.

80. Reiss, "Police Brutality," pp. 77–78.

The Judicial Process

Once an individual has been arrested by the police, he becomes eligible for further processing at the hands of official agents of the state. With his arrest, the police are in effect asserting that he is no longer to be treated as a law-abiding citizen but, rather, as a criminal. The change in status that arrest confirms is symbolized not only by physical detention but also by the warning that anything he says can and will be used against him in a court of law. Law-abiding citizens are given no such warning in their dealings with the police.

The judicial process can be thought of as a series of decision stages through which some, but not all, suspects will pass. Figure 12.1 shows the various stages in detail. Notice that there is considerable attrition as defendants pass from arrest to sentencing and implementation of punishment. Of course, jurisdictions differ in their rates of attrition, but even in felony cases it is not unusual to find dropout rates after arrest of 40 or 50 percent, and even higher.[1] In this chapter we will review the factors that influence this and other aspects of the criminal process after arrest.

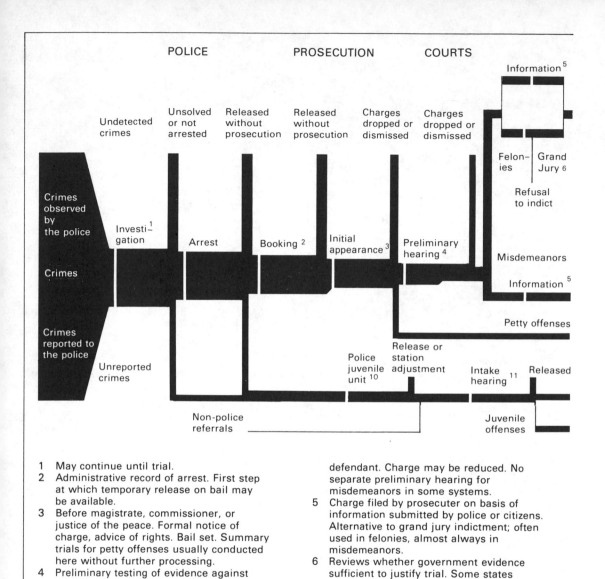

POLICE   PROSECUTION   COURTS

Information [5]

Undetected crimes

Unsolved or not arrested

Released without prosecution

Released without prosecution

Charges dropped or dismissed

Charges dropped or dismissed

Felon-ies | Grand Jury [6]

Refusal to indict

Crimes observed by the police

Investi-gation [1]

Arrest

Booking [2]

Initial appearance [3]

Preliminary hearing [4]

Misdemeanors

Crimes

Information [5]

Petty offenses

Crimes reported to the police

Unreported crimes

Police juvenile unit [10]

Release or station adjustment

Intake hearing [11]

Released

Non-police referrals

Juvenile offenses

Figure 12.1 A General View of the Criminal Justice System.

1 May continue until trial.
2 Administrative record of arrest. First step at which temporary release on bail may be available.
3 Before magistrate, commissioner, or justice of the peace. Formal notice of charge, advice of rights. Bail set. Summary trials for petty offenses usually conducted here without further processing.
4 Preliminary testing of evidence against

defendant. Charge may be reduced. No separate preliminary hearing for misdemeanors in some systems.
5 Charge filed by prosecuter on basis of information submitted by police or citizens. Alternative to grand jury indictment; often used in felonies, almost always in misdemeanors.
6 Reviews whether government evidence sufficient to justify trial. Some states

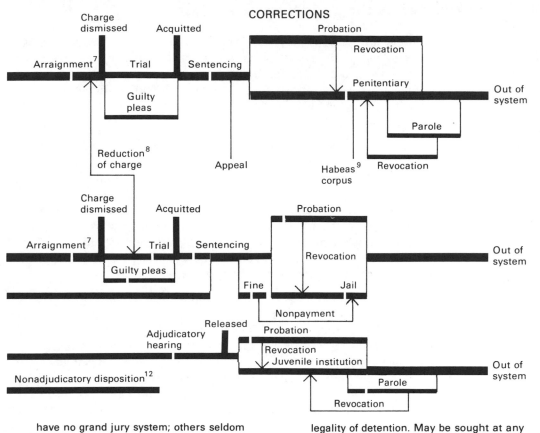

CORRECTIONS

have no grand jury system; others seldom use it.

7 Appearance for plea; defendant elects trial by judge or jury (if available); counsel for indigent usually appointed here in felonies. Often not at all on other cases.

8 Charge may be reduced at any time prior to trial in return for plea of guilty or for other reasons.

9 Challenge on constitutional grounds to legality of detention. May be sought at any point in process.

10 Police often hold informal hearings, dismiss or adjust many cases without further processing.

11 Probation officer decides desirability of further court action.

12 Welfare agency, social services, counseling, medical care, etc., for cases where adjudicatory handling not needed.

SOURCE: President's Commission on Law Enforcement and Administration of Justice, *The Challenge of Crime in a Free Society* (Washington, D.C.: U.S. Government Printing Office, 1967), pp. 8-9.

Overview of the Judicial Process

Different jurisdictions may use various procedures and terminologies in the handling of criminal suspects, but a general sense of the major decision stages in the American judicial process can be grasped from the following overview.[2] It mainly applies to adult felony offenders, but significant differences in the judicial handling of persons suspected of misdemeanors and petty crimes will be noted.

Initial Appearance Before a Magistrate   Within a reasonable time after arrest, (usually 48 hours), suspects must be brought before a court official, usually a magistrate, for consideration of bail. In minor cases such as drunkenness, disorderly conduct, vagrancy, traffic offenses, and violations of local ordinances, this initial appearance may also be a time when suspects can plead guilty to whatever charges the police have brought against them, and if they do so, a summary disposition is entered by the court. For those arrested on more serious charges, no plea or consideration of evidence is involved at this stage.

Determination of Charges   Following the initial appearance, assuming charges have not been dropped or dismissed, the prosecution must decide on what charges to pursue. Initial determination of charges is made in the light of police reports regarding the circumstances of the case. If the decision is made to prosecute, formal charges must be lodged against the suspect. Sometimes this is done through *grand jury* proceedings, in which the prosecution presents evidence in support of his case (but without the presence of the defendant or his counsel). If the grand jury agrees with the prosecution it hands down an *indictment* specifying the charges or it may reduce or alter the charges or grant no formal indictment. However, a grand jury rarely disagrees with the recommendations of the prosecution.

In states without a grand jury system, and in offenses not requiring grand jury proceedings, the prosecution formally presents charges before a magistrate or judge in a *preliminary hearing,* sometimes called an *information* proceeding. Unlike the grand jury situation, the defendant may challenge the evidence presented in support of the charges, and in some jurisdictions he may elect to waive the hearings altogether.

Arraignment and Plea   Upon indictment, or when bound over for trial on an information, a time is usually set for formal plea making. A judge asks the defendant for his plea, and if he accepts it a trial or sentencing date is set. A judge is not bound to accept a plea of guilty or nolo contendere (no contest); however, he *must* accept a plea of not guilty.

Trial   For those who have formally entered not guilty pleas, guilt or innocence is usually decided in a court trial. All defendants are entitled to a jury trial, though this right may be waived for most offenses in most states. Trial procedures, however, are basically the same regardless of whether or not a jury is sitting.

The trial is an *adversary* proceeding during which the prosecution and defense seek to convince the judge and jury that their presentation of the facts surrounding the case best accords with the truth. The onus of proof lies with the prosecution, who must demonstrate that the evidence implicates the defendant *beyond a reasonable doubt*. While trial proceedings are acted out within a fairly rigid set of rules, the presiding judge may rule on matters of procedure, evidence, testimony, and trial conduct. The judge cannot, however, overrule a jury's finding of not guilty.

Appeals　Upon conviction, the defendant has the right to appeal his case to a higher court. If an appeals court refuses to consider his case, or makes a negative ruling, the defendant may appeal to even higher courts. The end of the appeals road is the United States Supreme Court. The basis for an appeal may be procedural or evidentiary, or may involve basic questions of substantive law, such as the constitutionality of a particular criminal statute. In most jurisdictions, defendants also have the right to appeal sentences.

Sentencing　After conviction, the defendant faces sentencing. In some states, and for some offenses, a jury may set the sentence, while in other circumstances sentencing may be decided by a panel of judges. Usually, however, the trial judge decides the offender's fate. In most felony cases a time interval between conviction and sentencing is provided so that the defendant's background, present circumstances, and criminal record can be investigated. These investigations are intended as aids for the judge in his deliberations over sentencing alternatives, if these are available.

These are the major decision stages in the American judicial process. The decisions made at any one stage determine whether and how criminal suspects will move to the next one. Most suspects do not go through all the stages that are available to them. How and why the decisions are made, then, become central issues in determining what actually happens to those who enter the judicial process.

BAIL AND PRETRIAL DETENTION

Within a reasonable time after arrest, suspects must be accorded the opportunity to gain their release from custody, pending future proceedings against them. In Anglo-American law, the traditional route to freedom lies with the posting of a money bond. Those "bailed out" in this manner forfeit the amount of bail if they fail to appear at a specified later date.

To give someone the opportunity to post bail does not guarantee he will be released. For one thing, he must raise the necessary money. The actual amount of bail, whether $500 or $50,000, is beyond the reach of many arrested suspects. Those who cannot raise the bail themselves can turn to bondsmen and bonding agencies. For a fee, usually 10 to 20 percent of the bail, these bonding services guarantee the full amount of bail, permitting the release of those who hire them. The fee is not returnable, which means that the suspect is out of pocket whether or not he appears in court as scheduled. Only some states permit bondsmen to operate, and in those that do not the defendant is usually required to put up only 5 to 10 percent of the bail amount.

It might appear that bonding services make it easier for arrested suspects to secure their release. Indeed, this is true for some suspects. But it also happens that many people cannot raise even the bonding fee. Caleb Foote's pioneering study of bail practices in New York showed that 25 percent of all defendants failed to make bail at $500, 45 percent failed at $1,500, and 63 percent failed at $2,500.[3] Another study found that the percentage of felony suspects who could not pay bonding fees differed across the country, but in some areas it was as high as 80 to 90 percent.[4]

Those who cannot afford bail are punished for their lack of financial resources in a variety of ways. First, they are deprived of their freedom. Second, they are often placed in overcrowded and understaffed jail facilities, which provide few modest comforts, if any. Third, because they are incarcerated, they are deprived of those significant personal and social relationships they rely upon for support and emotional sustenance. Fourth, they lose some of the advantages that freedom brings when they seek legal services and prepare for the judicial proceedings ahead. Fifth, they are often forced to spend hours, days, and even months in the company of people they might normally have nothing to do with. Sixth, they are subject to a regimented daily routine that strips them of ordinary decision-making opportunities and undermines their identity. And seventh, they are deprived of privacy in dealing with personal affairs and suffer forced exposure to the personal activities of others. In sum, the jailed suspect suffers innumerable deprivations, despite the fact that he has not yet been legally declared criminal.

Bail Decision Making While some jurisdictions have predetermined limits governing the setting of bail, bail proceedings are generally characterized by on-the-spot decisions wherein considerable discretion is exercised. Police, prosecutors, and magistrates all influence bail decisions, and the amount of bail in any given case depends heavily on the factors influencing these legal authorities.

In Anglo-American procedural law, the fundamental consideration in setting bail has long been the question of nonappearance. The essential issue is whether or not the defendant will abscond once he is freed. But a judicial tradition has emerged over the years emphasizing other issues in addition to nonappearance. For example, considerable weight is traditionally given to the nature of the charges and the suspect's known criminal record.[5] Further, evidence from a recent study in England shows that bail decisions are often influenced by extralegal considerations that have no foundation in law, such as whether or not the suspect's freedom will impede further police inquiries and whether or not the prosecution feels that the accused is obviously guilty. In only 33 percent of the bail deliberations observed by the author did the prosecution mention the question of nonappearance.[6]

From a defendant's standpoint, the chances of receiving an unfavorable bail decision will tend to increase if he has a prior criminal record and if the current offense is a felony (especially one involving violence).[7] In addition, the recommendation of the prosecutor must be taken into account, for when this goes against the defendant the judge usually agrees with it. By agreeing with prosecution recommendations, the judge may hope to defuse potential criticism and can argue that others must share in the responsibility for the decision.[8] Of course, if the matter of bail is to be decided strictly on the basis of nonappearance, then the task is no simple one, and we should recognize the difficulties that magistrates face. Martin Friedland argues, "A system which requires security in advance produces an insoluble dilemma. In most cases it is impossible to pick a figure which is high enough to ensure the accused's appearance in court and yet low enough for him to raise; the two seldom, if ever, overlap."[9] On the other hand, recent evidence shows that few suspects flee or "willfully" fail to appear in court. Neither likelihood of a severe punishment nor high bond appears to have much effect on court appearances.[10]

PREVENTIVE DETENTION AND THE DANGEROUS OFFENDER

Over the years, considerable attention has been paid to the widespread European practice of refusing bail on the grounds that suspects pose a threat to the community if released. In American federal courts, preventive detention has generally been authorized when the accused is charged with a capital crime, when he is insane, or when he is an alien awaiting deportation proceedings.[11] In addition, federal judicial approval has been extended to bail denial in cases where there is a threat to witnesses or some other obstruction of justice.[12] State courts, however, have generally assumed greater leeway in the denial of bail; judicial opinion has consistently held that defendants in state courts have no automatic right to bail.

Whatever the legal and constitutional dilemmas posed by the bail issue, and there are many, judges who see fit to keep suspects in custody may do so indirectly by setting extremely high bail. In this way, the accused is typically prevented from securing his release because he is unable to raise bail. This practice is inherently discriminatory: "If the dangerous defendant can raise the bail sum, he goes free. By its nature, therefore, the system succeeds in retaining only the 'dangerous poor.' The 'dangerous rich' post bond and are released."[13]

Advocates of preventive detention are concerned that dangerous offenders will jeopardize the lives and property of members of the community. Certainly, some will, upon release, commit crimes they could not have committed if detained. Indeed, some suspects may commit crimes during the period between arrest and trial to pay off the bonding fees they have incurred in obtaining pretrial release.[14] But the crucial questions must be: Who is a dangerous suspect? and How is he identified? We are, unfortunately, far from answering these questions.

Perhaps the biggest practical difficulty lies in *crime prediction*. At the heart of the preventive-detention issue lies the anticipation that if released, dangerous suspects will in fact offend against community life and property before final disposition. Can judicial authorities predict such offenses with any degree of accuracy? Some recent evidence collected in Boston raises serious doubts about the efficacy of such prediction attempts. Using twenty-six variables to predict dangerousness, the authors found that only 5.7 percent of serious offenses could have been predicted. Further, only 0.75 percent of those arrested for violent or dangerous crimes were out on bail at the time of their arrest.[15]

Some might argue that if pretrial detention can prevent even one predatory or violent act, preventive detention serves a useful purpose. Against this view, however, is the specter of a judicial process operating on the basis of fear, speculation, and stereotypes.

Becoming a Legal Criminal

Legal confirmation of a suspect's criminality comes with his conviction in a court of law. Upon conviction, the defendant officially loses his status as a law-abiding citizen and is subject to punishment at the hands of the state. A conviction justifies the efforts of those who sought legal confirmation of guilt, most notably the police and prosecution:

> The policeman's triumph comes when the court vindicates his judgment by a conviction. . . . At any rate, a conviction reassures him of his own competence and at the same time of the worth of his job. . . . It provides for him a reassurance as to the correctness of his judgments.[16]

In America, all criminal defendants have the right to plead not guilty and to ask for trial by a jury of their peers. The trial provides the setting for the adversary proceedings that, in theory, are the heart of the Anglo-American judicial process. The trial is also the setting for review of previous actions against criminal suspects. It is the place where justice supposedly reigns; where fairness, impartiality, and due process guide men in their judgments about their fellows. As William Chambliss and Robert Seidman describe it:

It is in the courtroom, at the trial itself, that the majestic rights enshrined in the Constitution are upheld; it is there that evidence illegally obtained will be suppressed; it is there that the prosecution will be required to keep the high standard to which it is held; and it is there that the presence of counsel and judge will prevent oppression or overreaching by police or prosecution, however weak, humble, or lowly the accused may be.[17]

Fans of Perry Mason and other television counselors may be surprised to learn that *most criminal defendants never go to trial*. Instead, they plead guilty, virtually ensuring their own conviction. In fact, around 90 percent of all convictions are the result of guilty pleas.[18] This means that only about 10 percent of criminal convictions occur in the adversary setting of a public trial. What is generally touted as the cornerstone of the judicial process is, instead, little more than a faded trapping. If we insist on emphasizing the court trial as the setting of crucial decisions about guilt or innocence, and sometimes even of sentencing, then we are out of touch with the realities of the situation. To understand how criminal convictions usually come about and to understand how one becomes a legal criminal, we must focus on those pretrial phases of judicial decision making in which charges and pleas are considered.

THE DECISION TO PROSECUTE

For both defendants and police, the decision to prosecute is perhaps the most crucial in the entire criminal process. For defendants an unfavorable decision here often guarantees conviction; the only remaining question is whether something can be done to reduce the negative consequences that are likely to follow. For the police the decision to prosecute vindicates their judgment and efforts, though it may put their methods on the line. If there is no prosecution, there can be no adjudication of guilt or innocence, and certainly no official criminal punishment.

Many criminal cases that come before prosecutors are screened out at an early stage or end up being dismissed. Table 12.1 shows some recent figures from five American jurisdictions. In these cases there were more dismissals following arrests than either guilty pleas or trials.

Why do prosecutors decide not to pursue cases brought before them? Until recently only informed guesses could be made. Now, with the help of computerized information networks — most notably PROMIS, see page 493 — researchers can more accurately pinpoint the reasons behind such decisions and are able to make at least tentative geographical comparisons.

The decision not to prosecute is often made at an initial prosecution screening. Ignoring cases that are passed on to some other agency for prosecution (say, from the state to the federal level), two reasons for rejection appear most often: there are problems with the evidence and

Table 12.1 Felony attrition rates in five jurisdictions, 1977

JURISDICTION	REJECTED AT SCREENING	DROPPED OR DISMISSED AFTER FILING (%)	TOTAL ATTRITION RATE (%)
Cobb County, Georgia	18	11	29
District of Columbia	22	27	49
Salt Lake County, Utah	19	25	44
New Orleans	48	7	55
Los Angeles	40	12	52

SOURCE: Kathleen B. Brosi, *A Cross-City Comparison of Felony Case Processing* (Washington, D.C.: U.S. Government Printing Office, 1979) p. 7.

there are witness-related problems.[19] Evidence problems are most likely to involve either insufficient testimonial corroboration — willing witnesses could not substantiate the charges — or lack of physical evidence, such as stolen property or weapons. Recent comparisons across jurisdictions have found that relatively few cases are dropped because of due-process "technicalities," such as suspected violations of the rules governing police searches and seizures. One author writes: "While these issues may be substantial in terms of legal theory, they appear to have little impact on the overall flow of criminal cases after arrest. [In this study,] due process reasons accounted for only a small portion of the rejections at screening — from 1 to 9 percent."[20] When due process is an issue, it is most likely to surface in drug offense situations. The violation of due process here may well be a consequence of negative law enforcement attitudes toward drug offenders generally, coupled with the pressing need to secure physical evidence of possession or delivery.

Criminal charges may be dropped after cases have passed initial screening and after official charges have been filed. When this happens the major reasons are again either evidence- or witness-related. In many cities the failure of witnesses to appear in court or to make themselves available to the prosecution accounts for most of the dismissals and refusals to prosecute that arise after filing of charges.[21]

On the matter of witness cooperation it should be noted that designation of witnesses as "uncooperative" may be a result of prevailing offense stereotypes. That is, it may be that prosecutors associate certain offense situations with uncooperative witnesses and decide not to prosecute a given case because it fits the stereotype. An example that comes to mind is interpersonal assault. Here victims often consider the problem a personal matter, especially if it involves relatives or friends.[22] Many victims are unlikely to follow through with official complaints or appear as witnesses for that reason. Both police and prosecutors know this, and it colors their handling of assault cases. It is easy for them to ignore or drop such cases, citing lack of witness cooperation even when no attempt was actually made to establish that prospective witnesses would in fact be uncooperative if given the chance to testify.

Is there evidence of such a gap between prosecutor perceptions and witness intentions? Frank Cannavale sought to find out in a study of witness cooperation in Washington, D.C. His conclusion, carefully supported, was that "prosecutors were apparently unable to cut through to the true intentions of 23 percent or more of those they regarded as uncooperative and, therefore, recorded the existence of witness problems when these were premature judgments at best and incorrect decisions at worst."[23]

We should also recognize that the decision to prosecute is likely to be influenced by individuals and groups who are members of the larger community and are able to put pressure on the district attorney's office. In his study of prosecutors in King County, Washington, George Cole found that staff members routinely took steps to protect the district attorney from public criticism. These steps included manipulations of the bail system as well as the vigorous prosecution of certain forms of crime — for example, child molestation.[24] Needless to say, a prosecutor's charging practices can be expected to closely reflect community influences in those areas of enforcement where he is in substantial agreement with them.

NEGOTIATED JUSTICE

Since most defendants end up pleading guilty, criminal convictions are directly tied to those factors influencing decisions to enter a guilty plea. Many guilty pleas, probably most, are entered as a result of bargains, or negotiations, between the defendant, his counsel (if he has one), and the prosecution. To appreciate how the typical defendant assumes the legal identity of a criminal, let us consider the plea-bargaining process and its product, negotiated justice.

We have no way of knowing exactly what proportion of guilty pleas are entered as a result of bargains and other negotiations between relevant parties. For one thing, plea negotiations are often carried on in secrecy, and thus escape the scrutiny of those not directly involved or associated with the negotiators. In addition, when records of the negotiations are made they remain under the control of court officials and are often privileged information. Finally, the very nature of plea bargaining is such that parties to it have little to gain by making negotiations public and much to lose from it. From the defendant's standpoint, too much scrutiny might lead to a detrimental reappraisal of his legal situation. From the standpoint of the court officers, such scrutiny might bring adverse public or judicial reaction.

Confronted with these difficulties, researchers who seek an assessment of the extent of plea bargaining are forced to rely on the willingness of individual defendants, prosecutors, and defense attorneys to share with them their experiences at the bargaining table. The data thus gathered may not be representative of all jurisdictions and all types of criminal cases. Further, the accuracy of the data, and its validity, will depend in part on the accuracy and honesty of those supplying it. These are difficult conditions to appraise. Bearing all of this in mind, available evidence suggests that a majority of guilty pleas are founded in some sort of negotiation.[25]

The defendant may seek a number of bargains. Guilty pleas may be entered in exchange for a reduced charge; in exchange for a promise of leniency in sentencing; in exchange for concurrent consideration of multiple charges — that is, the defendant serves one sentence for a number of different crimes; or in exchange for dropped charges — that is, the defendant pleads guilty to one offense (usually the major one) and other charges are dropped.[26]

In addition to these bargains, a defendant might exchange a guilty plea for release on bail, or in order to avoid some future unpleasantness in his dealings with the law.[27] One prosecutor is quoted as saying:

> Defendants who are wanted in some other state like Arkansas or Louisiana, where prison conditions are known by them to be punitive, are very amenable to pleading guilty here [in Kansas]. When a defendant is picked up on a charge here and there is a hold order for Arkansas, I tell him: "Well, you can have a trial here or you can plead [guilty] here. Then again, maybe I'll just turn you over to Arkansas and forget the charges here." Invariably, he will decide to plead to the charges here in hope that he will not later be returned to Arkansas.[28]

Finally, there is a type of bargain that Arnold Enker calls a "tacit bargain."[29] Though no explicit negotiation is involved, defendants may plead guilty because they are aware that established court practices show leniency to those who plead guilty. Armed with this knowledge, they act as if a bargain had been struck. And considerable evidence from both America and abroad shows that it is quite common for judges to so "reward" those who plead guilty. Indeed, interviews conducted with both judges and prosecutors show that a majority expect defendants who plead guilty to receive lighter sentences. Most also feel that this is the way things *should* be.[30]

Apart from these potential advantages to pleading guilty, other considerations may influence a defendant's decision in this matter. These additional influences may surface whether or not a negotiation has been or can be entered into. Some defendants may be loath to bring their troubles to the attention of the public or friends and acquaintances. If they can avoid a trial they can usually avoid unwanted publicity. Other defendants may be aware that they undertake considerable risks in a trial with or without a jury.[31] The outcome of a trial is influenced by a host of factors, most beyond the defendant's control. Why suffer the uncertainties and risks of trial when a guilty plea, particularly if negotiated, leaves matters unaffected by courtroom drama and the vagaries of trial justice? For yet other defendants, a speedy resolution of their current difficulties can appear particularly attractive. If this can be accomplished with a guilty plea, why drag things out?

All of these advantages, pressures, and considerations are well known to prosecutors, judges, and others with roles in the judicial process. Those with the power to deal can muster an impressive array of threats and incentives to bring to bear on the suspect. If the stick doesn't work, the carrot might.

One particularly effective method prosecutors use to drive home the advantages of a guilty plea is found in the case of multiple charges. Where felony offenses are concerned, the prosecution commonly seeks a multiple-count indictment. If convicted on all counts, the defendant could well spend the rest of his days in the penitentiary. At the least, he will have a long conviction record. Here is an example of how a multiple-count indictment might read. The major charge is armed robbery; the others are lesser offenses:

Count 1. Robbery, 1st degree
Count 2. Assault, 2nd degree
Count 3. Assault, 3rd degree
Count 4. Grand larceny
Count 5. Carrying a dangerous weapon
Count 6. Petit larceny[32]

Clearly, the prosecutor is in a strong position if he can offer a defendant a means to escape charges on all six counts. In most cases, any such offer is difficult to refuse.

THE PROSECUTION AND THE GUILTY PLEA

The foregoing may have left the impression that prosecutors look with favor on guilty pleas and actually encourage negotiations to bring them about. Generally speaking, this is indeed the case. Some prosecutors even have handbooks available to guide their assistants in the bargaining process.[33]

Prosecutors, Abraham Blumberg suggests, are interested in obtaining guilty pleas and will seek negotiated pleas in preference to adversary proceedings. For one thing, he notes, "There is the almost impossible task of going through the elaborate procedures of a court trial for each case. The personnel and other resources of the prosecutor's office simply could not carry such an impossible burden."[34] Full court calendars put the prosecutor under considerable pressure to divert cases from the courtroom.[35]

Prosecutors are also faced with other pressures, many of which stem from the character of the judicial enterprise itself. Having but one role in an organized, goal-oriented complex of activities, the prosecution is subject to organizational demands beyond questions of time and resources. One such demand is *productivity*. As with the police, the prosecution is expected to demonstrate that its members are doing what they are paid to do, and such a demonstration requires something concrete. Convictions are concrete; a guilty plea is the easiest route to a conviction. Another organizational demand is *inter-role reciprocity*. No organization lasts long if its members act in such a way that mutual role obligations and expectations are undermined. The division of labor characterizing law enforcement and judicial administration necessitates that the actors meet the demands of interdependency. The police and prosecution, for instance, recognize their mutual dependency. If the police do not produce good busts, and repeatedly at that, the prosecutor's job is that much more difficult. By the same token, if the prosecution ties up the police in unnecessary court trials, the police job is more difficult. Police and prosecutors cooperate in numerous ways, not the least of which are in the areas of charges and pleas.

In his relationship with the world outside organized law enforcement, the prosecutor is subject to additional pressures. We have to remember that individuals and groups in the larger society have a vested interest in the judicial process. When this interest is centered on convictions, pressures to negotiate a plea may be felt by the prosecution. Such pressures might come, for example, from the victim of a crime. A desire for "satisfaction" may find expression in the badgering of the prosecutor handling the case. If the victim is an important member of the community, this may act as an added incentive for the prosecution to seek conviction via a negotiated plea. Other pressures may come from local politicians, area businessmen, or representatives of the news media who see in convictions evidence that community law enforcement is working.[36]

For all these reasons, negotiated guilty pleas look particularly attractive to the prosecution. But this does not mean that plea negotiations are inevitably devoid of any altruistic motivation. Indeed, some have argued that plea bargaining may provide an opportunity to humanize the judicial process, to make it more responsive to individual differences, needs, and circumstances.[37] An essential concern, however, is whether a prosecutor's decision to seek a guilty plea comes from a desire to achieve just and fair outcomes in a just and fair manner or from routinized organizational and extrajudicial pressures with little, if any, bearing on considerations of justice.

THE DEFENSE AND BARGAINED JUSTICE

Like prosecutors, defense attorneys actively seek guilty pleas. Indeed, they are often the first to suggest that their client plead guilty, and in many cases convince defendants to change their original not guilty plea to guilty.[38] Though a guilty plea inevitably means his client's criminal conviction, the defense attorney will argue that it is his professional obligation to do the best for his client, and if this is to be accomplished by "copping a plea," then so be it. The plea bargain is attractive, if not obligatory, when his client is guilty and the case against him strong enough to produce a conviction at trial. If a lighter sentence can be achieved through negotiation, then this is the route a responsible defense attorney is bound to take.

Yet this is not all of it. There are decided advantages to be gained from plea bargaining for the lawyer himself. In order to understand this, let us consider the practice of criminal law in America.

Criminal law is but one branch of law, and the attorneys who regularly work in this area make up only a small portion of the total number of lawyers in America. In fact, less than 20 percent of American lawyers specialize in or regularly handle criminal cases.[39] Those that do are generally ill prepared for what they will encounter when they begin their practice: according to one author, "most law students get only a cursory course in criminal law."[40] A study of New York City lawyers showed that those who regularly handle criminal cases are generally at the bottom of the attorneys' pecking order and are typically less well trained, less competent, and less likely to hold closely to established ethical standards when compared with noncriminal lawyers.[41] Many lawyers are reluctant to enter criminal work because it usually carries neither prestige nor substantial economic rewards. And if they are in private practice, they are reluctant to take time away from more prestigious and rewarding legal services. If and when they are drawn into the arena of criminal law, it is often because they are offered fees they find hard to refuse, because they have no choice (sometimes the case when indigent defendants are involved), or because the case is one that promises celebrity status for the lawyer handling it.[42]

The bulk of criminal cases are likely to be handled by one of two principal types of defense counsel: the *public defender* or the so-called *lawyer,* or *courthouse, regular.* The first works for the state and is charged with the defense of those who cannot afford a defense attorney of their own choosing. The latter is in private practice and molds his workday around the routine business of the police and courts. The lawyer regulars

are highly visible in the major urban centers of the nation; their offices — at times shared with bondsmen — line the backstreets near courthouses. They are also visible politically, with clubhouse ties reaching into judicial chambers and the prosecutor's office. The regulars make no effort to conceal their dependence upon police, bondsmen, jail personnel, as well as bailiffs, stenographers, prosecutors, and judges.[43]

The guilty plea is appealing to the typical defense counsel for various compelling reasons. For one thing, he is usually subject to many of the

The Halls of Justice or justice in the halls? For most defendants, the outcome is decided before they enter the courtroom.

same organizational demands and pressures that influence the prosecution. Whether public defender or private lawyer, the defense counsel's career is dependent on good relations with others in the immediate judicial system and those who are in a position to affect it. If he expects to stay in business he cannot afford to antagonize those he works with and depends on for information, support, and career advancement. Court organization is typically grounded, Blumberg asserts, in "pragmatic values, bureaucratic priorities, and administrative instruments" favoring maximum production, and defendants are manipulated to serve the professional interests of those within the organization.[44] According to another author:

> Legal officials are apt to follow the line of least resistance; to devise policies and practices which hold the greatest promise of rewarding the legal agencies and officials involved without undue organizational stress and strain.[45]

Those defense attorneys caught up in the ritual and routine of judicial behavior must follow the rules of the game or risk losing their insider status and the professional rewards that reciprocal obligations bring about. If they persist in bucking the system, sanctions will be applied. These may take various forms but will be most severe when they result in an attorney's exclusion from information and those conferences and deliberations that bear upon his role as defense counsel. If the recalcitrant attorney is employed by the state as a public defender, he can be fired or given such a hard time that resignation is about the only option left him. Chambliss and Seidman give the following account of a public defender who "took his position seriously," and sought adversary proceedings for his clients:

> Instead of pleading practically everybody guilty (as his predecessor had done), he began to try a relatively high proportion of his cases. The docket in the local trial court immediately slowed up. Out of three judges assigned to that particular bench, one began to spend all his time on criminal trials instead of a third of that time. . . . After about six months, this young Public Defender received a peremptory order to come to the state capitol to see the Chief Justice. The Chief Justice read him the riot act in terms of the need to avoid "frivolous" trials and the like, warning him of the necessity of "cooperating" with the prosecution and the judges. The Chief Justice was successful; the Public Defender resigned in disgust.[46]

There are obvious economic advantages to all of this. Playing the bargaining game enhances job security and furthers opportunities for getting ahead. In his King County, Washington, study, George Cole found that the criminal attorney's saleable product is *influence* rather than technical proficiency in the law: "Respondents hold the belief that clients are attracted partially on the basis of the attorney's reputation as a fixer, or as a shrewd bargainer."[47] In addition, private criminal lawyers don't make money in court but in their offices, on the phone, or in the offices of the prosecutor, where bargains are struck. Time is money, and time spent in court is the least profitable. The more clients you can handle in a given day, the more money you can make and the wider your contacts become.

JUDGES AND BARGAINED JUSTICE

Judges are by no means outsiders to the processes resulting in negotiated justice. Indeed, most authors agree that judges quite often take an active part in the bargaining. Newman provides numerous illustrations of judiciary involvement in bargained justice, although the extent of that involvement may vary according to the character of the bargain itself (whether it is for charge reduction or sentence leniency) and the jurisdiction in which the court operates.[48] For its part, the U.S. Supreme Court has consistently supported plea bargaining as an important element in American criminal procedure (see box on page 404).

It should come as no surprise that judges are routinely involved in bargained justice. After all, they, with the prosecution and defense, are actors in the same play. What is more, judges are subject to direct pressures from outside the immediate court organization. Their continued appointment or reelection depends on how well the court's business flows. When things get bogged down pressure from the media, their political bosses, and the higher judiciary can weigh heavily on their shoulders. Like the roles of prosecutor and defense attorney, the judge's role in the judicial process often leads him away from due process and toward an administration of the law best characterized as a cooperative endeavor aimed at the speedy, predictable confirmation of a suspect's criminal status.

THE FUTURE OF BARGAINED JUSTICE

Plea bargaining is pervasive and most people would probably laugh at the suggestion that its days are numbered — and they would probably be right. Yet in recent years more and more criticism has been heard about plea bargaining, both inside and outside legal circles. In one recent criminal justice text sixteen different criticisms are listed, and one could probably find more. The author of that text concludes:

> There is something deeply disturbing about a criminal justice system in which lawyers avoid the due process model like the plague, in which the outcome of cases depends on the personal interests and administrative convenience of the practitioners, and in which sentences are unrelated to the crimes committed or to the defendant's genuine correctional needs.[49]

There are signs, however, that some of the conventional wisdom about plea bargaining may have been off base. On the heels of increasing criticism of the system, some jurisdictions moved to abolish plea bargaining. Alaska was one of the first, with a complete ban in 1975. Other jurisdictions have adopted partial restrictions; for example, banning its use in cases involving career criminals, repeaters, and serious violators, or in cases involving specific heinous crimes such as rape or the killing of law enforcement personnel.

It appears that the effects of reduced bargaining were not exactly as expected, at least in Alaska. After the prohibition went into effect the number of court trials remained small, the court docket did not bog down (actually, cases were being processed faster than before), and the proportion of defendants pleading guilty remained pretty much the same as before the ban. If these findings were unexpected, so were the ones dealing with the severity of sentences. True, sentences for some classes of offenders did increase drastically — 237 percent for drug offenses; 117 percent for fraud. But in the case of burglary, larceny, and receiving stolen property, sentences actually *declined* for experienced, older offenders charged with more serious offenses and *increased* for young first offenders whose charges were the least serious in this group. Furthermore, the sentences given violent offenders remained basically unchanged.[50]

The full study has not been released as this text goes to press. These findings nevertheless suggest caution in anticipating the consequences of reduced plea bargaining. Certainly, it appears from the Alaska experience that the response of the judicial system cannot be taken for granted. Even so, doubts and cautions should not prevent the contemplation and testing of alternatives to the present system, however far-fetched they might seem. One author has recently demanded: "What is so inconceivable about a process which includes a trial (perhaps a shorter and neater trial) for *every* defendant?"[51] One thing a full return to the adversary system might promote is a redefinition by participants of the purpose of their activity. Instead of productivity, efficiency, and organizational self-perpetuation, the goals might bear some resemblance to the ideals of justice. Perhaps, too, the judicial process would look less like a con game to the many defendants whose fortunes are currently decided after a five-minute discussion with a public defender in some courthouse hallway or bullpen.[52] Jonathan Casper has expressed well the view held by many defendants — and undoubtedly many victims, too:

> The system as it operates in practice is seen by defendants in this study as an example of their life on the street. Outcomes do not seem to be determined by principles or careful consideration of persons, but by hustling, conning, manipulation, luck, fortitude, waiting them out, and the like. . . .
>
> How well you do in this world depends upon what you've got and how well you use it. The criminal justice system, like the streets, is a game of resource exploitation. The defendant typically has little in the way of resources and doesn't win. He can, though, with luck and skill, lose less than he might. In this way . . . the system has no real moral component in the eyes of the defendant. It is an extension of life on the street and the other participants — the police, defense attorney, the prosecutor, the judge — are themselves playing a game that is perceived as existing on the same moral level as that of the defendant.[53]

Sentencing

All offenders who are convicted of a crime face sentencing. In this section we shall look at the behavior of judges and at the constraints within which they operate. But a word of caution is necessary. Although, officially, it is the magistrate or judge who decides what sentence the convicted criminal must serve, in reality it is often the prosecutor who largely determines the sentence. This is so because he is in control of the charges that the defendant can be convicted of. A suspect who is arrested for armed robbery may, after plea negotiations, be formally charged with some other, lesser, offense. In this way the prosecutor has reduced the possible sentence. Furthermore, although judges are not bound to accept plea bargains that have been struck between defense and prosecution, they usually do, thus bowing once more to prosecutorial discretion.

SENTENCING DISPARITIES

The sentences handed down by judges for similar offenses are by no means uniform throughout the country, nor are they uniform within a single jurisdiction. There is, in short, considerable sentencing disparity in America.

The extent of the problem is only now being fully documented, though it has been recognized for years. One recent study of judges in New York, Connecticut, and Vermont (the U.S. Court of Appeals for the Second Circuit) used actual presentence reports by probation officers (see pages 407–410) and asked each judge to assign a sentence in twenty different cases. The range of sentences among the fifty judges interviewed was considerable, and the sentences for identical cases could not be predicted.[54] In a similar study, forty-seven Virginia judges were given identical descriptions of five criminal cases. They were asked to determine a verdict and assign a sentence as if the situation were real. There were high rates of agreement on the verdicts but wide variation in the sentences.[55] Using different methods, other studies have produced similar results.[56]

Sentencing disparities among judges are to be expected where there is an emphasis on individualized justice and where appropriately supportive sentencing structures are in force. For many years this has been true of most American jurisdictions. Consider the following eight sentencing structures for prison terms found around the country; all provide the judge with sentencing discretion:

1. Both maximum terms and minimum terms set by court within upper and lower limits set by law
2. Both maximum and minimum fixed by court (within legal limits), with minimum not to exceed some portion of the maximum
3. Maximum (within legal limits) set by court, minimum by law

4. Maximum fixed by law, minimum by court
5. Maximum and minimum set by law for each offense
6. Maximum set by law, minimum by parole board
7. Maximum fixed by court, no minimum
8. Minimum fixed by law, maximum by parole board[57]

Generally, then, judges do have some choice between different sentencing options for most crimes in most jurisdictions.

PRESENTENCE INVESTIGATIONS AND REPORTS

In both Europe and America, more and more attention is being given to the use of presentence investigations as an aid to sentencing. While rarely used in dealing with misdemeanants, presentence reports are intended to help the judge choose a sentence more appropriate to the particular case. In some states, a presentence investigation is mandatory; in others it is available at the request of the judge.

A presentence report contains information about the convicted offender considered relevant in guiding the judge toward an appropriate sentence, given the statutory framework for such decisions. The information is usually collected by probation officers or other trained social workers employed by the state. What is contained in the report will depend in part on the jurisdiction, in part on administrative policies, and in part on the experience, talents, hard work, competence, and perspectives of the investigators. "In theory [the report] is a neutral document, its purpose being neither adverse nor favorable to the sentencing fate of the defendant."[58] It is intended to provide accurate and relevant information on those aspects of an offender's personal and family history — police record, prior convictions, employment history, and family situation — that are thought to make a difference when it comes to sentencing alternatives.

In practice, presentence reports may be neither neutral and accurate nor filled with only relevant information. According to one recent study, reports often contain misinformation, prejudicial statements, and "facts" based on hearsay and rumor. Here are some illustrations, taken from presentence reports:

1. "While [the defendant] apparently never engaged in any serious criminal conduct before, and while he has never shown any tendency to use violence, it is rumored in the factory, and evidently widely believed, that about two years ago he murdered his boss's wife."
2. "His wife reports that he is given to murderous rages."
3. "In my opinion [as an experienced, graduate-trained probation and parole agent], he is the type of person who, if not checked soon, will kill somebody someday."
4. "There is a broad, deep base of sexual psychopathy in this boy. His offense may technically be burglary but he is basically a sex deviate."

5. "He is a loser, plain and simple. He is sexually inadequate, vocationally inadequate, and mentally inadequate. He has failed in everything — school, jobs, military service, with his family, and with his wife. He has even failed as a crook. There is absolutely no reason to think he can make it on probation and probably prison won't help him much. The only thing I can recommend is incarceration for as long as possible and then hope for the best."[59]

These selections illustrate the kinds of questionable information not uncommonly found in presentence reports. There is no reason to believe that all investigators go well beyond factual, objective, and relevant information. However, many probably do, for three reasons. First, many jurisdictions and administrative policies require or encourage investigators to recount feelings and attitudes, either their own or other people's, and to present opinions and recommendations.[60] Second, those who write the reports sooner or later look upon themselves as experts, professionals whose opinions are learned and should be taken seriously. Third, investigators are subject to organizational pressures; they are dependent on others, both in and out of the immediate court organization, and try to avoid rocking the boat. If the police, for example, are particularly anxious for a certain disposition, investigators may feel obliged to tilt their reports in the appropriate direction. Remember, participants in the judicial process work together, not in opposition.

Ralph Blankenship provides an intriguing analysis of how professionals in the field of social control attach special meanings to language used in the case records that accompany individuals throughout their official careers as deviants.[61] Presentence reports, probation records, prison records, and mental hospital records are put together by professionals who share language "registers," words and phrases having special meaning for them. When these professionals compile case records, they present an image of the subject that fits their perception of the criminal, psychotic, or delinquent reality: "the professional does not use his register to describe, but as a means of constructing his social reality."[62] Blankenship points out how direct quotes from labeled deviants give the appearance of letting the deviant tell his own story, but to those in the know they serve to discredit the story at the same time. What gets in, in the way of direct quotes is, of course, under the control of the person constructing the report.

Confidentiality For many years, presentence reports were for the judge's eyes only. The defendant or counsel were excluded from access to them. While the situation has changed somewhat in recent years, many jurisdictions retain the traditional approach.

The issue of confidentiality has sparked considerable debate, with little chance that it will be resolved one way or the other in the near future. On one side are those who claim that disclosure will invite retaliation by the defendant, will cause information sources to dry up, and will produce prolonged litigation as the defense seeks to challenge and cross-examine those who have collected or supplied the contents of the report. On the other are those who believe that any information to be used in sentence decision making must be subject to defense scrutiny, that confidentiality promotes backroom justice, and that the defendant must be assured of impartial and fair treatment by the state.[63]

Impact of Reports on Sentencing   All this matters little if presentence reports have no impact on actual sentences handed down. At least, it matters little from a pragmatic standpoint, though fundamental ethical and constitutional issues are involved, which do matter if justice is to be met. The question is, then, are judges influenced by presentence reports, and if so, to what extent?

Data dealing with the impact of presentence reports provide little basis for conclusive answers. Some studies, for example, show that presentence reports are influential in the sentencing process. Thus Carter and Wilkins found in their study in California that in all courts investigated, judges and probation officials were in broad agreement on major sentencing criteria and judges accepted 86 percent of investigators' recommendations.[64] Recent studies in England have found similar evidence of strong correlations between sentencing recommendations and actual sentences.[65]

On the other hand, Hogarth found evidence to suggest that the connection between presentence reports and sentencing decisions is by no means clear. Canadian magistrates, he found, are likely to use reports and other sources of information in a selective manner, when it is consistent with their own philosophy, attitudes, and preconceptions about the individual case.[66] As a specific source of information, however, presentence reports tended to be requested and used when judges already considered a case difficult, when they saw themselves as likely to give sentences out of keeping with their normal practice with respect to the offense involved. Hogarth speculates that the presentence report gives a judge the opportunity to justify a decision already made, rather than direct him in coming to his decision.[67]

Hogarth observes an important difference in the use and impact of presentence reports. He found that urban magistrates tended to react negatively to probation officer recommendations, while rural judges appeared more likely to accept the reports. He explains the difference by referring to the rural judge's easier work load, greater self-esteem and community status, greater informality, less punitive orientation, and to the closer ties between court and probation services in rural areas. In summing up the value of presentence reports, Hogarth concludes:

> . . . if the presentence report is to have the impact on sentencing that was originally intended, and indeed often assumed, certain favourable conditions for its proper use must exist. Magistrates must have the time to read reports carefully. They must also have the opportunity, when the need arises, to

discuss their contents informally with probation officers. Most important, they must have a set of attitudes and beliefs which are consistent with the rationale underlying the use of the presentence report, namely, the individualization of justice.[68]

EXTRALEGAL FACTORS IN SENTENCING

The existence of sentencing disparities would probably not be of so much concern were it not for the fact that much of the variation is thought to be the result of the judge's subjective beliefs, perceptions, fears, and attitudes rather than of objective features of the offense and offender as recognized in law. It appears that the widely divergent sentences imposed for essentially the same crime cannot be adequately accounted for by differences in the law, in the circumstances of the offense, or in the criminality of the offender. This state of affairs is found in other countries, too. What, then, are some of the extralegal factors thought to influence the sentencing decisions of judges?

Race and Class   Some weighty evidence supports the contention that sentencing decisions are influenced by social class and race. Reviewing years of American research, Wolfgang and Cohen find that "blacks usually receive longer prison terms than whites for most criminal offenses."[69] In his study of Norwegian conscientious objectors, Aubert found that unskilled workers were far more likely to be convicted, hence punished, than those with higher socioeconomic status.[70] Sellin found much evidence of racial bias in American sentencing practices.[71] In England, Chapman found numerous examples of clearly preferential treatment in the case of middle-class offenders,[72] whereas Hood found that middle-class judges gave more punitive sentences than those with working-class backgrounds.[73]

In many cases these differences appear to hold for offenses in general as well as for specific crimes. The impact of race and class has also been found in the sentences given juvenile offenders. In one study the records of 9,601 juvenile court dispositions in Philadelphia were analyzed. It was discovered that even when legal variables such as severity of offense and prior record were taken into account, blacks were more likely than whites to be prosecuted and institutionalized, and lower socioeconomic offenders were more severely penalized than others.[74]

In a study of early releases from prison under a "shock probation" program in Ohio,* Peterson and Friday found race to be the most important factor in determining releases in certain situations. For example, when the probation department had recommended against early release, whites were twice as likely as blacks to be released, even after controlling for a variety of legal variables.[75]

---

*Shock probation allows an incarcerated offender to appeal to the court of his conviction for early release from prison as a form of probation. He must appeal within sixty days of his original sentencing date.

Although the bulk of research seems to favor race and class as influences in sentencing, at least two studies have found contrary evidence. In his widely cited investigation, Green looked at the sentencing practices of twenty-one Philadelphia judges during the 1950s. After analyzing 1,437 sentences, he concluded that sentencing disparities, while considerable, were not significantly the result of extralegal factors. Instead, they were tied to variations in the nature of the offense charged, the number of charges, and the offender's prior record. Even though he found that whites were favored over blacks, the younger over the older offender, and females over males, Green argued that these differences were primarily due to differences in the pattern of criminality among the offenders.[76]

In their study of 10,488 defendants in South Carolina, North Carolina, and Florida during the late 1960s and early 1970s, Chiricos and Waldo found that "socioeconomic status of convicted criminal offenders is unrelated to the severity of the state's official sanction, as reflected in the length of prison terms assigned by the court."[77] The authors recognize a difficulty with their research, however. The distribution of offender socioeconomic status (SES) is heavily skewed toward the lower end of the status scale — only 3.4 percent had scores higher than 70 on a 100-point scale. As a result, it is debatable whether SES varies sufficiently to permit a test of the relationship between status differences and variations in sentencing. The authors try to resolve the problem, but it remains a serious drawback to the research.[78]

The evidence on status discrimination in sentencing permits no firm conclusions. Yet it is my view that even if there were incontestable evidence against the conventional wisdom that there is discrimination, the fact is that the penalties assigned by law to predominantly lower-class crimes (robbery, burglary, assault, heroin pushing) are, in general, higher than those for predominantly upper-class crime (corporate fraud, misrepresentation in advertising, restraint of trade, environmental crimes). This indicates built-in bias against lower-class offenders. True, penalties on the books are one thing and actual sentences another; still, this condition makes it probable that lower-class offenders will receive harsher penalties than higher-class criminals, even if the crimes are similar in consequence, or worse, even if occupational crimes have more serious consequences.

It should be borne in mind that evidence of status disparities in penalties does not prove that judges knowingly and intentionally favor one status group over another. Furthermore, we cannot fairly separate the judge from the broader sociocultural milieu in which he or she lives and works. We hardly encourage judicial equality when we allow some segments of society preferential consideration and opportunities while others are socially, economically, and politically disadvantaged. Nagel rightly argues: "As a basic and general matter . . . it should be pointed out that there would probably be no criminal procedure disparities if the opposed [status] groups did not exist or if the groups were not given differential treatment in society in general.''[79]

Community Characteristics   A person's attitudes and beliefs are shaped by a variety of influences. Some of the more important ones derive from the immediate social environment in which the person lives and works. Studies of judicial sentencing behavior bear this out. Almost all such studies show that it makes a great deal of difference where a judge lives and works. Hood found that judges in rural, or small town, communities were more inclined to sentence offenders to prison, this sentencing policy apparently fitting in well with community sentiments and the ''peaceful'' life-style of rural communities.[80] Emile Durkheim argued long ago that deviance stands out like a sore thumb in small, homogeneous, tradition-bound communities, and the collective sentiments that it threatens require immediate and forceful reaffirmation:

> We have only to note what happens, particularly in a small town, when some moral scandal has just been committed. They stop each other on the street, they visit each other, they seek to come together to talk of the event and wax indignant in common. . . .
>
> It is necessary that [solidarity] be affirmed at the very moment that it is contradicted, and the only means of affirming it is to express the unanimous aversion which crime continues to inspire, by an authentic act which can consist only in suffering inflicted upon the agent.[81]

Further evidence on the impact of community characteristics on sentencing suggests that the relationship is more complex than Hood's findings and Durkheim's interpretation would lead us to believe. Indeed, some evidence shows that, contrary to Hood's conclusion, sentencing in rural areas is less, not more, severe than that found in urban areas.[82] But Nagel found that sentences in rural areas are not less punitive for *all* offenses — rural courts were less punitive in assault cases but more so than urban and northern courts in cases involving larceny.[83]

The different authors do agree, however, that, whatever their direction, community characteristics cannot be ignored as influences on the sentencing behavior of judges. Those who pass sentence on others must live and work in a social setting that has the potential to be supportive or hostile. Since most judges in this country are appointed or elected in a decidedly political atmosphere, they cannot afford to antagonize those who have provided them with their jobs. Although, as Hogarth shows, some judges are able to isolate themselves from public opinion and pressures from different quarters, most probably cannot or find it unrewarding to do so. In this respect, judges are little different from other participants in the judicial process.

It is Hogarth's view that sentencing behavior largely boils down to a judge's particular judicial attitudes and penal philosophies. How a judge defines his role, what he sees as the purpose of punishment, how he perceives the various social and legal constraints to which he is subjected, how he views the relative merits of different sentencing options, all these subjective elements are brought to his sentencing decisions. Where we allow wide judicial discretion we can expect to find more room for the impact of attitude and philosophy. Within the boundaries of legal constraint, judges will attempt to organize their sentencing behavior in congruence with their perceptions of legal, situational, and social realities.[84]

CURBING JUDICIAL DISCRETION

No one argues that sentencing is easy or expects judges to behave like robots. Judges are human, and there is nothing that adequately prepares them for the awesome responsibility of deciding the fate of those found guilty of crimes. Whereas most experts acknowledge the need for some judicial discretion, they nevertheless support efforts to curtail it in the hope of reducing sentencing disparities and excesses.

Directed mostly toward the sentencing of felony offenders, whose crimes carry statutory prison terms of more than a year, these efforts have resulted in a variety of sentencing reforms. In some states juries are empowered to decide sentences; in others a panel of judges (often called a "sentencing council") is formed to consider penalties; in yet others a sentencing board, composed of lawyers, social workers, psychiatrists, and others with professional interest in the legal process, meets to decide sentences. The value of the last two methods lies mainly in the opportunities they provide for sharing views, philosophies, and knowledge about sentencing, thereby promoting greater uniformity than is found when judges act individually.

Sentencing Guidelines One promising reform consists of providing judges with guidelines based on a jurisdiction's actual sentencing practices so as to give structure to the individual exercise of discretion. Leslie Wilkins favors this approach and has devised reference tables that can be used to determine the average, or model, sentence given by area judges in cases of similar offense and offender circumstances (see table 12.2).[85]

Using information about the seriousness of the offense and the prior record and "social stability" of the offender, scores for offense and offender can be determined according to a prearranged formula. To find the model sentence for any particular combination of offense/offender scores, the judge simply finds the cell that lines up with his two scores in the table. Suppose an offender in Colorado has committed a Class 4 felony (say, a robbery) and is given an offense score of 6 and an offender score of 10. What would be the model sentence?

Wilkins considers the plan to be a middle course between the current lack of consistent policy and the much more restrictive system of mandatory flat sentencing described below. The model, or guideline, sentence

Table 12.2 Sentencing guidelines, felony 4, Denver

		OFFENDER SCORE				
		−1 −7	0 2	3 8	9 12	13+
OFFENSE SCORE	10–12	Indet. Min. 4–5 year max.	Indet. Min 8–10 year max.	Indet. Min. 8–10 year max.	Indet. Min. 8–10 year max.	Indet. Min. 8–10 year max.
	8–9	Out	3–5 month work project	Indet. Min. 3–4 year max.	Indet. Min. 8–10 year max.	Indet. Min. 8–10 year max.
	6–7	Out	Out	Indet. Min. 3–4 year max.	Indet. Min. 6–8 year max.	Indet. Min. 8–10 year max.
	3–5	Out	Out	Out	Indet. Min. 4–5 year max.	Indet. Min. 4–5 year max.
	1–2	Out	Out	Out	Out	Indet. Min. 3–4 year max.

SOURCE: Leslie T. Wilkins, Jack M. Kress, Don M. Gottfredson, Joseph C. Calpin, and Arthur M. Gelman, *Sentencing Guidelines: Structuring Judicial Discretion* (Washington, D.C., U.S. Government Printing Office, 1978), p. xv.

Note: Colorado uses a penal code that contains five levels of felonies (with Felony 1 being the most serious and Felony 5 the least serious) and three levels of misdemeanors. Typical crimes that fall within the Felony 4 category are manslaughter, robbery, and second degree burglary. The statutory designated maximum incarcerative sentence for a Felony 4 offense is 10 years. No minimum period of confinement is to be set by the court. The term "out" refers to a nonincarcerative type of sentence such as probation, deferred judgment, or deferred prosecution.

is to be considered advisory, but the judge is required to give written reasons if he decides to go outside the guidelines in a particular case. Wilkins and his coauthors see the plan "as a means to guide and structure — not eliminate — judicial discretion, so as to aid judges in reaching a fair and equitable sentencing decision."[86]

Determinate Sentencing Statutory changes in favor of determinate sentencing (sometimes called "flat" or "fixed-term" sentencing) have been one of the more notable products of concern over sentencing practices. The first state to enact fixed-term sentencing was Maine, in 1975. California, Illinois, Indiana, New Mexico, and Washington (in its 1977 juvenile code) soon followed suit.[87]

Determinate sentencing is advocated in many quarters as a solution to unfair (that is, excessively lenient or harsh) and disparate sentencing. It is supposed to virtually eliminate judicial discretion, but in some cases does so only *after* the judge has decided on a particular *type* of penalty (usually imprisonment). In other words, a judge is free to decide whether or not an offender should receive probation or some other penalty, but once the judge decides on prison, the law sets the term of imprisonment. The defendant serves a specified term with time off for good behavior; however, parole is abolished.

Slightly different is the *mandatory* sentencing system. Here imprisonment is *required* for certain offenses, usually those involving armed, violent, repeat, or drug offenders. Alabama, Colorado, Mississippi, North Carolina, Tennessee, and Virginia all have instituted some form of mandatory sentencing. Maine and Illinois have combined mandatory and fixed-term sentencing. Other states have retained combinations of mandatory and indeterminate sentencing or have made sentences fixed-term but not mandatory.[88]

As with any reform, this approach to sentencing has its critics. Some claim that discretion is not really curbed but is simply shifted from the judge to the prosecutor. Indeed, the California determinate-sentencing laws have been called a plea-bargainer's paradise, for they provide prosecutors with all kinds of leverage in securing guilty pleas.[89] Rather than receiving the sentences intended by the reformers, offenders escape them through the bargaining process. In addition, some critics argue that the mandatory sentences are uniformly too high and, despite rhetoric to the contrary, will be avoided by prosecutors and judges because correctional resources are inadequate to handle the influx of new prisoners.[90]

A recent study of the Indiana experience with determinate sentencing is instructive.[91] The new 1977 penal code provides for certain specific terms of imprisonment for seven classes of offense, with enhancement for aggravation (e.g., use of a weapon or brutality) and reduction for mitigation (e.g., victim precipitation). Under the code, for example, the maximum possible sentence for a Class A felony such as armed robbery or forcible rape would be thirty years *plus* twenty years in enhancement for aggravation; the minimum would be thirty years *minus* ten years in mitigation. Once in prison, the offender would be able to build up credit toward his future release in the form of "good time," thus reducing his actual time served.

The authors of the study point out that the code increases sentencing discretion in two ways. First, the enhancement and mitigation rules, coupled with other features of the code, greatly extend the bargaining flexibility of prosecutors who can play the carrot-and-stick game while pressuring for a plea. Under this system a lesser charge or fewer elements of aggravation add up to years off the sentence. Second, the use of credit time as the only way a sentence can be reduced once it is being served gives sentencing discretion to prison authorities. "Thus, a great deal of effective control over the inmate's sentence has been placed directly in the hands of the correctional officer who watches over him."[92]

"In fact," the authors go on, "that control has been formalized by the new law, and, even assuming the best intentions on the part of all concerned, the result may be a more repressive atmosphere for inmates."[93] Not only that, the authors show what could happen to first offenders under the new code as compared with the old. Even assuming the offenders had earned all the available credit time, they would still end up serving an estimated 47.4 percent *more* prison time if sentenced under the new penal code. In the case of some offenses the percentage difference is more, in others less. In two cases — negligent homicide and check forgery — offenders would serve less time under the new system.

The authors' own conclusion best summarizes the study. Although the evidence may look different in other jurisdictions, the case in favor of determinate sentencing is probably not helped, and we should probably be extremely cautious in advocating wholesale changes in the law, as some have done. For all its well-documented drawbacks, the indeterminate sentencing system, with its emphasis on judicial discretion and parole, may not have been improved upon:

> The new Indiana Penal Code provides such wide discretion, coupled with untenably heavy penalties, that a most likely result will be the creation and solidification of a formal system of decisions and rules that barely conceals a low-visibility, busy, and pragmatic system of informal decisions regulating the actual sentence, largely in the control of prosecutors, judges, and correctional officials. The new sentencing scheme may come to bear a strange resemblance to what reformers hoped to eliminate.[94]

References

1. Kathleen B. Brosi, *A Cross-City Comparison of Felony Case Processing* (Washington, D.C.: U.S. Government Printing Office, 1979), p. 14.
2. For more detailed discussion of the major decision stages, see Donald J. Newman, *Introduction to Criminal Justice* (Philadelphia: Lippincott, 1975), pp. 106–12; and Peter W. Lewis and Kenneth D. Peoples, *The Supreme Court and the Criminal Process — Cases and Comments* (Philadelphia: W. B. Saunders, 1978), pp. 73–90.
3. Caleb Foote, "A Study of the Administration of Bail in New York City," *University of Pennsylvania Law Review* 106 (1958), p. 633.
4. Lee Silverstein, "Bail in the State Courts — A Field Study and Report," *Minnesota Law Review* 50 (1966), pp. 621–31.
5. See Ronald L. Goldfarb, *Ransom: A Critique of the American Bail System* (New York: Harper and Row, 1965); Martin Friedland, *Detention Before Trial* (Toronto: University of Toronto Press, 1965).
6. A. Keith Bottemley, *Prison Before Trial* (London: G. Bells and Sons, 1970), pp. 59–73.
7. For similar findings in release decisions involving juveniles, see Lawrence E. Cohen and James R. Kluegel, "The Detention Decision: A Study of the Impart of Social Characteristics and Legal Factors in Two Metropolitan Juvenile Courts," *Social Forces* (1979), pp. 146–61.
8. See Frederic Suffet, "Bail Setting: A Study of Courtroom Interaction," *Crime and Delinquency* (1966), pp. 318–31.
9. Friedland, *Detention Before Trial*, p. 176.
10. *LEAA Newsletter* 8 (1979), p. 6.
11. Janet R. Altman and Richard O. Cunningham, "Preventive Detention," *George Washington University Law Review* 36 (1967), p. 178.
12. The President's Commission on Law Enforcement and the Administration of Justice, *Task Force Report: The Courts* (Washington, D.C.: U.S. Government Printing Office, 1967), p. 40.
13. Altman and Cunningham, "Preventive Detention," p. 179.
14. See William J. Chambliss, *Crime and the Legal Process* (New York: McGraw-Hill, 1969), p. 375.
15. Arthur R. Angel, "Preventive Detention: An Empirical Analysis," *Harvard Civil Rights–Civil Liberties Law Review* 6 (1971). pp. 309–32.
16. William A. Westley, *Violence and the Police: A Sociological Study of Law, Custom, and Morality* (Cambridge, Mass.: MIT Press, 1970), p. 178.
17. William J. Chambliss and Robert B. Seidman, *Law, Order, and Power* (Reading, Mass.: Addison-Wesley, 1971), pp. 398–99.
18. President's Commission, *Task Force Report: The Courts*, p. 4; also, Abraham S. Blumberg, *Criminal Justice* (Chicago: Quadrangle Books, 1970), p. 29.
19. See Brosi, *A Cross-City Comparison of Felony Case Processing*, pp. 16–28.
20. Ibid., pp. 18–19.
21. Ibid., p. 20. See also Frank J. Cannavale, Jr., *Witness Cooperation* (Lexington, Mass.: D. C. Heath, 1976), p. 25; Kristen J. Williams, "The Effects of Victim Characteristics on the Disposition of Violent Offenders," in William F.

McDonald, ed., *Criminal Justice and the Victim* (Beverly Hills, Calif.: Sage, 1976), pp. 177–213.

22. Michael J. Hindelang and Michael Gottfredson, "The Victim's Decision Not to Invoke the Criminal Justice Process," in McDonald, *Criminal Justice and the Victim*, pp. 57–78.

23. Cannavale, *Witness Cooperation*, appendix A, p. 50.

24. George F. Cole, "The Decision to Prosecute," *Law and Society Review* 4 (1970), pp. 331–43.

25. See Dominick R. Vetri, "Guilty-Plea Bargaining: Compromise by Prosecutors to Secure Guilty Pleas," *University of Pennsylvania Law Review* 112 (1964), pp. 896–908.

26. Donald J. Newman, "Pleading Guilty for Considerations: A Study of Bargain Justice," *Journal of Criminal Law, Criminology, and Police Science* 46 (1956), p. 787.

27. A. Keith Bottomley, *Decisions in the Penal Process* (London: Martin Robinson, 1973), p. 21.

28. Donald J. Newman, *Conviction: The Determination of Guilt or Innocence Without Trial* (Boston: Little, Brown, 1966), p. 85.

29. Arnold Enker, "Perspectives on Plea Bargaining," in President's Commission, *Task Force Report: The Courts*, appendix A, pp. 111–12.

30. See Alan J. Mendelsohn, "The Influence of Defendant's Plea on Judicial Determination of Sentence," *Yale Law Journal* 66 (1956), pp. 204–22; see also Vetri, "Guilty-Plea Bargaining: Compromises by Prosecutors to Secure Guilty Pleas," p. 907. For the situation abroad, consult Bottomley, *Decisions in the Penal Process*, pp. 120–22.

31. See Blumberg, *Criminal Justice*, pp. 55–56. See also Brosi, *A Cross-City Comparison of Felony Case Processing*.

32. From Blumberg, *Criminal Justice*, pp. 56–58.

33. Eugene H. Czajkoski, "Exposing the Quasi-Judicial Role of the Prosecutor's Office," *Federal Probation* 37 (1973), pp. 9–13.

34. Blumberg, *Criminal Justice*, p. 59.

35. See Donald M. McIntyre and David Lippman, "Prosecutors and Early Disposition of Felony Cases," *American Bar Association Law Journal* 56 (1970), pp. 1154–59.

36. See Chambliss and Seidman, *Law, Order, and Power*, pp. 400–3. Sudnow has shown, however, that public pressure sometimes leads prosecutors to reject pleas in favor of a trial. See David Sudnow, "Normal Crimes: Sociological Features of the Penal Code in the Public Defender Office," *Social Problems* 12 (1965), pp. 255–76.

37. See President's Commission, *Task Force Report: The Courts*, p. 10.

38. See Blumberg, *Criminal Justice*, pp. 92–93; Newman, "Pleading Guilty for Considerations," pp. 781–83.

39. Leonard Downie, Jr., *Justice Denied* (Baltimore: Penguin Books, 1972), pp. 166–68.

40. Ibid., p. 165.

41. See Jerome E. Carlin, *Lawyer's Ethics* (New York: Russell Sage, 1968).

42. Ibid. Also see Arthur Lewis Wood, *Criminal Lawyer* (New Haven: College and University Press, 1967); and Downie, *Justice Denied*, chapter 7.

43. Abraham S. Blumberg, "Lawyers with Convictions," *Transaction* (July 1967), p. 18.

44. Abraham S. Blumberg, "The Practice of Law as a Confidence Game: Organizational Cooptation of a Profession," *Law and Society Review* 1 (1967), p. 19.

45. Stuart L. Hills, *Crime, Power, and Morality* (Scranton, Pa.: Chandler, 1971), p. 27.

46. Chambliss and Seidman, *Law, Order, and Power*, p. 402.

47. Cole, "The Decision to Prosecute," p. 340.

48. See Newman, *Conviction*, chapters 7 and 8.

49. Gerald D. Robin, *Introduction to the Criminal Justice System* (New York: Harper and Row, 1980), p. 250.

50. *LEAA Newsletter* 8 (1979), p. 12.

51. John Griffiths, "Ideology in Criminal Procedure, or a Third 'Model' of the Criminal Process," *Yale Law Journal* 79 (1970), p. 397.

52. See Jonathan D. Casper, "Did You Have a Lawyer When You Went to Court? No I Had a Public Defender," *Yale Review of Law and Social Action* 1 (1971), pp. 4–9.

53. Jonathan D. Casper, *American Criminal Justice: The Defendant's Perspective* (Englewood Cliffs, N.J.: Prentice-Hall, 1972), p. 18.

54. "The Second Circuit Sentencing Study," U.S. Senate Hearings Before the Committee on the Judiciary, 94th Cong., 1974, pp. 8102–32. Cited in Robin, *Introduction to the Criminal Justice System*, pp. 297–98.

55. William Austin and Thomas A. Williams III, "A Survey of Judge's Responses to Simulated Legal Cases: Research Notes on Sentencing Disparity," *Journal of Criminal Law and Criminology* 68 (1977), pp. 306–10.

56. See Bottomley, *Decisions in the Penal Process*, chapter 4.

57. From Daniel Glaser, Fred Cohen, and Vincent O'Leary, "Sentencing and Parole Process," in Leonard Orland, ed., *Justice, Punishment and Treatment: The Correctional Process* (New York: Free Press, 1973).

58. Frank J. Remington, Donald J. Newman, Edward L. Kimball, Marygold Melli, and Herman Goldstein, *Criminal Justice Administration* (Indianapolis: Bobbs-Merrill, 1969), p. 696.

59. Ibid., pp. 697–98. For additional examples, see Newman, *Introduction to Criminal Justice*, pp. 246–58.

60. President's Commission, *Task Force Report: The Courts*, p. 22.

61. Ralph L. Blankenship, "Toward a Sociolinguistic Perspective on Deviance Labelling," *Sociology and Social Research* 58 (1974), pp. 253–61.

62. Ibid., p. 255.
63. See Remington et al., *Criminal Justice Administration*, pp. 702–10.
64. Robert M. Carter and Leslie T. Wilkins, "Some Factors in Sentencing Policy," *Journal of Criminal Law, Criminology, and Police Science* 58 (1967), pp. 503–14.
65. See Bottomley, *Decisions in the Penal Process*, pp. 164–66.
66. John Hogarth, *Sentencing as a Human Process* (Toronto: Toronto University Press, 1971), p. 324.
67. Ibid., p. 241–42.
68. Ibid., p. 262.
69. Marvin E. Wolfgang and Bernard Cohen, *Crime and Race* (New York: Institute of Human Relations Press, 1970), p. 80.
70. Vilhelm Aubert, "Conscientious Objectors Before the Norwegian Military Courts," in *Judicial Decision-Making*, ed. G. Schubert (New York: Free Press, 1963), pp. 207–11.
71. Thorsten Sellin, "Race Prejudice in the Administration of Justice," *American Journal of Sociology* 41 (1935), pp. 212–17.
72. Dennis Chapman, *Sociology and the Stereotype of the Criminal* (London: Tavistock, 1968).
73. Roger Hood, *Sentencing the Motoring Offender* (London: Heinemann, 1972); also his *Sentencing in Magistrates' Courts* (London: Stevens, 1962).
74. Terrence P. Thornberry, "Race, Socioeconomic Status and Sentencing in the Juvenile Justice System," *Journal of Criminal Law and Criminology* 64 (1973), pp. 90–98.
75. David M. Petersen and Paul C. Friday, "Early Release from Incarceration: Race as a Factor in the Use of 'Shock Probation,' " *Journal of Criminal Law and Criminology* 66 (1975), pp. 79–87.
76. Edward Green, *Judicial Attitudes in Sentencing* (London: Macmillan & Co., 1961). See also "Inter- and Intra-Racial Crime Relative to Sentencing," *Journal of Criminal Law, Criminology, and Police Science* 55 (1964), pp. 348–58. Mention should also be made of two studies by John Hagan, "Extra-Legal Attributes and Criminal Sentencing: An Assessment of Sociological View and Analysis," *Sociological Quarterly* 12 (1974), pp. 308–18; and "The Social and Legal Construction of Criminal Justice: A Study of the Pre-Sentencing Process," *Social Problems* 22 (1975), pp. 619–37. Hagan found differences to be attributable to legal variables, not race or class.
77. Theodore G. Chiricos and Gordon P. Waldo, "Socioeconomic Status and Criminal Sentencing: An Empirical Assessment of a Conflict Proposition," *American Sociological Review* 40 (1975), p. 766.
78. Ibid., pp. 758–59, footnote 14.
79. Stuart S. Nagel, "Disparities in Criminal Procedure," *UCLA Law Review* 14 (1967), p. 1296.
80. Hood, *Sentencing in Magistrates' Courts*, pp. 65–75.
81. Emile Durkheim, *The Division of Labor in Society* (New York: Free Press, 1964), pp. 102–8.
82. Hogarth, *Sentencing as a Human Process*, p. 320. See also pp. 218–23.
83. Nagel, "Disparities in Criminal Procedure."
84. Hogarth, *Sentencing as a Human Process*, pp. 209–10.
85. Leslie T. Wilkins, Jack M. Kress, Don M. Gottfredson, Joseph C. Calpin, and Arthur M. Gelman, *Sentencing Guidelines: Structuring Judicial Discretion* (Washington, D.C.: U.S. Government Printing Office, 1978).
86. Ibid., p. vii.
87. The Council of State Governments, *The Book of the States, 1978–1979*, (Lexington, Ky.: The Council of State Governments, 1978), p. 429.
88. Ibid.
89. Albert W. Alschuler, "Sentencing Reform and Prosecutorial Power: A Critique of Recent Proposals for 'Fixed' and 'Presumptive' Sentencing," in *Determinate Sentencing: Reform or Regression*, Proceedings of the Special Conference on Determinate Sentencing, University of California, Berkeley, June 2–3, 1977. (Washington, D.C.: U.S. Government Printing Office, 1978), p. 73.
90. Caleb Foote, "Deceptive Determinate Sentencing," in *Determinate Sentencing: Reform or Regression*, pp. 133–41.
91. Todd R. Clear, John D. Hewitt, and Robert M. Regoli, "Discretion and the Determinate Sentence: Its Distribution, Control, and Effect on Time Served," *Crime and Delinquency* 24 (1978), pp. 428–45.
92. Ibid., p. 440.
93. Ibid.
94. Ibid., p. 443.

Punishing the Criminal Offender

To do justice to the subject of criminal punishment would require an entire text. Since our space is limited, in this chapter we shall look at the meanings, objectives, and justifications of criminal punishment, as well as its major types. In chapter 14 we shall explore in more detail the nature and impact of imprisonment and the important problems of reformation and deterrence.

The Definition of Punishment

Punishment can be defined as any action designed to deprive a person or persons of things of value because of something that person has done or is thought to have done. According to Austin Turk, "examples of valued things include liberty, civil rights, skills, opportunities, material objects, less tangible forms of wealth, health, identity, life, and — perhaps most crucial — significant personal relationships."[1]

We say that punishment involves design, to emphasize that those who punish do so knowingly and intentionally. People may deprive others of valued things accidentally, without design, but to call this punishment ignores the purposive character of punitive reactions. Punishment is a reaction intended to deprive the punished of something the punisher assumes is valued. However, in addition to intended deprivations, a particular punishment may cause unintended deprivations, things the punishment is not specifically designed to produce. Though not a formal element of punishment as defined here, unintended deprivations ought not to be ignored in a discussion of punishment, for they are part of the reality of punitive reactions as experienced by those on the receiving end.

CRIMINAL PUNISHMENT

We need to specify the particulars of criminal punishment. There are three major categories of criminal punishment. The first category, *official criminal penalties,* consists of legal punishments, punishments provided for by law and imposed by lawful representatives of a state, community, or group according to the directives of law. Examples of official criminal penalties are fines, prison terms, and probation.

The second category of criminal punishment can be designated as *extralegal penalties.* These punishments, while not illegal, are not provided for by law nor designated as punishments to be applied by officials of the state. Extralegal criminal penalties are diverse; some examples are refusal to marry someone because of his or her criminality, denial of friendship on similar grounds, or nonphysical harassment of a prisoner by a guard.

The third category consists of *illegal penalties.* These are punishments that are themselves illegal (e.g., torture) or that are applied illegally (e.g., the lynching of a convicted murderer).

THE RELATIVITY OF PUNISHMENT

Punishment is a relative thing. It is relative, first, in the sense that what is a deprivation for one person or group may not be for another. For example, while most of us would probably consider a stay in jail as a significant deprivation, this view may not be held by everyone or by members of other societies. Second, it is relative in the sense that different people may have different views regarding which deprivations are more severe than others. While most of us would probably consider a jail sentence a more severe penalty than a fine, this view is apparently not shared by skid-row drunks. As the authors of one recent study contend, it is not uncommon for skid-row drunks to see fines as far more punitive than workhouse or jail terms.[2] For one thing, they see a jail sentence as an opportunity to recuperate from the ravages of their life; a fine, on the other hand, means giving up drinking money.

Punishment is also relative in terms of its imposition and the sorts of deprivations involved. At different times, and in different jurisdictions and cultures, certain types of deprivations have been imposed to the exclusion of others. Similarly, there are variations in the degree to which certain punishments are used. Some are used more frequently than others, and there are likely to be variations in the amount of deprivation depending on time, place, and situation. Like crime, punishment cannot be studied independently of the legal, cultural, political, and situational facets of social life.

Legal Punishment: Justification and Aims

When a convicted criminal is punished today, he is punished by the state in the name of its people. Crimes are conceived of as public wrongs, and in criminal law the state is the victim. The real injury to the real victim of a crime is formally ignored. The state prosecutes, the state adjudicates, and the state determines the possible penalties. The result, some authors have suggested, is that punishment has become "an abstract measure of justice," in the sense that the penalty for a crime is not assessed in terms of the real harm experienced by its immediate victims. Egon Bittner and Anthony Platt explain:

> The separation of the crime from the real grievance that it occasioned — except for purposes of proving the fact of its occurrence — makes its punishment an abstract measure of justice. This is so because we cannot look at the real harm to inform us about the gravity of the offence and we are not free to elect a punishment that has a direct compensatory relevance to the real harm. If to commit a crime means to offend society then it is not at all clear what the dues shall be that will expunge the offence and restore the violated order to its original state of integrity. The rule that someone who steals must spend some time in prison establishes a symbolic equivalence between act and sanction that is inherently arbitrary. The crime and the punishment do not stand in a reciprocal relationship, one causing a deficit and the other restoring the balance. Rather, they are, in a sense, analogous actions demonstrating that two wrongs can make a right.[3]

This situation, the authors maintain, raises the need for a moral justification of punishment that goes beyond the notion of victim compensation. Over the years, two major arguments have been offered in support of legal punishment. The first stresses the ideas of moral responsibility and just deserts, and is favored by the so-called *retributivists*. The second stresses the justification of punishment in terms of its capacity to deter or to reform. This view gained wide popularity through the efforts of the *utilitarians,* particularly Cesare Beccaria and Jeremy Bentham. Both perspectives seek to justify legal punishment in general and in its particular application.

RETRIBUTION

It is a mistake to believe, as many people apparently do, that retribution is synonymous with revenge.[4] Retributivists are quick to point out that their conception of legal punishment emphasizes the principles of justice and due process, not the subjective passions of punishers seeking vengeance. The principles of justice at the heart of retribution are that punishment is deserved when morally responsible persons are guilty of willfully violating the moral order as articulated in the laws of the society in which they claim membership. For its part, society has the moral right, and the duty, to punish the guilty. It has the right to punish because the integrity of its moral order has been violated; it has the duty to punish because not to do so negates the very idea of crime and renders moral responsibility meaningless. All of this does not mean that penalties will necessarily be severe. A distinguished panel of educators and lawyers, which recently concluded that the only just system of punishment is one based on retribution, proposed a maximum penalty for all crimes but murder of five years imprisonment.[5]

Retributivists see only one possible basis for justification of specific penalties for specific crimes. A specific penalty is justified when the guilty person has received a punishment reflecting the gravity of his offense. The two issues of guilt and making the punishment fit the crime provide the grounds for arguing that any particular legal punishment is a "just desert."

But how do we make the punishment fit the crime? Various possibilities have been offered: (1) make the punishment mirror the crime itself (*lex talionis,* an eye for an eye); (2) adjust the severity of penalties according to the social harm resulting from different offenses; and (3) link the penalties to the moral outrage or indignation felt by a majority of citizens.

From a practical standpoint, none of these possibilities offers much hope of realization. Even if all agreed that one particular possibility, or combination of possibilities, offered the best approach, translating the ideas involved into practice meets formidable difficulties. What kinds of penalties would accurately mirror robbing a bank of $20,000 or possessing 2 grams of heroin? On what basis are things considered socially harmful, and who makes the relevant judgments? Moral outrage may offer more hope, in that public sentiments can be tapped. In one recent attempt, wide agreement was found in rating the seriousness of 140 offenses.[6] Even so, a problem arises when it comes to determining actual penalties for actual crimes. Depending upon the circumstances surrounding two identical acts, the sense of moral outrage might well differ. Are we to expect judicial authorities to poll the public every time a criminal conviction is handed down? Surely this would be the only just way to deal with the problem of moral indignation.

Many retributivists favor moral outrage as the key issue in determining penalties, but how is that view articulated in America today? In other words, are we anywhere near making official penalties an accurate reflection of public sentiments? Evidence on the question is sparse, but what there is suggests that generally neither legal provisions for punishment nor actual penalty practices accord with public sentiments at all points. A number of studies show wide discrepancies between official views and actions and those supported by the public.[7] Most studies show, however, that the discrepancies vary according to offenses, so that while there is generally little evidence of strong agreement between official and public views, the differences may be slight where certain offenses are concerned. For example, occupational criminals tend to receive lighter sentences than the public would support. From the standpoint of those seeking to justify legal punishment practices in terms of public sentiments, available evidence suggests that America is some way from seeing "just deserts."

PREVENTION, REFORM, AND DETERRENCE

Today few people in the public eye speak of retribution when addressing the problem of punishment. This is certainly due in part to the popular misconception that retribution stands for revenge and all that that word implies. The emphasis today is almost always on punishment as a means of preventing crime, or in some way reducing it. Prevention is emphasized not only by politicians, public leaders, and professionals in the field of penal law, but also by many scholars. Indeed, some years ago a well-known American sociologist went so far as to say that preventing crime is "the sole justification [of punishment] known to the social scientist."[8] While this view can probably be disputed, the fact remains that many social scientists, probably most, believe that the justification of punishment lies in its preventive capabilities.

One of the first to outline this view was the Italian philosopher Cesare Beccaria, writing in the second half of the eighteenth century. In his monumental *Essay on Crimes and Punishments,* Beccaria argued that punishment can be justified as a legal device to prevent crimes provided it is applied fairly and openly. Beccaria was extremely concerned about the rampant injustices and unimaginable terrors characteristic of eighteenth-century law enforcement and penal practice. Yet he saw, too, that crime was apparently escalating and something had to be done. Punishment, applied fairly and properly, he thought, had to be the answer.[9]

A just punishment, in Beccaria's view, is one that is proportionate to the offense *and* sufficient to outweigh the pleasure derived from it. The second part is important, for it lies at the heart of the *utilitarian* doctrine, which Beccaria espoused, and helps explain how punishment prevents crime.

Simply put, the utilitarians argued in favor of a guiding principle: the greatest happiness for the greatest number. Any action has the capability of producing pleasure or happiness for someone, just as it can also produce pain. In seeking their pleasures people may cause others pleasure or pain; hence others' lives are often affected by our actions, and it behooves us to consider the impact of an action on the group as a whole. Whereas crime produces pleasure for its perpetrator, it produces pain for others — considered a bad or evil thing by utilitarians. Punishment also brings pain, so it, too, is a bad thing. Yet if by punishing the criminal we prevent crime, we give more pleasure to the group as a whole at the expense of those whose behavior is bad in the first place. We can justify the use of punishment along utilitarian lines, then, if the group as a whole is better off than if crime went unpunished.

This brings us to the ways in which punishment is conventionally thought to prevent crime. First, punishment is a way to *reform* criminals so that they will not commit crimes in the future. The original penitentiary was an early application of the idea that punishment reforms. Second, punishment is a way to prevent crime by *incapacitating* the offender so that he is in no position to engage in criminal activity. Death, banishment, and other penalties that remove an individual from access to opportunities to commit crimes are incapacitating penalties.

Third, there is the question of *deterrence*. The early utilitarians, especially Beccaria and his English counterpart, Jeremy Bentham, believed that punishment could be made to deter individuals from committing crime.[10] Like Beccaria, Bentham believed that punishment was justifiable if it prevented crime. The important remaining question is How? The answer, they believed, was fairly obvious: since people seek pleasure and avoid pain they will tend to avoid those things that bring pain, especially if the pain outweighs the actual or anticipated pleasure associated with them. Accordingly, punishment can prevent crime by its threat of pain. Simply put, people are scared away from crime by fear of punishment. We shall return to a more detailed analysis of the deterrence doctrine in chapter 14.

Official Criminal Penalties

The range of legal punishments throughout history has been vast. Whereas in most Western societies today there are three basic penalty types — physical detention, fines, and probation — not so long ago the list included all sorts of things: torture, branding and other public humiliations, maiming, deportation, banishment, loss of property and other economic goods, corporal punishment, forced labor, coerced penitence, self-denial, and, of course, death.

Official criminal penalties can best be approached as *types* of legal punishment. Sutherland and Cressey have provided a useful way to picture penalty types by enumerating four principal methods of punishment:

(1) removal from the group; (2) physical torture; (3) social degradation; and (4) financial loss.[11] Let us look more closely at the nature and use of official criminal penalties over the years.

REMOVAL FROM THE GROUP: DEATH

Death, banishment, transportation, and imprisonment are examples of removal penalties. At the least, these punishments remove an individual from his familiar everyday social interactions with family, friends, acquaintances, fellow workers, and other regular associates.

Death has been called "probably the most ancient of all forms of formal punishment," and "the pivotal criminal punishment in Western society from ancient times until the nineteenth century."[12] In early criminal codes, death was the penalty for a wide range of offenses. Both the ancient Mosaic code and that of Hammurapi prescribed death for witchcraft, incest, kidnapping, certain forms of theft, and negligence resulting in death.[13] In Greece, Rome, and among the Germanic tribes governed by the laws of Tacitus, death was also a common penalty, and Durkheim notes its extensive use by the ancient Egyptians, Assyrians, and Hindus.[14]

It has been said that during the reign of Henry VIII, 72,000 people were executed, many of them for trivial offenses.[15] We can never know if this figure is accurate since complete records have not survived, but it is certainly true that the medieval period saw an upsurge in the use of the death penalty in most of Europe. The popularity of this penalty seems to have reached a peak during the sixteenth century, when it dropped off only to rise to a new and higher peak by the end of the eighteenth century. At that time England had more than 200 capital offenses (some authors claim around 350). The list of capital crimes included arson, rape, sodomy, murder, forgery, highway robbery, pocket picking, shoplifting, burglary at night, stealing horses, cattle, and sheep, setting fire to coal mines, cutting down trees in a public avenue, destroying silk or velvet in the loom, sacrilege, mutiny, desertion, concealing the death of a bastard child, sending threatening letters, and returning from exile.[16] Until well into the nineteenth century, it was not uncommon for children to be hanged. By the 1840s, however, things took a turn away from death as the principal penalty. "Only" twenty offenses were designated as capital crimes, and the execution of young children became a thing of the past.

In America, capital punishment has traditionally been reserved for a mere handful of crimes in comparison to England. But even so, it was not limited to the kinds of violent and heinous offenses that today are commonly associated with such punishment. One of its earliest uses was as a punishment for sacrilege and witchcraft.

Methods of Execution   Today most countries rely on swift methods of execution that are thought to be painless — hanging, firing squad, electrocution, or asphyxiation.[17] But the history of capital punishment provides

Retribution, incapacitation, or deterrence? Here, especially, it makes a difference.

a good illustration of man's inhumanity to man. It was little more than one hundred years ago that England, then the world's most advanced nation, was still hanging, drawing, and quartering many of its condemned. This gruesome method of execution involved cutting out the entrails of the dying prisoner while he was hanging by the neck; after death his body was cut into sections and sometimes dragged through the streets. In Japan another gruesome form of execution was practiced only a few generations ago:

> The condemned were tied to a cross by ropes and then transfixed by light spears by the executioner. If the latter had been bribed heavily enough the first spear transfixed the heart. If not, the condemned passed through exquisite agony before death released them, the spears often being passed *slowly* through the body, so as to miss any immediately vital part.[18]

If we go back still further in history, we find an abundance of cruel and torturous methods of execution. Man's efforts in this regard have been limited only by his ingenuity and resourcefulness. According to ancient codes, and among many primitive peoples, death was often prolonged and agonizing, with stoning, burning at the stake, trampling to death, crucifixion, and impalement as favored techniques. During the medieval period, in France and Germany particularly, traitors, parricides, and those convicted of especially heinous crimes were killed on the wheel. This method of execution involved tying the condemned to the spokes of a large wheel. Since arms and legs will not naturally conform to a wheel's rim, the high point in the proceedings involved the breaking of the condemned man's limbs so they could be tied around the rim itself. The condemned were then left to die of exhaustion.[19]

Until recent times executions were generally carried out in public. As if it were not enough to die, and miserably at that, the condemned were made a public spectacle, which often had all the trappings of a family picnic, a fair, even a wedding.[20] Yet the cruelty and public aspects of capital punishment should not be viewed as indicative of some sort of perverse interest in the macabre and diabolical. On the contrary, the procedures were conditioned by history and culture, and based on what authorities felt were reasonable and practical concerns. Given sufficient variation in the kinds of offenses for which death could be imposed, the manner of execution could be varied to match or mirror in some way the nature and gravity of an offense. A particularly heinous crime would bring its perpetrator a crueler death than, say, a simple case of robbery. An effort to make the execution reflect the nature of the crime is illustrated by Graeme Newman: "Ploughing off of the head was a very early form of beheading for a person who trespassed across a boundary line. The offender was buried at the place of trespass up to the neck, and then a circular plough was driven over him, thus striking off the head.[21] Later this method was used for persons who illegally cut off the tops of trees.

Why execute in public? Here again there was reason behind the procedure. The issue was framed in terms of *deterrence* and *moral education*. The idea was that witnessing executions would deter observers from committing capital crimes by exploiting their fear of death, and further, it would reinforce in them the belief that the acts for which the condemned suffered were indeed wrong, sinful, and damnable.

Table 13.1 Abolition of the death penalty in the world community

JURISDICTION	DATE OF ABOLITION	JURISDICTION	DATE OF ABOLITION
San Marino	1848	Iceland	1940
Venezuela	1863	Switzerland[a]	1942
Mozambique	1867	India, Travencore	1944
Portugal	1867	Italy[a]	1944
Costa Rica	1880	Brazil[a]	1946
Netherlands[a]	1886[b]	West Germany	1949
Equador	1897	Finland[a]	1949
Norway[a]	1905[b]	Greenland	1954
Uruguay	1907	Honduras	1957
Colombia	1910	Netherlands, Antilles[a]	1957
Panama	1915	Bolivia	1961
Sweden[a]	1921	Monaco	1962
Argentina	1922	Great Britain	1965
Dominican Republic	1924	Northern Ireland	1966
Denmark[a]	1930	Austria	1968
Mexico[c]	1931		

SOURCE: Compiled from table 7.3 in William J. Bowers, *Executions in America* (Lexington, Mass.: D. C. Heath, 1974). Original source: Legal Defense Fund Brief for *Aikens* v. *California,* 406 U.S. 813: 92 S.Ct. 1931 (1972).

[a] Permits the death penalty during time of war or under military law

[b] Executed Nazi collaborators after World War II

[c] Twenty-nine of thirty-two states in Mexico abolished the death penalty between 1931 and 1970

Executions in America   As table 13.1 shows, many countries have abolished the death penalty altogether. As of the early 1970s, a small number of American states had done likewise: Michigan, Wisconsin, Maine, Minnesota, Alaska, Hawaii, Oregon, Iowa, West Virginia, New Jersey, and California. In addition, New York, Rhode Island, and Vermont have retained it only for one or two special cases, as when a "lifer" commits murder in prison.[22]

In America the last half century has witnessed a steady decrease in the use of the death penalty. Data collected by the Federal Bureau of Prisons show a total of 3,859 executions in the United States between 1930 and 1970. From a peak of around 170 executions a year during the 1930s, the number declined steadily over the following thirty years.[23] William Bowers suggests why:

> A number of factors operating within the judicial system appear to have played a part. These include increasing receptivity of federal courts to appeals in capital cases, growing concern among lawyers for the rights of criminal offenders, mounting reluctance of juries to hand down the death sentence and of governors and state penal authorities to schedule and carry out executions. These changes, in turn, may have been stimulated by accumulating

scientific evidence on the application and effectiveness of the death penalty, and changing moral standards in this country and abroad.[24]

Of those executions between 1930 and 1970, most were for murder (86.4 percent); rape accounted for 11.8 percent, with the remaining seventy cases (1.8 percent) split mainly between arson and kidnapping. Just over 2,300 executions (about 60 percent) occurred in the seventeen states of the South, as did all but 12 of the 455 executions for rape. Overall, more blacks than whites have been executed, and nearly 90 percent of those who died for rape were blacks.

These data clearly raise the question of racial discrimination in our use of the death penalty during recent history. We touched on this subject earlier, in chapter 4, but it seems appropriate to confront it once more. The charge of racial discrimination has been the main issue in the National Association for the Advancement of Colored People's (NAACP) long fight to have the death penalty abolished. Evidence accumulated on its behalf or independently during the period 1930 to 1960 seemed to support the contention.[25] More recently, William Bowers has added new evidence and interpretation in support of the charge. Following careful analysis of data going back as far as 1890, Bowers concludes that his findings point "unmistakably to a pattern of racial discrimination in the administration of capital punishment in America."[26] That discrimination has been concentrated in the South, he argues, where blacks have been executed for less serious crimes, as well as for crimes less often punished by death (e.g., rape), when committed by whites. Further, the blacks who have been executed were generally younger than their white counterparts and were more often executed without appeals.

The picture from northern and western regions of America shows considerably less evidence of racial discrimination in the imposition of the death penalty, but we find that those who end up being executed are characteristically of low social status. Robert M. Carter has drawn a composite sketch of the men executed in California over the years, and it shows us a person who from early childhood has had little going for him. Thirty-four years old when executed, the death penalty victim comes from a rural background of poverty and alcoholism. He will have been tagged delinquent at an early age, will drop out of school by age 14, and leave a broken home by 17. With few occupational skills he will drift from job to job and will soon be arrested for some unsophisticated, unplanned property crime. Convicted of the crime, his young marriage will break up and he will again be in and out of jobs and jail. Back to crime, this time with a partner, he will be arrested again, this time getting five years in prison. Out in two years and on parole with no marketable skills, he will work intermittently, drink more, and begin to think of himself as worthless, a no-good bum. The culmination of a life devoid of love and security comes quickly, as we find our frustrated criminal pulling a robbery for fast money, killing the gas station operator in the process. Caught three days later, he is sentenced to death and executed two years, eight months, and twenty-eight days after his arrest.[27]

Prospects for the Death Penalty in America   By the beginning of the 1970s it looked as if America might never execute a prisoner again. The last execution had been in 1967. In 1972 the Supreme Court ruled (in *Furman* v. *Georgia*) that the death penalty violated the Eighth Amendment prohibition against "cruel and unusual punishment." However, the majority of justices did not object to the death penalty per se but to the way it was being applied. According to the justices, the death penalty was being meted out in an arbitrary and often discriminatory fashion, with blacks and poor defendants usually the losers.

Advocates of the death penalty did not give up their cause, however. After the *Furman* v. *Georgia* ruling, many states immediately revised their death penalty statutes, hoping thereby to meet constitutional requirements. In 1976 the Supreme Court heard new arguments. In *Gregg* v. *Georgia*[28] a majority of seven justices held that the state of Georgia had achieved this objective, a finding also applied to Texas and Florida in companion cases. In the aftermath of *Furman,* thirty-four states had adopted new capital punishment statutes. Although at least one state, Ohio, had to go back to the drawing board with its new law when successfully challenged in the Supreme Court, it seems clear that executions are back with us. The January 1977 execution of Gary Gilmore by firing squad in a shed near Utah State Prison was the first execution in ten years. With a 1979 total of 567 inmates on death rows across the country, it is likely that we will see many more.[29]

The tenor of Supreme Court decisions in 1976 is mirrored in public attitudes toward capital punishment. A National Opinion Research Council survey of the same year showed that 65 percent of Americans favor capital punishment for murder. In fact, since 1969 there has been a rise in favorable attitudes toward this ultimate punishment. According to the author of a recent study, this rise can be linked to the emergence of a "law and order syndrome" showing heightened concern about crime, especially the kind of crime given floodlight publicity.[30] The periodic discovery of mass murderers and contract killers in our midst does much to bring on public clamor for the death penalty. In addition, constant talk of steadily increasing rates of violent crime turns those who are less moved by the sensational into supporters as well.

It should be pointed out, nevertheless, that things have not gone completely in favor of death penalty advocates, especially those who support mandatory death sentences for certain offenses. Some experts have argued that mandatory death sentences not only reflect society's proper revulsion at the occurrence of certain crimes — the killing of police officers, for example — but also serve to reduce discrimination in the administration of the death penalty. However, Bowers reports that mandatory sentencing affords no such promise.[31] For one thing, when faced with mandatory sentences, the alteration of charges may be all it takes to circumvent the spirit and intent of such laws. In addition, the Supreme Court, in *Woodson* v. *North Carolina* (1976)[32] and again in *Roberts* v. *Louisiana* (1977),[33] has ruled such mandatory death sentences as cruel and unusual punishment, in violation of the Eighth Amendment.

REMOVAL FROM THE GROUP: EXILE PENALTIES

Exile penalties such as transportation and banishment are rarely used today, though the deportation of aliens is a modern form of banishment. In more primitive times, banishment of wrongdoers from the tribal group or village community was a simple and effective means of ridding the group of undesirables. Often used as a substitute for death, it usually meant the same thing, for without the support and security of the group an individual soon fell prey to a hostile environment. Significantly, banishment rendered the offender an outcast not simply in territorial terms, but also in a normative sense. That is, those banished were considered outside the prevailing moral order, and as such, members of the group were under no obligation to treat them as they would each other. The banished could be slain on sight, and such action required no moral justification.[34]

As distant lands were opened to exploration and colonization, transportation emerged as a new criminal penalty. By the beginning of the seventeenth century, England and other colonial powers were making systematic use of transportation as they sought to achieve two goals by one means. While the home country could be rid of its dangerous classes, the developing colonies could benefit from a continuing supply of new laborers to tame the land. Hundreds of thousands of convicts were transported from England alone, first to America and then to Australia. An interesting glimpse of the reasoning behind Sir Joseph Banks's advocacy of Botany Bay as a new penal colony is provided by testimony before the House of Commons on April 1, 1779 (see box on pages 432–433). It was not until the second half of the nineteenth century that transportation was finally abolished.[35]

REMOVAL FROM THE GROUP: IMPRISONMENT

Today imprisonment is one of the principal official criminal penalties; however, its use as a specific punishment upon conviction of an offense is of relatively recent origin. Ancient societies rarely used physical detention, and when they did it was not as a punishment in itself, but rather (1) as a means of pretrial detention and surveillance, or (2) because offenders had not paid their fines, or (3) because secure physical confinement was

Joseph Banks, Esquire, being requested, in case it should be thought expedient to establish a Colony of convicted Felons in any distant Part of the Globe, from whence their Escape might be difficult, and where, from the Fertility of the Soil, they might be enabled to maintain themselves, after the First Year, with little or no Aid from the Mother County, to give his Opinion what Place would be most eligible for such Settlement? informed your Committee, That the Place which appeared to him best adapted for such a Purpose, was *Botany Bay,* on the Coast of *New Holland,* in the *Indian* Ocean, which was about Seven Months Voyage from *England;* that he apprehended there would be little Probability of any Opposition from the Natives, as, during his stay here, in the Year 1770, he saw very few, and did not think there were above Fifty in all the Neighbourhood, and had Reason to believe the Country was very thinly peopled; those he saw were naked, treacherous, and armed with Lances, but extremely cowardly, and constantly retired from our People when they made the least Appearance of Resistance: He was in this Bay in the End of *April* and Beginning of *May* 1770, when the Weather was mild and moderate; that the Climate, he apprehended, was similar to that about *Toulouse,* in the South of *France,* having found the Southern Hemisphere colder than the Northern, in such Proportion, that any given Climate in the Southern answered to one in the Northern about Ten Degrees nearer to the Pole; the Proportion of rich Soil was small in Comparison to the barren, but sufficient to support a very large Number of People; there were no tame Animals, and he saw no wild Ones during his Stay of Ten Days, but he observed the Dung of what were called *Kangourous,* which were about the Size of a middling Sheep, but very swift, and difficult to catch; some of those Animals he saw in another Part of the Bay, upon the same Continent; there were no Beasts of Prey, and he did not doubt but our Oxen and Sheep, if carried there, would thrive and increase; there was great Plenty of Fish, he took a large Quantity by hauling the Seine, and

necessary if certain kinds of penalties (torture, execution, banishment) were to be imposed.

According to Durkheim, prisons first gained a notable place in the punishment of criminals with the emergence of cities and a technology capable of constructing buildings large, private, and secure enough to operate as detention facilities on a regular basis. Early prisons were found in, or attached to, royal palaces, temples and churches, city walls, and even the private homes of court officials, members of the nobility, and others in positions of wealth and privilege.[36]

Once established, prisons soon took on a directly punitive role. Those unfortunate enough to be placed in them (often the foes of the powerful) were subjected to abominable degradations and deprivations. Forced to live with filth and vermin, the prisoners were fed hardly enough to keep them alive, and they were often held in shackles, iron collars, and other restraining devices. As Europe moved into the medieval period, prisons were admirably suited to the growing use of physical torture.

Today the essential accomplishment and ostensible raison d'être of prisons is to remove an offender from his normal habitat, to deprive him of his freedom. This modern conception of imprisonment gained ground during the eighteenth century, as penal reforms took shape both here and abroad.

struck several Stingrays, a kind of Skate, all very large; one weighed 336 Pounds. The Grass was long and luxuriant, and there were some eatable Vegetables, particularly a Sort of wild Spinage; the Country was well supplied with Water; there was Abundance of Timber and Fuel, sufficient for any Number of Buildings, which might be found necessary. Being asked, How a Colony of that Nature could be subsisted in the Beginning of their Establishment? he answered, They must certainly be furnished, at landing, with a full Year's Allowance of Victuals, Raiment, and Drink; with all Kinds of Tools for labouring the Earth, and building Houses; with Black Cattle, Sheep, Hogs, and Poultry; with Seeds of all Kinds of *European* Corn and Pulse; with Garden Seeds; with Arms and Ammunition for their Defence; and they should likewise have small Boats, Nets, and Fishing-tackle; all of which, except Arms and Ammunition, might be purchased at the *Cape of Good Hope;* and that afterwards, with a moderate Portion of Industry, they might, undoubtedly,

maintain themselves without any Assistance from *England.* He recommended sending a large Number of Persons, Two or Three hundred at least; their Escape would be very difficult, as the Country was far distant from any Part of the Globe inhabited by *Europeans.* And being asked, Whether he conceived the Mother Country was likely to reap any Benefit from a Colony established in *Botany Bay?* he replied, If the People formed among themselves a Civil Government, they would necessarily increase, and find Occasion for many *European* Commodities; and it was not to be doubted, that a Tract of Land such as *New Holland,* which was larger than the Whole of *Europe,* would furnish Matter of advantageous Return.

SOURCE: *House of Commons Journal,* 1 April 1779, vol. 37, p. 311. Reprinted in Lloyd Evans and Paul Nicholls, Eds., *Convicts and Colonial Society, 1788–1853* (New South Wales: Cassells, 1976) pp. 22–23.

Prison Developments in America[37]   The Walnut Street Jail in Philadelphia is usually identified as America's first state prison and its first penitentiary. Opened in 1773, the jail received its first state prisoner in 1790. This historic occasion rewarded the hard work and dedication of a group of Pennsylvania citizens, many of them Quakers. These citizens abhorred the cruelty and degradation of existing punishments and felt that an alternative could be devised that was both humane and reformative. The group embraced the Quaker view that criminals should be made to contemplate the evil of their ways in unrelieved solitude. Under conditions of solitary confinement day and night, the inmate would immerse himself in self-reflection and penitence — or so they asserted. Work, necessary for regeneration of the spirit, would be performed alone in one's cell.

Built inside the existing jail structure, the new penitentiary was an awesome place. Crude efforts were made to segregate women, capital offenders, and debtors, vagrants, and other petty criminals. The inmates were housed individually in tiny whitewashed cells measuring 6 feet wide, 8 feet long, and 9 feet high. A small grated window could be seen high up on the outside wall, and the toilet amenities consisted of a lead pipe in the corner of each cell. The convicts were preached to on a regular basis but were denied any form of recreation. For their part, the guards were forbidden to use chains or irons, weapons or canes.

Ten other states soon constructed prisons along the lines of Philadelphia's Walnut Street Jail.[38] Although particular procedures varied somewhat from state to state (in Massachusetts, for example, the guards were issued guns, bayonets, and cutlasses), the basic architectural design was the same, as was the emphasis on enforced solitude. Eventually, overcrowding in most of these early prisons forced administrators to give up on the idea of solitary confinement for all. Instead, it was used more and more for those who had violated prison rules.

Support for a penitentiary system embodying solitary confinement was reaffirmed in the 1820s when the Pennsylvania legislature authorized two new prisons — Western Penitentiary in Pittsburgh and Eastern Penitentiary in Philadelphia. The structures were monolithic, the cells small and ranged along the outside walls, and the solitude, for all intents and purposes, was total. Charles Dickens, on visiting Eastern Penitentiary, wrote of the inmate: "He sees the prison officer, but with that exception he never looks upon a human countenance or hears a human voice. He is a man buried alive; to be dug out in the slow round of years; and in the meantime dead to everything but torturing anxieties and horrible despair."[39]

The "Pennsylvania System" was tried and soon abandoned in New Jersey and Rhode Island. These states turned instead to what is known as the "Auburn System," after Auburn Prison in New York. In that prison, opened in 1817 but enlarged and modified by 1823, inmates were locked in separate cells at night but worked together in small groups during the day. Complete silence was maintained both day and night, however, and regimentation was complete. Architecturally, the prison contained tiered blocks of tiny cells with narrow galleries encircling them. All was surrounded by an outside wall of stone over 2½ feet thick. Almost all early American prisons were fashioned after Auburn. In contrast, most European and South American countries adopted the Pennsylvania system.

Another example of early prison design, this time from England, was the Panopticon Plan created by Jeremy Bentham. Called a "dinosaur of the penal world" by Goldfarb and Singer,[40] there are nevertheless some living examples, one at Joliet, Illinois. Basically, the panopticon consists of tiers of cells arranged along the outside of a large circular structure. Besides the innovative architecture, Bentham had plans for heating, care of prisoners, health and educational services, and food and clothing as well. Though thrilled with his invention, as it turned out Bentham found few takers.

The Reformatory Movement   From around 1870 to the early twentieth century, the so-called reformatory movement held sway in American corrections. The movement's principles were outlined at the first meeting of the American Prison Congress, in 1870, and included the idea that *reformation rather than suffering* should be the cornerstone of penal practice, and that *indeterminate sentences* should be adopted to enable authorities to release early, or keep longer, those inmates who had succeeded, or failed, in demonstrating their rehabilitation. Inmates were to be put into three classes, depending upon their achievements and conduct: (1) First Grade, meaning that they had earned sufficient "marks" to make them eligible for parole; (2) Second Grade, mostly for new entrants yet to show their true colors; and (3) Third Grade, for those whose disobedience and lack of improvement suggested the need for sterner measures.

The first prison organized to apply these principles was the Elmira Reformatory in New York, opened in 1876. Elmira was primarily designed for young first offenders, 16 to 30 years old. Its superintendent was Zebulon Brockway, a confident and determined administrator who left no stone unturned in his efforts to prove the success of this new penology.[41] Encouraged by early results and the prospect of doing something successful in the battle against crime, other states soon followed suit, and by 1913 some eighteen state reformatories had been organized around the country.[42]

Yet the old style of harsh prison discipline, hard labor, and strict regimentation continued to dominate prison life. At least sixteen major state prisons of the Auburn variety — including Menard in Illinois, Folsom in California, Walla Walla in Washington State, and Brushy Mountain in Tennessee, all in operation today — were opened between 1870 and 1900. By the 1900s the reformatory movement was on the decline. It failed for a number of reasons: (1) lack of high quality leadership and staff, especially in the key area of education; (2) continued acceptance, despite the rhetoric, of the idea that the prison experience should be punishing; (3) lack of recognition that reformation and architecture might somehow be related — the reformatories were by and large monolithic stone fortresses; (4) overcrowding, which led to a breakdown in the already clumsy efforts at classification, grading, and behavior modification; (5) overemphasis on the custodial functions of prison by administrators; and, perhaps most important, (6) lack of official commitment to the movement in the form of supporting policy and resources.

Prisons Today In America today we see an agglomeration of prison philosophies, goals, and architectures. There has, in fact, been little consequential innovation over the last fifty years. With the exception of so-called community corrections, discussed in the following chapter, the form and character of detention as punishment are pretty much what they were decades ago.

There are some 250 prisons housing adult offenders and administered by either state governments or the Federal Bureau of Prisons. In 1969 an attempt at classification was made. At that time, about 70 percent of the 214,000 inmates were housed in "work-oriented" prisons, about 23 percent in "rehabilitation-oriented" institutions, and about 7 percent in

Table 13.2 Characteristics of Adult Inmates in State Prisons

CHARACTERISTICS	PERCENTAGE	CHARACTERISTICS	PERCENTAGE
Sex		*Employment status*	
Male	97	*(month prior to arrest)*	
Female	3	Employed	68
		Unemployed	32
Race			
White	53	*Occupation*	
Black	47	Blue collar	82
		White collar	15
Age			
Under 20	8	*Personal income*	
20–24	30	Under $4,000	42
25–29	23	$4,000–$5,999	18
30–34	14	$6,000–$9,999	18
35–39	9	$10,000 or more	14
40–49	10		
50 and over	5	*Marital status*	
		Never married	48
Education		Sometime married	28
8th grade or less	26	Currently married	24
1–3 yrs. high school	35		
4 yrs. high school	28		
1–3 yrs. college	8		
4 yrs. or more college	1		

SOURCE: National Prisoner Statistics, *Special Report: Profile of State Prison Inmates: Sociodemographic Findings from the 1974 Survey of Inmates of State Correctional Facilities,* SD-NPS-SR-4 (Washington, D.C.: U.S. Government Printing Office, 1979).

"special-function" institutions such as prison hospitals. Thirty-one of the rehabilitation prisons housed women, 58 housed men. Of the 77 maximum security prisons in 1969, 12 were built before 1850, 33 between 1850 and 1899, and 32 since 1900.[43] In 1976, some 50,000 adult felons were serving time in maximum security prisons built before 1900. That figure represents almost one-fifth of all adult inmates in state and federal prisons on any day that year.[44]

During the mid-1970s, most of the almost 200,000 inmates in state prisons were serving time for robbery (23 percent), burglary (18 percent), or homicide (14 percent). The next largest category was drug offenses (10 percent).[45] (It will be interesting to see whether this picture changes with the supposed "softening up" of reactions to many drug offenses.) Table 13.2 shows additional data on inmate populations in state prisons in 1974. We see that the typical inmate was a young adult male who had not completed high school, and whose personal income prior to incarceration was less than $6,000 a year. Conventional wisdom notwithstanding, the typical prison inmate will have been employed immediately prior to his arrest. As for race, blacks are clearly overrepresented in our prisons. Blacks account for 12 percent of the nation's population, but they make up 47 percent of its state prison population.

For some years prior to the mid 1970s the U.S. prison population had remained fairly stable, at around 200,000 adult inmates. By 1974, however, it was clear the picture was changing. In that year the total adult prison population jumped from a 1973 figure of 204,211 to 218,466 inmates. By 1976 there were 263,291 inmates; of these, 9,983 were women, compared to 6,684 women in 1973 — an increase of 50 percent in just three years. Looking at the *rate* of incarceration, that is, the number of prisoners per 100,000 civilian population, we see that in 1973 the rate was 97.8 and the next year it was 103.6; by 1976 it had grown to 123, a considerable increase over the 1973 level.[46]

One penologist, John Conrad, sees the rise in inmate populations as stemming from a new "hard line" in the administration of justice.[47] He suggests it has resulted from a combination of things: first, an escalation in public anger at the criminal; second, an increase in public disenchantment with social meliorism, represented in part by widespread use of probation and parole and in recent advocacy of community corrections; and finally, rising crime rates in urban areas have helped exacerbate already high levels of social conflict in our cities. Once again, perhaps, we are seeing a manifestation of the law-and-order syndrome noted earlier with respect to the death penalty.

Juvenile Detention Adults are not the only ones who can be imprisoned for violating the law. Children, in most states as young as 13, can be incarcerated in detention facilities for periods up to a year or more.

According to the latest census of detention facilities, there are 992 publicly operated institutions for juvenile custody.[48] Almost half are regarded as "open," which is to say there are minimal in-house physical and staff controls and there is a good deal of accessibility to the surrounding community. Even so, 228 institutions are classified as "strict," or maximum security, and more than 400 reported allowing no community access at all.

Over the past decade most states have experienced a decline in the number of juveniles held in public facilities. This reflects recent efforts to divert juvenile offenders, especially those charged with noncriminal offenses, from the path to detention. Yet we must be careful in judging this apparent decline in juvenile incarcerations. It now appears that there has been a *rise* in the housing of juveniles in *private* facilities (ranches, boarding houses, group homes, shelters, and so forth) — about 7 percent from 1975 to 1977, according to government estimates.[49] Of course, many of these private facilities have none of the characteristics we associate with prisons or reformatories, but some do. Andrew Scull tells us that in Massachusetts during the early 1970s, when efforts were being made to close all state reform schools, some of the juveniles handed over to private agencies were eventually housed in the very state facilities that had been newly vacated![50]

The decarceration trend may continue, but the odds are against it. The law-and-order syndrome that has apparently led to reaffirmation of the death penalty and to increased rates of adult incarceration is unlikely to leave untouched the juvenile offender, who after all is responsible for a sizable portion of the nation's street crime. As of December 31, 1977, there were nearly 46,000 juveniles housed in public facilities and 30,000 in what amounts to private custody.[51] These figures can be expected to rise, and to rise faster than the corresponding increase in the overall juvenile population. It is possible that construction of new detention facilities will be delayed, as calls for cuts in government spending are heeded in state and federal legislatures. In the long run, however, there will almost certainly be new construction to alleviate overcrowding and to satisfy the law-and-order advocates.

Jail as Punishment   Jail time is generally used as punishment only for those convicted of misdemeanors and petty offenses. Sometimes a judge will allow time spent in jail while awaiting trial and sentencing to be counted toward the eventual sentence. If less than a year is left for a felony offender, he will usually serve out his time in jail.

A February 1978 census of jail populations discovered that 158,394 people were being held in the nation's 3,493 jails. Of these, *40 percent had not been convicted of a crime*. These inmates were awaiting formal adjudication proceedings; most had simply been unable to make bail. The remaining 60 percent were serving out sentences, awaiting transfer to prison or other correctional facility, or involved in post-conviction proceedings of one sort or another. The vast majority of jail inmates were found to be young men in their early twenties. Most had not completed high school. Slightly less than half were black, while only 6 percent were women.[52]

Urban jails in general are overcrowded places lacking even modest amenities. Critics contend that jail time is generally more punitive, dangerous, and degrading than time in a maximum security prison. There is, in addition, the mixing of technically innocent people with convicted offenders, not to mention petty offenders with hardened criminals. Experienced convicts say they would rather do their time anywhere but in jail.

Physical Torture

At one time or another most societies have used torture as a criminal punishment. Often, however, torture was an addition to some other punishment, such as removal from the group. The physical aggravation often attached to the death penalty is one good example, and the mutilation used for branding is another.

As a penalty alone, not in addition to another, physical torture has mainly taken the form of flogging or whipping. A variety of instruments have been used, ranging from the cat-o'-nine-tails to the birch. Flogging is probably one of the oldest criminal penalties. It is known to have been practiced by the ancient Jews, and it was a common feature of Roman and Greek punishment. In England, flogging was long considered the accepted penalty for vagrants, vagabonds, and beggars, and its use extends as far back as Anglo-Saxon times. Under the Anglo-Saxon kings, the lash was sometimes an alternative to monetary compensation, and was prescribed mainly for slaves who worked, traveled, or ate on forbidden days. Both abroad and in America, flogging continued to be an official criminal penalty until well into the twentieth century, though most jurisdictions have now abolished it.

While the term *corporal punishment* is traditionally used to refer to floggings, the historical connotation of torture has emphasized the maximization of pain and suffering. If we think about torture as practiced in the old days we probably picture monstrous gadgets designed to inflict the severest of physical torments. As a matter of fact, we need not go too far back in history to find evidence of such punishments.

Physical torture became a fixture of Western penal law during the fifteenth century, and remained so until well into the eighteenth century. In England, torture was always held to be illegal as a penalty for crime, but this did not stop its use. On the contrary, torture was used extensively, both as a punishment for crimes committed and as a device for the extraction of guilty pleas and confessions. Torture as a punishment mainly took the form of mutilation. As a device for obtaining confessions and pleas, it involved all the trappings of a chamber of horrors.

The torture devices of medieval Europe ranged from thumbscrews to such monstrous devices as the rack and the "scavenger's daughter." The rack, as Vincent Price fans well know, stretches its victims; the scavenger's daughter rolls them up into a ball:

> On the rack the prisoner seemed in danger of having the fingers torn from his hands, the toes from his feet, the hands from the arms, the feet from the legs, the forearms from the upper arms, the legs from the trunk. Every ligament was strained, every joint loosened in its socket; and if the sufferer remained obstinate when released, he was brought back to undergo the same cruelties with the added horror of past experience and with a diminished fortitude and physical power. In the Scavenger's Daughter, on the other hand, the pain was caused by an ingenious process of compression. The legs were forced back to the thighs, the thighs were pressed onto the belly, and the whole body was placed within two iron bands which the torturers drew together with all their strength until the miserable human being lost all form but that of a globe. Blood was forced out of the tips of the fingers and toes, the

nostrils and mouth; and the ribs and breastbone were commonly broken in by the pressure.[53]

In colonial America and in England, another form of torture widely used to exact confessions and pleas was the so-called *peine forte et dure* (the strong and hard pain). Heavy weights were placed on the suspect's chest so as to make every breath excruciatingly painful. Usually the torture was used on those who stood mute at their trials, and at least one American colonist is known to have died under the presses during the Salem witch hunt.[54]

Though such physical tortures have been outlawed in Anglo-American law for at least 150 years, recent disclosures indicate that cruel and vicious physical abuse has not disappeared from our prison systems. Apart from the frequently cited beatings and floggings administered in the name of discipline, we now know that in at least one state prison system physical atrocities were common for recalcitrant inmates. In the late 1960s, Tom Murton, then head of the Arkansas prison system, revealed case after case of physical torture. Perhaps the most startling of all the atrocities was the systematic use of a device named after an Arkansas prison farm, the "Tucker telephone." This was an electrical device capable of inflicting excruciating pain on its victims. Wires from the "telephone" were attached to the genitals and feet of inmates, who were then "rung up" with an electrical charge.[55]

Social Degradation

The humiliation and shame that may routinely accompany disclosure of a person's criminal status have been explicitly promoted in some legal punishments. Over the centuries, penalties designed to degrade the offender have taken various forms, but all operate on the principle that those punished suffer the additional torment of stigmatization and accompanying status loss.

Some forms of degradation also incorporate elements of physical torture, such as mutilation and its offshoot, branding. Branding and mutilation flourished during the medieval period and remained important legal punishments until the end of the eighteenth century. Mutilations included dismemberment, loss of ears, eyes, tongue, nose, and lips, and a multitude of other disfigurements. However, there seems to have been little specification as to which offenses were to be punished by mutilation or branding, it being largely a matter of judicial discretion. In colonial America, maiming and branding were used quite frequently for a variety of offenses, including burglary, robbery, religious crimes, and hog stealing.[56]

Less permanent degradations were suffered in the pillory and stocks, though they were not always less painful. Designed to maximize exposure to public ridicule, these devices were in use at least as early as the thirteenth century. In 1406, the English Parliament made it mandatory for each village and town to erect a set of stocks. The only difference between the two devices, both of which were placed in some prominent public place, was that in the pillory the prisoner stood with his arms and head protruding from the crosslike apparatus, but in the stocks he sat so that his feet protruded as well. Any offender so punished was left at the mercy of passersby and any crowd that might have gathered to witness the spectacle. Often the offender had to undergo the additional embarrassment of having his or her hair cut off.

The stocks and pillory were used extensively in England and America for those convicted of minor crimes such as drunkenness, disorderly conduct, prostitution, petty theft, blasphemy, cheating, lying, swearing, and threatening. Sometimes the offender was flogged while locked in the device, and sometimes he was left in it for days. While not a pleasant experience by any standard, what was worse for many was the outright cruelty of the crowds gathered about them. During the seventeenth and eighteenth centuries in England, violence toward the offenders became commonplace. As one commentator described a typical scene: "The mob no sooner saw the prisoners exposed in the pillory than they pelted them with stones, brickbats, dead dogs and cats, and other things."[57] Some punished in the stocks and pillories died as a result of crowd violence, one reason these penalties were abolished in the early nineteenth century.

Variations on the pillory have appeared over the years. In Sweden, for example, those convicted of misdemeanors were sometimes tied upon a wooden horse and left to the derision of the locals.[58] In both England and colonial America the "ducking (or cucking) stool" was often used to punish those who made a nuisance of themselves by gossiping, spreading rumors, and so forth. The ducking stool was a chairlike device the offender sat in while he — or as was most often the case, she — was lowered into a pool of stagnant water.

Although we no longer brand, maim, or duck criminal offenders, many nations continue to include social degradation penalties among their legal punishments. Usually, these modern degradations involve the removal of civil or other rights, and they are specified in law as *automatic penalties on conviction for certain offenses.* They are imposed regardless of the other punishments handed down by the courts. In some jurisdictions, the deprivations extend into the areas of employment, citizenship, inheritance, other property rights, and even marriage.[59] In America, most states give these automatic penalties to felony offenders, who usually lose, temporarily or permanently, their right to vote and their right to hold public office or work in certain occupations. States differ as to how long these deprivations remain in effect. If standards recently proposed are adopted, states may soon repeal all mandatory provisions depriving offenders of civil rights or other attributes of citizenship.[60]

HIDDEN DEGRADATIONS

Criminal punishments often contain less visible degradations — less visible, that is, to the general public. The shame and humiliation suffered by their victims, however, are nonetheless an important aspect of the experience.

Probation is one such penalty — and it *is* a penalty, despite what many people think. The American Bar Association defines probation as "a sentence not involving confinement which imposes conditions and retains authority in the sentencing court to modify the conditions of sentence or to re-sentence the offender if he violates the conditions."[61] More and more criminal offenders are being placed on probation, often as an alternative to fines or incarceration. In the mid-1960s, approximately half of all convicted persons were put on probation; today the figure is estimated to be more than 60 percent. The number of adults and juveniles under state probation supervision on September 1, 1976, was 1,251,918, a rate of 583 per 100,000 population.[62] In Florida, where the use of probation in felony cases has increased tremendously, the period 1967 to 1974 showed an increase of over 500 percent; 79 percent of felony offenders were given probation as all or part of their sentence in 1974.[63]

When placed on supervised probation (the usual case) the probationer is often required to fulfill a variety of demeaning stipulations or conditions. The conditions of probation are often left to the discretion of courts and probation services, though they have in some cases been legislated and thus made part of the official criminal code. The degradations lie in these conditions. Probationers have been told they must attend church; must not marry without permission; must not drive a car, even if needed for work; must spend their evenings and days in ways dictated by probation officers; must spend their earnings only in certain ways; must not travel certain distances, or to certain places; must dress in ways that conform to community standards; or must not smoke or drink.[64]

Social degradation is incorporated in yet another experience many criminal offenders face: parole. Parole is a conditional release from a prison or other correctional facility. It is granted by parole agencies at some point before the maximum term of a prison sentence is served. While many might not think parole a punishment, the truth is that parolees are not treated as if their punishment has ended. Instead, they are subject to all kinds of deprivations, most intended to humiliate and degrade. Parolees are often required to lead an exemplary life, much more so than we expect of ordinary citizens, while at the same time many of the important elements of a productive, successful, responsible, and meaningful social existence are denied them. The parolee is not free to move around. He cannot choose his own friends, associates, or even employment. He has little privacy. He can make few substantive decisions without first getting permission. He has no effective control over his daily life and yet is required to demonstrate that he can in fact control his life. Rather than encourage the development of a favorable self-image, the conditions of parole often undermine the parolee's sense of worth, reduce his status in the eyes of those he cares about, and lock him into a condition of dependency.[65]

Critics of the parole system point to the parole decisions themselves as the cause of many problems. Who gets parole is very often a decision in the hands of political appointees who look for evidence that the inmate has fulfilled the expectations of prison administrators. The parole applicant who can show that he has been a model prisoner often has the advantage over others, some of whom may in fact have made a serious commitment to going straight but nevertheless failed to impress prison officials that they held the right social attitudes and rule-abiding orientation while incarcerated.[66] For inmates facing long prison terms, a favorable parole decision is so desirable that it puts considerable pressure on them to hustle and con their way through the prison experience in the hopes of selling their "new decency" to officials.

The manner in which parole hearings are carried out differs from state to state. Whereas some are seemingly very concerned that the inmate receive the best shot at a successful hearing, others deny any procedural benefits. A recent survey of American parole practices found that twenty-nine states denied the inmate legal representation and thirty generally allowed no witnesses. In addition, twenty-eight states keep no verbatim record of the proceedings, twenty-eight do not allow any appeal, and five provide no written explanation of their decision.[67]

PUBLIC REACTIONS AND DEGRADATION

Stigmatizing those identified as criminals also has a degrading effect; extralegal punishments usually occur when people have trouble with the law. Arrest, conviction, and sentencing are authoritative actions that mark people as different from, and inferior to, those recognized as straight, law-abiding, upright, and thoroughly decent citizens. Tagged as suspects, criminals, ex-cons, or ex-offenders by law enforcement agencies, those officially processed as criminals must contend with the stigma such labels carry with them. They are now outsiders, persons perceived as untrustworthy, suspicious, and threatening. Others can respond to them in punitive ways precisely because of their redefined social identity, an identity that emphasizes their criminality to the exclusion of other personal attributes.[68]

In addition to official criminal penalties, then, convicted persons often face the hostility and fear of those who know about their troubles and redefine their identity accordingly. In effect, the punishments imposed by family, friends, acquaintances, workmates, employers, landlords, and a host of others degrade the person identified as criminal. He is no longer a person worthy of marriage, friendship, a job, or a place in the community.

The likelihood of extralegal punishments being imposed on a criminal offender depends on a host of factors. Most important are the nature of his alleged offense, his reputation in the community, and the severity of the legal punishments meted out to him. If an offense is regarded as serious, if the offender has low preconviction status in the community, and if the authorities have punished him severely, further punishment at the hands of the community has ready support. His social image is redefined downward with ease since he has little going for him, and everything fits neatly into place. Things may be different if a person is convicted of an offense generally regarded as minor, if he had high status in the community before his conviction, and if the authorities treat him lightly, for then the public may be reluctant even to label him criminal, let alone subject him to further deprivations. The feeling that he is different and inferior is less easy to accept. According to one author, the people least likely to be stigmatized by the criminal process and to suffer punitive consequences are those in business, politics, and the professions who commit occupational crimes.[69] In short, those most likely to suffer deprivations at the hands of the public are those who fit the prevailing stereotype of the criminal. Those who fit that stereotype may find that a mere arrest record, with no subsequent conviction, is all it takes for others to react punitively.[70]

Financial Penalties

Today fines are the most commonly imposed criminal penalties. Although no accurate national data exist, estimates usually place fines at around 75 percent of all criminal convictions. In other countries, too, the fine is the most widely used criminal penalty.[71]

The fine has existed in penal law for centuries. The Anglo-Saxons first systematically used financial penalties. Monetary payments in the form of damages or compensation were made to the victims of wrongs. Monetary compensation replaced the long-standing tradition of self-help justice that allowed victims to retaliate directly against those who wronged them, often with disruptive and bloody consequences. Some authors have argued that the threat to group life and property posed by victim retaliation was an important factor in the development and initial popularity of financial penalties.[72]

As time passed and the distinction between criminal law and civil law emerged along with centralized political authority and the state, use of monetary penalties escalated and took new shape. By the thirteenth century, the king received the payments in criminal cases, and victims of wrongs could receive compensation only through civil courts. The growing popularity of the fine is partly explained by the fact that financial penalties were an important source of revenue for the royal treasury. More recently, fines have been supported on similar grounds, though it is now the state and local governments that benefit from the added income. Fines are regarded with favor because they are inexpensive to impose, can be paid back if wrongly imposed, can be readily adjusted according to the gravity of the offense and the financial capacity of the offenders, and can be substituted for more stigmatizing and incapacitating punishments such as imprisonment.

The use of the fine as a legal punishment has not escaped criticism. Much current criticism focuses on the use of jail and prison terms as penalties imposed for nonpayment of fines, and on the built-in inequities that characterize monetary punishments. Recent studies show, for example, that around 50 percent of those fined end up in jail or prison for nonpayment. These are usually the poor.[73] In effect, the imposition of fines discriminates against those with low incomes and insecure financial status. Further, nonpayment often entails additional suffering avoided by those who can pay their fines. A jail term may mean loss of job and loss of housing, not to mention the multitude of other deprivations incurred through incarceration. By contrast, fines are a relative boon to those who can afford them and thus avoid these alternative punishments. Fines are imposed extensively in cases involving consumer fraud, antitrust violations, and a host of occupational crimes. For the middle-class offender or the corporation a fine is often akin to a slap on the wrist, and in light of prevailing criminal stereotypes, merely reinforces the view that it is the "dross of society," the "dangerous classes" who belong in jail. Not surprisingly, those who are imprisoned, whether for nonpayment of fines or for other reasons, are indeed from the lower status levels. In 1972, for example, out of 141,600 adult jail inmates, around two-thirds had not graduated high school, and well over half had incomes under $3,000.[74]

References

1. Austin T. Turk, *Criminality and Legal Order* (Chicago: Rand McNally, 1969), p. 19.
2. See Keith Lovald and Helger R. Stub, "The Revolving Door: Reactions of Chronic Drunkenness Offenders to Court Sanctions," *Journal of Criminal Law, Criminology and Police Science* 59 (1968), pp. 525–30.
3. Egon Bittner and Anthony M. Platt, "The Meaning of Punishment," *Issues in Criminology* 2 (1966), p. 81.
4. See Stanley E. Grupp, ed., *Theories of Punishment* (Bloomington: Indiana University Press, 1971); also, Gertrude Ezorsky, ed., *Philosophical Perspectives on Punishment* (Albany: State University of New York Press, 1972).
5. See Andrew von Hirsch, *Doing Justice: The Choice of Punishments* (New York: Hill and Wang, 1976), p. 136.
6. Peter H. Rossi, Emily Waite, Christine E. Bose, and Richard E. Berk, "The Seriousness of Crimes: Normative Structure and Individual Differences," *American Sociological Review* 39 (1974), pp. 224–37.
7. For example, Donald J. Newman, "Public Attitudes Toward a Form of White Collar Crime," *Social Problems* 4 (1957), pp. 228–32; Arnold M.

Rose and Arthur E. Prell, "Does the Punishment Fit the Crime?" *American Journal of Sociology* 61 (1955), pp. 247–59; Don Gibbons, "Crime and Punishment: A Study in Social Attitudes," *Social Forces* 47 (1969), pp. 391–97.

8. E. A. Ross, *Social Control* (New York: Macmillan, 1929), p. 108.

9. Cesare Beccaria, *Essay on Crimes and Punishments,* trans. Henry Paolucci (New York: Bobbs-Merrill, 1963).

10. Jeremy Bentham, *The Principles of Morals and Legislation* (New York: Hafner Publishing, 1948).

11. Edwin H. Sutherland and Donald R. Cressey, *Criminology,* 9th ed., (Philadelphia: Lippincott, 1974), p. 303.

12. Graeme Newman, *The Punishment Response* (Philadelphia: Lippincott, 1978), p. 27.

13. See Gerhard O. W. Mueller, "Tort, Crime, and the Primitive," *Journal of Criminal Law, Criminology, and Police Science* 46 (1955), pp. 316–19.

14. Emile Durkheim, "Deux lois de l'évolution pénale," *l'Anné Sociologique* IV (1900), pp. 65–93, mimeographed translation.

15. E. Roy Calvert, *Capital Punishment in the Twentieth Century* (1927; repr. New York: Kennikat Press, 1971), p. 4.

16. See William Blackstone, *Commentaries on the Laws of England,* vol. IV (Boston: Beacon Press, 1962).

17. See Clarence H. Patrick, "The Status of Capital Punishment: A World Perspective," *Journal of Criminal Law, Criminology, and Police Science* 56 (1965), pp. 397–411.

18. John Lawrence, *A History of Capital Punishment* (New York: Citadel Press, 1960), p. 223.

19. Ibid., p. 227.

20. See Douglas Hay et al., eds., *Albion's Fatal Tree: Crime and Society in Eighteenth Century England* (London: Allen Lowe, 1975), p. 114.

21. Newman, *The Punishment Response,* pp. 31–32.

22. For the most detailed analysis of executions in America, including a listing of every American legally executed from 1864 to 1967, see William J. Bowers, *Executions in America* (Lexington, Mass.: D. C. Heath, 1974).

23. These data come from National Prisoner Statistics, "Capital Punishment, 1930–1970," *Bulletin No. 46* (1971).

24. Bowers, *Executions in America,* p. 29.

25. See Charles S. Mangum, *The Legal Status of the Negro* (Chapel Hill: University of North Carolina Press, 1940); Guy B. Johnson, "The Negro and Crime," *The Annals* 277 (1941), pp. 93–104; Harold Garfinkel, "Research Note on Inter- and Intra-Racial Homicides," *Social Forces* 27 (1949), pp. 369–81; Frank E. Hartung, "Trends in the Use of Capital Punishment," *The Annals* 284 (1952), pp. 8–23; Marvin E. Wolfgang, Arlene Kelly, and Hans C. Nolde, "Comparison of the Executed and the Commuted among Admissions to Death Row," *Journal of Criminal Law, Criminology, and Police Science* 53 (1962), pp. 301–11; and Marvin E. Wolfgang and Marc Riedel, "Race, Judicial Discretion, and the Death Penalty," *The Annals* 407 (1973), pp. 119–33.

26. Bowers, *Executions in America,* p. 102.

27. Robert M. Carter, "The Johnny Cain Story: A Composite of Men Executed in California," *Issues in Criminology* 1 (1965), pp. 66–76.

28. 428 U.S. 153 (1976).

29. For state-by-state data on prisoners sentenced to death, see National Prisoner Statistics Bulletin, "Capital Punishment 1979," Advance Report, June 1980, SO-NPS-CP-8A (Washington, D.C.: U.S. Government Printing Office, 1980).

30. Joseph H. Rankin, "Changing Attitudes toward Capital Punishment," *Social Forces* 58 (1979), pp. 194–211.

31. Bowers, *Executions in America,* p. 104.

32. 428 U.S. 280 (1976).

33. 431 U.S. 633 (1977) (per curiam).

34. See Bittner and Platt, "The Meaning of Punishment," p. 85.

35. For more on banishment and transportation see Anthony Babbington, *The Power to Silence* (London: Robert Maxwell, 1968), chapters 11 and 12. For the Australian experience, see Lloyd Evans and Paul Nicholls, eds., *Convicts and Colonial Society, 1788–1853* (New South Wales: Cassells, 1976).

36. Durkheim, "Deux lois de l'évolution pénale."

37. For more detailed reviews consult: Howard Gill, *The Attorney General's Survey of Release Procedures* (Washington, D.C.: U.S. Government Printing Office, 1940); Ronald L. Goldfarb and Linda R. Singer, *After Conviction* (New York: Simon and Schuster, 1973); and David Fogel, *. . . We Are the Living Proof, . . .* 2nd ed. (Cincinnati: Anderson, 1979).

38. These states were: New York, New Jersey, Kentucky, Virginia, Massachusetts, Vermont, Maryland, New Hampshire, Ohio, and Georgia.

39. Charles Dickens, *American Notes,* pp. 155–56. Cited in Goldfarb and Singer, *After Conviction,* p. 26.

40. Goldfarb and Singer, *After Conviction,* p. 32.

41. See his own account: Zebulon R. Brockway, *Fifty Years of Prison Service: An Autobiography* (1912; repr. Montclair, N.J.: Patterson Smith, 1969).

42. The states were: New York, Michigan, Massachusetts, Pennsylvania, Minnesota, Colorado, Illinois, Kansas, Ohio, Indiana, Wisconsin, New Jersey, Washington, Oklahoma, Maine, Wyoming, Nebraska, and Connecticut.

43. Joint Commission on Correctional Manpower and Training, *Manpower and Training in Correctional Institutions* (Washington, D.C.: U.S. Government Printing Office, 1969). Figures cited in Goldfarb and Singer, *After Conviction,* p. 49.

44. Gordon Hawkins, *The Prison: Policy and Prac-*

tice (Chicago: University of Chicago Press, 1976), p. 42.

45. See National Prisoner Statistics, *Special Report: Profile of State Prison Inmates: Sociodemographic Findings from the 1974 Survey of Inmates of State Correctional Facilities*, #SD-NPS-SR-4 (Washington, D.C.: U.S. Government Printing Office, 1979).

46. U.S. Department of Justice, "Prisoners in State and Federal Institutions," *National Prisoner Statistics Bulletin* #SD-NPS-PSF2, 3, and 4.

47. John P. Conrad, "We Should Never Have Promised a Hospital," *Federal Probation* (1975).

48. U.S. Department of Justice, *Children in Custody: Advance Report on the 1977 Census of Public Juvenile Facilities*, #SD-JD-SA (Washington, D.C.: U.S. Government Printing Office, 1979).

49. Ibid., p. 1, note 1.

50. Andrew T. Scull, *Decarceration: Community Treatment and the Deviant — A Radical View* (Englewood Cliffs, N.J.: Prentice-Hall, 1977), p. 53.

51. *Children in Custody*, p. 1.

52. U.S. Department of Justice, *LEAA Newsletter* 8 (1979), p. 3.

53. Luke Owen Pike, *A History of Crime in England*, vol. II (Montclair, N.J.: Patterson Smith, 1968), pp. 87–88.

54. Kai T. Erickson, *Wayward Puritans* (New York: Wiley, 1966), p. 149.

55. Tom Murton and Joe Hyams, *Accomplices to the Crime: The Arkansas Prison Scandal* (New York: Grove Press, 1969).

56. See Alice M. Earle, *Curious Punishments of Bygone Days* (1896; repr. Montclair, N.J.: Patterson Smith, 1969), pp. 138–48.

57. Babbington, *The Power to Silence*, p. 13.

58. J. T. James, *Journal of a Tour*, vol. 1 (London: John Murray, 1817), pp. 236–39.

59. See Mirjam R. Damaska, "Adverse Legal Consequences of Conviction and Their Removal: A Comparative Study," *Journal of Criminal Law, Criminology, and Police Science* 59 (1968), pp. 347–60 and 542–68.

60. Standard 16.17, in National Advisory Commission on Criminal Justice Standards and Goals, *Corrections* (Washington, D.C.: U.S. Government Printing Office, 1973), p. 593.

61. American Bar Association, *Standards Relating to Probation* (New York: Institute of Judicial Administration, 1970), p. 9.

62. U.S. Department of Justice, *State and Local Probation and Parole Systems*, #SD-P-1 (Washington, D.C.: U.S. Government Printing Office, 1978), p. 40.

63. Scull, *Decarceration*, p. 47.

64. See Carl H. Imlay and Charles R. Glasheen, "See What Conditions Your Conditions Are In," *Federal Probation* 35 (1971), pp. 3–11; Eugene H. Czajkoski, "Exposing the Quasi-Judicial Role of the Probation Office," *Federal Probation* 37 (1973), pp. 9–13.

65. For a study of parole experiences in California, see Rosemary J. Erickson, Wayman J. Crow, Louis A. Zurcher, and Archie V. Connett, *Paroled but Not Free* (New York: Behavioral Publications, 1973).

66. See A. Keith Bottomley, "Parole Decisions in a Long-Term Closed Prison," *British Journal of Criminology* 13 (1973), pp. 26–40.

67. Vincent O'Leary and Kathleen Hanrahan, "Law and Practice in Parole Proceedings: A National Survey," *Criminal Law Bulletin* 13 (1977), summary tables, pp. 205–11.

68. See Erving Goffman, *Stigma: Notes on the Management of Spoiled Identity* (Englewood Cliffs, N.J.: Prentice-Hall, 1963); and Shlomo Shoham, *The Mark of Cain* (Dobbs Ferry, N.Y.: Citadel, 1970).

69. Shoham, *The Mark of Cain*, pp. 61–64. See also Richard D. Schwartz and Jerome A. Skolnick, "Two Studies of Legal Stigma," *Social Problems* 10 (1962), pp. 133–43; Dennis Chapman, *Sociology and the Stereotype of the Criminal* (London: Tavistock, 1968). For some contrary evidence, see Garland F. White, "Public Response to Hypothetical Crimes: Effects of Offender and Victim Status and the Seriousness of the Offense on Punitive Reactions," *Social Forces* 53 (1975), pp. 411–19; and Ralph Wahrman, "Status, Deviance, and Sanctions," *Pacific Sociological Review* (1970), pp. 229–40.

70. Albert G. Hess and Fré le Poole, "Abuse of the Record of Arrest Not Leading to Conviction," *Crime and Delinquency* 13 (1967), pp. 494–505.

71. Ralph Davidson, "The Promiscuous Fine," *Criminal Law Quarterly* 8 (1965), pp. 74–76.

72. Ibid. Also, C. Ray Jeffery, "Criminal Justice and Social Change," in *Society and the Law*, ed. F. James Davis et al. (New York: Free Press, 1962), pp. 265–66.

73. "Fining the Indigent," *Columbia Law Review* 71 (1971), pp. 1281–1308.

74. U.S. Bureau of the Census, *Statistical Abstract, 1975* (Washington, D.C.: U.S. Government Printing Office, 1976), p. 163.

Consequences of Punishment

When we punish someone our action signifies disapproval of both the offending act and the person who commits it. If we are staunch retributivists we are uninterested in the consequences of the punishment; our concern lies with questions of guilt and just deserts. We want the guilty to suffer a punishment commensurate with the severity of the offense — no more, no less. If, on the other hand, we are advocates of the view that punishment can prevent crime, then the consequences of punishment will be uppermost in our minds. We want the punishment to *work,* that is, to prevent further crime.

As mentioned in the previous chapter, modern American penal policy has given center stage to advocates of either reform and rehabilitation or deterrence. By and large, retribution is played down. Yet at the same time that our policies have emphasized the crime-preventive functions of punishment, criminological theory and research have been raising this warning: far from preventing crime and deviance, punishment may actually *encourage* their occurrence. The work of Tannenbaum, Lemert, and others discussed in chapter 2 illustrates this thinking. Essentially, the theory is that individuals may react and adjust to punishing experiences, eventually becoming precisely what the punishment is designed to prevent: a more committed criminal.[1]

Obviously, the consequences of punishment bear serious thought. It is possible that in punishment we have a contributing factor in the etiology of criminal behavior. In this chapter we shall examine the consequences of punishment, keeping in mind that while it may prevent some people from committing crimes, it may also encourage the commission of crimes by others.

How Punishment Can Prevent Crime

In his important contribution to the literature on criminal punishment, Jack Gibbs identifies ten different ways punishment can prevent crimes.[2] *First,* certain forms of punishment *incapacitate* potential offenders by removing or diminishing the opportunities to commit crimes. Incapacitation is absolute when an offender is executed, but a relative matter for other forms of punishment. Consider imprisonment: although putting someone behind bars reduces the opportunity to commit crimes, it does not rule out all manner of offenses and may actually encourage some; for example, homosexual rape. In Gibbs's view, changes in penal policy since 1800 have brought about a decline in the incapacitating value of legal punishments: initially executions declined in favor of imprisonment, and, more recently, imprisonment declined in favor of fines and probation.[3]

Second, some punishments can prevent crimes because they place offenders under *surveillance.* The conditions of probation and parole often have this effect. Punitive surveillance can work to prevent crimes simply because it increases the visibility of an offender's behavior. Gibbs acknowledges, however, that surveillance of probationers and parolees probably does not prevent a substantial amount of crime.[4]

Enculturation is the *third* preventive mechanism associated with punishment. The idea is that people acquire knowledge that a certain behavior is illegal by experiencing, witnessing, reading about, or being told of punishment for doing it, and this knowledge furthers their respect for the law.[5] Simply put, people refrain from committing a criminal act because they have learned that it is wrong or bad through the punitive response to it. The punishment establishes the criminality of the act, and that fact (or belief) is reason for refraining from doing it. Clearly, for punishment to so prevent crime we have to be dealing with people who accept the precept of "obedience to law."

The *fourth* crime-preventive mechanism of punishment is *reformation,* the idea that the experience of punishment alters an offender's behavior: he or she "no longer contemplates criminal acts."[6] Essentially, the argument supports the notion that punishment conveys to some offenders a sense of shame and remorse, and it is this that promotes subsequent conformity. Even an arrest, Gibbs notes, may produce a "moral jolt," as we saw in the case of amateur shoplifters (see page 190).

In his discussion of reformation, Gibbs notes that the terms *reformation* and *rehabilitation* have usually been considered interchangeable. He argues that "the meanings of the terms should be distinguished. Criminal rehabilitation is the alteration of an offender's behavior by nonpunitive means, so that he or she no longer violates laws. Criminal reformation is the alteration of an offender's behavior *through punishment,* so that he or she no longer violates laws."[7] Recalling our discussion of imprisonment in the preceding chapter, early American prison systems clearly emphasized reformation of offenders. Modern correctional practice tends to favor the rehabilitation of offenders; programs of work release, halfway houses, and other features are efforts in this direction. Later in this chapter we shall return to the issue of rehabilitation.

The *fifth* way in which punishment can prevent crime is through *normative validation*. This notion echoes an argument advanced many years ago by Emile Durkheim. He saw in punishment the opportunity to reaffirm, possibly intensify, condemnation of an act.[8] Indeed, this is a "function" of punishment, according to Durkheim.[9] When we punish we remind the sufferer, *and also ourselves and others who know of it,* that the rule of law is valid, that violation of it continues to be condemned. So normative validation means the maintenance or enhancement through punishment of already existing (but perhaps weakening) condemnation of certain behaviors.

Sixth is *retribution*. This may come as a surprise, especially since our discussion in chapter 13 specifically distinguished between punishment as retribution and punishment as crime prevention. Gibbs asserts that where there exists a demand that the guilty be punished, not to do so would encourage private vengeance, the extreme form of which is armed vigilantism.

> Even in societies with "law," the certainty and severity of punishment could become so negligible that the citizens would seek personal retribution; and what the injured party would take to be justifiable vengeance could be criminal assault, criminal homicide, robbery, extortion, kidnapping, or theft. So no imagination is required to see that retribution "outside the law" generates crimes. Hence, retribution through legal punishments may prevent crimes.[10]

Stigmatization is Gibbs's *seventh* crime-preventive mechanism in punishment. Because it identifies a perpetrator as "criminal" — often publicly and dramatically — punishment "thereby becomes a *criterion* for subsequent social condemnation. The punished individual faces the prospects of incontestable divorce, loss of job, denial of alternative employment opportunities, exclusion from voluntary associations, and termination of all manner of other social relations (e.g., friendships, romantic attachments, kinship ties)."[11] An individual may refrain from crime not because of the punishment itself but, rather, because of the anticipated stigmatization. It seems that Gibbs is splitting hairs, but the point is well taken: different kinds of punishment can produce different stigmatizing effects, just as the same punishments can when inflicted in different ways. Presumably, the stigmatizing impact of public punishment is greater than that of private or secretive punishment. Another important issue concerns the fact that stigmatizing effects may be linked to class or ethnic status: blacks, Chicanos, and low-income people "are less prone to view punishment as a stigma than are upper-class Anglos," Gibbs suggests.[12] In any event, recognition of the crime-preventive possibilities of stigmatization clearly influenced the invention and adoption of certain methods of punishment, as we saw in the earlier discussion of social degradation penalties.

The *eighth* preventive mechanism in punishment is *normative insulation*. Recall for a moment Sutherland's theory of differential association: that people may learn attitudes and values favorable to law violation in their intimate associations with others. Presumably, the more we associate intimately with persons who are not law-abiding, the more we are likely to adopt their normative orientation.[13] If we could somehow escape their influence, perhaps our own normative orientations would be more law-abiding. In Gibbs's view at least three punishments have the effect of insulating us from the normative influence of offenders: execution, imprisonment, and banishment.[14]

Habituation, the *ninth* way in which punishment is thought to prevent crime, has been discussed by Zimring and Hawkins, among others.[15] These authors argue that people develop the habit of conforming to the law; apparently they conform quite uncritically. Punishment comes in because it contributes both to the development and maintenance of habits. Recent efforts to reduce the speed at which Americans drive on the nation's highways are examples of the effects of habituation. By all accounts many drivers are not abiding by the 55-mile-per-hour speed limit, but driving *is* slower than it was before the change in law took place, especially in states with systematic enforcement. Though it is difficult to separate habituation from deterrence, habituation is implied when drivers tend to follow speed limits in the absence of patrolling police, or after enforcement has abruptly ended for some reason.[16]

Deterrence is the *tenth* way in which punishment can prevent crime. Before discussing this preventive mechanism, it is appropriate to ask whether current evidence favors, among those enumerated above, any one particular mechanism over another. Gibbs's presentation is rather discouraging here for it is clear that there has been very little research dealing with any of the preceding nine crime-preventive mechanisms.[17] Gibbs also makes it clear that research to establish if and how they do work is obstructed by conceptual and methodological problems, especially when efforts are made to separate out the effects, if any, of deterrence.

Obviously, if we think only of individual offenders who are caught and convicted, then incapacitation through execution would be a sure way to prevent *their* further criminality. It is preposterous to suggest this remedy for all types of offenses, and it would certainly be rejected by some even for premeditated murder. For any other type of punishment, incapacitation is a matter of degree. Among the other conventional penalties that are imposed in the Western world, only imprisonment can be considered incapacitating, and then only temporarily in most cases. Indeed, it is possible that in some instances a prison sentence provides opportunities to acquire additional skills and abilities that may be put to criminal use upon release. It is doubtful that this is a major consequence of imprisonment, but the idea is part of the conventional wisdom, and we shall return to it again for further consideration.

Some scholars consider stigmatization to be among the most important effects of conviction and punishment. Shlomo Shoham writes:

> . . . the social stigma of conviction is probably the most potent deterrent to potential offenders. A person who is not a professional or habitual criminal or a lawyer is rarely aware of the exact or even the approximate penalty he is likely to suffer for the offense he is about to commit, though he is, of course, aware of the possibility of detection and punishment. The fear of stigma is probably much stronger than the fear of punishment for the average law-abiding citizen. He is afraid of losing his job, of being ostracized by his business associates and friends, of the possible alienation of members of his family, of having to leave his neighborhood or even his town.[18]

Once again, however, we must acknowledge the other side of the coin. Gibbs reminds us that "stigmatization may generate secondary deviance or result in definitions favorable to crime through differential association. In the case of secondary deviance, the offender identifies himself as a criminal not only because of punishment but also because of subsequent stigmatization." In the case of differential association, stigmatization may bar the offender from "normal" social relations, forcing him to "turn to those who attach no stigma to punishment, and they are likely to be sources of definitions favorable to crime."[19]

One of the ways teachers, judges, and other authorities attempt to explain their choice of punishment is: "I'm going to make an example out of you!" This remark may be thought of as an attempt to raise fear in others who are potential offenders; in this case we would correctly think of deterrence. There is more to the remark, however, for it also shows the colors of normative validation. The speaker is alerting others to the fact that punishments such as this *will be* applied to violations such as that. "Take note. Those in my position intend to enforce that rule and this is the kind of punishment you can expect." The intended audience — a class of schoolchildren, workers in a factory, people in general — are reminded both how they ought to behave and what the appropriate reaction will be if they don't.

In the minds of many, normative validation must surely rank as the major goal in punishment. Certainly, if we can reinforce and perhaps even intensify conformity to the law, then we will see less violation of it. Yet strangely enough, a vital ingredient is often missing when it comes to the punishment of crime: publicity. Gibbs argues:

> If punishments validate laws and thereby reduce the crime rate, they do so only to the extent that they are publicized. But in the United States and many other countries, actual punishments are not publicized systematically, and the citizenry is informed only at the whim of the news media. The situation is all the more remarkable because publicizing punishments might further both normative validation and deterrence.[20]

One might well ask, Have we really given normative validation a chance? The answer is probably no.

A Closer Look at Deterrence

In the preceding chapter we spoke rather generally about deterrence, the tenth way in which punishment can prevent crime. A more detailed discussion is in order for two reasons: (1) there appears to be widespread belief that it works, a view held by many experts as well as by members of the public; and (2) deterrence has become a major research focus in criminology, giving it not only scientific standing as a cause célèbre, but also a tremendous amount of empirical scrutiny, which is not the case with the other nine preventive mechanisms.

The emergence of deterrence as an object of considerable research interest over the last decade or so shows how topics once put aside as dead issues can reemerge to claim the limelight. By the 1950s many social scientists clearly viewed deterrence as passé. After all, study after study had purported to demonstrate a lack of evidence that fear of punishment deters potential criminals. This was argued even for the ultimate punishmant, death.[21] It was easy for some to say, "If fear of death does not deter people, how can we expect lesser penalties to act as deterrents to crime?"

The reemergence of deterrence as a major issue also illustrates the intimate connection between theory and research. As we saw in chapter 2, the late 1950s and early 1960s witnessed growing theoretical interest in reactions to crime and deviance. The so-called labeling perspective grew up around the idea that reactions might somehow contribute to crime. Thus reactions to crime and deviance received a new lease on life, this time as *independent variables* in the analysis of crime. Far from deterring crime, perhaps punishment helps cause it.

This issue could not be resolved by reference to previous research partly because that research focused primarily on one type of punishment (death) and one type of crime (homicide). Even if the death penalty does not in some way deter homicide, perhaps other kinds of punishment deter (or help cause) other kinds of crime. So, careful analysis of questions pertaining to the relationship (if any) between crime and its punishment required new research ventures. These, it turned out, gave rise to new theoretical issues, among them conceptual distinctions dealing with types of deterrence, types of crime and criminals, and various dimensions of punishment.

TYPES OF DETERRENCE

It has become conventional to distinguish between *specific* (or *individual,* or *special*) deterrence and *general* deterrence.[22] The distinction recognizes two classes of potential offenders who may refrain from crime because they fear punitive sanctions: (1) those who have directly experienced punishment for a crime or crimes they committed in the past — specific deterrence; and (2) those who have not experienced punishment but are deterred from crime by the threat of punishment — general deterrence.

The distinction is important because the deterrent effect of experienced punishments may be quite different from that of threatened punishments. Even so, not all authors agree with this conventional distinction between specific and general deterrence, and it in no way exhausts typological possibilities.[23] For example, Jack Gibbs distinguishes between *absolute* and *restrictive* deterrence. Some people refrain from a particular criminal activity *throughout their lives* because they fear punishment (absolute deterrence), whereas others may modify or curtail their criminal activities *for a period of time* because they see a growing risk of punishment if they persist (restrictive deterrence). Typological refinements of this sort not only reveal the complexities of deterrence; they also serve to guide theory and research into new, possibly fruitful directions.

TYPES OF CRIMES AND TYPES OF OFFENDERS

Criminologists have recognized that punishment may deter only some offenders who commit only certain crimes.[24] Regarding type of crimes, William Chambliss believes an important distinction can be made between instrumental crimes and expressive crimes.[25] *Instrumental crimes* are those directed toward some material end: burglary, occupational crimes, tax evasion, parking violations, robbery, and so on. *Expressive crimes* constitute ends in themselves; they articulate desires: most murders and assaults, drunkenness, most sex offenses, consumption of illicit drugs, and so forth. In Chambliss's view, the deterrent effect of punishment may well be greater for instrumental crimes, since these activities typically involve some degree of planning and risk assessment (though sometimes not much). Expressive crimes, on the other hand, are often impulsive and emotional; people about to commit them respond to pressures of the moment, not to what might happen to them in the future.

Andenaes presents another effort to distinguish types of offenses.[26] He adopts the classic dichotomy of *mala in se* crimes and *mala prohibita* crimes (see page 13). This distinction recognizes that some offenses are "evil in themselves" or inherently immoral, whereas others are "evil because prohibited." Examples of *mala in se* crimes are robbery, murder, rape, and arson; examples of *mala prohibita* crimes are drug offenses, traffic violations, and many occupational crimes. Andenaes's argument is that *mala in se* crimes support and are supported by the moral codes of society, whereas crimes that are simply illegal stand on the law alone. Accordingly, if people conform to prohibitions of the latter sort, it is more likely a result of deterrence (that is, fear of punishment) rather than of any moral imperative, as would be expected in the case of crimes that are evil in themselves. Needless to say, Chambliss and Andenaes cannot both be right, for some offenses, such as burglary and robbery, would appear in the "less deterrable" column for Andenaes but the "more deterrable" column for Chambliss. Nevertheless, some combination of properties might yet work. It is possible, for example, that crimes that are both instrumental and *mala prohibita* are most deterrable, and offenses that are both expressive and *mala in se* are least deterrable. There appears to have been no research examining this specific issue.

When all is said and done, we may need to know a lot more about the offender when organizing our ideas about deterrence. After all, it is *people* who are deterred and not the acts they commit. Perhaps some people are more amenable to deterrence than others. Chambliss offers some insights here, too. He suggests that we distinguish between persons who have a relatively high commitment to crime as a way of life and those with a relatively low commitment. Those involved in crime on a regular, perhaps even professional, basis are usually caught up in subcultures providing group support for their activities, and crime is for them a way of life. Such offenders are less likely to be deterred, Chambliss argues, for criminal penalties are something they have learned to live with, and the threat of them may be offset by the supportive role played by subcultural peers. The typical shoplifter, naive check forger, tax evader, or other occasional offender, on the other hand, does not think of himself as a criminal and receives little direct group support for his criminal activity. Fear of punishment may well prove an important factor in turning such low commitment individuals away from crime, especially if they have already experienced punishment.

If we put all three distinctions together, then, the following predictions could serve as objects of further investigation: 1. *Fear of punishment is most likely to deter low commitment individuals who engage in* mala prohibita *crimes that are also instrumental crimes.* 2. *Fear of punishment is least likely to deter high commitment individuals who engage in* mala in se *crimes that are also expressive crimes.*

THE NORMATIVE, ACTUAL, AND COGNITIVE SIDES OF PUNISHMENT

Turning to punishment itself, there are at least three sides to criminal penalties. The *normative* side specifies what is supposed to happen according to law when various offenses are committed. The *actual* side deals with what really happens to convicted criminals. The *cognitive* side includes people's perceptions of what happens to criminals.[27]

The deterrence doctrine presumes an inverse correlation between measurable aspects of punishment (identified in the following section) and criminal activity: the more severe the punishment for a crime, the lower the rate of that crime. But what side of punishment are we talking about? Early deterrence research focused primarily on statutory provisions (whether or not the death penalty is prescribed for certain offenses), ignoring the important possibility that it is not punishment *on the books* that people fear, but further experiences with *actual* punishment or the threat of such experiences.

Much recent research has put right the earlier lack of attention to actual punishments[28]; but we have not yet corrected the imbalance concerning perceptions of punishment.[29] This neglect is something of a mystery, since the essential mechanisms presumed to motivate potential offenders to refrain from crime are threat, fear, and risk. These are subjective matters, based on knowledge and beliefs about punishment. It is evidence of the long-standing neglect of this side of punishment when readers have to be reminded as recently as 1977 that the deterrence doctrine is a *psychological* theory, properly tested only with evidence on perceptions.[30]

PROPERTIES OF PUNISHMENT

We now examine the various aspects of punishment considered relevant in tests of the deterrence thesis. In their early work, Beccaria and Bentham made a significant contribution to the development of ideas about deterrence when they focused attention on three properties of punishment.[31] They recognized that criminal penalties can be more or less *certain,* more or less *severe,* and more or less *swift* in their imposition. Though a little vague on the matter, Bentham and Beccaria must be understood as saying that the deterrent impact of punishment will be greater the more certain, severe, and swift the penalties. Of the three properties, severity of punishment was considered less important than the others, a view quickly adopted by many scholars for obvious reasons:

one can deemphasize the clearly punitive side of crime control while still maintaining that punishment can prevent crime if imposed with certainty and celerity.

Except for one or two very recent efforts, hardly any research has been done that speaks to the issue of celerity.[32] This is sad, for it was a problem close to Beccaria's heart. Not only did he denounce the Italian practice of detaining criminal defendants for months, sometimes years, before adjudication and sentencing, but he also considered it vital to impose penalties as soon as possible so that the connection between offense and penalty was not weakened or obscured by the passage of time. Both seem admirable concerns.

When we discussed perceptions of punishment, we meant perceptions of the severity, certainty, and celerity of criminal penalties. Some authors have recently pointed out, however, that whereas legal punishments are clearly of central concern in the study of crime, there are various extra-legal penalties that are often brought to bear on criminal offenders. Loss of job, ostracism, even physical abuse may be imposed as sanctions by persons having no legal role in the judicial process. Further, it could be that extralegal penalties have a more crucial role in deterrence than legal punishments. Not fearing the threat of legal sanctions, or at least not letting that fear influence his behavior, a potential offender may refrain from committing a crime because he fears the social condemnation of friends, relatives, or peers. Indeed, recent studies that have investigated this possibility find some support for it.[33] Yet, to complicate matters, William Minor finds that in the case of at least one offense (tax fraud), the measured deterrent effect is from formal (legal) sanctions, not informal (extralegal) ones.[34]

THE PROBLEM OF CAUSALITY

One final issue deserves mention before we summarize the findings of deterrence research. That issue is causality, which can be rephrased as the "chicken or the egg" dilemma. A number of writers on deterrence have alerted their readers to the fact that a negative (or inverse) relationship between punishment and crime does not necessarily support the deterrence argument. Far from crime being influenced by punishment, it might be that things are the other way around. David Greenberg explains how:

> For example, when crime rates are high relative to police and court resources, law enforcement resources might stretch thin, reducing the chances of a crime leading to arrest or conviction. There is evidence that clearance rates fall when police resources fail to keep pace with mounting crime rates. Lower prison sentences might also result if reduced prosecutor resources and larger backlogs in the court lead to plea bargains more favorable to the defendant. In urbanized areas, where crime rates tend to be exceptionally

high, budgetary and reform group pressures may result in more highly developed probation services and higher judicial utilization of probation than in rural areas. These effects would lead to negative relationships between crime rates and measures of punishment certainty and severity, but the direction of causality would be the opposite of that assumed by deterrence theory.[35]

This problem also extends to research on the relationship between perceptions of punishment and self-reported criminality. Although some recent research attempts to place the variables in the "right" order, that is, where perceptions influence behavior rather than the other way around, the fact that this is accomplished by asking people to recall their *past perceptions,* or predict their *future behavior,* raises the likelihood of distortions. Indeed, Minor reports one study that shows perceptions do not remain stable over time. This raises doubts about tests of deterrence that ask people to recall earlier conduct and then relate those reports to current perceptions as if they have remained the same since the earlier behavior.[36]

Does Fear of Punishment Really Prevent Crime?

Where does all this leave us? Certainly, deterrence is a complex matter, far too complicated for us to do it justice in a few pages. Nevertheless, one is tempted to hope that with the hundreds of studies completed during the past few years some answers to the question, Does punishment deter crime? can be given with confidence.

Regrettably, this seems not to be the case. Although most authors agree that any rejection of the deterrence doctrine is premature, few are willing to accept it. We are confronted by a vast array of conflicting findings. This results in part from differing research methodologies, but it is also due to problems with the nature of the data and their interpretation, as well as to the complexities inherent in the subject.

To the lay person, the inability of the scientific community to substantiate or reject the conventional wisdom that punishment deters — especially if it is swift, certain, and severe — must be difficult to understand. In the minds of most people the issue is simple and must therefore be simple to resolve; people either are or are not influenced by fear of punishment. Each of us can surely come up with our own illustrations of deterrence at work, but researchers have found the going very rough indeed. In fact, the further they delve into the subject, the more complex it seems to become. Where twenty-five years ago reputable scientists were willing to fling aside the deterrence doctrine as disproved, none would do so today. All of this makes the subject an exciting and challenging area of research in criminology.

It would be misleading, however, to conclude this brief discussion of deterrence without noticing one ray of light that keeps breaking through the inconclusive haze. It concerns the *certainty* of punishment. While there are (of course!) exceptions to this, it appears on balance that *the more certain the imposition of punishment actually is, or is perceived to be, the lower the level of crime.*[37] For those who want to believe in deterrence, this will no doubt be taken as firm confirmation of the doctrine's validity. That would be a mistake, for the jury is still out on the question of certainty of punishment, as indeed it is on almost all other deterrence issues. When all is said and done, the most difficult and pressing task for criminology is to separate deterrence effects from the nine other preventive possibilities of punishment.

Reformation and Rehabilitation: Do They Work?

It has become conventional to speak of "corrections" when referring to the organized efforts of governments to deal with convicted offenders whose sentences involve incarceration or some form of direct supervision. Hence the American Correctional Association is primarily composed of professionals in prison, parole, probation, or community treatment jobs. The word *corrections* means just what you would expect: to put right someone who has gone wrong.

Needless to say, if you are trying to change someone it helps if you have a firm idea of what "right" looks like. In primitive societies, or in those headed by totalitarian regimes, it is relatively easy to assert what is right and wrong, for attitudes and behaviors tend to be cast in the same mold and are confined within narrow limits. But in modern complex societies, definitions of right and wrong, of what is desirable and what is not, are harder to pin down and consensus is unlikely. When there is no strongly entrenched sense of what right is, the goal of corrections is largely what those in charge of it say it is. When correctional decision makers support parole applications, for example, it is because the applicant conforms to their image of a "corrected" person.

It should be clear from this that investigations into whether or not reformation and rehabilitation work are likely to be hampered from the start. Certainly, investigators cannot assume that their view of a successful correctional outcome is the same as that of practitioners in the field. Nor can they assume that the officially designated goals of reformation and rehabilitation, whatever they may be, are the same as those held by the people who are actually running things. Whatever the formal goals of an organizatoin, invariably there are informal ones to contend with.

MEASURING THE SUCCESS OF REFORMATION AND REHABILITATION

It is important to keep in mind that no one has yet managed to isolate the effects of reformation and rehabilitation from those of other forces affecting the behavior of ex-offenders. Apart from the other possible consequences of punishment (stigmatization, incapacitation, deterrence, and so on), there are many things likely to influence someone's behavior after release from prison or correctional supervision. Most of these are beyond the control of correctional authorities. There is nothing they can do about an offender's past record of crimes, age at first offense, race or sex, job history, marital status, or past experiences with the authorities.[38]

It is, then, extremely difficult to demonstrate a direct link between an offender's experiences with reformation and rehabilitation and his subsequent attitudes and behavior. Nevertheless, criminologists rightly persist in their efforts to evaluate correctional outcomes, and they do so primarily by looking at *recidivism*. The word means relapse into crime, hence recidivists are those who once again commit crime. The rate of recidivism would be the proportion of offenders in a population who relapsed into crime, who committed a new crime (or crimes) after having been "corrected." The focus on recidivism implies that correctional programs are successful to the degree that ex-offenders who have been through them stay that way — in other words, do not relapse into crime.

There are actually a number of different ways of picturing recidivism, and it is a criticism of existing approaches that this fact has not been adequately emphasized. To illustrate, let us imagine a hypothetical offender, George, who has been arrested and convicted of armed robbery and has gone through the correctional process, including specific efforts to reform and rehabilitate him. Now it is possible that one or more of the following statements will apply to George.

During the rest of his lifetime, George

(1a) *never* again commits armed robbery.
(1b) commits armed robbery *once* again.
(1c) commits armed robbery *more than once* again.

(2a) *never* commits an offense *similar to* armed robbery (that is, one involving instrumental use of violence).
(2b) commits a similar offense *once*.
(2c) commits a similar offense *more than once* again.

(3a) *never* commits a *more serious* offense than armed robbery.
(3b) commits a more serious offense *once*.
(3c) commits a more serious offense *more than once*.

(4a) *never* commits a *less serious* offense than armed robbery.
(4b) commits a less serious offense *once*.
(4c) commits a less serious offense *more than once*.

We could have chosen any other offense as a reference point; however, minor offenses rarely result in any organized efforts at reform and rehabilitation (except, perhaps, in the case of young juvenile offenders), and, among other serious crimes, armed robbery almost always results in correctional supervision for those who are convicted.

Now consider various recidivism possibilities. If George belongs in categories 1a, 2a, 3a, and 4a, he has clearly *not* relapsed into crime of any sort. He might be called "absolutely reformed" or "absolutely rehabilitated," depending on the context of correctional efforts. On the other hand, George might fall into the combined categories 1c, 2c, 3c, and 4c. In this case we have a disaster: George has not only relapsed into the same crime more than once, but into similar crimes, more serious crimes, and less serious crimes as well. In between these two extremes there are seventy-nine other possibilities. Here are three, picked at random:

1. George never again commits armed robbery, but commits a similar offense once, a more serious offense once, and many less serious offenses (1a, 2b, 3b, 4c).
2. George commits armed robbery once again, but no other offenses at all (1b, 2a, 3a, 4a).
3. George never again commits armed robbery, never commits a similar or more serious offense, and commits a less serious offense only once (1a, 2a, 3a, 4b).

Visualizing recidivism in this way — as a matter of kind and degree rather than mere presence or absence — promises a more enlightened approach to evaluating correctional outcomes, and can help in the construction of specific programs of rehabilitation and reform. Although total eradication of recidivism may be held to by a few fanatics as the goal of corrections, more reasonable designs might stress eradication of only certain forms of criminality (say, those involving violence) and reductions in the probability that offenders will "graduate" to more serious crimes than those for which they have been punished.

RATES OF RECIDIVISM

Accurate information on recidivism is notoriously hard to come by. If relapse into crime is taken in its broadest sense, then *any* new criminal behavior, no matter how petty, would be evidence of a person's recidivism. But finding out about that crime is no easy task, as we learned in chapter 3. Furthermore, simply to show that someone has *not* been arrested (much less not convicted) does not prove he has stayed clear of crime. To prove it, we would need an observer at his elbow at all times. Indeed, parolees may well take extra effort to hide their further involvement in crime, knowing that if they are merely suspected of new offenses they risk being returned to prison.

Most recidivism studies have focused on returns to prison. If a former inmate is sent back to prison, it is often taken as evidence of the failure of reform and rehabilitation; therefore, low rates of recidivism (measured by reimprisonment) are taken as evidence of correctional successes. It turns out that neither of these interpretations is sound. People are often sent back to prison for technical violations of the conditions of their parole, *not* for new crimes. On the basis of recent national survey data on male parolees, David Greenberg writes that "many of the returnees were sent back to prison for behavior that is not forbidden to the general public, for suspicion of an offense where guilt was not proved in court, and at least sometimes when the parolee had already been tried and acquitted."[39] Only 25 percent of those returned to prison during their first year on parole were reimprisoned for new felony offenses.

In addition, understandable concern over recidivism should not obscure the fact that (1) only a small proportion of convicted offenders actually serve time in prison, and (2) those who do generally have long histories of involvement in crime. Indeed, a 1974 survey found that over 71 percent of the nation's prison inmates had had some prior correctional experience, either as a juvenile or as an adult.[40] Viewed in this light, recidivism rates based on prison paroles cannot fairly be used as generalizations for all criminal offenders or even for those who have had non-prison experience with reformation or rehabilitation. Relapses into crime by ex-inmates may tell us something about reform efforts *in prison* — though this is doubtful — but they certainly tell us nothing about correctional efforts carried out in nonprison contexts.

Needless to say, low recidivism rates do not mean that inmates are "corrected." Even if we exclude problems of discovery, that is, of establishing whether or not they have committed new crimes, we cannot be sure that ex-inmates would have committed new crimes had they not been subjected to correction. For all these reasons, then, it is difficult to interpret the findings on reimprisonment. The problem is exacerbated when we discover that estimates of reimprisonment rates vary from 35 percent of ex-inmates to more than 65 percent.[41]

As far as the issue of recidivism is concerned, it appears that most experts are pessimistic about the chances of ex-inmates going straight. And it is not just that they relapse into petty crimes; Gibbs suggests that no criminologist would find it surprising if the rate of *felony* recidivism were as high as 80 percent.[42]

PRISONS AND REHABILITATION

There are several schools of thought concerning the connection between correctional efforts and recidivism. There are those who argue that reform and rehabilitation simply will not work in a prison setting. Part of the problem relates to prison organization and management: "Wardens are paid for running quiet prisons, not for reforming inmates. Any attempt to establish rehabilitation programs in prison are opposed by both staff and inmates because it makes life more difficult for all concerned."[43] Another author has observed that, rhetoric to the contrary, "the actual experience of imprisonment for most persons imprisoned in this country in this century has been simply punitive."[44] Furthermore, prisons isolate inmates from the communities into which they will later return, often by hundreds of miles. A 1971 survey by William Nagel found even the newest correctional facilities for men located in sparsely populated areas, far from the largest cities in their states.[45] Prison construction is largely a matter of politics — it means money and jobs for some, danger and deviance to others — almost never a matter of what is best for the inmate.

In the early 1970s Badillo and Haynes observed that New York State could boast the highest concentration of psychologists and psychiatrists in the world. Yet the state's penal system had none on its regular staff, and there were only sixty for the entire American prison system. Further, of the nation's correctional budget, only five cents of every dollar was actually spent on "correcting" inmates. Badillo and Haynes concluded: "We do not have in America, and never have had, any rehabilitation program on a significant scale for a significant length of time."[46] This is the "we haven't done enough" argument, and it has many adherents. The solution, they suggest, "is simply a more full-hearted commitment to the strategy of treatment."[47]

From another side comes the view that physical confinement breeds its own version of tyranny, expressed in the relationship between guards and prisoners and between prisoners themselves. Philip Zimbardo's well-known experiment in the basement of a Stanford University building has helped document what he calls the *pathology of imprisonment* (see box on pages 464–465). One manifestation of the tyranny has been the use of prisoners in research involving drugs, shock therapy, and even psychosurgery. In "Clockwork Orange in a California Prison," R. T. Trotter describes three brain operations performed in 1968 on inmates of Vacaville State Penitentiary.[48] In his doctoral dissertation, Richard Speiglman has documented the use of powerful depressants such as Thorazine, Prolixin, and Acetine in the California prison system.[49] Whether in this form or in day-to-day prison life, the tyranny of confinement is viewed by many as antithetical to reform and rehabilitation. No amount of behavior modification, drug therapy, group counseling, or correctional techniques can overcome the pathology of imprisonment. *"Prisoners adjust to the environment of the prison, not to the environment of free men,"* C. Ray Jeffery claims; like many others he advocates the community, not the prison, as the key to rehabilitation.[50]

Halfway Houses One outgrowth of growing interest in community-based alternatives to prison has been the *halfway house* movement. Although it began over a hundred years ago with the purpose of providing temporary shelter, food, clothing, and counsel to ex-offenders, the movement really got going in the 1950s and early 1960s. Today no single description adequately conveys the myriad forms the nation's halfway houses have taken. Sometimes called community treatment centers, the

PATHOLOGY OF IMPRISONMENT

I was recently released from solitary confinement after being held therein for 37 months [months!]. A silent system was imposed upon me and to even whisper to the man in the next cell resulted in being beaten by guards, sprayed with chemical mace, blackjacked, stomped and thrown into a strip-cell naked to sleep on a concrete floor without bedding, covering, wash basin or even a toilet. The floor served as toilet and bed, and even there the silent system was enforced. To let a moan escape your lips because of the pain and discomfort . . . resulted in another beating. I spent not days, but months there during my 37 months in solitary. . . . I have filed every writ possible against the administrative acts of brutality. The state courts have all denied the petitions. Because of my refusal to let the things die down and forget all that happened during my 37 months in solitary . . . I am the most hated prisoner in [this] penitentiary, and called a "hard-core incorrigible."

Maybe I am an incorrigible, but if true, it's because I would rather die than to accept being treated as less than a human being. I have never complained of my prison sentence as being unjustified except through legal means of appeals. I have never put a knife on a guard's throat and demanded my release. I know that thieves must be punished and I don't justify stealing, even though I am a thief myself. But now I don't think I will be a thief when I am released. No, I'm not rehabilitated. It's just that I no longer think of becoming wealthy by stealing. I now only think of killing — killing those who have beaten me and treated me as if I were a dog. I hope and pray for the sake of my own soul and future life of freedom that I am able to overcome the bitterness and hatred which eats daily at my soul, but I know that to overcome it will not be easy.

This eloquent plea for prison reform — for humane treatment of human beings, for the basic dignity that is the right of every American — came to me secretly in a letter from a prisoner who cannot be identified because he is still in a state correctional institution. He sent it to me because he read of an experiment I recently conducted at Stanford University. In an attempt to understand just what it means psychologically to be a prisoner or a prison guard, Craig Haney, Curt Banks, Dave

facilities provide housing for psychiatric patients, delinquent children, alcoholics and other problem drug users, neglected children, homeless adults, the mentally retarded, as well as criminal offenders.[51]

Early halfway houses were not really part of the correctional system, but today there are close ties between the two, for these reasons: (1) recognition among those involved in community corrections that their very survival and success depend in large part upon a close association with mainstream corrections, and (2) increasing state and federal involvement in community corrections.[52] The correctional bureaucracy is vast and now encompasses the community as well as the more traditional institutions.

The idea that the best rehabilitative possibilities lie in the community has been challenged by at least one penologist. Nora Klapmuts has argued that enthusiasm for community treatment reflects some shaky reasoning:

If prisons do not rehabilitate, and if the goal of correction is to reduce recidivism through integration of offender and community, it seems axiomatic that treating the offender without removing him from society will be more effective. Unfortunately, while one may express the opinion that, since prisons are not effective (a validated observation) then one *might as well* retain offenders in the community, one cannot assume without the support of adequate research that the best rehabilitative possibilities are to be found in the community. The most rigorous research designs generally have found that offenders eligible for supervision in the community in lieu of incarceration do

Jaffe and I created our own prison. We carefully screened over 70 volunteers who answered an ad in a Palo Alto city newspaper and ended up with about two dozen young men who were selected to be part of this study. They were mature, emotionally stable, normal, intelligent college students from middle-class homes throughout the United States and Canada. They appeared to represent the cream of the crop of this generation. None had any criminal record and all were relatively homogeneous on many dimensions initially.

Half were arbitrarily designated as prisoners by a flip of a coin, the others as guards. These were the roles they were to play in our simulated prison. The guards were made aware of the potential seriousness and danger of the situation and their own vulnerability. They made up their own formal rules for maintaining law, order and respect, and were generally free to improvise new ones during their eight-hour, three-man shifts. The prisoners were unexpectedly picked up at their homes by a city policeman in a squad car, searched, handcuffed, fingerprinted, booked at the Palo Alto station house and taken blindfolded to our jail. There they were stripped, deloused, put into a uniform, given a number and put into a cell with two other prisoners where they expected to live for the next two weeks. The pay was good ($15 a day) and their motivation was to make money.

We observed and recorded on videotape the events that occurred in the prison, and we interviewed and tested the prisoners and guards at various points throughout the study. Some of the videotapes of the actual encounters between the prisoners and guards were seen on the NBC News feature "Chronolog" on November 26, 1971.

At the end of only six days we had to close down our mock prison because what we saw was frightening. It was no longer apparent to most of the subjects (or to us) where reality ended and their roles began. The majority had indeed become prisoners or guards, no longer able to clearly differentiate between role playing and self. There were dramatic changes in virtually every aspect of their behavior, thinking and feeling. In less than a week the experience of imprisonment undid (temporarily) a lifetime of learning; human

as well in the community as they do in prison or training school. When intervening variables are controlled, recidivism rates usually appear to be about the same.[53]

Where community corrections clearly has the edge over imprisonment is in the opportunity it provides for an offender's continuation of many of the social relationships that free people take for granted. Another particularly damaging aspect of imprisonment is that the removal of an individual from society interrupts his normal or expected progress through the cycles of life, especially those pertaining to work. Martinson reminds us that most inmates are young and would normally be embarking on a series of important economic and social "moves" in life to ensure their "making it." It is not the prison regimen or efforts at rehabilitation that really affect recidivism rates but, rather, the degree to which those important moves are interrupted. It doesn't take long to be left behind in a highly technological age.[54]

The Effects of Imprisonment: A Closer Look

As we observed in the preceding chapter, America's prison population has been increasing over the past few years. Whatever the merits of decarceration and community corrections, it is clear that prisons remain

values were suspended, self-concepts were challenged and the ugliest, most base, pathological side of human nature surfaced. We were horrified because we saw some boys (guards) treat others as if they were despicable animals, taking pleasure in cruelty, while other boys (prisoners) became servile, dehumanized robots who thought only of escape, of their own individual survival and of their mounting hatred for the guards.

We had to release three prisoners in the first four days because they had such acute situational traumatic reactions as hysterical crying, confusion in thinking and severe depression. Others begged to be paroled, and all but three were willing to forfeit all the money they had earned if they could be paroled. By then (the fifth day) they had been so programmed to think of themselves as prisoners that when their request for parole was denied, they returned docilely to their cells. Now, had they been thinking as college students acting in an oppressive experiment, they would have quit once they no longer wanted the $15 a day we used as our only incentive. However, the reality was not

quitting an experiment but "being paroled by the parole board from the Stanford County Jail." By the last days, the earlier solidarity among the prisoners (systematically broken by the guards) dissolved into "each man for himself." Finally, when one of their fellows was put in solitary confinement (a small closet) for refusing to eat, the prisoners were given a choice by one of the guards: give up their blankets and the incorrigible prisoner would be let out, or keep their blankets and he would be kept in all night. They voted to keep their blankets and to abandon their brother.

About a third of the guards became tyrannical in their arbitrary use of power, in enjoying their control over other people. They were corrupted by the power of their roles and became quite inventive in their techniques of breaking the spirit of the prisoners and making them feel they were worthless. Some of the guards merely did their jobs as tough but fair correctional officers, and several were good guards from the prisoners' point of view since they did them small favors and were friendly. However, no good guard ever interfered with a command by any of the bad

an important feature of this country's reaction to at least some crimes and some criminals. In fact, America's imprisonment rates are highest among industrialized democracies (see table 14.1).

What of the charge that far from "correcting" criminals and preventing crime, prisons may actually be contributing to the rate of crime through their effects on inmates? In an age and country where rationality is thought to rule, it would certainly be ironic if one of our major forms of punishment helped produce precisely what it was thought to prevent. Worse still, we depend on it more and more.

The problem boils down to the following questions. Are people different when they leave prison from what they were when they arrived? Are different effects witnessed for different types of prisons? The quest for answers is made easier if we know about what really goes on in prison.

THE "PAINS OF IMPRISONMENT"

In a study of life in a maximum security prison, Gresham Sykes wrote about the "pains of imprisonment."[55] He observed, as others had before him, that prison means much more than mere deprivation of freedom. First, there is a deep sense of rejection by the free community. Every day the inmate remains cut off from society he or she is reminded of this rejection, and the psychological toll is heavy. Second, prisons are not hotels, as some seem to think, but are places of involuntary confinement

guards; they never intervened on the side of the prisoners, they never told the others to ease off because it was only an experiment, and they never even came to me as prison superintendent or experimenter in charge to complain. In part, they were good because the others were bad; they needed the others to help establish their own egos in a positive light. In a sense, the good guards perpetuated the prison more than the other guards because their own needs to be liked prevented them from disobeying or violating the implicit guards' code. At the same time, the act of befriending the prisoners created a social reality which made the prisoners less likely to rebel.

By the end of the week the experiment had become a reality, as if it were a Pirandello play directed by Kafka that just keeps going after the audience has left. The consultant for our prison, Carlo Prescott, an ex-convict with 16 years of imprisonment in California's jails, would get so depressed and furious each time he visited our prison, because of its psychological similarity to his experiences, that he would have to leave. A Catholic priest who was a former prison chaplain

in Washington, D.C. talked to our prisoners after four days and said they were just like the other first-timers he had seen.

But in the end, I called off the experiment not because of the horror I saw out there in the prison yard, but because of the horror of realizing that *I* could have easily traded places with the most brutal guard or become the weakest prisoner full of hatred at being so powerless that I could not eat, sleep or go to the toilet without permission of the authorities. *I* could have become Calley at My Lai, George Jackson at San Quentin, one of the men at Attica or the prisoner quoted at the beginning of this article.

SOURCE: Philip G. Zimbardo, "The Pathology of Imprisonment." Published by permission of Transaction, Inc. *Society*, vol. 9, no. 6 pp. 4–8. Copyright © 1972 by Transaction, Inc.

that lack most of the amenities that Americans take for granted. The prisoner lives — for an average of three years, according to recent surveys[56] — under extreme material deprivation. In the larger society the possession and use of myriad goods and services is taken as a sign of one's status; not to have them, or not to be able to control their use if you do, marks the individual as a loser, an incompetent, a person lacking worth.

Deprivation of heterosexual relationships is a third pain of imprison-

Table 14.1 Imprisonment rates of industrialized democracies

United States (average rate; figures vary from 4.3 in Vermont to 25.0 in Louisiana)	21.5	New Zealand	9.7
		West Germany	8.1
		Denmark	5.4
Canada	9.0	France	5.2
England and Wales	8.15	Italy	5.1
Australia (average rate; figures vary from 4.09 in Victoria to 8.5 in Western Australia)	6.65	Sweden	4.3
		Norway	4.0
		Holland	1.8

SOURCE: *Corrections Compendium* xi (February-March 1978), p. 12. Reprinted by permission.

Note: Rate represents number of prisoners per 10,000 population (1976).

ment. The inmate is "figuratively castrated by involuntary celibacy."[57] Apart from the physical pleasure that sex has undoubtedly brought most inmates in their time of freedom, there is the psychic pleasure that sex involves; both are officially denied the inmate of most prisons.

Fourth, there is the deprivation of autonomy, the lack of independence that is typical of "total institutions" such as prisons, mental hospitals, and military installations. There are rules and regulations to cover virtually everything. Seemingly, the inmate's most trivial actions are brought under the control of someone else. Discussing why loss of autonomy should be so painful to inmates, Sykes has recently written:

> It is possible that the loss of autonomy is particularly painful in American society because of the insecurities produced by the delays, the conditionality, and the uneven progress so often experienced in gaining adult status. It is also possible that many criminals have had great difficulties in adjusting to figures of authority and so find the many restraints of prison life especially threatening as earlier psychological struggles are reactivated in more virulent form.[58]

The fifth and final pain of imprisonment identified by Sykes is forced association with other criminals, often for long periods of time and always under conditions of deprivation. This involuntary association has many aspects, but those likely to be most threatening are those that undermine an inmate's sense of physical security. In a recent analysis of prison violence, Hans Toch draws a stark picture of this facet of prison life:

> Jails and prisons . . . have a climate of violence which has no free-world counterpart. Inmates are terrorized by other inmates, and spend years in fear of harm. Some inmates request segregation, others lock themselves in, and some are hermits by choice. Many inmates injure themselves.
>
> The "testing out" of new arrivals by their peers leaves many a first offender feeling vulnerable. Rumors of danger are rife. In jails, inmates who have already spent time in the "pen," or who claim to know what happens there, spread horrifying tales about brutality. Recipients of such accounts arrive in prison expecting to struggle for their survival. Such fears cause problems beyond the immediately obvious ones. In prison, fear is a stigma of weakness, and it marks men as fair game for exploitation. . . . Inmate norms contain implicit threats of violence. Unpaid debts call for violence; group loyalties prescribe retaliation for slights to group members. There is also the norm of "fight or flight": Beleaguered inmates are told (by both fellow inmates and staff) to do battle unless they wish to seek refuge in segregation.[59]

It is worth noting that Toch warns of the probability that prison violence will increase as a result of recent trends in criminal justice. The emphasis on decarceration has resulted in primarily the violent and hard-core offenders getting prison terms. Hence prisons are being filled with inmates who are aggressive, tough, or bitter. By the same token, determinate sentences and tougher parole policies have reduced the stakes that in-

A GUARD'S FIRST NIGHT ON THE JOB

. . . When I arrived for my first shift, 3 to 11 p.m., I had not had a minute of training except for a one-hour orientation lecture the previous day. I was a "fish," a rookie guard, and very much out of my depth.

A veteran officer welcomed the "fish" and told us: "Remember, these guys don't have anything to do all day, 24 hours a day, but think of ways to make you mad. No matter what happens, don't lose your cool. Don't lose your cool!"

I had been assigned to the segregation unit, containing 215 inmates who are the most trouble. It was an assignment nobody wanted.

To get there, I passed through seven sets of bars. My uniform was my only ticket through each of them. Even on my first day, I was not asked for any identification, searched, or sent through a metal detector. I could have been carrying weapons, drugs, or any other contraband. I couldn't believe this was what's meant by a maximum-security institution. In the week I worked at Pontiac, I was subjected to only one check, and that one was cursory.

The segregation unit consists of five tiers, or galleries. Each is about 300 feet long and has 44 cells. The walkways are about 3½ feet wide, with the cells on one side and a rail and cyclone fencing on the other. As I walked along one gallery, I noticed that my elbows could touch cell bars and fencing at the same time. That made me easy pickings for anybody reaching out of a cell.

The first thing [they] told me was that a guard must never go out on a gallery by himself. You've got no weapons with which to defend yourself, not even a radio to summon help. All you've got is the man with whom you're working.

My partner that first night was Bill Hill, a soft-spoken six-year veteran who immediately told me to take the cigarettes out of my shirt pocket because the inmates would steal them. Same for my pen, he said — or "They'll grab it and stab you."

We were told to serve dinner on the third tier, and Hill quickly tried to fill me in on the facts of prison life. That's when I learned about cookies and the importance they have to the inmates.

"They're going to try and grab them, they're going to try and steal them any way they can," he said. "Remember, you only have enough cookies for the gallery, and if you let them get away, you'll have to explain to the guys at the end why there weren't any for them."

Hill then checked out the meal, groaning when he saw the drippy ravioli and stewed tomatoes. "We're going to be wearing this," he remarked, before deciding to simply discard the tomatoes. We served nothing to drink. In my first six days at Pontiac, I never saw an inmate served a beverage.

Hill instructed me to put on plastic gloves before we served the meal. In view of the trash and waste through which we'd be wheeling the food cart, I thought he was joking. He wasn't.

---

mates have in remaining nonviolent. Being passive, quiet, obedient, and nonaggressive is no longer good for an early release.[60]

VICTIMIZATION OF PRISONERS

Sociologist Lee Bowker has depicted the inmate experience as one of *victimization,* "a continuous process extending through all hours of the day and the night."[61] Any transaction is seen as victimizing when "a relatively more powerful individual receives more goods, services, or other advantages from a relatively less powerful individual through the coercive exercise of superior strength, skill, or other power resources."[62] Victimization of prisoners involves four systems, according to Bowker: the biological, the psychological, the economic, and the social. A brief look at these levels of victimization will provide further insights into the prison experience.

"Some inmates don't like white hands touching their food," he explained.

Everything went routinely as we served the first 20 cells, and I wasn't surprised when every inmate asked for extra cookies.

Suddenly, a huge arm shot through the bars of one cell and began swinging a metal rod at Hill. As he ducked away, the inmate snared the cookie box.

From the other side of the cart, I lunged to grab the cookies — and was grabbed in turn. A powerful hand from the cell behind me was pulling my arm. As I jerked away, objects began crashing about, and a metal can struck me in the back.

Until that moment I had been apprehensive. Now I was scared. The food cart virtually trapped me, blocking my retreat.

Whirling around, I noticed that mirrors were being held out of every cell so the inmates could watch the ruckus. I didn't realize the mirrors were plastic and became terrified that the inmates would start smashing them to cut me up.

The ordinary din of the cell house had turned into a deafening roar. For the length of the tier, arms stretched into the walkway, making grabbing motions. Some of the inmates swung brooms about.

"Let's get out of here — now!" Hill barked. Wheeling the food cart between us, we made a hasty retreat.

Downstairs, we reported what had happened. My heart was thumping; my legs felt weak. Inside the plastic gloves, my hands were soaked with sweat. Yet the attack on us wasn't considered unusual by the other guards, especially in segregation. That was strictly routine, and we didn't even file a report.

What was more shocking was to be sent immediately back to the same tier to pass out medication. But as I passed the cells from which we'd been attacked, the men in them simply requested their medicine. It was as if what had happened minutes before was already ancient history.

Biological Victimization Included here are murder, rape, and assault. Bowker contends that biological victimization is more likely to characterize relationships between inmates than guard-inmate relationships. On occasion, perhaps more so than we think, inmates are assaulted by guards and guards by inmates. As a matter of fact, recent discussions of prison life have spoken of a "trench warfare climate," and have taken special note of the physical intimidation of guards by inmates (see box on pages 469–471).[63] Inmates are often prepared for violence, as evidenced by the routine carrying of assaultive devices such as knives and iron bars (called "headknockers").[64]

Homosexual rape and other sexual assaults have long been associated with prison life, and the reasons are not hard to find. Both satisfaction of physiological need and the display of power and domination that such behavior exhibits can be linked to the pains of imprisonment. While no accurate data exist on the frequency of sexual assaults in prison, most authorities consider the behavior widespread and repetitive. In one recent study of sexual assaults in the sheriff's vans and jails of Philadelphia, Alan Davis estimated that 2,000 rapes had occurred in a twenty-six-month period in the late 1960s.[65] The exchange of sex for protection has been widely documented both here and abroad. In a twist to this common theme, Davis discovered that many of the aggressors he interviewed felt they had to continue participating in gang rapes to avoid becoming victims

From another cell, however, an inmate began raging at us. "Get my medication," he said. "Get it now, or I'm going to kill you." I was learning that whatever you're handing out, everybody wants it, and those who don't get it frequently respond by threatening to kill or maim you. Another fact of prison life.

Passing cell No. 632, I saw that a prisoner I had helped take to the hospital before dinner was back in his cell. When we took him out, he had been disabled by mace and was very wobbly. Hill and I had been extremely gentle, handcuffing him carefully, then practically carrying him down the stairs. As we went by his cell this time, he tossed a cup of liquid on us.

Back downstairs, I learned I would be going back to that tier for a third time, to finish serving dinner. This time, we planned to slip in the other side of the tier so we wouldn't have to pass the trouble cells. The plates were already prepared.

"Just get in there and give them their food and get out," Hill said. I could see he was nervous, which made me even more so. "Don't stop for anything. If you get hit, just back off, 'cause if they snare you or hook you some way and get you against the bars, they'll hurt you real bad."

Everything went smoothly. Inmates in the three most troublesome cells were not getting dinner, so they hurled some garbage at us. But that's something else I had learned: Getting no worse than garbage thrown at you is the prison equivalent of everything going smoothly.

SOURCE: Excerpted from an article by William Recktenwald, *St. Louis Globe-Democrat*, Nov. 13, 1978. Reprinted by permission of the Chicago Tribune–New York News Syndicate, Inc.

themselves.[66] As for women's prisons, it appears that sex is probably more widespread than in men's prisons, but it is less directly related to demonstrations of power and domination.[67]

Bowker suggests that there may be even more violence in juvenile institutions than in adult ones.[68] If true, one explanation could be that youths are still in that period of life where proving oneself, especially one's masculinity, is an important concern. Life in the detention home and reformatory is an extension of life on the street, but a more concentrated one, as it were. The opportunities for asserting (or failing to assert) one's manliness are probably more frequent and the constant surveillance by adult keepers merely increases the likelihood that demonstrations of "coolness," "toughness," and independence will be highly valued in interpersonal relationships.

Psychological Victimization Combined with other forms of victimization, this primarily consists of manipulation and intimidation for the purposes of achieving status, prestige, authority, and power. The new prisoner (often called a "fish") is likely to be scared, confused, and vulnerable to demands made by more experienced cons. Among the types of psychological victimization described in one study of a juvenile institution are "threat-gestures," "ranking," and "scapegoating."[69] Bowker describes them this way:

In threat-gestures, threatening verbal commands and denigrating gestures are used to keep lower status boys in a constant state of psychological turmoil. Ranking is the use of verbal insults to remind weak boys of their social inferiority. Scapegoating combines threat-gestures, ranking, and physical aggression toward certain individuals who have come to permanently occupy positions at the bottom of the social hierarchy. Once a boy has been manipulated into the scapegoat role, it is very unlikely that he will be able to reestablish himself as a viable member of the community of prisoners.[70]

There are various ways in which guards and other staff members victimize prisoners through manipulation and intimidation. It is the guards who control the flow of information and materials inside the prison. They are in an excellent position to intimidate and disrupt the psychic equilibrium of prisoners. Refusing to allow inmates to shower, make telephone calls, receive mail when it comes, and eat certain foods are deprivations that take on added significance in a prison setting. Similarly, purposely deceiving and exploiting inmates by breaking promises and using information against them intensify the pains of imprisonment.

Economic Victimization   Bowker correctly observes that "enforced material deprivation encourages the formation of a sub rosa economy within the prison."[71] Economic transactions between inmates and between inmates and guards involve all sorts of goods and services, from sex to drugs to books to wages. We earlier mentioned the use of inmates for drug research as an aspect of the tyranny of imprisonment; Bowker sees it as an example of economic victimization.

In addition, there is constant thievery of personal possessions whenever inmates' backs are turned, and simply getting commissary purchases back to one's cell may entail running a gauntlet of would-be robbers. Those inmates who give up any attempt to protect their economic rights become fair game for exploitation and harassment.

The prison bureaucracy is not above blatant forms of economic victimization. The idea that prisons could be a source of productive labor goes back a long way. In the seventeenth century the English geared their jails and workhouses to convict labor. Georg Rusche and Otto Kirchheimer have argued that prison labor grew in popularity during the early period of capitalistic expansion, when the suppy of free labor was unstable and at times dwindled to precarious levels. In their view, it was one further example of the exploitative nature of capitalism.[72] Not surprisingly, profit making remained in the forefront of American interest in convict labor; both private and public enterprises took quick advantage of the cheap labor afforded by the prison system.

Public discussions on the uses of prison labor have tended to emphasize one or more of the following as governing principles: (1) that work be punishment *in addition* to deprivation of freedom, (2) that work be an antidote to idleness (the Quaker view), and (3) that work be a tool of rehabilitation and reform.[73] The question of economic exploitation looms when we consider the material benefits accruing from the work, regardless of its purpose. Who gets what? Who really benefits? There can be no doubt that there is a tremendous labor potential in our prisons — one author estimates its value at over $1 billion[74] — but there must surely be justice in its development and use. Today many prisoners are paid no wages for their work, and those that are receive little more than a pittance. Perhaps if work in prison helped inmates secure valuable work skills, habits, attitudes, and future jobs on the outside, wages would seem less important; but these are considered only remote possibilities by most authorities. Hawkins reminds us that real learning can only take place in settings approximating those in the outside world.[75]

Even so, it is worth pointing out that economic victimization through the prison labor system is not inevitable. A recent assessment of Nordic prison labor programs offers hope for the future.[76] In Finland, for example, efforts are directed at making prison as much like the outside as possible. Though they emerged in the late 1940s in response to labor shortages — further support for Rusche and Kirchheimer — the Finnish labor colonies have apparently lost whatever taint of exploitation that fact might have given them. There are no guards as such, no bars, no outer walls; inmates wear civilian clothes, are referred to as workers, and are allowed family visits on weekends. They are paid the minimum trade union rates, sometimes more, from which the prison deducts 25 percent to pay for their keep and whatever special items (like saunas) they use. Only about 10 percent of Finland's prison population can be found in the labor colonies, however. And those that are generally have committed misdemeanors or are first offenders.

In Sweden, inmates are transferred from a more traditional closed prison to a modern one at Tillberga. Resembling a modern factory (though it has a thirty-foot fence around it), Tillberga has single-story dormitories housing twenty-four inmates, each in their own room with their own key. A strong work ethic is mixed with economic reward. Pay is set at the minimum wage, with about one-third deducted for expenses; however, the inmates do get wage increases, as would workers on the outside. The results of all this must await further research. Both Finnish and Swedish efforts are encouraging, if for no other reason than they appear to reduce the impact of economic victimization in prison settings.

Social Victimization   By this Bowker means the victimization of prisoner groups rather than specific individuals.[77] He identifies three bases for the victimization: race and ethnicity, religion and ideology, and nature of offense.

In Bowker's view racial and ethnic group victimization is the most significant and widespread. It used to be that the minority black inmates were the object of victimization; now it appears that in many prisons it is the whites, especially the middle-class whites, who are victimized by black inmates.[78] Leo Carroll's research at a New England state prison confirms the direction of interracial aggression, as does a more recent study of Stateville, the Illinois penitentiary at Joliet.[79] In Stateville, James Jacobs found four highly cohesive gangs whose reputation and power dominated interracial contacts and radiated throughout the prison. The Black P. Stone Nation, the Devil's Disciples, and the Vicelords are black gangs; the Latin Kings is made up of Hispanic inmates. Their exploitation of other prisoners is extensive.

Certain offenders are singled out for special victimization by other inmates. In particular, child molesters, child rapists, and homosexuals are at the bottom of the pecking order and consequently come in for the most systematic victimization by other inmates as well as guards. In contrast, violent offenders who commit murder, adult rape, and robbery stand at the top of the hierarchy; unless they subsequently demonstrate otherwise, their reputations for being tough and cool stand them in good stead in this world dominated by street-wise felons. As for the victimization of particular religious or ideological groups, which Bowker calls commonplace, Black Muslims and members of the Native American Church are the most likely sufferers. Until recently, when "court decisions forced some degree of religious freedom, minority group religions were . . . outlawed by prison administrators on the grounds that they were both illegitimate and a danger to the custody operations of the institutions."[80]

PRISON SUBCULTURES AND PRISONIZATION

We have reviewed some pretty unpleasant facets of prison life in the last few pages. Although it is important to bear in mind that all prisons are not alike, the pains of imprisonment and various forms of prisoner victimization are present to some extent in all institutions.[81] Most maximum security prisons in this country and in Europe are monolithic, forbidding structures, primarily housing those offenders who have been deemed dangerous to others and who have extensive histories of criminal involvement. It is in precisely such prisons that we would expect to find the most brutalizing effects of incarceration.

Those who have investigated prison life speak of the adaptations that inmates make to the pains of imprisonment. Among these is the development of *inmate subcultures,* consisting of particular values, social roles, and norms. Studies have found different subcultural characteristics from one prison to the next, but there is little argument about their existence and importance in prison life.[82]

There *is* extensive debate among authorities over the so-called prisonization issue. Donald Clemmer was the first to use the term in 1940. He defined *prisonization* as "the taking on in greater or lesser degree of the folkways, mores, customs, and general culture of the penitentiary." It is a process of assimilation, wherein newcomers come to adopt, and are adopted into, the subcultural elements of prison existence. Most important for Clemmer, prisonization implies a *change* in the attitudes, values, and behaviors of those who are imprisoned: they become more antisocial, more criminal. It is a variation of the "prisons as schools of crime" argument, and Clemmer thought that one of the most important determinants of prisonization is length of sentence; the longer the sentence, the more complete the prisonization.[83]

Gordon Hawkins has identified three lines of criticism.[84] First, there is the assumption that prisonization is directly related to time spent in prison. A number of authors have found a "U-shaped" pattern or curve, where prisonization apparently fades as time passes. From being antisocial and nonconformist during the bulk of their stay, inmates become more social and conformist in the months prior to their release.[85] Other studies have found little evidence of any increase in prisonization as time passes.[86] There are, as always, conflicting findings, but as Hawkins notes, Clemmer's prisonization hypothesis is placed in doubt.

Second, the prisonization hypothesis does not place sufficient emphasis on variations in prison organization. A number of studies have shown that inmate attitudes and behaviors are much more positive in treatment-oriented prisons than in custody-oriented institutions.[87] A recent comparison of twenty-five prisons in five countries (the United States, Mexico, Spain, West Germany, and Great Britain) found substantial variation in prisonization (measured by adherence to inmate codes). The nonpunitive, humanitarian milieu of treatment prisons was less conducive to prisonization than the degrading, punitive milieu of custody prisons; however, a majority of inmates in all but two prisons saw a prisonized subculture within the institutional population, though this perception was more likely the more prisonized the respondent. Whereas this might be interpreted as evidence of considerable inmate solidarity, it was apparent that in all prisons the inmate respondents *overestimated* other inmates' adherence to the inmate subculture.[88] In fact, some studies have shown little actual solidarity among prison inmates.[89]

Finally, there is the criticism that far from being indigenous (a functional adaptation to prison life itself), inmate subcultures may in fact be *largely imported from outside*. The importation view has been advocated by John Irwin and Donald Cressey, among others, and has received recent support in the cross-cultural study mentioned in the previous paragraph.[90] In that study it was found that inexperienced prison newcomers tended to resist prisonization and held the least antisocial attitudes *when in maximum security prisons*. Jacobs's study of inmate gangs at Stateville penitentiary in Illinois also provides support for the importation model. Here the prison served not only to preserve the street norms and organization of the gangs, but also to strengthen them. When incarcerated, gang members brought with them the essential features of the parent gangs; the same people who were the leaders on Chicago streets were the leaders in prison.[91]

Hawkins concludes his analysis of the prisonization question with a great deal of pessimism and no little skepticism about the benefits of imprisonment. Prisons, he argues, probably do not have a lasting impact on convicts; they merely provide a setting in which earlier-acquired predispositions can be acted out and perhaps strengthened:

> One starts with doubt about the reformative effects of imprisonment on the ground that inmates are being prisonized and in effect criminalized. One concludes with doubt about the crimogenic effects of imprisonment on grounds which imply not merely that inmates are not being corrupted but rather that neither their attitudes nor their behavior are being affected in any significant fashion by the experience of imprisonment.[92]

The view that prisons neither reform nor criminalize most inmates is reiterated by John Irwin, himself an ex-convict. Speaking of the "Big House" — those monolithic, maximum security prisons whose heyday stretched over sixty years through the 1940s — Irwin concludes that the experience "did not reform prisoners or teach many persons crime. It embittered many. It stupefied thousands."[93]

By all accounts the correctional future looks bleak. There may be more prison disorder and rioting such as that which occurred at New Mexico State Penitentiary early in 1980.

According to Irwin, two factors helped promote the prison unrest that culminated in the earlier revolts at the Missouri State Penitentiary and at Attica, New York, and that set the scene for the turmoil of the 1970s. First, prisons began housing more and more blacks, who by the 1960s were becoming more assertive, and finally militant. This fueled white fears and prejudices, stirring up more tension between the races. Second, many inmates grew disenchanted with rehabilitation and its promise: "After years of embracing rehabilitation's basic tenets, submitting themselves to treatment strategies, and then leaving prison with new hope for a better future, they discovered and reported back that their outside lives had not changed."[94] Prisoners, educated by the very programs they came to despise, spread their indictment of rehabilitation and taught themselves to "see through things," and to fight "the system."

Today, Irwin believes, a new prison hero has emerged: the "convict."

> The convict or hog stands ready to kill to protect himself, maintains strong loyalties to some small groups of other convicts (invariably of his own race), and will rob and attack or at least tolerate his friends' robbing and attacking other weak independents or their foes. He openly and stubbornly opposes the administration, even if this results in harsh punishment. Finally, he is

The 1980 riot at New Mexico State Penitentiary left thirty-three prisoners dead at the hands of their fellow inmates. Is there a solution to the pains and pathology of imprisonment?

extremely assertive of his masculine sexuality, even though he may occasionally make use of the prison homosexuals or, less often, enter into more permanent sexual alliance with a kid. . . . To circulate in this world, the convict world, one must act like a convict and, with few exceptions, have some type of affiliation with a powerful racial clique or gang."[95]

Prisons today are full of hate, with "dope fiends, pimps, bikers, [and] street gang members" competing for power and respect.[96] It is hard to imagine that anyone can emerge from prison and "go straight."

References

1. See chapter 2, pp. 45–48.
2. Jack P. Gibbs, *Crime, Punishment, and Deterrence* (New York: Elsevier, 1975), pp. 57–93.
3. Ibid., p. 59.
4. Ibid., p. 66.
5. Ibid., pp. 68–69.
6. Ibid., p. 72.
7. Ibid.
8. Emile Durkheim, *The Division of Labor in Society* (New York: Free Press, 1964), pp. 98–108.
9. Ibid.; see also Emile Durkheim, *The Rules of Sociological Method* (New York: Free Press, 1964.)
10. Gibbs, *Crime, Punishment and Deterrence*, p. 83.
11. Ibid., p. 84.
12. Ibid., p. 85.
13. See chapter 2 of this text, pp. 39–40.
14. Gibbs, *Crime, Punishment and Deterrence*, p. 87.
15. See Franklin E. Zimring and Gordon J. Hawkins, *Deterrence: The Legal Threat in Crime Control* (Chicago: University of Chicago Press, 1973), p. 85.
16. Gibbs, *Crime, Punishment and Deterrence*, p. 90.
17. Ibid., pp. 59–61.
18. Shlomo Shoham, *The Mark of Cain* (Dobbs Ferry, N.Y.: Citadel, 1970), p. 9.
19. Gibbs, *Crime and Punishment and Deterrence*, pp. 85–86.
20. Ibid., p. 82.
21. See, for example, E. Roy Calvert, *Capital Punishment in the Twentieth Century* (1927; repr. New York: Kennikat Press, 1971); Leonard Savitz, "A Study in Capital Punishment," *Journal of Criminal Law, Criminology, and Police Science* 59 (1958), pp. 328–41; Karl F. Schuessler, "The Deterrent Influence of the Death Penalty," *The Annals* 284 (1952), pp. 54–62; George B. Vold, "Can the Death Penalty Prevent Crime?" *Prison Journal* (1932), pp. 3–8. For more recent evidence, see William C. Bailey, "Murder and the Death Penalty," *Journal of Criminal Law and Criminology* 65 (1974), pp. 416–23; and Robert Nash Parker and M. Dwayne Smith, "Deterrence, Poverty, and Type of Homicide," *American Journal of Sociology* 85 (1979), pp. 614–24.
22. See Johannes Andenaes, *Punishment and Deterrence* (Ann Arbor: University of Michigan Press, 1974), especially appendixes 1 and 2.
23. See, for example, William J. Chambliss, "Types of Deviance and the Effectiveness of Legal Sanctions," *Wisconsin Law Review* (1967), pp. 703–19.
24. See, for example, Gordon P. Waldo and Theodore G. Chiricos, "Perceived Legal Sanctions and Self-Reported Criminality: A Neglected Approach to Deterrence Research," *Social Problems* 19 (1972), pp. 527–40; Johannes Andenaes, "Deterrence and Specific Offenses," in his *Punishment and Deterrence*, pp. 84–104; Theodore G. Chiricos and Gordon P. Waldo, "Punishment and Crime: An Evaluation of Some Empirical Evidence," *Social Problems* 18 (1970), pp. 200–17; Richard D. Schwartz and Sonya Orleans, "On Legal Sanctions," *University of Chicago Law Review* 34 (1967), pp. 274–300; and Richard T. Salem and William J. Bowers, "Severity of Formal Sanctions as a Deterrent to Deviant Behavior," *Law and Society Review* 5 (1970), pp. 21–40.
25. Chambliss, "Types of Deviance." See also his *Crime and the Legal Process* (New York: McGraw-Hill, 1969), pp. 368–72.
26. Johannes Andenaes, "The General Preventive Effects of Punishment," *University of Pennsylvania Law Review* 114 (1966), pp. 949–83.
27. See Alexander L. Clark and Jack P. Gibbs, "Social Control: A Reformulation," *Social Problems* 12 (1965), pp. 398–415.
28. For example, see William J. Chambliss, "The Deterrent Influence of Punishment," *Crime and Delinquency* 12 (1966), pp. 70–75; Jack P. Gibbs, "Crime, Punishment and Deterrence," *Southwestern Social Science Quarterly* 48 (1968), pp. 515–30; and Charles R. Tittle, "Crime Rates and Legal Sanctions," *Social Problems* 16 (1969), pp. 408–23.
29. Studies now available include Dorothy Miller et al., "Public Knowledge of Criminal Penalties: A Research Report," in *Theories of Punishment*, ed. Stanley F. Grupp (Bloomington: Indiana University Press, 1971), pp. 205–26; Waldo and Chiricos, "Perceived Legal Sanctions and Self-Reported Criminality"; Gary F. Jensen, "Crime Doesn't Pay: Correlates of a Shared Misunderstanding," *Social Problems* 17 (1969), pp. 189–201; Maynard L. Erickson, Jack P. Gibbs, and Gary F. Jensen, "The Deterrence Doctrine and the Perceived Certainty of Legal Punishments," *American Sociological Review* 42 (1977), pp. 305–17; W. William Minor, "Deterrence Research: Problems of Theory and Method," in *Preventing Crime*, ed. James A. Cramer (Beverly Hills, Calif.: Sage, 1978), pp. 21–45.
30. Erickson, Gibbs, and Jensen, "The Deterrence Doctrine and Perceived Certainty of Legal Punishments," p. 305.
31. See Cesare Beccaria, *On Crimes and Punishment*, trans. Henry Paolucci (New York: Bobbs-Merrill, 1963); and Jeremy Bentham, *The Principles of Morals and Legislation* (New York: Hafner Publishing, 1948).
32. For recent work see Alfred Blumstein, Jacqueline Cohen, and Daniel Nagin, eds., *Deterrence and Incapacitation: Estimating the Effects of Crimi-*

nal Sanctions on Crime Rates (Washington, D.C.: National Academy of Science, 1978).

33. See Linda S. Anderson, Theodore G. Chiricos, and Gordon P. Waldo, "Formal and Informal Sanctions: A Comparison of Deterrent Effects," *Social Problems* 25 (1977), pp. 103–14; Charles R. Tittle, "Sanction, Fear and the Maintenance of Order," *Social Forces* 55 (1977), pp. 579–96.

34. Minor, "Deterrence Research: Problems of Theory and Method," p. 35.

35. David F. Greenberg, "Crime Deterrence Research and Social Policy," in *Modelling the Criminal Justice System,* ed., Stuart S. Nagel (Beverly Hills, Calif.: Sage, 1977), pp. 286–87. See also, David F. Greenberg, *Mathematical Criminology* (New Brunswick, N.J., Rutgers University Press, n.d.), pp. 36–41.

36. Minor, "Deterrence Research: Problems of Theory and Method," p. 28.

37. For reviews of the research see Blumstein, Cohen, and Nagin, *Deterrence and Incapacitation,* especially pp. 95–139; Gibbs, *Crime, Punishment and Deterrence,* chapter 5.

38. A point Gresham M. Sykes has also made. See his *Criminology* (New York: Harcourt Brace Jovanovich, 1978), p. 564, note 48.

39. David Greenberg, "The Incapacitative Effect of Imprisonment: Some Estimates," *Law and Society Review* 9 (1975), p. 551.

40. U.S. Department of Justice, *Survey of Inmates of State Correctional Facilities, 1974 — Advance Report,* National Prisoner Statistics Special Report, No. 50-NPS-SR-2 (Washington, D.C.: U.S. Government Printing Office, 1976), p. 35.

41. See Daniel Glaser, *The Effectiveness of a Prison and Parole System* (Indianapolis: Bobbs-Merrill, 1964); Martinson, "What Works? Questions and Answers about Prison Reform," *The Public Interest* 35 (1974), pp. 22–54; Gene Kassebaum, David Ward, and Daniel M. Wilner, *Prison Treatment and Parole Survival* (New York: Wiley, 1971); John Conrad, *Crime and Its Correction* (Berkeley: University of California Press, 1970); and Greenberg, "The Incapacitative Effect of Imprisonment: Some Estimates."

42. Gibbs, *Crime, Punishment and Deterrence,* p. 74.

43. C. Ray Jeffery, *Crime Prevention through Environmental Design* (Beverly Hills, Calif.: Sage, 1977), p. 88.

44. Gordon Hawkins, *The Prison: Policy and Practice* (Chicago: University of Chicago Press, 1976), p. 48.

45. See William G. Nagel, *The New Red Barn: A Critical Look at the Modern American Prison* (New York: Walker, 1973), pp. 38–50.

46. Herman Badillo and Milton Haynes, *A Bill of No Rights: Attica and the American Prison System* (New York: Outerbridge and Lazard, 1972), pp. 178–79.

47. Martinson, "What Works?" p. 49.

48. R. T. Trotter, "Clockwork Orange in a California Prison," *Science News* 101 (1972), pp. 174–75. On other methods of human modification in total institutions, see Nicholas N. Kittrie, *The Right to Be Different: Deviance and Enforced Therapy* (Baltimore: Penguin Books, 1973), pp. 297–339.

49. Richard Speiglman, "Building the Walls Inside: Medicine, Corrections, and the State Apparatus for Repression" (Ph.D. diss., University of California, Berkeley, 1976).

50. Jeffery, *Crime Prevention Through Environmental Design,* p. 86.

51. John M. McCartt and Thomas J. Mangogna, "The History of Halfway Houses in the United States," and "Overview of Issues Relating to Halfway Houses and Community Treatment Centers," both in Robert M. Carter and Leslie T. Wilkins, eds., *Probation, Parole, and Community Corrections* 2nd ed. (New York: Wiley, 1976), pp. 544–67.

52. See Ibid., pp. 554–55.

53. Nora Klapmuts, "Community Alternatives to Prison," in Robert G. Leger and John R. Stratton, eds., *The Sociology of Corrections: A Book of Readings* (New York: Wiley, 1977), p. 439 (author's italics).

54. Robert Martinson, "The Paradox of Prison Reform," *New Republic* 166 (1972). Cited in Klapmuts, "Community Alternatives to Prison," pp. 414–15.

55. Gresham M. Sykes, *The Society of Captives* (Princeton, N.J.: Princeton University Press, 1958), chapter 4.

56. U.S. Department of Justice, *LEAA Newsletter* 8 (1979), p. 7.

57. Sykes, *Criminology,* p. 523.

58. Ibid., p. 525.

59. Hans Toch, *Police, Prisons, and the Problem of Violence* (Rockville, Md.: National Institute of Mental Health, 1977), p. 53.

60. Ibid., pp. 61–62.

61. Lee H. Bowker, "Victimization in Correctional Institutions: An Interdisciplinary Analysis." Paper presented at the annual meeting of the Academy of Criminal Justice Sciences, New Orleans, March 1978, p. 1.

62. Ibid., p. 2.

63. Toch, *Police, Prisons, and the Problem of Violence,* pp. 65–67; James B. Jacobs and Harold G. Retsky's "Prison Guard," *Urban Life and Culture* 4 (1975), pp. 5–29. Unfortunately, little is known about the guards' perceptions of prison life. Gordon Hawkins has called prison guards the "invisible men" in prison research, a point echoed by David Kogel. See Hawkins, *The Prison: Policy and Practice,* pp. 81–98; Fogel, ". . . We Are the Living Proof . . ." pp. 70–82.

64. See Anthony L. Guenther, "Compensations in a Total Institution: The Forms and Functions of Contraband," *Crime and Delinquency* (1975), pp.

243–54. We might note that the carrying of weapons was common in the 1800s, too. See W. David Lewis, *From Newgate to Dannemora* (Ithaca, N.Y.: Cornell University Press, 1965), p. 131.

65. Alan J. Davis, "Sexual Assaults in the Philadelphia Prison System and Sheriffs' Vans," *Transaction* 6 (1968), pp. 9–16.

66. Ibid.

67. The major studies of women's prisons are David A. Ward and Eugene Kassebaum, *Women's Prisons: Sex and Social Structure* (Chicago: Aldine, 1965); Rose Giallombardo, *Society of Women: A Study of a Woman's Prison* (New York: Wiley, 1966); Esther Heffernan, *Making It in Prison: The Square, the Cool, and the Life* (New York: Wiley Interscience, 1972). See also Nanci Koser Wilson, "Styles of Doing Time in a Co-Ed Prison: Masculine and Feminine Alternatives," in Dennis Szabo and Susan Katzenelson, eds., *Offenders and Corrections* (New York: Praeger, 1978), pp. 53–71.

68. Bowker, "Victimization in Correctional Institutions," p. 4.

69. Howard W. Polsky, *Cottage Six* (New York: Wiley, 1962), pp. 55–67.

70. Bowker, "Victimization in Correctional Institutions," p. 7.

71. Ibid., p. 11.

72. Georg Rusche and Otto Kirchheimer, *Punishment and Social Structure* (1938; repr. New York: Russell and Russell, 1968), pp. 24–52.

73. Hawkins, *The Prison*, pp. 115–16.

74. Neil M. Singer, *The Value of Inmate Manpower* (Washington, D.C.: American Bar Association, 1973). Cited in Hawkins, *The Prison*, p. 121.

75. Ibid., p. 121.

76. Peter Wickman, "Industrial Wages for Prisoners in Finland and Sweden," in Dennis Szabo and Susan Katzenelson, *Offenders and Corrections*, pp. 141–51.

77. Bowker, "Victimization in Correctional Institutions," p. 14.

78. Ibid., p. 16.

79. See Leo Carroll, *Hacks, Blacks, and Cons: Race Relations in a Maximum Security Prison* (Lexington, Mass.: D. C. Heath, 1974); James B. Jacobs, "Street Gangs behind Bars," *Social Problems* 21 (1974), pp. 395–409; also, his more complete account: *Stateville: The Penitentiary in Mass Society* (Chicago: University of Chicago Press, 1977).

80. Bowker, "Victimization in Correctional Institutions," p. 15. See also James B. Jacobs, "Stratification and Conflict among Prison Inmates," *Journal of Criminal Law and Criminology* 66 (1976), pp. 476–82.

81. Two scholars have recently emphasized that not all prisons *systems* are alike, either. They advocate more detailed investigations of what effects system variations have on prison realities. See Eric H. Steele and James B. Jacobs, "A Theory

of Prison Systems," *Crime and Delinquency* (1975), pp. 149–62.

82. The list of studies giving details of inmate subcultures is vast. One extensive review of the literature is Lee H. Bowker, *Prisoner Subcultures* (Lexington, Mass.: D. C. Heath, 1977). Some of the classic studies are: Norman S. Hayner and Ellis Ash, "The Prisoner Community as a Social Group," *American Sociological Review* 4 (1939), pp. 362–69; also their "The Prison as a Community," *American Sociological Review* 5 (1940), pp. 577–83. Donald Clemmer, *The Prison Community* (New York: Holt, Rinehart and Winston, 1940); Clarence Schrag, "Leadership among Prison Inmates," *American Sociological Review* 19 (1954), pp. 37–42, and his "A Preliminary Criminal Typology," *Pacific Sociological Review* 4 (1961), pp. 11–16. Gresham M. Sykes and Sheldon L. Messinger, "The Inmate Social System," in Richard A. Cloward et al., eds., *Theoretical Studies in The Social Organization of the Prison* (New York: Social Sciences Research Council, 1960), pp. 5–19. John Irwin, *The Felon* (Englewood Cliffs, N.J.: Prentice-Hall, 1970).

83. Clemmer, *The Prison Community*.

84. Hawkins, *The Prison*, pp. 63–80.

85. See Stanton Wheeler, "Socialization in Correctional Communities," *American Sociological Review* 26 (1961), pp. 697–712; Peter Garabedian, "Social Roles and Processes of Socialization in the Prison Community," *Social Problems* 11 (1963), pp. 139–52.

86. Robert Atchley and M. Patrick McCabe, "Socialization in Correctional Communities: A Replication," *American Sociological Review* 33 (1968), pp. 774–85. See also Charles Wellford, "Factors Associated with Adoption of an Inmate Code: A Study of Normative Socialization," *Journal of Criminal Law, Criminology, and Police Science* 58 (1967), pp. 197–203.

87. See David Street, "The Inmate Group in Custodial and Treatment Settings," *American Sociological Review* 30 (1965), pp. 40–55; Robert D. Vinter and Charles Perrow, *Organization for Treatment in a Comparative Study of Organizations for Delinquents* (New York: Free Press, 1966); Bernard B. Berk, "Organizational Goals and Inmate Organization," *American Sociological Review* 31 (1966), pp. 522–34. Oscar Grusky, "Organization Goals and the Behavior of Informal Leaders," *American Journal of Sociology* 65 (1966), pp. 59–67.

88. Ronald L. Akers, Norman S. Hayner, and Werner Gruninger, "Prisonization in Five Countries: Type of Prison and Inmate Characteristics," in Szabo and Katzenelson, *Offenders and Corrections*, pp. 90–115.

89. See Thomas Mathieson, *The Defenses of the Weak* (London: Tavistock, 1965).

90. See John Irwin and Donald R. Cressey, "Thieves,

Convicts and the Inmate Culture," *Social Problems* 10 (1962), pp. 142–55; Wellford, "Factors Associated with Adoption of an Inmate Code"; Jacobs, "Street Gangs behind Bars"; Barry Schwartz, "Pre-Institutional Versus Situational Influence in a Correctional Community," *Journal of Criminal Law, Criminology, and Police Sci-* L. Akers, Norman S. Hayner, and Werner Gruninger, "Homosexual and Drug Behavior in Prison: A Test of the Functional and Importation Models of the Inmate System," *Social Problems* 21 (1974), pp. 410–22; Charles W. Thomas, "The-oretical Perspectives on Prisonization: A Comparison of the Importation and Deprivation Models," *Journal of Criminal Law and Criminology* 68 (1977), pp. 135–45.

91. Jacobs, "Street Gangs behind Bars." Also his *Stateville: The Penitentiary in Mass Society*.
92. Hawkins, *The Prison*, pp. 72–73.
93. John Irwin, *Prisons in Turmoil* (Boston: Little, Brown, 1980), p. 21.
94. Ibid., p. 63.
95. Ibid., p. 195.
96. Ibid., p. 181.

Crime and Public Policy

In the course of this text we have seen abundant evidence of the close connection between crime and politics. This connection is seen in the basic fact that "the criminal law, courts, and prisons are instruments of government, created and funded by government, and administered by government functionaries."[1] Passing laws, deciding about law enforcement practices, adopting modes of punishment, and deploying money and resources to deal with crime are all political actions. In this final chapter we shall look more closely at the politics of crime as manifested in public policy — the decisions and practices adopted by those in or employed by government. Public policy impinges upon all aspects of the crime scene. Its impact begins with official decisions about what and whom to identify as criminal, and continues through all phases of the criminal process.

The Underpinnings of Public Policy

Many things shape public policy, whether on crime or anything else. Not least among these influences are the attitudes, beliefs, ideas, and assumptions about crime of those in positions of political power and influence. These attitudes and beliefs constitute the ideological underpinnings of policy and shape the positions taken on specific issues. The particular ideology underlying public policy is not always obvious, but it is there nonetheless and actual policy decisions cannot be divorced from it. As Walter Miller has observed, "Ideology is the permanent hidden agenda of criminal justice."[2]

The same ideology is not, of course, shared by everyone, nor does a particular ideology necessarily retain its influence over time. Policies will change as time passes. We can also expect that the policies created, adopted, and implemented at any particular time will not meet with the approval of all who have an opinion on crime.

Different assumptions and beliefs about criminal matters have achieved prominence throughout history and across cultures. The ideologies embodying these assumptions and beliefs have sometimes stimulated policy change and sometimes reinforced existing policies; sometimes they have had little or no effect on public policy. Whether or not a particular ideology does influence policy depends on many things; most important are the social status and degree of political power and influence of those subscribing to it.

Attempts to identify and classify beliefs and assumptions about crime have been few; recently, a number of authors have sought to correct this deficiency.[3] Walter Miller offers one of the most detailed statements on major ideological positions. He used as his data source public statements (verbal or written) on criminal matters made by a variety of Americans, including novelists, sociologists, journalists, legislators, other government officials, lawyers, policemen, clergymen, historians, and labor leaders.[4]

Miller placed the different ideological positions he was able to identify on a one-dimensional scale:

	Leftist			Centrist			Rightist			
5	4	3	2	1	0	1	2	3	4	5
	radical							conservative		

The most extreme ideological positions were given the value 5. More moderate ones ranged between the extreme left and extreme right positions. The ideological position *left 3* is more leftist than position *left 1,* but less leftist than position *left 5.* Each ideological position identified by Miller concerns a specific crime issue and is made up of assumptions and beliefs about that issue. (See box on pp. 484–487.)

IDEOLOGICAL POSITIONS ON CRIMINAL JUSTICE ISSUES

1. Opinions on the causes of crime and the locus of responsibility for it:

Left 5. Behavior designated as "crime" by the ruling classes is an inevitable product of a fundamentally corrupt and unjust society. True crime is the behavior of those who perpetuate, control, and profit from an exploitative and brutalizing system. . . . [Those labeled "criminals" by the establishment] bear no responsibility for what the state defines as crime; they are forced into such actions as justifiable responses to deliberate policies of oppression, discrimination, and exploitation.

Right 5. Crime and violence are a direct product of a massive conspiracy by highly organized and well-financed radical forces seeking deliberately to overthrow the society. Their basic method is an intensive and unrelenting attack on the fundamental moral values of the society, and their vehicle is that sector of the populace sufficiently low in intelligence, moral virtue, self-control, and judgment as to serve readily as their puppets by constantly engaging in those violent and predatory crimes best calculated to destroy the social order. . . .

Left 3. Public officials and agencies with responsibility for crime and criminals must share with damaging social conditions major blame for criminality. By allocating pitifully inadequate resources to criminal justice agencies the government virtually assures that they will be manned by poorly qualified, punitive, moralistic personnel who are granted vast amounts of arbitrary coercive power. These persons use this power to stigmatize, degrade and brutalize those who come under their jurisdiction, thus permitting them few options other than continued criminality. Society also manifests enormous reluctance to allocate the resources necessary to ameliorate the root causes of crime — poverty, urban deterioration, blocked educational and job opportunities — and further enhances crime by maintaining widespread systems of segregation. . . .

Right 3. The root cause of crime is a massive erosion of the fundamental values which traditionally have served to deter criminality, and a concomitant flouting of the established authority which has traditionally served to constrain it. The most extreme manifestations of this phenomenon are found among . . . the young, minorities, and the poor. Among these groups and elsewhere there have arisen special sets of alternative values or "countercultures" which actually provide direct support for the violation of the legal and moral norms of law-abiding society. A major role in the alarming increase in crime and violence is played by certain elitist groups of left-oriented media writers, educators, jurists, lawyers, and others who contribute directly to criminality by publicizing, disseminating, and supporting these crime-engendering values.

2. Assumptions and beliefs concerning the proper methods of dealing with offenders:

Left 4. All but a very small proportion of those

Miller observes that there are convergences and divergences, consistencies and inconsistencies, among and within the various ideological positions. He also notes that while the statements might reflect the gist of someone's ideology, that person is unlikely to feel comfortable with all the statements exactly as phrased. But most interesting is his observation that both left and right can be reduced to basic governing principles or values, and that few Americans would quarrel with them since they are "intrinsic aspects of our national ideals":

For the right, the paramount value is order — an ordered society based on a pervasive and binding morality — and the paramount danger is disorder — social, moral and political. For the left, the paramount value is justice — a just society based on a fair and equitable distribution of power, wealth,

who come under the jurisdiction of criminal justice agencies pose no real danger to society, and are entitled to full and unconditional freedom in the community at all stages of the criminal justice process. . . . Criminal justice processing as currently conducted is essentially brutalizing — particularly institutional incarceration, which should be entirely abolished. "Rehabilitation" under institutional auspices is a complete illusion; it has not worked, never will work, and must be abandoned as a policy objective. Accused persons, prisoners, and members of the general public subject to the arbitrary and punitive policies of police and other officials must be provided full rights and resources to protect their interests — including citizen control of police operations, full access to legal resources, fully developed grievance mechanisms, and the like.

Right 4. Dangerous or habitual criminals should be subject to genuine punishment of maximum severity, including capital punishment where called for, and extended prison terms (including life imprisonment) with airtight guarantees that these be fully served. Probation and parole defeat the purposes of public protection and should be eliminated. . . . To speak of "rights" of persons who have chosen deliberately to forfeit them by engaging in crime is a travesty, and malefactors should receive the punishment they deserve without interference by leftists working to obstruct the processes of justice. "Rehabilitation" as a policy is simply a weakly disguised method of pampering criminals, and has no place whatever in a proper system of criminal justice. Fully

adequate facilities for detection, apprehension, and effective restraint of criminals should be granted those police and other criminal justice personnel who realize that their principal mission is swift and unequivocal retribution against wrongdoers and their permanent removal from society to secure the full protection of the law-abiding.

Left 2. Since the behavior of most of those who commit crimes is symptomatic of social or psychological forces over which they have little control, ameliorative efforts must be conducted within the framework of a comprehensive strategy of services which combines individually oriented clinical services and beneficial social programs. . . . Institutional programs organized around the concept of the therapeutic community can be most effective in helping certain kinds of persons, such as drug users, for whom external constraints can be a useful part of the rehabilitative process. Rehabilitation rather than punishment must be the major objective in dealing with offenders. . . . Where imprisonment is indicated, sentences should be as short as possible, and inmates should be accorded the rights and respect due all human beings.

Right 2. Lawbreakers should be subject to fair but firm penalties based on the protection of society, but taking into account as well the future of the offender. Successful rehabilitation is an important objective since a reformed criminal no longer presents a threat to society. Rehabilitation should center on the moral reeducation of the offender, and instill in him the respect for

prestige, and privilege — and the paramount evil is injustice — the concentration of valued social resources in the hands of a privileged minority. . . .

Stripped of the passion of ideological conflict, the issue between the two sides could be viewed as a disagreement over the relative priority of two valuable conditions: whether *order with justice,* or *justice with order* should be the guiding principle of the criminal justice enterprise.[5]

The Impact of Ideology on Crime Policy

The expectation that ideology influences public policy is based on the assumption that a person's views or theories about an issue guide him in

authority and basic moral values which are the best safeguards against continued crime. These aims can be furthered by prison programs which demand hard work and strict discipline. . . . Sentences should be sufficiently long as to both adequately penalize the offender and insure sufficient time for effective rehabilitation. . . .

3. Positions regarding the proper operating policies of criminal justice agencies:

Left 5. The whole apparatus of so-called "law-enforcement" is in fact simply the domestic military apparatus used by the ruling classes to maintain themselves in power, and to inflict harassment, confinement, injury or death on those who protest injustice by challenging the arbitrary regulations devised by the militarists and monopolists to protect their interests. To talk of "reforming" such a system is farcical; the only conceivable method of eliminating the intolerable injustices inherent in this kind of society is the total and forceful overthrow of the entire system, including its so-called "law-enforcement" arm. All acts which serve this end, including elimination of members of the oppressor police force, serve to hasten the inevitable collapse of the system and the victory of progressive forces.

Right 5. Maximum possible resources must be provided those law enforcement officials who realize that their basic mission is the protection of society and maintenance of security for the law-abiding citizen. In addition to increases in manpower, law-enforcement personnel must be provided with the most modern, efficient and lethal weaponry available, and the technological capacity (communications, computerization, electronic surveillance, aerial pursuit capability) to deliver maximum force and facilities possible to points of need — the detection, pursuit, and arrest of criminals, and in particular the control of terrorism and violence conducted or incited by radical forces.

Left 3. The more efficiency gained by law enforcement agencies through improvements in technology, communications, management, and so on, the greater the likelihood of harassment, intimidation, and discrimination directed against the poor and minorities. Improvements in police services . . . should be achieved by abandoning antiquated selection and recruitment policies which are designed to obtain secure employment for low-quality personnel and which systematically discriminate against the minorities and culturally disadvantaged. . . . The outmoded military model with its rigid hierarchical distinctions found among the police and other agencies should be eliminated, and a democratic organizational model put in its place. The police must see their proper function as service to the community. . . . [L]aw enforcement agencies should stringently limit access to information concerning offenders, especially younger ones, and much of such information should be destroyed. . . . The major burden of corrections should be removed from the institutions, which are crime-breeding and dehumanizing, and placed directly in the

structuring his subsequent actions toward it.[6] But in the realm of policy it all depends on whose ideology we are talking about.

Those whose views and theories about criminal matters are most likely to be articulated in policy are persons in occupations dealing directly with such matters — legislators, government officials, judges, police officials, lawyers, prison officials, and others whose work routinely brings them into contact with law, crime, and criminals. Also included are persons with acknowledged expertise in the study of criminality and law — psychologists, psychiatrists, criminologists, sociologists, lawyers, and economists.

Ideological positions are likely to reflect actual work experiences and the effects of the socialization process normally associated with entering an occupation. We saw the importance of these experiences in our discussion of the police "working personality" (pages 368–369). Since these

communities, to which all offenders must at some point return.

Right 3. Law enforcement agencies must be provided all the resources necessary to deal promptly and decisively with crime and violence. . . . The right of the police to stringently and effectively enforce the law must be protected from misguided legalistic interference. . . . The scope of the criminal law must be expanded rather than reduced; there is no such thing as "victimless" crime; the welfare of all law-abiding people and the moral basis of society itself are victimized by crimes such as pornography, prostitution, homosexuality, and drug use, and offenders must be vigorously pursued, prosecuted, and penalized. Attempts to prevent crime by pouring massive amounts of tax dollars into slum communities are worse than useless, since such people can absorb limitless welfare "benefits" with no appreciable effect on their criminal propensities. Communities must resist attempts to open up their streets and homes to hardened criminals through halfway houses and other forms of "community corrections."

Left 1. There must be better coordination of existing criminal justice facilities and functions so as to better focus available services on the whole individual. . . . Coordination and liaison must also increase between the criminal justice agencies and the general welfare services of the community, which have much to contribute both in the way of crime prevention and rehabilitation of criminals. Local politicians often frustrate the purposes of reform by consuming resources in

patronage, graft, and the financial support of entrenched local interests, so the federal government must take the lead in financing and overseeing criminal justice reform efforts. . . .

Right 1. The operations of the police should be made more efficient, in part through increased use of modern managerial principles and information processing techniques. Police protection should focus more directly on the local community. . . . Prison reform is important, but innovations should be instituted gradually and with great caution, and the old should not be discarded until the new is fully proven to be adequate. . . . The federal government must assume a major role in providing the leadership and financial resources necessary to effective law-enforcement and crime control.

SOURCE: Walter B. Miller, Appendix to "Ideology and Criminal Justice Policy: Some Current Issues," *Journal of Criminal Law and Criminology* 64 (June 1973), pp. 155–162. Reprinted by permission.

experiences are not the same for all crime-related occupations or for all persons in a particular occupation, and since the backgrounds, current status, and prior experiences of those entering various occupations will be different, we should expect ideological differences among persons working in the field of crime. We can also anticipate differences in the intensity of particular ideological positions and emotional commitment to them. Miller's impressions of four crime-related professions — the police, the judiciary, corrections, and academic criminology — support these expectations. For example, the police are not only rightist, but substantially so; academic criminologists, on the other hand, are substantially leftist.

Miller also found ideological differences in the *same* crime-related professions: "Judges show enormous variation in ideological predilections, probably covering the full range from right five to left four."[7] (Remember the earlier discussion of factors influencing sentencing and the important effect of differences in penal philosophy and the personal attitudes of judges toward crime issues — see pages 412–413). This means that in policy we are likely to find strains, as competing ideological positions are more or less articulated.[8] Assuming that at least some of those persons holding different assumptions and beliefs about criminal matters do influence policy decisions, we should expect to see different crime strategies in the same policy framework.

Looking at the last hundred years or so, it is evident that public policy on criminal matters has indeed incorporated competing crime strategies. Two "ideal type" models of organized reactions to crime and criminals have been identified. One rests heavily on *order with justice,* the other on *justice with order.* While neither model is meant to portray reality in all its detail and complexity, both are drawn from criminal justice in action and emphasize what are thought to be fundamental divergences in assumptions and beliefs about the correct way to deal with criminals. The models were first suggested by Herbert L. Packer; he calls them the *crime control model* and the *due process model.*[9]

Order with Justice: The Crime Control Model According to Packer, the ideology underlying the crime control model emphasizes repression of conduct defined as criminal as the most important function of the criminal process:

> The failure of law enforcement to bring criminal conduct under tight control is viewed as leading to the breakdown of public order and thence to the disappearance of an important condition of human freedom. If the laws go unenforced — which is to say, if it is perceived that there is a high percentage of failure to apprehend and convict in the criminal process — a general disregard for legal controls tends to develop. The law-abiding citizen then becomes the victim of all sorts of unjustifiable invasions of his interests. His security of person and property is sharply diminished, and, therefore, so is his liberty to function as a member of society. The claim ultimately is that the criminal process is a positive guarantor of social freedom.[10]

To support this ideology the crime control model pays the most attention to the capacity of the criminal justice system to catch, prosecute, convict, and dispose of a high proportion of criminal offenders. With its emphasis on a high rate of apprehension and conviction, and given limited resources, the crime control model places a premium on speed and finality. Speed is enhanced when cases can be processed informally and when procedure is uniform or standardized; finality is secured when the occasions for challenge are minimized. To ensure that challenges are kept to a minimum, the model also demands that those who work in criminal justice assume that those apprehended are in fact guilty. This places heavy emphasis on the quality of administrative fact finding and the coordination of agency tasks and role responsibilities. Success is gauged by how expeditiously nonoffenders are screened out of the process and offenders passed through to final disposition. Packer likens the crime control model to an assembly-line conveyor belt, down which an endless stream of cases flows, to be processed by workers performing routinized, but essential, tasks.

Justice with Order: The Due Process Model   Whereas the crime control model resembles an assembly line, Packer visualizes the due process model as an obstacle course: "Each of its successive stages is designed to present formidable obstacles to carrying the accused any further along in the process."[11] The ideology underlying the due process model is not diametrically opposed to that of the crime control model — it does not rest, for instance, on the view that the repression of crime is undesirable. Rather, it emphasizes a different set of concerns.

The due process model sees the crime control function as subordinate to ideals of justice. This model emphasizes ensuring that facts about the accused are subjected to formal scrutiny; ensuring that the accused is afforded an impartial hearing under adversary procedures; ensuring that coercive and stigmatizing powers are not abused by those in an official position to exercise them; maintaining the presumption of innocence until guilt is legally proven; ensuring that all defendants are given equal protection under the law, including the chance to adequately defend themselves; and ensuring that suspects and convicted offenders are accorded the kind of treatment that supports their dignity and autonomy as human beings. The emphasis, then, is on justice first.

The First Priority Is Order

American public policy on criminal matters today, as it has been for decades, is dominated by the ideology and practices of the crime control model. For many years we have seen abundant evidence of this; for example, the proliferation of public and private police forces whose primary goal is the detection and apprehension of criminals and the defense of order. We have seen continued efforts to create and enforce laws dealing with moral questions and essentially private behavior. We have seen the increasing efforts to unite and coordinate crime control at the federal, state, and local levels. We have seen a growing emphasis on informality in the criminal process, best exemplified in the extensive use of plea bargaining. We have seen continued efforts to promote efficiency, productivity, and professionalism in the activities and personnel of our law enforcement agencies. We have seen, conversely, a paucity of judicial decisions supporting due process values, and few serious efforts to organize and fund programs to ensure equal protection under the law and to guarantee the dignity and autonomy of all who come into contact with the enforcement agencies of government.

The dominant crime control model with its emphasis on establishing order through efficient legal repression had its roots in events of the 1950s and 1960s and in the way those in positions of power and influence interpreted them. Early in the 1950s, America entered a phase of domestic conflict against a background of cold war tensions. Many Americans visualized a communist (or black) subversive under every bed. The McCarthy era, coupled with large-scale migration from rural to urban areas and growing racial tensions as blacks moved closer to full civil rights, presented the image that a breakdown of public order was imminent, or had already arrived. Published reports of increased social disorganization in the cities and rising crime rates helped complete the picture.

In the 1960s, public order was given new shocks. President Kennedy was assassinated in 1963. The "American way" was mocked by strange people, among them hippies and long-haired rock and folk musicians. Suddenly the universities — previously bastions of middle-class morality and purpose — seemed to be overrun by pot-smoking, acid-dropping weirdos who preferred free love and the words of Timothy Leary to fraternities and respectable careers. Riots erupted in Watts, followed by more riots in nearly every major city. Then came more assassinations, more riots, the Black Panthers, the Students for a Democratic Society, campus demonstrations and sit-ins, violence at the Democratic National Convention in Chicago, and new evidence of sharply rising rates of street crime.

Some thought America was under siege. Crime became the number-one problem in the minds of many, if not most, citizens. In 1965 President Lyndon Johnson encouraged people to think this way: he launched the war on crime, asserting that Americans "must arrest and reverse the trend toward lawlessness."[12] He called for urgent steps toward more and better law enforcement, with increased federal involvement in crime control. To get the ball rolling and to lend force to the sense of urgency, Johnson established the President's Commission on Law Enforcement and the Administration of Justice, a commission to be "composed of men and women of distinction who share my belief that we need to know more about the prevention and control of crime."[13]

This commission, and later ones dealing with crime and public order, confirmed that urgent steps toward more efficient crime control were necessary to win the war on crime and reestablish order. Priority was given to the repression of threats to public order and middle-class morality. This came as no surprise to some authors, who pointed out that commission members were overwhelmingly drawn from the established business, political, legal, and religious elites, constituencies with a large stake in the preservation of order and the existing political, legal, and economic structure of American society.[14]

Legislative support for emphasizing order through crime control came in 1968 when Congress passed the Omnibus Crime Control and Safe Streets Act. The act has subsequently been revised and extended, but its basic thrust has remained the same: to channel federal resources and efforts into a massive campaign against lawlessness, particularly the lawlessness of the street criminal, the political activist, and the military dissenter. Under Title 1 of the act, Congress established the Law Enforcement Assistance Administration (LEAA) under the Department of Justice. Through this move, Congress extended federal involvement in and control over the enforcement activities of state and local governments, and helped establish what were to become the primary crime strategies throughout the nation. Although the Constitution specifically places the major responsibility for criminal matters in the hands of the states, the federal government was able to assume considerable power and influence in such matters.

THE LEAA

When it was established in 1968, the rationale and purpose of the LEAA was expressed as follows (note how well this mandate fits the crime control model and its underlying ideology):

> Congress finds that the high incidence of crime in the United States threatens the peace, security and general welfare of the Nation and its citizens. To prevent crime and to insure the greater safety of the people, law enforcement efforts must be better coordinated, intensified, and made more effective at all levels of government. . . .
>
> It is the purpose of this Title to (1) encourage States and units of general local government to prepare and adopt comprehensive plans based on their evaluation of State and local problems of law enforcement; (2) authorize grants to States and units of local government in order to improve and strengthen law enforcement; and (3) encourage research and development directed toward the improvement of law enforcement and the development of new methods for the prevention and reduction of crime and the detection and apprehension of criminals.[15]

To help LEAA carry out its mandate, Congress allocated just over $60 million for its operations in 1969. Since then LEAA has been one of the fastest growing federal agencies; its annual budget quickly reached half a billion dollars (in 1971), then climbed over $800 million, and by 1976 it stood at $1.015 billion.[16] (As a result of numerous criticisms of agency practices during the 1970s, however, Congress voted LEAA only $486 million for 1980. It remains to be seen whether the budget will climb again in the future.) Most of this money has gone to programs and research projects designed to upgrade the efficiency, productivity, and organization of police agencies. LEAA funds have been used to purchase new and sophisticated police equipment (from weapons and ammunition to vehicles, computers, and bulletproof clothing); to train patrolmen and reorganize police departments; to finance management training programs and operations research; to fund research at universities and private institutes into scientific and technological innovations to aid the war on crime; and to plan future policy throughout the various levels of the legal process.[17] (Federal support of criminal justice research comes largely through the National Institute of Law Enforcement and Criminal Justice. Insofar as government funded research reflects and supports government policy, one can see in criminal justice research further evidence of the conservative bent of national crime policy.[18] High priority areas for future research are deterrence, career criminals, prosecution, and sentencing.)

SCIENCE, TECHNOLOGY, AND THE MILITARY

One of LEAA's major contributions to the crime control effort has been the funding of programs designed to advance the application of science and technology to law enforcement problems. LEAA's predecessor, the Office of Law Enforcement Assistance, had funded a special Task Force to report on science and technology. As part of the 1967 President's Crime Commission, the Task Force reviewed and evaluated the past and potential contributions to crime control from science and technology. The Task Force concluded that these areas should be exploited to the fullest extent possible, with the federal government assuming leadership and the major fiscal role.[19]

Congress responded to the Task Force recommendations by including within the 1968 Omnibus Crime Control Act provisions for a research institute, under the authority of LEAA, which would sponsor and fund scientific research and technological development. Thus was established the National Institute of Law Enforcement and Criminal Justice, and by 1974 its annual budget had reached more than $40 million.[20] The money for research and development, coupled with the much larger funds of LEAA's grant programs ($900 million in 1976) and those available from other federal agencies (such as the National Institute of Mental Health), has given the federal government considerable power and influence in the application of science and technology to crime control. Also, enforcement agencies previously too poor to attempt serious rationalization of their crime control activities have now been able to pursue more directly and vigorously the strategies of order through legal repression.

Information Systems   The development of sophisticated systems to handle information about crime has been one of LEAA's major contributions to crime control. Most of these systems center around electronics, with the computer a key element; all have been designed with one central aim — to improve detection, apprehension, and conviction rates.

Today computers are a fact of life in America; few, if any, of us have escaped them. The value of computers in law enforcement was recognized early in their development, but high cost and the expense of running them put them beyond the reach of most agencies. But the federal government could afford them, and the FBI was one of the first agencies to put them to use. Today the FBI's National Crime Information Center (NCIC) is hooked up to teleprinters in most of the nation's law enforcement agencies. Computers, and the electronic technology that goes with them, now provide immediate access to millions of bits of information about crime, suspects, and offenders; this information can be stored, manipulated, retrieved, and passed on at a moment's notice.

Recent developments in information systems, about which LEAA is particularly proud, are worth noting, for they tell us about what our government considers important in its effort at crime control.

SEARCH. The LEAA describes SEARCH (Systems for Electronic Analysis and Retrieval of Criminal Histories) as "an interstate computerized network which when fully operational will allow an immediate check among participating states to find whether a suspect has a criminal history in any of them, and to obtain an up-to-date summary of that history."[21] By 1972, SEARCH had a membership of fifty states, plus the District of Columbia, Puerto Rico, and the Virgin Islands. In 1974, SEARCH was made a nonprofit corporation: SEARCH Group Incorporated.

NALECOM. Under a $500,000 grant, the Jet Propulsion Laboratory (part of NASA) "is performing an analysis for the design, development, and operational implementation of a communications system that will meet tomorrow's needs."[22] NALECOM (National Law Enforcement Communications) is intended to upgrade and supersede the information systems currently making up NCIC and NILETS (the National Law Enforcement Telecommunications System). It is anticipated that NALECOM will produce a system capable of instant transmission of fingerprints and graphic information on suspects.

PROMIS. This computer-based information system was developed for use by prosecutors (PROMIS stands for Prosecutor's Management Information System). Its purpose is to provide prosecutors with immediate access to intimate information about a defendant's criminal history, and to information about court caseload, court activity, and how the case stacks up against past and current cases in terms of such things as the seriousness of the alleged crime. The ultimate goal is to standardize prosecutorial actions and to reduce the inefficiency of big-city prosecuting offices. LEAA notes in support of the system that, after its implementation in Washington, D.C., a 25 percent increase in the conviction rate for "serious misdemeanor cases" was achieved.[23]

SWAT — A Military Offshoot The threats to order posed by riots, demonstrations, hijackings, and acts of terrorism during the last few years were met in the government by calls for the application of military technology and tactics to domestic crime problems. These calls were supported by the Task Force report on science and technology, which urged the same line. One well-known product of this concern has been SWAT,

- $400,000 to the King County, Washington, Department of Public Safety to establish an Integrated Criminal Apprehension Program.
- $248,852 to Reading, Pennsylvania, to develop an Integrated Criminal Apprehension Program.
- $138,915 to the Alaska Department of Law to develop a variety of victim/witness services.
- $275,481 to Seattle, Washington, to establish a citywide crime prevention program.
- $394,761 to New York City to establish a Night Time Jury Trials Program for felony criminal cases in King's County (Brooklyn).
- $149,329 to the North Carolina Department of Crime Control and Public Safety to implement an Offender-Based State Corrections Information System.
- $399,910 to the New York County, New York, District Attorney's Office to establish a court delay reduction program.
- $250,000 to the Fort Worth, Texas, Police Department to coordinate a wide-ranging crime prevention program in eight sections of the city.
- $131,531 to Positive Futures, Inc., Washington, D.C., to help historically black colleges and universities get more involved in criminal justice programs.
- $195,996 to the Waimanalo Council of Community Organizations, Waimanalo, Hawaii, to help establish a community crime prevention program.
- $72,568 to the Mississippi Judicial Council to design a plan for restructuring the state's chancery and circuit courts.
- $75,000 to New Jersey to develop an Offender-Based State Corrections Information System.
- $250,114 to the State University of New York, Albany, to upgrade criminal justice education programs serving communities with large minority populations.
- $345,204 to New Hampshire to renovate its state prison.
- $176,994 to the Orleans Parish Criminal Sheriff's Office, New Orleans, Louisiana, to implement a jail population control plan.
- $65,348 to Talladega College, Talladega, Alabama, to add a criminal justice degree program to its curriculum.
- $124,479 to Research Triangle Institute, Raleigh, North Carolina, to examine six neighborhoods in Atlanta, Georgia, to determine why some urban neighborhoods remain safe and secure, despite their proximity to high crime areas, and why others do not.
- $100,000 to the Lansdowne Mental Health Center, Ashland, Kentucky, to expand its family violence program.
- $74,410 to Cincinnati, Ohio, to train state and local staffs of Treatment Alternatives to Street Crime (TASC) programs at the National TASC Training Center.
- $63,270 to the National College of District Attorneys, Houston, Texas, to train some 200 prosecutors in arson prosecution.
- $400,885 to the Missouri Supreme Court to continue its support of the court's

Special Weapons and Tactics. SWAT became familiar to Americans when ABC ran an adventure series of the same name, based on the Los Angeles Police Department's SWAT teams.

SWAT was initiated in Los Angeles in late 1967 "in response to the increased incidence of urban violence, and in particular the emergence of the sniper as a threat to police operations, the appearance of the political assassin, and the threat of guerrilla warfare."[24] The SWAT concept was based on the Marine Corps model of antiguerrilla military tactics and organization. In Los Angeles, and later elsewhere, SWAT teams of five- or six-man squads were assembled for intensive training in the precise and lethal operations of guerrilla combat. Each man was expected to handle any task that conditions might require and to use effectively any of the various devices and weapons with which the teams were equipped, including "automatic rifles, semi-automatic shotguns, gas masks, gas can-

implementation of a new judicial article, a new criminal code, and a speedy trial statute.

- $650,000 to Vera Institute of Justice to continue research on the relationship of unemployment and crime.
- $97,688 to the National Legal Aid and Defender Association to design an information system for public defenders that includes a method for weighting cases to help assign case loads.
- $397,423 to Studies of Justice, Inc., Washington, D.C., to furnish legal services to prisoners in Alabama and North Carolina.
- $395,433 to the Police Executive Research Forum to analyze the management training needs of police departments and conduct a four-week pilot training program for 40 senior police managers.
- $224,933 to Social Issues Research Associates, Berkeley, California, to analyze factors influencing the granting or revoking of parole.
- $156,292 to Southern Illinois University's Center for the Study of Crime, Delinquency and Corrections to research the nature and patterns of homicide in the United States.
- $197,809 to the University of Southern California to compare data from two studies on crime and delinquency conducted separately in Philadelphia and Copenhagen, Denmark.
- $349,991 to the Rand Corporation to find out how and to what extent criminal justice research findings are eventually transformed into policy and practice in criminal justice agencies.

- $299,927 to the Institute of Policy Analysis, Eugene, Oregon, to assess the new Washington state juvenile code.
- $199,971 to the National Retired Teachers Association/American Association of Retired Persons to develop and test a plan for police departments to use senior citizens in a support role in the crime analysis process.
- $150,895 to the Socio-Environmental Research Center, Milwaukee, Wisconsin, to develop data collection techniques and models for violent crime.
- $666,667 to the Florida Department of Health and Rehabilitative Services, Tallahassee, to provide diversion services for youths convicted of property crimes and repeat misdemeanors.
- $105,000 to the Delaware State Police, Dover, to redesign and upgrade the state's Uniform Crime Reporting System.
- $365,329 to four Indiana cities and the Indiana State Police to establish Managing Criminal Investigations programs.
- $268,642 to Florida and $270,000 to Maryland to begin a two-year test of sentencing guidelines on a multijurisdictional basis.
- $184,761 to the Victim-Witness Assistance Program, San Francisco, California, to focus on ways to stop family violence by helping both victims and offenders.

SOURCE: *LEAA Newsletter* 8 (November 1979), p. 14.

isters, smoke devices, ropes, pry bars, manhole hooks, and walkie talkies."[25]

Most SWAT activities center on the protection of police and fire personnel, the rescue of hostages, the nonviolent apprehension of barricaded suspects, and the protection of public officials. The notorious May 14, 1974, shootout in Los Angeles, involving twenty-nine SWAT members and resulting in the deaths of six suspected Symbionese Liberation Army members, has tended to obscure the fact that before that time SWAT teams had fired weapons on only a handful of occasions. Even so, the proliferation of military-style police units, heavily armed and specifically trained to use violence on their fellow citizens, criminals or otherwise, in the name of order lends a flavor to domestic law enforcement that makes it hard to contest the claim that rightist ideology emphasizing order through repression is the major force behind public policy on crime.

Heavy LEAA funding of crime control research and technological developments is likely to continue through the next decade (see box on pages 494–495). Yet at least one evaluation expert questions the expectation that new technology will significantly improve crime prevention and control. George Kelling notes that with the possible exception of radios and bulletproof vests, "there is no evidence that any technological devices have significantly improved the effectiveness of police service."[26]

Public Policy and Criminal Stereotypes

President Johnson, in calling for a war on crime, and Congress, in passing the Omnibus Crime Control and Safe Streets Act, drew attention only to certain crimes and certain criminals. Despite using such broad expressions as "lawlessness in America," they considered the real crime problem to be the overt threats to public order and prevailing institutions represented in street crimes — muggings, forcible rapes, burglaries, assaults, and armed robberies — and the activities of junkies and dope pushers, militant activists and other so-called radicals. Except for the last two groups the bulk of those identified as the real threat to law and order are lower-class individuals living mostly in the poverty areas of the nation's cities.

Nineteenth-century officials dubbed such persons "the dangerous classes." Today, as then, policy makers focus crime control efforts on the relatively poor, uneducated, and powerless members of society. Describing the situation over the years, William Chambliss asserted:

> The lower-class person is (1) more likely to be scrutinized and therefore to be observed in any violation of the law; (2) more likely to be arrested if discovered under suspicious circumstances; (3) more likely to spend the time between arrest and trial in jail; (4) more likely to come to trial; (5) more likely to be found guilty; and (6) if found guilty, more likely to receive harsh punishment than his middle-class counterpart. Even after the sentence is passed, the built-in biases continue — among those sentenced to death for murder, lower-class persons are more likely to be executed than are the others.'[27]

This is not a new situation, nor is it characteristic only of America or other capitalistic countries. In Nigeria, for example, the tendency has also been for law in action to single out as criminals those lacking money or influence.[28] Further, the picture has been the same throughout history. Those low in status and relatively powerless have traditionally been the persons most likely to be labeled criminal and most likely to receive the almost undivided coercive attention of the state.

Because current crime policies show no evidence of changing their focus, people have no incentive to alter their long-held stereotypes of the criminal. On the contrary, *current policies merely reinforce these stereo-*

types. The American citizen is encouraged to view the streets as the unsafe turf of the criminal class. He is encouraged to believe that drug pushers and heroin addicts pose a serious and constant threat to his security and well-being and to that of the nation as a whole (President Richard Nixon once remarked, "The drug problem has assumed the dimensions of a national emergency").[29] He is encouraged to distrust his less-well-off neighbors, to spy on them (LEAA has spent considerable money supporting programs encouraging people to be the eyes and ears of the police), and to demand speedy and harsh disposition when they are charged with criminal offenses.

The targets of crime policy, meanwhile, are encouraged to view themselves as subjugated and oppressed by the authorities and to see their illegal actions as political crimes.[30] They feel that they are oppressed because they lack political power and that their "crimes" are legitimate reactions to this political condition. Crime control policy further alienates and aggravates the disadvantaged segments of society when they realize that middle-class criminality escapes the serious attention of the state. That it had escaped serious attention until recently is evidenced by the paucity of government programs aimed at detecting and apprehending those who commit occupational crimes. With all of the money spent on projects and programs dealing with drugs, burglary, robbery, and street crimes generally, the LEAA in 1975 reported only two funded projects specifically dealing with the prosecution of crimes of fraud.[31] In its *Sixth Annual Report* (for 1974), LEAA reported spending a mere $30,000 (out of more than $483 million) on one consumer fraud prosecution unit in one state (Vermont).[32] That report made no other mention of efforts to control occupational crime. This should come as no real surprise, however. The National Advisory Commission on Criminal Justice Standards and Goals set, as a primary goal for 1983, a 50 percent reduction in the rates of street crimes committed by strangers — rape, murder, aggravated assault, robbery, and burglary — and a 50 percent reduction in the rates of robbery and burglary, whether committed by a stranger or a friend or acquaintance. The commission had little to say about occupational crimes in its six reports and more than 400 recommendations.

This is not to say that street crimes should receive no attention, or even that they should receive less attention than they do. The issue is how much and what kind of attention they receive relative to other forms of criminality. The relative lack of attention authorities give to occupational crime is hard to justify when we consider its impact on society. This inattention reinforces prevailing stereotypes about the middle-class criminal. For when a middle-class offender is apprehended, unusual as that is, the view seems to be that he must be ill or disturbed, since real criminals do not come from his class:

> . . . the middle-class offender does not *need* to steal and is, therefore, in a different category from the working-class offender who is assumed to *need*

to steal and must, therefore, be prevented by the threat of prosecution. . . . Underlying the attitudes expressed by the police, the prosecution, and the magistrates and judges is the belief that the wealthy do not need to commit crimes, especially crimes of theft, so that if they do it is because of physical ill health, mental illness, or evil influence.[33]

Since our policies make the detection, apprehension, and harsh punishment of occupational criminals rare, they confirm the belief that only the rare middle-class person turns to crime. We are encouraged to continue thinking that crime is a lower-class phenomenon.

An extreme version of this view is presented in Jeffrey Reiman's recent book, *The Rich Get Richer and the Poor Get Prison*.[34] Reiman believes that the criminal justice system has failed to reduce crime and protect society precisely because that failure "serves the interests of the rich and powerful in America." How can that be? Reiman asserts that this failure performs an ideological service by funneling discontent toward those depicted as responsible for rising crime — the poor, the black, the lower classes — and away from the rich and powerful. At the same time, the system focuses on individual wrongdoing rather than the institutions that make up the social order, thus "implicitly conveying the message that the social conditions in which crime occurred are not responsible for the crime." If social conditions are not responsible for crime, then cries for fundamental change in the social order are without substance; the "radical" threat can be resisted by a united middle class urging support of prevailing government policies and practices. When crime is not lower class, it is the political crime of lower-class sympathizers.

POLITICAL CRIME

Political crime is difficult to define, partly because there is virtually no formal recognition of it in substantive criminal law. In recent years, however, some consensus in criminological literature has emerged, and the emphasis is clearly on a definition incorporating two elements: (1) the acts have been defined by the authorities as crimes; and (2) they are interpreted (either by the perpetrators or by officialdom) as designed to bring about or influence change in the political system or its policies. Clinard and Quinney identify political crimes as "treason, sedition, espionage, sabotage, military draft violations, war collaboration, radicalism, and various other forms of protest which may be defined as criminal."[35] These crimes sometimes appear no different from traditional crimes — murder, kidnapping, or theft. The true political criminal has been characterized as one whose illegal actions express a commitment to a cause going beyond personal gain or satisfaction, for example the overthrow of a political regime.[36]

Over the centuries, governments everywhere have reacted vigorously to those they see as posing a threat to the viability of their control. Those in power and those with access to it do all they can to protect their favored position and the existing order supporting it. One thing they do is create laws proscribing subversive conduct:

> The history of attempts to outlaw certain groups and ideas that are felt to threaten the viability of the state is the history of the use of law to protect the state. All nations have such laws and use them at various times to prevent attempts to change the distribution of power in society. These laws are by their very nature repressive of free communication and have been the product of times of national crisis. American examples of such efforts include the Sedition Act of 1798, criminal anarchy laws and criminal syndicalism laws enacted in the early twentieth century, the Smith Act of 1940, the McCarren Act of 1950, and the "Rap Brown" portion of the 1968 Omnibus Bill.[37]

While times of national crisis, real or imagined, spur legislative action and concentrated enforcement activities, times of relative domestic tranquillity do not normally result in the repeal of crisis legislation. In fact, the tendency is for repressive legislation to accumulate, so that as new crises occur the state has the force of old and new coercive measures. Francis Allen observes:

> Typically, laws proscribing political behavior are enacted in periods of strong public feeling, sometimes bordering on hysteria. Typically, too, such periods, although recurrent, are short-lived. Nothing is so dead as yesterday's red scare; but the veering of public attention away from the subject that earlier produced hysteria weakens the impetus to repeal or modify the legislation passed in a state of public excitement. The result is to confer a kind of immortality on such laws, making some available for continued application by an unobserved bureaucracy, and maintaining all for use in the next period of public agitation. When the next period arrives, not only are the old laws likely to be applied, but they may also stimulate new legislative adventures in repression and crime definition.[38]

The events of the past few decades signified a time of national crisis to those in government. The result was a concerted effort on the part of the authorities to crack down on demonstrations, civil disorders, radicals, militant activists, and any individual thought, rightly or wrongly, to constitute a threat to the establishment and the validity of its laws. Old laws were reused and new ones passed. Lists of subversives were compiled in secret and circulated around various government agencies. The federal government, in particular, drew upon its vast resources in the crime control field and began operations involving the FBI, the CIA, the IRS, the Justice Department, the White House, and a motley crew of informers and *agents provocateurs*.[39] The full extent of the government's repressive measures will never be known; however, recent revelations have forcefully demonstrated that some viewed breaking the law to catch lawbreakers as an acceptable practice. How ironic that "law and order" should have been the rallying cry of those pursuing such practices.

Due Process

We have argued that the ideology of order through repression has dominated public policy for many decades. Yet that policy has not been totally devoid of strategies ensuring human rights and dignities and furthering the cause of justice. To be sure, such strategies have offered poor competition for crime control interests, yet they have been significant enough for those with rightist leanings to bitterly assert that criminals are being "mollycoddled" and that the hands of the police and courts are tied. These comments are usually directed at those seeking to ensure due process for criminal suspects and defendants or advocating increased use of probation, pretrial release, therapy, or community-based corrections as opposed to harsher forms of punishment and other repressive and degrading practices.

The doctrine of *due process of law* originated with the signing of the Magna Charta in 1215. This document set out the terms of an agreement between King John and the English barons. It was a charter of liberties and rights designed by the barons to counteract the threat that the state would abuse its coercive powers in dealing with them. The king promised that "no man shall be arrested, or imprisoned, or disseized [deprived of his lands], or outlawed, or exiled, or in any way molested; nor will we proceed against him unless by the lawful judgment of his peers or by the law of the land."[40]

In America, the legal document outlining due process of law is the Constitution, particularly the Fourth, Fifth, Sixth, Eighth, and Fourteenth amendments. The essential provisions of these amendments are:

Fourth Amendment: "The right of the people to be secure in their persons, houses, papers, and effects, against unreasonable searches and seizures, shall not be violated, and no Warrants shall issue, but upon probable cause, supported by Oath or affirmation, and particularly describing the place to be searched, and the persons or things to be seized."

Fifth Amendment: "No person shall . . . be subject for the same offence to be twice put in jeopardy of life or limb; nor shall be compelled in any criminal case to be a witness against himself, nor be deprived of life, liberty, or property, without due process of law. . . ."

Sixth Amendment: "In all criminal prosecutions, the accused shall enjoy the right to a speedy and public trial, by an impartial jury . . . ; to be confronted with the witnesses against him; to have compulsory process for obtaining Witnesses in his favor, and to have the assistance of counsel for his defence."

Eighth Amendment: "Excessive bail shall not be required, nor excessive fines imposed, nor cruel and unusual punishments inflicted."

Fourteenth Amendment: ". . . No State shall make or enforce any law which shall abridge the privileges or immunities of citizens of the United States; nor shall any State deprive any person of life, liberty, or property, without due process of law; nor deny to any person within its jurisdiction the equal protection of the laws."

The United States Supreme Court has the responsibility to rule on constitutional matters; over the years practitioners in law and the criminal process have turned to this august body for guidance. The Supreme Court reacts to requests for rulings on constitutional questions rather than initiating them, so its decisions are always set against a backdrop of existing controversy and legal debate. Also, its rulings are not fixed; it may rule one way and later rule another way on the same question. This fact explains why basic policy questions often return again and again for rulings by the Court. It also explains why the composition of the Court is such an important issue, and why, when a President makes a new appointment, the ratification process in Congress is often so heated: whoever is appointed could shift the direction of Court rulings. For this reason the Supreme Court cannot be divorced from politics and the prevailing ideologies held by those in positions of power and influence.

Rulings in support of due process values have been few and far between, taking the history of the Court as a whole. Even over the last seventy years a supportive ruling has been so unlikely that when one does occur it has been greeted with considerable fuss. Should a number of such rulings come from any particular Court, the Court is honored with the reputation of being "liberal" or "radical."

Some significant due process rulings have been made, however. One was *Weeks* v. *United States* (1914), in which the court established the "exclusionary rule," arguing that evidence obtained illegally by the police must be excluded from subsequent criminal proceedings. In *Rochin* v. *California* (1952) the Court ruled that the sanctity of a person's body is inviolate, and attempts to remove from it evidence for a conviction (in this case, narcotics pumped from a suspect's stomach were used to convict him) constitute illegal search and seizure. In *Mapp* v. *Ohio* (1961) the Court ruled that neither state nor federal courts can accept evidence obtained in violation of the constitutional requirements of reasonable search and seizure. In *Gideon* v. *Wainwright* (1963) the Court ruled that any indigent defendant should be allowed free legal counsel. In *Escobedo* v. *Illinois* (1964) *Gideon* was extended to include right to counsel at the time of interrogation. In *Miranda* v. *Arizona* (1966), it was ruled that upon arrest, the police must notify the suspect of his rights during interrogation, his right to counsel, and the possible uses of evidence obtained during interrogation. In *Katz* v. *United States* (1967) the Court ruled that a court order is required to use electronic surveillance. In *Duncan* v. *Louisiana* (1968) the Court reaffirmed the right to a jury trial regardless of the legal seriousness of the offense. In *Witherspoon* v. *Illinois* (1968) the Court reaffirmed that the jury must be impartial. *Chimel* v. *California* (1969) restricted the physical vicinity subject to search without a warrant to that within the "immediate control" (reach) of a suspect. Other rulings have been mentioned in previous chapters.

Many of these significant due process decisions came out of the last few years of the Warren Court (named after its chief justice, Earl Warren). (The Warren Court's last major decision in the realm of criminal affairs, *Terry* v. *Ohio* (1968), was the first of a number of subsequent decisions seeming to reverse the trend in support of due process for which that Court had become famous. In this decision, eight justices agreed (only Justice Douglas dissented) that a police officer may frisk (make a search of outer clothing) a suspect when he "observes unusual conduct which leads him reasonably to conclude in the light of his experience that criminal activity may be afoot and that the persons with whom he is dealing may be armed and presently dangerous." In his dissenting opinion Justice Douglas argued that he could not see how such a search could be constitutional under the Fourth Amendment, since the question of "probable cause" was ignored. Douglas found no basis for concluding that the officer had probable cause for believing that a crime was being committed, had been committed, or was about to be committed by the defendants in the case at hand.)[41]

The Warren Court made many enemies by its due process decisions:

> Unfortunately for the Court, its attempts to set policy for the justice system came at a time of rising crime (or so it was widely perceived) and in a decade marked by political violence and protest, urban riots, and the assassination of a President, his brother, and two black leaders. People associated court decisions with this rising tide of violence; the justices were accused of "coddling criminals" and "handcuffing the police" and generally blamed for the breakdown of law and order, notwithstanding the lack of any empirical connection between judicial decisions and crime rates. Public opinion strongly opposed those court decisions which received major publicity, particularly the *Miranda* decision which set forth the rules for the interrogation of suspects. Law and order generally, and the Supreme Court's role specifically, became a major issue in the 1968 presidential campaign and the winning candidate announced his intention by future appointments to redress the balance between "the forces of peace and the forces of crime." Congress responded by its most effective recent attack upon the Court, including passage of a law to reverse several court decisions and passage of an omnibus crime bill for the District of Columbia providing for the preventive detention of dangerous criminals awaiting trial and allowing police officers in the pursuit of narcotics offenders to enter private dwellings without knocking.[42]

The Court's decisions did not sit well with the crime control ideology or with those working in the criminal justice system. As it happens, however, the power of the Supreme Court to make policy is far greater than its power to see that policy actually put into practice. This is best evidenced by the fact that even after the *Miranda* decision had been put into force, its provisions were still being ignored by a substantial number of Washington, D.C. police officers.[43] Police discretionary powers are quite vast, so Court decisions are not always the best guide to what actually goes on. As Joel Grossman and Richard Wells note, "There have been significant changes in the formal rules which govern the criminal process, but a substantially lower level of real change."[44]

The Rehabilitative Ideal and the Therapeutic State

Just as the Warren Court was accused of tying the hands of the crime control apparatus, those advocating rehabilitation and treatment rather than punishment have been accused of coddling criminals and wanting to turn prisons into country clubs and hotels. Few policy issues generate more heated debate than the question of what to do with, to, or for criminal offenders.

Historically, the established policy both here and abroad has been to emphasize punishment as the appropriate way to deal with criminals. Yet during the last seventy-five years or so a trend away from strictly punitive measures has taken place. This can be seen in the increased use of probation, parole, community-based corrections, and various programs designed to "treat" offenders. Treatment programs cover the gamut of therapeutic approaches — from psychotherapy to reality therapy, behavior modification, chemotherapy, transactional analysis, and group therapy.

The trend toward rehabilitation and treatment cannot be explained by any one cause; it seems to be rooted in a number of things. First, nineteenth-century positivism led many to view criminality as a problem amenable to scientific analysis and solution. Another factor was the growing number of scholars and practitioners who questioned the deterrent efficacy of traditional ways of dealing with criminals. Some held that crime was the result not of free will and wickedness, but of "sickness" brought on by genetic or environmental conditions. Also, humanitarians condemned existing policies as harsh and cruel. Perhaps most important, practitioners and theorists in the developing fields of psychology and psychiatry saw in the criminal — a deviant — the perfect opportunity to put their theories into practice. What actually allowed the "rehabilitative ideal" to make inroads into crime policy, more than anything else, was the fact that its advocates held the view that crime was injurious to society and promised to provide new defenses against it.[45]

JUVENILE JUSTICE

It is by no means coincidental that at the same time governments were becoming aware of the rehabilitative promise new approaches to the question of juvenile justice were surfacing. Juvenile courts were established under the *parens patriae* doctrine; their avowed purpose was to care for, rather than punish, the delinquent. The doctrine placed "little or no emphasis . . . upon an individual's guilt of a particular crime; but much weight is given to his physical, mental, or social shortcomings. In dealing with the deviant, under the new system, society is said to be acting in a parental role . . . seeking not to punish but to change or socialize the nonconformist through treatment or therapy."[46]

Illinois was the first state to establish a juvenile court (in Cook County in 1899), and by the end of World War II every state had passed legislation providing for the special handling of juveniles (usually defined as those under 17) following the *parens patriae* doctrine. As the juvenile court system unfolded, its typical features were: (1) private hearings before designated officials — judge or probation officer — and parents or guardian only; (2) informal hearings, because the court trial atmosphere was considered inappropriate given the state's parental role; (3) no juries and usually no counsel, either for the prosecution or defense; (4) no cross-examination of one's accusers; (5) no sentence — the preferred term was "adjudication" or "disposition"; and (6) no punishment — the preferred expression was "treatment" or "care."

THE THERAPEUTIC STATE

Based on *parens patriae* and individualized treatment, juvenile justice became part of the trend toward what some authors have called the "therapeutic state" — a state in which therapy is a tool governments use to control deviants and enforce conformity to rules. Today therapy for social control purposes is found in the areas of mental health, alcoholism, drug addiction, psychotherapy, juvenile delinquency, and adult crime. In some of these areas citizens may volunteer for treatment; in all of them, however, the state may make treatment compulsory. According to Nicholas Kittrie, the trend has been divestment: the criminal law has been forced to relinquish its jurisdiction over areas formerly its concern alone.[47] Freed from the criminal law, these areas are also freed from the constraints to which the state is subject in criminal matters. In other words, the state has emerged largely unfettered in its expanding role of *parens patriae*. A considerable danger has thus been created by the trend toward rehabilitation and therapy. In its dealings with nonconformists, the state need pay no attention to due process and the rights and dignities of its citizens.

This serious danger has in fact proved real, leading some observers to demand that the rehabilitative ideal be exposed for what it has turned out to be — another tool of repression, but a more insidious one. Critical studies of juvenile justice in action and of the use of therapy in prisons and mental institutions[48] show that whatever the original aims and expectations might have been, the "welfare and health components of the therapeutic power have served as subterfuge for circumventing traditional limitations against excesses of state power."[49] Under the guise of therapy, rehabilitation, and reform, criminals of every age, sometimes only suspects, have been incarcerated under indeterminate sentences, forced to undergo treatment of all kinds, used as guinea pigs in therapeutic experiments, and even brainwashed. The fact that many of these "offenders'' — particularly juveniles and those adjudged mentally ill — found themselves in therapy programs without due process of law makes the abuses all the worse, and the policies supporting them all the more repressive.

RECENT DEVELOPMENTS

Some recent developments may well presage movement away from rehabilitation therapy and some of the abuses we have briefly discussed. Many state legislatures are currently considering mandatory flat prison sentences as a replacement for indeterminate sentences. This means an offender would have to be released upon completion of the term of his sentence and could not be held for rehabilitative purposes (pages 414–416). A trend toward more lengthy prison terms may also be developing, and the longer a person must stay in prison the less justifiable, or useful, would be attempts at therapy. Also, the feeling is widespread that rehabilitation has no effect whatever on the overall crime rate, and with the rebirth of scholarly interest in punishment as a deterrent, this could mean a return to punishment as the cornerstone of official reactions to crime.

Recent court decisions have reaffirmed the importance of due process for juveniles and have also outlawed some of the commonplace abuses in the nation's jails and prisons under the guise of treatment. In *Kent* v. *United States* (1966), the Supreme Court argued that a juvenile could not be transferred to an adult criminal court without a hearing and that he had right to counsel. Justice Abe Fortas wrote the majority opinion and observed in his preliminaries that ''there may be grounds for concern that the child receives the worst of both worlds: that he gets neither the protections accorded to adults nor the solicitous care and regenerative treatment postulated for children.''[50] This decision was followed by the more significant case, *in re Gault* (1967). Here the Court extended to juvenile court proceedings the right to counsel, the right to confront one's accusers, the right to remain silent, and the right to speedy notification of the charges.

Some recent federal court decisions have laid down restrictions on what can be done with offenders and suspects incarcerated for therapy. After the atrocities at the Cummings and Tucker prison farms in Arkansas became known in the late 1960s, one federal court ruled that the conditions at the prisons constituted cruel and unusual punishment. Another federal court ruled in Michigan that psychosurgery could not be performed on an inmate without his informed consent. These and other recent decisions may curb therapeutic abuses, but when all is said and done, some questions still must be answered, and the answers are as yet wanting. Nicholas Kittrie enumerates some of the more compelling questions:

Foremost is the question of the basic balance between society's right to protect and improve itself in its members through preventive measures, and the individual's right to be left alone. How much of a social hazard must be demonstrated before society may step in and subject a deviant to therapy? May society seek to remedy one's status or personality over one's objections? . . .

Beyond the substantive questions regarding the exercise of therapeutic sanctions looms the question of procedural due process. . . . Should there be a right to a hearing and counsel? . . . Should the state be required to disclose the medical record upon which it proceeds against an individual? Should the term of therapeutic treatment be determinate or indeterminate? Should social sanctions depend on the availability of treatment? Should the individual against whom sanctions are exercised have the legal right to demand effective treatment?[51]

Francis Allen asks another important question: what are we trying to produce with our efforts at rehabilitation, and by what scale of values do we determine the ends of therapy?[52] This question is perhaps the most important of all.

Future Policy

What about the future? What can we expect from our government? Will policy remain dominated by rightist ideology and practices? Will more emphasis be placed on doing something about occupational crime or will we see a continued policy bias in favor of the suppression of lower-class criminality? Will significant moves be made toward the decriminalization of victimless crimes or will governments continue to enact and enforce laws dealing with homosexuality, drugs, prostitution, and the like? Will serious efforts be made to curb the discretionary powers of the police or will we see attempts to extend them? Will the therapeutic state become more powerful or less powerful?

At the time of this writing we are still feeling the effects of Watergate, which alerted many Americans to the abuses of power that are possible, perhaps probable, in government circles. President Carter promised a fresh look at crime and has bemoaned the tendency of past crime policy to reinforce the traditional stereotype of the criminal. Because of these things perhaps the next few years will see considerable attention paid to justice with order, rather than order with justice. Perhaps money and resources will now be channeled to improving the quality of life for all Americans, especially the poor and disadvantaged, rather than into drug enforcement, police agencies, the suppression of dissent, or prisons.

Rather than speculating on changes in policy it is more realistic, and sobering, to consider what is unlikely to change in the foreseeable future. Some very basic conditions seem destined to remain largely unchanged.

First, the demand for order will remain. Second, the state will still rely on law as its major tool in maintaining order. Third, the established elites will continue to hold the trump card in policy decision making. Fourth, officials will look toward science and technology for answers to questions about crime. Fifth, as always, organizations seek their own perpetuation, so the criminal justice bureaucracy will continue to exist in its present form, if not expand yet further. And sixth, punishment will probably remain the cornerstone of reactions to crime.

The persistence of these conditions does not bode well for any radical changes in crime policy; but changes have been and are going to be made. Although the basic strategy in crime control has been unchanged — focusing considerable resources on burglary and other forms of predominantly lower-class crime — tactical changes have occurred in recent years. Resources are being channeled into citizen-participation programs such as Operation Identification (also known as TRAP, Project Bandit, Thwart-a-Thief, and Theft Guard).[53]

SUGGESTIONS FOR CHANGE: SOME EXAMPLES

This does not mean that no serious thought has been given to fundamental policy changes or that such changes have not been suggested. Though academic criminologists have not given sufficient attention to public policy, some have advanced quite radical proposals. Some proposals cover the gamut of policy issues, while others deal with select problems such as police patrolling techniques, use of probation, or the legislation of morality. A detailed discussion of proposed reforms is impossible here, but it is fitting to conclude our analysis of crime in America by mentioning at least some of them. Most belong to the ideological left, and some are more radical than others. There is little chance that the latter will be adopted by government agencies because the more radical policy proposals call for fundamental changes in the structure of American society and a redefinition of crime itself:

> [A] radical perspective defines crime as a violation of politically-defined human rights: the truly egalitarian rights to decent food and shelter, to human dignity and self-determination, rather than the so-called right to compete for an unequal share of wealth and power. A socialist, human-rights definition of crime frees us to examine imperialism, racism, capitalism, sexism and other systems of exploitation which contribute to human misery and deprive people of their human potentiality. The State and legal apparatus, rather than directing our investigations, should be a central focus of investigation as a crimogenic institution, involved in corruption, deception and crimes of genocide (Watergate, Indochina, etc.). Under the legal definition of crime, the solutions are primarily aimed at controlling the victims of exploitation (poor, third world, youth, women) who, as a consequence of their oppression, are channeled through the criminal justice system. Under a radical, human-rights

A SAMPLING OF THE MORRIS-HAWKINS PROPOSALS FOR REFORM OF CRIMINAL JUSTICE POLICY

Criminal Definitions

1. **Drunkenness.** Public drunkenness shall cease to be a criminal offense.
2. **Narcotics and drug abuse.** Neither the acquisition, purchase, possession, nor the use of any drug will be a criminal offense. The sale of some drugs other than by a licensed chemist (druggist) and on prescription will be criminally proscribed: proof of possession of excessive quantities may be evidence of a sale or of intent to sell.
3. **Gambling.** No form of gambling will be prohibited by the criminal law; certain fraudulent and cheating gambling practices will remain criminal.
4. **Disorderly conduct and vagrancy.** Disorderly conduct and vagrancy laws will be replaced by laws precisely stipulating the conduct proscribed and defining the circumstances in which the police should intervene.
5. **Abortion.** Abortion performed by a qualified medical practitioner in a registered hospital shall cease to be a criminal offense.
6. **Sexual behavior.** Sexual activities between consenting adults in private will not be subject to the criminal law. Adultery, fornication, illicit cohabitation, statutory rape and carnal knowledge, bigamy, incest, sodomy, bestiality, homosexuality, prostitution, pornography, and obscenity; in all of these the role of the criminal law is excessive.
7. **Juvenile delinquency.** The juvenile court should retain jurisdiction only over conduct by children which would be criminal were they adult.

Punishment and Treatment

1. The money bail system shall be abolished. All but a small number of offenders who present high risk of flight or criminal acts prior to trial shall be granted pretrial release upon such conditions and restrictions as the court may think necessary and with stringent penalties for failure to appear.

---

definition, the solution to "crime" lies in the revolutionary transformation of society and the elimination of economic and political systems of exploitation.[54]

One specific policy reform advanced by radical criminologists is the dismantling of government crime information systems. These are viewed as oppressive instruments of state power and are considered easily abused to the detriment of human rights and dignities.[55] Another proposal is disarming the police, especially removing military hardware. But beyond such specific proposals, the radical alternative remains a collection of rather vague assertions to the effect that what is required is a revolutionary move toward democratic socialism, as opposed to the state socialism of the USSR and Sweden, minimizing the rule of law and allowing the people to determine their destiny, not the state with its ruling-class priorities. Quinney's recent statements are representative of the radical alternative:

> Our praxis is one of thought and action — reflecting upon the world and acting to transform it. We can free ourselves from the oppression of the age only as we combine our thoughts and our actions, turning each back upon the other. Our theory and our practice are formed in the struggle to make a socialist society. This is the critical life.[56]

The radical alternative rejects anything but the total transformation of society, hence its advocates look unsympathetically on the more moder-

2. Unless cause to the contrary can be shown, treatment of offenders shall be community based.

3. For a felony, no term of imprisonment of less than one year shall be imposed by the courts.

4. All correctional authorities shall develop community treatment programs for offenders, providing special intensive treatment as an alternative to institutionalization.

5. All correctional authorities shall make an immediate start on prison plans designed to reduce the size of penal institutions, develop modern industrial programs, and expand work-release, graduated release, and furloughs for prisoners.

6. All state and federal laws restricting the sale of prison-made products shall be repealed.

7. All local jails and other correctional facilities including probation and parole services shall be integrated within unitary state correctional systems.

8. All correctional authorities shall recruit additional probation and parole officers as needed for an average ratio of thirty-five offenders per officer.

9. Parole and probation services shall be made available in all jurisdictions for felons, juveniles, and such adult misdemeanants as need or can profit from them.

10. Every release from a penal institution for felons and for such categories of misdemeanants as the correctional authorities see fit shall be on parole for a fixed period of between one and five years.

SOURCE: Norval Morris and Gordon Hawkins, *The Honest Politician's Guide to Crime Control* (Chicago: University of Chicago Press, 1970), pp. 3, 112–113. Reprinted by permission of the University of Chicago Press. Copyright © 1969, 1970 by the University of Chicago. All rights reserved.

Note: This is just a sampling of the proposals advanced by these authors. I have chosen criminal definitions and punishment and treatment because they represent the two ends, so to speak, of the criminal process.

ate policy reforms suggested by colleagues. In fact, they see both liberal and conservative proposals as essentially identical, that is, as promoting the interests of a capitalist economy. This may well be, but unless one is a diehard radical, the reforms advocated by moderate leftists and their conservative counterparts are significantly different in terms of their effect on the American scene. Conservatives would expand the scope of the criminal law; leftists would reduce it. Conservatives would opt for more severe punishments; leftists would continue the search for alternatives to punishment. Conservatives would support increased efforts to detect and apprehend conventional criminals; leftists would emphasize the prevention of crime, especially occupational crimes committed by those in business and politics. Conservatives would support the use of law to enforce essentially private morality; leftists would not.

Most academic criminologists are moderate leftists. Norval Morris and Gordon Hawkins offer the most sweeping policy reforms (see box above). They begin by questioning the proper scope of criminal law and then progress through all stages of the legal process for both adults and juveniles. They believe that we now know enough about crime to find a cure for it: "not a sudden potion nor a lightning panacea but rather a legislative and administrative regimen which would substantially reduce the impact of crime."[57] Their cure, the authors contend, is realistic and would reduce both the incidence of crime and the fear of crime.

Somewhat more limited in scope are the proposals offered by John

Griffiths and Edwin Schur. Griffiths, for example, contends that a third model of the criminal process should be given serious consideration in criminal justice policy making. Arguing that Packer's crime control and due process models can be reduced to the same basic premise — that a state of battle exists between the state and the individual — Griffiths proposes an alternative, the "family model." According to this model, the state and the individual are not at odds; rather, the focus is on reconciliation. The model assumes that "criminals are just people who are deemed to have offended — that we are all of us actually or potentially criminal — that 'criminals' are not a special kind or class of people with a unique relation to the State."[58] In such a system, criminal justice would be a matter of seeking a cooperative, constructive, conciliatory outcome involving the interests of all parties, the state, the offender, and the victim. Griffiths observes that this was in fact the unfulfilled promise of juvenile justice under the *parens patriae* doctrine. But,

> very little effort was ever made, by the society as a whole, to implement it. Facilities, staffs, funds, and the like have never been nearly adequate to the needs of children. The "process" has been one of rush, routine, crowding, arbitrariness and often squalor and even brutality. There has never been any real commitment to a non-hostile attitude. Children have been shuffled off into dreary institutions where they can be exiled and forgotten — just like criminals — and the label "delinquent" and all of its euphemistic alternatives have persisted in memories, police and court records, and so forth, as permanent badges of obloquy.[59]

Two reform approaches offer hope of cleaning up the mess of juvenile justice. One stresses the removal from juvenile statutes of "status offenses," acts that would not be crimes if committed by adults. Children in many states can be labeled delinquent for truancy, curfew violations, running away, being "ungovernable," being sexually active, associating with bad company, and a host of other "sins." These, it is argued, should not be the focus of coercive repression on the part of the state. The second line of reform relates to the first and concerns the appropriate strategy for dealing with juveniles in trouble. The strategy is called "radical non-intervention" and is described here by Schur, one of its major proponents:

> In radical non-intervention delinquents are seen not as having special personal characteristics, nor even as being subject to socioeconomic constraints, but rather as *suffering from contingencies.* Youthful "misconduct," it is argued, is extremely common; delinquents are youths who, for a variety of reasons, drift into disapproved forms of behavior and are caught and "processed." A great deal of the labeling of delinquents is socially unnecessary and counterproductive. Policies should be adopted, therefore, that accept a greater diversity in youth behavior; special delinquency laws should be exceedingly narrow in scope or abolished completely along with preventive efforts that single out specific individuals and programs that employ "com-

pulsory treatment." . . . The crucial objection is to compulsion; even "therapy" — while it does not provide a major solution to delinquency problems — is quite compatible, provided the individual submits to it voluntarily.[60]

Future policy is likely to incorporate those reforms permitting lawmakers and criminal justice practitioners to retain both their ideological commitment to order and their jobs. Radical changes are unlikely in the foreseeable future.

One of the most substantial impediments to radical change, and even to moderate changes if they cause dismantling of existing programs and agencies, is a general resistance to any change that might result in the loss of status and jobs and of existing benefits associated with crime and existing efforts to deal with it. Karl Marx in in the nineteenth century and Charles Reasons and Russell Kaplan in 1975 have argued this point. Marx noted, with much irony, how crime and criminals "benefited" society:

> The criminal produces not only crimes but also criminal law and in addition to this the inevitable compendium in which [the] professor throws his lectures onto the general market as "commodities." This brings with it augmentation of national wealth. . . . The criminal, moreover, produces the whole of the police and of criminal justice, constables, judges, hangmen, juries, etc.; and all these different lines of business . . . create new needs and new ways of satisfying them. Torture alone has given rise to the most ingenious mechanical inventions, and employed many honourable craftsmen in the production of its instruments. . . . In this way . . . the criminal comes in as one of those natural "counterweights" which bring about a correct balance and open up a whole perspective of "useful" occupations.
>
> The effects of the criminal on the development of productive power can be shown in detail. Would locks ever have reached their present degree of excellence had there been no thieves? Would the making of bank-notes have reached its present perfection had there been no forgers? Would the microscope have found its way into the sphere of ordinary commerce but for trading frauds? Doesn't practical chemistry owe just as much to adulteration of commodities and the efforts to show it up as to the honest zeal for production?[61]

Marx's point is that respectable people make a living off crime and criminals even while they castigate them. An entire industry grew around crime, hence radical change would actually undermine this industry and is likely to be resisted. Reasons and Kaplan argue that efforts to do away with prisons, among other things, will be resisted because of the jobs they create, the scientific research they benefit and support, the reduction of unemployment rates they can produce, and the prison-related occupations they support.[62] Some argue that even if a viable plan were devised to prevent or significantly reduce crime, it would be resisted by the very same people who consider crime a problem. This was the case during the witch hunts of medieval Europe. Some of the very people who heartily condemned witchcraft saw to it that the crime of witchcraft flourished rather than disappeared. They helped create witchcraft (all it needed was to point the finger at someone), for in witchcraft lay their own status and prosperity as witch finders, witch hunters, witch watchers, torturers, executioners, and judges.[63] While the crime scene in America may change in character, some people will always ensure that crime continues to be a problem — and those people will not always be the criminals.

References

1. Francis A. Allen, *The Crimes of Politics* (Cambridge, Mass.: Harvard University Press, 1974), p. 4.
2. Walter B. Miller, "Ideology and Criminal Justice Policy: Some Current Issues," *Journal of Criminal Law and Criminology* 64 (1973), p. 142.
3. Ibid., pp. 141–62. See also Clarice S. Stoll, "Images of Man and Social Control," *Social Forces* 47 (1968), pp. 119–27; Richard Quinney, "The Ideology of Law: Notes for a Radical Alternative to Legal Oppression," *Issues in Criminology* 7 (1972), pp. 1–35; and Gresham M. Sykes, "The Future of Criminality," *American Behavioral Scientist* 15 (1972), pp. 409–19.
4. Miller, "Ideology and Criminal Justice Policy," p. 143.
5. Ibid., p. 148.
6. Stoll, "Images of Man and Social Control," p. 121.
7. Miller, "Ideology and Criminal Justice Policy," p. 150.
8. See Stoll, "Images of Man and Social Control," pp. 122–26.
9. Herbert L. Packer, "Two Models of the Criminal Process," *University of Pennsylvania Law Review* 62 (1964), pp. 1–68; see also his *The Limits of the Criminal Sanction* (Stanford, Calif.: Stanford University Press, 1968).
10. Packer, *The Limits of the Criminal Sanction,* p. 158.
11. Ibid., p. 163.
12. "Crime, Its Prevalence, and Measures of Prevention." Message from the President of the United States, House of Representatives, 89th Cong., March 1965, Document No. 103; cited in Richard Quinney, *Critique of Legal Order: Crime Control in Capitalist Society* (Boston: Little, Brown, 1974), p. 60.
13. Ibid.
14. Anthony M. Platt, ed., *The Politics of Riot Commissions* (New York: Macmillan, 1971), p. 20; see also Quinney, *Critique of Legal Order,* pp. 60–75.
15. Cited in Quinney, *Critique of Legal Order,* p. 101.
16. U.S. Department of Justice, *The LEAA: A Partnership for Crime Control* (Washington, D.C.: U.S. Government Printing Office, 1976), p. 42.
17. For complete details, see the LEAA *Annual Report,* published each year by the Superintendent of Documents, U.S. Government Printing Office.
18. See Daniel Glaser, "The Federal Government and Criminal Justice Research," *Federal Probation* 41 (1977), pp. 9–14; Walter C. Reckless and Harry E. Allen, "Developing a National Crime Policy: The Impact of Politics on Crime in America," in *Criminology: New Concerns,* Edward Sagarin, ed. (Beverly Hills, Calif.: Sage, 1979), pp. 129–38.
19. See President's Commission on Law Enforcement and the Administration of Justice, *Task Force Report: Science and Technology* (Washington, D.C.: U.S. Government Printing Office, 1967).
20. LEAA, *Sixth Annual Report,* 1974 (Washington, D.C.: U.S. Government Printing Office, 1975), p. 60.
21. LEAA, *Safe Streets: The LEAA Program at Work* (Washington, D.C.: U.S. Government Printing Office, 1971), p. 25.
22. LEAA, *Sixth Annual Report,* p. 78.
23. Ibid., p. 80.
24. Center for Research on Criminal Justice, *The Iron Fist and the Velvet Glove* (Berkeley, Calif.: Center for Research on Criminal Justice, 1975), p. 48.
25. Ibid.
26. George L. Kelling, "Police Field Services and Crime: The Presumed Effects of a Capacity," *Crime and Delinquency* 24 (1978), pp. 182–83.
27. William J. Chambliss, *Crime and the Legal Process* (New York: McGraw-Hill, 1969), p. 86; see also Robert Lefcourt, ed., *Law Against the People* (New York: Random House, 1971), p. 22.
28. See William J. Chambliss, "The Political Economy of Crime: A Comparative Study of Nigeria and the U.S.A.," in *Critical Criminology,* eds. Ian Taylor, Paul Walton, and Jock Young (London: Routledge and Kegan Paul, 1975), pp. 167–79.
   Routledge and Kegan Paul), 1975), pp. 167–79.
29. Cited in *Safe Streets: The LEAA Program at Work,* p. 19.
30. Allen, *The Crimes of Politics,* pp. 75–76.
31. National Institute of Law Enforcement and Crim-

inal Justice, *Exemplary Projects: The Prosecution of Economic Crimes* (Washington, D.C.: U.S. Government Printing Office, 1975).

32. LEAA, *Sixth Annual Report,* p. 175.

33. Dennis Chapman, *Sociology and the Stereotype of the Criminal* (London: Tavistock, 1968), pp. 72–75.

34. Jeffrey H. Reiman, *The Rich Get Richer and the Poor Get Prison* (New York: Wiley, 1979), pp. 139–67.

35. Marshall B. Clinard and Richard Quinney, eds., *Criminal Behavior Systems: A Typology* (New York: Holt, Rinehart and Winston, 1967), p. 15.

36. See Stephen Schafer, "The Concept of the Political Criminal," *Journal of Criminal Law, Criminology, and Police Science* 62 (1971), pp. 380–87. See also W. William Minor, "Political Crime, Political Justice, and Political Prisoners," *Criminology* 12 (1975), pp. 385–97.

37. Charles E. Reasons, ed., *The Criminologist: Crime and the Criminal* (Pacific Palisades, Calif.: Goodyear Publishing, 1974), p. 158.

38. Allen, *The Crimes of Politics,* pp. 47–48.

39. Use of informers and *agents provocateurs* is discussed in Gary T. Marx, "Thoughts on a Neglected Category of Social Movement Participant: The Agent Provocateur and Informer," *American Journal of Sociology* 80 (1974), pp. 402–42. See also Andrew Karmen, "Agents Provocateurs in the Contemporary Leftist Movement," in *The Criminologist,* ed., Reasons, pp. 209–26.

40. Cited in George F. Cole, *The American System of Criminal Justice* (North Scituate, Mass.: Duxbury Press, 1975), p. 105.

41. 392 U.S. 1 (1968).

42. Joel B. Grossman and Richard S. Wells, *Constitutional Law and Judicial Policy Making* (New York: Wiley, 1972), p. 434.

43. See Richard J. Medalie, Leonard Zeitz, and Paul Alexander, "Custodial Police Interrogation in Our Nation's Capital: The Attempt to Implement Miranda," *Michigan Law Review* 66 (1968), pp. 1347–79.

44. Grossman and Wells, *Constitutional Law,* p. 441.

45. Francis Allen, "Criminal Justice, Legal Values, and the Rehabilitative Ideal," *Journal of Criminal Law, Criminology, and Police Science* 50 (1959), pp. 226–36.

46. Nicholas N. Kittrie, *The Right to Be Different: Deviance and Enforced Therapy* (Baltimore: Penguin Books, 1973), p. 3.

47. See ibid., pp. 4–8.

48. For juvenile studies see Aaron V. Cicourel, *The Social Organization of Juvenile Justice* (New York: Wiley, 1968); Michael H. Langley, "The Juvenile Court: The Making of a Delinquent," *Law and Society Review* 7 (1972), pp. 273–98; and Kittrie, *The Right to Be Different,* chapter 3. Studies of institutional therapy include Jessica Mitford, *Kind and Usual Punishment* (New York: Knopf, 1973); Gene G. Kassebaum, David Ward, and Daniel Wilner, *Prison Treatment and Parole Survival* (New York: Wiley, 1970); and Erving Goffman, *Asylums* (Garden City, N.Y.: Doubleday, 1961).

49. Kittrie, *The Right to Be Different,* p. 379.

50. 383 U.S. 541 (1966), p. 556.

51. Kittrie, *The Right to Be Different,* pp. 47–48.

52. Allen, "Criminal Justice, Legal Values, and the Rehabilitative Ideal," p. 226.

53. Thomas W. White, Katryna J. Regan, John D. Waller, Joseph S. Wholey, *Police Burglary Prevention Programs* (Washington, D.C.: National Institute of Law Enforcement and Criminal Justice, 1975), p. 26.

54. Tony Platt, "Prospects for a Radical Criminology in the USA," in *Critical Criminology,* ed. Taylor et al., p. 103.

55. Center for Research on Criminal Justice, *The Iron Fist and the Velvet Glove,* pp. 116–36; Jeff Gerth, "The Americanization of 1984," *Sundance Magazine* 1 (1972), pp. 58–65.

56. Quinney, *Critique of Legal Order,* pp. 197–98.

57. Norval Morris and Gordon Hawkins, *The Honest Politician's Guide to Crime Control* (Chicago: University of Chicago Press, 1970), p. ix.

58. John Griffiths, "Ideology in Criminal Procedure, or a Third Model of the Criminal Process," *Yale Law Journal* 79 (1979), p. 374.

59. Ibid., p. 400.

60. Edwin M. Schur, *Radical Non-Intervention: Rethinking the Delinquency Problem* (Englewood Cliffs, N.J.: Prentice-Hall, 1973), p. 23.

61. Karl Marx, *Theories of Surplus Value,* vol. 1 (Moscow: Foreign Languages Publishing House, 1969), pp. 387–88.

62. Charles E. Reasons and Russell L. Kaplan, "Tear Down the Walls? — Some Functions of Prisons," *Crime and Delinquency* 21 (1975), pp. 360–72.

63. Elliot P. Currie, "Crimes without Criminals: Witchcraft and Its Control in Renaissance Europe," *Law and Society Review* 3 (1968), pp. 20–22.

Appendix

Throughout the text you will come across references to various criminal offenses. Each of the chapters in part II deals with the historical development of relevant offenses, and an effort is made to acquaint the reader with contemporary criminal law definitions. However, the FBI maintains its own offense classification and definitional system. When FBI data are presented for certain offenses, the conception of that offense may not strictly agree with dominant criminal law definitions, and sometimes the FBI includes in its offense categories a number of discrete criminal law offenses. So that you will know exactly how the FBI defines any particular offense category, the following list of FBI offenses is presented.* Use it as a reference when you deal with FBI data.

FBI Part I Offenses

Criminal Homicide: (a) Murder and nonnegligent manslaughter: all willful felonious homicide as distinguished from death caused by negligence. *Excludes* attempt to kill, suicide, accidental death, or justifiable homicide. (b) Manslaughter by negligence: any death that police investigation established was primarily attributable to gross negligence of some individual other than the victim.

Forcible Rape: The carnal knowledge of a female, forcibly and against her will in the categories of rape by force, assault by rape, and attempted rape. *Excludes* statutory offenses (no force used, victim under age of consent).

Robbery: Stealing or taking of anything of value from the care, custody, or control of a person by force or violence or by putting in fear, such as strong-arm robbery, stickup, armed robbery, assault to rob, and attempt to rob.

* From FBI *Uniform Crime Reports,* 1973 (Washington D.C.: U.S. Government Printing Office, 1974), pp. 55–56.

Burglary, breaking or entering: Burglary, housebreaking, safecracking, or any breaking or unlawful entry of a structure with the intent to commit a felony or a theft. Includes attempted forcible entry.

Aggravated assault: Assault with intent to kill or for the purpose of inflicting severe bodily injury by shooting, cutting, stabbing, maiming, poisoning, scalding, or the use of acids, explosives, or other means. *Excludes* simple assault.

Larceny-theft (except auto theft): The unlawful taking, carrying, leading, or riding away of property from the possession or constructive possession of another. *Excludes* embezzlement, con games, forgery, worthless checks, etc.

Auto theft: Unlawful taking or stealing or attempted theft of a motor vehicle. Specifically excluded from this category are motor boats, construction equipment, airplanes, and farming equipment.

Arson: Willful or malicious burning with or without intent to defraud. Includes attempts.

FBI Part II Offenses

Other assaults (simple): Assaults that are not of an aggravated nature.

Forgery and counterfeiting: Making, altering, uttering, or possessing, with intent to defraud; anything false that is made to appear true. Includes attempts.

Fraud: Fraudulent conversion and obtaining money or property by false pretenses. Includes bad checks except forgeries and counterfeiting. Also includes larceny by bailee.

Embezzlement: Misappropriation or misapplication of money or property entrusted to person's care, custody, or control.

Stolen property — buying, receiving, possessing: Buying, receiving, and possessing stolen property, and attempts.

Vandalism: Willful or malicious destruction, injury, disfigurement, or defacement of property without consent of owner or person having custody or control.

Weapons — carrying, possessing, etc.: All violations of regulations or statutes controlling the carrying, using, possession, furnishing, and manufacturing of deadly weapons or silencers. Includes attempts.

Prostitution and commercialized vice: Sex offenses of a commercial nature and attempts, such as prostitution, keeping a bawdy house, procuring, or transporting women for immoral purposes.

Sex offenses (except forcible rape and last category): Statutory rape, offenses against chastity, common decency, morals, and the like. Includes attempts.

---

* The first data collection is available in the October 1980 publication of *Uniform Crime Reports*.

Narcotic drug laws: Offenses relating to narcotic drugs, such as unlawful possession, sale, use, growing, manufacturing, and making of narcotic drugs.

Gambling: Promoting, permitting, or engaging in gambling.

Offenses against the family and children: Nonsupport, neglect, abuse, etc.

Driving under the influence: Driving or operating any motor vehicle while drunk or under the influence of alcohol or narcotics.

Liquor laws: State or local liquor law violations, except drunkenness and driving under the influence.

Drunkenness: Drunkenness or intoxication.

Disorderly conduct: Breach of the peace.

Vagrancy: Vagabondage, begging, loitering, etc.

Suspicion: Arrest for no specific offense and release without formal charges being placed. [It is interesting that the FBI considers suspicion an offense. See chapter 11 for a discussion of police views of suspicion.]

Curfew and loitering laws (juveniles): Offenses relating to violation of local curfew or loitering ordinances where such laws exist.

Runaway (juveniles): Limited to juveniles taken into protective custody as runaways under provisions of local statutes.

Photograph Acknowledgments

Chapter 1 page 2 Fred Conrad; page 17 Franklin Wing/Stock, Boston, Inc.

Chapter 2 page 21 © Ken Robert Buck; page 46 Leo De Wys, Inc.

Chapter 3 page 66 Cary Wolinsky/Stock, Boston, Inc.; page 75 United Press International Photo

Chapter 4 page 98 © Bob Combs/Rapho-Photo Researchers, Inc.; page 108 © John Garrett 1978/Woodfin Camp and Associates; page 118 © Bob Adelman/Magnum Photos, Inc.

Chapter 5 page 138 James Motlow/Jeroboam; page 152 Lauren Dale

Chapter 6 page 168 Gilles Peress/© Magnum Photos, Inc.; page 188 © Josephus Daniels/Photo Researchers, Inc.

Chapter 7 page 205 J. P. Laffont/Sygma; page 223 Jean-Paul Paireault/Gamma-Liason

Chapter 8 page 250 Douglas Corry/Leo De Wys, Inc.; page 265 Church Fishmann/Leo De Wys, Inc.

Chapter 9 page 281 Frank Siteman/The Picture Cube; page 294 Ken Regan Camera 5; page 305 Ken Robert Buck/Stock, Boston, Inc.

Chapter 10 page 314 © 1977 Peter Menzel/Stock, Boston, Inc.; page 341 Burt Glinn/© Magnum Photos, Inc.

Chapter 11 page 356 © Susan Kuklin 1979/Photo Researchers, Inc.; page 364 Norman A. Sylvia/The Providence Journal

Chapter 12 page 387 Fred Ward/Black Star; page 402 Francis Miller/© Time, Inc.

Chapter 13 page 419 © 1978 Eric A. Roth/The Picture Cube; page 426 © Danny Lyon/Magnum Photos, Inc.

Chapter 14 page 448 © Andrew Brilliant/The Picture Cube; page 477 Barbaraellen Koch/The New Mexican

Chapter 15 page 482 L. Andrews/© Magnum Photos, Inc.

Name Index

Brodie, H. Keith H., 312
Bromberg, Walter, 134
Brosi, Kathleen, 396, 416, 418
Brown, Brenda A., 350
Brown, Richard Maxwell, 134
Brownmiller, Susan, 349, 350, 351
Bryan, James H., 346, 351
Bryant, Clifton D., 351
Bullock, Henry Allen, 131, 137
Burgess, E. W., 33
Burgess, Robert L., 41–42, 63, 114, 135
Burt, Cyril, 31–32, 62

Calhoun, George, 11, 19
Calpin, Joseph C., 414, 418
Calvert, Roy E., 446, 478
Cameron, Mary Owen, 189, 190, 203
Cannavale, Frank J. Jr., 397, 416, 417
Carey, James T., 312
Carlin, Jerome E., 417
Carroll, Leo, 474, 480
Carter, Robert M., 409, 418, 429–430, 446
Casey, John J., 312
Casper, Jonathan D., 405, 417
Casteneda, Carlos, 311
Cavan, Sherri, 351
Center for Research on Criminal Justice, 512
Chafee, Zachariah, Jr., 386
Chambers, Carl D., 311, 312
Chambliss, William J., 61, 93, 172, 174, 202, 379, 386, 394, 402, 416, 418, 454–455, 478, 496, 512
Chapman, Dennis, 72–73, 94, 370, 385, 410, 418, 513
Chappell, Duncan, 203, 330, 350
Chein, Isidore, 312
Chimbos, Peter D., 203
Chilton, Roland J., 63
Chiricos, Theodore G., 411, 418, 478, 479
Chodorkoff, Bernard, 116, 135
Christensen, Cornelia V., 351
Christensen, Harold T., 350
Cicourel, Aaron V., 513
Clark, Alexander L., 478
Clark, John P., 63, 94
Clear, Todd R., 418
Clemmer, Donald, 474–475, 480
Clinard, Marshall B., 126, 136, 243, 248, 350, 351, 498, 513
Cloward, Richard A., 37–38, 63
Cobern, Morris, 384
Cohen, Albert K., 32–33, 36–37, 62, 63
Cohen, Bernard, 137, 410, 418
Cohen, Fred, 417
Cohen, Jacqueline, 478, 479

Cohen, Lawrence E., 416
Coke, Sir Edward, 317
Cole, George F., 397, 403, 417, 513
Colquhoun, Patrick, 359, 384
Conklin, John E., 145, 149–151, 153–154, 166, 203, 244, 247, 249, 253, 278
Connett, Archie V., 447
Conrad, John P., 437, 447, 479
Cooper, Phillip, 136, 137
Cortes, Juan B., 62
Council of State Governments, 418
Cramer, James A., 478
Cressey, Donald R., 10, 19, 33, 40, 61, 62, 63, 93, 202, 210, 213, 214–215, 216, 247, 251–252, 255, 265, 266, 273–274, 278, 279, 280, 300, 312, 424–425, 446, 475, 480
Critchley, T. A., 384
Crotty, William J., 135
Crow, Wayman J., 447
Crowther, Betty, 311
Cumming, Elaine, 385
Cumming, Ian, 385
Cunningham, Richard O., 416
Currie, Elliott P., 249, 513
Curtis, Lynn, 350
Cutler, James E., 134
Czajkoski, Eugene H., 417, 447

Dale, Robert, 166
Damanska, Mirjan R., 447
D'Antonio, William V., 63
Darwin, Charles, 25
Davidson, Ralph, 447
Davis, Alan J., 480
Davis, E. Eugene, 19
Davis, F. James, 8, 19, 447
Defleur, Lois B., 63
Defleur, Melvin L., 63
Defrancis, Vincent, 351
Denfeld, Duane, 166, 203
Dentler, Robert A., 94
Dershowitz, Alan, 249
Dickens, Charles, 434, 446
Dinitz, Simon, 44, 62, 64
Dirks, Raymond L., 248
Dobin, Henry, 313
Doleisch, Wolfgang, 203
Dollard, John, 117, 135, 312
Doob, L., 135
Dorman, Michael, 279
Douglas, Jack D., 351, 385
Douglas, William O., 502
Downie, Leonard Jr., 417
Doyle, James C., 248
Driver, Edwin D., 386
Dugdale, Richard L., 61
Dunn, Christopher S., 313, 384

Durkheim, Emile, 6, 19, 34, 35, 37, 62, 100, 134, 412, 418, 425, 432, 446, 450, 478

Earle, Alice M., 447
Edelhertz, Herbert, 207, 213, 247, 249
Edell, Laura, 385
Eder, George Jackson, 136
Edwards, John N., 351
Edwards, Loren E., 203
Einstadter, Werner J., 157, 163, 166
Elliott, Delbert S., 63, 79, 94
Ellis, Albert, 351
Ellis, Rosalind D., 312
Empey, Lamar T., 63, 94
Engels, Frederick, 52, 64
England, Ralph W., 64
Enker, Arnold, 398, 417
Epps, Edgar, 63
Erickson, Kai T., 20, 45, 47, 64, 134, 447
Erickson, Maynard L., 63, 94, 478
Erickson, Rosemary J., 447
Esselzstyn, C., 351
Evans, Lloyd, 433, 446
Evans-Pritchard, E. E., 11, 19
Eysenck, H. J., 62
Ezorsky, Gertrude, 447

Fahey, Richard P., 136
Farberman, Harvey A., 248
Faris, Robert E. L., 62
Farrington, David P., 94
Federal Bureau of Investigation (FBI), 81–90, 94, 104, 105, 106, 107, 126, 132, 134, 143–145, 147–148, 153, 158, 166, 173, 306, 313, 324–325
Feldman, Roger A., 134
Ferdinand, Theodore N., 350
Ferracuti, Franco, 121–122, 126–127, 134, 135
Ferri, Enrico, 21, 26, 31
Finger, Charles J., 166
Fisher, Joseph C., 134
Fitch, J. H., 352
Flanagan, Timothy J., 19, 94, 166
Fogel, David, 446
Foldessy, Edward P., 204
Fooner, Michael, 94
Foote, Caleb, 392, 416, 418
Fort, Joel, 313
Fortas, Abe, 505
Foster, Henry H. Jr., 19
Fourth International Criminological Congress, 203
Fox, Richard, G., 61
Francis, Roy G., 137
Freidland, Martin, 393, 416
Freud, Sigmund, 115–116

Stoll, Clarice S., 512
Stouffer, Samuel A., 192, 203
Stratton, John R., 63, 479
Straus, Murray A., 19, 135
Street, David, 480
Stub, Helger R., 445
Sudnow, David, 417
Suffet, Frederic, 416
Sultan, Cynthia G., 136, 137
Sutherland, Edwin H., 10, 19, 21, 33, 39–42, 60, 61, 93, 173–174, 175, 177, 202, 203, 204, 206, 210, 224, 229, 243, 247, 248, 249, 351, 424–425, 446, 451
Sutter, Alan G., 312
Sutton, L. Paul, 31
Svalastoga, Kaare, 135
Sykes, Gresham M., 44–45, 61, 65, 215, 466–469, 479, 480
Szabo, Dennis, 480

Taft, Donald R., 64
Takagi, Paul, 129, 136, 137
Tangri, Sandra S., 64
Tannenbaum, Frank, 46–47, 64
Tappan, Paul W., 16, 20
Taylor, G. Rattray, 349
Taylor, Ian, 64, 65
Taylor, Norman, 311
Teeters, Negley, 23
Terry, C. E., 283–284, 311, 312
Thomas, Charles W., 481
Thomas, D. A., 336–337, 351
Thompson, Hunter, 124
Thornberry, Terrence P., 418
Thrasher, Frederick M., 62
Tifft, Larry L., 94
Time, 279, 345, 351
Tinklenberg, Jared, 313
Tittle, Charles R., 478, 479
Toby, Jackson, 136, 192–193, 203
Toch, Hans, 468, 479
Tompkins, John S., 256, 272, 279, 280
Trasler, Gordon, 62
Triplett, Frank, 166
Trotter, R. T., 463, 479
Tumin, Melvin M., 102, 108–109, 115, 134, 135, 136, 166, 350
Turk, Austin T., 19, 20, 49–50, 61, 64, 93, 167, 384, 419, 445
Turner, J. W. Cecil, 202, 247

Turner, R. E., 351
Tyler, Gus, 258, 278, 279

Union of Radical Criminologists, 57
United Nations, 111
United States Bureau of the Census, 447
United States Bureau of Prisons, 428, 446
United States Chamber of Commerce, 247, 248
United States Department of Justice, 19, 184, 313, 325, 447

Valachi, Joseph, 253, 261, 279
Valentine, Alan, 165, 351
Van Bemmelen, J. M., 64
Van den Berghe, Pierre L., 114, 135
Vander Zanden, James W., 135
Velerde, Albert J., 351
Verrko, Veli, 135
Vetri, Dominick R., 417
Vinter, Robert D., 480
Vold, George B., 27–28, 31, 61, 62, 155, 166, 478
Von Hentig, Hans, 109, 135
Von Hirsch, Andrew, 445
Voss, Harwin L., 63, 94, 134

Wahrman, Ralph, 447
Waite, Emily, 136
Wald, Patricia M., 313
Waldo, Gordon P., 136, 411, 418, 478, 479
Walker, Nigel, 93, 94
Wallace, Robert, 204
Waller, John D., 513
Wallerstein, James S., 94
Walsh, Marilyn, 203, 249
Walton, Paul, 64, 65
Walton, Robert P., 312
Waltz, Jon R., 203
Ward, David A., 135, 479, 480
Ward, Renee E., 135
Warlick, Mark, 351
Wasserstein, Bruce, 248
Weber, Marvin Glenn, 234, 248
Weber, Max, 8–9, 19
Weinberg, Martin S., 203, 348, 352
Weiner, Norman, 385
Weir, Adrianne W., 94, 165

Weis, Kurt, 94, 350
Weiss, Joseph G., 94
Wellford, Charles, 64, 480, 481
Wells, Kenneth M., 384
Wells, Richard S., 384, 502, 513
Wenninger, Eugene P., 63
Werthman, Carl, 385, 405
West, D. J., 94
Westley, William A., 136, 416
Weston, Paul B., 384
Wheeler, Stanton, 65, 349
White, Garland F., 447
White, Leslie A., 351
White, Thomas W., 513
White, Walter, 134
Whitman, Howard, 151, 166
Wholey, Joseph S., 513
Wickman, Peter, 480
Wilkins, Leslie T., 409, 413–414, 418
Williams, Colin J., 348, 352
Williams, Kristen M., 166, 416
Williams, Thomas A., 417
Wilner, Daniel, 479
Wilson, James Q., 385
Wilson, Nancy Koser, 480
Winick, Charles, 351
Wiseman, Jacqueline P., 308, 313, 385
Wolfgang, Marvin E., 61, 64, 93, 106, 108, 109, 110, 121–123, 126–127, 128, 134, 135, 136, 137, 166, 410, 418, 446
Wolin, Sheldon S., 134
Wood, Arthur Lewis, 417
Wright, Helena, 349
Wyle, Clement, 94

Yablonsky, Lewis, 62, 63, 122–123, 124–125, 135, 136, 236, 245, 248, 249
Yale Law Journal, 337, 351
Yochelson, Samuel, 19, 29, 30
Young, James H., 248
Young, Jock, 64, 65
Young, Wayland, 351
Youngblood, Clifford W., 248

Zeitz, Leonard, 513
Zilboorg, Gregory, 62
Zimbardo, Philip G., 463, 464–467
Zimring, Franklin E., 107, 134, 478
Zurcher, Louis A., 447

Subject Index